Subclassing and Hooking
with Visual Basic

Stephen Teilhet

O'REILLY®

Beijing · Cambridge · Farnham · Köln · Paris · Sebastopol · Taipei · Tokyo

Subclassing and Hooking with Visual Basic
by Stephen Teilhet

Copyright © 2001 O'Reilly & Associates, Inc. All rights reserved.
Printed in the United States of America.

Published by O'Reilly & Associates, Inc., 101 Morris Street, Sebastopol, CA 95472.

Editor: Ron Petrusha

Production Editors: Leanne Clarke Soylemez and Matt Hutchinson

Cover Designer: Ellie Volckhausen

Printing History:

    June 2001:   First Edition.

Library of Congress Cataloging-in-Publication Data

    Subclassing and Hooking with Visual Basic.
        p. cm.
      ISBN 0-596-00118-5
        1. Microsoft Visual BASIC 2. BASIC (Computer program language) I. Title:
    Subclassing & hooking with Visual Basic

QA76.73 .B967 2001
005.26'8--dc21   2001033096

ISBN: 0-596-00118-5

[M]

Dedicated to Kandis, Patrick, and Nicholas

Table of Contents

Preface

I came about the idea to write this book when I noticed that there was no one place you could go to learn about subclassing and hooking. Originally, these two subjects were geared toward more advanced C++ developers. Visual Basic (VB) developers were never able to use either of these techniques in a pure VB solution until the advent of Versions 5 and 6, when the language allowed developers to tap into subclassing and hooking techniques. Unfortunately, there remained a problem of insufficient information to help the VB developer understand how, when, where, and why to use these techniques.

In doing some research, I came to the realization that few VB developers had a solid grasp of these techniques. In fact, these techniques were being underused and even misused. Developers were creating incredibly complex and hard-to-maintain code, code that could be greatly simplified if the programmer had only taken advantage of subclassing, hooking, or even both techniques in tandem. This book is meant not only to teach subclassing and hooking techniques, but also to be a single resource from which developers can get information and answers to their questions about these techniques.

Who This Book Is For

This book is for the VB developer who wants a better understanding of subclassing and hooking, as well as knowledge of how to incorporate these techniques into his projects. You need not be an advanced VB developer to learn how to effectively use subclassing and hooking. The beginning of this book lays a solid foundation that will bring the beginning or intermediate developer up to speed.

In understanding subclassing and hooking, you must delve deep into the internals of the Windows operating system. This deeper understanding of Windows enables you not only to gain an understanding of subclassing and hooking, but also to learn more about the messaging system, which is the heart of the Windows operating system. In the process, you'll become a better programmer whether or not you commonly use subclassing and hooking in your applications.

You will need to utilize many of the Win32 application programming interface (API) functions to write subclassing and hooking applications. Therefore, a good knowledge of the Win32 API functions and how they are used within VB is necessary. You can find definitions for most of these API functions, constants, and structures using the API Text Viewer, which ships with Visual Studio 6. However, several API functions, constants, and structure definitions are missing from this viewer. You can find this missing information by searching through both the C++ *Windows.h* and *WinUser.h* header files. Additionally, I have provided definitions for the various API functions, constants, and structures used within this book in Appendixes A, B, and C.

I will focus on using the Visual Basic language in this book. All the subclassing code and most of the hooking code will be written in VB. The limitations of VB come into play when developers try to write system-wide hooks. System-wide hooks require a true Win32 dynamic link library (DLL) to be created, something that VB does not support (it enables you to generate only COM DLLs). Visual C++ will enter the picture at this point. The Visual C++ code will be kept to a minimum so that you can focus on using VB to implement hooks.

The code in this book was written and tested using Visual Basic Version 6 Service Pack 3, Visual Basic.NET Beta 1, and Visual C++ Version 6 Service Pack 3. The following operating systems were used while writing this book and its examples: Windows 98, Windows NT 4 Service Pack 4, and Windows 2000 Service Pack 1. There are subtle differences in these operating systems that affect how subclassing and hooking operate on each system. These differences are noted in this book wherever they will affect the developer.

How This Book Is Structured

This book is grouped into four distinct sections. The first is the introductory section, which contains information about the Windows operating system and the basics of subclassing and hooking. This section lays the foundation that will enable you to completely grasp the rest of the material in this book. This section contains the following chapters:

Chapter 1, *Introduction*

This chapter defines subclassing and hooking and gives several examples of how each can be used effectively. In addition, the tools used in this book are explained. The tools include the following:

— Spy++, which enables us to view information about processes, windows, and messages. This tool comes as part of the Visual Studio Version 6 development environment.

— The *Dbgwproc.dll* DLL, which enables us to more easily debug sub-classing code within projects written in Versions 5 or 6 of VB. This tool can be downloaded from *http://msdn.microsoft.com/vbasic/downloads/ controls.asp.*

— Microsoft System Information, which enables us to see the installed hooks in a Windows 98 system. This tool can be accessed from the Help → About Microsoft Visual Basic… menu item on the Visual Basic main menu bar. When the About dialog box appears, click the System Info… button to view the Microsoft System Information tool.

— SmartCheck, developed by Compuware Numega Labs, which enables us to watch under the hood as a VB project runs. A 14-day trial version of this software is available from Compuware Numega Labs at *http://www. numega.com/evaluations/default.asp.*

Chapter 2, *Windows System-Specific Information*

This chapter contains information on Windows' processes, threads, windows, and messaging system, as well as how they relate to subclassing and hooking.

Chapter 3, *The Basics of Subclassing and Hooks*

This chapter starts out with a discussion of how subclassing operates and the different types of subclassing at your disposal, and is followed by a discussion of how hooking operates. Finally, the pros and cons of using subclassing and hooks are laid out for you.

The second section covers the technique of subclassing and its variations. The process of subclassing VB forms is discussed, along with subclassing controls, common dialog boxes, and ActiveX controls that you create. Adding to this, global subclassing and superclassing are discussed at length, along with debugging your subclassing code. This section contains the following chapters:

Chapter 4, *Subclassing*

A discussion of the **AddressOf** operator is presented first, followed by an in-depth discussion of the various types of subclassing, along with examples of each type. Tips for using subclassing are presented throughout this chapter.

Chapter 5, *Subclassing the Windows Common Dialog Boxes*

A crash course on using the Windows Common Dialog APIs is presented first. Next, the technique of subclassing the Open and Save As common dialogs is discussed and examples are provided. Finally, the chapter finishes with a discussion of subclassing each of the other common dialogs.

Chapter 6, *ActiveX Controls and Subclassing*
> This chapter discusses how to subclass a third-party ActiveX control and an ActiveX control that we create in VB. Next follows a discussion of subclassing a UserControl from within an ActiveX control that is created in VB. This chapter finishes by creating an ActiveX control that is used to subclass a VB form.

Chapter 7, *Superclassing*
> The technique of superclassing a window is discussed and examples are provided, and the differences and similarities between superclassing and other types of subclassing are noted.

Chapter 8, *Debugging Techniques for Subclassing*
> This chapter presents various techniques used to debug your subclassing application. Along with this discussion, several of the previously mentioned tools are discussed in more detail.

The third section covers the technique of hooking. Fifteen different types of hooks are discussed, each in its own chapter (except for the mouse and low-level keyboard hooks, which are grouped with the regular mouse and keyboard hooks, respectively). This section contains the following chapters:

Chapter 9, *WH_CALLWNDPROC*
> The `WH_CALLWNDPROC` hook is presented in this chapter, along with details of its operation, examples, and things to watch out for when using it.

Chapter 10, *WH_CALLWNDPROCRET*
> The `WH_CALLWNDPROCRET` hook is presented in this chapter, along with details of its operation, examples, and things to watch out for when using it.

Chapter 11, *WH_GETMESSAGE*
> The `WH_GETMESSAGE` hook is presented in this chapter, along with details of its operation, examples, and things to watch out for when using it.

Chapter 12, *WH_KEYBOARD and WH_KEYBOARD_LL*
> The `WH_KEYBOARD` and `WH_KEYBOARD_LL` hooks are presented in this chapter, along with details of their operation, examples, and things to watch out for when using them.

Chapter 13, *WH_MOUSE and WH_MOUSE_LL*
> The `WH_MOUSE` and `WH_MOUSE_LL` hooks are presented in this chapter, along with details of their operation, examples, and things to watch out for when using them.

Chapter 14, *WH_FOREGROUNDIDLE*
> The `WH_FOREGROUNDIDLE` hook is presented in this chapter, along with details of its operation, examples, and things to watch out for when using it.

Chapter 15, *WH_MSGFILTER*

> The `WH_MSGFILTER` hook is presented in this chapter, along with details of its operation, examples, and things to watch out for when using it.

Chapter 16, *WH_SYSMSGFILTER*

> The `WH_SYSMSGFILTER` hook is presented in this chapter, along with details of its operation, examples, and things to watch out for when using it.

Chapter 17, *WH_SHELL*

> The `WH_SHELL` hook is presented in this chapter, along with details of its operation, examples, and things to watch out for when using it.

Chapter 18, *WH_CBT*

> The `WH_CBT` hook is presented in this chapter, along with details of its operation, examples, and things to watch out for when using it.

Chapter 19, *WH_JOURNALRECORD*

> The `WH_JOURNALRECORD` hook is presented in this chapter, along with details of its operation, examples, and things to watch out for when using it.

Chapter 20, *WH_JOURNALPLAYBACK*

> The `WH_JOURNALPLAYBACK` hook is presented in this chapter, along with details of its operation, examples, and things to watch out for when using it. A discussion of how this hook is used in tandem with the WH_JOURNAL-RECORD hook also is provided.

Chapter 21, *WH_DEBUG*

> The `WH_DEBUG` hook is presented in this chapter, along with details of its operation, examples, and things to watch out for when using it. Also discussed are ways to enhance the debugging of hooks in your applications.

The fourth and final section covers the techniques of subclassing and hooking as they apply to the new VB.NET language. This section contains the following chapters:

Chapter 22, *Subclassing .NET WinForms*

> The various techniques of subclassing using the new VB.NET language are presented in this chapter, along with examples.

Chapter 23, *Implementing Hooks in VB.NET*

> This chapter discusses how to use hooks with the new VB.NET language. Examples using various hooks also are provided.

Obtaining the Sample Code

The example VB source code from *Subclassing and Hooking with Visual Basic* is freely downloadable from the O'Reilly & Associates web site at *vb.oreilly.com*. Just follow the link to the book's title page and then click the *Examples* link. The downloadable code will be updated to reflect the most recent beta or production release of the VB.NET platform.

Conventions Used in This Book

Throughout this book, we have used the following typographic conventions:

Constant width

> Indicates a language construct such as a language statement, a constant, or an expression. Interface names appear in constant width. Lines of code also appear in constant width, as do function and method prototypes.

Constant width bold

> Indicates user input in code sections.

Italic

> Represents intrinsic and application-defined functions, the names of system elements such as directories and files, and Internet resources such as web documents. New terms also are italicized when they are first introduced.

Constant width italic

> Indicates replaceable parameter names in prototypes or command syntax, and indicates variable and parameter names in body text.

The owl icon designates a note, which is an important aside to the nearby text.

The turkey icon designates a warning relating to the nearby text.

How to Contact Us

We have tested and verified all the information in this book to the best of our ability, but you might find that features have changed (or even that we have made mistakes!). Please let us know about any errors you find, as well as your suggestions for future editions, by writing to:

> O'Reilly & Associates, Inc.
> 101 Morris St.
> Sebastopol, CA 95472
> (800) 998-9938 (in the U.S. or Canada)
> (707) 829-0515 (international/local)
> (707) 829-0104 (fax)

You also can send messages electronically. To be put on our mailing list or to request a catalog, send email to:

> *nuts@oreilly.com*

To ask technical questions or comment on the book, send email to:

> *bookquestions@oreilly.com*

For technical information on Visual Basic programming, to participate in Visual Basic discussion forums, or to acquaint yourself with O'Reilly's line of Visual Basic books, you can access the O'Reilly Visual Basic web site at:

> *http://vb.oreilly.com*

Acknowledgments

I first want to thank Ron Petrusha, my editor, for taking a chance on an unproven author. This is the first book that I have written, and it has been a very fulfilling experience. Under Ron's constant guidance and direction, I have grown considerably in my skill and understanding of the intricacies of writing.

I cannot thank my wife enough; she has been there, enabling me in every way possible to complete this project. Without her, I might have dismissed the idea of writing this book early on, thinking that it would be too far out of my grasp. Hearing her enthusiasm while telling others about the book that I was writing always renewed my determination and energy to finish this book.

I want to thank Mom and Dad for their support and the many long-distance phone calls they made to make sure that I was still on schedule.

I would like to thank William J. Steele, a Microsoft consultant, for taking time out of his busy schedule to discuss some of the questions and theories that I came up with while in the process of writing this book.

The technical reviewers, Daniel Creeron and J.P. Hamilton, did a wonderful job of reviewing the book's technical material. This was no easy job, and I thank them for their valuable feedback.

Finally, I would like to thank Jessamyn Read for doing a great job in transforming the illustrations that I came up with into their final form.

I

Introducing Subclassing and Hooking

This section will lay the basis for developing applications that incorporate sub-classing and hooking by examining the Windows family of operating systems as messaging systems. We'll also explore what subclassing and hooking involves, how they differ, and why you'd want to use one technique rather than another. Finally, we'll look at some software tools that you can use both to better understand the operation of Windows, as well as to gather information about how your subclassed windows or hooks are performing.

1

Introduction

Windows is a message-based system. This means that every action you take while using the system creates one or more messages to carry out the action. These messages are passed between objects within the system. These messages also carry with them information that gives the recipient more detail on how to interpret and act upon the message.

Clicking a button control provides a good messaging example. This produces not only the message for the mouse button click, but also a wide array of other messages. These include messages to repaint the button in its depressed state, notification messages to inform other objects of the button's change in state, messages to determine the state of the mouse cursor, as well as others. Even a simple act such as moving the mouse or pressing a key on the keyboard can produce an astonishing number of messages.

In addition to communicating user actions, Windows also uses messages internally to do housekeeping. Messages need to be sent to update the time and date, to notify other objects of a change in state, and even to notify applications when system resources are exhausted.

The Windows messaging system is the heart of the operating system. As a result, the messaging system is very complex.

Subclassing and the Windows hooking mechanism operate on messages within the messaging system. This makes subclassing and hooking two very powerful techniques. With them, we can manipulate, modify, or even discard messages bound for other objects within the operating system and, in the process, change the way in which the system behaves. As you might already have guessed, a thorough understanding of the messaging system is critical to mastering the techniques of subclassing and hooking.

Along with this power comes responsibility. It is up to the developer to make sure that he or she is using these techniques correctly. Windows is very unforgiving if these techniques are used incorrectly.

Subclassing

Subclassing techniques deal with intercepting messages bound for one or more windows or controls. These messages are intercepted before they can reach their destination window. The intercepted message can be left in its original state or modified. Afterward, the message can be sent to its original destination or discarded.

By intercepting messages in this manner, we can have a powerful influence on how the window or control will react to the messages it receives. Consider, for example, right-clicking the Visual Basic (VB) text box control. This action causes a default pop-up menu to be displayed containing the following menu items: Undo, Cut, Copy, Paste, Delete, and Select All. Replacing this menu with one of our own is a fairly simple task using subclassing. Subclassing has many other uses as well, such as:

- Determining when a window is being activated or deactivated and responding to this change

- Responding to new menu items that are manually added to the system menu of a window

- Displaying descriptions of menu items as the mouse moves across them

- Disallowing a user to move or resize a window

- Allowing a user to move or resize a window within specified boundaries

- Determining where the mouse cursor is and responding accordingly

- Modifying the look of a window or control

- Changing the way a combo box operates

- Determining when the display resolution has been changed

- Monitoring the system for a low system-resource condition

- Modifying or disallowing keystrokes sent to a window or control

- Modifying how a window or control is painted on the screen

Subclassing opens up a wealth of possibilities to the VB developer—possibilities that ordinarily are completely unavailable, or at least are not easy to implement.

There are three types of subclassing, all of which I will discuss. The first is *instance subclassing*, which makes it possible to intercept messages for a single instance of a window or control. This type of subclassing is the most commonly used. It is used to control, for example, the user's ability to size a single instance of a window. The second is *global subclassing*, which makes it possible to intercept messages for one or more windows or controls that are all created from the same window class. All windows derive from some type of class; these classes describe the fundamental look and behavior of windows created from them. Take, for example, a standard button control; each instance of this control derives from a BUTTON class. Using global subclassing, we can change the behavior of the class. This in turn allows us to intercept messages from all window or control instances created from this class. Using global subclassing we can control the user's ability to size any window created from a particular class. The third type of subclassing, *superclassing*, is a close relative of global subclassing. Superclassing also has the ability to intercept messages for one or more windows or controls. The difference is that a brand-new window class is created to facilitate this type of subclassing. Similar to global subclassing, superclassing allows users to size a window to be controlled.

The Window Hooking Mechanism

The *window hooking mechanism*, or hooks, also deals with intercepting messages, but at a much broader scope than subclassing. Hooking allows us to intercept messages at various set points within the operating system. For example, we can intercept a message before and after a window has processed it.

There are several different kinds of hooks, each with their own special purpose and location within the operating system. They are:

```
WH_CALLWNDPROC
WH_CALLWNDPROCRET
WH_CBT
WH_DEBUG
WH_FOREGROUNDIDLE
WH_GETMESSAGE
WH_JOURNALPLAYBACK
WH_JOURNALRECORD
WH_KEYBOARD
WH_KEYBOARD_LL
WH_MOUSE
WH_MOUSE_LL
WH_MSGFILTER
WH_SYSMSGFILTER
WH_SHELL
```

Hooks, unlike subclassing, can have an application scope or a system-wide scope. By this, I mean a single hook can intercept specific messages within a single application, or it can be set up to intercept those same messages for all applications running in the system. Hooks give us control over the system, which cannot be achieved with subclassing. The following are just a few of the uses for hooks:

- Modifying messages sent to dialog boxes, scroll bars, menus, or message boxes

- Subclassing a window that resides in a separate process

- Creating a macro recorder that can play back the recorded macro as well

- Developing computer-based training (CBT) applications

- Capturing and modifying mouse or keyboard messages at a system level

- Providing a help function key for menu items and message boxes

- Creating a utility similar to Spy++

- Creating an automated testing application

- Determining when an application is idle

- Modifying mouse buttons and keystrokes for a particular application, or for all applications

- Modifying ALT+TAB and ALT+ESC key functionality

I will discuss all the hooks listed here, as well as show how to apply them to a single application or to all applications running in the system, in Chapters 9 through 21.

Tools to Aid Us in Our Efforts

Along with using these advanced techniques, effectively implementing subclassing and hooking in our development work requires that we employ debugging tools beyond the capabilities of the VB debugger.

While developing the projects for this book, I used several software utilities as well as other professional applications that I built. Although you can successfully build applications that subclass various windows or that hook into certain message streams without these utilities, I do not suggest doing so. These utilities give you, the developer, a valuable insight into what is happening inside the system while running your projects in the VB integrated development environment (IDE) and especially at runtime. You will be able to see things operate in a way that is unavailable to you by just using the Visual Basic or Visual C++ development environments.

I would go as far as saying that some of these utilities are necessary to understand how subclassing and hooks work. Otherwise, you will only be blindly plugging code into an application, not fully understanding why you are doing it and what is happening behind the scenes. When the application locks up, debugging it will be frustrating and possibly futile. What I am stressing here is that we, as programmers, must aspire to have an understanding of what we are doing. Without this understanding we cannot hope to reach the more advanced areas of our discipline. Having an understanding of how subclassing and hooks work and interact with the rest of the Windows system will allow you to build successful applications.

I will describe the utilities that I use in the following sections. Although this book will not include a tutorial for operating these utilities, there is some very good documentation in the Microsoft Developer Network Library (MSDN) for Spy++ and PView. The NuMega tools come with their own documentation. Note that some of these tools display different information depending on which operating system you are using (e.g., Windows 9x, NT, or 2000).

Spy++

The Spy++ utility is included in the Win32 Software Development Kit (SDK) as well as in Microsoft Visual Studio.

I have used this utility the most, except maybe for NuMega's SmartCheck utility. Spy++ is one of the most valuable tools when implementing subclassing and superclassing. Spy++ can provide you with all the information you need to verify the state of the application before and after a subclassing operation, as well as all the message information being passed to and from a window. Spy++ is described as a tool for "spying" on different parts of the operating system. This means you can watch as processes, threads, and windows contained within the threads are created and destroyed. Also, you can get valuable information on these objects, some of which is contained within the structures used to create them. But even more useful is the ability to watch in real time as messages flow throughout the system. This, in my opinion, is the most powerful feature of this tool.

Spy++ is a Multiple Document Interface (MDI) application. Let's start up Spy++ and quickly run through the windows and menus, just to become familiar with getting around in the tool. Each child window within Spy++ displays information on processes, threads, top-level windows, or messages. Let's start with the Processes window and work our way down.

When Spy++ is started, it will take a snapshot of the system at that point in time. (This does not apply to spying on messages; messages are displayed as soon as they arrive at the window.) Any time an application is started or ended, or its state changes, you should refresh the display by pressing the F5 key. This will allow you to view the most current state of the system.

The Processes window, which is shown in Figure 1-1, is opened automatically when Spy++ is launched, and displays a list of currently running processes in the system in a tree hierarchy. You can drill down through the processes, which are displayed with a two-gear icon, into the threads within a process, displayed with a single-gear icon. If a thread contains any top-level windows, you can drill down into these windows as well. *Top-level windows* are windows that have the desktop window as their only window. The top-level windows are displayed with a rectangular window icon. Each item in the tree can be double-clicked to display a dialog box that displays its properties. Within each properties dialog box, except for the Processes Properties dialog, there are hyperlinks to facilitate the process of drilling up and down through processes, threads, windows, and messages. Each item can be right-clicked as well to display a pop-up menu for that item. A separate pop-up menu is displayed for processes, threads, windows, and messages.

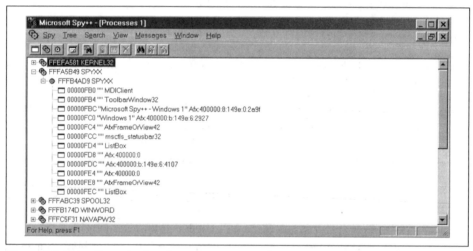

Figure 1-1. Using Spy++ to view the processes currently running

If your primary interest is examining the running threads rather than the processes, you can open the Threads window by selecting the Threads option from the Spy menu. The Threads window, which is shown in Figure 1-2, displays a list of currently running threads in all processes in the system, sorted by thread ID. The display is similar to the Processes window, except that the Processes level has been removed and the running threads are now at the top of the hierarchy. You can double-click and right-click the items in the list, just as in the Processes window.

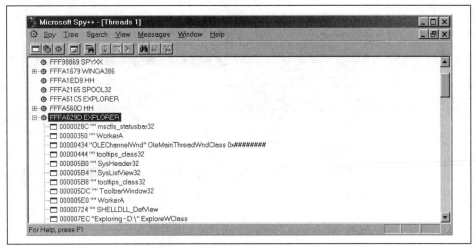

Figure 1-2. Using Spy++ to view the running threads of all running processes

Finally, if you're interested in the windows handled by the system and its applications, you can use the Windows window, which also is opened when Spy++ starts. The Windows window, which is shown in Figure 1-3, operates like the Processes and Threads windows and displays a list of all currently running top-level windows and their child windows. With this information, you can see how an application's designer arranged the user interface (UI) for each application.

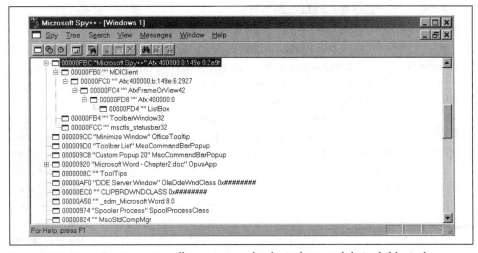

Figure 1-3. Using Spy++ to view all running top-level windows and their child windows

Finally, the Messages window, which is shown in Figure 1-4, is the window that we will be most interested in for the applications that we will be building throughout this book.

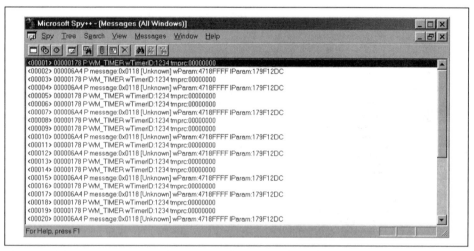

Figure 1-4. Using Spy++ to view the messages being sent throughout the system

Clicking the Messages → Options... menu item displays the Message Options dialog box. This dialog contains the following three tabs.

The Windows tab

Determines which windows will be watched. Dragging the Finder icon and dropping it onto a window will select that window's messages to be displayed in Spy++. The checkboxes in the Additional Windows frame allow you to view messages for additional windows.

The Messages tab

Because watching every message for every window in the system would produce far too much information to digest, this tab allows you to choose which messages to display. The Messages to View list box displays every message that can be watched. The checkboxes in the Message Groups frame, to the right of the list box, correspond to separate groups of related messages. Most of the checkboxes are self-explanatory; for example, mouse messages correlate with the Mouse checkbox. The Non-Client checkbox relates to messages that usually have the letters NC in them. NC stands for non-client. These messages describe actions originating from the non-client area of a window, such as the title bars and/or a border that is being resized. The General checkbox relates to the messages commonly used in a window, such as WM_COMMAND, WM_TIMER, or WM_PAINT. The Registered checkbox watches for messages defined by the developer using the *RegisterWindowMessage* application programming interface (API) function. The Unknown checkbox watches for messages that are defined to be in the range of zero to one less than the WM_USER constant (&H400). These are message identifiers that are reserved for the system to use. The Registered checkbox watches for messages that are defined to be equal to or greater than the WM_USER constant. These are application-defined messages. After you select all the messages you want to watch, it is a good idea to check the Save Settings as Default checkbox; this way, you will not have to go back every time and re-select the appropriate messages.

The Output tab

This tab allows you some control over the message information displayed by Spy++. For this tab, I usually check all the checkboxes grouped in the Show in Message Log frame, and increase the value in the Lines Maximum text box to an appropriate value (somewhere around 3,000). Checking all these checkboxes will display the maximum amount of information about a message. We will not need the Message Origin Time and Message Mouse Position checkboxes until later, when we look into using journaling hooks. Checking the Save Settings as Default checkbox is a good idea here as well.

After selecting which messages to view for which windows, clicking Messages → Start Logging will allow Spy++ to start displaying the messages that you have selected in the Messages window. The first column of the Messages window will display a line number to denote the order of the messages. The next column is the window handle that the message was directed to. The third column is for message codes. A message code could be displayed as a P, S, s, or R. A message code of P means that this message was posted to the window's message queue, and that the posting application has continued to execute code and it is not waiting for a return code to be sent back. An S means that the message was sent to this window using the *SendMessage* API function or one of its derivatives, such as *SendMessageCallback*. *SendMessage* will wait for a return value to be passed back to it before continuing to execute code in the calling application. Every message with a code of S is followed by that same message with a code of R. A message code of R means that a return value has been passed back to the caller. A message code of s means that the return value cannot be accessed due to a security restriction. The next column in the Messages window displays the actual message name. This name might be preceded by one or more periods. Each period is a nesting level. This means that a message could be received by the window procedure that, in turn, might fire off several other messages, each of which could be handled before the original message completes processing. If you watched for every message for a particular window, you would notice that some messages having a code of S (sent messages) are not immediately followed by the returned message. Instead several other nested messages might be fired off, each being preceded by one or more periods. It would look something like this in Spy++:

```
000301B0  S  WM_NCACTIVATE
000301B0  S  .WM_GETTEXT
000301B0  R  .WM_GETTEXT
000301B0  R  WM_NCACTIVATE
```

Values following the message will describe in detail the *wParam* and *lParam* parameters. This description depends on the type of message. By checking the Decoded Message Parameters and Decoded Return Values checkboxes in the Message Options dialog box, you will be able to see a useful description of the *wParam*, *lParam*, and return values of each message.

If you double-click a message, the Message Properties dialog box appears. This dialog basically displays the same information that is present in the Messages child window, but it adds two useful features. The first is the Window Handle field in the dialog box, which is a hypertext link to the window properties. Clicking this field will take you to the Window Properties dialog box for the window with that particular handle. The second is that, if a message contains a pointer to a string or a structure, the Message Properties dialog box displays the actual text in the case of a string or the members and their values in the case of a structure.

Clicking Messages → Stop Logging will stop Spy++ from displaying messages.

Using Spy++ to examine a VB application

The parent of all windows is the Desktop window; this window will always be at the top of the hierarchy. Below that window are all the parent windows within each running application. To view the window information for your VB application, search through the list for any parent windows containing the text ThunderRT6FormDC. The caption of your window should be to the left of ThunderRT6FormDC (e.g., "Chapter 4—Subclassing Example" ThunderRT6FormDC). ThunderRT6FormDC is the name of the class from which this form was created. Any form that your application creates will be created from this class and will be considered a parent window. The next level below the parent is the child window. Child windows are usually controls contained within a VB form. Any VB-intrinsic control class will be prepended with the word **ThunderRT#.** Hence, a command button would be called ThunderRT6CommandButton in Version 6 of VB. Child windows can be parents to other child windows, as happens when controls (such as a PictureBox control) contain controls. Each container control is the parent to the child control(s) that it contains.

If you run a simple VB executable (EXE), you will notice that several different hidden windows are running within the same process as your EXE. These hidden windows are VBBubbleRT6, OleMainThreadWndClass 0x########, VBMsoStdCompMgr, ThunderRT6Main, OleDdeWndClass 0x########, and VBFocusRT6.

Every VB application has a hidden top-level window to which all messages and events are initially sent. This window is derived from the class called **ThunderRT6Main.** This window owns all other VB forms in the application.

OleMainThreadWndName is a hidden window derived from the `OleMainThreadWndClass 0x########` class. It is created by COM to handle message marshaling between COM components.

The `VBMsoStdCompMgr` class is the basis for several controls developed for Microsoft Office. For example, the Microsoft Office development team created the default toolbar that all windows now use. The letters "Mso" contained in VBMsoStdCompMgr stand for Microsoft Office. While running an application in the VB IDE, this class will drop the VB in its name and be displayed as MsoStdCompMgr instead.

The window created from the `VBFocusRT6` class is an invisible proxy form for windowless or lightweight controls. This proxy form is used to receive keyboard, mouse, and system messages for these controls.

All VB form and control classes are superclasses of the `VBBubbleRT6` class, which is also a superclass of the `ThunderRT6Main` class. The `VBBubbleRT6` class is responsible for forwarding messages to the appropriate window.

If you bring up a VB application (EXE) in Spy++, you might notice that all windows beginning with the word ThunderRT6 have the same window procedure and class window procedure, except for ThunderRT6Main. To see this, look at the Window Proc field in the General and Class tabs of the Window Properties dialog box. The reason all window procedures use the same function pointer is that all classes beginning with the word ThunderRT6, except for `ThunderRT6Main`, are derived from the same base class, `VBBubbleRT6`. In other words, `ThunderRT6CommandButton`, `ThunderRT6FormDC`, etc., are all superclasses of the base class, `VBBubbleRT6`. Other third-party controls will have different window procedures because these controls were created from different window classes.

Another interesting thing to notice is the construction of the ThunderRT6ComboBox control. When viewing a control created from this class, you can drill down one level deeper to discover a standard Windows edit control. (This is not a VB control because the class name is not prefixed with the word Thunder). This shows that a ThunderRT6ComboBox control consists of a VB-defined combo box and a standard Windows edit control. This information will come in handy if you ever need to subclass a VB combo box.

If you double-click a window in the hierarchy, Spy++ opens the Window Properties dialog, which contains information about that particular window. There are five tabs in this dialog box: General, Styles, Windows, Class, and Process. The General tab has several items of interest. The Window Caption displays the caption of a form or button. Some windows, such as the text box control, do not have captions. The Window Handle is the unique, system-wide handle of the selected window. This value is always passed on to the window's window procedure to identify which window the message was directed to. When watching messages with Spy++, it is sometimes helpful, especially when debugging, to match up the window handle in the message to an actual window. This will show you which window is receiving the message. The Window Proc is another very valuable field on this tab; this is the field we change to subclass a window. Do not confuse it with the class window procedure, which is contained only within the class and not the window instance. Before subclassing a window, check out the value of its Window Proc. After subclassing a window, recheck this value (don't forget to hit F5 to refresh the view). You'll notice that it has changed and is now pointing to the window procedure we defined in our code (BAS) module. After removing the subclass, check this value again and notice that it has been returned to its original number.

The Styles tab has two list boxes, one containing Window Styles and the other containing Extended Styles. These styles have an indirect effect on the messages that a window sends and receives; for details, see the documentation on the MSDN CD-ROM. The Windows tab contains the window handles to the selected window's parent, the first child, and any owner windows of that particular window. The parent window handle is useful to determine to which window a notification message will be sent. The owner window of any VB application is the window created from the `ThunderRT6Main` class. The handles listed on this tab are hyperlinks to the windows that they reference. Clicking the hyperlink displays the properties of that window in the Window Properties dialog box.

The Class tab is also very useful for determining subclassing information. The Class Name is the name given to this class when it was registered with the system. The Class Atom is the unique 16-bit integer value that identifies this class; it is returned from the call to *RegisterClassEx*. Every class also has styles similar to a window style. The `CD_DBLCLKS`, `CS_HREDRAW`, `CS_VREDRAW`, and `CS_SAVEBITS` class styles can have an effect on the messages sent and received by a window. There is one more bit of critical information on this tab: the Window Proc field, which translates to the window procedure of the class, not the window. Using this field, we can determine when a window has been subclassed. All we have to do is see whether the Window Proc values on the General and Class tabs match. If they do, the window has not been subclassed. If they are different, the window is subclassed. Global subclassing and superclassing are two techniques that will modify the class window procedure directly.

This completes the whirlwind tour of Spy++. If you do nothing else, familiarize yourself with this utility. Even if you never use subclassing or hooks, you can still use this utility to debug application message flow, as well as watch and learn how an application is set up and operates within the system.

NuMega SmartCheck

SmartCheck, developed by NuMega (*http://www.numega.com*), is a tool designed to help developers track down bugs and correct them. As an additional bonus, with this tool you can take a look under the hood of a compiled VB application and watch how it works. To tell you how to use it would require more than just one chapter. I will leave that subject to the documentation provided with the tool.

SmartCheck really shines when your application throws a General Protection Fault (GPF). If you have ever had the pleasure of tracking down a GPF in VB without any tools, you will understand what I mean. Because VB hides many lower-level system operations from the developer, it is difficult to determine why a piece of code will produce a GPF, and if it happens at random intervals, it is nearly impossible to figure out. SmartCheck goes over each executing line of code with a fine–toothed comb. That way, it is possible to see a problem such as a string returned from an API call that is overwriting its bounds and setting up a time bomb that will eventually blow up in your face. Try finding that problem yourself without any tools.

SmartCheck tracks all sorts of items such as API calls, bad calls to intrinsic VB functions, value coercion problems, messages, memory leaks, hooks, and much more. We will be paying close attention to the hooks, messages, and API calls that SmartCheck will be watching throughout the book.

Dbgwproc.dll

This is a dynamic link library (DLL) that you can get from the Microsoft web site that helps with troubleshooting VB applications that use subclassing. As we shall see later, debugging a VB application that uses the subclassing and hooking techniques described in this book is difficult because, having circumvented VB's own protective mechanisms, you cannot go very far with the debugging tools VB provides. *Dbgwproc.dll* is a tool that, when your application is running in debug mode, will allow you to trace through your application without crashing. You can find this tool on the Microsoft web site at *http://msdn.microsoft.com/vbasic/downloads/controls.asp*. I will talk about this tool in Chapter 8.

Microsoft System Information

This utility can be run under Windows 98 by selecting Start → Programs → Accessories → System Tools → System Information. Sadly, the System Information application provided with Windows NT/2000 does not show this information.

This tool can display all the system-wide hooks that are currently installed in the system. To do this, expand the path System Information → Software Environment

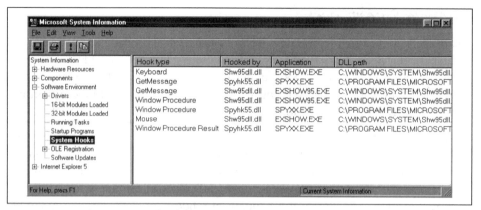

Figure 1-5. Displaying system hooks in Microsoft System Information

→ System Hooks. This will give us insight into applications that use system-wide hooks to do their work. In the Applications column in Figure 1-5, you see three entries for *SPYXX.EXE*, which is the Spy++ utility that we discussed previously. We can see that it installs three system-wide hooks: GetMessage, Window Procedure, and Window Procedure Result. We will discuss system-wide hooks, including these three types of hooks, throughout Part III of this book. This utility also can be used to make sure that our applications are installing our system-wide hooks correctly. Unfortunately, this is all the information about hooks that it can give us.

A Word of Warning

The techniques presented in this book make extensive use of the Win32 API and pointers. As you know, VB does not give us direct access to pointers. Instead we must use API functions to convert these pointers into information that VB can use.

As with using pointers in C, we must also take care when handling pointers in VB. Failing to do so will result in your application behaving unpredictably or crashing.

Incorrectly setting up and calling Win32 API functions is another source of problems. To function correctly, API functions must not only be declared correctly in VB, but also have their arguments passed in properly.

I will not be covering in any great detail how to set up and call Win32 API functions in this book. It is up to you to make sure the API functions that you use are declared and used properly. For more information on the topic of Win32 API functions, you can read Steven Roman's book entitled *Win32 API Programming With Visual Basic*, published by O'Reilly & Associates.

2

Windows System-Specific Information

Before delving into the guts of subclassing and using hooks, we must first learn how the Windows messaging system works. This chapter is not going to teach you all the details of processes, threads, or some of the other Windows objects encountered while programming the operating system. Instead, I will concentrate on the particulars of the Windows operating system only insofar as they apply to the subject of this book.

Understanding how the Windows messaging subsystem works is a necessary first step toward learning how to correctly design and implement subclassing and hooks through Visual Basic (VB). In fact, this holds true for using subclassing or hooks in any language, but it is more important in VB because VB shields the developer from going too deeply into the Windows internals. This is a double-edged sword. On one hand, VB makes it very simple to construct applications that might take much more time and effort in a different language such as C++. On the other hand, not being able to easily get intimate with the lower levels of the Windows operating system makes the task of debugging and implementing advanced functionality into our applications more difficult. Knowledge of what is happening in the system, where it is happening, and why it is happening is essential to constructing and debugging your applications.

Tinkering with the Windows messaging system is neither straightforward nor easy. One wrong line of code, one misplaced pointer—even exiting your application early—could easily bring down the entire system. Creating invalid page faults as well as freezing an application or your entire system is easy to do when adding subclassing and/or hooks to an application. This is the main reason why some developers shy away from using these tools and sometimes even downplay their usefulness. Armed with the information in this book, you will be able to consistently use these tools to add advanced functionality to your applications with a minimum of pain and confusion.

With that said, this chapter will focus mainly on explaining the underlying Windows messaging system: what is it, how it works, as well as what makes up a message and how to interpret it. This will give you, the developer, a solid foundation on which to build throughout the rest of the chapters.

Inside a Windows Application

This section focuses on the areas that are of greatest interest to us in using subclassing and hooks effectively. If you are interested in learning more about these subjects, pick up a copy of *Win32 API Programming with Visual Basic* by Steven Roman. He gives these topics a very thorough explanation.

Window Relationships

All windows are related in some way to one or more other windows. The most common type of window relationship is the parent-child relationship. Other types of relationships include owner-owned and top-level windows. Although information on the relationship of one window to another is not a requirement to understanding subclassing or hooks, it is very helpful. This information will come into play more as I discuss subclassing the common dialog boxes and as I get into the specifics of hooks, such as the WH_SHELL hook. For example, the WH_SHELL hook only provides information on top-level, unowned windows.

Central to defining the relationship among windows is the concept of *Z-order*. When windows are drawn on the screen, only one window can be active at any time. This active window receives user input through the mouse and keyboard. This window also overlaps all other displayed windows on the screen. The windows below the active window are stacked one on top of the other; this is illustrated in Figure 2-1. You can think of this stack of windows as being similar to a stack of paper. The piece of paper on the top of the stack is the topmost piece of paper. The next piece of paper is located below the topmost piece, the third piece down is located below the second one, and so on and so forth.

A Z-order defines where a window is currently at in the stack of windows. Making a window the active window will place it at the top of the Z-order. Using the Z-order, we can determine which window will be given the focus when the current window is minimized. The window given the focus will be the next window down, starting from the top of the Z-order.

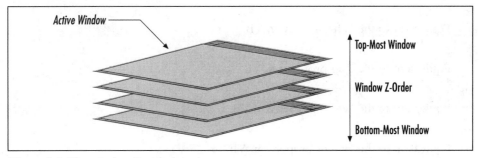

Figure 2-1. The window Z-order

The Z-order also describes the ordering of controls within a window. If two controls overlap and the first is higher on the Z-order than the second, the first control is drawn on top of the second control.

The Z-order can be manipulated through the *SetWindowPos* application programming interface (API) function. This is the VB declaration for this function:

```
Public Declare Function SetWindowPos Lib "user32" Alias "SetWindowPos" _
       (ByVal hwnd As Long, ByVal hWndInsertAfter As Long, _
       ByVal x As Long, ByVal y As Long, ByVal cx As Long, _
       ByVal cy As Long, ByVal wFlags As Long) As Long
```

Definitions of this function's parameters are:

hwnd
 The handle of the window being modified.

hWndInsertAfter
 The handle of the window that comes before this window in the Z-order. This argument also can take the following constants:

 HWND_BOTTOM (1)
  Places the window at the bottom of the Z-order.

 HWND_NOTOPMOST (-2)
  For topmost windows, places the window above all nontopmost windows (that is, behind all topmost windows). For nontopmost windows, the flag has no effect.

 HWND_TOP (0)
  Places the window at the top of the Z-order.

 HWND_TOPMOST (-1)
  Places the window above all nontopmost windows and maintains the window's topmost position, even if it loses the focus (an option typically indicated on menus as "always on top").

x

Equivalent to the Left property in VB.

y

Equivalent to the Top property in VB.

cx

Equivalent to the Width property in VB.

cy

Equivalent to the Height property in VB.

wFlags

Flags that specify the sizing and positioning attributes. If multiple flags are present, they can be logically `Ored` together. Some of the possible flags are:

SWP_DRAWFRAME *(32)*

Draws a frame around the window.

SWP_HIDEWINDOW *(128)*

Hides the window.

SWP_NOACTIVATE *(16)*

Does not activate the window. Otherwise, *SetWindowPos* by default activates the window.

SWP_NOMOVE *(2)*

Retains the window's current position (i.e., ignores the *x* and *y* parameters).

SWP_NOOWNERZORDER *(512)*

Leaves the owner window's position in the Z-order unchanged.

SWP_NOREPOSITION *(512)*

The same as the SWP_NOOWNERZORDER flag.

SWP_NOSIZE *(1)*

Retains the current window size (ignores the *cx* and *cy* parameters).

SWP_NOZORDER *(4)*

Retains the current Z-order (ignores the *hWndInsertAfter* parameter).

SWP_SHOWWINDOW *(64)*

Displays the window.

This function is successful when the return value is nonzero. You can set a window to be always on top in VB using the *SetWindowPos* function, as this code illustrates:

```
SetTopMostWindow = SetWindowPos(Form1.hwnd, HWND_TOPMOST, 0, 0, 0, 0, _
    SWP_NOMOVE OR SWP_NOSIZE)
```

When the Windows operating system is started, a desktop window is created. This is a special window on which all other windows are drawn. This window is also at the top of the window hierarchy. This window is the parent to all other top-level windows in the system.

A parent window can have one or more windows as its children. These child windows are contained within their parent window; that is to say, the child windows are drawn within the client area of the parent. A common example of a child window is a control that is placed on a form. The control is the child window and the form is its parent.

It is possible for a child window to have child windows of its own. A VB picture box control could have several button controls as its child windows, for example. These buttons would be drawn within the bounds of the picture box. Any button or part of a button located outside of the picture box would not be drawn (the bottom would be clipped). The button child controls would consider the picture box control their parent window, even though the picture box control is itself a child of a form. Child windows have these attributes:

- They must have a single parent window.
- They are drawn relative to the upper-left point in the parent's client area.
- They cannot have a menu.
- Any portion of the child window outside of the parent's client area is hidden or clipped.

Parent windows have these attributes:

- They can have many child windows.
- They can have a menu.
- They can be top-level windows.
- When a parent window is shown, destroyed, moved, or hidden, the same happens to the child window.

A *top-level window* is a window that has the desktop window as its parent window. Every window has a handle to its parent window. Top-level windows must have the desktop window handle as their parent window handle. Note that a parent window can be considered a top-level window, but a child window cannot. Top-level windows have these attributes:

- Only one top-level window can be active at any one time.
- An application can have more than one top-level window.
- When the user manipulates a child window (possibly a control), the top-level window associated with the child window (its parent) is activated.

The last window relationship I will discuss is the owner-owned relationship. Only top-level windows can be owned by or be owners of other top-level windows. Owned windows have these attributes:

- Owned windows are always higher in the Z-order than their owners.

- Owned windows are hidden when their owners are hidden.

- Owned windows are not hidden when their owners are minimized.

- Only top-level windows can be owner windows.

What Are All These Handles For?

All objects have a handle. A handle is simply a long datatype that contains a number identifying an object. To use an object in the Windows operating system, you first need to get its handle.

Handles are vital to using subclassing and hooks. When subclassing a window, the handle to that window must first be obtained. The hWnd property in VB makes this task a trivial one. This handle is then sent to a Win32 API function called *SetWindowLongPtr* to initiate as well as to remove the subclassing. *SetWindowLongPtr* is described in more detail in Chapter 3.

Handles are also vital to using hooks. All hooks, when installed, are identified by a hook handle. One of the more important uses for this handle is to remove the hook—failing to remove a hook before the application stops creates a nasty problem. A special type of hook called a system-wide hook uses a module handle to identify the dynamic link library (DLL) module that has installed the hook. System-wide hooks and their usage are a complex topic, and more discussion is devoted to it in Chapter 3.

In VB, forms and many controls have an hWnd property that contains the window handle. Also, several different API functions can be called from VB to get handles to various other objects. For our purposes, we will be using three main handles. They are the window handle (hWnd), the module handle (hModule or hInstance), and the hook handle (hHook). They are described next.

hWnd

The system assigns an hWnd to each window upon creation. Every window in the system has its own unique window handle. This handle is unique even across processes. A message uses this window handle to find its way to the destination window to which the message was directed. To illustrate, when a mouse is clicked over a button, the mouse-click event is converted into a message, and the hWnd of the button is included within the message structure. This message passes through the Windows messaging system and arrives at the window to which the event was first directed.

A window handle can be retrieved in VB by using the form or control's hWnd property. You also can use several Windows API functions to obtain an hWnd. The *FindWindow* API function is used to find a top-level window handle given a specific class name and window name. The *FindWindow* function is declared in VB as follows:

```
Public Declare Function FindWindow Lib "user32" Alias "FindWindowA" _
    (ByVal lpClassName As String, ByVal lpWindowName As String) As Long
```

The function's parameters are:

lpClassName
 A string that contains the window class name of the window being searched for

lpWindowName
 A string that contains the window name of the window being searched for

This function returns the hWnd of the first top-level window that matches the criteria. A zero is returned if this function finds no windows matching the specified criteria. If more than one window is found, the window highest in the Z-order is returned.

To obtain the handle to the desktop window, the *GetDesktopWindow* API function is used. This function is declared in VB as follows:

```
Public Declare Function GetDesktopWindow Lib "user32" _
    Alias "GetDesktopWindow" () As Long
```

This function takes no arguments and returns the desktop window handle.

Another useful function to obtain an *hwnd* is the *GetWindow* API function. This function is declared in VB as follows:

```
Public Declare Function GetWindow Lib "user32" Alias "GetWindow" _
    (ByVal hwnd As Long, ByVal wCmd As Long) As Long
```

Its parameters are:

hwnd
 The handle of a window used as a starting point.

wCmd
 Defines the relationship between the window provided by the *hwnd* argument and the window handle to be returned by this function.

A window handle is returned based on its relationship with the window provided in the *hwnd* argument. The relationship is determined by the *wCmd* constant; if no window meets the criteria defined by *wCmd*, the function returns either 0 or *hwnd*. The *wCmd* argument can contain any of the following values:

GW_CHILD *(5)*

The returned window handle is the first child window found in the Z-order.

GW_ENABLEDPOPUP *(6)*

The returned window handle is a pop-up window owned by the window represented by the *hwnd* argument. For Windows 2000 only.

GW_HWNDFIRST *(0)*

The returned window handle is the first in the Z-order with the same window type (topmost, top-level, or child) as the window represented by the *hwnd* argument.

GW_HWNDLAST *(1)*

The returned window handle is the last in the Z-order with the same window type (topmost, top-level, or child) as the window represented by the *hwnd* argument.

GW_HWNDNEXT *(2)*

The returned window handle is next in the Z-order with the same window type (topmost, top-level, or child) as the window represented by the *hwnd* argument.

GW_HWNDPREV *(3)*

The returned window handle is previous in the Z-order with the same window type (topmost, top-level, or child) as the window represented by the *hwnd* argument.

GW_OWNER *(4)*

The returned window handle is the owner of the window represented by the *hwnd* argument.

By first using the *GetDesktopWindow* or *FindWindow* function, you can obtain a handle that can be used by the *GetWindow* function to find a related window.

hInstance

An hInstance is a handle to a specific running instance of your application. Every application has an instance handle, which is provided by the system. If an application is running more than once on the same system, the instance handle to each application will be different to distinguish one instance from all other instances. This handle is passed into the window class structure during creation of a window to track which module created and registered a window. Also, when a DLL is linked to the application at runtime, it receives an instance handle from the system.

To obtain the instance handle of a VB application, use the App.hInstance property. You also can use the *GetWindowLong* API function to retrieve the instance handle of any VB or non-VB application. All that is needed for this function is a window handle belonging to the application whose instance handle you need. The *GetWindowLong* function is declared in VB as follows:

```
Public Declare Function GetWindowLong Lib "user32" _
        Alias "GetWindowLongA" _
        (ByVal hwnd As Long, ByVal nIndex As Long) As Long
```

Its parameters are:

hwnd

A window handle.

nIndex

A constant that determines the type of value that this function will return. The GWL_HINSTANCE constant (or –6) must be provided to the *nIndex* parameter to return the application's instance handle.

The following code fragment uses this function to return an instance handle of an application containing Form1:

```
Const GWL_HINSTANCE = -6
hInstance = GetWindowLong(Form1.hwnd, GWL_HINSTANCE)
```

Multiple instances of an application or DLL use the same code segment (assuming the base addresses where they are loaded into the process are the same), but they use different data segments. The hInstance handle is used to identify the data segments for each module. This means that it is possible for each DLL to use the same code but different sets of variables.

The hInstance handle is not global in scope, as is the case with the hWnd handle. This handle is valid only within a single process.

In Win32, an hInstance and an hModule are exactly the same. According to Microsoft's documentation, both the hInstance and the hModule point to the base address at which the executable (EXE) or the DLL module is loaded within the process.

One last point about handles. Never store the handle of an object in a global variable. This is because if the object is destroyed, the handle stored in the global variable will point to nothing. This will cause an error when using the invalid handle in your code. Other things could happen, such as the creation of a new object that's assigned this handle. This is possible because Windows reuses handle IDs. When using handles in your code, get the handle as late as possible and then use it. This will guarantee that the handle is valid when you use it.

hHook

Every hook that you create needs a handle that identifies it. Like the hWnd window handle, the hHook handle value is unique to the entire system. As the name implies, the hHook handle will be used only with hooks, not with subclassing.

To get a handle to a hook, we must use the *SetWindowHookEx* API function, the Win32 hook installation function; in other words, we retrieve the handle to a hook when that hook is defined. The *SetWindowHookEx* function is declared in VB as follows:

```
Public Declare Function SetWindowsHookEx Lib "user32" _
    Alias "SetWindowsHookExA" _
    (ByVal idHook As Long, ByVal lpfn As Long, _
    ByVal hmod As Long, ByVal dwThreadId As Long) As Long
```

It has the following parameters:

idHook

This is the identifier of the type of hook that is being installed (e.g., GetMessage hook, CBT hook, Debug hook, etc.)

lpfn

A pointer to the hook callback function.

hmod

The handle of the DLL containing the hook callback function. If this is NULL, the hook callback function is not contained within a DLL. Instead, it is contained in the application's (EXE's) code.

dwThreadId

The ID of the application thread that contains the hook callback function. If this is NULL, the hook callback function is contained within a DLL (see *hmod*).

The return value of this function is the handle to the newly created hook. This handle needs to be stored so that it can later be used to remove the hook. This is one case where you need to store a handle for later use. You can do this because you are in control of this handle's creation and destruction; the other handles mentioned here are controlled by the system.

Processes

Understanding processes inside and out is not a requirement for being able to learn and understand the material in this book, although a simple understanding is helpful. The information presented here on processes is only a high-level overview.

All applications require a process to run within. A process is a 4Gb virtual address space that contains the application, all its modules, the application's resources, and at least one thread of execution. The application's modules include such things as the main executable (**.EXE*), DLLs (**.DLL*), drivers (**.DRV*), and ActiveX controls (**.OCX*). Application resources include but are not limited to dialogs, fonts, files, handles to objects, and bitmap files. Threads are described in the next section.

Perhaps the most striking feature of a process is that everything encapsulated within it is considered private to the rest of the running processes. This keeps one process from invading one or more other processes and causing them to crash. There are, however, methods in Windows that provide the ability to pierce that veil of secrecy. Methods such as file mapping, injecting code (DLLs) into other processes, and other interprocess communication (IPC) techniques allow processes to communicate and interact with each other.

Threads

Threads operate only within a process. Each process has one main thread and potentially many other worker threads performing other tasks within the process. The threads within a process actually execute code; the process itself does not execute code. Every thread also has its own message queue. Actually, I should clarify this statement. Threads are created initially without a message queue; this is done to speed up system performance. A message queue is created only when the thread is about to use the User32 or GDI32 modules, as is done when a new window is created. Immediately before the first window is created, a message queue is created for that thread.

If more than one window is created in this thread, the message queue uses the hWnd element of the message structure to determine which window will receive each particular message. For more detail on Windows messages, see "Inside the Windows Messaging System" later in this chapter. For now, it's important to understand that only threads contain message queues; processes do not have message queues.

The Internals of a Window

Window has a broader meaning than the conventional use of the term. To the operating system, a window can be the desktop window, an application's top-level window, any child windows of the top-level window, dialog boxes, message boxes, or controls. The main similarity among these windows is that they all have a window procedure that can receive messages from its owning thread's message queue and act on them. All windows contain a default window procedure that is defined in the window class.

Using Spy++, we can provide evidence that controls placed on a window are in fact windows themselves. First, create a simple VB application with a few controls on it. Next, compile and run the application. Start Spy++ and press the CTRL+W keys to display the list of currently running windows. The top level of the window tree in Spy++ contains the Desktop, which is a window. The next level down contains a list of all top-level windows in the system. We can find our VB application's main window in this list and then drill down to the next level to view all its child windows. These child windows are the controls that we placed on the VB form. By double-clicking one of these control windows, we can view its Properties dialog box. In the dialog box, we notice that each control has its own window procedure, which we can see in the Window Proc field on the Class tab of the dialog box, as shown in Figure 2-2.

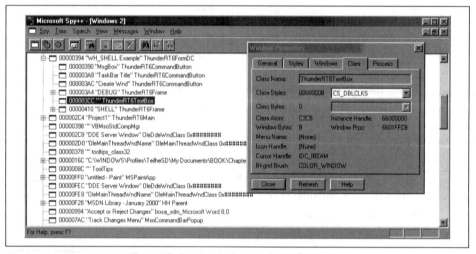

Figure 2-2. Spy++ output for a text box control in a VB application

The window class

Every window is created from something called a window class. This is somewhat similar to the type of class that we use in VB or C++, but it is not the same. A *window class* is nothing more than a structure of elements describing the base information that every window needs. This information consists of things common to all windows, such as the type of cursor to display, the window's icon, even the look and feel of the window itself. When we create a window in C/C++, we start by filling the `WNDCLASSEX` structure with the necessary information. The `WNDCLASSEX` structure is defined in Visual C++ as follows:

```
typedef struct _WNDCLASSEX {
    UINT        cbSize;
    UINT        style;
    WNDPROC     lpfnWndProc;
```

```
    int        cbClsExtra;
    int        cbWndExtra;
    HINSTANCE  hInstance;
    HICON      hIcon;
    HCURSOR    hCursor;
    HBRUSH     hbrBackground;
    LPCTSTR    lpszMenuName;
    LPCTSTR    lpszClassName;
    HICON      hIconSm;
} WNDCLASSEX, *PWNDCLASSEX;
```

This equivalent structure in VB is as follows:

```
Public Type WNDCLASSEX
    cbSize As Long
    style As Long
    lpfnWndProc As Long
    cbClsExtra As Long
    cbWndExtra As Long
    hInstance As Long
    hIcon As Long
    hCursor As Long
    hbrBackground As Long
    lpszMenuName As String
    lpszClassName As String
    hIconSm As Long
End Type
```

The members of the WNDCLASSEX structure are:

cbSize

The size of this structure.

style

A combination of class style constants ORed together. These styles determine the fundamental look and operation of a window created from this class. For example, the **CS_NOCLOSE** constant disables the Close option on the class's window menu, while the **CS_HREDRAW** constant forces a redraw of the window whenever the width of its client area changes.

lpfnWndProc

The function pointer to the window procedure for this class.

cbClsExtra

The amount of extra space to add to the end of the class structure. The developer uses this to store class-related information.

cbWndExtra

The amount of extra space to add to the end of the window structure. The developer uses this to store window-related information.

hInstance

> The instance handle of the module that contains the window procedure for this class.

hIcon

> The handle to an icon resource.

hCursor

> The handle to a cursor resource.

hbrBackground

> The handle to a brush or a color value used to paint the background of the window created from this class.

lpszMenuName

> The null-terminated string that defines the menu resource.

lpsqClassName

> The null-terminated string or class atom defining the name of the class. This value must be unique.

hIconSm

> The handle to the small icon resource.

After the WNDCLASSEX structure is defined, we register this class by using the *RegisterClassEx* API function. Its VB declaration is:

```
Public Declare Function RegisterClassEx Lib "user32" _
        Alias "RegisterClassExA" _
        (pcWndClassEx As WNDCLASSEX) As Integer
```

The single parameter to *RegisterClassEx* is:

pcWndClassEx

> A pointer to the WNDCLASSEX structure

This function returns a class atom, which is a unique identifier to the newly registered class. At this point, we can proceed to actually create a window of this class by calling the *CreateWindowEx* API function, the VB declaration for which is:

```
Public Declare Function CreateWindowEx Lib "user32" _
        Alias "CreateWindowExA" _
        (ByVal dwExStyle As Long, ByVal lpClassName As String, _
        ByVal lpWindowName As String, ByVal dwStyle As Long, _
        ByVal x As Long, ByVal y As Long, _
        ByVal nWidth As Long, ByVal nHeight As Long, _
        ByVal hWndParent As Long, ByVal hMenu As Long, _
        ByVal hInstance As Long, lpParam As Any) As Long
```

The parameters of *CreateWindowEx* are:

dwExStyle

A combination of extended window style constants ORed together. The constants include WS_EX_ACCEPTFILES, which indicates that the window accepts drag-drop files; WS_EX_CONTEXTHELP, which includes a question mark that appears in the window's title bar; WS_EX_DLGMODALFRAME, which creates a window with a double border; or WS_EX_MDICHILD, which creates an Multiple Document Interface (MDI) child window.

lpClassName

The class name or class atom returned by *RegisterClassEx*.

lpWindowName

If the window has a title bar, this is the window caption. If no title bar exists, this is the text for the control (e.g., the text string displayed for a checkbox).

dwStyle

A combination of window style constants and control style constants ORed together. Some style constants include WS_CAPTION, to create a window with a title bar; WS_DISABLED, to create a window that is initially disabled; WS_MAXIMIZEBOX, to include a maximize button on the window; or WS_SIZEBOX, to create a window that has a sizing border. Control constants include BUTTON, COMBOBOX, EDIT, LISTBOX, MDICLIENT, RICHEDIT_CLASS, SCROLLBAR, and STATIC.

x

Equivalent to the Left property of a VB window.

y

Equivalent to the Top property of a VB window.

nWidth

Equivalent to the Width property of a VB window.

nheight

Equivalent to the Height property of a VB window.

hWndParent

A handle to this window's parent or owner window.

hMenu

A handle to the default window's menu resource.

hInstance

The instance handle of the module that is associated with this window.

lpParam

> A pointer to user-defined data. This pointer is stored to the *lpCreateParams* member of the CREATESTRUCT structure, a structure generated by the operating system using the parameters passed to the *CreateWindowEx* function and, in turn, passed in the *lParam* parameter of the WM_CREATE message.

This function returns a handle to the window (hWnd), which allows us to manipulate the created window.

VB completely hides all the mechanics of window creation from the developer. It is easier to see how class and window creation works in Visual C++. Therefore, the code that follows will be written in Visual C++.

When writing a simple Windows application in Visual C++, you first create and register a new window class, as shown in Example 2-1. This class will be used to create the main window for our application. When the class is created, a function pointer to the window procedure for this new window needs to be provided in the *lpfnWndProc* member. For this example, the window procedure for this window will be the *WndProc* function. Finally, the class is registered using *RegisterClass*.

Example 2-1. Creating and Registering a Window Class

```
WinClass.lpszClassName = "NewWindowClass";
WinClass.lpfnWndProc = WndProc;
WinClass.style = CS_OWNDC | CS_VREDRAW | CS_HREDRAW;
WinClass.hInstance = hInstance;
WinClass.hIcon = LoadIcon( NULL, IDI_APPLICATION );
WinClass.hCursor = LoadCursor( NULL, IDC_ARROW );
WinClass.hbrBackground = (HBRUSH)( COLOR_WINDOW+1 );
WinClass.lpszMenuName = NULL;
WinClass.cbClsExtra = 0;
WinClass.cbWndExtra = 0;

RegisterClassEx( &WinClass );
```

Next, a window is created from this class and displayed, as shown in Example 2-2. The *CreateWindow* function is used to create the window. Because this function will not display the window, we have to use the *ShowWindow* API function to tell the window to display itself.

Example 2-2. Displaying a Window Created from a Window Class

```
hWnd = CreateWindowEx( WS_EX_LTRREADING,
            "NewWindowClass",
            "Main Window",
            WS_OVERLAPPEDWINDOW,
            0,
            0,
            CW_USEDEFAULT,
```

Example 2-2. Displaying a Window Created from a Window Class (continued)

```
            CW_USEDEFAULT,
            hOwner,
            NULL,
            hInstance,
            NULL );
```

```
ShowWindow( hWnd_Main, SW_SHOW );
```

ShowWindow is defined in VB as follows:

```
    Public Declare Function ShowWindow Lib "user32" Alias "ShowWindow" _
          (ByVal hwnd As Long, ByVal nCmdShow As Long) As Long
```

Its parameters are:

hwnd

> The handle of the window to be shown.

nCmdShow

> A constant specifying how the window is displayed. Constants include SW_
> FORCEMINIMIZE (for Windows 2000 only), SW_HIDE, SW_MAXIMIZE, SW_
> MINIMIZE, SW_RESTORE, SW_SHOW, and SW_SHOWDEFAULT.

This function returns a zero if this window was previously hidden. A non-zero value is returned otherwise.

You might be saying to yourself, "I've never had to do that in VB." That's because to create a window, VB must go through the process for you. VB developers are shielded from using a window class to create new windows. You can still access the class through VB using API functions such as *GetClassLong* or *SetClassLong*. Chapter 7 goes into depth on using these and other APIs to create a window class and, in turn, to create one or more windows from that class.

In the WNDCLASSEX structure, the window class element that we will focus on is *lpfnWndProc*. This is a pointer to the default window procedure that all windows must have to receive messages. The default window procedure defined here is pivotal in subclassing as well as in superclassing, another technique similar to subclassing. We will discuss both topics at length in Part II of this book.

Because all windows are created from classes, it stands to reason that some system-wide classes describe windows that are intrinsic to the Windows operating system. Table 2-1 lists these system-wide classes.

Table 2-1. System-wide Window Classes

Class Name	Description
Button	The button class
ComboBox	The combo box class

Table 2-1. System-wide Window Classes (continued)

Class Name	Description
Edit	The edit control class
ListBox	The list box class
MDIClient	The MDI client window class
ScrollBar	The scroll bar class
Static	The static control class
ComboLBox	The list box class that is contained in a combo box
DDEMLEvent	The DDEML events class (Windows NT/2000)
Message	The message-only window class (Windows 2000)
#32768	The menu class
#32769	The desktop window class
#32770	The dialog box class
#32771	The task switch window class
#32772	The icon titles class (Windows NT/2000)

These classes are created by the operating system and can be used by every running process. These classes cannot be destroyed by an application. This type of class has a system-wide or global scope—hence its name, system-wide class. This means that any application or DLL currently running in the system can use most of these classes to create new windows. (Even though the last eight items in Table 2-1 are system-wide, they are available only to the system. The developer cannot use these classes to create windows.)

There are two more types of classes, each having a more limited scope. The first type of class is the *application global class*. This class is created and registered by a module (DLL or EXE) within the process by placing the CS_GLOBALCLASS constant in the *style* element of the WNDCLASSEX structure. This type of class is registered and used only within a single process. All modules within that process have the ability to create new windows using this type of class.

The second type of class is the local class. The local class is created and registered by a single module (EXE or DLL). This type of class is available only to the module that registered it. Excluding the CS_GLOBALCLASS constant from the *style* member of the WNDCLASSEX class structure allows you to create this type of class.

When you are using the SPY++ program to watch your VB applications, you will notice that VB uses classes prepended with the word "Thunder". Looking at Figure 2-3, you can see that there are several Thunder classes:

ThunderRT6FormDC
   The class for all VB forms.

ThunderRT6CommandButton

  The class for all VB buttons.

ThunderTR6TextBox

  The class for all VB text boxes.

ThunderRT6Main

  The class for the form that owns all VB top-level windows. This window is always hidden.

Depending on the version of VB you are using, ThunderRT5 or ThunderRT6 can be prepended to the class name. The letters in RT# denote the word "runtime", and the number denotes the version of VB. The number is not added for versions of VB earlier than 5. Also, when running in the IDE, there is no RT#, just the word Thunder. Thunder was the code name for VB when it was first being developed at Microsoft.

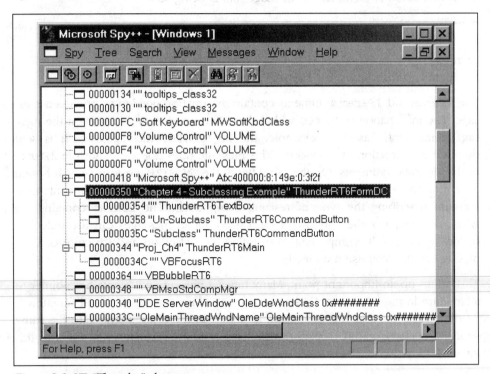

Figure 2-3. VB "Thunder" classes

The window procedure

All windows must have a window procedure to process incoming messages from their thread's message queue. A window procedure is basically a function that receives the window's message passed in as a Long, along with any parameters associated with the message as arguments. The body of this function is simply a

large case statement that provides the appropriate functionality for each message
that the developer is interested in. All window procedures have the following prototype:

```
LRESULT CALLBACK WindowProc(
    HWND hwnd,
    UINT uMsg,
    WPARAM wParam,
    LPARAM lParam
);
```

The window procedure has the following parameters:

hwnd

   The handle of the window to which the message is directed

uMsg

   A constant that identifies the message that is being sent

wParam

   Extra information that the message can contain

lParam

   Extra information that the message can contain

The *wParam* and *lParam* arguments contain information needed to process a message. The information contained within these two arguments depends on the message being sent. Take, for example, the WM_DESTROY message, which is sent
during the destruction of a window. This message does not use either the *lParam*
or the *wParam* arguments. On the other hand, the WM_SIZE message, which is sent
after a window has been resized, uses both arguments. The *wParam* contains a
constant describing the type of resizing being done. The *lParam* contains the
width and height of the window being resized. Other messages can use only one
of the arguments. It is important to examine the definition and structure of each
message so that you use it correctly.

This brings up an important point. Many times a message will contain a pointer to
a structure in the *wParam* or *lParam* arguments. The *CopyMemory* API function is
used to place the structure pointed to by either of these arguments into the same
structure declared in VB. The *CopyMemory* procedure declaration in VB is as follows:

```
Public Declare Sub CopyMemory Lib "kernel32" Alias "RtlMoveMemory" _
        (Destination As Any, Source As Any, ByVal Length As Long)
```

Its parameters are:

Destination

   The destination address to which the information is to be copied

Source
> The source address from which the information is to be copied

Length
> The length in bytes of the information to be copied

Example 2-3 is a short example using *CopyMemory* to get a structure returned from the *GetClassInfoEx* API function. The first four lines dimension the variables that are used. The **WNDCLASSEX** structure will be copied from memory using the pointer stored in the structOrigBttnClass variable and placed into the structCopy-BttnClass variable. The next line of code uses *GetClassInfoEx* to retrieve the class structure for the system-wide **BUTTON** class. The structOrigBttnClass variable now contains a pointer to the **WNDCLASSEX** structure. Before we can use this structure, we have to use the *CopyMemory* function to copy the structure pointed to by structOrigBttnClass into the structCopyBttnClass variable. The last line of code uses the structCopyBttnClass variable to retrieve the *lpfnwndproc* member data and place it into a separate variable.

Example 2-3. Using the CopyMemory Procedure

```
Dim structOrigBttnClass As WNDCLASSEX
Dim structCopyBttnClass As WNDCLASSEX
Dim m_OrigBttnWinProc as Long
Dim lRetVal As Long

'Get original Window's button class
lRetVal = GetClassInfoEx(App.hInstance, "BUTTON", structOrigBttnClass)

'Get a copy of its elements
CopyMemory structCopyBttnClass, structOrigBttnClass, LenB(structOrigBttnClass)

'Get original button window procedure and save it
m_OrigBttnWinProc = structCopyBttnClass.lpfnwndproc
```

CopyMemory also can be used for pointers to null-terminated strings that are passed back to VB applications. Understanding and using *CopyMemory* is a requirement for manipulating messages that contain pointers to structures as well as strings.

To resume our discussion of the window procedure, for a window procedure to be able to process messages, it must first be fed the messages. A message loop is used for this purpose. In short, a *message loop* runs for the entire lifetime of the thread to which it is attached. It continually checks the thread message queue for messages and then passes them on to the window procedure. I will explain this in more detail later in this chapter. For now, Example 2-4 shows the Visual C++ code used to create a message loop.

Example 2-4. A Message Loop

```
while( GetMessage( &msg, NULL, 0, 0 ) ) //Get msg from queue
{
    TranslateMessage( &msg ); //Necessary for keyboard input
    DispatchMessage( &msg ); //Sends msg to window procedure
}
```

In a Visual C++ application, a window procedure looks something like Example 2-5. In a real-world application, the `switch` statement (analogous to a VB `Select Case` statement) would handle many more messages.

Example 2-5. A Window Procedure

```
LRESULT CALLBACK WndProc( HWND hWnd,
                UINT umsg,
                WPARAM wParam,
                LPARAM lParam )
{
    switch ( umsg )
    (
        case WM_COMMAND:
            //Do work here
            break;
        case WM_DESTROY:
            PostQuitMessage( 0 );
            return 0;
        default:
    }

    return( DefWindowProc( hWnd, umsg, wParam, lParam ));
}
```

As you can see, most of the *WndProc* window procedure is taken up by a `switch` statement. Hundreds of messages can be passed to a window procedure. In a real-world application written in C++, a window procedure could become very large.

A very important observation must be made about this window procedure. Notice that, by default, the *DefWindowProc* API function is called at the very end of this window procedure. This function is declared in VB as follows:

```
Public Declare Function DefWindowProc Lib "user32" _
        Alias "DefWindowProcA" _
        (ByVal hwnd As Long, ByVal wMsg As Long, _
        ByVal wParam As Long, ByVal lParam As Long) As Long
```

Its parameters are:

hwnd

The handle of the window to which the message is directed.

uMsg

A constant that identifies the message that is being sent.

wParam

Extra information that the message can contain. This value is determined by the message.

lParam

Extra information that the message can contain. This value is determined by the message.

The return value also depends on the message. As you might notice, these arguments are the same in number and type as the arguments in the *WndProc* window procedure. These arguments are simply passed through to this function. This function calls the *default window procedure*, which provides the minimum functionality for all windows.

Window procedures, for nearly all messages, must call the default window procedure. Failing to do so can mean that certain messages might not be handled correctly. The previous code example for the WndProc function calls *DefWindowProc* after processing the WM_COMMAND message, but not after the WM_DESTROY message. The WM_DESTROY message calls *PostQuitMessage*, which simply informs the thread that it is time to be destroyed. At this point, any of this window's child windows are first destroyed, then the window is deactivated, and keyboard and mouse input are not accepted. The window and any other objects it owns are finally removed from memory.

The *DefWindowProc* function is not called because, for this message, it would not be desirable to allow other actions to occur while this window is being destroyed. During the process of destroying a window, the hWnd of that window also is destroyed. The *DefWindowProc* might cause other messages to be fired off that can slow down or interfere with the destruction process. Potentially, messages could be waiting in the message queue to be processed by the window procedure relating to this hWnd. If a message ends up in the thread's message queue with the handle to a window that has been destroyed, a General Protection Fault (GPF) could occur when the message loop tries to process this message.

On the other hand, if certain messages are not passed on to the default window procedure, the application might not behave correctly. Imagine trying to resize or move a window when the resize and move messages are not being passed on to the default window procedure for processing. It would seem as if the application was frozen. As you can see, it is imperative to pass the messages on to the default window procedure, unless you handle all the low-level functionality of the default window procedure in the window procedure you develop. This is not recommended.

When a system, mouse, or keyboard event sends a message to a specific window, it is handled by the window procedure for that window. The procedure can perform some action based on the message, or if the messaged is not handled, it is passed on to the default window procedure through the *DefWindowProc* API function for default processing.

It is interesting to note that when more than one window is created from a single class, each window has the same window procedure. This is because the class member *lpfnWndProc*, which is inherited by each window, is pointing to the same memory location. Now this procedure is what makes our window functional. Unfortunately, this window procedure is not as readily available to the VB developer to be modified as it is to the Visual C++ developer. To override or change the default behavior of a window, we need to subclass the window—or, in other words, to change the *lpfnWndProc* member to point to a window procedure that we create.

Creating a simple window application with Visual C++

Because VB tends to obscure most of the details of a Windows application's operation, it is useful to look at the Visual C++ code for a very simple application that displays a plain window, which is shown in Example 2-6. The application consists of only two functions. The first, the *WinMain* function, is the entry point to a Windows application. This function is called by the system, which provides values as arguments of this function as well. The function's arguments are:

hIinstance
  The instance handle for the current instance of the application.

hPrevInstance
  Win32 applications always set this to NULL.

lpszCmdLine
  The command line parameters passed in to this application.

nCmdShow
  Determines how this window is initially displayed to the user.

The second function, *WndProc*, is the application's window procedure.

Example 2-6. A Simple Windows Application Written in C++

```
int PASCAL WinMain( HINSTANCE hInstance,
            HINSTANCE hPrevInstance,
            LPSTR lpszCmdLine,
            int nCmdShow )
{
    WNDCLASS WinClass;
    MSG msg;
    HWND hWnd;

    WinClass.lpszClassName = "NewWindowClass";
    WinClass.lpfnWndProc = WndProc;
```

Example 2-6. A Simple Windows Application Written in C++ (continued)

```
    WinClass.style = CS_OWNDC | CS_VREDRAW | CS_HREDRAW;
    WinClass.hInstance = hInstance;
    WinClass.hIcon = LoadIcon( NULL, IDI_APPLICATION );
    WinClass.hCursor = LoadCursor( NULL, IDC_ARROW );
    WinClass.hbrBackground = (HBRUSH)( COLOR_WINDOW+1 );
    WinClass.lpszMenuName = NULL;
    WinClass.cbClsExtra = 0;
    WinClass.cbWndExtra = 0;

    RegisterClassEx( &WinClass );//Register this class

    HWnd = CreateWindowEx( WS_EX_LTRREADING,
            "NewWindowClass",
            "Main Window",
            WS_OVERLAPPEDWINDOW,
            0,
            0,
            CW_USEDEFAULT,
            CW_USEDEFAULT,
            hOwner,
            NULL,
            hInstance,
            NULL );

    ShowWindow( hWnd, SW_SHOW ); //Show the created window

    while( GetMessage( &msg, NULL, 0, 0 ) ) //Get msg from queue
    {
        TranslateMessage( &msg ); //Necessary for keyboard input
        DispatchMessage( &msg ); //Sends msg to window procedure
    }

    return msg.wParam;
}

LRESULT CALLBACK WndProc( HWND hWnd,
                UINT umsg,
                WPARAM wParam,
                LPARAM lParam )
{
    switch ( umsg )
    {
        case WM_COMMAND:
            //Do work here
            break;
        case WM_DESTROY:
            PostQuitMessage( 0 );
            return 0;
        default:
    }

    return( DefWindowProc( hWnd, umsg, wParam, lParam ));
}
```

Inside the Windows Messaging System

The messaging system is at the core of the Windows operating system. Without messages, the operating system would be about as useful as a pile of rocks. Subclassing and hooks operate on the messaging system; this is why it is so important to understand messaging as it applies to the Windows operating system. In this section, I will discuss each separate mechanism within the messaging system to give you an idea of how these pieces relate and operate together to send messages from a source to a destination window. Figure 2-4 shows how the messaging system works.

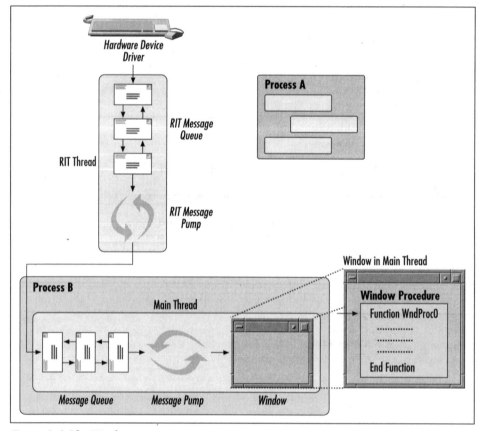

Figure 2-4. The Windows messaging system

The Raw Input Thread

The operating system upon bootup creates one thread for itself, called the *raw input thread* (RIT). There is only one of this type of thread in the system. This thread contains a system message queue used to receive hardware events such as mouse clicks and keyboard keypresses. It can collect events from these hardware devices through device drivers. A *device driver* is basically a type of DLL that acts as the translator between the hardware device and the Windows system. This allows hardware devices to communicate with the system. A device driver sits and waits for input from the hardware device for which it is associated. After it gets some type of input, it interrupts the system and sends a hardware event to the system message queue on the RIT. The RIT takes the hardware event off of its system message queue and converts it to a standard Windows message. The RIT posts the message to the correct thread's (or threads') message queue. The last step in the process is for the thread's message queue to deliver the message to the correct window procedure.

Let's take, for example, a mouse-button click that is generated by the user. The mouse driver gathers information about the mouse and places it into a **MSG** structure, defined as follows:

```
typedef struct tagMSG {
    HWND    hwnd;
    UINT    message;
    WPARAM  wParam;
    LPARAM  lParam;
    DWORD   time;
    POINT   pt;
} MSG, *PMSG;
```

The **MSG** structure has the following elements:

hwnd

The handle of the window to which the message is directed.

message

The message to be passed to this window. All window messages are constants, which are defined in the Win32 Software Development Kit (SDK) header files. The header files *WINUSER.H* and *WINABLE.H* contain most of these constants.

wParam and lParam

Many messages make use of the *wParam* and *lParam* elements to pass in extra information to the receiving window procedure. This extra information depends on the message. For example, it could indicate which mouse button was pressed, or if the Ctrl key was pressed in combination with the currently pressed key. Some messages need to pass much more information than is possible with the *wParam* and *lParam* arguments. To get around this limitation, some messages have special structures associated with them. Pointers to these structures are passed in either the *lParam* or *wParam* elements.

Each message has its own identity—that is, the way one message fills in the **MSG** structure is not the way every message will fill it in. Most messages have their own information that must be passed on to the receiving window. There-fore, become familiar with the message that you are going to be trapping before you write the code or you might be in for a surprise.

time

Represents when the message was posted. *time* is equal to the number of clock ticks since the computer has been running. So, to find the amount of time that has elapsed between messages, just subtract the previous message's time member from the current message's time member. The time member will play an important role when we start using journal hooks.

pt

A pointer to a POINT structure. The *pt* member points to a structure containing the mouse cursor coordinates when this message was generated.

To continue with our example, the window handle to the window on which the mouse was clicked is placed in the *hwnd* member. The appropriate message identifier is placed in the *message* member of this structure. In this case, it would be the WM_LBUTTONDOWN message. Information about the area of the window that the mouse was over when the click was generated and which mouse button was pressed is placed in the *wParam* and *lParam* members. The *time* member contains the time that this message was sent. The *pt* member contains the mouse coordinates at the point in time when the mouse button was clicked. This MSG data item is then sent to the RIT system message queue. When the RIT detects this message being sent to its system message queue, it wakes up and processes that message. The RIT then broadcasts this message to all Windows message queues. The message loop for each message queue determines if this message needs to be processed and, if so, which window will do the processing. The *hwnd* member of the MSG structure is used to determine which window procedure will process this message.

The System Message Queue

The system message queue is a single queue that is part of the raw input thread that receives messages from the keyboard, mouse, and other hardware devices via the hardware's device driver. It is similar to a thread's message queue.

Thread Message Queues

A single message queue is contained within each thread of a process. This message queue receives messages from within the thread, from other threads, and from the RIT. The message queue is basically a *doubly linked list*, with each node in the list containing a single message. This is illustrated in Figure 2-5. A doubly linked list consists of nodes that contain pointers to both the previous node in the list as well as the next node in the list. Using these pointers, it is possible to traverse the linked list in both a forward and backward direction.

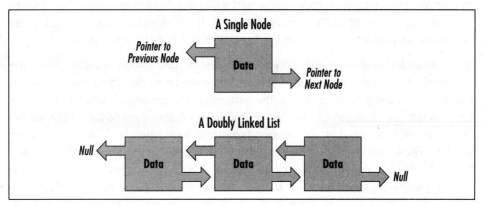

Figure 2-5. The Windows message queue as a doubly linked list

The message queue also acts as a First In First Out (FIFO) queue. Therefore, messages are pulled from the queue in the same order as they were put into the queue. Mechanisms are in place which allow messages to be skipped or even removed without being sent to a window. These mechanisms are accessed through the *GetMessage* API function.

Message Loops

The message queue itself only queues up messages; it does not send them anywhere. The thread needs a way to get these messages from the queue and send them to the correct window. This is where the message loop—sometimes called the message pump—enters the picture. The message loop is what enables the messages to be sent from a thread's message queue to the correct window procedure within that thread. As previously mentioned, a typical message loop looks like this in Visual C++:

```
while( GetMessage( &msg, NULL, 0, 0 ) )
{
    TranslateMessage( &msg );
    DispatchMessage( &msg );
}
```

These loops are constantly polling the message queue for messages that relate to windows within the thread. After a message is found, it is sent to the correct window. The message loop uses the *hWnd* element of the message structure (the message structure is introduced in the next section) to identify which window to send the message to. As usual, VB hides this functionality from the developer as well.

Even though only three lines of code are in the message loop, a lot goes on here. First, the while loop will run for the life of the thread. This is because *GetMessage* will always return a non-zero value, which evaluates to true in Visual C++, except when it receives a WM_QUIT message. The WM_QUIT message returns a zero and causes the loop to be exited. After the loop is exited, the thread terminates.

The *TranslateMessage* API function relates only to messages originating from the keyboard. This function translates virtual key messages into character messages, which are in turn posted back into the same thread's message queue. This means that when a key is pressed, a virtual key message combination of WM_KEYDOWN followed by WM_KEYUP is sent to the message queue associated with that window by the RIT. These messages contain the virtual key code identifying the pressed key on the keyboard. *TranslateMessage* will create a WM_CHAR message. This message is then placed back on the queue from which the WM_KEYDOWN and WM_KEYUP messages originated. This information will become more useful as we start hooking keyboard messages.

Lastly, the *DispatchMessage* API function is called. The *DispatchMessage* function does exactly that: it dispatches the message to the window with the same hWnd as in the message structure. If the hWnd is NULL, *DispatchMessage* ignores the message and returns. If hWnd is equal to HWND_TOPMOST, all top-level windows in the system—and not just within the process—will receive this message.

Messages

A message has the structure:

```
typedef struct tagMSG {
    HWND    hwnd;
    UINT    message;
    WPARAM  wParam;
    LPARAM  lParam;
    DWORD   time;
    POINT   pt;
} MSG, *PMSG;
```

The MSG structure elements were defined earlier in this chapter in the section "The Raw Input Thread."

If you compare the arguments of the window procedure with the MSG structure, you will notice two arguments missing in the window procedure. The *time* and *pt* values are not sent to the window procedure. Fortunately, two API calls allow you to retrieve the *time* and *pt* elements information manually; they are *GetMessageTime* and *GetMessagePos*.

The Different Types of Messages

There are many different types of messages in the Windows operating system. The message constants contained in the message element of the MSG structure have a prefix followed by an underscore and then the name of the message. For example, messages relating to the combo-box control are prefixed by CB, while messages relating to mouse, keyboard, clipboard, scrollbar, and several other controls have the prefix WM. A list of message prefixes appears in Table 2-2.

Table 2-2. Windows Message Prefixes

Prefix	Message Type	Prefix	Message Type
ABM	Application desktop toolbar	MCM	Month calendar control
BM	Button control	PBM	Progress bar
CB	Combo-box control	PGM	Pager control
CBEM	Extended combo-box control	PSM	Property sheet
CDM	Common dialog box	RB	Rebar control
DBT	Device	SB	Status bar window
DL	Drag list box	SBM	Scroll bar control
DM	Default push-button control	STM	Static control
DTM	Date and time picker control	TB	Toolbar
EM	Edit control	TBM	Trackbar
HDM	Header control	TCM	Tab control
HKM	Hot key control	TTM	Tooltip control
IPM	Internet protocol (IP) address control	TVM	Tree-view control
LB	List box control	UDM	Up-down control
LVM	List view control	WM	General window

Performance Considerations

When implementing subclasses and hooks, performance is a critical factor. Too much code executing within a hook or a subclassed window could easily bring performance down below an unacceptable level. Keep this in the front of your mind when writing the code to handle subclassing and hooks. System-wide hooks have the most potential to degrade performance. I will discuss where these performance bottlenecks can arise as we progress through this book.

3

The Basics
of Subclassing
and Hooks

This chapter will introduce how subclassing and hooks operate. I will use bits and pieces of code, instead of complete examples, so that we can focus on the basics of hooking and subclassing. The finer details of the code will be covered in the remainder of this book.

This chapter is broken up into two sections. The first section deals with subclassing and how it works, as well as what it is useful for. The second section deals with the hooking mechanism in a similar fashion. Of the two languages I use, I will focus as much as possible on Visual Basic (VB) and use Visual C++ only when VB has reached its limits.

What Is Subclassing?

The idea behind subclassing is simple; implementing it is not so simple. Subclassing is, in simple terms, the creation of a new window procedure, which is inserted into the message stream just before the default window procedure that every window initially starts out with. I use the term *message stream* to denote the path a message takes from its source to its destination.

This is not to say that subclassing is not dangerous when implemented incorrectly or without regard to other processes running in the operating system. But by understanding the messaging system and following its rules, we can safely use subclassing.

The dangers of subclassing are what stop many programmers from learning and using subclassing in their projects. The foremost danger with subclassing is causing a General Protection Fault (GPF). GPFs are critical errors that will either cause your application/system to stop functioning or cause the application/system to shut down. If you are running an application in the VB IDE and it causes a

GPF, not only is the application shut down, but also the IDE. This is because both are running in the same process, and a GPF will cause that process to terminate.

Several things cause GPFs. They include:

- Using a pointer variable that points to an invalid location in memory
- Trying to read from memory that is not accessible from the application (e.g., in a separate process memory space)
- Trying to write to memory that is not accessible from the application (e.g., in a separate process memory space)
- Reading or writing past an array or string boundary
- Incorrectly calling a dynamic link library (DLL) function

GPFs are elusive problems for the VB programmer to track down; in fact, they're even elusive problems for the C++ programmer to track down. That is why using tools such as NuMega Bounds Checker and Microsoft Spy++ (which are discussed in Chapter 1) are necessary when tracking down hard-to-find problems such as these.

The most prevalent reason that GPFs are caused in subclassing or hooking applications is the use of invalid pointers. An *invalid pointer* is a variable that contains the address to a memory location that was not allocated correctly by the application. Subclassing and hooking rely heavily on pointers—specifically, on function pointers used to access callback functions, and on pointers to data returned in a message argument. Visual Basic developers ordinarily do not have to deal with pointers in the same way as Visual C++ programmers do. Pointers are well hidden in the VB environment. But through the manipulation of message parameters and the use of more advanced application programming interface (API) functions, the VB developer soon finds herself neck-deep in pointers. Take, for example, the *GetClassInfoEx* API function that was introduced in Chapter 2. The third and final argument to this function is a pointer to a **WNDCLASSEX** structure. Without knowledge of how to use the *CopyMemory* API function to get to the structure, the VB programmer is lost.

Another reason for GPFs in these types of applications is that VB uses Windows API functions extensively to make subclassing and hooking work. Making a simple error in calling an API function could easily result in a GPF. Errors in calling API functions usually occur because of declaring or calling an API function incorrectly. Two of the most common sources of errors in calling Win32 API functions include:

- Failing to use **ByVal** correctly in the declaration of an API function
- Passing in a string to an API function that is not correctly terminated with a **NULL**

As I take you through each step of the process, I will point out the pitfalls and potential trouble areas that you will encounter. However, by reading this book and following its guidelines for subclassing, you will gain the skills needed to safely incorporate subclassing and hooking into your applications.

How Does Subclassing Work?

As I said, subclassing involves inserting a user-defined window procedure right before the default window procedure is called.

So, the object that we are subclassing must have a window procedure. This means that we will be dealing with windows—though the term "window" is to be understood very broadly: we can subclass a VB form as well as a button, combo box, or even a scrollbar. ActiveX controls we create ourselves through VB also can be subclassed just like any other window in the operating system can.

There are two caveats pertaining to the previous paragraph. For a window to be subclassed it must have a window handle (hWnd). This hWnd is sent as an argument to the *SetWindowLongPtr* API function, which will be described in detail later in this chapter. If the control has no hWnd, the call to *SetWindowLongPtr* will fail. Windowless (or lightweight) controls do not have window handles and therefore cannot be subclassed. The following controls have no window handle and are considered windowless:

- Label

- Line

- Shape

- Image

- WLCheck Control (contained in *MSWLess.OCX* shipped with VB 6)

- WLCombo Control (contained in *MSWLess.OCX* shipped with VB 6)

- WLCommand Control (contained in *MSWLess.OCX* shipped with VB 6)

- WLFrame Control (contained in *MSWLess.OCX* shipped with VB 6)

- WLHScroll Control (contained in *MSWLess.OCX* shipped with VB 6)

- WLVScroll Control (contained in *MSWLess.OCX* shipped with VB 6)

- WLList Control (contained in *MSWLess.OCX* shipped with VB 6)

- WLOption Control (contained in *MSWLess.OCX* shipped with VB 6)

- WLText Control (contained in *MSWLess.OCX* shipped with VB 6)

The second caveat is that any window outside of the process that is performing the subclassing cannot be subclassed. In other words, process A cannot subclass a window in process B. This is because the address space of a process is off limits to all other processes. This limitation protects applications from writing or reading memory within another application's address space. Doing so could cause a GPF, which would crash the offending application, and possibly others.

As we saw in Chapter 2, all windows derive from a window class. This window class has the *lpfnWndProc* element in its structure. *lpfnWndProc* is a pointer to a function—that is, it contains the address of a function, in this case the address of the default window procedure that was created when the window class was registered. (Function pointers will be discussed in greater depth in Chapter 4.) Every message directed to this window will be sent to the window procedure pointed to by the *lpfnWndProc* function pointer. This function pointer is the key to subclassing. Our main mission is to change the *lpfnWndProc* function pointer to point to a window procedure that we create. Figure 3-1 illustrates this part of the process. As Figure 3-1 shows, the default window procedure is not destroyed. It still plays an active role in handling messages.

Before we modify the *lpfnWndProc* function pointer, we need to have a function for it to point to. So, the first bit of code we need to write is our own window procedure. This custom code is responsible for handling all messages or just specific messages in the way that you want, and, by implication, in a way that's different from the default window procedure. (Otherwise, what would be the point of subclassing?) This code usually takes the form of a large **Select Case** statement, which we'll omit in this chapter. It does not matter what we call the procedure, so I'll use the generic name of *WinProc*. The parameters and return value are very important to the proper operation of this new window procedure. Remember, the message loop will be calling our new window procedure, so it expects the same function signature as the default window procedure. As we saw in Chapter 2, the default window procedure has the following C language prototype:

```
LRESULT CALLBACK WindowProc(
    HWND HWND,        // handle to window
    UINT uMsg,        // message identifier
    WPARAM wParam,    // first message parameter
    LPARAM lParam     // second message parameter
);
```

We can translate this into VB as follows:

```
Public Function WinProc( _
        ByVal hwnd As Long, _
        ByVal uMsg As Long, _
        ByVal wParam As Long, _
        ByVal lParam As Long) As Long

End Function
```

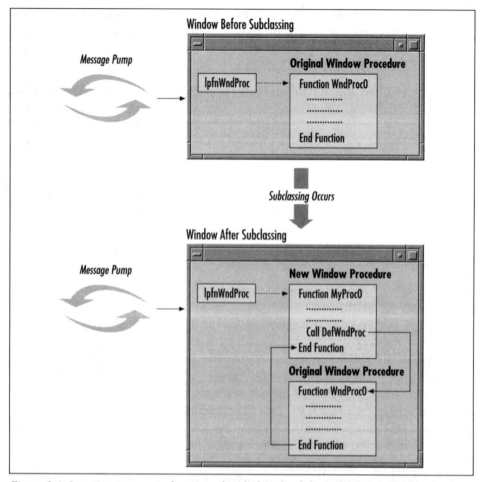

Figure 3-1. Inserting a new window procedure before the default window procedure during subclassing

Of course, this function has no code, so it is pretty much useless at this point. In fact, it can be worse than useless, as we will see a little later; this function can cause some or all open applications to stop responding to input.

Now we have a new window procedure, but no way of using it. To use it, we need to place it before the default message procedure in the message stream. For this purpose, we can call the *SetWindowLongPtr* API function, which modifies a particular attribute of a specific window. (The Win16 and Win32 APIs also include another function, *SetWindowLong*, that you can use to insert your new window procedure. However, we do not recommend its use because it makes conversion to 64-bit Windows difficult. See the sidebar on 64-bit compatibility later in this section.) The VB declaration for the *SetWindowLongPtr* API function is:

```
Declare Function SetWindowLongPtr Lib "user32" Alias "SetWindowLongA" _
        (ByVal hwnd As Long, _
        ByVal nIndex As Long, _
        ByVal dwNewLong As Long) As Long
```

The function has the following parameters:

hWnd

> The handle of the window whose attribute is to be modified. It can be obtained by retrieving the value of a form or control's hWnd property.

nIndex

> A Long indicating the window attribute to be modified. A number of values are possible, though the value used to replace a window procedure is GWLP_WNDPROC, or −4. (Note that you must use the **Const** statement to define the constant yourself if you choose to use it.)

dwNewLong

> The replacement value. For a subclassed window, this parameter represents the address of the new window procedure. You can get the address of your new window procedure by passing its name as an argument to the **AddressOf** operator.

If the call to *SetWindowLongPtr* succeeds, the function returns the original value before replacement (in this case, the original address of the window procedure). If it fails, it returns zero.

The way this function is used to subclass a window is shown below:

```
Private lOrigWinProc as Long

Sub Form1_Load()
    lOrigWinProc = SetWindowLongPtr(Form1.hwnd, _
        GWLP_WNDPROC, AddressOf WinProc)
End Sub
```

This code subclasses the Form1 window in a VB application. The first argument to *SetWindowLongPtr* is the handle to the window to be subclassed. The second argument is the GWLP_WNDPROC constant, which tells *SetWindowLongPtr* that we are going to replace the pointer to the window procedure of the Form1 window. The value of GWLP_WNDPROC is −4. The third argument is the pointer to our new window procedure. This last argument uses the **AddressOf** operator, introduced in VB 5, to provide a pointer to our new window procedure function. (The **AddressOf** operator is what VB developers were waiting for to use function callbacks and subclassing in their applications without relying on third-party products. We will discuss it in greater depth in Chapter 4.) After the *SetWindowLongPtr* function has succeeded, it returns the window's original window procedure pointer. Do not change or discard the value of this pointer, or else the original

64-bit Compatibility

To make your applications portable to the upcoming 64-bit Windows operating system, you must follow some simple rules. Before continuing, you might want to install the latest Platform Software Development Kit or SDK (there is also a new Platform Device Driver Kit, or DDK) from the Microsoft web site at *http://msdn.microsoft.com.* This is a rather large file, but you can download and install only the pieces that are of interest to you. If you are going to program solely in the VB environment, it is optional for you to download this information. Be forewarned, though, that any documents containing 64-bit Windows topics are subject to change.

Microsoft is making the transition from 32-bit to 64-bit as easy as possible for the developer. Theoretically, if you follow these seven rules, your code should compile and run on both platforms. These rules are geared toward the Visual C++ developer. The rules are as follows:

1. Pointers cannot be cast to `int`, `long`, `ULONG`, or `DWORD` types.

2. If a 32-bit pointer is necessary, use only the *PtrToLong* and *PtrToUlong* functions in the *Basetsd.h* header file to truncate 64-bit pointers to 32-bit pointers. Note that converting a 64-bit pointer to a 32-bit pointer is extremely dangerous because the upper half of the pointer's information is removed.

3. Take care when casting a pointer returned from an API function. Casting a returned pointer could corrupt it.

4. Using the `DWORD` datatype for polymorphic input parameters to a function will cause problems; instead, use the `UINT_PTR` or `PVOID` datatypes.

5. Replace these API calls:

   ```
   GetWindowLong
   SetWindowLong
   GetClassLong
   SetClassLong
   ```

   with these API calls:

   ```
   GetWindowLongPtr
   SetWindowLongPtr
   GetClassLongPtr
   SetClassLongPtr
   ```

6. When accessing the extra bytes of a class or window, use the `FIELD_OFFSET` macro to get the offset value for the data you need. The *cbClsExtra* and *cbWndExtra* members of the `WNDCLASSEX` structure allocate memory for these extra bytes.

—Continued—

7. LPARAM, WPARAM, and LRESULT are all 64 bits wide. Do not use DWORD, ULONG, UINT, INT, int, or long datatypes with these types because they might truncate them.

The most obvious change between 32-bit and 64-bit systems is the datatypes. A 32-bit pointer is 32 bits wide; a 64-bit pointer is 64 bits wide. This allows for a great deal more memory to be accessed by a single process—16 terabytes, to be exact.

The new Platform SDK also contains a syntax checker which works with the Visual C++ compiler to detect problems in your code that will make it difficult to port from 32-bit code to 64-bit code.

As for VB developers, we currently need to make only one change to our code to allow us to run our applications on 32-bit as well as 64-bit Windows operating systems. The changed code is shown here:

```
#If Win32 Then
    Private Declare Function SetWindowLongPtr Lib "user32" _
        Alias "SetWindowLongA" _
        (ByVal hwnd As Long, ByVal nIndex As Long, _
      ByVal dwNewLong As Long) As Long
    Private Declare Function SetClassLongPtr Lib "user32" _
        Alias "SetClassLongA" __
        (ByVal hwnd As Long, ByVal nIndex As Long, _
      ByVal dwNewLong As Long) As Long
    Private Const GWL_HINSTANCE = (-6)
    Private Const GWL_WNDPROC = (-4)
    Private Const GWL_USERDATA = (-21)
    Private Const GWL_HWNDPARENT = (-8)
    Private Const GCL_MENUNAME = (-8)
    Private Const GCL_HBRBACKGROUND = (-10)
    Private Const GCL_HCURSOR = (-12)
    Private Const GCL_HICONSM = (-34)
    Private Const GCL_HMODULE = (-16)
    Private Const GCL_WNDPROC = (-24)
    Private Const DWL_MSGRESULT = 0
    Private Const DWL_DLGPROC = 4
    Private Const DWL_USER = 8
#ElseIf Not Win16 And Not Win32 Then
    Private Declare Function SetWindowLongPtr Lib "user32" __
        Alias "SetWindowLongPtrA" __
        (ByVal hwnd As Long, ByVal nIndex As Long, _
      ByVal dwNewLong As Long) As Long
    Private Declare Function SetClassLongPtr Lib "user32" _
        Alias "SetClassLongAPtrA" __
        (ByVal hwnd As Long, ByVal nIndex As Long, _
      ByVal dwNewLong As Long) As Long
    Private Const GWLP_HINSTANCE = (-6)
```

—Continued—

```
        Private Const GWLP_WNDPROC = (-4)
        Private Const GWLP_USERDATA = (-21)
        Private Const GWLP_HWNDPARENT = (-8)
        Private Const GWLP_ID = (-12)
        Private Const GCLP_MENUNAME = (-8)
        Private Const GCLP_HBRBACKGROUND = (-10)
        Private Const GCLP_HCURSOR = (-12)
        Private Const GCLP_HICONSM = (-34)
        Private Const GCLP_HMODULE = (-16)
        Private Const GCLP_WNDPROC = (-24)
        Private Const DWLP_MSGRESULT = 0
        Private Const DWLP_DLGPROC = 8
        Private Const DWLP_USER = 16
    #End If
```

SetWindowLongPtr and *SetClassLongPtr* are both defined to be in *User32.DLL* regardless of the platform. The only difference in the 32-bit and 64-bit VB API declarations is the alias, which points to the exported function name in *User32. DLL*. This code will allow your applications to port easily to the 64-bit Windows operating system.

Note that the Microsoft documentation for Win64 is subject to change; therefore, the code presented here also is subject to change.

window procedure will be lost. We need to keep this safely tucked away in the *lOrigWinProc* variable for use later.

OK, so now we have our own window procedure in place. This means that the *lpfnWndProc* function pointer is currently pointing to our new window procedure function called *WinProc*, and that the default window procedure will not be used. However, this is highly undesirable: the default window procedure contains the minimal amount of code required to use a window. For instance, the default window procedure contains the code to paint the window on the screen when it receives a WM_PAINT message. We need to make sure that this painting functionality works, or else the window will stop painting itself. We could handle this by adding all the necessary code to our own window procedure, though this is an unnecessary duplication of code. Instead, it's much easier and more efficient to simply send the WM_PAINT message on to the default message procedure.

In other words, to get the minimal functionality out of our new window procedure, we need to pass to the default window procedure the message that *WinProc*, our custom message handler, receives. This guarantees us that the default functionality of our Form1 window will still be in place when we use it. We can do this by calling the *CallWindowProc* API function, which is declared as follows:

```
Public Declare Function CallWindowProc Lib "user32" _
        Alias "CallWindowProcA" _
        (ByVal lPrevWndFunc As Long, _
        ByVal hWnd As Long, _
        ByVal Msg As Long, _
        ByVal wParam As Long, _
        ByVal lParam As Long) As Long
```

CallWindowProc has the following parameters:

lPrevWndFunc

A pointer to the window procedure to be called. In the case of our example, this is a pointer to the default window procedure that we saved in the *lOrigWinProc* variable when inserting the new window procedure into the message stream.

hWnd, Msg, wParam, and lParam

These parameters match perfectly, in number and in type, to the parameters in the *WinProc* function. They simply allow the message information to be passed on to the default window procedure.

This function's return value depends on the type of message (identified by the *Msg* argument) processed.

After inserting this function into our *WinProc* function, *WndProc* looks like this:

```
Public Function WinProc (ByVal hwnd As Long, _
                ByVal uMsg As Long, _
                ByVal wParam As Long, _
                ByVal lParam As Long) As Long

    'Select Case structure to handle messages goes here.

    WinProc = CallWinProc(lOrigWinProc, hwnd, uMsg, wParam, lParam)
End Function
```

With our custom window procedure in place, we can do some really powerful things. Every message directed to this window passes through this function. A `Select Case` statement can be set up to trap for certain messages, such as the `WM_MOUSEMOVE` message, or we can just monitor all messages coming into this window. Watching and even manipulating the messages that are passed to this function allow us more flexibility to develop powerful and feature-rich applications than by just using the events that VB makes available to us.

Messages can be handled in one of three different ways:

- The message can be ignored and passed through to the default window procedure, as in the code sample above.

- The message can be discarded so that it is not passed to the default window procedure at all. Be very careful, though, that in stopping the message from being passed on to the default window procedure you do not stop your application from functioning correctly.

• The message can be modified and passed on to the default window procedure. Not all messages should be modified.

Presumably, it is also possible to modify the message and not pass it on to the default message procedure, but that would accomplish nothing.

A message also can be passed on to the default window procedure at different times within our *WinProc* function:

• If we place the call to the *CallWinProc* API function after our message handling code, we can affect the message before it reaches the default window procedure. This is shown in the previous code example.

• If we place the call to the *CallWinProc* API function before our message handling code, the default functionality for the message remains intact. The code would then look like this:

```
Public Function WinProc (ByVal hwnd As Long, _
                         ByVal uMsg As Long, _
                         ByVal wParam As Long, _
                         ByVal lParam As Long) As Long

    WinProc = CallWinProc(lOrigWinProc, hwnd, uMsg, wParam, lParam)

    'Select Case structure to handle messages goes here.
End Function
```

After the default window procedure returns control to our *WinProc* function, we can examine the message as well as the state of the window to determine if anything more needs to be done.

The last part of subclassing involves removing the subclassed window procedure from the message stream. This must occur prior to unloading the window from memory or ending the application. In removing the subclassed window procedure from the message stream, the pointer to the original window procedure (represented in our example by *lOrigWinProc*) must be restored. Otherwise, the next time a message is directed toward that window and the window procedure is called, *lpfnWndProc* will point to an invalid memory location, and we all know what that means: GPF. To remove the new window procedure that we created, simply use the *SetWindowLongPtr* API function similarly to the way you used it to subclass the window but with a slight change. Instead of the last argument being **AddressOf WinProc**, as it was in the Form1_Load event, you need to supply the *lOrigWinProc* variable as an argument. The code is shown below:

```
Sub Form1_Unload()
    Dim lReturnValue as Long
```

```
        LReturnValue = SetWindowLongPtr(Form1.hwnd, GWLP_WNDPROC, lOrigWinProc)
    End Sub
```

After the original value that was in the *lpfnWndProc* element of the window class is restored, the window can be closed down safely.

That is how subclassing works. There is not much code involved here; most of the coding will deal with specific messages that the *WinProc* function is watching for. Chapter 4 will deal with the code involved in subclassing a window in more detail.

The Types of Subclassing

Our discussion of subclassing in the last section illustrated just one type of subclassing. However, you can choose from two different types of subclassing, which we'll examine in this section.

Instance subclassing

When we call the *SetWindowLongPtr* function, as we did in the previous section, we subclass a specific window denoted by the window handle passed to the *hwnd* parameter of *SetWindowLongPtr*. The window has already been created when we insert the new window procedure into the class structure. Therefore, we are only modifying a copy of the window class information associated with this particular window. This is called *instance subclassing*. Only one instance of the window has been subclassed.

For example, using *SetWindowLongPtr*, we can subclass Form1, as we did in the previous code samples. If this same project had a second form named Form2, that form would continue to rely exclusively on its original window procedure for message processing. It is not affected by the call to *SetWindowLongPtr* that replaced Form1's window procedure. To subclass Form2 correctly, some changes will have to be made to the original code. The new code to subclass both forms would look like this:

```
Sub Form1_Load()
    lOrigWinProc = SetWindowLongPtr(Form1.hwnd, _
            GWLP_WNDPROC, AddressOf WinProc)

    lOrigWinProc2 = SetWindowLongPtr(Form2.hwnd, _
            GWLP_WNDPROC, AddressOf WinProc)
End Sub
```

The new code makes two separate calls to *SetWindowLongPtr* for each window that is to be subclassed. Notice also that the original window procedure is saved into two separate variables (*lOrigWinProc and lOrigWinProc2*) so that each is not lost.

It is possible for the same subclassed window procedure, *WinProc*, to be used for both forms, or a second subclassed window procedure could be created for

Form2. This decision will depend on whether Form2's functionality will be the same as Form1's. If the *WinProc* function is used for both forms, it will be modified to look like this:

```
Public Function WinProc (ByVal hwnd As Long, _
                ByVal uMsg As Long, _
                ByVal wParam As Long, _
                ByVal lParam As Long) As Long

    'Select Case structure to handle messages goes here.

    If hwnd = Form1.hwnd then
        WinProc = CallWinProc(lOrigWinProc, hwnd, _
                    uMsg, wParam, lParam)
    ElseIf hwnd = Form2.hwnd then
        WinProc = CallWinProc(lOrigWinProc2, hwnd, _
                    uMsg, wParam, lParam)
    End If
End Function
```

This function uses the *hwnd* argument passed in to the *WinProc* function to determine which original window procedure should be called.

If a new subclass window procedure is created for Form2, it will look like this:

```
Public Function WinProc2 (ByVal hwnd As Long, _
                ByVal uMsg As Long, _
                ByVal wParam As Long, _
                ByVal lParam As Long) As Long

    'Select Case structure to handle messages goes here.

    WinProc2 = CallWinProc(lOrigWinProc2, hwnd, _
                uMsg, wParam, lParam)
End Function
```

Note that we need to pass `AddressOf WinProc2` instead of `AddressOf WinProc` to the *SetWindowLongPtr* function used to subclass Form2.

The code to remove the subclassing on both windows is as follows:

```
Sub Form1_Unload()
    Dim lReturnValue as Long

    lReturnValue = SetWindowLongPtr(Form1.hwnd, GWLP_WNDPROC, lOrigWinProc)

    lReturnValue = SetWindowLongPtr(Form2.hwnd, GWLP_WNDPROC, lOrigWinProc2)
End Sub
```

Global subclassing

Instead of supplying a new window procedure on a window-by-window basis, you can simply modify the window procedure of a window class directly; this technique is called *global subclassing*. It differs from instance subclassing in that the actual window class—and not the copy of the class information a window gets when it is first created—is being modified directly. This means that any window created with this modified class will automatically use the window procedure whose pointer you provided to this class. However, any windows that were created from this class before it was modified will use the original class's window procedure.

This confirms, incidentally, that when any window is created from a window class, that class's information is embedded into the newly created window structure. When we subclass a window, we modify the *lpfnWndProc* class element embedded in the window. When we globally subclass, we modify the *lpfnWndProc* element within the class itself. New windows created from this class will then inherit the changes to the class. Figure 3-2 illustrates global subclassing.

To globally subclass a window, you call the *SetClassLongPtr* function. The VB declaration of this function follows:

```
Public Declare Function SetClassLongPtr Lib "user32" Alias "SetClassLongA" _
    (ByVal hwnd As Long, ByVal nIndex As Long, _
    ByVal dwNewLong As Long) As Long
```

The *SetClassLongPtr* function has the following parameters:

hwnd

The handle to a window that was created using the class we want to modify. It can be obtained by retrieving the value of a form or control's hWnd property.

nIndex

A Long indicating the window attribute to be modified. A number of values are possible, though the value used to tell this function to modify the window procedure is GCLP_WNDPROC, or –24. (Note that you must use the Const statement to define the constant yourself if you choose to use it.)

dwNewLong

The replacement value. For a subclassed window, this parameter represents the address of the new window procedure. You can get the address of your new window procedure by passing its name as an argument to the AddressOf operator.

The return value of this function will be the original value in the class structure that was replaced with the value in the *dwNewLong* argument. For our purposes, this function will return either a zero if an error occurred, or the address of the original class window procedure if it was successful.

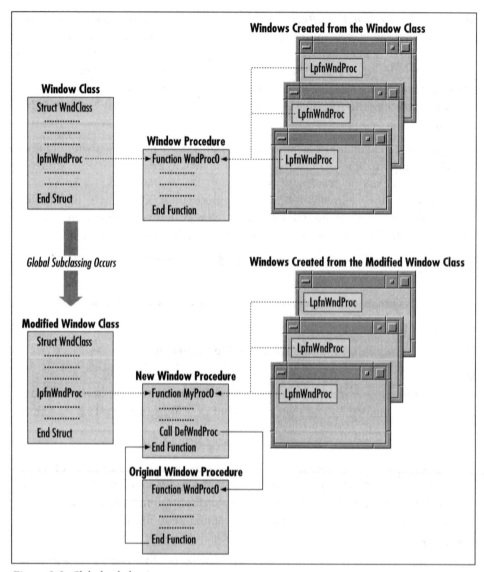

Figure 3-2. Global subclassing

The steps to perform global subclassing closely follow the steps for instance subclassing. This code will initiate global subclassing:

```
Private lOrigClsProc as Long

Sub Form1_Load()
    Load frmHidden

    lOrigClsProc = SetClassLongPtr(frmHidden.hwnd, _
        GCLP_WNDPROC, AddressOf ClsProc)
End Sub
```

The first line of this function will load a hidden form called frmHidden into memory. The hWnd of this form is used in the first argument to the *SetClassLongPtr* function. To use this function to modify a class's structure, we need to give it a handle to a window that was created using this class. The function uses this handle to get indirectly to the class structure in memory. This handle also is used when removing the global subclass. Therefore, this window is hidden to protect it from being closed by the user, which would render the hWnd needed for global subclassing invalid.

The last parameter of the *SetClassLongPtr* function sends the address of the *ClsProc* function that we define in our VB code. This function will basically look like this:

```
Public Function ClsProc (ByVal hwnd As Long, _
                ByVal uMsg As Long, _
                ByVal wParam As Long, _
                ByVal lParam As Long) As Long

    'Select Case structure to handle messages goes here.

    ClsProc = CallWinProc(lOrigClsProc, hwnd, uMsg, wParam, lParam)
End Function
```

Nothing is new here. Notice that the original class window procedure must be called here, as it is with instance subclassing. This ensures that the default processing will occur for any messages sent to this function.

The messages that pass through this function can be handled in one of three different ways, similar to instance subclassing:

- The message can be ignored and passed on to the *CallWinProc* function.
- The message can be discarded before calling the *CallWinProc* function.
- The message arguments can be modified and then passed on to the *CallWinProc* function.

The message also can be passed to the *CallWinProc* function at different times.

- The message can be processed and then sent to the *CallWinProc* function.
- The message can be sent to the *CallWinProc* function and then processed.

The final step to global subclassing is to restore the original class window procedure to the class with a code fragment such as the following:

```
Sub Form1_Unload()
    Dim lReturnValue as Long

    lReturnValue = SetClassLongPtr(frmHidden.hwnd, _
            GCLP_WNDPROC, lOrigClsProc)
End Sub
```

This function calls *SetClassLongPtr* using the same window handle that was used to initiate global subclassing. The only difference is that the address of the original class window procedure is being passed into the last argument of this function, thus restoring the class to its original state.

Global subclassing brings with it a whole new set of uses as well as problems. Chapter 4 will deal with this subject more thoroughly.

Superclassing

We can go one step further and create our own window class that inherits from an existing window class. This is called *superclassing*. You create this new window class by filling in a new window class structure with the information obtained from an existing class. The existing class most likely is a class that Windows provides.

When filling the new class structure with the existing class's information, it is imperative to retrieve and save the original class's `lpfnWndProc` function pointer because it provides our new class with the essential base functionality. The other class elements can be filled with data needed to define the new window class. In particular, the `lpszClassName` element of the new window class structure must contain a unique string that will define this class. From this newly created class, we in turn use the technique of global subclassing to change the `lpfnWndProc` window procedure function pointer to point to a new window procedure that we define. Figure 3-3 illustrates superclassing.

The new class—or, as it is sometimes called, the superclass—should have a unique class name, with a single exception; it is also possible to name this superclass with one of the system-wide class names listed here:

Button
> The button control class

ComboBox
> The combo-box control class

Edit
> The edit control class

ListBox
> The list box control class

MDIClient
> The MDI client window class

ScrollBar
> The scroll bar control class

Static
> The static control class

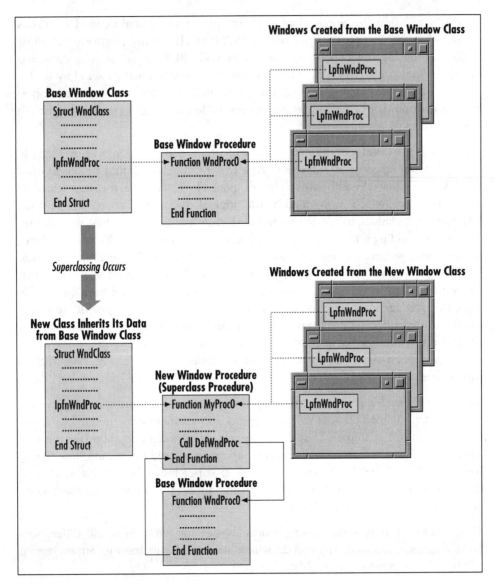

Figure 3-3. How superclassing works

For example, I could create a superclass with the name of BUTTON, which is an existing system-wide class name. When I create a window from a BUTTON class, the system searches the process for any local classes with a class name of BUTTON before searching for any system-wide classes with this name. The order in which Windows will search for classes is:

1. Any application local classes with the same class name within the process

2. Any application global classes with the same class name within the process

3. All system-wide classes

Windows will find the application local- or application global-defined BUTTON superclass before it finds the system-wide BUTTON class. This, in effect, will allow us to override the functionality of the system-wide BUTTON class. The danger is that the system-wide BUTTON class can never be used to create a window in this process; instead, the superclass will always be used. If a new version of the operating system modifies or removes this system-wide class, the superclass might not work correctly, if at all.

Superclassing a developer-defined class (which is a superclass in and of itself) in an application is generally redundant. A new window class should be based on a window class that already exists. This original class will give the new class its default behavior, which is provided by the original class' window procedure. If we now use superclassing to create another new class using the class that we just created, we are adding a new layer of complexity to our application. This added layer can be a maintenance nightmare, especially if the developers maintaining the code have no documentation to inform them how the code is supposed to work. It can also hurt performance because now when a message is sent to a window of this class, the message must be passed from the superclassed window procedure to the developer-defined class window procedure and then passed once more to the original class's window procedure. In a sense, you are superclassing a class which has already been superclassed (Class B superclasses a base class A; class C then superclasses Class B).

Instead, the developer should look for a way of using superclassing to modify only a system-defined class. If the two superclasses cannot be merged into a single superclass in our example of superclassing a developer-defined class (i.e., class B merged with class C), a second, separate superclass should be created, one that is based on the original base class (i.e., class B superclasses base class A, class C superclasses base class A). This will lessen the application's complexity and keep performance at an acceptable level.

This is basically how superclassing works. Notice the similarities and differences between Figure 3-3 and Figure 3-2, which illustrated subclassing. Superclassing will be discussed more thoroughly in Chapter 7.

Why Do We Use Subclassing?

We use subclassing to add or modify the functionality of any application window (and most VB controls) when that functionality cannot be added or modified in a robust way by using the VB language alone. Some examples of subclassing include:

- Adding text to the status bar that describes which menu item the mouse is currently over.

- Indicating what part of a window's non-client region the mouse is over. This could be the title bar, the Close button, a window border, etc. Note that the MouseOver event in a VB form captures mouse events only in the client area of the form, not in the nonclient area.

- Restricting the user's ability to move or resize a form or dialog.

- Instead of writing new code to mimic the common dialog controls, you can subclass them and add your own functionality, such as a file viewer for the Open dialog box that allows you to preview specific types of files.

- Windows can be monitored to determine when they become active or inactive.

- Through subclassing, you can modify the way a window is drawn by capturing the paint messages (`WM_DRAWITEM`, `WM_PAINT`, `WM_NCPAINT`, etc.).

- Pop-up menus displayed when right-clicking text boxes can be replaced with menus of your own design.

- An application similar to Spy++ can be developed to watch messages sent to a particular window or windows within a single process.

What Are Hooks?

The Microsoft documentation defines hooks in this manner:

> A *hook* is a point in the system message-handling mechanism where an application can install a subroutine to monitor the message traffic in the system and process certain types of messages before they reach the target window procedure.

One more thing should be added to this definition. The addition I have made is in italics:

> A *hook* is a point in the system message-handling mechanism where an application can install a subroutine to monitor the message traffic in the system and process certain types of messages before they reach the target window procedure, *as well as after they are processed by the target window procedure.*

The subroutine that is installed at a hook point is typically called a *filter function*. A filter function is analogous to a window procedure in that it can receive and process messages. When these filter functions are placed into the message stream at a hook point by using the *SetWindowHookEx* API function (which will be defined later in this chapter), it is called *installing* a hook. A *hook point* is a system-defined point in the message stream at which a filter function can be installed. These hook points cannot be changed.

Hooks are similar to subclassing in that both intercept messages, although this is where most of the similarities end. You might think of hooks as extensions to subclassing. If a problem cannot be solved with subclassing, look into using hooks to augment or even replace subclassing. It is highly possible that several hooks could be used in combination to solve a problem.

The fundamental characteristic of all types of subclassing is that a new developer-defined window procedure is created which intercepts messages before the original window procedure has a chance to receive them. This new window procedure then decides how to handle the message and whether it will be passed on to the original window procedure.

Hooks intercept messages at various set locations in the operating system. The WH_GETMESSAGE hook can intercept messages immediately before they arrive at their destination window procedure, similar to subclassing. The WH_CALLWNDPROCRET hook can intercept messages after being processed by a window procedure. The WH_JOURNALRECORD hook intercepts messages after being sent from the raw input thread (RIT) but before they arrive at their destination thread's message queue.

Hooks have more specific functionality than subclassing does. The WH_CBT hook is a good illustration of this. Although this hook can be used for several different types of tasks, it was created to make the process of creating computer-based training (CBT) applications easier and more robust. This hook can be used to watch the actions a user performs in the system. The hook can then give feedback to the CBT application about whether the user is performing the action correctly. The hook accomplishes this by capturing messages relating to window activation, creation, destruction, minimization, maximization, movement, and sizing, as well as mouse and keyboard activity. This is just a sampling of the messages that this hook can receive.

Table 3-1 presents many of the similarities and differences among subclassing and hooking.

Table 3-1. Comparison Between Subclassing and Hooking

Subclassing	Hooks
Intercepts messages.	Intercepts messages.
The basic steps are to write a subclassed window procedure, call *SetWindowLongPtr* or *SetClassLongPtr* to initiate subclassing, and then use the same function to terminate the subclassing.	The basic steps are to write a hook filter function, call *SetWindowsHookEx* to install the hook, and then use *UnhookWindowsHookEx* to terminate the hooking.
Can cause serious GPFs if implemented incorrectly.	Can cause serious GPFs if implemented incorrectly.
Can pass messages on to the original window procedure of the subclassed window.	Can pass messages on to the next hook in a chain of hooks.

Table 3-1. Comparison Between Subclassing and Hooking (continued)

Subclassing	Hooks
Captures every type of message that is bound for its window.	Specific types of messages can be captured, or every message in the system can be captured.
All window procedure functions accept these arguments: *hwnd*, *Msg*, *lParam*, and *wParam*.	All hook filter functions accept these arguments: *code*, *lParam*, and *wParam*.
Subclassing is performed at one point in the system, immediately before the original window procedure.	Hook points are located at various places spread throughout the messaging system.
Windows in a separate process cannot be subclassed.	Hooks can operate on a single window in a process, or on all windows in all processes.
Uses a subclassed window procedure to process messages.	Uses a hook filter function to process messages.
The subclassed window procedure is a callback function.	The hook filter function is a callback function.
A single window can be subclassed multiple times.	A single hook can have multiple filter functions chained to it.

There are 15 different types of hooks to choose from. There is also a 16th hook called WH_HARDWARE, but it is not currently implemented in Windows. The 16 documented hook types are:

WH_CALLWNDPROC

Called before a message reaches a window procedure.

WH_CALLWNDPROCRET

Called after a window procedure finishes processing a message.

WH_CBT

Captures messages that make it easier for the developer to create CBT applications.

WH_DEBUG

Called every time another hook function is about to be called. This hook function is always called first, which makes it useful in debugging hook function calls.

WH_FOREGROUNDIDLE

Called when there are no pending messages in the current thread's message queue.

WH_GETMESSAGE

Called immediately before the *GetMessage* or *PeekMessage* API functions return a message.

WH_JOURNALRECORD

Captures all mouse and keyboard messages before they can arrive at their destination window procedure.

WH_JOURNALPLAYBACK

Plays back the messages recorded with the WH_JOURNALRECORD hook.

WH_KEYBOARD

Captures specific keyboard messages after they are posted to a thread's message queue but before they are processed by a window procedure.

WH_KEYBOARD_LL

Captures specific keyboard messages before they are posted to a thread's message queue.

WH_MOUSE

Captures mouse messages after they are posted to a thread's message queue but before they are processed by a window procedure.

WH_MOUSE_LL

Captures specific mouse messages before they are posted to a thread's message queue.

WH_MSGFILTER

Called whenever a dialog box, a message box, a scrollbar control, or a menu receives a message. This hook also is called when the user presses the ALT+TAB or ALT+ESC keys. This hook receives these messages only for a single thread.

WH_SYSMSGFILTER

The system-wide or global hook equivalent to WH_MSGFILTER. This filter receives messages from all threads running in the system.

WH_SHELL

Called when an action is performed on a top-level window.

WH_HARDWARE

Not implemented in Win32.

It should be noted that low-level hooks—those with _LL appended to the hook name—are available only in Windows 2000 and Windows NT Service Pack 3 or higher.

Each hook resides at various places throughout the Windows messaging system. All hooks are placed by the operating system and cannot be moved to a different spot in the messaging system. Think of a hook as an opening in the messaging system. As messages flow throughout the operating system, they pass through one or more of these hook points or *openings*. A hook alone is useless to the developer unless a filter function is attached to the hook. A filter function is similar in concept to the *WinProc* window procedure that we created in the subclassing section. The filter function is then attached to the hook. At this point, any messages that go through this hook are passed on to the attached filter function before being sent on to their next destination. Hooking is illustrated in Figure 3-4.

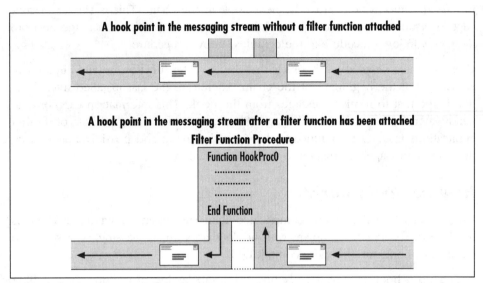

Figure 3-4. A hook point in the system before and after a filter function is attached to it

If more than one application attaches a filter function to a hook, the filter functions are chained together. This is called a *filter function chain*; it is illustrated in Figure 3-5.

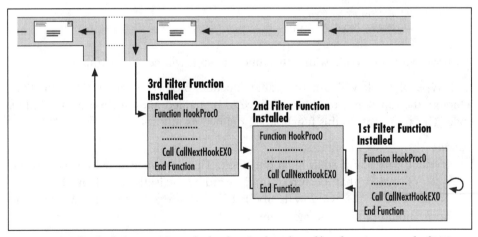

Figure 3-5. A hook chain in action; the hook point has three filter functions attached to it

The operating system maintains this filter chain internally so that we do not have to bother checking for the existence of other filter functions and inserting and removing our filter functions from the chain. The only thing we have to remember is that other applications might have installed filter functions to the same hook that we are using. Thus, when we are done processing in our filter function, we need to pass the information on to the next hook in the chain. This is similar in concept to a subclassed window passing the information about the message on from the new window procedure to the default window procedure.

One additional detail about hooks is that the last filter function installed in a chain is installed at the beginning of the chain. Therefore, the last installed filter function is the first to receive messages from the hook. This information can come in handy later if you install more than one filter function for a single hook, or if other applications install a filter function that is misbehaving and possibly not relaying the correct message information to your filter function.

How Do Hooks Work?

Using hooks is a little more complicated than subclassing a window. There is much more flexibility and power with hooks than with subclassing, so it stands to reason that hooks will be more complicated.

Setting up a hook is similar to setting up a subclassing procedure. First, a filter function needs to be written. Although a filter function is similar to a window procedure, the parameters it takes are completely different. A filter function has the following prototype:

```
Public Function MessageProc(
       ByVal uCode As Long, _
       ByVal wParam As Long, _
       lParam As Long) As Long
End Function
```

For now there is no code within this function, so it will not do anything.

Each type of hook will use this same function prototype for its filter function, although the function itself does not have to be named *MessageProc*, as it is in this code. The arguments to this function are defined as follows:

ucode

Identifies an action specific to the hook. This argument usually specifies the type of action that occurred (e.g., window activation), when the action occurred (e.g., the window is about to be destroyed), or even whether the hook should process the message.

wparam

The value is dependent on the type of hook. This argument usually contains information relating to a message such as an hWhWndnd, virtual key code, system command value, or ID of the captured message.

lparam

>   The value is dependent on the type of hook. This argument usually contains a pointer to a structure that relates to the message that was captured.

Next, after the filter function has been written, the hook needs to be installed. This is done using the *SetWindowsHookEx* API function. This API function is declared in VB as follows:

```
Declare Function SetWindowsHookEx Lib "user32" Alias "SetWindowsHookExA" _
                        (ByVal idHook As Long, _
                        ByVal lpfn As Long, _
                        ByVal hmod As Long, _
                        ByVal dwThreadId As Long) As Long
```

Its parameters are as follows:

hHook

>   A constant that defines the type of hook procedure that we are installing.

lpfn

>   A pointer to the filter function that we have previously written.

hmod

>   If the hook filter function resides in a DLL, this argument contains the handle to this DLL. The DLL handle can be obtained in a VB application through the **App.hInstance** property. If the hook filter function resides in the application code and not in a DLL, this argument is set to **NULL**.

dwThreadId

>   If the hook filter function resides in the application code and not in a DLL, this argument is set to the thread ID in which the hook filter function resides. If the hook filter function resides in a DLL, this argument is zero.

>   VB standard EXE applications are single-threaded by default. To get the ID of the thread that contains the hook filter function, you use **App.ThreadID**. If a VB application uses the *CreateThread* API function to spawn multiple threads, the **App.ThreadID** property will return the thread ID of the currently executing thread (the topic of creating threads in VB is beyond the scope of this book). In other words, if a VB application creates two threads and separate calls to **App.ThreadID** are made in each thread, you will get back two different thread IDs. To get the thread ID of the thread containing the code for the hook filter function, you must call **App.ThreadID** within the same thread that contains the hook filter function. If a thread terminates, its ID is no longer valid.

>   For a Visual C++ application, the *GetCurrentThreadID* API function also will return the ID of the currently running thread. *GetCurrentThreadID* takes no arguments and returns a Long value, which is the thread ID.

If the call to *SetWindowsHookEx* is successful in installing the filter function in the filter function chain, the return value will be a handle to the hook's filter function. If *SetWindowsHookEx* returns a zero, an error has occurred.

We use this API function as shown below to install a message filter hook:

```
Private hHook as Long

Sub Form1_Load()
    hHook = SetWindowsHookEx(WH_MSGFILTER, _
                 AddressOf MessageProc, _
                 0, _
                 App.ThreadID)
End Sub
```

hHook is a variable of type Long that stores the returned hook handle. We will need it to access the handle stored to this variable in the filter function and in the function responsible for unhooking the filter function from the hook point.

We also need to add a function to our filter function that will call the next filter function in the chain. This is the *CallNextHookEx* API function, which is declared in VB as shown:

```
Private Declare Function CallNextHookEx Lib "user32"_
        (ByVal hHook As Long, _
        ByVal ncode As Long, _
        ByVal wParam As Long, _
        lParam As Any) As Long
```

The function has the following parameters:

hHook
> The handle to the hook. This hook handle is returned by the *SetWindowHookEx* function.

ncode
> A constant identifying the hook code.

wParam
> The *wParam* argument passed into the hook filter function. The value of this argument is dependent on the message that it is associated with.

lParam
> The *lParam* argument passed into the hook filter function. The value of this argument is dependent on the message that it is associated with.

The return value is dependent on the type of hook that is installed.

This API function is similar to the *CallWinProc* API function used in subclassing. It will pass on this filter function's parameters to the next filter function in the chain, if there is one. You never know if someone else has already installed a filter function for the same hook as you have, so to be polite, we pass the parameters on to the next filter function.

When this function is placed in the filter function, it will look like this in our code:

```
Public Function MessageProc(ByVal uCode As Long, _
    ByVal wParam As Long, _
    lParam As Long) As Long
    'Code to handle messages goes here.

    MessageProc = CallNextHookEx(hHook, uCode, wParam, lParam)
End Function
```

This filter function will intercept messages, but it does not do anything useful with them.

Hooking, like subclassing, allows you to do one of three things with the intercepted message:

- The message information can be ignored and passed through to the next hook function in the chain.

- The message can be discarded so that the next filter function in the chain will not be called. This could be very dangerous because another application might already have a filter function installed for this same hook and it might need to know about the message that you just discarded.

- The message information can be modified and passed on to the next filter function in the chain. Not all hooks allow you to modify the message's information, though.

As with most things in Windows, after you use it, you must clean up after yourself. After all, we don't leave the refrigerator door open after getting out a glass of milk. So, too, must we always be careful to clean up after ourselves when using hooks. To release a filter function from the hook chain gracefully, we must use the *UnhookWindowsHookEx* API function. The VB declaration of this API function is:

```
Private Declare Function UnhookWindowsHookEx Lib "user32" _
    (ByVal hHook As Long) As Long
```

Its single parameter is:

hHook

The handle to the hook. This hook handle is returned by the *SetWindowHookEx* function.

The code to unhook the filter function is shown below:

```
Sub Form1_Unload()
    Dim lReturnVal As Long
    lReturnVal = UnhookWindowsHookEx(hHook)
End Sub
```

The *UnhookWindowsHookEx* API function will remove the hook's filter function from the chain that is associated with the hook handle *hHook*. Remember, the handle *hHook* was returned by the *SetWindowsHookEx* API function.

These are the basics of using a hook. Though the mechanics of creating and releasing a hook are the same regardless of hook type, each of the 15 types of hook functions are very different from one another, and all play unique roles within the system. In Part III of this book, I have dedicated a chapter to each hook function to further discuss their application and operation.

Hook Scope

A hook can be installed to intercept messages for one thread in one process or for all threads in all processes running in the system. The scope of a hook depends on where it resides (in an application or a DLL) and how it is created with the *SetWindowsHookEx* API function. The third and fourth parameters of this function determine the scope of the hook.

Thread-specific

When a hook only intercepts messages that pertain to a single thread, the hook has thread-specific scope. These hooks can reside in a DLL but usually reside in the application (EXE). The thread-specific hooks we will be installing using VB will reside in the application's EXE code, not in a DLL. Thread-specific hooks must set the *hmod* parameter of the *SetWindowsHookEx* function to zero, meaning that the hook filter function will be located within the code running in a thread inside the application. The *dwThreadId* parameter is set equal to the thread ID of the application that will install the filter function.

Hooks that can have thread-specific scope are:

- WH_CALLWNDPROC
- WH_CALLWNDPROCRET
- WH_CBT
- WH_DEBUG
- WH_FOREGROUNDIDLE
- WH_GETMESSAGE
- WH_KEYBOARD
- WH_MOUSE
- WH_MSGFILTER
- WH_SHELL

System-wide

Hooks that can intercept messages dispatched to all threads in the system are considered to have global or system-wide scope. The filter functions for these types of hooks must be contained within a Win32 DLL.

To create a system-wide hook, *SetWindowHookEx* is called with the *hmod* argument set to the DLL handle and the *dwThreadID* argument set to NULL. Setting the *dwThreadID* argument to NULL informs the system that this hook should be installed for every thread running in every process. If this argument is set to a valid thread ID, the system installs a hook specifically for the thread having this ID. When the system creates this hook, it injects or maps the DLL with the handle found in the *hmod* argument into every running process on the system. To be more precise, when the system is alerted that a system-wide filter function needs to be called for the first time by a thread, the system will determine if the DLL containing the hook filter function has been mapped into the process containing that thread. If it cannot be located, it is mapped into the process at this point. This allows each process to have its own mapping of the hook filter function code contained within the DLL.

Now that a DLL is injected into every process that is running in the system, we have the problem of removing or unmapping the DLL from each process space when we remove the hook. Fortunately, Windows takes care of this for us when *UnhookWindowsHookEx* is called. This function iterates through every process that is currently running in the system and decrements the locks held on each DLL by one. If no other resource holds a lock on the DLL, it is automatically unmapped from the process space.

All hooks can have system-wide scope. The following hooks, however, can be used only as system-wide hooks:

- WH_JOURNALPLAYBACK
- WH_JOURNALRECORD
- WH_MOUSE_LL
- WH_KEYBOARD_LL
- WH_SYSMSGFILTER

Why Do We Use Hooks?

Hooks, like subclassing, are used to augment applications with functionality that can't be programmed through standard techniques. If it were not for hooks, some system features would be inaccessible to the VB programmer and, to a lesser extent, to the Visual C++ programmer.

Hooks allow us to write programs that:

- Provide function key support to dialog boxes within our application, including messages boxes, which are a special type of modal dialog box.

- Record and play back mouse actions and keystrokes, similar to the macro recorder found in Microsoft Excel and Microsoft Word.

- Watch for one or more messages within an application or the system, and act on just those specific messages. Programs of this type, such as Spy++, make extensive use of hooks.

- CBT applications would be difficult, if not impossible, to create without using special hooks designed for CBT applications.

- Automated testing applications are another type of application that uses many of the hooks in Windows.

- Subclassing a window in another process can be mimicked by using hooks.

As you can see, there are many good uses for hooks.

Deciding Between Hooking or Subclassing

When deciding whether to implement subclassing or hooking, there are many factors to consider. Each technique has its own pros and cons. One of the main factors to consider is performance. A system-wide hook is the worst offender. There are two big performance detractors for this type of hook. The first is that the hook will incur processing overhead for each application in the system, regardless of whether the application makes use of the hook. Remember, the DLL containing the hook function is injected into every running process on the system. The second problem is that a system-wide hook will serialize all messages that pertain to the specific hook. This means that instead of messages going directly into the message queues, they are first routed through the installed hook's filter function, which resides in the DLL. These messages pass through the DLL in a serialized fashion, one after the other.

Thread-specific hooks can be serious offenders as well, but the performance hit is about the same as with subclassing. This is because both techniques involve capturing messages for only one particular thread. This places significantly less stress on the system than capturing messages for every running thread in the system. Instance subclassing offers the best performance of the various techniques because only messages for a single window are captured.

Table 3-2 and Table 3-3 detail the main pros and cons of using hooks and subclassing.

Table 3-2. Pros and Cons of Using Hooks

Pros	Cons
Allows VB access to more powerful functionality not otherwise available.	Degrades performance more than subclassing.
Can operate on a single window in a process.	System-wide hooks must be placed in a Win32 DLL, which is injected into every process which calls the hook filter function.
Can operate on multiple windows in multiple processes.	The Win32 DLL used in system-wide hooking cannot be forcibly removed from each process after the hook is uninstalled.
Fifteen different types of hooks can be utilized.	If a preceding hook does not pass a message along to your hook, it will never know that the message was sent.
More than one filter function can be installed for a single hook.	
It is possible to, in effect, subclass a window in a separate process by using the WH_ GETMESSAGE hook.	

Table 3-3. Pros and Cons of Using Subclassing

Pros	Cons
Allows VB access to more powerful functionality not otherwise available.	Can operate only on windows within a single process.
Are less of a burden on the system than hooks.	Can possibly degrade performance.
A single window can be subclassed multiple times.	If critical messages are not passed back to the original window procedure, the application might seem as if it is frozen.
Multiple windows of the same class can be subclassed with a single call to *SetClassLongPtr.*	Multiple windows having different classes cannot be subclassed with a single call to *SetClassLongPtr;* this function must be called separately for each class.
A single class can be subclassed using global subclassing or superclassing.	

Regardless of how sound your choice of technique, though, badly written code will cause any of these techniques to greatly degrade performance. Each of the chapters in Part II and Part III also will show where performance can be affected by incorrectly or poorly written code.

II

Subclassing and Superclassing

In this section, we'll explore techniques for subclassing windows, dialog boxes, and ActiveX controls. In addition, we'll explore the related technique of superclassing. Finally, because subclassed and superclassed applications are often unstable because of the developer's failure (for whatever reason) to follow all the rules of subclassing and superclassing, we'll examine techniques for debugging an application and detecting what is causing the application to behave in unintended ways.

4

Subclassing

This chapter takes you deeper into the subject of subclassing, starting off with a discussion of the `AddressOf` operator. A fair amount of discussion is given to this operator because it plays a pivotal role in using Visual Basic (VB) to subclass windows. Presented next will be the two types of subclassing—instance and global subclassing. Their similarities, differences, and applications are discussed at length. Code examples will be presented for both types of subclassing. These examples are meant to be for illustration only; such things as error handling code will be omitted for clarity.

As we progress through this chapter I will be placing the key points and rules of subclassing in bold type. These points and rules will be summarized at the conclusion of the chapter.

The AddressOf Operator

The `AddressOf` operator, first introduced in Version 5 of VB, gave developers limited access to pointers, a feature that VB effectively hides from them but that is essential to high-end development environments such as Visual C++. The `AddressOf` operator greatly increases the potential of a VB application. As we shall see, though, there are always bumps in the road when implementing more advanced functionality, and `AddressOf` has several of them.

`AddressOf` provides the VB developer with a simple way of using function pointers without relying on another language. A *function pointer* is simply a variable that contains the memory location of a single function. In other words, this variable points to a function. Now, instead of having to use the function name to call the function, we can instead use the function pointer to call the function.

A *callback* or *callback function* is the function which the function pointer references. Code that receives a function pointer can use it to call back (hence the name "callback") to that function. Usually, these callback functions are small in size because they might be called many times per second and affect application performance.

Function pointers and callback functions are mainly used for asynchronous processing and with the enumeration application programming interface (API) functions. *EnumWindows*, *EnumChildWindows*, and *EnumDesktopWindows* are just some of Windows' enumeration API functions. These functions each take a function pointer in their argument list. This function pointer is used to invoke a callback function for each item—a window, in this case—found by the API function. We'll look at some examples of enumeration functions and asynchronous processing later in this section.

Using AddressOf

The rules defining how `AddressOf` must be used greatly limit its functionality and make it far less powerful than many VB developers had originally hoped. It seems that Microsoft's plans for introducing VB developers to function pointers was primarily meant to allow access to Windows API functions that were previously unusable. Great, but what about using function pointers within a pure VB application? By this I mean calling a VB function and passing it a function pointer using `AddressOf`. This called function would accept the function pointer and use it to directly call a callback function. The answer is that `AddressOf` cannot be used in this manner. Disappointing, yes, but we still have the use of many API functions that were previously unusable.

There are several other limitations and problems to watch out for when using `AddressOf` in your applications. `AddressOf` must be placed immediately before a function name in an argument list for a called function. For example:

```
Call DLLFunction(hwnd, 0, AddressOf VBCallbackFunction)
```

This argument must be the name of a previously defined function. Because any kind of pointer is useless outside of the process that created it, it makes sense that the function that `AddressOf` precedes must be in the same process.

`AddressOf` can be used only with VB functions, subs, and properties. You cannot use it to get a pointer to an API function that you have declared in your code using the `Declare` statement. For example, you cannot do the following:

```
RetVal = EnumWindows(AddressOf EnumChildWindows, 0)
```

EnumChildWindows is a Windows-defined API function, not a VB function, sub, or property. This will cause an error when compiling your application.

It would be nice if the function whose pointer we pass using the `AddressOf` operator could reside anywhere in our VB application, but unfortunately, this is not permitted.

It is also important that any function that is passed a function pointer knows exactly how to call the callback function. The parameter lists of the callback function and the code that will be calling it must match exactly in number and in type.

Perhaps the most significant limitation of using callbacks is that the function pointed to by the `AddressOf` operator must reside in a code (BAS) module, rather than a form (FRM) or class (CLS) module. Of course, we can call functions within the CLS or FRM files from the callback in the BAS module, but our problem remains that we cannot cleanly package our callback function into an object.

Callback functions (including subclassed window procedures) must reside in a BAS module.

You might wonder why this limitation exists. FRM and CLS modules are considerably different from BAS modules: only one copy of the data in a BAS module is stored in the application's process space, while FRM and CLS module data can be instantiated multiple times, with each copy of the object having its own data. Along with instantiating a FRM or CLS module, you also can destroy it by setting it to equal `Nothing`, as follows:

```
Set CObj = Nothing
```

This, in effect, removes all traces of that instance of the object from the process's address space. Think how much trouble we could get ourselves into if we destroyed an object that contained the subclassed window procedure before we had replaced it with the original window procedure. The results would be disastrous. Similar problems would arise if we tried to use *SetWindowLongPtr* to insert the subclassed window procedure from an object that had not been created.

Within the BAS module, the callback procedures should be defined as `Public`. A public function in a BAS module is always visible from anywhere in the application. A public function in a FRM or CLS module is only visible when you have successfully created an object variable referencing that object (FRM or CLS module).

Define a callback function (including a subclassed window procedure) as `Public`.

There is one last problem with allowing callback functions to reside in FRM or CLS modules: they use vtables to get to their functions. A FRM or CLS module is basically a Component Object Model (COM) object—that is, they adhere to the COM standards. This means that an extra level of abstraction exists to get to that object's public functions. BAS modules, because they are not COM objects, do not have this extra layer of abstraction, and therefore their public functions are directly accessible from anywhere in the application's code.

Finally, it's important to understand that, when you pass a function pointer using `AddressOf`, you are arranging for some routine (usually a function in the Win32 API) that's external to your application to temporarily pass flow control to a routine in your own application (that is, to the callback function). Because from your point of view this external routine is a black box that's beyond your control, you should not raise any errors in the callback function that are propagated back to the calling routine. You should use `On Error Resume Next` to bypass the error. If necessary, you can check the Err object to see if an error has been raised while still inside the VB callback function. If one has been raised, you should handle it immediately, clear the error, and continue on.

Use `On Error Resume Next` for error handling in the callback function.

Callbacks and Enumeration Functions

To see how callback functions work with the Win32 enumeration functions, let's use *EnumChildWindows* in a simple example. *EnumChildWindows* is declared in VB in the following manner:

```
Public Declare Function EnumChildWindows Lib "user32" Alias "EnumChildWindows" _
        (ByVal hWndParent As Long, ByVal lpEnumFunc As Long, _
        ByVal lParam As Long) As Long
```

Its parameters are:

hWndParent
    The handle to the parent window whose child windows we want to enumerate

lpEnumFunc
    A pointer to a callback function

lParam
    Any other data that needs to be sent to the callback function

To use this function, a callback procedure needs to be written. The callback function for this example will be called *EnumProc*. The documentation for *EnumChildWindows* also describes this callback function in detail. It must have the prototype:

```
Public Function EnumProc(ByVal hWnd As Long, lParam As Long) As Long
```

This function takes two arguments. The first, *hWnd*, is a handle to a window in the enumeration list. The second argument is *lParam*, which receives a developer-defined value. Because it is passed by reference, this value also is passed back to the calling routine. Using this argument, one can pass information into and out of this callback function. To continue enumerating windows, this function should return **TRUE**; to stop enumerating them, it should return **FALSE**. Thus, a very simple *EnumProc* callback function appears as follows:

```
Public Function EnumProc(ByVal hWnd As Long, lParam As Long) As Long
    'Do work here

    EnumProc = True
End Function
```

Now that we have a callback function, we can write the code to call the *EnumChildWindows* function. The first argument to this function is **AddressOf** *EnumProc*. This evaluates to a function pointer, which points to the *EnumProc* function. The second argument is zero, which is passed in to the *lParam* argument for the *EnumProc* function:

```
Sub Main()
    RetVal = EnumChildWindows(AddressOf EnumProc, 0)
End Sub
```

When this program is run it will call *EnumChildWindows*. This function, in turn, calls the *EnumProc* callback function once for every top-level window currently running in the system. When *EnumWindows* is finished processing, it returns control to the *Main* function.

Callbacks and Asynchronous Processing

Asynchronous processing is different from an enumeration function. *Asynchronous processing* allows code in the main application to call a function and then immediately return and continue execution of the main application's code before the function's code has finished processing. With it you can write code that allows a user to perform some time-consuming task, such as sorting a large amount of information, and the user will be able to continue using the same application without waiting for the sorting to finish. This gives the user the illusion of a fast application even though the sorting might take quite some time.

A callback function can be called during the sorting process to determine if the user has canceled the action. In processing involving large nested loops, you can use a function pointer to call a callback function, which determines if the user has clicked a Cancel button. If so, the callback function returns a status code informing the sorting routine that the user wants to cancel the sorting operation. The operation is canceled and the application proceeds onward.

A callback function also could be called to inform the application of the sorting operation's progress. The application could then update status information displayed to the user that keeps the user informed of how much work still needs to be done by the sort routine.

Figure 4-1 illustrates the order in which functions are called for a VB application implementing asynchronous processing. In step 1, a function (*Main*) in the BAS file calls a function in a dynamic link library (DLL) and passes it a function pointer to the *CB* callback function, also within the BAS file. In step 2, the DLL function (*DLLFunct*) uses this function pointer to call the function *CB* in the BAS file during its processing. This function might notify the main application of the status of the *DLLFunct* function or determine if the user wants to cancel its operation. In step 3, the *CB* function finishes processing and immediately returns control to the *DLLFunct* function. In step 4, the *DLLFunct* function returns control to the *Main* function in the BAS file.

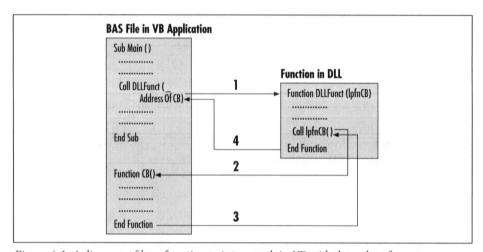

Figure 4-1. A diagram of how function pointers work in VB with the order of events

As I mentioned in Chapter 2, the `lpfnWndProc` member of the window class structure is a function pointer to the window procedure. The `lpfn` prefix tells us that this is a Long pointer to a function.

There is one problem with the application and DLL in Figure 4-1. The application stops executing as soon as it calls *DLLFunct* from the BAS file. The application is waiting for the *DLLFunct* function to return. The code in the callback function, *CB*, will still execute every time it is called, but for all practical purposes the VB application is waiting for the DLL to finish execution. To solve this problem and make the application truly asynchronous, we need to start a new thread in the DLL and use this thread to execute the *DLLFunct* function code. The only change to Figure 4-1 is the addition of a new function that is called from the *Main* subroutine in place of the *DLLFunct* DLL function. This new function would create a new thread, run the *DLLFunct* code on this thread, and immediately return control to the *Main* subroutine in the BAS file. With the addition of this new function, our VB application can continue running as if the *DLLFunct* procedure had never been called.

AddressOf and Subclassing

With subclassing, we will be using the **AddressOf** operator to get a function pointer to our new window procedure. This new window procedure is the callback function that the window message loop calls first, after receiving a message. The code required to implement **AddressOf** is quite simple. First you code the callback function:

```
Public Function NewWndProc(ByVal hWnd As Long, _
                    ByVal uMsg As Long, _
                    ByVal wParam As Long, _
                    ByVal lParam As Long) as Long
     'Your code goes here
End Function
```

This function will eventually serve as our new subclassed window procedure. Next we use the **AddressOf** operator to pass a pointer referring to this function into the Win32 *SetWindowLongPtr* function. The *SetWindowLongPtr* function call will look like this:

```
m_lOrigWndProc = SetWindowLongPtr(hWnd, GWLP_WNDPROC, AddressOf NewWndProc)
```

SetWindowLongPtr is described in detail in Chapter 3. This single line of code effectively subclasses the window that has *hWnd* as its handle. It accomplishes this by replacing the function pointer to the original window procedure with a function pointer to our *NewWndProc* function, acquired by using the **AddressOf** operator. The *SetWindowLongPtr* function will then return the pointer to the original window procedure to the calling function.

This window is now subclassed. Any messages sent to this window will be sent to the *NewWndProc* function. Instead of simply calling this function a callback function, it is usually called a *subclassed window procedure.* Any window procedure or subclassed window procedure is just a callback function used specifically to process window messages. This is why they are called window procedures instead of callback functions.

As we noted, any routine that is passed a function pointer must know exactly how to call the callback function. This is not too hard in the case of subclassing because all window procedures take the same number and type of arguments. If we deviate from this, our code will not work and will eventually crash the process that it is running in. It is not only necessary to match the function parameters, but it is also wise to understand how the calling function and the callback function work. This knowledge will help to prevent passing bad data to a callback function, which could cause problems ranging from simple logic errors to more troublesome General Protection Fault (GPF) problems. This also allows us to correctly handle data returned from a callback function.

Some Subclassing Tips

As we've seen, subclassing involves creating a particular kind of callback function, one that is called by a window's event loop. Hence, the general tips that we've presented for callback functions (such as defining the callback as a Public function in a BAS module and using On Error Resume Next for error handling in the callback function) apply as well to subclassed window procedures. In addition, though, two tips and pitfalls that are unique to subclassing are worth mentioning.

First, remember that all messages for a window are passed through its subclassed window procedure. As a result, the subclassed window procedure (as well as a hook's filter function) can potentially be called hundreds or even thousands of times per second. If large amounts of code are executed in the window procedure for many of the messages, the performance of the application will degrade considerably. This makes it critically important to avoid doing too much work within a callback function. Performing file I/O in either type of procedure is one type of operation that could take up an unusually long amount of time to finish because of relatively slow disk access. If such long processes are included within these callback functions, the results could be less than satisfactory.

Do as little work as possible in the subclassed window procedure.

Second, never use the *DoEvents* function inside the window procedure. *DoEvents* will halt processing to allow other queued messages to be processed. Using this function inside a window procedure stops processing for that particular message. The problem occurs when a new message is sent to the window procedure before the previous message can finish processing. The first message yields to the second message, the second message yields to the third message, and so on. The outcome of this is unpredictable because messages might be processed out of order, or not be processed at all.

 Do not use the *DoEvents* function within any window procedure.

Finally, stepping through a subclassing application in break mode from within the VB IDE is problematic. Doing so can cause the application, as well as the VB IDE, to freeze. This makes it much more difficult to debug these types of applications. Debugging applications using subclassing is discussed in depth in Chapter 8.

 Stepping through a subclassing application in the IDE can be problematic.

Instance Subclassing: An Example

As we saw in Chapter 3, instance subclassing involves using the *SetWindowLongPtr* function to replace the window procedure of a specific window instance.

In this section, we'll write our first simple subclassing application. The application will have two buttons, one to subclass the VB form and another to remove the subclass. The only other control will be a multiline text box that will display messages as they are sent to this form. I will add some more functionality to this application in the example following this one.

Let's start with the layout of the form. It's rather simple; the nondefault properties are listed in Table 4-1, and the form is displayed in Figure 4-2.

Table 4-1. Nondefault Properties of Form and Controls for Subclassing Example

Object	Property Name	Property Value
frmCh4	Caption	"Chapter 4—Subclassing Example"
frmCh4	ClientHeight	3612
frmCh4	ClientLeft	48
frmCh4	ClientTop	336
frmCh4	ClientWidth	6960
Text1	Height	3372

Table 4-1. Nondefault Properties of Form and Controls for Subclassing Example (continued)

Object	Property Name	Property Value
Text1	Left	1560
Text1	MultiLine	-1 'True'
Text1	ScrollBars	2 'Vertical'
Text1	Top	120
Text1	Width	5292
cmdUnSubclass	Caption	"Un-Subclass"
cmdUnSubclass	Height	372
cmdUnSubclass	Left	120
cmdUnSubclass	Top	600
cmdUnSubclass	Width	1332
cmdSubclass	Caption	"Subclass"
cmdSubclass	Height	372
cmdSubclass	Left	120
cmdSubclass	Top	120
cmdSubclass	Width	1332

Here is how it will work. The text box is initially blank. When you click the Subclass button, messages that are sent to the window procedure for the VB form will display in the text box. Each line in the text box is a separate message. In our first cut at this project, messages will be displaying faster than you can read them. (We will discuss the number and frequency of messages sent to a window later in this chapter.) To remove the subclass procedure, simply click the Un-Subclass button; the messages will stop displaying.

The code will include functionality to handle problems such as clicking the Subclass button more than once and clicking the Un-Subclass button when no subclass procedure has been installed. There is also another problem that needs to be handled: prematurely ending the application before clicking the Un-Subclass button. In other words, you cannot stop an application cleanly without first removing any subclassed window procedure that has been installed. Ending an application any other way will cause a GPF to occur.

To demonstrate this, let's assume that we forget to restore the original window procedure before shutting down the application. The subclassed window will continue to call our subclassed window procedure even as the application is being destroyed. While the application is being destroyed, the code within the BAS module that contains the subclassed window procedure is removed from memory. If the subclassed window receives any messages passed to it, such as `WM_DESTROY` (the message indicating that the window is about to be destroyed), the window

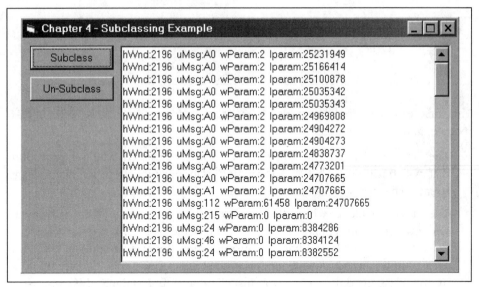

Figure 4-2. The first example subclassing application

tries to call the subclassed window procedure using its function pointer. If the code for this subclassed window procedure has been removed from memory, this function pointer will point to unallocated memory and cause a GPF.

Do not end an application before removing all subclassed window procedures.

I should mention here that the **End** statement in VB will crash your application. The **End** statement forces the application to stop dead in its tracks. This means that any unload events for the Form or Terminate events for the class modules will not execute. The Unload and Terminate events provide the perfect place to clean up the application and prepare it to shut down properly. These events are our last lines of defense. It is here that I will place code to make absolutely sure that the application can shut down without a crash.

Using the **End** statement bypasses these events and has the potential to create serious problems. Calling the **End** statement after cleaning up your application and preparing it to shut down would be fine, but being good programmers, we would not use the **End** statement anyway, right? As a note, the Stop button in the VB IDE will act the same as using the **End** statement.

Do not use the **End** statement in your code or the Stop button in the VB IDE.

This first example application will consist of a form (see Figure 4-2), a BAS module, and a class module:

- The BAS module, as you guessed, holds the subclassed window procedure that will be installed before the original window procedure in the message stream. This, for now, is the extent of the code in the BAS module.

- The class module is where the code to install and uninstall the subclassed window procedure contained in the BAS module resides. It would be nice to place the new subclassed window procedure in the class module as well, but as we know, the **AddressOf** operator does not support this. By placing code in the class module to control installing and uninstalling the subclassed window procedure, we are able to ensure that the application will function properly. By calling a public function in the class, we can install the subclassed windows procedure. But what if something goes wrong and either we forget to remove the subclassed window procedure or the application encounters an unhandled error? In either case, the class is destroyed before the form. The code that is placed in the **Class_Terminate** event will allow the application to remove the subclassed window procedure and shut down gracefully.

A discussion of each module follows.

The Class Module

A good starting point is the code for the class module, which is named CSubclass. The private constants, the variables, and the Windows API function will be declared in the declarations section of the module, as follows:

```
Private Declare Function SetWindowLongPtr Lib "user32" Alias "SetWindowLongA" _
        (ByVal hwnd As Long, _
        ByVal nIndex As Long, _
        ByVal dwNewLong As Long) As Long

Private Const GWLP_WNDPROC = -4

Private m_lOrigWndProc As Long
Private m_hwnd As Long
```

SetWindowLongPtr will be used to do the actual subclassing. The **GWLP_WNDPROC** constant is used as an argument to *SetWindowLongPtr* and indicates that the window's procedure is being replaced. The last two private member variables will hold data pertaining to the window being subclassed.

Two variables also are declared in the class module's declarations section. The variable **m_hwnd** holds the window handle of the subclassed window, and the *m_lOrigWndProc* variable holds the original window procedure for that same window. The `Class_Initialize` event, which is shown in Example 4-1, is used to initialize these two private member variables to zero.

Example 4-1. The Class_Initialize Event Procedure

```
Private Sub Class_Initialize()
    m_lOrigClassProc = 0
    m_hwnd = 0
End Sub
```

Two public properties are needed for the two private member variables **m_hwnd** and *m_lOrigWndProc*; these are shown in Example 4-2.

Example 4-2. Properties of the CSubClass Class

```
Public Property Get OrigWndProc() As Long
    OrigWndProc = m_lOrigWndProc
End Property

Public Property Let hwnd(Handle As Long)
    m_hwnd = Handle
End Property
```

The address of the original window procedure contained in the member variable *m_lOrigWndProc* needs to be available to the subclassed window procedure in the BAS file. The first property that we expose in this class, `OrigWndProc`, will take care of this requirement. The second property is used only by an external function to set the *m_hwnd* member variable. The class needs to know the window (*m_hwnd*) in which to install and remove the subclassed window procedure.

Now that we have the class data wrapped up, we can get to the meat of the class code. The public function that will actually perform the subclassing is shown in Example 4-3.

Example 4-3. The EnableSubclass Function

```
Public Function EnableSubclass() As Boolean
    If m_lOrigWndProc > 0 Then
        'Already subclassed
        '  Do not allow to subclass a 2nd time
        MsgBox "Error: Already subclassed"
    Else
        m_lOrigWndProc = SetWindowLongPtr(m_hwnd, _
                        GWLP_WNDPROC, _
                        AddressOf Module1.NewWndProc)
    End If

    If m_lOrigWndProc > 0 Then
```

Example 4-3. The EnableSubclass Function (continued)

```
        EnableSubclass = True
    Else
        EnableSubclass = False
    End If
End Function
```

When this function is called, we want to check the *m_lOrigWndProc* member variable to find out if it contains a number other than zero. If it does, we know that this window has been subclassed and should not be subclassed a second time. If the window were to be subclassed more than once using the code in this example, we would lose the function pointer to our original window procedure. Without this pointer to the original window procedure, the application will crash when it is shut down. Let me explain why in a little more detail.

Looking at Figure 4-3, we see why subclassing a window more than once will lead to a crash. The *m_lOrigWndProc* member variable is first initialized to zero to indicate that no subclassing has occurred. When the window is subclassed using *SetWindowLongPtr*, the pointer to the original window procedure is stored in this variable. Removing the subclass at this point will be successful. If instead the window is subclassed a second time, and then we try to remove the subclassing, the application will crash, and we will get a message similar to this:

```
    PROJ_CH4 caused a stack fault in module MSVBVM60.DLL at 0167:66023e13.
```

A stack fault occurs when memory is accessed beyond the limits of the stack. The *stack* is a linked list used by function calls to store information that goes out of scope. Every thread has its own stack space. The stack space for any one thread can be up to 1MB in size. Information can only be inserted (pushed) onto the top of the stack or retrieved (popped) from the top of the stack. This is a First In, Last Out (FILO) type of structure. VB uses the stack mainly to store function arguments and local variables declared in functions.

Information such as global and static variables is stored in the application's default heap. A *heap* is a block of memory set aside by the application to store information. Heap memory is accessible throughout the entire application, and therefore provides an excellent area to store global and static variables. Variables of this type never go out of scope, and thus require no stack space.

Variables local to a function go out of scope when calling another function. This is necessary to prevent variables local to one function from being modified from within another function. The stack provides a way to save the calling function's local variables while the called function is executing. Upon returning from the called function the calling function's local variables are restored properly.

Function arguments also are pushed onto the stack. Arguments declared as **ByVal** have their actual data placed on the stack. Arguments declared as **ByRef** have pointers to the data placed on the stack. For `ByRef` arguments, the called function obtains a pointer to the actual data and can subsequently modify the actual data. `ByVal` arguments only pass a copy of the data to a function. The copy can be modified without also changing the value within the calling function.

To demonstrate this, a function *foo* is called in VB from the function *Call_foo*.

```
Private Function Call_foo(strX as string, lngY as Long) as long
    Dim intZ as Integer

    intZ = 1
    strX = "NULL"
    lngY = 100

    Debug.Print "Before Call"
    RetVal = foo(strX, lngY)
    Debug.Print "After Call"
End Function
```

The arguments to the function *foo* are placed at the top of the stack. For this function, both `strX` and `lngY` are placed on the stack. Though it is not passed to the *foo* function, the integer `intZ` also is placed on the stack because it is local in scope to the *Call_foo* function. The stack would look something like this:

```
Top of Stack ->     intZ = 1
                    lngY = pointer to the value of lngY
                    strX = "NULL"
```

Next, the function *foo* is called, and the system starts executing code in this function. Remember that the variables local to the function *Call_foo* are now out of scope. The *foo* function is as follows:

```
Private Function foo(ByVal in_strX as string, ByRef in_lngY as Long) as long
    StrX = "Text"
    LngY = 700
End Function
```

When **End Function** is encountered, execution is returned to the *Call_foo* function. The information on the stack is removed and the *Call_foo* local variables are restored. In this case:

- `intZ` will still equal 1 because this local variable was only stored on the stack.

- `lngY` will equal 700 because the pointer was passed in to the function *foo*.

- `strX` will equal `NULL` because only a copy of this variable was modified in the function *foo*.

Now that we understand how the stack works, we can better understand the stack fault problem. When a function is called, various data related to that function is placed on the stack. When a function returns, the data placed on the stack is removed and the memory is freed so that it can be used again. If that function never returns, the information on the stack will remain and the memory will not be freed.

The problem with losing a function pointer to a window procedure is illustrated in Figure 4-3, a step-by-step example that shows the values of the original window procedure (*m_lOrigWndProc*) and the pointer to the correct window procedure (*lpfnWndProc*). The address &H10001F0B points to the original window procedure, &H202020BB points to the first subclassed window procedure, and &H300F0022 points to the second subclassed window procedure. If you notice when our second subclassed window procedure is called, it thinks that the first subclassed window procedure is the original window procedure (see Step 3 in Figure 4-3). *CallWindowProc* will use the pointer stored in the variable *m_lOrigWndProc* to call the first subclassed window. Actually, this would be fine except for the fact that we do not have the function pointer to the original window procedure. This function pointer was lost when we subclassed this window a second time. Unfortunately, the code now thinks that the first subclassed window procedure is the original window procedure. When *CallWindowProc* is executed in the first window procedure, it calls itself because the function pointer in the variable *m_lOrigWndProc* is pointing to itself. This sets up a really nasty recursive function call in which the first subclassed window procedure keeps calling itself and never returns. This will continue to happen until the stack fills up and then tries to write past its boundary, causing a stack fault.

Never lose the function pointer to the original window procedure for the subclassed window.

To correct this problem, the address of each window procedure (including the original one) has to be saved. These values could possibly be stored in an array. When the second subclassed window procedure calls the *CallWindowProc* function, this array would be use to look up the next subclassed window procedure to call. In this case, it would be the first window procedure. After the first window procedure is finished, the original window procedure would be called. The original window procedure should be stored in this array as well.

There are two things to keep in mind with subclassing a window multiple times. First, the window procedures should be called in the reverse order in which they were installed. For example, the last installed subclassed window procedure should be called first, the second installed window procedure should be called next, and so on. Second, when removing the subclassed window procedures, they must be removed in the reverse order from which they were installed. Adhering to these rules will ensure that problems resulting from the interaction between sub-classed window procedures are at a minimum.

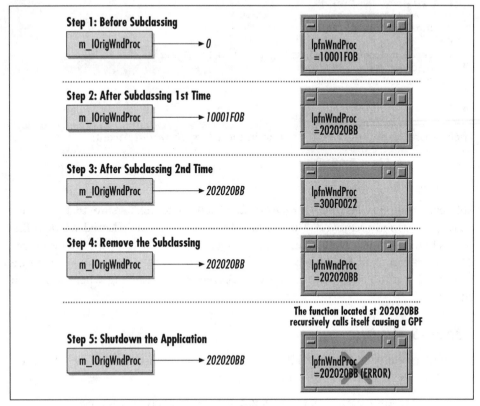

Figure 4-3. Losing the function pointer to a window procedure

Getting back to our *EnableSubclass* method, if no subclassing has occurred, *SetWindowLongPtr* is called to place our new subclassed window procedure into the message stream just before the original window procedure. This function will return a success or error status to the calling function.

The next function in this class is the *DisableSubclass* method, which is shown in Example 4-4. This function removes the installed subclassed window procedure and returns a success or error status. Once again the `m_lOrigWndProc` member variable is checked to see if in fact a subclassed window procedure has been installed. A value of zero means that none has been installed. If the value is non-zero, *SetWindowLongPtr* is called, this time with the `m_lOrigWndProc` variable passed in the last argument to the function. The subclassed window procedure is removed from the message stream. This will have the effect of resetting the window to the way it operated before the subclassing was performed.

Example 4-4. The DisableSubclass Method

```
Public Function DisableSubclass() As Boolean
    If m_lOrigWndProc = 0 Then
        'Do not remove subclass - none exist
        DisableSubclass = False
    Else
        SetwindowlongPtr m_hwnd, GWLP_WNDPROC, m_lOrigWndProc
        m_lOrigWndProc = 0
        DisableSubclass = True
    End If
End Function
```

There is one last bit of code to look at in the *Class_Terminate* event:

```
Private Sub Class_Terminate()
    Call DisableSubclass
End Sub
```

This code simply calls the *DisableSubclass* method to make sure that the sub-classing is properly removed. This event is fired before the subclassed window finishes shutting down. Note that, because *DisableSubclass* tests the value of *m_lOrigWndProc* to make sure that subclassing is in effect, we do not need to be concerned that the class Terminate event will remove subclassing when none is in effect.

The BAS Module

The BAS module defines several API functions and constants that will be used throughout the project. They are as follows:

```
Public Declare Function CallWindowProc Lib "user32" Alias "CallWindowProcA" _
        (ByVal lpPrevWndFunc As Long, ByVal hwnd As Long, _
        ByVal Msg As Long, ByVal wParam As Long, ByVal lParam As Long) As Long

Public Declare Sub CopyMemory Lib "kernel32" Alias "RtlMoveMemory" _
        (Destination As Any, Source As Any, ByVal Length As Long)

Public Declare Function DefWindowProc Lib "user32" Alias "DefWindowProcA" _
        (ByVal hwnd As Long, ByVal wMsg As Long, ByVal wParam As Long, _
        ByVal lParam As Long) As Long

Public Const WM_CTLCOLOREDIT = &H133
Public Const WM_SETCURSOR = &H20
Public Const WM_NCHITTEST = &H84
Public Const WM_MOUSEMOVE = &H200
Public Const WM_NCLBUTTONDOWN = &HA1
Public Const WMSZ_BOTTOM = 6
Public Const WM_SIZING = &H214
Public Const HTMINBUTTON = 8
Public Const WM_SYSCOMMAND = &H112
Public Const SC_MINIMIZE = &HF020&
```

```
Public Type POINTAPI
        x As Long
        y As Long
End Type

Public Type MINMAXINFO
        ptReserved As POINTAPI
        ptMaxSize As POINTAPI
        ptMaxPosition As POINTAPI
        ptMinTrackSize As POINTAPI
        ptMaxTrackSize As POINTAPI
End Type
```

The BAS module contains only two items of interest: the public declaration of the class module variable and the subclassed window procedure. The code for the first item is:

```
Dim CSubClsApp As CSubclass
```

The object variable needs to be declared as a global variable in the BAS module. It is then instantiated in the **Form_Load** event, as follows:

```
Set CSubClsApp = New CSubclass
```

If you declare the variable in the form module, the application works fine until it is stopped without first clicking the Un-Subclass button. The problem is that the form module is destroyed before the BAS module containing the subclassed window procedure is destroyed. The subclassed window procedure has a reference to the form module's text box. We all know that when you access a control on a form that is not loaded, Windows automatically loads the form. This, in turn, creates a new **CSubClsApp** object. The first **CSubClsApp** object is destroyed along with its *m_lOrigWndProc* variable. When the application tries to finish shutting down, the original window procedure is not restored. At this point the window is still sending messages to the subclassed window procedure in the BAS module. The BAS module is then removed from memory, which invalidates the function pointer to the subclassed window procedure. Now this function pointer is pointing to garbage. When a message is sent to this window, the application tries to call the subclassed window procedure function using this invalid pointer, and the application crashes.

The subclassed window procedure in the BAS module is the heart of the subclassing operation. This is where we can do all our magic. Basically, this subclassed window procedure displays all messages sent to the window by writing the subclassed window procedure's parameters to the text box on the form. The following line of code does this:

```
frmCh4.txtMessages.Text = frmCh4.txtMessages.Text & _
        "hWnd:" & hwnd & _
        " uMsg:" & Hex$(uMsg) & _
```

```
        "   wParam:" & wParam & _
        "   lparam:" & lParam & vbNewLine
```

If this is the only line of code in the subclassed window procedure (excluding the call to the *CallWindowProc* API function), every message sent to this window will display in the text box. The number of messages and the speed at which they are displayed are overwhelming. To make things more readable, let's prevent some of the more frequent messages from displaying so that we can better see what is going on by modifying our code as follows:

```
If uMsg = WM_CTLCOLOREDIT Or _
        uMsg = WM_SETCURSOR Or _
        uMsg = WM_NCHITTEST Or _
        uMsg = WM_MOUSEMOVE Then
    'Skip displaying these messages
Else
    frmCh4.txtMessages.Text = frmCh4.txtMessages.Text & _
        "   hWnd:" & hwnd & _
        "   uMsg:" & Hex$(uMsg) & _
        "   wParam:" & wParam & _
        "   lparam:" & lParam & vbNewLine
End If
```

Adding this **If-Then-Else** statement to filter out the more frequent messages makes the remaining messages easier to read.

The final subclassed window procedure is shown in Example 4-5.

Example 4-5. NewWndProc, the Subclassed Window Procedure

```
Public Function NewWndProc(ByVal hwnd As Long, ByVal uMsg As Long, _
                ByVal wParam As Long, ByVal lParam As Long) As Long
   If uMsg = WM_CTLCOLOREDIT Or _
      uMsg = WM_SETCURSOR Or _
      uMsg = WM_NCHITTEST Or _
      uMsg = WM_MOUSEMOVE Then
        'Skip displaying these messages
   Else
   frmCh4.txtMessages.Text = frmCh4.txtMessages.Text & _
           "hWnd:" & hwnd & _
        "   uMsg:" & Hex$(uMsg) & _
        "   wParam:" & wParam & _
        "   lparam:" & lParam & vbNewLine
   End If

    'Pass message to the default window procedure
    NewWndProc = CallWindowProc(CSubClsApp.OrigWndProc, hwnd, uMsg, wParam, lParam)
End Function
```

When you run the finished application, if you remove the **If...Else...End If** construct so that all messages are listed in the text box, you'll discover that far too many messages are generated for you to meaningfully read and analyze. To understand why these messages are being sent so frequently, let's examine the purpose of each message that we are deliberately ignoring. Every time a new line of information is written to the text box and displayed, the text box must repaint itself. The WM_CTLCOLOREDIT message is sent by the multiline text box to its parent window (the one which we are subclassing) every time the text box wants to repaint itself. The parent (subclassed) window uses this information to direct the repainting of the text box control.

The WM_SETCURSOR message is sent to the window directly under the mouse cursor whenever the mouse is moved over that window. You can get an idea of the number of WM_SETCURSOR messages the window receives just by removing the check for this message and then moving the mouse back and forth over the subclassed window.

The WM_NCHITTEST message is similar to the WM_SETCURSOR message because it is sent to the window whenever the mouse is moved. The WM_NCHITTEST message also is sent to the window whenever any mouse button event (a mouse button down message, a mouse button up message, and others) occurs as well. This message is sent to the window before the actual mouse messages (e.g., WM_LBUTTONDOWN, WM_LBUTTONUP, WM_MOUSEMOVE, etc.). The WM_NCHITTEST message determines where the mouse event occurred on the window. This information aids the system in determining how to process the subsequent mouse message. For example, WM_NCHITTEST can determine if the mouse event occurred in the client or nonclient area of a window. If the left mouse button was pressed in a nonclient portion of a window, the WM_NCLBUTTONDOWN message would be sent. If the same mouse event occurred in the client area of a window, the WM_LBUTTONDOWN message would be sent.

The final message that will not be displayed is the WM_MOUSEMOVE message. At first glance it might seem that this message is the same as the WM_SETCURSOR message. Both are sent for mouse move events. The difference is in each message's parameters. The WM_MOUSEMOVE message has parameters to determine if a mouse button is depressed. This message can be useful when subclassing a window to modify its drag-and-drop operations.

You should experiment by allowing specific messages or all messages to be displayed in the text box. This will give you an indication of the number of messages a window will receive every second of its existence.

The Form Module

The code for the form module, which is shown in Example 4-6, is very simple. When the form loads, it creates an object instance of the CSubclass class and sets its hWnd property. When the Subclass button is clicked, the subclassing object

(CSubClsApp) will subclass the window identified by the `CSubClsApp.hwnd`
property. This is performed in the *CSubClsApp.EnableSubclass* function. When the
Un-Subclass button is clicked, the subclassing code is removed by calling the
CSubClsApp.DisableSubclass function. Finally, the object we created is destroyed
when we unload this window. This allows the code in the `CSubclass_`
`Terminate` event to remove any subclassing so that the application can shut
down without crashing.

Example 4-6. Code for the frmCh4 Form

```
Private Sub Form_Load()
    Set CSubClsApp = New CSubclass
    CSubClsApp.hwnd = Me.hwnd
End Sub

Private Sub cmdSubclass_Click()
    Call CSubClsApp.EnableSubclass
End Sub

Private Sub cmdUnSubclass_Click()
    Call CSubClsApp.DisableSubclass
End Sub

Private Sub Form_QueryUnload(Cancel As Integer, UnloadMode As Integer)
    Set CSubClsApp = Nothing
End Sub
```

Doing Something Interesting

Although this is a good exercise in learning how to subclass a window, we are not
doing anything useful here. In this section, I will show you how to allow a user to
resize only one side of a window without resizing any other portion of the
window. Also, I will override the default window's minimize functionality by capturing messages specific to window minimization. By intercepting these messages,
we can force the window to roll up or hide itself in any other way that we want
when the user tries to minimize the window.

Overriding window resizing

The first thing we must do, before writing any code, is figure out which message
or messages to capture. I usually use the Spy++ tool in conjunction with the
Microsoft Developer Network (MSDN) CD-ROM. I use the Spy++ tool to watch for
specific messages or for patterns of messages. Then I look up their meanings in
the MSDN. You also could do the reverse and figure out which messages you will
need to watch for by looking up messages specific to the type of window you are
subclassing in the MSDN. Then, using Spy++, watch for these specific messages.

Thoroughly research the messages that you will be trapping in the subclassed window procedure. Each message has its own idiosyncrasies.

Usually it takes more than one message to perform an action in Windows. Take, for example, resizing a window. During this operation, many messages are sent to and from a window when it is going through the resizing process. The following is a list of the messages sent and their order for the sizing process:

```
WM_NCLBUTTONDOWN                    - Posted
WM_SYSCOMMAND                       - Sent
     WM_ENTERSIZEMOVE               - Sent
     WM_ENTERSIZEMOVE               - Received
     WM_SIZING                      - Sent
     WM_SIZING                      - Received
     WM_WINDOWPOSCHANGING           - Sent
          WM_GETMINMAXINFO          - Sent
          WM_GETMINMAXINFO          - Received
     WM_WINDOWPOSCHANGING           - Received
     WM_WINDOWPOSCHANGED            - Sent
     WM_SIZE                        - Sent
          (Window is repainted)
     WM_SIZE                        - Received
     WM_WINDOWPOSCHANGED            - Received
     WM_EXITSIZEMOVE                - Sent
     WM_EXITSIZEMOVE                - Received
WM_SYSCOMMAND                       - Received
```

The process starts with the user clicking the left mouse button over a window border and dragging that border to resize it. A WM_NCLBUTTONDOWN message is posted to this window in response to the user clicking and holding down the left mouse button. This message contains information about which border the mouse is over in its *wParam* argument. This message is then passed on to the *DefWindowProc* function after the window procedure has finished processing it. *DefWindowProc* determines if a sizing operation needs to be initiated. If so, *DefWindowProc* sends a WM_SYSCOMMAND message to the message queue of the window being resized. The *wParam* member for this message contains the value SC_SIZE, which informs the window that it is being sized. The *lParam* member contains the mouse cursor's *x* and *y* position. At this point, the user is holding the left mouse button down while dragging a border of the window. All messages from this point are nested within the WM_SYSCOMMAND message. In other words, the window procedure does not return immediately when it is passed this message; instead, other messages are sent in response to this message.

The only message that is posted is WM_NCLBUTTONDOWN; all other messages for the sizing process are sent to the window. The difference is that posted messages are sent to the window's message queue, while sent messages are sent directly to the window procedure for immediate processing. The *DefWindowProc* function sends these messages to the window so that they can be processed before any pending messages in the queue. When sizing a window, the system does not want any other messages to interfere with this operation.

In response to the `WM_SYSCOMMAND` message, *DefWindowProc* sends the `WM_ENTERSIZEMOVE` message to the window. This message informs the window that it has entered a sizing or moving modal loop. While in this modal loop, the window is forced to process only positioning or sizing messages. This puts all other messages that could adversely affect the sizing or positioning of a window on hold. This modal loop runs from within the *DefWindowProc* function. While in this loop, the function will only send messages to the window relating to the sizing process.

After sending the `WM_ENTERSIZEMOVE` message, the *DefWindowProc* function sends the `WM_SIZING` message to the window. The *wParam* member for this message contains the window border that is being sized. The *lParam* member contains a pointer to a RECT structure, which defines the dimension and position of the window. The window procedure sends this message to the *DefWindowProc* function when it is finished processing it.

Next, *DefWindowProc* sends the `WM_WINDOWPOSCHANGING` message containing the new values for the window size, position, and Z-order. This message contains a pointer to the `WINDOWPOS` structure in the *lParam* member and `NULL` in the *wParam* member. The `WINDOWPOS` structure contains the size, position, and Z-order values of the window. These values can be modified to override the default sizing, moving, and Z-order behaviors.

In response to the `WM_WINDOWPOSCHANGING` message, *DefWindowProc* sends a `WM_GETMINMAXINFO` message to the window being sized. This message allows the application to validate the window size and position before proceeding. This message contains a pointer to this structure defining the default values for this window's maximized position, maximized size, and tracking size in the *lParam* member. The values in this structure can be modified to control the outcome of the sizing or moving operation. The *wParam* member contains a `NULL`.

Next, *DefWindowProc* sends the `WM_WINDOWPOSCHANGED` message. This message is similar to the `WM_WINDOWPOSCHANGING` message, except that the size, position, and Z-order of the window have been changed. The *lParam* and *wParam* members are exactly the same for both messages. Modifications made to the `WINDOWPOS` structure contained in the *lParam* member of this message will have no effect on the window.

When the user releases the left mouse button, the WM_SIZE message is sent by *DefWindowProc* informing the window that the user is finished sizing the window. The *lParam* member of this message contains the SIZE_RESTORED flag, which informs the window that it has been resized. The *wParam* member contains the new width and height of the client area of this window. More messages are sent to reposition and repaint the newly sized window. Finally, a WM_EXITSIZEMOVE message is sent by *DefWindowProc* to the window, forcing the window to exit the sizing modal loop and allow other messages in the message queue to be processed normally. This message contains NULLs in its *wParam* and *lParam* members. It is here that the WM_SYSCOMMAND message returns from the *DefWindowProc* function and the window is once again able to pull messages from its message queue.

Many actions performed on a window consist of a series of messages. Consider creating a window, destroying a window, maximizing a window, or even activating a window. This does not mean that all actions that take place are this complex, but be prepared to dig in to the messages and their definitions.

To determine which messages I was interested in, I set up Spy++ to watch for General messages and Non-Client messages for a particular window. Then I pressed the F8 key to allow Spy++ to start logging messages. I activated the window that was being spied on and resized a border. As soon as I was done, I stopped Spy++ from logging any more messages. Many messages were fired, but fortunately many of these were duplicates from such actions as moving the mouse. WM_NCHITTEST is one of the messages that appear multiple times. As I mentioned earlier in this chapter, in the section "The BAS Module," this message is directly related to mouse actions. Because mouse actions are required for sizing a window border (clicking the mouse button and dragging the window border), this message is of importance. Looking down through the list of messages, I noticed the spot where sizing and repainting messages started to appear (e.g., WM_SIZING, WM_WINDOWPOSCHANGED, WM_SIZE, etc.). This is the area where the window resizing took place. At the beginning of the resizing operation, a WM_NCLBUTTONDOWN message is posted with the parameter HTBOTTOM. This means that the left mouse button was clicked while the cursor was over the bottom border of the window (HTBOTTOM).

So, now that we have a sense of the sequence of messages involved in resizing a window, we can write a window procedure that will only allow the window's bottom border to be resized. This procedure, which is shown in Example 4-7, uses *CallWindowProc* to pass all messages on to the original window procedure, with a single exception: any WM_NCLBUTTONDOWN message whose *wParam* member has a value other than HTBOTTOM (indicating that the user is attempting to resize the top, left, right, top right, top left, bottom right, or bottom left borders) is handled by our window procedure alone. It adds a line to the text box ("Skipping the resize process") and returns a 0, indicating that processing of the message is complete. As a result, the default sizing behavior occurs only when the *wParam* of this message is equal to HTBOTTOM. Otherwise, the default sizing routine is not called.

Example 4-7. Window Procedure to Allow Resizing of Only the Bottom Window Border

```
Public Function NewWndProc(ByVal hwnd As Long, ByVal uMsg As Long, _
            ByVal wParam As Long, ByVal lParam As Long) As Long
    If uMsg = WM_NCLBUTTONDOWN And _
      (wParam = HTLEFT Or wParam = HTRIGHT Or _
     wParam = HTTOP Or wParam = HTTOPLEFT Or _
     wParam = HTTOPRIGHT Or wParam = HTBOTTOMLEFT Or _
     wParam = HTBOTTOMRIGHT) Then
        frmCh4.txtMessages.Text = frmCh4.txtMessages.Text & _
            "Skipping the resize process" & vbNewLine
        NewWndProc = 0
    Else
        NewWndProc = CallWindowProc(CSubClsApp.OrigWndProc, _
            hwnd, uMsg, wParam, lParam)
    End If
End Function
```

To allow the window to perform the default processing for a message, it must be passed on to the original window procedure (*CallWindowProc*) or to the default window procedure (*DefWindowProc*).

There is one problem, though. If you click the system menu of the subclassed window, choose the Size menu item, and then size any window border, our code will not stop any but the bottom border from being resized. For some reason, our code is not being executed. Why is this? Start up Spy++ and watch the Non-Client and General messages (select these two on the Messages tab of the Message Options dialog box) when resizing the window using the Size system menu item. A large number of WM_NCHITTEST messages will appear. Oddly, no WM_NCLBUTTONDOWN messages appear. Sizing the window borders using the Size menu item bypasses the WM_NCLBUTTONDOWN message. Spy++ shows that this is because when we resize a window by clicking and dragging with the mouse, the WM_NCLBUTTONDOWN message is what causes the WM_SYSCOMMAND message to be fired with a *wParam* value of SC_SIZE. When we resize the window by using the Size menu item, the WM_SYSCOMMAND message with the SC_SIZE *wParam* value is automatically posted to the window's message queue. Thus, because the window is already in the sizing modal loop, the WM_NCLBUTTONDOWN message is unnecessary.

To solve our dilemma, we could remove the Size menu item from the system menu, but a solution that does not force us to modify other behaviors just to fix the immediate problem is preferable. These short-term solutions are short cuts and have caused problems for many a developer later on in the development cycle. Instead, in such cases, more research and more observation usually helps. You might notice in the Spy++ output that one message is always used in the sizing process: WM_SIZING. This message, similar to WM_NCLBUTTONDOWN, contains a constant identifying the border that is being sized in the *wParam* member. The *lParam* member is a pointer to a RECT structure defining the new size of the window.

Limiting window sizing to the bottom border is straightforward. We'll use the *GetWindowRect* API function to get the current size and position of the window. Remember, the window has not been sized at this point. *GetWindowRect* is defined in VB as follows:

```
Private Declare Function GetWindowRect Lib "user32" _
        (ByVal hwnd As Long, lpRect As RECT) As Long
```

Its parameters are:

hwnd

   The handle of the window

lpRect

   A pointer to a RECT structure

A RECT structure is defined in VB as follows:

```
Public Type RECT
            Left As Long          'Equal to the Left property of a form
            Top As Long           'Equal to the Top property of a form
            Right As Long         'Equal to the Width property of a form
            Bottom As Long        'Equal to the Height property of a form
    End Type
```

GetWindowRect is used to get the previous position and size of the window. This information is used to replace the data pointed to by the *lParam* member of the WM_SIZING message structure in all situations except when the bottom border is being sized. The code to do this is shown in Example 4-8.

Example 4-8. Window Procedure to Handle Resizing with the System Menu

```
Public Function NewWndProc(ByVal hwnd As Long, ByVal uMsg As Long, _
        ByVal wParam As Long, ByVal lParam As Long) As Long

    Dim RectStruct As RECT
    Dim OrigRectStruct As RECT

    If uMsg = WM_SIZING And wParam <> WMSZ_BOTTOM Then   'Do not size
        'Get new window dimensions
        CopyMemory RectStruct, ByVal lParam, LenB(RectStruct)
```

Example 4-8. Window Procedure to Handle Resizing with the System Menu (continued)

```
    'Get original window dimensions
    GetWindowRect hwnd, OrigRectStruct

    'Do not allow these sides to be sized
    RectStruct.Top = OrigRectStruct.Top
    RectStruct.Left = OrigRectStruct.Left
    RectStruct.Right = OrigRectStruct.Right

    'Set new window dimensions
    CopyMemory ByVal lParam, RectStruct, LenB(RectStruct)
  End If

  NewWndProc = CallWindowProc(CSubClsApp.OrigWndProc, hwnd, uMsg, wParam, lParam)
End Function
```

CopyMemory is used to retrieve and set the *lParam* member of the WM_SIZING message structure.

Overriding a window's minimize behavior

For this next example, we will override the minimize behavior of the window. In short, when the Minimize button on the windows title bar is clicked, the default window behavior is replaced with a new behavior. Instead of minimizing the window, our window procedure will roll up the window so that only the title bar is showing. The result will look similar to Figure 4-4.

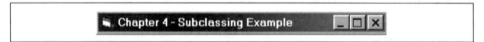

Figure 4-4. The rolled-up window

Let's start with the WM_NCLBUTTONDOWN message once again. This message provides great information on where the mouse is located when the left mouse button is pressed. This time, we are looking for the *wParam* parameter to contain the HTMINBUTTON constant. This means that the left mouse button has been clicked on the Minimize button on the window's title bar. As a note, we want to make sure that our code is not executed when the window is maximized, and that instead the default functionality is executed. If we were to try to change the height of the window while it is maximized, a GPF would occur in the application. We prevent this by checking to make sure that the frmCh4.WindowState property is not equal to vbMaximized. The first cut of the code in the subclassed window procedure looks like Example 4-9.

Example 4-9. Window Procedure to Change the Default Minimize Behavior

```
Public Function NewWndProc(ByVal hwnd As Long, ByVal uMsg As Long, _
            ByVal wParam As Long, ByVal lParam As Long) As Long
   If uMsg = WM_NCLBUTTONDOWN And _
    wParam = HTMINBUTTON And _
```

Example 4-9. Window Procedure to Change the Default Minimize Behavior (continued)

```
        frmCh4.WindowState <> vbMaximized Then
            frmCh4.Height = 30
            NewWndProc = 0
    Else
    'Pass message to the default window procedure
            NewWndProc = CallWindowProc(CSubClsApp.OrigWndProc, _
                            hwnd, uMsg, wParam, lParam))
    End If
End Function
```

If we use this code, our window will roll up when the Minimize button on the title bar is clicked. There are two problems with this approach. The first is similar to the previous example: the Minimize menu item in the system menu still minimizes the window without executing our code to roll it up. The second problem is that the Minimize button is not visually depressed when it is clicked. The cause of this second problem is that the code to draw the button in the depressed state is in the default window procedure. If you notice, the default window procedure is never called in our subclassed window procedure if the user clicks the Minimize button. In addition, there is a third minor problem. When the window is subclassed and rolled up, the restore functionality is not available. This is because the restore functionality is available only when the window is in the minimized state. In this case, the window is still in the normal state when it is rolled up; therefore, the Restore button and the Restore menu item are not available.

Instead of focusing on the cause of the minimization action, we will focus on the result of clicking the Minimize button. Clearly, the `WM_SYSCOMMAND` message with the `SC_MINIMIZE` value for the *wParam* argument is what instigates the minimization action. Let's use this message to trigger our roll-up functionality. The code for this solution is shown in Example 4-10.

Example 4-10. Minimizing a Window Using the WM_SYSCOMMAND Message

```
Public Function NewWndProc(ByVal hwnd As Long, ByVal uMsg As Long, _
            ByVal wParam As Long, ByVal lParam As Long) As Long

    Dim SizingStruct As MINMAXINFO

    If uMsg = WM_SYSCOMMAND Then
        If wParam = SC_MINIMIZE Then
            If frmCh4.WindowState <> vbMaximized Then
                'Do not process message - instead do our own work
                frmCh4.Height = 30
            Else
                'Handle this however you want
            End If

            NewWndProc = 0
        Else
            NewWndProc = DefWindowProc(hwnd, uMsg, wParam, lParam)
```

Example 4-10. Minimizing a Window Using the WM_SYSCOMMAND Message (continued)

```
        End if
    Else
        'Pass message to the default window procedure
        NewWndProc = CallWindowProc(CSubClsApp.OrigWndProc, _
                               hwnd, uMsg, wParam, lParam)
    End If
End Function
```

This code works as it should. This is not to say that the WM_NCLBUTTONDOWN message is problematic. Instead, I wanted to show you how I arrived at my conclusions as well as show examples of capturing different messages. As you can see from these last two examples, modifying the default behavior of a window can become a daunting task.

Global Subclassing

Global subclassing revolves around the same principles as instance subclassing. With global subclassing, though, we are going to go one level deeper before performing the subclassing. By this I mean that the modifications to the window procedure function pointer will occur in the class itself, not the individual window created from the class. Only those windows created from the class after the subclassing has occurred will use the new subclassed window procedure. When I mention subclassing in this section, I am referring to global subclassing.

 Instance subclassing affects a specific window and its window procedure. Global subclassing affects every window created from a window class that has had its class window procedure modified.

Unlike instance subclassing, global subclassing can capture the window creation messages—and, more specifically, WM_CREATE and WM_NCCREATE. When a window is created, the WM_NCCREATE message is sent first to the window to finish creating its nonclient area in memory. The WM_CREATE message is sent next to finish creating the window's client area in memory. Note that the window is still not displayed on the screen at this point. Other messages still need to be sent to the window to position, size, and paint it on the desktop.

The reason that instance subclassing cannot capture these messages is that when instance subclassing occurs, the window has already been created. Therefore, the window creation messages have already been processed. Global subclassing, on the other hand, occurs before a window is created. The subclassed window procedure is in place at the point when the window is created. Therefore, all window creation messages are captured.

Global subclassing allows the window creation messages to be processed. Instance subclassing does not have this ability.

To see how global subclassing differs from instance subclassing, we'll examine the modifications needed to change the previous instance subclassing example (rolling up the form using the window procedure shown in Example 4-10) to perform global subclassing.

Changes to the Class

The only real change to the class module is that you must swap *SetWindowLongPtr* for the *SetClassLongPtr* API function. This change will provide the `lpfnWndProc` member of the class structure with a pointer to our new window procedure. Along with using this new API function, there is also a new constant, `GCLP_CLSPROC`. This constant tells *SetClassLongPtr* to modify the `lpfnWndProc` function pointer in the class structure to point to a new window procedure that we define.

To call *SetClassLongPtr*, we need to replace the following declarations and constants:

```
Private Declare Function SetWindowLongPtr Lib "user32" Alias "SetWindowLongA" _
        (ByVal hwnd As Long, _
        ByVal nIndex As Long, _
        ByVal dwNewLong As Long) As Long

Private Const GWLP_WNDPROC = -4
```

with these:

```
Private Declare Function SetClassLongPtr Lib "user32" Alias "SetClassLongA" _
        (ByVal hwnd As Long, ByVal nIndex As Long, ByVal dwNewLong As Long) As Long

Private Const GCLP_CLSPROC = (-24)
```

In addition, you must change the *EnableSubclass* function in our class module to use:

```
m_lOrigClassProc = SetClassLongPtr(m_hwnd, GCLP_CLSPROC, _
        AddressOf Module1.NewClassProc)
```

instead of:

```
m_lOrigClassProc = SetwindowlongPtr(m_hwnd, GWLP_WNDPROC, _
        AddressOf Module1.NewWndProc)
```

The same must be done for the *DisableSubclass* function. It should use:

```
SetClassLongPtr m_hwnd, GCLP_CLSPROC, m_lOrigClassProc
```

instead of:

```
SetWindowlongPtr m_hwnd, GWLP_WNDPROC, m_lOrigClassProc
```

Additionally, all references to the *m_lOrigWndProc* member variable should be changed to *m_lOrigClassProc*.

The *SetClassLongPtr* API function allows us to modify the structure of a class as long as we have a handle to the window that was created from this class. This means that before we can globally subclass a window class, we must first create a new window from that class. The window handle from this window is used in the first argument of the *SetClassLongPtr* function.

This example will create the window before globally subclassing the class. Usually, this window is hidden from the user so that the user does not inadvertently close the window and destroy its handle. This handle is also what we need to remove the global subclassing and restore the application to its initial state. Otherwise, the application would crash.

Global subclassing requires that a window, usually hidden, is created and its hWnd used for global subclassing. This window must remain in memory for the life of the application.

A minor modification is needed in the *DisableSubclass* function. The modification might seem minor, but it will have a big impact on whether the example will work. Look at the following line in the *DisableSubclass* function:

```
m_lOrigClassProc = 0
```

This line must be removed. If the reason for this is not apparent at first, let me explain. The object created from the CSubclass class holds the window handle (*m_hwnd*) of the original window we created before modifying the class. We need to keep this handle for the lifetime of the application. We also have the pointer to the original class procedure (*m_lOrigClassProc*), which we need to keep for the lifetime of the application. This is because when we modify a class through global subclassing and then create new windows from the modified class, those new windows can exist for the lifetime of the application.

When a message is sent to the globally subclassed window, that window will look up its own modified window procedure and call it. In this example, that window procedure would be the *NewClassProc* function in our BAS module. The problem doesn't lie here, though. It lies at the end of the window procedure, where we try to call the original class procedure. Remember, the class was subclassed, not the window.

When a window is created from the modified class, the window procedure it receives from the class is considered to be that window's original window procedure. If we had intentionally removed the global subclass and the code had set the `m_lOrigClassProc` variable to 0 (as it would in instance subclassing), *CallWindowProc* would try to dereference a NULL pointer to get the address of the original window procedure. You might have thought that just because the global subclassing had been removed, all windows would suddenly revert to calling their original window procedure. This is not the case because the `lpfnWndProc` member of the window structure of preexisting windows is not modified by the call to *SetClassLongPtr*. Whenever a message is sent to a globally subclassed window, it still tries to call our *NewClassProc* function and, in turn, the original window procedure (indicated by `m_lOrigClassProc`). This is illustrated in Figure 4-5. This diagram will be discussed in more detail later in this chapter.

These are the only modifications that we will make to this class.

 Do not lose the hWnd and original window procedure contained in the CSubclass class when implementing global subclassing.

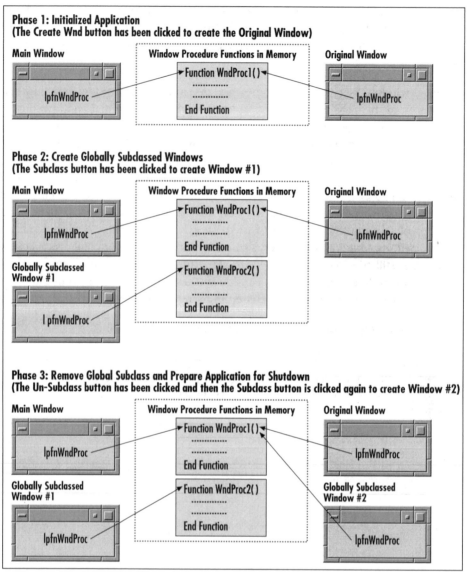

Figure 4-5. The lifetime of the globally subclassed example application where WndProc1 is the window procedure of the unmodified class and WndProc2 is the window procedure of the modified class

The final code for the class is shown in Example 4-11, with revised lines in bold-face.

Example 4-11. Modified CSubclass.cls Module for the Global Subclassing Example

```
#If Win32 Then
    Private Declare Function SetWindowLongPtr Lib "user32" Alias "SetWindowLongA" _
```

```
FocusWindow = 0
For I = 0 To Forms.Count - 1
    If Forms(I).hwnd = hwnd Then
        FocusWindow = I
        Exit For
    End If
Next I
```

Global subclassing will allow more than one window to use the same subclassed window procedure. This can be very powerful because it allows us to add functionality to a number of similar windows without having to write subclassing code for each separate window, as we would with instance subclassing. The problem is that all the windows that have been globally subclassed will use the same window procedure (*NewClassProc*). So the trick is to determine which window the message is bound for. This is easier than it looks. Remember, we are always passed a hWnd window handle in our subclassed window procedure. We can use the *hwnd* argument to set up a loop iterating through each window of the project to determine which window we need to work with; of course, this is not the optimal solution. Whenever we need to set the form height property of this window, for example, we could simply use the following code:

```
Forms(FocusWindow).Height = 30
```

The window procedure then needs to be modified so that we perform our operations on the window in the *FocusWindow* ordinal position in the Forms collection. Example 4-12 shows the complete window procedure, with revised lines indicated in boldface.

Example 4-12. The Window Procedure for the Global Subclassing Example

```
Public Function NewClassProc(ByVal hwnd As Long, ByVal uMsg As Long, _
            ByVal wParam As Long, ByVal lParam As Long) As Long

    Dim I As Integer
    Dim FocusWindow As Long

    NewClassProc = CallWindowProc(CSubClsApp.OrigWndProc, hwnd, uMsg, _
                        wParam, lParam)
    For I = 0 To Forms.Count - 1
        If Forms(I).hwnd = hwnd Then
            FocusWindow = I
            Exit For
        End If
    Next I

    'Modify the windows default processing if necessary
    If uMsg = WM_SYSCOMMAND And FocusWindow <> 0 Then
        If wParam = SC_MINIMIZE Then
            If Forms(FocusWindow).WindowState <> vbMaximized Then
                'Do not process message - instead do our own work
                Forms(FocusWindow).Height = 30
```

Example 4-12. The Window Procedure for the Global Subclassing Example (continued)

```
                End If
                NewClassProc = 0
        Else
                NewClassProc = CallWindowProc(CSubClsApp.OrigWndProc, hwnd, uMsg, _
                                              wParam, lParam)
        End If
    Else
        'Pass message to default handler
        NewClassProc = CallWindowProc(CSubClsApp.OrigWndProc, hwnd, uMsg, _
                                      wParam, lParam)
    End If
End Function
```

 All globally subclassed windows will call the same subclassed window procedure in your BAS module. This means that your window procedure must be able to determine which window the message is intended for.

Changes to the Form

The number of code changes that must be made to the form are substantial. Most notably, the order of events needed to install and uninstall the global subclass must be changed. Also, there is a new button on the form called Create Wnd. This button will create a form; we use this form's handle to initiate global subclassing. The main form looks the same as the form used in the instance subclassing examples, except for the addition of this new button. In addition to these changes, a brand-new form named frmGlobalSub is added to the project. This new form has no code associated with it, and only its Caption property is changed to read "Globally Subclassed Form". This new form is used to provide the hWnd that is used in the call to *SetClassLongPtr*.

Example 4-13 shows the code behind the new button, which is named cmdCreateWnd. This button-click event first creates a new form from the frmGlobalSub form that was added to the project. In a real-life application, this window would be hidden from the user. Next, an instance of the CSubclass class is created and initialized with the handle of the window just created. Finally, this button is disabled. This is to remove the user's ability to create another window and a new CSubclass object.

Example 4-13. The Create Wnd Button's Click Event Procedure

```
Private Sub cmdCreateWnd_Click()
    'Create new form
    Dim CGSubForm As New frmGlobalSub
```

Example 4-13. The Create Wnd Button's Click Event Procedure (continued)

```
    CGSubForm.Caption = "Original Window"
    CGSubForm.Visible = True

    'Create subclassing object
    Set CSubClsApp = New CSubclass
    CSubClsApp.hwnd = CGSubForm.hwnd

    'Do not create a second instance, we will lose the original hwnd
    cmdCreateWnd.Enabled = False
End Sub
```

The Click event procedure for the Subclass button is entirely new; it is shown in Example 4-14. The code checks to make sure that a window has been created that can be used to initiate global subclassing. This is done by making sure that the cmdCreateWnd button has been disabled. If it has been disabled, the *EnableSubclass* public method in the **CSubclass** object is called. This method will use *SetClassLongPtr* to modify the **lpfnWndProc** member of the class structure. The last thing this method does is create a new form using the modified class.

Example 4-14. The cmdSubclass_Click Event Procedure

```
Private Sub cmdSubclass_Click()

    Dim NewForm As frmGlobalSub

    If cmdCreateWnd.Enabled = False Then
        Call CSubClsApp.EnableSubclass

        Set NewForm = New frmGlobalSub
        NewForm.Show
    Else
        MsgBox "Click on the 'Create Wnd' button to create a window to subclass."
    End If
End Sub
```

This button can be clicked multiple times to create multiple globally subclassed windows without crashing the application. This is because the *EnableSubclass* method will call the *SetClassLongPtr* API function only once. After this method has successfully been called, it knows not to call *SetClassLongPtr* a second time. Calling *SetClassLongPtr* a second time would cause us to lose the function pointer (**m_lOrigClassProc**) to the original window procedure in the class.

The Un-Subclass button still calls the *DisableSubclass* public method of the **CSubclass** class. The only difference is that it now checks to see if the cmdCreateWnd button has been disabled before calling the *DisableSubclass* method. Its single line of code then appears as follows:

```
    If Not Me.cmdCreateWnd.Enabled Then Call CSubClsApp.DisableSubclass
```

All the code in the Form_Load event should be removed.

Next, add the following code before the existing code in the *Form_QueryUnload* event procedure:

```
'Remove all child windows to prevent a GPF
Dim I As Integer
For I = Forms.Count - 1 To 0 Step -1
    If Forms(I).Caption <> "Chapter 4 - Subclassing Example" And _
            Forms(I).Caption <> "Original Window" Then
        Unload Forms(I)
    End If
Next I
```

This event still destroys the **CSubClsApp** object, but certain processing must now happen before and after the **CSubClsApp** object destruction. Before the class is destroyed, all globally subclassed windows must be unloaded. This code destroys only the globally subclassed windows; destroying any other window would cause our application to crash. Because we know what the window captions will contain, it is a simple matter of looping through all the current windows in the application and only unloading the ones that have been globally subclassed. We do not want to unload the main form because it is already in the process of being unloaded. Neither do we want to unload the original window because, as I mentioned earlier, we would lose our window handle (*m_hwnd*) that is needed to release the global subclassing.

Instead of using the form's caption to determine if the window has been globally subclassed, you might want to store an array of window handles. You can then loop through this array and unload each window in the array. When using this method, make absolutely certain that you unload every globally subclassed window or your application could crash.

After the class has been destroyed, the original window can be destroyed. The following code, which should be added to the end of the *Form_QueryUnload* procedure, does just that:

```
'Remove the original window to clean up
For I = Forms.Count - 1 To 0 Step -1
    If Forms(I).Caption = "Original Window" Then
    Unload Forms(I)
    End If
Next I
```

Unload all globally subclassed forms before destroying the CSubclass object. Unload the original window that is used to get the hWnd to initiate global subclassing only after destroying the CSubclass object.

Example 4-15 shows the complete window procedure, with revised lines indicated in boldface.

Example 4-15. The Modified frmCh4.frm Module for the Global Subclassing Example

```
Private Sub cmdCreateWnd_Click()
    'Create new form
    Dim CGSubForm As New frmGlobalSub
    CGSubForm.Caption = "Original Window"
    CGSubForm.Visible = True

    'Create subclassing object
    Set CSubClsApp = New CSubclass
    CSubClsApp.hwnd = CGSubForm.hwnd

    'Do not create a second instance, we will lose the original hwnd
    cmdCreateWnd.Enabled = False
End Sub

Private Sub cmdSubclass_Click()
    If cmdCreateWnd.Enabled = False Then
        Call CSubClsApp.EnableSubclass

        Set NewForm = New frmGlobalSub
        NewForm.Show
    Else
        MsgBox "Click on the 'Create Wnd' button to create a window to subclass."
    End If
End Sub

Private Sub cmdUnSubclass_Click()
    If cmdCreateWnd.Enabled = False Then
        Call CSubClsApp.DisableSubclass
    Else
        MsgBox "Click on the 'Create Wnd' button to create a window to subclass."
    End If
End Sub

Private Sub Form_QueryUnload(Cancel As Integer, UnloadMode As Integer)
    'Remove all child windows to prevent a GPF
    Dim I As Integer
    For I = Forms.Count - 1 To 0 Step -1
        If Forms(I).Caption <> "Chapter 4 - Subclassing Example" _
        And Forms(I).Caption <> "Original Window" Then
            Unload Forms(I)
        End If
    Next I

    'Make sure class is destroyed here
    Set CSubClsApp = Nothing

    'Remove the original window to clean up
    For I = Forms.Count - 1 To 0 Step -1
```

Example 4-15. The Modified frmCh4.frm Module for the Global Subclassing Example (continued)

```
        If Forms(I).Caption = "Original Window" Then
            Unload Forms(I)
        End If
    Next I
End Sub
```

Quite a few code changes and additions were made to the form module, but global subclassing does operate a bit differently than instance subclassing.

How It All Works

When you run this code, the global subclassing application is easy to use; here are the steps you follow to use this application:

1. Click the Create Wnd button.

2. Click the Subclass button. (This button can be clicked multiple times to create globally subclassed windows.)

3. Closing the application can be done in one of two ways:

    a. Click the Un-Subclass button and then close the application.

    b. Close the application without clicking the Un-Subclass button.

When you click the Create Wnd button, a new window is created with the caption "Original Window". This window's handle is needed by *SetClassLongPtr* to initiate global subclassing. This is also the window that is usually hidden from the user. Now the application has all the information it needs for global subclassing.

When the user clicks the Subclass button, a new window is created and displayed. This window has the caption "Globally Subclassed Form". Here's the interesting part. When you click the Minimize button on the title bar of the window with the caption "Original Window", the window is minimized as it normally would be. When you click the Minimize button for the window with the caption "Globally Subclassed Form", the form rolls up instead of being minimized. That's not all. If you click the Subclass button repeatedly, new windows will be displayed with the caption "Globally Subclassed Form". Each new window will also roll up when the Minimize button is clicked.

Instead of performing instance subclassing on each window separately, which would be a lot of work, we have altered the base functionality of every window to suit our needs. Clicking the Un-Subclass button and closing the application will destroy all the created windows and restore the original *lpfnWndProc* function pointer in the form window class.

Now that you know how to use this example application, let's take a look at what is going on behind the scenes. Nothing of real interest happens when the application is first started. Clicking the Create Wnd button only sets up the application for global subclassing. At this point, no subclassing of any kind has occurred. The application will be displayed on the screen similar to Figure 4-6.

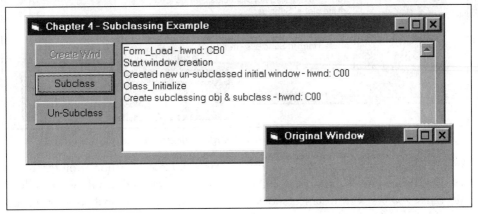

Figure 4-6. Screenshot of the example application after clicking the Create Wnd button

Nothing much has happened so far. Neither window has been modified, so they each will use their own default window procedure. The state of the application can be seen in Figure 4-7.

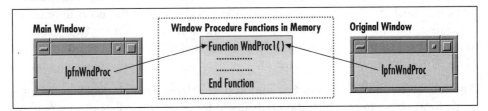

Figure 4-7. State of the application after clicking the Create Wnd button

The next step is to click the Subclass button. This creates a new window, and the application now appears as in Figure 4-8.

The code for the Subclass button calls the *EnableSubclass* public method of the **CSubclass** class. The *EnableSubclass* method will use *SetClassLongPtr* to modify the class that was used to create the original window (from here on out, when I use the term "original window" I am referring to the window with the caption "Original Window"). The class that this function modifies is **ThunderRT6FormDC**. The *SetClassLongPtr* API function requires a window handle (*m_hwnd*) to modify the function pointer to the class window procedure. This window handle must be taken from a window created from the class that we want to globally subclass.

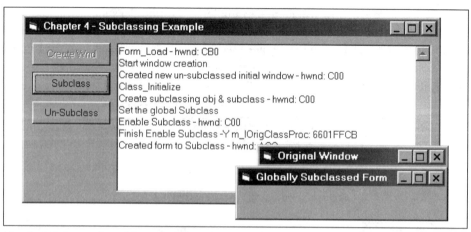

Figure 4-8. Screenshot of the example application after clicking the Subclass button

After calling *SetClassLongPtr*, the class' `lpfnWndProc` function pointer to its window procedure is now pointing to our new subclassed window procedure, *NewClassProc*. As with instance subclassing, we retain the original window procedure in the `m_lOrigClassProc` member variable so that we can restore the class to its original state.

Because the class was globally subclassed after the original window was created, the original window will continue using the pointer to the class's original window procedure (this is the same pointer that is contained in the m_lOrigClassProc member variable). When the original window was created, the class information used to create this window was copied into the window structure. The pointer to this window's window procedure is no longer tied to the class's window procedure. Therefore, it remains unchanged.

The second thing that the Subclass button does is create a new window from the same form object from which the original window was created. This new window uses the function pointer to the window procedure that is now contained in the modified class. Therefore, when you click the Minimize button for the original window, the window is actually minimized the way Windows intended, and when you click the Minimize button of the new window, it rolls up instead of minimizes. Figure 4-9 shows the state of the application at this point.

Each time the Subclass button is clicked, a new window is created. This new window will use the same class that we previously modified. Therefore, each new window will roll up as well.

The next step is to click the Un-Subclass button. The screen should look something similar to Figure 4-10. The code behind this button calls the *DisableSubclass* public member function of the `CSubclass` class. The only action *DisableSubclass*

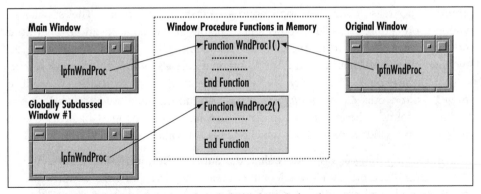

Figure 4-9. State of the application after clicking the Subclass button

performs is to call *SetClassLongPtr*, which removes the global subclass. If you observe the functionality of each created window, you will notice that the way they function has not changed, even though the global subclass has been removed. This is because only the class structure has changed; not the window structure of each existing window. If you minimize the original window, it still works the way the Windows operating system intended it to work. Each new window created after the Subclass button was clicked retains the roll-up functionality.

 Global subclassing affects the class structure, not the window structure of existing windows.

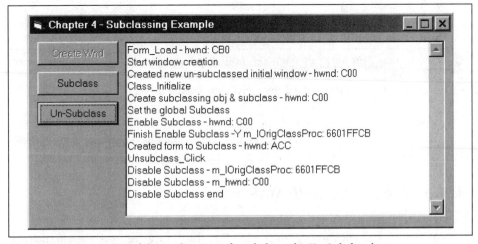

Figure 4-10. Screenshot of the application after clicking the Un-Subclass button

There is no reason for this application to crash at this point. The subclassed window procedure *NewClassProc* is still available at the same location. Therefore, no function pointers are pointing to invalid memory locations. We still have the member variable that contains the original class's window procedure (*m_ lOrigClassProc*). That way, when our subclassed window procedure, *NewClassProc*, calls *CallWindowProc* to pass on the message, a valid window procedure is found. The modified window class has been changed back to use its original class window procedure, which is also still valid.

The interesting thing to do now is click the Subclass button again. Because the *m_ lOrigClassProc* member variable still contains the class's original window procedure, the code will not allow *SetClassLongPtr* to be called a second time. This way we are assured of not losing the original class's window procedure. After bypassing the call to set another global subclass, the code creates a new window. This window inherits its properties from the restored window class, which now has its original class window procedure. The newly created window uses this window procedure as its default. Clicking the Minimize button of this new window will minimize it the way Windows intended it to be minimized. This is shown in Figure 4-11.

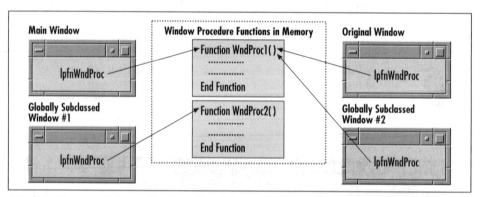

Figure 4-11. State of the application after clicking the Un-Subclass button (the Globally Subclassed Window #2 is created after removing the global subclass with the SetClassLongPtr API function; notice that it uses the unmodified class's window procedure as its own)

It is also important to note that if the application is closed before the global subclass is removed, the `CSubclass` class will automatically remove the global subclass when the class is destroyed. This prevents our application from crashing.

Behind the Scenes with Spy++

To see how this application works from the inside, let's use the Spy++ utility to spy on the global subclassing example. For this purpose, you should use the application's compiled EXE, rather than running it from the development environment. The information that you see in Spy++ for an application that is running in the development environment most likely will not be correct because of the way VB handles the `AddressOf` operator while running an application in the IDE. Note, though, that when running this example on your computer you will not see the memory addresses and handles that I use here. I am using these values to show you the relationships between classes and their windows.

First, let's start up the global subclassing example and then run Spy++. View the application's windows by selecting the Spy → Windows menu item or by pressing Ctrl-W. Find the line which has the window caption followed by the word ThunderRT6Main (i.e., "Chapter 4—Subclassing Example" ThunderRT6Main). I will refer to this window as the *main form*. At this point, the main window is displayed, and the information we gather from the General and Class tabs of the Windows Properties dialog box is as follows:

```
Window Caption = "Chapter 4 - Subclassing Example"
hWnd = 00190444
Wnd Proc = 6601FFCB
Class Name = ThunderRT6FormDC
Class Wnd Proc = 6601FFCB
```

A window has been created and displayed; that is about it. Next, click the Create Wnd button on the main form, then switch to Spy++ and press F5 to refresh the Spy++ display. A new window is displayed with the following attributes:

```
Window Caption = "Original Window"
hWnd = 00460536
Wnd Proc = 6601FFCB
Class Name = ThunderRT6FormDC
Class Wnd Proc = 6601FFCB
```

The main window's attributes remain the same as before you clicked the Create Wnd button. Now everything is in place for us to successfully perform global subclassing. Here comes the interesting part. Click the Subclass button on the main form. Now let's take a look at the attributes of all three windows:

```
Window Caption = "Chapter 4 - Subclassing Example"
hWnd = 00190444
Wnd Proc = 6601FFCB
Class Name = ThunderRT6FormDC
Class Wnd Proc = 004050C5

Window Caption = "Original Window"
hWnd = 00460536
Wnd Proc = 6601FFCB
Class Name = ThunderRT6FormDC
Class Wnd Proc = 004050C5

Window Caption = "Globally Subclassed Form"
hWnd = 00D5053E
Wnd Proc = 004050C5
```

```
Class Name = ThunderRT6FormDC
Class Wnd Proc = 004050C5
```

As you might notice, the Class Wnd Proc field changed from **6601FFCB** to **004050C5**. This field was changed through the *SetClassLongPtr* function. This Class Wnd Proc field is the same for all windows. This is correct because the class information is stored separately from the window information. By looking at this information, you can see that the first two windows that were created remained unchanged—they continue to use their old window procedures. The third window is using the new window procedure (Wnd Proc) from the **ThunderRT6FormDC** class. This is because the first two windows were created using the original class information, while the third window was created after we modified the class's window procedure. If we create more global subclassed windows, their information is the same as the window with the caption "Globally Subclassed Form" (except, of course, for the window handle, which must be unique for all windows).

Now click the Un-Subclass button on the main form. Switch to Spy++, press F5 to refresh its display, and now view each window's information. The new window information is as follows:

```
Window Caption = "Chapter 4 - Subclassing Example"
hWnd = 00190444
Wnd Proc = 6601FFCB
Class Name = ThunderRT6FormDC
Class Wnd Proc = 6601FFCB

Window Caption = "Original Window"
hWnd = 00460536
Wnd Proc = 6601FFCB
Class Name = ThunderRT6FormDC
Class Wnd Proc = 6601FFCB

Window Caption = "Globally Subclassed Form"
hWnd = 00D5053E
Wnd Proc = 004050C5
Class Name = ThunderRT6FormDC
Class Wnd Proc = 6601FFCB
```

The class's window procedure has been changed back to its original value. This value was kept in the *m_lOrigClassProc* member variable in the **CSubclass** class. Even though the class's window procedure is changed back, each window's window procedure remains as it was before clicking the Un-Subclass button. Every window whose Wnd Proc field points to the original window procedure will act like a normal window. Every window whose Wnd Proc field points to the new window procedure that we created will use our modified functionality.

Here is the tricky part, which can bring your application crashing down around you if you are not careful: because each window's window procedure remains the same, subclassed windows will still call the globally subclassed window procedure, *NewClassProc*. The *NewClassProc* window procedure still needs to know the original window procedure to call whenever it receives a message. If we get rid of the value in the *m_lOrigClassProc* member variable, the application will crash because *m_lOrigClassProc* would then point to an invalid location in memory. So, we need to protect the *m_lOrigClassProc* member variable from being modified in any way.

What happens if the Subclass button is clicked at this point? If we click it, a new window appears with the caption "Globally Subclassed Form". This form has the following attributes:

```
Window Caption = "Globally Subclassed Form"
hWnd = 3B5E042C
Wnd Proc = 6601FFCB
Class Name = ThunderRT6FormDC
Class Wnd Proc = 6601FFCB
```

The example code bypasses the call to *SetClassLongPtr* and instead creates a window from the current **ThunderRT6FormDC** class. This window will not have the modified window behavior (notice the value for the Wnd Proc field).

Summary of Key Points in Subclassing

This chapter presented a great deal of information about subclassing. Before proceeding on to the following chapters, make sure that you have a solid grasp of the concepts presented in this chapter. These concepts will be used throughout the rest of the book. To help with this, the following is a list of key points mentioned in the course of this chapter:

- Use **On Error Resume Next** for error handling in the subclassed window procedure.

- Do as little work as possible in the subclassed window procedure.

- Stepping through a subclassing application in the IDE can be problematic.

- Subclassed window procedures and other callback functions must reside in a BAS module.

- Define the subclassed window procedure and any other callback functions as Public.

- Do not end an application before removing all subclassed window procedures.

- Do not use the **End** statement in your code or the Stop button in the VB IDE.

- Never lose the function pointer to the original window procedure for the subclassed window.

- Do not use the *DoEvents* function within any window procedure.

- Thoroughly research the messages that you will be trapping in the subclassed window procedure. Each message has its own little quirks.

- To allow the window to perform the default processing for a message, it must be passed on to the original window procedure (*CallWindowProc*) or to the default window procedure (*DefWindowProc*).

- Instance subclassing affects a specific window and its window procedure. Global subclassing affects every window created from a window class that has had its class window procedure modified.

- Global subclassing allows window creation messages to be processed. Instance subclassing does not have this ability.

- Global subclassing requires that a window, usually hidden, will be created and its hWnd used for global subclassing. This window must remain in memory for the life of the application.

- Do not lose the hWnd and original window procedure contained in the CSubclass class when implementing global subclassing.

- All globally subclassed windows will call the same subclassed window procedure in your BAS module.

- Unload all globally subclassed forms before destroying the CSubclass object. Unload the original window, used to get the hWnd to initiate global subclassing, after destroying the CSubclass object.

- Global subclassing affects the class structure, not the window structure.

5

Subclassing the Windows Common Dialog Boxes

This chapter will focus on subclassing, but in a more specific area. In this chapter I will show you how to subclass the Windows common dialogs. Subclassing is the term commonly used to describe what we will be doing in this chapter, but as we shall see, the term might not be entirely accurate. The Open, Save As, Print, Page Setup, Print Property Sheet, Font, Help, Find, Replace, and Color dialogs are all part of the standard dialogs that ship with the Windows operating system. These dialogs are found in *comdlg32.dll*. Most of them also are encapsulated in an ActiveX control called the Common Dialog control.

Visual Basic (VB) can use either *comdlg32.dll* or the Common Dialog control to create and manipulate these dialog boxes. Using the Common Dialog control hides much of the complexity of using the common dialogs. However, if you want to subclass a common dialog, you have to use *comdlg32.dll* directly. Throughout this chapter I will be using *comdlg32.dll* to create and manipulate the common dialog boxes that we will subclass.

You might wonder why you would want to subclass one of the Windows common dialogs, especially because modifying a common dialog is usually the exception rather than the rule. But sometimes modifying a common dialog box is a more efficient approach to solving a problem, especially when the developer needs more control over a user's interaction with a common dialog box. Instead of creating a whole new Save As or Print Setup dialog box from scratch, we can use the functionality of the Save As common dialog box and augment, customize, or modify its behavior. This saves the developer many hours of re-creating a common dialog by leveraging the prebuilt code within *comdlg32.dll*.

In this chapter, we'll build an example application (see Figure 5-1) that focuses on teaching the fundamentals of subclassing a common dialog box. The common dialog used in this application is the Save As dialog, which we'll modify to perform a simple function by adding four controls to it: a checkbox, a drop-down list box, a text box, and a button. (The button is the only control that serves no real purpose, except to display a message box. I just wanted to add it in this example to show you how to use a button control in a subclassed common dialog box.) Essentially, our sample application will transform the Save As dialog into a rudimentary Export As dialog box, as shown in Figure 5-2. This subclassed common dialog box will take a text file containing several columns of words or numbers and delimit each word or number with a character or characters of the user's choice. The drop-down list box contains a list of standard delimiters that the user can choose from.

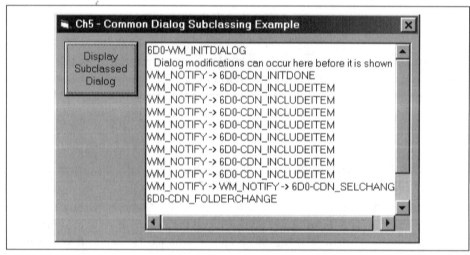

Figure 5-1. The main application window

 The dialog we'll work with is the Explorer-style Save As dialog, as opposed to the outdated old-style Save As dialog box used in earlier versions of Windows. I chose the Save As dialog box because it is almost identical to the Open dialog box, and these two common dialogs are also the most widely used in applications.

Checking the Use Predefined Delimiter checkbox displays the drop-down list box and hides the text box. When the checkbox is unchecked, the drop-down list box is hidden and the text box is displayed. This text box is available to allow the user to enter a delimiting character of his or her choice. Now, I know that I could place the delimiting functionality outside of the common dialog box and everything would work just fine. On the other hand, by encapsulating this functionality within

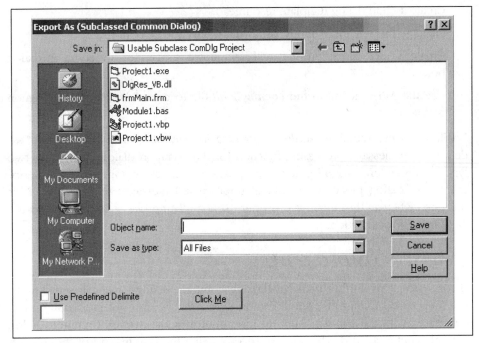

Figure 5-2. The subclassed common dialog box

a common dialog box, other developers can use the same exporting code just by instantiating this common dialog box.

The rest of the common dialog controls retain their default functionality. As an added feature, every time a message of interest is captured by our dialog hook procedure, it will be displayed in the multiline text box on the main application window. The main application window is displayed in Figure 5-1.

The other common dialog boxes work like the Open and Save As dialogs, although each has its own special characteristics. Two features that differ between common dialog boxes are the application programming interface (API) functions used to create the dialogs, and the structures that hold the dialog's information. Even with these differences, the same basic rules can be followed to subclass all common dialogs.

How Common Dialog Box Subclassing Works

Subclassing a common dialog box is not as easy as subclassing a window. A few extra steps are involved. The four main steps are:

1. Create a child dialog template resource.

2. Package this resource in a dynamic link library (DLL), optional

3. Create a hook procedure that will intercept messages for the common dialog box.

4. Use the API function in the *comdlg32.dll* file to create the modified common dialog.

I will be using the term *dialog procedure* instead of "window procedure" to describe the message processing function for the common dialog box. These two types of procedures, for all practical purposes, are the same. One small difference is that the dialog procedure sends all unprocessed messages to the *DefDlgProc* function, whereas the window procedure sends all unprocessed messages to the *DefWindowProc* function.

Using the COMDLG32.DLL

Before going any further with subclassing common dialogs, we will see how to use the *comdlg32.dll* APIs. The common dialog that we use for subclassing must be created with the *comdlg32.dll* API instead of with the ActiveX Common Dialog control (*comdlg32.ocx*). The consequence of using the DLL instead of the ActiveX control (OCX) is mainly added complexity: all the details that the OCX hid from us are now up to us to handle. The good thing is that there is no longer a performance penalty for having to load the *comdlg32.ocx*, and this file will not have to be shipped along with your final application.

The common dialog box relies on *comdlg32.dll* for much more that just its creation. This DLL provides the dialog procedure for the dialog (a *dialog procedure* does for a dialog what a window procedure does for a window). This DLL also contains the default dialog resources needed to describe the common dialog box. This is why we must add our own dialog template resource to the common dialog box instead of just modifying the common dialog box resource directly. The DLL also handles message routing within the common dialog boxes.

For our example, we'll create a Save As common dialog box. As we'll see, using the *comdlg32.dll* to create common dialog boxes by hand is not as hard as it sounds. To start off, the *GetSaveFileName* API function and the OPENFILENAME structure must be defined. The *GetSaveFileName* function, which opens the Save As common dialog, is declared as follows:

```
Private Declare Function GetSaveFileName Lib "comdlg32.dll" _
    Alias "GetSaveFileNameA" (pSavefilename As OPENFILENAME) As Long
```

Its single parameter is:

pSaveFilename

A pointer to an OPENFILENAME structure

The *GetSaveFileName* API function takes the OPENFILENAME structure as its only parameter and uses it to create and display the Save As common dialog box. This function will return zero if there is an error, if the Close button on the titlebar was clicked, or if the Cancel button was clicked.

The OPENFILENAME structure is declared as follows:

```
Private Type OPENFILENAME
    lStructSize As Long
    hwndOwner As Long
    hInstance As Long
    lpstrFilter As String
    lpstrCustomFilter As String
    nMaxCustFilter As Long
    nFilterIndex As Long
    lpstrFile As String
    nMaxFile As Long
    lpstrFileTitle As String
    nMaxFileTitle As Long
    lpstrInitialDir As String
    lpstrTitle As String
    flags As Long
    nFileOffset As Integer
    nFileExtension As Integer
    lpstrDefExt As String
    lCustData As Long
    lpfnHook As Long
    lpTemplateName As String
    pvReserved As Long
    dwReserved As Long
    FlagsEx As Long
End Type
```

It has the following members:

lStructSize

Size of this structure. It should be set to Len(OPENFILENAME).

hwndOwner

The handle of the dialog's owning window. It can be zero if no window owns this dialog.

hInstance

The handle to the object that contains the dialog template resource. For this example, this is a handle to our resource DLL. To get this handle, the *LoadLibrary* API function is used. This function takes one parameter: the path and filename of the DLL. *LoadLibrary* returns the handle to the DLL.

lpstrFilter

A string defining the filters, if any, used in the dialog box's Save As Type drop-down list. The filter is in the format *{filter name}|{filter}*. The filter name is a name for the filter, such as "All Files". The filter is an expression used to describe the filter, such as "*.*". Therefore, the code to describe this filter would look like the following:

```
OPENFILENAME.lpstrFilter = "AllFiles | *.*"
```

lpstrCustomFilter

The last filter chosen by the user.

nMaxCustFilter

The size of *lpstrCustomFilter*.

nFilterIndex

The index of the chosen filter.

lpstrFile

When initializing the dialog, this member contains the default text for the File Name edit control. When the user selects a file and exits the dialog box, this member contains the complete path of the selected file.

nMaxFile

The size of *lpstrFile*.

lpstrFileTitle

The filename and extension of only the returned file.

nMaxFileTitle

The size of *lpstrFileTitle*.

lpstrInitialDir

The default path for the dialog box when it is initialized.

lpstrTitle

The title of the dialog box.

Flags

Various flags used to initialize the dialog box. Some of the more commonly used flags are:

OFN_ALLOWMULTISELECT (&H200)

Allows the user to select more than one file.

OFN_EXPLORER (&H80000)

Creates a new Explorer-style common dialog box.

OFN_FILEMUSTEXIST (&H1000)

To open a file, the file must exist or an error is raised.

OFN_HIDEREADONLY (&H04)

The Read Only checkbox on the dialog is hidden.

OFN_NOVALIDATE (&H100)

The file and path are not validated during processing by the dialog.

OFN_PATHMUSTEXIST (&H800)

The path chosen in the dialog must exist, or an error is raised.

OFN_SHOWHELP (&H10)

The Help button is displayed.

OFN_ENABLEHOOK (&H20)

Used for subclassing; enables the use of a dialog hook procedure.

OFN_ENABLETEMPLATE (&H40)

Used for subclassing; enables the use of a resource in either a .RES or .DLL format.

OFN_ENABLETEMPLATEHANDLE (&H80)

Used for subclassing; enables the use of a resource stored in memory.

OFN_ENABLEINCLUDENOTIFY (&H400000)

Used for subclassing; enables the dialog to send the CDN_INCLUDEITEM notification.

nFileOffset

The position of the first character of the filename in *lpstrFile*. This member is zero-based.

nFileExtension

The position of the first character of the filename extension in *lpstrFile*. This member is zero-based.

lpstrDefExt

The file extension appended to the filename, if one is not provided.

lCustData

Extra data that can be sent to the dialog hook procedure via the WM_INITDIALOG message. When this message is sent to the hook procedure, it contains a pointer to this structure in the *lParam* parameter of this message.

lpfnHook

The pointer to our dialog hook procedure.

lpTemplateName

The dialog template resource ID.

pvReserved

Reserved by the system.

dwReserved

Reserved by the system.

FlagsEx

Setting this flag to zero allows the Places bar to be displayed on the common dialog box; setting this flag to any other number prevents this bar from displaying. The Places bar is located on the lefthand side of the Open and Save As common dialog boxes under Windows 2000 and contains shortcuts to commonly used folders, such as Desktop, History, My Documents, My Computer, and My Network Places.

The OPENFILENAME structure contains information needed to initialize the Save As common dialog box. After the *GetSaveFileName* function returns, the OPENFILENAME structure is returned with some member values changed. The *lpstrFileTitle* member for this structure returns information about the file and extension the user has selected or typed into the Save As dialog box. The *lpstrFile* member returns the entire path and filename for the selected or typed-in filename.

Although the OPENFILENAME structure and the *GetSaveFileName* API function are used for the Save As dialog box, most every other common dialog box is created using a different structure and a different API function. The structure names and API function calls for these other common dialogs are listed in Table 5-1.

Table 5-1. Structures and Functions for All Common Dialog Boxes

Common Dialog Type	Dialog Structure	Dialog Creation Function
Open	OPENFILENAME	*GetOpenFileName*
Save As	OPENFILENAME	*GetSaveFileName*
Color	CHOOSECOLOR	*ChooseColor*
Font	CHOOSEFONT	*ChooseFont*
Print	PRINTDLG	*PrintDlg*
Print Property Sheet (Win2000)	PRINTDLGEX	*PrintDlgEx*
Page Setup	PAGESETUPDLG	*PageSetupDlg*
Find	FINDREPLACE	*FindText*
Replace	FINDREPLACE	*ReplaceText*

The code in Example 5-1 shows how to initialize the OPENFILENAME structure and call the *GetSaveFileName* API function. To use this code, create a new VB Standard EXE project and add a button called Command1 to the form. None of the default properties needs to be changed for either the form or the button. Next, insert this code into the form's code window. Run the project and click the button. A Save As dialog box will appear with the title "Common Dialog Example".

Example 5-1. Opening the Save As Common Dialog

```
Private Declare Function GetSaveFileName Lib "comdlg32.dll" Alias _
    "GetSaveFileNameA" (pOpenfilename As OpenFilename) As Long
```

Example 5-1. Opening the Save As Common Dialog (continued)

```
Private Type OpenFilename
    lStructSize As Long
    hwndOwner As Long
    hInstance As Long
    lpstrFilter As String
    lpstrCustomFilter As String
    nMaxCustFilter As Long
    nFilterIndex As Long
    lpstrFile As String
    nMaxFile As Long
    lpstrFileTitle As String
    nMaxFileTitle As Long
    lpstrInitialDir As String
    lpstrTitle As String
    flags As Long
    nFileOffset As Integer
    nFileExtension As Integer
    lpstrDefExt As String
    lCustData As Long
    lpfnHook As Long
    lpTemplateName As Long
    pvReserved As Long
    dwReserved As Long
    FlagsEx As Long
End Type


Private Sub Command1_Click()
    Dim SaveAsDlgStruct As OpenFilename
    Dim lRetVal As Long

    'Initialize data structure
    SaveAsDlgStruct.lStructSize = Len(SaveAsDlgStruct)
    SaveAsDlgStruct.hwndOwner = Me.hWnd
    SaveAsDlgStruct.lpstrFilter = "All Files" & Chr$(0) & "*.*" & Chr$(0) & Chr$(0)
    SaveAsDlgStruct.lpstrFile = Chr$(0) & Space(255)
    SaveAsDlgStruct.nMaxFile = Len(SaveAsDlgStruct.lpstrFile) - 1
    SaveAsDlgStruct.nFilterIndex = 1
    SaveAsDlgStruct.lpstrInitialDir = "C:\"
    SaveAsDlgStruct.lpstrTitle = "Common Dialog Example"
    SaveAsDlgStruct.flags = 0
    SaveAsDlgStruct.FlagsEx = 0

    'Call API function to create the common dialog box
    lRetVal = GetSaveFileName(SaveAsDlgStruct)

    'Determine and act on the return value
    If lRetVal = 0 Then
        Debug.Print "The Cancel button was clicked or an error occured"
    Else
        Debug.Print Trim(SaveAsDlgStruct.lpstrFile) & " is the file to be saved"
    End If
End Sub
```

Basically three steps are involved in this code sample:

1. Initialize the OPENFILENAME structure. Many of the members in this structure are familiar to you if you have used the ActiveX common dialog control. Some will not be familiar. One of the members that might not be familiar to you is *lStructSize*, which must be set to the length of the entire structure; this ensures that the *GetSaveFileName* function will not write to memory past the bounds of this structure. The *hwndOwner* member is the handle to the window that owns this common dialog box; in our case, it is equal to frmMain.hwnd.

2. Call the *GetSaveFileName* function to create and display the dialog box.

3. Retrieve the path and filename of the selected file based on the return value of *GetSaveFileName*.

The code here does not do much more than the *comdlg32.ocx* control would do. The difference is that using the *comdlg32.ocx* control decreases the amount of code that we have to write for this example. This example does not allow the common dialog to be subclassed. To implement a common dialog hook procedure to intercept messages and a dialog template resource to modify the user interface (UI) of the common dialog, we must learn a little more about the *comdlg32.dll* and the way it functions.

The Resource File

The first step in subclassing a common dialog box involves creating a dialog resource that will be stored in a resource file. VB requires the resource file to have an extension of .RES. This file contains information on each individual resource stored within it. Many types of resources can be stored in this file; some of the main types of resources used by Windows are:

Strings
Cursors
Accelerator tables
Bitmaps
Dialogs
Icons
Menus
Fonts
User-defined resources

All resources in Windows follow a standardized format. Each resource has a unique identifier (a constant called a *resource id*) that is used by an application to manipulate that particular resource. For the application to use the resource, this identifier must be defined in your VB application as well as in the resource file. If you use a resource editor, the resource ID is provided to you. Finally, the resource file contains the actual data that constitutes the resource.

Resource files can be created by hand, but it is much easier to create them through a resource-editing tool. Visual C++ has such a tool called the Resource Editor that can produce standard Windows resources. This is the tool I will use in this chapter, but you can use what is most familiar to you.

Using resource files can improve application response time. Instead of loading all resources at one time, you can load individual resources as they are needed. Take, for instance, images on a form in VB. If the images were stored on the form, they would all be loaded into memory when the form was loaded into memory. If, instead, the images were in a resource file separate from the form, the form could load itself into memory and then load the images into memory one by one as needed.

Another useful feature of resource files is the ability to internationalize an application with minimal changes to the application itself. If all strings used by an application reside in a single resource file, that file could be translated into another language and then recompiled into the application. This would allow the application to support multiple languages without the developer having to touch the application or any of its code. Of course, for this to work to its fullest potential, all strings—including field identifiers, all captions, static text for any form or control, and any message box and dialog text, just to mention a few—must reside in the resource file.

In this chapter, we will not focus on these two uses of resource files. Rather, we will be using the resource file for the purpose of storing a dialog resource that defines the controls we are adding to the dialog and their placement. The resource will then be included in the standard common dialog box as a child dialog window. For reference, I will call this resource a *dialog template resource file.*

In this chapter I refer to both a parent and a child dialog window. The parent dialog window is the original dialog window that we intend to subclass, and the dialog template resource file describes the child dialog window. For a visual description, see Figure 5-3, which is a subclassed Save As dialog. The parent dialog is the window containing all the original controls for this dialog. The child dialog is the window indicated by the dotted line; this is where the controls we added are placed. The child dialog is superimposed onto the parent dialog, and the upper-left coordinate of the child dialog begins at location 0,0 of the common dialog's client area.

Subclassing a common dialog box allows us to intercept messages to control the look and behavior of the dialog. The dialog resource allows us to add controls to the existing common dialog box. Using subclassing, we also can intercept messages from these new controls added by the resource template. It is possible to subclass a common dialog box without first creating a dialog resource. If a dialog resource is not implemented, the look of the common dialog will not be modified from its original appearance.

We need to create this dialog template resource file because it is not possible to directly modify the default dialog template for the Explorer-style Open and Save As common dialog boxes. Every common dialog box has a default dialog template that determines where controls are placed on the dialog and what each control's properties are set to. Most common dialog default templates are contained in a header (*.h*) file that is accessible by the developer (more on these header files later in this chapter). These header files can be modified and recompiled to change the default appearance of the dialog. However, the default dialog templates for the Explorer-style Open and Save As dialogs are compiled into the *comdlg32.dll* file and, therefore, are not accessible.

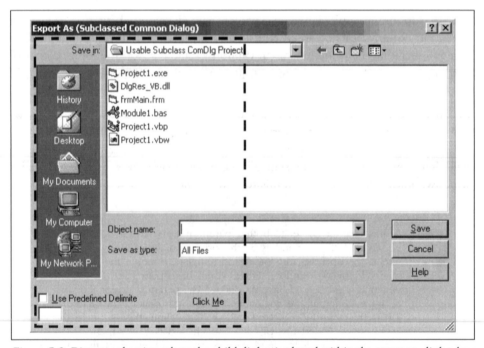

Figure 5-3. Diagram showing where the child dialog is placed within the common dialog box

The common dialog box will treat the dialog template resource that we create as a child window to itself, as Figure 5-3 shows. Any time I reference either the child dialog template resource or the dialog template resource, I am speaking of the dialog resource that is contained within the resource file (.RES) or the .DLL.

Multiple resources can be contained within a single .RES file. So, if you need to modify more than one common dialog or modify one common dialog in several different ways, all the dialog template resources can be placed within a single .RES file. When placing multiple resources within a single .RES file, make sure that a unique ID identifies each resource. Placing multiple resources in a single resource file is necessary because VB allows only one resource file per project. Adding a second file will produce an error, and it will not be added to the project.

Creating a Dialog Resource File Using VB and Visual C++

Though you could create the dialog resource using only Visual C++, I will show you how to use VB to start out the process. For those of you more comfortable using the Visual C++ dialog editor, feel free to use only that editor. For those of you who develop mainly in VB, you might feel more comfortable using the dialog (form) editor in VB. It does not matter which tool is used to start the process of creating the dialog resource.

In VB, create a new Standard EXE project and place the four controls that we are adding to the common dialog box (a checkbox, a drop-down list box, a text box, and a command button) on the form, as shown in Figure 5-4. The nondefault properties of the controls are listed in Table 5-2 and the nondefault properties of the form are listed in Table 5-3.

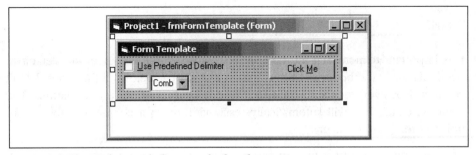

Figure 5-4. The VB form with the controls placed on it

Table 5-2. Nondefault Properties of the Controls

Control Name	Property Name	Property Value
Check1	Caption	&Use Predefined Delimiter
Check1	Top	60

Table 5-2. Nondefault Properties of the Controls (continued)

Control Name	Property Name	Property Value
Check1	Left	120
Check1	Height	252
Check1	Width	2112
Text1	Top	360
Text1	Left	120
Text1	Height	288
Text1	Width	492
Combo1	Style	Dropdown Combo
Combo1	Top	360
Combo1	Left	660
Combo1	Height	288
Combo1	Width	792
Button1	Caption	Click &Me
Button1	Top	60
Button1	Left	3060
Button1	Height	372
Button1	Width	1332

Table 5-3. Nondefault Properties of the Form

Property	Value
Name	frmFormTemplate
Top	0
Left	0
Height	1200
Width	4605

It is important to note that all the controls placed in the resource will default to being placed at the bottom of the common dialog box, below all the other default controls. However, they still retain the same relative position to one another. The common dialog box will automatically resize its form to accommodate these controls (more about this later).

After placing the controls in their proper place on the VB form, save the project. The project filenames are listed in Table 5-4.

Table 5-4. Filenames for the VB Project

Filename	Description
FrmFormTemplate.frm	Contains the form named frmFormTemplate
VB_Form_RES.vbp	Project file

This VB form will be imported into the Visual C++ editor so that a dialog template resource can be created from it.

Next, start up Visual C++ and click the File → New... menu item. In the New dialog, select the Files tab. This tab contains individual items that can be created within the Visual C++ environment. Select the Resource Template item in the list box, type the name of the resource template, **DlgRes**, in the File Name text box (don't include a file extension), and type the location where you want this file to be saved in the Location text box. Click the OK button.

A new window opens up in the Visual C++ IDE with an empty resource file in it. This resource file has the name of the file you typed into the File Name text box in the New dialog, followed by a *.rct* extension. Right-click this item and choose the Import... option from the pop-up menu. This will open the Import Resource dialog box. First, select Visual Basic Forms (.frm) from the Files of Type drop-down box. Then find and select the form file that we just created in VB (*FrmFormTemplate.frm*). The Visual C++ dialog editor will convert this file to one that it can use and display it in its own editor. When creating this example application, I noticed that the drop-down list box was not imported from the VB form. I am not sure why this happened, but if this occurs on your project, simply re-add the control using the Visual C++ editor in the same way as you would in VB.

We must make a few critical modifications to this form. Right-click the form and select Properties from the pop-up menu. The Dialog Properties dialog will appear. On the General tab, remove any text from the Caption text box. Also, make sure that the X Pos and Y Pos text boxes contain a zero. Most of the time there will be no reason to modify the value in the ID drop-down combo box. On the Styles tab, the Style drop-down box should contain the item Child. The Border drop-down box should contain the item None. The "Clip siblings" checkbox should be checked.

Setting the Style drop-down box to Child gives this dialog a style of WS_CHILD. This style informs Windows that this is a child window. Child windows are contained within a parent window. In this case, our dialog template will be a child window of the common dialog box, which is the parent. The coordinate system for the child window originates at the top-left corner of the parent window's client area. Also, any part of the child window that is outside of the parent window's client area is clipped or hidden. Failure to make this a child window will most likely cause the dialog template controls not to display.

Checking the "Clip siblings" checkbox gives this child window a window style of WS_CLIPSIBLINGS. This style will not allow any of the controls on the child dialog box to paint on top of the controls on the default common dialog box.

On the More Styles tab, the only boxes that should be checked are the Visible checkbox, the 3D-look checkbox, and the Control checkbox. The last two tabs are the Extended Styles tab and the More Extended Styles tab. These tabs contain several checkboxes, all of which should be unchecked.

The Control checkbox on the More Styles tab sets the DS_CONTROL style. This style allows the user to use the TAB key to move between the controls on the parent dialog window and those of the child window defined from the dialog template resources. It also allows the user to use any accelerator keys defined in the child window. Basically, this style makes fully integrating our dialog template resource into the common dialog box much easier.

The 3D-look checkbox sets the DS_3DLOOK style. A window using this style draws its controls with a 3D border, and the font for the window will be nonbold as well. This style is required only for applications compiled to run under versions of Windows NT below 3.1. Windows 9x and Windows NT versions 3.1 and above do not require this style to be set; the 3D look and feel is automatically applied to windows running under these operating systems.

The properties should be checked for each control on this dialog as well. For each control, it is a good idea to check the "Tab stop" and Visible checkboxes on the General tab of the Properties dialog box. Also, for checkbox controls, the Auto checkbox on the Styles tab should be checked as well. The Auto checkbox sets the BS_AUTOCHECKBOX style for the checkbox. This style will automatically toggle the checkbox to be checked or unchecked every time a user clicks it.

This is about all that needs to be done in the Visual C++ dialog editor. Save your work and exit Visual C++. If the editor creates a file with an extension other than .RES, you should click the File → Save As... menu item and choose to save the file as type *.RES. The resource file (.RES) created by Visual C++ will be used by our application to modify the look of the common dialog box.

Because it is much easier to use a tool such as the dialog editor in Visual C++ to create the dialog template resource, I am not going to devote time to showing you how to create a dialog resource by hand. If you are interested, you can save the dialog template as a Resource Script (RC) file by clicking File → Save As... in the Visual C++ editor and choosing to save your dialog template as an RC (*.rc) file. Open this file in Notepad and examine the results. The section that is commented with the word "Dialog" is the section where your dialog resource is actually defined. The resource compiler (*RC.EXE*) that ships with Visual Studio can be used to compile this *.rc* file. This is a command line utility that takes a *.rc* file and creates a *.res* file that can be linked to your application by the Visual C++ linker.

It also will be helpful to save the file as a resource script. When a resource is saved as a resource script file, a *resource.h* C++ header file is created. In this file are all the constants that you need in your application to reference the dialog template resource and the controls that you placed on this resource. These constants will need to be declared in your VB subclassing application.

Manipulating Control Placement on the Dialog

Following the steps above allows you to create a resource that will be displayed at the default location in the common dialog box. This default location will always be at the bottom of the dialog box. The common dialog box will be resized to accommodate all the controls on the child dialog template. In the case of our sample application, this is precisely what we want; as Figure 5-3 shows, all the controls from our resource file should appear in the lower-left corner of the Save As dialog.

This placement poses a problem if any controls must be placed on the left side, right side, or top of the common dialog box. However, there is a way to tell the common dialog box where you want to place these controls: you can include a static text control in your custom dialog box template (in VB, the static text control is represented by the Label control) and assign in the identifier `stc32`. (This value is defined in the *Dlgs.h* header file, which is a Windows-supplied header file that contains definitions needed for Windows dialogs.) When a child window has a control whose identifier is `stc32`, Windows will place the parent window's controls in the area defined by the `stc32` control, and will place the child window's controls so that they have the same position as they do relative to the `stc32` control. Windows also will add the necessary space to the left, right, bottom, and top of the dialog box to accommodate the additional controls.

A quick example (which you don't have to create for yourself) shows how this works. Imagine that we create a form that has four command buttons and a Label control. When we import it into the Visual C++ resource editor, it appears as in Figure 5-5. Note that our Label control in VB becomes a static text control in Visual C++. This control will define the area of the common dialog box where the default controls are placed. By placing our new controls around this label control, we allow these controls to be drawn relative to the default controls on the common dialog box. Windows will try to maintain the correlation that the default controls have to the static text control.

To do this, use the static text control's Properties dialog to change its control identifier to `stc32`. As I've mentioned, this value is predefined in the Windows dialog header file, *Dlgs.h*. In VB, this constant is defined as:

```
Const stc32 = &H45F
```

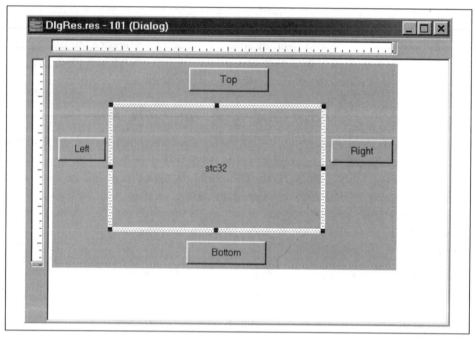

Figure 5-5. The dialog template resource with the stc32 label added

In Visual C++, `stc32` is defined as:

```
#define stc32        0x045f
```

Figure 5-6 shows how Windows uses the static text control to define where the
new controls are placed. Windows tries to place all the standard controls in the
common dialog box inside the static text control. The top left coordinate of the
area containing the default common dialog controls is placed at the same location
as the top left coordinate of the static text control. If the static text control can
hold all the default dialog controls, all is fine. If, instead, the static text control is
too small, the height and width of the static text control are increased until all the
default dialog controls can be placed within it. The new controls that are added to
the common dialog will retain their position relative to the top left corner of the
`stc32` static text control. This means that any controls placed above the static text
control will be placed above the default controls in the dialog, controls placed to
the right of the static text control will be placed to the right of the default controls
in the dialog, and so on. The common dialog box will resize itself to accommodate the new controls.

Using the Resource

After the resource file (.RES) is created, there are two ways to use it within a subclassing application in VB. The first way is to simply add the resource file to the

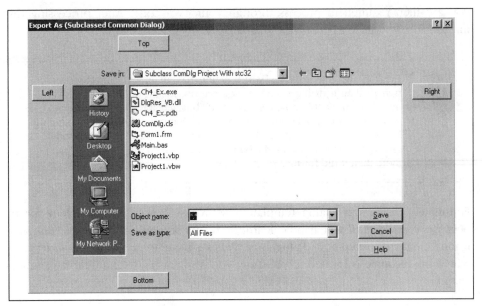

Figure 5-6. The common dialog box created with the dialog template in Figure 5-3

application. The second way is to add the resource file to a DLL and load the resource from this DLL. There is a reason for using each method to incorporate a resource into a project. If an application is running in the IDE at design time, the resource must be in a DLL. When the application is running as a standalone EXE, the resource can be embedded into the EXE as a .RES file, or it can be contained within a DLL. This is a limitation of VB, not of the resource file.

No other application can access the dialog template resource if it is embedded within this application as a .RES file because they are running in separate processes. Placing a resource in a separate DLL allows multiple applications to access the same resources. A single application also can access multiple resource DLLs.

VB has three functions for loading and using resources: *LoadResString*, *LoadResData*, and *LoadResPicture*. Although *LoadResString* and *LoadResPicture* are functions that load particular kinds of data (strings and images, respectively) from resource files, *LoadResData* is a general-purpose function for retrieving items from resource files. Its syntax is:

```
LoadResData(resID, resType)
```

where **resID** is the identifier of the resource, and **resType** is an integer that identifies the type of resource that's being loaded. To load a dialog resource, you supply the *LoadResData* function with a **resType** value of 5, indicating that this is a dialog resource. Unfortunately, this method only returns an array of bytes, which you are then required to process through your own code. After processing this information, you have to create the dialog manually through your code.

> Even though the *LoadResData* function has an index value to support loading a dialog resource, you are not meant to use it this way in VB. I know this might sound odd, but see the Microsoft article entitled "LoadResData Function Does Not Support All Formats." The ID of this article is Q171731 in the Microsoft Developer Network (MSDN) knowledgebase. Maybe this article will clarify things for you more than it did for me.

Fortunately, using our dialog template resource will not be a problem for us because *comdlg32.dll* will handle loading and incorporating the dialog template resource into the common dialog box. All we have to do is tell *comdlg32.dll* where the resource is located. I will show you how this is done a little later in this chapter.

Embedding the Resource in the EXE

Embedding a resource in an executable is a fairly straightforward process. The resource (.RES) file needs to be added to the project by using the Project → Add File menu option, and then the project needs to be compiled into an executable.

Embedding the resource into an EXE might simplify the coding required and might even increase performance over placing the resource into a DLL. One problem with this method is that the application must be recompiled any time one or more resources are changed. This could pose a problem if the EXE file has to be updated on several different machines every time it is recompiled. Use your own judgment when deciding whether to place the resource(s) into the EXE or into the DLL.

Using a Resource in a DLL

A more flexible method for adding a resource to an application is to package it within a DLL. We can create this DLL in two ways. One is to use Visual C++ to create the DLL, and the other is to use VB. That's right—we can create a resource DLL from within VB alone. I will go through the creation of a resource DLL from both development environments.

Creating a Visual C++ resource DLL

To create a C++ resource DLL, follow these steps:

1. Open Visual C++ and select the File → New… menu item. This will display the New dialog box.

2. On the Projects tab, select the item Win32 Dynamic-Link Library in the list, and enter the name of the DLL in the Project Name field and the location in the Location field. Click the OK button.

3. A DLL creation wizard dialog will be displayed. Select the "A simple DLL project" radio button, then click the Finish button.

4. The New Project Information dialog appears. Click the OK button and the resource DLL project will be created.

5. To add the resource to this project, locate the Resource Files folder in the project window in File view and right-click it. Select the "Add Files to Folders..." menu item. The Insert Files Into Project dialog box is displayed.

6. Select Resource Files in the Files of Type drop-down box, then find and select the .RES file that you previously created in your resource editor of choice. Click the OK button.

7. The resource is now added to your C++ DLL. Compile this DLL and the resource will be available to other applications.

This is the simplest way that I have found to create a resource DLL in Visual C++.

Creating a VB resource DLL

There is not much involved in creating a resource DLL from VB. First, start up VB and create a new ActiveX DLL project. When VB creates this project, it also creates a class module called Class1 within the project. Even though there is no code in this class, it will need to remain in the project because VB requires that any ActiveX object (EXE, DLL, or Control) must contain a class module to load the object correctly into memory. Otherwise, you will get a compiler error ("No creatable public component detected") when trying to compile or run this project.

The steps to add a resource file to a VB project are:

1. Open a new ActiveX DLL project in the VB IDE. (The Startup Object property of the project is set to None by default for a resource DLL.)

2. Right-click the Project explorer window and select the Add → Add File... menu item in the pop-up menu. This will display the Add File dialog box.

3. In the Files of Type drop-down box, select the Resource Files (*.res) item, then find and select the resource file that you want to add to the project and click the Open button.

4. Compile the DLL.

To see the resource file, locate the Related Documents node in the Project Explorer window and expand that branch. The resource filename is displayed under this node.

VB does not provide a way to directly edit resources within the IDE. An add-in ships with VB to allow the creation and editing of resource files, but even this add-in will not let you create or edit dialog template resources. This limitation prevents us from creating the resource entirely within the VB environment.

Creating the Subclassing Application

The application we will create in this section subclasses the Save As common dialog box. This application has one form module called *frmMain.frm*, which is displayed in Figure 5-7. The nondefault properties of this form are listed in Table 5-5. The form contains a command button control called Command1 and a text box control called Edit1.

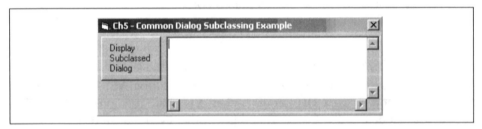

Figure 5-7. The main form of the sample application

Table 5-5. Nondefault Properties of frmMain and Its Controls

Control Name	Property Name	Property Value
frmMain	Caption	Ch5 - Common Dialog Subclassing Example
frmMain	BorderStyle	3-Fixed Dialog
frmMain	Top	0
frmMain	Left	0
frmMain	Height	3420
frmMain	Width	5760
Command1	Caption	Display Subclassed Dialog
Command1	Top	60
Command1	Left	60
Command1	Height	852
Command1	Width	1212
txtMsg	Multiline	True
txtMsg	Top	60

Table 5-5. Nondefault Properties of frmMain and Its Controls (continued)

Control Name	Property Name	Property Value
txtMsg	Left	1380
txtMsg	Height	2952
txtMsg	Width	4272

Clicking the button control creates a Save As common dialog box, subclasses it, and displays it. The Save As dialog is modified to include the extra controls that are contained in our resource DLL. This dialog is displayed in Figure 5-8.

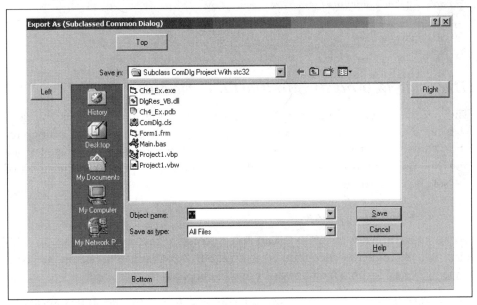

Figure 5-8. The subclassed Save As common dialog box

The first thing you might notice about this new dialog is that the caption of this dialog has been changed to "Export As (Subclassed Common Dialog)". Additional UI changes derive from the child dialog template used to create the controls at the bottom of the dialog box. These controls have no real functionality. The button control with the caption "Click Me" simply displays a message box indicating that the button has been clicked. The Use Predefined Delimiter checkbox allows the user to switch between displaying an edit box (shown in Figure 5-8) and a drop-down list box. If this were a real working example, the edit box would allow a user to enter in a delimiter of his or her own choice. However, if the checkbox is checked, the drop-down list box is displayed, allowing the user to choose from four predefined delimiters.

This project consists of a form (*frmMain.frm*) and a code module (*Module1.bas*). It also uses the resource DLL that was created earlier in this chapter. The resource DLL is named *DlgRes_VB.DLL*.

The Code Behind the frmMain.frm Module

Not much code is contained in the form—only behind the Command1 button that calls the *Start* procedure in the *Module1.bas* module. The code for the form is shown in Example 5-2.

Example 5-2. The Command1_Click Event Procedure

```
Private Sub Command1_Click()
    Call Start(Me.hwnd)
End Sub
```

The Code Behind the Module1.bas Module

This section describes the code that creates the dialog and performs the subclassing. I will start out by describing some of the finer points of the dialog creation structure as it relates to subclassing the common dialog. Next, I will show you the code for this module, and finally, I will end with a detailed discussion of the subclass procedure.

The dialog creation structure

To be created, every common dialog has a structure that must be filled in with data. For the Save As dialog, this is the OPENFILENAME structure. Before we continue, we must become familiar with a few members in this structure.

The *Flags* member contains specific flags used to define the appearance and behavior of this common dialog box. The flags that you will need to be concerned about when subclassing the Save As common dialog (Const statements for all of which should be added to your project) are:

OFN_ENABLEHOOK *(&H20)*
> Allows the common dialog hook procedure to be called only if the *lpfnHook* structure member points to a hook procedure.

OFN_ENABLETEMPLATE *(&H40)*
> When the dialog template resource is contained within the application or within a resource DLL, this flag indicates that the *hInstance* member of the structure is set to the instance handle of the application (App.hInstance).

OFN_ENABLETEMPLATEHANDLE *(&H80)*
> When the dialog template resource is already set in a section of memory, this flag can be used to obtain that resource. In this case, the *hInstance* structure

member needs to be set to the handle of the memory object for the common dialog to be displayed correctly. This flag overrides the `OFN_ENABLETEMPLATE` flag if both are set.

OFN_EXPLORER (&H800000)

This flag is required to display the new Explorer-style common dialog boxes seen in Windows NT Version 4 and Windows 9x. This flag also must be set when adding a hook procedure or a dialog template to an Open or Save As common dialog box. To stay current with your UI, I suggest that you always use this flag.

OFN_ENABLEINCLUDENOTIFY (&H400000)

Enables the common dialog box to send `CDN_INCLUDEITEM` notification messages to the hook procedure defined in the *lpfnHook* structure member. This message is sent once for each item in a folder when the user opens that specific folder in the Open or Save As common dialog boxes. In the hook procedure, a zero can be returned if you do not want that item to be displayed in the file listview control of the common dialog box. Otherwise, send a nonzero value to display the item in this control. This flag is used only in Windows 2000; Windows NT and Windows 9x do not use this flag. This notification code will still be sent to the dialog hook procedure in Windows NT and 9x, but the return value means nothing to these operating systems.

For the purpose of our subclassing example, I will be setting the `OFN_EXPLORER`, `OFN_ENABLEHOOK`, `OFN_ENABLETEMPLATE`, and `OFN_ENABLEINCLUDENOTIFY` flags. Because the dialog template resource is in a DLL, the `OFN_ENABLETEMPLATE` flag must be used instead of the `OFN_ENABLETEMPLATEHANDLE` flag. The `OFN_ENABLEINCLUDENOTIFY` flag is set to ensure forward compatibility with Windows 2000.

The *lpfnHook* member in the `OPENFILENAME` structure holds a function pointer to the common dialog hook procedure. There is one problem here: in VB, we use the `AddressOf` operator to get a function pointer. The `AddressOf` operator must be used in the parameter list of a function call. We need a way for VB to get the function pointer to our hook procedure into this member of the structure. `AddressOf` was not specifically designed to do this, but there is an interesting workaround for this problem. As we know, this code will produce an error:

```
Dim FunctPtr As Long
FunctPtr = AddressOf OFNHookProc
```

Instead, we need to create a function such as the following one that returns the address parameter (in this example it is *FunctAddr*) passed in to this function:

```
Function SaveAsProc(FunctAddr As Long) As Long
    SaveAsProc= FunctAddr
End Function
```

This function is then called using the following line of code:

```
Dim FunctPtr As Long
FunctPtr = SaveAsProc(AddressOf OFNHookProc)
```

This line calls *SaveAsProc* and passes to it the address of the *SaveAsProc* function. This function will reside in one of our code (BAS) modules. The function simply passes back the address of the *OFNHookProc* function to the *FunctPtr* variable. Now that we have a valid value in the *FunctPtr* variable, we can simply set the *lpfnHook* structure member equal to the *FunctPtr* variable.

The common dialog box uses the *lpTemplateName* member only if the OFN_ ENABLETEMPLATE flag is set in the *Flags* member of the OPENFILENAME structure. To place a value in the *lpTemplateName* member, we first need to go back to the resource file that we created in the Visual C++ resource editor. When we saved this file as a resource script (giving the resource file an extension of *.rc*), the resource editor also created a *resource.h* header file. Opening this file reveals the constants for the dialog template itself, as well as for each control on this dialog. This information is presented as a list of #define statements in the *resource.h* file. The #defines found in the *resource.h* file for the example presented in this chapter are:

```
#define IDD_DIALOG1                     101
#define IDC_EDIT1                       1000
#define IDC_CHECK1                      1001
#define IDC_BUTTON1                     1002
#define IDC_COMBO1                      1003
```

We need to copy all these #defines and add them as Const statements to our *Module1.bas* module. The VB code looks something like this:

```
Const IDD_DIALOG1 = 101
Const IDC_EDIT1 = 1000
Const IDC_CHECK1 = 1001
Const IDC_BUTTON1 = 1002
Const IDC_COMBO1 = 1003
```

The IDD_DIALOG1 constant is the one we are looking for. This constant is the identifier for the dialog template resource that we want to add to the common dialog box. The *lpTemplateName* member needs to be set equal to this constant so that Windows will know which dialog resource in the application's process space to add to the default common dialog box. The minimum requirement to add a dialog template resource to a common dialog is to set the OFN_ENABLETEMPLATE flag in the *Flags* member of the OPENFILENAME structure and also to set the *lpTemplateName* member of this same structure to the dialog template resource ID found in the *resource.h* file. Otherwise, an error will be raised when the system tries to find a valid dialog resource.

The last structure member I want to look at is not required for subclassing a common dialog box, but it can be useful in sending information back and forth from the application to the common dialog box. This is the *lCustData* member, which can contain data of type Long or a pointer. The reason I am including it here is that this data is available to the dialog hook procedure when a message that the hook intercepts contains a pointer to this OPENFILENAME structure. Take, for instance, the CDN_INITDONE message that is sent to the dialog hook procedure when it is finished placing the controls on the dialog box. This message has an *lParam* parameter that contains a pointer to an OFNOTIFY structure. The OFNOTIFY structure contains a pointer to the OPENFILENAME structure within its *lpOFN* member. The data saved by the application in the *lCustData* member of the OPENFILENAME structure is thus available to the dialog hook procedure through this message, as well as through any other message that has a pointer to the OPENFILENAME structure.

The members of the OPENFILENAME structure also are updated when controls return from the *GetSaveFileName* function. The *lCustData* member of this structure can be changed within the dialog hook procedure. When this structure is passed back to the calling application, it can retrieve any information that the dialog hook procedure has placed there. This can be useful in solving the problem of passing information back and forth between the main application and its common dialog box, and especially its Cancel button.

The code for the Module1.bas module

The code for this module is shown in Example 5-3.

Example 5-3. Code for the Module1.bas Module

```
'-------------------------------------------
'  Create and subclass the Save As
'  Common dialog box
'-------------------------------------------

Sub Start(OwnerHWnd As Long)
    Dim CommonDialogStruct As OpenFilename
    Dim RetVal As Long

    With CommonDialogStruct
        .lStructSize = Len(CommonDialogStruct)
        .hwndOwner = OwnerHWnd
        .lpfnHook = GetAddressOf(AddressOf SaveAsProc)
        .lpTemplateName = IDD_DIALOG1
        .lpstrFilter = "All Files" & Chr$(0) & "*.*" & Chr$(0) & Chr$(0)
        .nFilterIndex = 1
        .lpstrFile = Chr$(0) & Space(255)
        .nMaxFile = Len(.lpstrFile) - 1
        .lpstrTitle = "Export As (Subclassed Common Dialog)"
```

Example 5-3. Code for the Module1.bas Module (continued)

```
       .flags = OFN_FILEMUSTEXIST Or _
               OFN_SHOWHELP Or _
               OFN_EXPLORER Or _
               OFN_ENABLEHOOK Or _
               OFN_ENABLETEMPLATE Or _
               OFN_ENABLEINCLUDENOTIFY
       .hInstance = LoadLibrary(App.Path & "\DlgRes_VB.dll")
       .FlagsEx = 0
   End With

   RetVal = GetSaveFileName(CommonDialogStruct)

   If RetVal = 0 Then
      MsgBox "The Cancel button was clicked"
   ElseIf RetVal = 1 Then
      MsgBox Trim(CommonDialogStruct.lpstrFile)
   Else
      'error
      MsgBox CommDlgExtendedError
   End If

   FreeLibrary (CommonDialogStruct.hInstance)
End Sub


'---------------------------------------------
' Helper functions
'---------------------------------------------


Function GetAddressOf(ByVal ProcAddr As Long) As Long
   GetAddressOf = ProcAddr
End Function

Public Function GetHiWord(ByRef Value As Long) As Long
   If (Value And &H80000000) = &H80000000 Then
      GetHiWord = ((Value And &H7FFF0000) \ &H10000) Or &H8000&
   Else
      GetHiWord = (Value And &HFFFF0000) \ &H10000
   End If
End Function

Public Function GetLoWord(ByRef Value As Long) As Long
   GetLoWord = (Value And &HFFFF&)
End Function


'---------------------------------------------
' The Subclass Procedure
'---------------------------------------------


Public Function SaveAsProc(ByVal hwnd As Long, ByVal uMsg As Long, _
              ByVal wParam As Long, ByVal lParam As Long) As Long
   Dim NMHStruct As NMHDR
   Dim lContext As Long
```

Example 5-3. Code for the Module1.bas Module (continued)

```
Dim lTemp As Long
Dim lNotificationCode As Long
Dim lControlID As Long
Dim hCtrl As Long
Dim lRetVal As Long

SaveAsProc = 0

Select Case uMsg
    Case WM_INITDIALOG
        frmMain.txtMsg.Text = frmMain.txtMsg.Text & Hex$(hwnd) & "-WM_INITDIALOG" & _
                            vbNewLine
        frmMain.txtMsg.Text = frmMain.txtMsg.Text & "Dialog modifications can " & _
                            "occur here before it is shown" & vbNewLine

        DoEvents

        'Init the combo box items
        hCtrl = GetDlgItem(hwnd, IDC_COMBO1)
        lRetVal = SendMessageStr(hCtrl, CB_INSERTSTRING, 0&, "-")
        lRetVal = SendMessageLong(hCtrl, CB_SETITEMDATA, 0&, 0&)
        lRetVal = SendMessageStr(hCtrl, CB_INSERTSTRING, 1&, ";")
        lRetVal = SendMessageLong(hCtrl, CB_SETITEMDATA, 1&, 1&)
        lRetVal = SendMessageStr(hCtrl, CB_INSERTSTRING, 2&, ":")
        lRetVal = SendMessageLong(hCtrl, CB_SETITEMDATA, 2&, 2&)
        lRetVal = SendMessageStr(hCtrl, CB_INSERTSTRING, 3&, ",")
        lRetVal = SendMessageLong(hCtrl, CB_SETITEMDATA, 3&, 3&)
        lRetVal = SendMessageLong(hCtrl, CB_SETCURSEL, -1&, 0&)
    Case WM_NOTIFY
        frmMain.txtMsg.Text = frmMain.txtMsg.Text & "WM_NOTIFY -> "
        DoEvents

        CopyMemory NMHStruct, ByVal lParam, LenB(NMHStruct)

        Select Case NMHStruct.code
            Case CDN_INCLUDEITEM
                frmMain.txtMsg.Text = frmMain.txtMsg.Text & Hex$(hwnd) & _
                                "-CDN_INCLUDEITEM" & vbNewLine

                DoEvents
            Case CDN_INITDONE
                frmMain.txtMsg.Text = frmMain.txtMsg.Text & Hex$(hwnd) & _
                                "-CDN_INITDONE" & vbNewLine

                DoEvents
            Case CDN_SELCHANGE
                frmMain.txtMsg.Text = frmMain.txtMsg.Text & Hex$(hwnd) & _
                                "-CDN_SELCHANGE" & vbNewLine

                DoEvents
            Case CDN_FOLDERCHANGE
                frmMain.txtMsg.Text = frmMain.txtMsg.Text & Hex$(hwnd) & _
                                "-CDN_FOLDERCHANGE" & vbNewLine

                DoEvents
            Case CDN_HELP
                frmMain.txtMsg.Text = frmMain.txtMsg.Text & Hex$(hwnd) & _
```

Example 5-3. Code for the Module1.bas Module (continued)

```
                                             "-CDN_HELP" & vbNewLine
                    DoEvents
                Case CDN_FILEOK
                    frmMain.txtMsg.Text = frmMain.txtMsg.Text & Hex$(hwnd) & _
                                       "-CDN_FILEOK" & vbNewLine
                    DoEvents
                Case CDN_SHAREVIOLATION
                    frmMain.txtMsg.Text = frmMain.txtMsg.Text & Hex$(hwnd) & _
                                          "-CDN_SHAREVIOLATION" & vbNewLine
                    DoEvents
                Case CDN_TYPECHANGE
                    frmMain.txtMsg.Text = frmMain.txtMsg.Text & Hex$(hwnd) & _
                                       "-CDN_TYPECHANGE" & vbNewLine
                    DoEvents
                Case Else
                    frmMain.txtMsg.Text = frmMain.txtMsg.Text & Hex$(hwnd) & _
                                       "-" & CStr(uMsg) & "   " & vbNewLine
            End Select
        Case WM_COMMAND
            lNotificationCode = GetHiWord(wParam)
            Select Case lNotificationCode
                Case EN_CHANGE
                    lControlID = GetLoWord(wParam)
                    Select Case lControlID
                      Case IDC_EDIT1
                          frmMain.txtMsg.Text = frmMain.txtMsg.Text & Hex$(hwnd) _
                                    & "-IDC_EDIT1 -> EN_CHANGED" & vbNewLine
                          DoEvents
                    End Select
                Case EN_KILLFOCUS
                    lControlID = GetLoWord(wParam)
                    Select Case lControlID
                      Case IDC_EDIT1
                          frmMain.txtMsg.Text = frmMain.txtMsg.Text & Hex$(hwnd) & _
                                    "-IDC_EDIT1 -> EN_KILLFOCUS" & vbNewLine
                          DoEvents
                    End Select
                Case EN_SETFOCUS
                    lControlID = GetLoWord(wParam)
                    Select Case lControlID
                      Case IDC_EDIT1
                          frmMain.txtMsg.Text = frmMain.txtMsg.Text & Hex$(hwnd) & _
                                    "-IDC_EDIT1 -> EN_SETFOCUS" & vbNewLine
                          DoEvents
                    End Select
                Case BN_CLICKED
                    lControlID = GetLoWord(wParam)
                    Select Case lControlID
                      Case IDC_BUTTON1
                          frmMain.txtMsg.Text = frmMain.txtMsg.Text & Hex$(hwnd) & _
                                     "-IDC_BUTTON1 -> BN_CLICKED" & vbNewLine
                          DoEvents
```

Example 5-3. Code for the Module1.bas Module (continued)

```
                        'A message box is not a really good thing
                        'to have in a hook function
                        MsgBox "The button has been clicked!"
                    Case IDC_CHECK1
                        frmMain.txtMsg.Text = frmMain.txtMsg.Text & Hex$(hwnd) & _
                                "-IDC_CHECK1 -> BN_CLICKED" & vbNewLine
                        DoEvents

                        'Do something to the UI
                        If CBool(SendMessageLong(lParam, BM_GETCHECK, 0&, 0&)) Then
                            hCtrl = GetDlgItem(hwnd, IDC_EDIT1)
                            Call ShowWindow(hCtrl, SW_HIDE)

                            hCtrl = GetDlgItem(hwnd, IDC_COMBO1)
                            Call ShowWindow(hCtrl, SW_SHOW)
                        Else
                            hCtrl = GetDlgItem(hwnd, IDC_COMBO1)
                            Call ShowWindow(hCtrl, SW_HIDE)

                            hCtrl = GetDlgItem(hwnd, IDC_EDIT1)
                            Call ShowWindow(hCtrl, SW_SHOW)
                        End If
                    End Select
                Case CBN_CLOSEUP
                    lControlID = GetLoWord(wParam)
                    Select Case lControlID
                Case IDC_COMBO1
                    frmMain.txtMsg.Text = frmMain.txtMsg.Text & Hex$(hwnd) & _
                                "-IDC_COMBO1 -> CBN_CLOSEUP" & vbNewLine
                    DoEvents
                End Select
            Case Else
                frmMain.txtMsg.Text = frmMain.txtMsg.Text & _
                            "Unhandled notification message - " & vbNewLine
            DoEvents
            End Select
        Case WM_DESTROY
            frmMain.txtMsg.Text = frmMain.txtMsg.Text & Hex$(hwnd) & _
                        "-WM_DESTROY" & vbNewLine
        Case WM_NCDESTROY
            frmMain.txtMsg.Text = frmMain.txtMsg.Text & Hex$(hwnd) & _
                        "-WM_NCDESTROY" & vbNewLine
    End Select
End Function
```

The *Start* procedure initializes the **OPENFILENAME** structure, calls the Win32 *GetSaveFileName* function, and unloads the resource DLL after the subclassed common dialog is closed. The *SaveAsProc* procedure is the dialog hook procedure; in the next section, we'll discuss how the dialog hook procedure works and how messages are passed on it.

The dialog hook procedure

Capturing messages from the dialog template resource is the job of the *dialog hook procedure*. The dialog hook procedure is similar to the subclassed window procedure that we discussed in the earlier chapters. But we do not call it a subclassed dialog procedure because a subclassed dialog procedure captures messages bound for a dialog before the dialog's original window procedure can process the message. The subclassed window procedure then passes the message on to the original window procedure through the *CallWindowProc* API call. The dialog hook procedure that we will use in this chapter captures messages before they reach the dialog procedure *and* after they have been processed by the dialog procedure. The dialog hook procedure will capture notification messages sent by the common dialog box and messages for the controls added to the dialog template resource.

The *comdlg32.dll* file will handle routing messages to the default dialog procedure so that the dialog hook procedure will not have to. Instead of calling an API function to pass the message on, as it would do in a subclassed window procedure, the dialog hook procedure returns a value indicating whether it processed the message.

Hook procedure names for each type of common dialog box are listed in Table 5-6. These are standard names; you can use your own names for these dialog hook procedures if you want.

Table 5-6. Hook Procedures for Each Type of Common Dialog Box

Common Dialog Type	Hook Procedure Name (Recommended)
Color	*CCHookProc*
Find	*FRHookProc*
Replace	*FRHookProc*
Font	*CFHookProc*
Open	*OFNHookProc*
Save As	*OFNHookProc*
Print	*PrintHookProc*
Page Setup	*PageSetupHook* or *PagePaintHook*

Note in Table 5-6 that the Page Setup dialog box is now used instead of the out-dated Print Setup dialog box. Also, the Page Setup common dialog box can have two hooks. *PageSetupHook* is the dialog hook procedure used to receive messages from the child dialog controls and to receive notification codes from the parent dialog. This hook procedure is similar to the other hook procedures listed in this table. The *PagePaintHook* procedure allows modifications to be made to the sample page object found in the Page Setup common dialog box. With this second hook procedure, the messages to draw margins, paper sizes, and envelope items can be intercepted and changed.

The parent dialog box does not send messages originating from the default controls to the dialog hook procedure. Instead, notification messages are sent to the dialog hook procedure which allow it to get information about a subset of the user's actions within the parent dialog box. For example, when the user changes folders in an Open common dialog box, every mouse or keyboard event is not passed in to the dialog hook procedure; rather, a notification code (CDN_FOLDERCHANGE) is sent to the hook via the WM_NOTIFY message described shortly.

To see how messaging works in a subclassed common dialog box, see Figure 5-9. In this diagram, a control on the child dialog will send a notification code wrapped in a WM_COMMAND message to its parent (#1). The child dialog then passes this WM_COMMAND message on to the dialog hook procedure (#2). The dialog hook procedure might or might not pass the WM_COMMAND message on to the default dialog procedure (#3), depending on its return value.

The parent dialog box will receive notifications from its child controls (#4). These notifications go to the default dialog procedure (#5), unless they are special dialog hook notification codes wrapped inside a WM_NOTIFY message. These messages need to be sent first to the dialog hook procedure and then on to the default dialog procedure (#5).

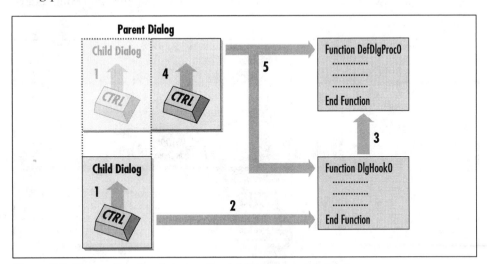

Figure 5-9. The message flow between the child and parent dialog boxes

We will want to intercept and possibly handle four main types of messages in the dialog hook procedure. These are initialization, notification, ActiveX control, and shutdown messages. They are explained in more detail in the next four sections.

Dialog initialization

Dialog initialization involves loading combo boxes and list boxes with default data, placing controls, sizing controls, as well as executing other types of initializations that you might want to perform. You can perform your initializations at two points in the dialog hook procedure. The first occurs when the hook procedure receives the WM_INITDIALOG message; this is where I chose to do the initializations in Example 5-3. The second is during the CDN_INITDONE notification, which is contained in a structure pointed to by the *lParam* parameter of the WM_NOTIFY message. As a note, the WM_INITDIALOG message is sent first to the default common dialog box (the parent), then a second separate WM_INITDIALOG message is sent to the child dialog. The parent dialog box will always receive the WM_INITDIALOG message before the child dialog receives its WM_INITDIALOG message. Also, WM_INITDIALOG is the only message that is processed first by the default dialog box procedure and then sent to the dialog hook procedure. All other messages will be received by the dialog hook procedure first. The hook procedure then decides whether to pass them on to the default dialog procedure.

Figure 5-10 describes this process. The WM_INITDIALOG message is sent first to the default dialog procedure (#1). After the default dialog procedure is done initializing, it passes the WM_INITDIALOG message on to the hook procedure (#2). Lastly, the CDN_INITDONE notification code is sent to the hook procedure (#3). The CDN_INITDONE notification is sent by the child dialog upon completing its initialization.

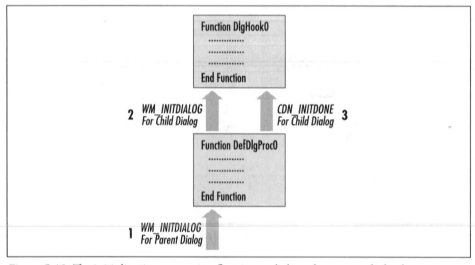

Figure 5-10. The initialization messaging flow in a subclassed common dialog box

When deciding where in the hook procedure to put your initialization code, consider these points. The WM_INITDIALOG message is sent to the hook procedure before the CDN_INITDONE message. Both messages are sent to the hook procedure before the dialog is displayed. The CDN_INITDONE is not really a message in and of itself; instead, it is a notification code that is contained within the WM_NOTIFY message sent to the dialog hook procedure informing it of its status. This message is also specific to the Explorer-style Open and Save As common dialog boxes. It is not sent as a notification by any other common dialog box.

A very important difference between these two messages is the point at which the common dialog box is initially sized. When the WM_INITDIALOG message is sent, the common dialog box has not been sized to accommodate the new controls contained in the dialog template resource. After the CDN_INITDONE notification is sent, the common dialog box has been resized to include the new controls in the dialog template resource. This difference will come in handy when modifying the size and position of the common dialog and its controls during its creation. As a rule of thumb, keep code to resize and position the common dialog box in the CDN_INITDONE notification.

The final difference between these two messages is that the return value for the dialog hook procedure is ignored when processing the CDN_INITDONE notification. The return value for the dialog hook procedure is not ignored when processing the WM_INITDIALOG message. The return value for the dialog hook procedure can be either TRUE or FALSE for this message. If it is FALSE, the keyboard focus is set to the first control in the tab order of the common dialog box that is visible, enabled, and has the WS_TABSTOP style. If it is FALSE, the keyboard focus is set to the control that has an hWnd value equal to the value in the *wParam* value of this message. The *wParam* parameter contains the hWnd of the control that is to receive keyboard focus when the common dialog is displayed.

Common actions performed in the dialog hook procedure are to query and modify control properties. For this, you need to know the control's handle. This is a fairly simple task. Just use the GetDlgItem API function:

```
Public Declare Function GetDlgItem Lib "user32" Alias "GetDlgItem" _
    (ByVal hDlg As Long, ByVal nIDDlgItem As Long) As Long
```

Its parameters are:

hDlg
    The handle to the dialog box where the control is located; this is either the default common dialog box or the child dialog box.

nIDDlgItem
    The ID of the control in the resource file.

This API function returns the handle of the control that you specify.

To get the handle of a control you want to deal with on the child dialog box, you need to set the *hDlg* parameter of this API function equal to the handle of the child dialog box. The handle for the child dialog box is stored in the *hwnd* parameter passed in to the dialog hook function. The second parameter, *nIDDlgItem*, is the ID of the control whose handle you need to get. A list of the child dialog boxes' control IDs is found in the *resource.h* file created earlier.

This is fine for controls in the child dialog box, but what if you need to find a control's handle that is located on the parent dialog box? To do this, we need to use the *GetParent* API function before calling *GetDlgItem*. *GetParent* is defined as follows:

```
Public Declare Function GetParent Lib "user32" Alias "GetParent" _
    (ByVal hwnd As Long) As Long
```

Its single parameter is:

hwnd

   The handle of the child window

GetParent returns the handle of that child's parent window. We then use this handle in the *hDlg* parameter of the *GetDlgItem* function. The *nIDDlgItem* parameter uses a predefined value. The predefined control ID values for the Open and Save As common dialog boxes are:

```
Public Const chx1 = &H410       'Read-only checkbox
Public Const cmb1 = &H470       'File type filters drop-down combo box
Public Const cmb2 = &H471       'Current drive and folder drop-down combo box
Public Const cmb13 = &H47C      'Current selected file drop-down combo box
                                '  (Used for Windows 2000)
Public Const edt1 = &H480       'Current selected file edit box
                                '  (Used in previous versions of Windows)
Public Const lst1 = &H460       'Displays contents of the selected drive or
                                '  folder, this is a list box
Public Const stc1 = &H440       'Label for lst1 control
Public Const stc2 = &H441       'Label for cmb1 control
Public Const stc3 = &H442       'Label for edt1 control
Public Const stc4 = &H443       'Label for cmb2 control
Public Const IDOK = 1           'The default dialog OK button
                                '  (will not have OK in its caption)
Public Const IDCANCEL = 2       'The dialog cancel button
Public Const pshHelp = psh15    'The dialog help button
```

Additional control IDs not listed here are used in the other types of common dialog boxes. Using Spy++, we can find the control IDs for these other common dialog controls. The values for all common dialog box controls also can be found in the *Dlgs.h* header file.

To find a control ID with Spy++, open an instance of the common dialog box and find it in the Windows list in Spy++. Find the control to which you need to get an ID and double-click it. The Window Properties dialog box will appear. Locate the Control ID field on the General tab. This is the highlighted control's ID. The Control ID field is visible only for controls, not for other types of windows. Note that these constants could change in future releases of the Windows operating system. This could cause compatibility issues for your application in the future.

After we have the handle to the control that we are interested in, we can use the *SendMessage, SendMessageStr,* or *SendMessageLong* API functions to send messages to those controls. Some of the messages that we can send, which are specific to the common dialog boxes, are:

```
'Initial Values
Public Const WM_USER = &H400
Public Const CDM_FIRST = (WM_USER + 100)

'Gets the full path and name of the selected file
Public Const CDM_GETFILEPATH = (CDM_FIRST + &H1)

'Gets the list of item ID's for the current folder
Public Const CDM_GETFOLDERIDLIST = (CDM_FIRST + &H3)

'Gets the current path on the selected folder
Public Const CDM_GETFOLDERPATH = (CDM_FIRST + &H2)

'Gets only the name of the selected file and its extension
Public Const CDM_GETSPEC = (CDM_FIRST + &H0)

'Allows a control to be hidden
Public Const CDM_HIDECONTROL = (CDM_FIRST + &H5)

'Allows text in a control to be changed
Public Const CDM_SETCONTROLTEXT = (CDM_FIRST + &H4)

'Allows the default file name extension to be set
Public Const CDM_SETDEFEXT = (CDM_FIRST + &H6)
```

Most of these messages are useful only in the Open and Save As common dialog boxes.

Other control-specific messages can be sent as well. For the list of messages specific to a control, see the Microsoft Platform Software Development Kit (SDK) documentation in the MSDN.

Processing dialog box notification messages

The parent common dialog is able to send several different notification messages to its hook procedure indicating that an action has occurred. These notification messages are contained in a WM_NOTIFY message that has information in both its *lParam* and *wParam* parameters. The *lParam* parameter contains the ID of the control that is sending this message to its parent. The control IDs can be found in the *Resource.h* file for our dialog template resource. The *wParam* parameter contains a pointer to a NMHDR structure. The NMHDR structure is defined in VB as follows:

```
Private Type NMHDR
    hwndFrom As Long
    idfrom As Long
    code As Long
End Type
```

Its members are:

hwndFrom

   The handle to the control sending this notification message

idfrom

   The identifier of the control sending this notification message

code

   A code identifying the type of notification

The *wParam* parameter contains the control ID of the control that sent the message. The Microsoft documentation states that the control ID in this parameter is not guaranteed to be unique; instead, use the *hwndFrom* or *idfrom* values found in the NMHDR structure pointed to by the *lParam* parameter of this message.

Common dialog boxes can send several different types of notification codes. Because the dialog box controls themselves cannot send notification messages to the hook procedure, the common dialog box has a set of these notification messages that it can send to the hook procedure. Each code is defined below:

CDN_FILEOK

   The user has selected an item and then clicked the OK button (which is actually the default button of the common dialog box), or double-clicked a file in the listview control.

CDN_FOLDERCHANGE

   The user has moved to a different folder.

CDN_HELP

The dialog Help button was clicked.

CDN_INCLUDEITEM

(Windows 2000 only.) If the `OFN_ENABLEINCLUDENOTIFY` flag was set in the `OPENFILENAME` structure, this notification is sent to the dialog hook procedure once for every folder and file displayed in the Open or Save As common dialog box. Returning a nonzero value from the dialog hook procedure for this message prevents the dialog from displaying that file or folder; returning a zero allows the file or folder to be displayed. This notification will be sent in Windows 98 and Windows NT, but returning either a zero or nonzero value will have no effect.

CDN_INITDONE

This notification is sent upon completion of the `WM_INITDIALOG` message that is sent to this child dialog box. When this notification message has been sent, all the controls will be placed on the common dialog and the dialog will be set to its final size. At this point, the system is done placing and sizing the controls as well as the dialog, and you can safely rearrange and size the controls and the dialog itself.

CDN_SELCHANGE

This notification is sent whenever a user changes the current selection in the listview control.

CDN_SHAREVIOLATION

If the OK button is clicked and a sharing violation occurs on this file, this notification is sent. To prevent an error and to force the common dialog box to return the locked file, simply return a nonzero value for the dialog hook procedure.

CDN_TYPECHANGE

This notification is sent when the user changes the file currently selected to a file of a different type. Switching selection between files of the same type will not force this notification to be sent.

The source of these notification messages is apparent from the prefix applied to the notification code name. The `CDN` prefix tells you that these messages are Common Dialog Notification messages. The individual controls do not send these notification messages. Only the dialog itself sends these messages.

As you might have noticed, some of these notification codes will be sent only from the Open or Save As common dialog boxes. If you are expecting a notification from the dialog box and you are not receiving one, make sure that the correct flags have been set in the *Flags* member of the `OPENFILENAME` structure. The

OFN_EXPLORER flag is required to allow notifications to be sent from Explorer-Style Open and Save As dialog boxes.

To access the NMHDR structure in VB, you will need to use the *CopyMemory* API function. The following code fragment uses the *CopyMemory* function to copy the structure pointed to by the *lParam* parameter into the NMHDR structure defined in VB:

```
Dim udtNM As NMHDR
CopyMemory udtNM, ByVal lParam, LenB(NMHDR)
```

Processing messages from the controls on the child dialog box

If you place new controls on the common dialog via the dialog template resource, obviously you will want to be able to make them do something. To make the controls function, we need to be able to catch messages that they send, such as the button click message (BN_CLICK). To catch messages such as these, we need to watch for the WM_COMMAND message in the dialog hook procedure. The *wParam* parameter of the WM_COMMAND message contains two pieces of information. The notification code is contained in the high-order word of the *wParam* parameter. The low-order word contains the control's ID. The control IDs are specified in the C++ *resource.h* header file that we created at the beginning of this chapter. The *lParam* parameter contains the hWnd of the control that sent this message. If a control did not send this message, this parameter is NULL.

When an action is performed on a control in the child dialog box, messages are routed in the manner illustrated earlier in Figure 5-9. For example, if the user clicks a button that was added to the child dialog box:

1. The button notifies its parent, which is the child dialog created from the dialog template resource, that it has been clicked. This notification is packaged in a WM_COMMAND message, not the WM_NOTIFY message used for parent dialog control notifications.

2. The dialog hook procedure receives the notification message packaged in a WM_COMMAND message.

3. The dialog hook procedure uses the high-order word of the *wParam* parameter to get the notification code. This code is processed in a Select Case statement.

4. The low-order word of the *wParam* parameter is used to get the ID of the control. This ID also is processed in a Select Case statement which is nested within the previous Select Case statement.

5. After the dialog hook procedure is finished processing this message, it can send it on to the default dialog procedure by returning a zero.

Extracting the High- and Low-Order Words

To get the high-order word of the *wParam* parameter, just mask off its low-order word. You must determine if the sign bit is set; the sign bit determines the method used to mask off the low-order word. To determine the value of the sign bit, simply AND the value with &H80000000. The code used to do this is:

```
Public Function GetHiWord(ByRef Value As Long) As Long
    If (Value And &H80000000) = &H80000000 Then
        GetHiWord = ((Value And &H7FFF0000) \ &H10000) Or &H8000&
    Else
        GetHiWord = (Value And &HFFFF0000) \ &H10000
    End If
End Function
```

To get the low-order word of *wParam*, the high-order word must be masked off. The sign bit does not have any bearing on this function. The code that accomplishes this is:

```
Public Function GetLoWord(ByRef Value As Long) As Long
    GetLoWord = (Value And &HFFFF&)
End Function
```

The most common way of responding to the controls that have been added to the common dialog box is to set up nested `Select Case` statements. The code used in the example for this chapter looks similar to the outline of a `Select Case` statement shown here:

```
Select Case uMsg
    Case WM_COMMAND
        lNotificationCode = Get_HiWord(wParam)
        Select Case lNotificationCode
        Case BN_CLICKED
            lControlID = Get_LoWord(wParam)
            Select Case lControlID
            Case IDC_BUTTON1
                'Do button click work here
            End Select
        End Select
End Select
```

The outer `Select Case` statement will test for the WM_COMMAND message being sent in the *uMsg* parameter of the dialog hook procedure. The first nested `Select Case` statement will test the high-order word of *wParam* for specific notification codes (BN_CLICKED in the code above). Then the innermost nested `Select Case` statement will test for a specific control ID (this is IDC_BUTTON1 in the previous code). The control ID is obtained from the low-order word of the *wParam* parameter for the message. Now the control can do something in response to the notification message. To determine which notification messages can be sent by a particular control, see the Microsoft Platform SDK documentation.

The default controls on the parent dialog also have control IDs (these were listed earlier in this chapter). Trying to intercept messages sent from these default controls does not work because those messages are sent straight to the dialog procedure and not to our dialog hook procedure.

Processing the dialog shutdown messages

We can shut down the dialog either by forcing it to close using Alt-F4, by using the Close button on the dialog titlebar, by clicking the OK button, or by clicking the Cancel button. When the user closes the dialog, two messages appear that you can intercept in the dialog hook procedure: WM_DESTROY and WM_NCDESTROY. The WM_DESTROY message is sent to the dialog box first, and then the WM_NCDESTROY message follows it. The WM_DESTROY message is sent to the window as its client area is removed from memory and after the dialog box has been removed from the screen. The WM_NCDESTROY message is sent to the dialog to let it know that its nonclient area is being removed from memory.

Cleanup code can be placed in the CDN_FILEOK notification code handler located in the dialog hook procedure. If the user closes the dialog in any way other than clicking the OK button, an error is raised. The application receives the error and must handle it.

Default message processing

You have to do almost nothing for default message processing. This is because the dialog hook procedure processes messages differently than a typical subclassed window procedure or even a typical hook procedure.

The only thing you must do is return either a zero (FALSE) or a nonzero (TRUE) value from the hook procedure. A return value of zero or False indicates that the default dialog procedure should process this message. A nonzero or True return value indicates that the default dialog procedure must not process this message. The value returned from the dialog hook procedure really depends on the message itself and sometimes on the actions taken in the hook procedure. To determine what to return in the hook procedure, examine the message definitions and their requirements for returned values. One thing you should do is set the default return value for this dialog hook procedure to zero and then, if it is required, change that value to nonzero on a per-message basis.

Subclassing Common Dialog Boxes Other Than Open and Save As

The previous material covered subclassing the Explorer-style Open and Save As common dialog boxes. This section covers subclassing all other types of common dialog boxes. The techniques in this section pertain to these common dialogs:

Color
Font
Print
Print Property Sheet (Win2000)
Page Setup
Find
Replace

The Dialog Template Resource

The foremost difference between the Open and Save As common dialogs and the remaining common dialogs is how the dialog template resource is created. With the Open and Save As common dialogs, a separate child dialog had to be created and integrated into the parent common dialog box. This is necessary because the dialog resource for these two common dialogs is embedded in the *comdlg32.dll*. Not so with these other common dialog boxes. Their dialog resources are available in C++ header files (**.h*) and in resource (**.dlg*) files. The header files contain all the control IDs for each control on these dialogs. The resource files contain the actual dialog resource. Table 5-7 lists all resource IDs, header files, and resource files that each common dialog box uses. These files are shipped with the Visual C++ development environment.

Table 5-7. Resource IDs, Header Files, and Resource Files of the Common Dialog Boxes

Dialog type	Resource ID	Resource File	Header File
Color	DLG_COLOR	*Color.dlg*	*ColorDlg.h*
Font	FORMATDLGORD31	*Font.dlg*	*Dlgs.h*
Print	PRINTDLGORD	*Prnsetup.dlg*	*Dlgs.h*
Print Setup	PRNSETUPDLGORD	*Prnsetup.dlg*	*Dlgs.h*
Page Setup	PAGESETUPDLGORD	*Prnsetup.dlg*	*Dlgs.h*
Print Property Sheet	PRINTDLGEXORD	*Prnsetup.dlg*	*Dlgs.h*
Find	FINDDLGORD	*Findtext.dlg*	*Dlgs.h*
Replace	REPLACEDLGORD	*Findtext.dlg*	*Dlgs.h*

Creating a dialog resource file

I will use the Color common dialog box to illustrate how to create a dialog resource for these common dialogs. After the resource file is created, it can be placed either in a resource DLL and loaded into the project via *LoadLibrary,* or in a .RES file and embedded into the VB project.

The first step is to open Visual C++ and create a resource file similar to the way you created the resource file for the Save As example application. After the file is created, immediately save the empty file as a resource script file—that is, with a *.rc* extension. Note that no resources were added to the file.

Next, open the *COLOR.DLG* file located in the *Include* directory in the Visual C++ directory. Copy just the text that makes up the resource script for the Color common dialog box from this file onto the Clipboard. The portion of the file that is copied is shown in Example 5-4.

Example 5-4. Code from the COLOR.DLG Resource Script

```
CHOOSECOLOR DIALOG DISCARDABLE  2, 0, 298, 210
STYLE DS_MODALFRAME | DS_3DLOOK | DS_CONTEXTHELP | WS_POPUP | WS_CAPTION |
    WS_SYSMENU
CAPTION "Color"
FONT 8, "MS Shell Dlg"
BEGIN
    LTEXT           "&Basic colors:",IDC_STATIC,4,4,140,9
    CONTROL         "",COLOR_BOX1,"Static",SS_SIMPLE | WS_GROUP | WS_TABSTOP,
                    4,14,140,86
    LTEXT           "&Custom colors:",IDC_STATIC,4,106,140,9
    CONTROL         "",COLOR_CUSTOM1,"Static",SS_SIMPLE | WS_GROUP |
                    WS_TABSTOP,4,116,140,28
    PUSHBUTTON      "&Define Custom Colors >>",COLOR_MIX,4,150,140,14,
                    WS_GROUP
    DEFPUSHBUTTON   "OK",IDOK,4,166,44,14,WS_GROUP
    PUSHBUTTON      "Cancel",IDCANCEL,52,166,44,14,WS_GROUP
    PUSHBUTTON      "&Help",1038,100,166,44,14,WS_GROUP
    CONTROL         "",COLOR_RAINBOW,"Static",SS_SIMPLE | SS_SUNKEN,152,4,
                    118,116
    CONTROL         "",COLOR_LUMSCROLL,"Static",SS_SIMPLE | SS_SUNKEN,280,4,
                    8,116
    CONTROL         "",COLOR_CURRENT,"Static",SS_SIMPLE | SS_SUNKEN,152,124,
                    40,26
    PUSHBUTTON      "&o",COLOR_SOLID,300,200,6,14,WS_GROUP
    RTEXT           "Color",COLOR_SOLID_LEFT,152,151,20,9
    LTEXT           "|S&olid",COLOR_SOLID_RIGHT,172,151,20,9
    RTEXT           "Hu&e:",COLOR_HUEACCEL,194,126,20,9
    EDITTEXT        COLOR_HUE,216,124,18,12,WS_GROUP
    RTEXT           "&Sat:",COLOR_SATACCEL,194,140,20,9
    EDITTEXT        COLOR_SAT,216,138,18,12,WS_GROUP
    RTEXT           "&Lum:",COLOR_LUMACCEL,194,154,20,9
    EDITTEXT        COLOR_LUM,216,152,18,12,WS_GROUP
    RTEXT           "&Red:",COLOR_REDACCEL,243,126,24,9
```

Example 5-4. Code from the COLOR.DLG Resource Script (continued)

```
        EDITTEXT        COLOR_RED,269,124,18,12,WS_GROUP
        RTEXT           "&Green:",COLOR_GREENACCEL,243,140,24,9
        EDITTEXT        COLOR_GREEN,269,138,18,12,WS_GROUP
        RTEXT           "Bl&ue:",COLOR_BLUEACCEL,243,154,24,9
        EDITTEXT        COLOR_BLUE,269,152,18,12,WS_GROUP
        PUSHBUTTON      "&Add to Custom Colors",COLOR_ADD,152,166,142,14,
                        WS_GROUP
        PUSHBUTTON      "Test Button",IDC_BUTTON1,31,188,87,14
END
```

Paste this script into the *.rc* file that you just created in Visual C++ between the section commented with:

```
//////////////////////////////////////////////////////////////////////
// English (U.S.) resources
```

and the section commented with:

```
//////////////////////////////////////////////////////////////////////
//
// TEXTINCLUDE
//
```

Save and close this *.rc* file.

Next, open the *Resource.h* file that was created by the Visual C++ resource editor along with the *.rc* file. Add the ID for the common dialog to the top of this file. The ID for the Color dialog is:

```
#define CHOOSECOLOR                 10
```

Next, find the *colordlg.h* header file for the original Color common dialog box. Open this file in Notepad and copy all the **#define** statements into the *Resource.h* file that you just created. These **#define** statements describe the existing controls on the Color common dialog box.

Now you can open this resource in Visual C++ and the dialog resource will appear in the editor; double-click the resource to open it. I increased the height of this dialog box and added a button to the bottom of it, as shown in Figure 5-11.

The ID that is given to this new button is 1000. This needs to be manually added to the top of the *resource.h* file as well. The code will look like this:

```
#define IDC_BUTTON1                 1000
```

Save this resource as a RES file. The steps to add this resource to the application are the same as in the previous Save As common dialog subclassing example.

The Color common dialog

The Color common dialog box allows the user to choose a predefined color or a user-defined color. The dialog allows the user to define a color not available in the preset list of colors.

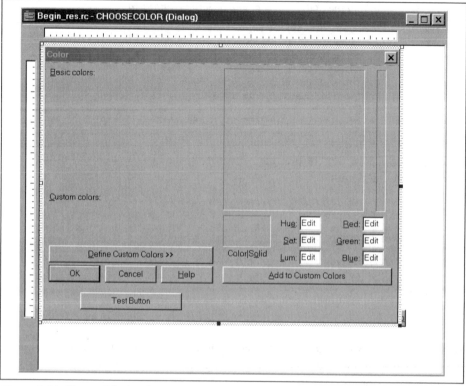

Figure 5-11. The modified Color common dialog box resource

To create this common dialog, initialize the **CHOOSECOLOR** structure. This structure is defined in VB as follows:

```
Public Type CHOOSECOLOR
        lStructSize As Long          ' size of this structure
        hwndOwner As Long            ' owning window
        hInstance As Long            ' instance handle
        rgbResult As Long            ' user chose color returned to application
        lpCustColors As Long         ' pointer to array of COLORREF structures
        flags As Long                ' one or more flags OR'ed together
        lCustData As Long            ' app-defined data passed in to the hook
        lpfnHook As Long             ' pointer to dialog hook procedure
        lpTemplateName As long       ' choose color dialog template name End Type
```

The members that are related to subclassing are:

hInstance

> The instance handle of the object that contains the dialog resource. This is usually set equal to the **App.hInstance** property.

flags

> Flags describing this common dialog box. The **CC_ENABLETEMPLATE** and **CC_ENABLEHOOK** flags must use a modified template and a dialog hook function.

lpfnHook

A pointer to the developer-defined dialog hook function.

lpTemplateName

The ID of the modified dialog resource.

This structure is passed in to the *ChooseColor* API function to create and display the Color common dialog box. This function is declared as follows:

```
Public Declare Function ChooseColor Lib "comdlg32.dll" Alias "ChooseColorA" _
      (pChoosecolor As CHOOSECOLOR) As Long
```

The *Start* procedure we created in the previous example that subclassed the Save As common dialog can be modified, as shown in Example 5-5, to use the CHOOSECOLOR structure and the *ChooseColorDlg* function to create the subclassed Color common dialog. The code modifications appear in boldface. The code is modified to use the CHOOSECOLOR structure and the *ChooseColorDlg* function to create this dialog. These are the modifications that must be made to allow the code for the Save As example to work with the Color dialog as well as with the other common dialogs that I will be describing next.

Example 5-5. The Start Procedure Modified to Subclass the Color Common Dialog

```
Sub Start(OwnerHWnd As Long)
    Dim CommonDialogStruct As CHOOSECOLOR
    Dim RetVal As Long

    With CommonDialogStruct
        .lStructSize = Len(CommonDialogStruct)
        .hwndOwner = OwnerHWnd
        .lpfnHook = GetAddressOf(AddressOf DlgProc)
        .lpTemplateName = IDD_DIALOG1
        .hInstance = LoadLibrary(App.Path & "\DlgRes_VB.dll")
        .flags = OFN_ENABLEHOOK Or _
                 OFN_ENABLETEMPLATE Or _
                 OFN_ENABLEINCLUDENOTIFY
    End With

    RetVal = ChooseColor(CommonDialogStruct)

    If RetVal = 0 Then
        MsgBox "The Cancel button was clicked"
    ElseIf RetVal = 1 Then
        MsgBox Trim(CommonDialogStruct.rgbResult)
    Else
        'error
        MsgBox CommDlgExtendedError
    End If

    FreeLibrary (CommonDialogStruct.hInstance)
End Sub
```

The Font common dialog

The Font common dialog box allows the user to choose a font as well as the properties for that font. Properties include style, size, effects, and color.

To create this common dialog, initialize the **CHOOSEFONT** structure. This structure is defined in VB as follows:

```
Public Type CHOOSEFONT
        lStructSize As Long                  ' size of this structure
        hwndOwner As Long                    ' calling window's handle
        hdc As Long                          ' printer DC/IC
        lpLogFont As Long                    ' pointer to the LOGFONT structure
        iPointSize As Long                   ' 10 * size in points of selected font
        flags As Long                        ' one or more flags OR'ed together
        rgbColors As Long                    ' returned text color
        lCustData As Long                    ' data passed to hook
        lpfnHook As Long                     ' pointer to hook
        lpTemplateName As String             ' custom template name
        hInstance As Long                    ' instance handle of EXE that
                                             '    contains custom dlg. template
        lpszStyle As String                  ' style field here
                                             '    must be LF_FACESIZE or bigger
        nFontType As Integer                 ' same value reported to the EnumFonts
                                             '    call back with the extra FONTTYPE_
                                             '    bits added
        MISSING_ALIGNMENT As Integer         '
        nSizeMin As Long                     ' minimum pt size allowed
        nSizeMax As Long                     ' max pt size allowed
    End Type
```

Its members that relate to subclassing are:

hInstance

> The instance handle of the object that contains the dialog resource. This is usually set equal to the **App.hInstance** property.

flags

> Flags describing this common dialog box. The **CF_ENABLETEMPLATE** and **CF_ENABLEHOOK** flags must be set to use a modified template and a dialog hook function.

lpfnHook

> A pointer to the developer-defined dialog hook function.

lpTemplateName

> The ID of the modified dialog resource.

This structure is passed in to the *ChooseFontDlg* API function to create and display the Font common dialog box. This function is declared as follows:

```
Public Declare Function ChooseFont Lib "comdlg32.dll" Alias "ChooseFontA" _
    (pChoosefont As CHOOSEFONT) As Long
```

The Print common dialog

The Print common dialog box allows the user to choose from an assortment of options for a particular print job. Options include the printer to send the job to, the number of times to print the job, and the pages that can be printed in the document. This common dialog is available to all 32-bit Windows operating systems.

To create this common dialog, initialize the **PRINTSTRUCT** structure. A Print Setup dialog box rather than the Print common dialog box also can be displayed by setting the **PD_PRINTSETUP** flag in the *flags* member of this structure. For new development, this common dialog should not be used; instead, use the Page Setup common dialog, described next. The **PRINTDLG** structure is defined in VB as follows:

```
Public Type PRINTDLG
        lStructSize As Long              ' size of this structure
        hwndOwner As Long                ' owning window
        hDevMode As Long                 ' pointer to DEVMODE structure
        hDevNames As Long                ' pointer to DEVNAMES structure
        hdc As Long                      ' handle to a device context
        flags As Long                    ' one or more flags OR'ed together
        nFromPage As Integer             ' start page
        nToPage As Integer               ' ending page
        nMinPage As Integer              ' minimum start page number
        nMaxPage As Integer              ' maximin ending page number
        nCopies As Integer               ' number of copies
        hInstance As Long                ' instance handle
        lCustData As Long                ' app-defined data passed in to the hook
        lpfnPrintHook As Long            ' pointer to print hook
        lpfnSetupHook As Long            ' pointer to setup hook
        lpPrintTemplateName As Long      ' print template name (in resource file)
        lpSetupTemplateName As Long      ' setup template name (in resource file)
        hPrintTemplate As Long           ' print template name (in memory object)
        hSetupTemplate As Long           ' setup template name(in memory object)
    End Type
```

The following members of the **PRINTDLG** structure are related to subclassing:

hInstance
> The instance handle of the object that contains the dialog resource. This is usually set equal to the **App.hInstance** property.

flags
> Flags describing this common dialog box. The **PD_ENABLEPRINTTEMPLATE** flag must be set to use a modified template for the Print dialog box. The **PD_ENABLESETUPTEMPLATE** flag must be set to use a modified template for the Print Setup dialog box.

lpfnPrintHook

A pointer to the developer-defined dialog hook function.

lpfnSetupHook

A pointer to the developer-defined dialog hook function.

lpPrintTemplateName

The ID of the modified Print dialog resource.

lpSetupTemplateName

The ID of the modified Print Setup dialog resource.

This structure is passed to the *PrintDlg* API function to create and display the Print common dialog box. This function is declared as follows:

```
Public Declare Function PrintDlg Lib "comdlg32.dll" Alias "PrintDlgA" _
    (pPrintdlg As PRINTDLG) As Long
```

The Page Setup common dialog

The Page Setup common dialog box allows the user to choose the printing properties for a particular print job. Properties include the paper size, paper source, orientation, and margin sizes.

To create this common dialog, initialize the PAGESETUPDLG structure. This structure is defined in VB as follows:

```
Public Type PAGESETUPDLG
        lStructSize As Long                   ' size of this structure
        hwndOwner As Long                     ' owning window
        hDevMode As Long                      ' pointer to DEVMODE structure
        hDevNames As Long                     ' pointer to DEVNAMES structure
        flags As Long                         ' one or more flags OR'ed together
        ptPaperSize As POINTAPI               ' pointer to a POINTAPI structure
        rtMinMargin As Rect                   ' minimum sizes of the margins
        rtMargin As Rect                      ' actual sizes of the margins
        hInstance As Long                     ' instance handle
        lCustData As Long                     ' app-defined data passed in to the hook
        lpfnPageSetupHook As Long             ' pointer to page setup dialog hook
        lpfnPagePaintHook As Long             ' pointer to sample page dialog hook
        lpPageSetupTemplateName As Long       ' page setup template name
        hPageSetupTemplate As Long            ' handle to page setup template
    End Type
```

It has the following members that are related to subclassing:

hInstance

The instance handle of the object that contains the dialog resource. This is usually set equal to the App.hInstance property.

flags

Flags describing this common dialog box. The `PSD_ENABLEPAGE-SETUPTEMPLATE` flag must be set to use a modified template. The `PSD_ENABLEPAGESETUPHOOK` flag must be set to use the page setup hook pointed to by the *lpfnPageSetupHook* function pointer. The `PSD_ENABLEPAGEPAINTHOOK` flag must be set to use the page setup hook pointed to by the *lpfnPagePaintHook* function pointer.

lpfnPageSetupHook

The pointer to the developer-defined dialog hook function.

lpfnPagePaintHook

The pointer to the developer-defined dialog hook function, which specifically intercepts the painting messages for the sample page object on this dialog box.

lpPrintTemplateName

The ID of the modified dialog resource.

This structure is passed in to the *PageSetupDlg* API function to create and display the Page Setup common dialog box. This function is declared as follows:

```
Public Declare Function PageSetupDlg Lib "comdlg32.dll" Alias "PageSetupDlgA" _
    (pPagesetupdlg As PAGESETUPDLG) As Long
```

The Print Property Sheet common dialog

The Print Property Sheet common dialog box allows the user to choose from an assortment of properties for a particular print job. Options included on this dialog are similar to the options on the Print common dialog box, with the additional options to print only the current page and to print more than one range of pages for a single document. This common dialog replaces the Print common dialog box on Windows 2000 and greater platforms.

To create this common dialog, initialize the **PRINTDLGEX** structure. This structure is declared in VB as follows:

```
Public Type PRINTDLGEX
        lStructSize As Long          ' size of this structure
        hwndOwner As Long            ' owning window
        hDevMode As Long             ' pointer to DEVMODE structure
        hDevNames As Long            ' pointer to DEVNAMES structure
        hdc As Long                  ' handle to a device context
        flags As Long                ' one or more flags OR'ed together
        flags2 As Long               ' must be set to zero
        Exclusionflags As Long       ' excludes ctrls. from prn. Drv. Prop. page
        nPageRanges As Long          ' number of page ranges
        nMaxPageRanges As Long       ' size of lpPageRanges
```

```
            lpPageRanges As Long        ' pointer to array of PRINTPAGERANGE struct's
            nMinPage As Integer         ' minimum start page number
            nMaxPage As Integer         ' maximin ending page number
            nCopies As Integer          ' number of copies
            hInstance As Long           ' instance handle
            lpPrintTemplateName As Long ' dialog template for General tab
            lpCallback As Long          ' pointer to a callback object
            nPropertyPages As Long      ' number of property page handles
            lphPropertyPagesAs String   ' pointer to array ofproperty page handles
            nnStartPage As Long         ' property page initially displayed
            dwResultAction As Long      ' returns the results of actions in this dlg.
    End Type
```

Its members that are related to subclassing are:

hInstance

The instance handle of the object that contains the dialog resource. This is usually set equal to the **App.hInstance** property.

flags

Flags describing this common dialog box. The **PD_ENABLEPRINTTEMPLATE** flag must be set to use a modified dialog template for the General tab.

lpCallback

A pointer to the developer-defined dialog hook function.

lpPrintTemplateName

The ID of the modified dialog resource for the General tab.

This structure is passed in to the *PrintDlgEx* API function to create and display the Print Property Sheet common dialog. This function is declared as follows:

```
Public Declare Function PrintDlgEx Lib "comdlg32.dll" Alias "PrintDlgA" _
        (pPrintdlg As PRINTDLGEX) As Long
```

The **PRINTDLGEXORD** dialog template located in the *PrnSetup.dlg* template file should be modified. This dialog template will be displayed on the lower portion of the General tab.

There is no member within the **PRINTDLGEX** structure to add the typical dialog hook function pointer, as there is with the structures for the other types of common dialog boxes. Instead, an *lpCallback* member is available. This member holds a pointer to a Component Object Model (COM) object, which implements the **IPrintDialogCallback** interface. This interface contains three methods that are called to pass information back to the application implementing the callback. Code is added to these three methods allowing messages sent to the modified dialog resource to be handled. The three methods are:

InitDone

Called when the General tab has finished initializing. Its prototype is:

```
HRESULT InitDone();
    HWND hDlg,
```

```
        UINT uMsg,
        WPARAM wParam,
        LPARAM lParam,
        LRESULT *pResult);
```

SelectionChanged

Called when the user selects a different printer on the General tab. Its prototype is:

```
HRESULT SelectionChanged();
        HWND hDlg,
        UINT uMsg,
        WPARAM wParam,
        LPARAM lParam,
        LRESULT *pResult);
```

HandleMessage

Intercepts any messages sent to the modified dialog resource located on the General tab. Its prototype is:

```
HRESULT HandleMessage(
        HWND hDlg,
        UINT uMsg,
        WPARAM wParam,
        LPARAM lParam,
        LRESULT *pResult);
```

with the following parameters:

hDlg

Handle to the modified dialog resource on the General tab.

uMsg

Message ID received by the modified dialog resource.

wParam

Extra information sent with the message, dependent on the type of message.

lParam

Extra information sent with the message, dependent on the type of message.

pResult

Pointer to a value that equals **TRUE** if the message was processed in this method. This value equals **FALSE** if the message was not processed.

This function returns **S_OK** to stop the *PrintDlgEx* function from performing its default functionality for this message. A return value of **S_FALSE** allows the *PrintDlgEx* function to finish performing its default handling of this message.

The Find common dialog

The Find common dialog box allows a user to search for a whole or partial word in the displayed text. The user controls the direction and the case sensitivity of the search. This dialog and the Replace dialog are the only two common dialog boxes that are modeless.

To create this common dialog, initialize the **FINDREPLACE** structure. This structure is defined in VB as follows:

```
Public Type FINDREPLACE
        lStructSize As Long              ' size of this struct
        hwndOwner As Long                ' handle to owning window
        hInstance As Long                ' instance handle of.EXE that
                                         '    contains cust. dlg. template
        flags As Long                    ' one or more flags OR'ed together
        lpstrFindWhat As String          ' pointer to search string
        lpstrReplaceWith As String       ' pointer to replace string
        wFindWhatLen As Integer          ' size of find buffer
        wReplaceWithLen As Integer       ' size of replace buffer
        lCustData As Long                ' custom data passed to hook function
        lpfnHook As Long                 ' pointer to hook function
        lpTemplateName As Long           ' custom template name
End Type
```

The **FINDREPLACE** members related to subclassing are:

hInstance

> The instance handle of the object that contains the dialog resource. This is usually set equal to the *App.hInstance* property.

flags

> Flags describing this common dialog box. The **FR_ENABLETEMPLATE** and **FR_ENABLEHOOK** flags must be set to use a modified template and a dialog hook function.

lpfnHook

> The pointer to the developer-defined dialog hook function.

lpTemplateName

> The ID of the modified dialog resource.

This structure is passed to the *FindText* API function to create and display the Find common dialog box. This function is declared as follows:

```
Public Declare Function FindText Lib "comdlg32.dll" Alias "FindTextA " _
    (pFindreplace As FINDREPLACE) As Long
```

The Replace common dialog

The Replace common dialog box allows a user to search for and replace a whole or partial word in the displayed text. The user controls the case sensitivity of the search. Two edit boxes are provided, one for the text to be replaced and one for the replacement text. Buttons are provided on this dialog to allow searching for text to be replaced, replacing the selected text, replacing all text in the document at once, and canceling the dialog. This dialog and the Find dialog are the only two common dialog boxes that are modeless.

To create this common dialog, initialize the **FINDREPLACE** structure. This structure is defined in VB as follows:

```
Public Type FINDREPLACE
        lStructSize As Long         ' size of this struct
        hwndOwner As Long           ' handle to owning window
        hInstance As Long           ' instance handle of .EXE that
                                    '   contains cust. dlg. template
        flags As Long               ' one or more flags OR'ed together
        lpstrFindWhat As String     ' pointer to search string
        lpstrReplaceWith As String  ' pointer to replace string
        wFindWhatLen As Integer     ' size of find buffer
        wReplaceWithLen As Integer  ' size of replace buffer
        lCustData As Long           ' custom data passed to hook function
        lpfnHook As Long            ' pointer to hook function
        lpTemplateName As Long      ' custom template name
    End Type
```

The members of **FINDREPLACE** that are related to subclassing are:

hInstance

> The instance handle of the object that contains the dialog resource. This is usually set equal to the **App.hInstance** property.

flags

> Flags describing this common dialog box. The **FR_ENABLETEMPLATE** and **FR_ENABLEHOOK** flags must be set to use a modified template and a dialog hook function.

lpfnHook

> The pointer to the developer-defined dialog hook function.

lpTemplateName

> The ID of the modified dialog resource.

This structure is passed in to the *ReplaceText* API function to create and display the Replace common dialog box. This function is declared as follows:

```
Public Declare Function ReplaceText Lib "comdlg32.dll" Alias "ReplaceTextA" _
        (pFindreplace As FINDREPLACE) As Long
```

Receiving Notification and Control Messages from the Dialog

The basic structure of the dialog hook procedure for these common dialog boxes remains the same as the one provided with the Save As example. Note, though, that several of the common dialogs use messages specific to their own operation. For example, the Open and Save As dialogs use the **CDN_FOLDERCHANGE** message to indicate that the user has changed folders in the dialog; this message does not apply to the other common dialogs.

What follows is a list of messages specific to each common dialog; the Color dialog implements the following messages:

COLOROKSTRING

> Sent when the user clicks the dialog's OK button. If the dialog hook procedure returns a 0, the selected color is rejected, and the dialog stays open.

SETRGBSTRING

> This message can be sent by the dialog hook procedure to force a color to be selected in the dialog box.

To use either message, the message must first be manually registered by your application using the *RegisterWindowMessage* function. This function is declared as follows:

```
Public Declare Function RegisterWindowMessage Lib "user32" _
        Alias "RegisterWindowMessageA" _
        (ByVal lpString As String) As Long
```

The function's single parameter is:

lpString

> A null-terminated string that identifies the new message

The function returns a unique number identifying the message in the range of &HC000 to &HFFFF. Messages in this range are global to the system; therefore, after a message is registered, any application can use it. If a zero is returned, the message failed to register. When registered, the new message can be sent using *SendMessage* or *PostMessage*. The dialog hook procedure also can intercept it.

The following is the code used to register these two Color dialog messages:

```
Dim ClrOKMsg as Long
Dim SetRGBMsg as Long

ClrOKMsg = RegisterWindowMessage("COLOROKSTRING")
SetRGBMsg = RegisterWindowMessage("SETRGBSTRING")
```

The Font dialog implements the following messages:

WM_CHOOSEFONT_GETLOGFONT

> This message can be sent by the dialog hook procedure to return information on the currently selected font.

WM_CHOOSEFONT_SETLOGFONT

> This message can be sent by the dialog hook procedure to set the selected font.

WM_CHOOSEFONT_SETFLAGS

This message can be sent by the dialog hook procedure to change the flags currently set in the CHOOSEFONT structure.

The Open and Save As dialogs implement the following messages:

CDN_FILEOK

The Open or Save button was clicked.

CDN_FOLDERCHANGE

The currently selected folder has changed.

CDN_HELP

The Help button was clicked.

CDN_INITDONE

The dialog has finished its initialization, including processing the WM_ INITDIALOG message.

CDN_SELCHANGE

A new file or folder has been selected.

CDN_SHAREVIOLATION

A sharing violation has occurred while trying to save or open the selected file.

CDN_TYPECHANGE

A new file type has been selected.

All these messages are sent to the dialog as a parameter of the WM_NOTIFY message. The Save As and Open dialog boxes are the only two that support these notification messages.

The following Select Case code block should be used in the dialog hook procedure only when using either the Save As or Open dialogs:

```
Select Case uMsg
    Case WM_NOTIFY
        CopyMemory NMHStruct, ByVal lParam, LenB(NMHStruct)

        Select Case NMHStruct.code
            Case CDN_INCLUDEITEM
                frmMain.txtMsg.Text = frmMain.txtMsg.Text & Hex$(hwnd) & _
                "-CDN_INCLUDEITEM" & vbNewLine
                DoEvents
            Case CDN_INITDONE
                frmMain.txtMsg.Text = frmMain.txtMsg.Text & Hex$(hwnd) & _
                "-CDN_INITDONE" & vbNewLine
                DoEvents
            Case CDN_SELCHANGE
                frmMain.txtMsg.Text = frmMain.txtMsg.Text & Hex$(hwnd) & _
                "-CDN_SELCHANGE" & vbNewLine
                DoEvents
            Case CDN_FOLDERCHANGE
```

```
                    frmMain.txtMsg.Text = frmMain.txtMsg.Text & Hex$(hwnd) & _
                      "-CDN_FOLDERCHANGE" & vbNewLine
                    DoEvents
                Case CDN_HELP
                    frmMain.txtMsg.Text = frmMain.txtMsg.Text & Hex$(hwnd) & _
                      "-CDN_HELP" & vbNewLine
                    DoEvents
                Case CDN_FILEOK
                    frmMain.txtMsg.Text = frmMain.txtMsg.Text & Hex$(hwnd) & _
                      "-CDN_FILEOK" & vbNewLine
                    DoEvents
                Case CDN_SHAREVIOLATION
                    frmMain.txtMsg.Text = frmMain.txtMsg.Text & Hex$(hwnd) & _
                      "-CDN_SHAREVIOLATION" & vbNewLine
                    DoEvents
                Case CDN_TYPECHANGE
                    frmMain.txtMsg.Text = frmMain.txtMsg.Text & Hex$(hwnd) & _
                      "-CDN_TYPECHANGE" & vbNewLine
                    DoEvents
                Case Else
                    frmMain.txtMsg.Text = frmMain.txtMsg.Text & Hex$(hwnd) & _
                      "-" & CStr(uMsg) & "    " & vbNewLine
            End Select

        'Other Case statements...

    End Select
```

For the Page Setup dialog, if the PSD_ENABLEPAGEPAINTHOOK flag is set in the
PAGESETUPDLG flags member, a second hook function can be implemented. This
hook function intercepts the following messages, which modify the look of the
sample page image at the top of this common dialog box:

WM_PSD_PAGESETUPDLG

Contains information regarding the paper size, paper orientation, and type of
printer device.

WM_PSD_FULLPAGERECT

Contains a RECT structure defining the location and size of the sample page
image.

WM_PSD_MINMARGINRECT

Contains a RECT structure defining the location and minimum size of the rectangle indicating the margin.

WM_PSD_MARGINRECT

Contains a RECT structure defining the location and size of the rectangle indicating the margin.

WM_PSD_GREEKTEXTRECT

Contains a RECT structure defining the location and size of the rectangle containing the Greek text.

WM_PSD_ENVSTAMPRECT

Contains a RECT structure defining the location and size of the rectangle indicating the envelope and stamp. This message is sent only for envelope print jobs.

WM_PSD_YAFULLPAGERECT

Contains a RECT structure defining the location and minimum size of the rectangle indicating an envelope's return address. This message is sent only for envelope print jobs.

The Find and Replace dialogs implement the following message:

FINDMSGSTRING

Sent by the Find or Replace dialog box to the window procedure of the window that owns either of these common dialogs. This message is sent in response to the user clicking the Replace, Replace All, or Find Next button. This message also is sent to inform the owning window that the user has closed this dialog.

This message also must be registered with the *RegisterWindowMessage* function. The owning window can be subclassed to watch for this message.

Problems Subclassing the Find and Replace Common Dialogs

The Find and Replace common dialog boxes operate differently than all other common dialog boxes in one respect. These common dialogs are modeless. This means that code will continue executing in the calling procedure; it will not wait for the dialog to be closed. For a modeless dialog to work properly, Windows requires that the *IsDialogMessage* API function be used in the main message loop of the application. The *IsDialogMessage* API function basically does the work of the *TranslateMessage* and the *DispatchMessage* API functions, but for modeless dialog boxes. Therefore, if *IsDialogMessage* returns a TRUE value, it has processed the message and the *TranslateMessage* and the *DispatchMessage* API functions should not be called. The *IsDialogMessage* API function's main purpose is to provide default dialog keyboard processing for the modeless dialog box. Modal dialog boxes automatically support default dialog keyboard processing. Here is the list of default dialog keyboard keys processed by the *IsDialogMessage* API function:

ALT+mnemonic

Moves the focus to the first control in the tab order after the static control containing this mnemonic

DOWN

Moves the focus to the next control

UP

Moves the focus to the previous control

ENTER

Simulates clicking the OK button

ESC

Simulates clicking the Cancel button

LEFT

Moves the focus to the previous control

RIGHT

Moves the focus to the next control

TAB

Moves the focus to the next control

SHIFT+TAB

Moves the focus to the previous control

Mnemonic (performs same action as the ALT+mnemonic key combination)

Moves the focus to the first control in the tab order after the static control containing this mnemonic

Unfortunately, it is not possible to add the *IsDialogMessage* API function to the main message loop of a VB application. The main message loop for a VB application is located in **ThunderRT6Main**. In a Visual C++ application, the main message loop of an application that uses modeless dialog boxes would look something like this:

```
while (GetMessage(&msg, NULL, 0, 0))
{
        if (NULL == hDlgCurrent || !IsDialogMessage(hDlgCurrent, &msg))
        {
            TranslateMessage(&msg);
            DispatchMessage(&msg);
        }
}
```

Using Spy++ to Peer into the Common Dialog Subclassing Application

Start the Chapter 5 example and then run Spy++. Click the button in the example application to display the subclassed Save As common dialog box. Locate the example application and the Export As subclassed common dialog box in the Windows child window of Spy++. The Export As common dialog box will be labeled "Export As (Subclassed Common Dialog)". It also will contain the text #32770 after the window caption. This value is the class name for a window's dialog box. Double-click this dialog box to display the Window Properties dialog box. This class name also can be found on the Class tab of the Window Properties dialog box.

If you expand the branch for the Export As common dialog, you will see all the controls that make up that common dialog box. It is here that you can find the IDs for all the dialog's controls. You also will see a window in this list with no caption and the class name of #32770. This is the child dialog of the common dialog box, created from the dialog template resource. If you look at the window procedure for this child dialog and compare it to the window procedure of its parent dialog box, you will see that they are the same. Therefore, we can deduce that all messages for the parent and the child dialog boxes are handled in one window procedure. This window procedure is the same for the dialog box (General tab) as it is for the class (Class tab). This means that this window (dialog) procedure has not been subclassed. So, the dialog hook procedure really is a hook and not a subclassed dialog procedure.

If you expand the branch for the child dialog box, you will see all the controls that you placed on your dialog template resource. The class names for the controls are not preceded by the word "Thunder", even if you did import the VB form into the Visual C++ resource editor. Therefore, they will all have different window procedures with respect to their classes.

Using the Windows tab of the Window Properties dialog box, we can verify that the original common dialog box is the parent to the child dialog box created from the resource file. To do this, double-click the child dialog box and find the handle value in the Parent Window field on the Windows tab. Compare this to the handle of the default common dialog box. They are the same.

—Continued—

For a VB application, there is a way around this. The WH_GETMESSAGE hook must be used to trap messages sent to the dialog box before they reach the dialog box's dialog procedure. This hook is installed while handling the WM_ INITDIALOG message and it is uninstalled while handling the WM_DESTROY message. The WH_GETMESSAGE hook function then waits for keyboard messages to arrive. When a keyboard message arrives, it sends it to the *IsDialogMessage* API function. If this API function returns TRUE, it has processed the message, and the keyboard message should not be passed on to the default dialog procedure. If it returns FALSE, it did not process the message, and the default dialog procedure needs to process this message. The WH_ GETMESSAGE hook function is discussed in Chapter 11.

6

ActiveX Controls and Subclassing

This chapter deals with the different ways of using subclassing with an ActiveX control. It covers the following topics:

- Subclassing a third-party ActiveX control

- Subclassing an ActiveX control that you created

- Subclassing a UserControl from within the Visual Basic (VB) control

- Subclassing a VB form from one or more ActiveX controls

Subclassing a Third-Party ActiveX Control

This is the easiest of the four types of subclassing discussed in this chapter. Subclassing a third-party ActiveX control is exactly the same as subclassing a VB form. There is no difference because the system sees both the control and the form as windows. Using *SetWindowLongPtr*, you would subclass the control just like you would any other window:

```
Private Sub Form_Load()
    gCtrlWndProc = SetWindowLongPtr(Button1.GetHwnd, GWL_WNDPROC, AddressOf
CtrlProc)
End Sub
```

You set up the subclass function just like you would any other subclass function: by passing the window message on to the original window procedure by way of *CallWindowProc*, as the following subclass function indicates:

```
Public Function CtrlProc(ByVal hWnd As Long, ByVal uMsg As Long, _
                ByVal wParam As Long, ByVal lParam As Long) As Long
    'Do subclassing work here
```

```
gCtrlWndProc = SetWindowLongPtr(Button1.GetHwnd, GWL_WNDPROC, _
                               AddressOf CtrlProc)
```

Using *SetWindowLongPtr*, the subclass procedure is removed from the control, similar to removing the subclass procedure from any other window:

```
Private Sub Form_Unload(Cancel As Integer)
    Dim RetVal As Long
    RetVal = SetWindowLongPtr(Button1.GetHwnd, GWL_WNDPROC, gCtrlWndProc)
End Sub
```

Now that we can subclass a control, we will move on to subclassing a control that we create within the VB environment.

Subclassing an ActiveX Control Created in VB

Subclassing an ActiveX control that we create through VB is similar to subclassing a third-party control. However, we must overcome one small hurdle first. The problem is that the UserControl module's **hwnd** property is not visible outside of the UserControl module.

You can overcome this problem in two ways. First, you can use the *FindWindowEx* function to get the handle to the control. This function is declared in this manner in VB:

```
Private Declare Function FindWindowEx Lib "user32" Alias "FindWindowExA" _
    (ByVal hWnd1 As Long, ByVal hWnd2 As Long, _
    ByVal lpsz1 As String, ByVal lpsz2 As String) As Long
```

The function has the following parameters:

hWnd1

> The hWnd of the parent window to the window that you want to find. The function uses this parameter as a starting point for searching for the target window. If **Null**, the function uses the desktop as the parent window.

hWnd2

> The hWnd of any child windows to the window specified by the *hWnd1* parameter. If a valid child window handle is provided, this function starts searching through all the windows that are children to the window specified by this parameter.

lpsz1

> The class name or class atom of the window that we are searching for.

lpsz2

> The caption of the window that we are searching for.

If this function succeeds, the hWnd of the window is returned; otherwise, a zero is returned, indicating failure.

Example 6-1 shows the code to find the hWnd of a VB-created ActiveX control.

Example 6-1. Finding the Window Handle of an ActiveX Control Created with VB

```
Private Sub Form_Load()
    Dim retval As Long

    'Use the ThunderUserControlDC class if you are running inside of the IDE
    retval = FindWindowEx(Form1.hWnd, 0, "ThunderRT6UserControlDC", vbNullString)
End Sub
```

The first argument to the *FindWindowEx* function is the handle to the form where the UserControl exists. The second argument is zero because the UserControl is not a child window of another control on the form. If the UserControl were contained inside another control on the form, the second parameter, *hWnd2*, would contain the hWnd of this control.

The third argument is the class name of the UserControl. You find the class name using Spy++. Remember that the class name is different when running inside the IDE as opposed to running in a standalone executable. The class name for a User-Control running in the IDE is **ThunderUserControlDC**; the class name for a User-Control running in a standalone executable is **ThunderRT6UserControlDC**.

The last argument is **vbNullString**. You use this because the UserControl has no caption. We can validate this as well through Spy++, as shown in Figure 6-1.

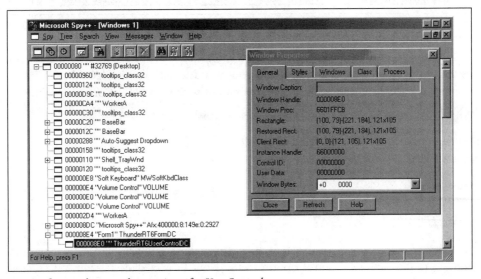

Figure 6-1. Looking at the caption of a UserControl

As noted previously, you can get the hWnd of a UserControl in another way. If you use the Object Browser included with VB to look through the properties of the UserControl module, you'll find that it exposes an **hwnd** property, as Figure 6-2 illustrates. Unfortunately, it is not visible from outside the control.

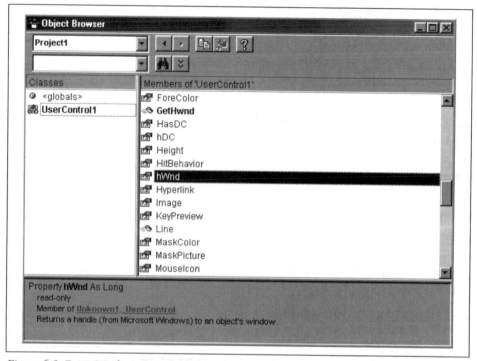

Figure 6-2. Browsing the UserControl object

To circumvent this problem, I provided a public function that exposes the hWnd of the control. Example 6-2 shows the code used to expose the hWnd of a User-Control. As a note, this code must be contained within the UserControl module to access its **hwnd** property.

Example 6-2. Retrieving the hWnd of a UserControl

```
Public Function GetHwnd()
    GetHwnd = hWnd
End Function
```

Creating the Control

Let's see how this works by creating a simple ActiveX control. Start a new project and select the ActiveX Control option in the New Project dialog. After VB creates the project, it will contain a single UserControl module called UserControl1. The file for the UserControl1 module is called *UserControl1.ctl*.

First, select a background color that will show up against a form background. In this case, I used the Properties window to set the BackColor property to Green. Next, place the code shown in Example 6-2 into UserControl1. This allows the application that is subclassing this control to access its hWnd. Next, we will begin to create the application that subclasses this control.

Creating the Project to Subclass the Control

To subclass the ActiveX control we created, we need a container to host the control. First, add a Standard EXE project to the ActiveX control project we created previously. The new project will be created with a form module called Form1. Next, add a *.bas* module to the new project. This *.bas* module will contain the subclass procedure for the control.

Before the ActiveX control that we created can be hosted in the form in the second project, it must be compiled into an *.ocx*. The control will now appear in the Toolbox tool window. Place an instance of the control in the Form1 module. Also add a button (Command1) and a text box (Text1) to the form. Figure 6-3 shows the final form.

Table 6-1 presents the nondefault properties of the form and its controls.

Table 6-1. Nondefault Properties of the Form and Its Controls

Object	Property Name	Property Value
Form	Caption	"Subclass a VB-Created ActiveX Ctrl"
Form	Top	330
Form	Left	45
Form	Height	4005
Form	Width	4800
UserControl	Name	UserControl1
UserControl	Top	60
UserControl	Left	60
UserControl	Height	1095
UserControl	Width	1335
Command Button1	Name	Command1
Command Button1	Caption	"Subclass"
Command Button1	Top	1320
Command Button1	Left	60
Command Button1	Height	375
Command Button1	Width	1335
TextBox	Name	Text1

Table 6-1. Nondefault Properties of the Form and Its Controls (continued)

Object	Property Name	Property Value
TextBox	MultiLine	True
TextBox	Top	60
TextBox	Left	1500
TextBox	Height	3495
TextBox	Width	3135

Next, add the code shown in Example 6-3 to the Click event of the Command1 button control contained on the Form1 module. This code uses the *GetHwnd* public method of the UserControl1 to retrieve its hWnd. This value is used in the *SetWindowLongPtr* function to subclass the ActiveX control.

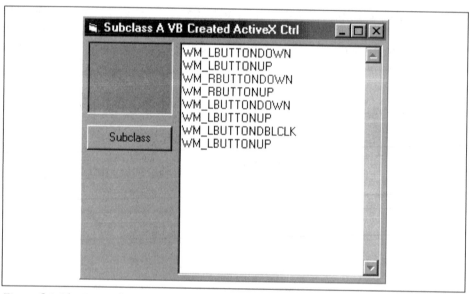

Figure 6-3. The Form1 form, which hosts the ActiveX control that we created

Example 6-3. The Command1_Click Event Procedure

```
Private Sub Command1_Click()
    Form1.Text1.Text = ""
    gCtrlWndProc = SetWindowLongPtr(UserControl1.GetHwnd, GWLP_WNDPROC, _
                AddressOf CtrlProc)
End Sub
```

Add the code shown in Example 6-4 to the *Form_Unload* subroutine to remove the subclass procedure from the ActiveX control. This is the only code that you need to add to the Form1 module.

Example 6-4. The Form_Unload Event Procedure

```
Private Sub Form_Unload(Cancel As Integer)
    Dim RetVal As Long
    RetVal = SetWindowLongPtr(UserControl12.GetHwnd, GWLP_WNDPROC, gCtrlWndProc)
End Sub
```

Next, we'll add the code shown in Example 6-5 to the *Module1.bas* module. This *.bas* module contains the application programming interface (API) declarations, variables, and constants needed to implement subclassing; it also contains the subclass procedure. A global variable, *gCtrlWndProc*, is defined that contains a pointer to the original ActiveX control's window procedure.

Example 6-5. Code for the Module1.bas Module

```
Public Declare Function SetWindowLongPtr Lib "user32" Alias "SetWindowLongA" _
         (ByVal hWnd As Long, ByVal nIndex As Long, ByVal dwNewLong As Long) As Long
Public Declare Function CallWindowProc Lib "user32" Alias "CallWindowProcA" _
         (ByVal lpPrevWndFunc As Long, ByVal hWnd As Long, ByVal Msg As Long, _
         ByVal wParam As Long, ByVal lParam As Long) As Long

Public Const GWLP_WNDPROC = (-4)
Public Const GWLP_USERDATA = (-21)
Public Const WM_MOUSEACTIVATE = &H21
Public Const WM_LBUTTONUP = &H202
Public Const WM_LBUTTONDOWN = &H201
Public Const WM_LBUTTONDBLCLK = &H203
Public Const WM_RBUTTONDBLCLK = &H206
Public Const WM_RBUTTONDOWN = &H204
Public Const WM_RBUTTONUP = &H205

Public gCtrlWndProc As Long


Public Function CtrlProc(ByVal hWnd As Long, ByVal uMsg As Long, _
               ByVal wParam As Long, ByVal lParam As Long) As Long
    Select Case uMsg
        Case WM_LBUTTONUP
            Form1.Text1.Text = Form1.Text1.Text & "WM_LBUTTONUP" & vbNewLine
        Case WM_LBUTTONDOWN
            Form1.Text1.Text = Form1.Text1.Text & "WM_LBUTTONDOWN" & vbNewLine
        Case WM_LBUTTONDBLCLK
            Form1.Text1.Text = Form1.Text1.Text & "WM_LBUTTONDBLCLK" & vbNewLine
        Case WM_RBUTTONUP
            Form1.Text1.Text = Form1.Text1.Text & "WM_RBUTTONUP" & vbNewLine
        Case WM_RBUTTONDOWN
            Form1.Text1.Text = Form1.Text1.Text & "WM_RBUTTONDOWN" & vbNewLine
        Case WM_RBUTTONDBLCLK
            Form1.Text1.Text = Form1.Text1.Text & "WM_RBUTTONDBLCLK" & vbNewLine
    End Select

    CtrlProc = CallWindowProc(gCtrlWndProc, hWnd, uMsg, wParam, ByVal lParam)
End Function
```

The *CtrlProc* subclass procedure contains code that will write out text to the Text1 text box whenever the right or left mouse button is single-clicked or double-clicked while over the subclassed control.

To use this application, click the Subclass button to allow the form to subclass the VB ActiveX control. After the control is subclassed, you can right- or left-click the control with the mouse, and the Text1 text box will display the mouse buttons that were clicked. Double-click events also are tracked by the subclass procedure. Notice that when you double-click either the right or left mouse buttons, you see the following pattern:

```
WM_LBUTTONDOWN
WM_LBUTTONUP
WM_LBUTTONDBLCLK
WM_LBUTTONUP
```

The reason for this pattern is detailed in Chapter 13 on the `WH_MOUSE` mouse hook.

This is how you subclass an ActiveX control created in VB. The only thing you must do beyond normal subclassing is to get the hWnd of the control either by using the *FindWindowEx* function or by adding a public method to the UserControl that exposes the hWnd of the control.

Subclassing a UserControl from Within a VB-Created ActiveX Control

The UserControl is the base on which you create your control. You can subclass the UserControl while creating your own ActiveX control. For example, you might need to watch for specific mouse or keyboard events that are directed to your control. To watch for these and any other messages, you need to subclass the UserControl.

Subclassing a UserControl when only one control is on the form at any one time is easy. In fact, it is not much different from subclassing any other window. The problem occurs when more than one of the subclassed controls exists on a form at any one time.

To see what I mean, let's examine a little more of how subclassing works with a VB ActiveX control. The subclass procedure must exist in a *.bas* module, and one instance of this module exists for every control that is instantiated. However, one instance of a UserControl module is created for each instance of the control. When the control is subclassed, a message will first be sent to the only function in the *.bas* module that is acting as the subclass procedure for all instances of the control. This procedure must then know which instance of the UserControl module to forward the message to so that it can be processed. After the message is processed, it must be sent to the original window procedure of that instance of the control. If the message is not forwarded to the correct original window procedure, all instances of the control might seem as though they are not processing any messages.

To be able to direct the message to the original window procedure of the correct control, we must store a pointer to each control. This pointer is used to pass the message on to a function that exists within the correct instance of the control—or, more specifically, within the correct instance of the UserControl module. The best place to store this pointer is in the UserData section of each control. Then, as each control is subclassed, it will store a reference to itself in its own UserData section. Every window has a UserData section in which to store information pertinent to itself. You place data in the UserData section through *SetWindowLongPtr* in this fashion:

```
Call SetWindowLongPtr(hWnd, GWLP_USERDATA, 100)
```

You access data from the UserData section through *GetWindowLongPtr* in this manner:

```
pUserData = GetWindowLongPtr(hWnd, GWLP_USERDATA)
```

You use *SetWindowLongPtr* to store a pointer to the control, right after the control is subclassed. The line of code that does this is:

```
Call SetWindowLongPtr(hWnd, GWLP_USERDATA, ObjPtr(Me))
```

Every time the subclass function in the *.bas* module is called, it uses the hWnd value that is passed in to it to retrieve a pointer to the control through the *GetWindowLongPtr* function. The line of code that does this is:

```
pUserData = GetWindowLongPtr(hWnd, GWLP_USERDATA)
```

pUserData will receive the value contained in the UserData section of the control corresponding to the hWnd value passed in to it. This value is then cast to a UserControl1 object type so that a function on it can be called to handle the message sent to it. You use *CopyMemory* to copy the value of the *pUserData* variable—which, by the way, points to the vtable of the control—into a variable of type UserControl1. The code to do this is:

```
CopyMemory ctlRefToCtrl, pUserData, 4
```

Now the variable *ctlRefToCtrl* points to the correct instance of the control to which we need to pass the intercepted message. Using this variable, the *CtrlProc* function can be called on that instance of the control. This function processes the message and passes it on to the original window procedure of that control:

```
MainCtrlProc = ctlRefToCtrl.CtrlProc(hWnd, Msg, wParam, lParam)
```

When this function returns, the *ctlRefToCtrl* variable must be cleaned up as follows:

```
CopyMemory ctlRefToCtrl, 0&, 4
Set ctlRefToCtrl = Nothing
```

For a diagram of how this works, see Figure 6-4.

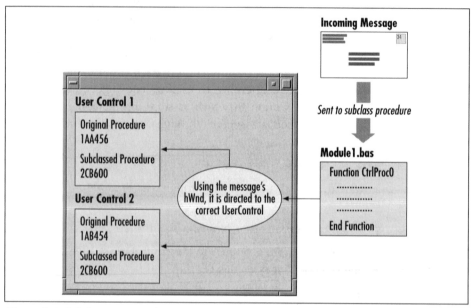

Figure 6-4. Subclassing more than one UserControl

You might notice that we used the *ObjPtr* function to get a pointer to an instance of the control. This is an undocumented function in VB that takes an object as its only parameter and returns a pointer to that object. Interestingly, this function will not increment the reference count of the object or control. This will be useful in the last section of this chapter, where we'll be using more than one control to subclass the same form.

Creating the Control

The ActiveX control that we will create consists of only a UserControl and no other constituent controls. The subclass procedure watches for mouse clicks and changes the background color of the control to a specific color depending on the type of mouse message intercepted.

The UserControl module

To create the ActiveX control, create an ActiveX Control project in VB, then open the UserControl1's code module so that you can add code to it.

First, declare a private variable, *m_OrigCtrlProc*, to hold the address of the original window procedure for the control instance:

```
Private m_OrigCtrlProc As Long
```

Also, declare a private variable, *m_hwndCtrl*, to contain the handle to the control instance:

```
Private m_hwndCtrl As Long
```

The `UserControl_Initialize` event occurs when the control is first created but before it is sited on the container. It is useful to note that this event also is fired at design time. Therefore, we can use this event to call the function to subclass the control both at runtime and while it is in the IDE, as shown in Example 6-6.

Example 6-6. The UserControl_Initialize Event Procedure

```
Private Sub UserControl_Initialize()
    SubClass
End Sub
```

The `UserControl_Terminate` event occurs after the control is unsited from its container but immediately before the control is destroyed. This event also is fired during design time when you close the child window that contains the form this control is sited on in the IDE. Because you must remove a subclass procedure before the subclassed window is destroyed, it is a good idea to place the code to remove the subclass procedure in the Terminate event. If the code to remove the subclass procedure is not executed, memory leaks or a General Protection Fault (GPF) might result every time the control is destroyed in the IDE or in a compiled application. Therefore, we'll use this event to remove the subclass from the control, as Example 6-7 shows.

Example 6-7. The UserControl_Terminate Event Procedure

```
Private Sub UserControl_Terminate()
    RemoveSubClass
End Sub
```

The *SubClass* function in the UserControl module performs the subclassing; it is shown in Example 6-8. It checks the *m_OrigCtrlProc* variable to determine if the control was already subclassed. If it was, the control cannot be subclassed a second time. Next, it uses *SetWindowLongPtr* to subclass the control. *MainCtrlProc* is the subclass procedure, and it is contained in the *Module1.bas* module in the control project (this module is discussed in the next section). The final thing this function does is critical to the correct operation of the subclassed control. It uses *SetWindowLongPtr* to store a pointer to the instance of this control in its own UserData section. This allows a pointer to this control to be retrieved when you only have the hWnd to the control itself.

Example 6-8. The SubClass Function to Perform the Subclassing

```
Private Sub SubClass()
    If m_OrigCtrlProc = 0 Then
        m_OrigCtrlProc = SetWindowLongPtr(hWnd, GWLP_WNDPROC, AddressOf MainCtrlProc)
        m_hwndCtrl = hWnd

        Call SetWindowLongPtr(hWnd, GWLP_USERDATA, ObjPtr(Me))
    End If
End Sub
```

The *RemoveSubClass* function shown in Example 6-9 uses *SetWindowLongPtr* to remove the subclass procedure from the control instance. It sets *m_OrigCtrlProc* back to zero to indicate that the subclass procedure was removed from the control.

Example 6-9. The RemoveSubClass Function to Remove the Subclassing

```
Private Sub RemoveSubClass()
    If m_OrigCtrlProc <> 0 Then
        SetWindowLongPtr m_hwndCtrl, GWLP_WNDPROC, m_OrigCtrlProc
        m_OrigCtrlProc = 0
    End If
End Sub
```

The *CtrlProc* function shown in Example 6-10 acts as the subclass procedure. This procedure changes the background color of the control any time a right or left mouse-button message is intercepted. Notice that the function is declared as a **Friend** function. This allows functions within the scope of the project to access this function, but denies access to functions outside of this project. This prevents any function within the application that is hosting this control from calling this function. You can make this a public function, but if you did, it would be visible for the world to see and call.

Example 6-10. CtrlProc, the Subclass Procedure

```
Friend Function CtrlProc(ByVal hWnd As Long, ByVal uMsg As Long, _
                ByVal wParam As Long, ByVal lParam As Long) As Long
    Select Case uMsg
        Case WM_LBUTTONDBLCLK
            UserControl.BackColor = vbBlue
        Case WM_LBUTTONDOWN
            UserControl.BackColor = vbRed
        Case WM_LBUTTONUP
            UserControl.BackColor = vbCyan
        Case WM_RBUTTONDBLCLK
            UserControl.BackColor = vbGreen
        Case WM_RBUTTONDOWN
            UserControl.BackColor = vbWhite
        Case WM_RBUTTONUP
            UserControl.BackColor = vbBlack
    End Select
```

Example 6-10. CtrlProc, the Subclass Procedure (continued)

```
    CtrlProc = CallWindowProc(m_OrigCtrlProc, hWnd, uMsg, wParam, ByVal lParam)
End Function
```

The Module1.bas module

Since our subclass procedure must reside outside of the UserControl module itself, add a code module to the project. By default, VB will name it Module1.

Declare a constant in the *Module1.bas* module to allow the *SetWindowLongPtr* function to place data into the control's UserData section:

```
    Public Const GWLP_USERDATA = (-21)
```

Define the **ctrlRefToCtrl** variable as follows:

```
    Dim ctlRefToCtrl As UserControl1
```

The **ctlRefToCtrl** variable contains a reference to the UserControl1 object. You use this reference to call a function in a particular instance of a control. You must use the UserControl1 type; you cannot use a type such as Object or Control.

Next, add the **pUserData** variable, which holds an address to the UserData section of the control:

```
    Dim pUserData As Long
```

The *MainCtrlProc* function shown in Example 6-11 acts as the central subclass procedure that initially is called. This function uses the hWnd value passed to it to get the data stored in the UserData section of the instance of the control that the hWnd value refers to. It uses the pointer stored in the UserData section of this window to determine which instance of the *CtrlProc* function is called in the UserControl1 module.

Example 6-11. The MainCtrlProc Function

```
Public Function MainCtrlProc(ByVal hWnd As Long, ByVal Msg As Long, _
        ByVal wParam As Long, ByVal lParam As Long) As Long
    pUserData = GetWindowLong(hWnd, GWLP_USERDATA)

    CopyMemory ctlRefToCtrl, pUserData, 4
    MainCtrlProc = ctlRefToCtrl.CtrlProc(hWnd, Msg, wParam, lParam)
    CopyMemory ctlRefToCtrl, 0&, 4

    Set ctlRefToCtrl = Nothing
End Function
```

Any time any instance of a subclassed control receives a message, the message is sent to this window procedure. This window procedure calls *GetWindowLong* to obtain the UserData information for the control that the message is being sent to. Remember that when the control is subclassed, a reference to is stored in the User-

Data section of the control. The subclass procedure is sent the hWnd of the control that the message is being sent to. We can use this hWnd value in the *GetWindowLong* function to obtain a reference to the control. To actually use this reference, we must copy it to a variable of the same type as the reference. Using *CopyMemory*, we can copy to the `ctlRefToCtrl` variable the reference contained in the *pUserData* variable, which is of type *UserControl*. Now the *ctlRefToCtrl* variable points to the control that the message is being sent to. This variable is used to call the *CtrlProc* function on the instance of the control that is being passed the message. The function on the control instance does its work and returns. It uses *CopyMemory* to remove the reference contained in the `ctlRefToCtrl` variable. Then it sets the `ctlRefToCtrl` variable to Nothing.

Hosting the Control

To host the control, you simply compile the ActiveX control project into an ActiveX control (OCX) and then create a separate standard EXE project to host the control. This project will be created with one form initially. Place the OCX on this form. Note that if the standard EXE project is not in the same project group, you will have to set a reference to the new control using the Components dialog box.

Place at least two controls on the form. You do not need to write any code. Compile the project and then run it. The form in the example will look like the one in Figure 6-5. The controls are automatically subclassed when the application is started. The subclassing is automatically removed when the application ends. Clicking each control changes the background color of each control independently of the other.

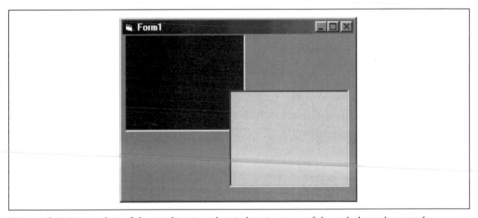

Figure 6-5. Screenshot of the application that is hosting two of the subclassed controls

When you click the left mouse button over a control, the background color will change according to the message received. The color will change to red when you depress the left mouse button and to cyan when you release the button. If you depress the left mouse button and hold it down, you will see the control change to red. When you double-click the left mouse button, the subclass procedure will receive mouse messages in the following order:

```
WM_LBUTTONDOWN
WM_LBUTTONUP
WM_LBUTTONDBLCLK
WM_LBUTTONUP
```

The control changes color for each message. If you double-click the left mouse button and hold it down on the second click, you will notice that the color changes to blue. When you release it, the color changes back to cyan.

Creating an ActiveX Control That Subclasses Other Windows

We need to examine one last situation: creating an ActiveX control that subclasses the form that it is sited on. This gives us a way to encapsulate a subclassing routine that we can literally drop onto a form and have it work without requiring that the user of the control to do anything. The user does not even have to set any properties on the control. This is a good way to distribute common subclassing functionality between project developers without every developer having to know the intricacies of subclassing a form. For instance, if every form in an application needed to know whether a laptop's battery was getting low on power, you could create a control that subclasses the form onto which it is dropped and then watches for the WM_POWERBROADCAST message.

Using a control to subclass the form onto which it is dropped has several problems. First, when one control is dropped onto the form, it immediately subclasses the form and stores its original window procedure. This is fine, but when a developer drops another control onto the same form, the new control subclasses the form a second time and stores what it thinks is the form's original window procedure. Instead, it is storing the address to the subclass procedure of the first control. Actually, the application will seem to work until you close it. When you close the application, the operating system does not destroy the controls in the reverse order in which they were created; instead, it destroys them in no guaranteed order. Therefore, the form's original window procedure might or might not be restored. Most likely it will not. This will cause the application to crash.

Creating the First Version of the Control

Let's start with the code that is contained in the *Module1.bas* module; it is shown in Example 6-12.

Example 6-12. Code in the Module1.bas Module

```
Private SubClassedForm_hWnd As Long          'hWnd of the VB Form
Private CtrlInstance_Ptr As Long             'Pointer to instance of Ctrl
Private SubClassedForm_OrigWndProc As Long   'Original WndProc of VB Form

Public Function SubClass(hForm As Long, pSubClassCtrl As UserControl1) As Boolean
    SubClass = False

    If SubClassedForm_hWnd = 0 Then
        SubClass = True

        SubClassedForm_hWnd = hForm
        CtrlInstance_Ptr = ObjPtr(pSubClassCtrl)
        SubClassedForm_OrigWndProc = SetWindowLongPtr(hForm, GWL_WNDPROC, _
                             AddressOf VBFormWndProc)
    End If
End Function

Public Sub UnSubClass()
    Call SetWindowLongPtr(SubClassedForm_hWnd, GWL_WNDPROC, _
                     SubClassedForm_OrigWndProc)
End Sub

Private Function VBFormWndProc(ByVal hWnd As Long, ByVal wMsg As Long, _
        ByVal wParam As Long, ByVal lParam As Long) As Long
    Dim oObject As UserControl1

    'Create the object and call the form proc in the object
    Call CopyMemory(oObject, CtrlInstance_Ptr, 4)
    VBFormWndProc = oObject.HandleMessage(SubClassedForm_OrigWndProc, _
                     hWnd, wMsg, wParam, lParam)
    Call CopyMemory(oObject, 0&, 4)
End Function
```

The module defines the following three private member variables:

SubClassedForm_hWnd

Holds the handle to the window that is being subclassed by the control.

CtrlInstance_Ptr

Holds a pointer to the instance of the control. The *.bas* module's subclass procedure uses this to determine which control to send the message to.

SubClassedForm_OrigWndProc

Holds the original window procedure of the subclassed form.

This *.bas* module contains three functions: one that subclasses the container form, one that removes the subclass procedure from the container form, and one that contains the central subclass procedure.

The *SubClass* function actually does the subclassing. This function takes the form handle to the subclassed form (hForm) and the pointer to the control that is trying to perform the subclassing. If the *SubClassedForm_hWnd* variable contains zero, the form has not yet been subclassed. In this case, this control subclasses the form, thereby placing the original window procedure in the *SubClassedForm_OrigWndProc* variable and the pointer to itself in the *CtrlInstance_Ptr* variable. The subclassed form hwnd also is stored in the *SubClassedForm_hWnd* variable.

The *UnSubClass* function removes the subclass procedure from the container form. *SetWindowLongPtr* is called with the original window procedure to the container form.

VBFormWndProc acts as the subclass procedure. This is the function that intercepts the message before it is actually sent to the window. This function creates a pointer to the control that should receive the message by using *CopyMemory* and then calls the function on that instance of the control that can handle the message. In this case, the *HandleMessage* function (shown in Example 6-13) will handle the message sent to it. This technique is the same as was used previously to allow each control instance to receive the intercepted message.

Example 6-13 shows the code for the *UserControl1.ctl* module of the control.

Example 6-13. Code for the UserControl1.ctl Module

```
Private Const WM_LBUTTONDOWN = &H201
Private Const WM_LBUTTONUP = &H202

Private SubclassingCtrl As Boolean

Private Sub UserControl_Initialize()
    SubclassingCtrl = False
End Sub

Friend Function HandleMessage(ByVal plOldProc As Long, ByVal hWnd As Long, _
        ByVal wMsg As Long, ByVal wParam As Long, ByVal lParam As Long) As Long
    Select Case wMsg
        Case WM_LBUTTONDOWN
            UserControl.BackColor = vbBlue
        Case WM_LBUTTONUP
            UserControl.BackColor = vbWhite
    End Select

    HandleMessage = CallWindowProc(plOldProc, hWnd, wMsg, wParam, lParam)
End Function

Private Sub UserControl_ReadProperties(PropBag As PropertyBag)
    SubclassingCtrl = SubClass(UserControl.Parent.hWnd, Me)
End Sub

Private Sub UserControl_Terminate()
    If SubclassingCtrl Then Call UnSubClass
End Sub
```

This module has one private member variable, *SubClassingCtrl*. This variable acts as a flag that determines whether this instance of the control is the one that actually subclassed the form and, therefore, holds the original window procedure. This variable is set in the *UserControl_ReadProperties* event, which tries to subclass the form. If successful, this member variable is set to TRUE; otherwise, it is set to FALSE.

The *UserControl_Initialize* event is fired first when the control is sited. This event simply initializes the *SubclassingCtrl* member variable.

The *UserControl_ReadProperties* event is fired after the *UserControl_Initialize* event fires. This event calls the method in the *.bas* module to subclass the container form. It sends the *SubClass* function the hWnd of the parent—or container—window and a pointer to itself (the Me pointer).

The *UserControl_Terminate* event is fired before the control is destroyed. This function removes the subclass procedure from the form only if this instance is responsible for installing the subclass procedure. As a note, controls are always destroyed before their containing window; this means that the form will never be destroyed before the subclass procedure is removed.

The *HandleMessage* function handles the messages sent to the window on a per-control basis. This function simply sets the background color of the control depending on whether the left mouse button is pressed or released.

This code can now be compiled into an ActiveX control and placed on a form. The test form, shown in Figure 6-6, has three of these controls dropped onto it. Note that the test form and its project contain no code; the ActiveX control does all the work.

Running the application, we notice that when we click the left mouse button on the client area of the form, a single control changes colors according to the mouse clicks. The control that changes color is the control that initially subclassed the form.

Clicking the nonclient area of the form produces WM_NCLBUTTONDOWN and WM_NCLBUTTONUP messages, which we do not capture. Clicking any of the ActiveX controls will not force the one control to change background colors either. This is because the mouse-click message is not passed on from the container to the control.

If we placed these controls within another control—say, a PictureBox control—where the PictureBox control was a child to the form, the application would still work the same. That is, the one control would still change colors only when the client area of the form was clicked, not when the client area of the PictureBox was clicked.

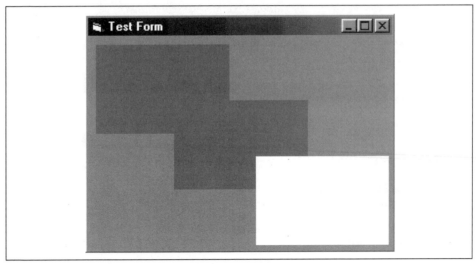

Figure 6-6. The test form for the ActiveX control

Creating the Second Version of the Control

The previous design for the control has one slight flaw—only one control on the form will intercept messages that are sent to the form. This means that even though the other controls exist on the form, they do nothing of any use. If you merely want to prevent problems when a developer inadvertently adds more than one control to a form, this design might be sufficient. If, instead, you want every subclassing control to receive messages, we must make some changes to the current control.

It is possible to allow the intercepted message to be passed into all forms simultaneously. This also introduces some problems that we must deal with. I will discuss these problems as I describe the required code changes to allow all controls to receive the form's messages.

Example 6-14 presents the modified code for the *Module1.bas* module.

Example 6-14. Modified Code for the Module1.bas Module

```
Private SubClassedForm_hWnd As Long          'hWnd of the VB Form
Private CtrlInstance_Ptr(5) As Long          'Array of Pointers
Private SubClassedForm_OrigWndProc As Long   'Original WndProc of VB Form

Private Next_CtrlInstance As Integer


Public Function SubClass(hForm As Long, pSubClassCtrl As UserControl1) As Boolean
    Dim Temp As Long
    Dim I As Integer

    SubClass = False
```

Example 6-14. Modified Code for the Module1.bas Module (continued)

```
    If Next_CtrlInstance > 5 Then
        MsgBox "No more controls can subclass the form"
    Else
        If SubClassedForm_hWnd = 0 Then
            Next_CtrlInstance = 0
            For I = 0 To 5
                CtrlInstance_Ptr(I) = 0
            Next I
            SubClassedForm_OrigWndProc = SetWindowLongPtr(hForm, GWL_WNDPROC, _
                        AddressOf VBFormWndProc)
        End If

        SubClassedForm_hWnd = hForm
        CtrlInstance_Ptr(Next_CtrlInstance) = ObjPtr(pSubClassCtrl)

        Next_CtrlInstance = Next_CtrlInstance + 1
        SubClass = True
    End If
End Function

Public Sub UnSubClass()
    Dim I As Integer

    If SubClassedForm_OrigWndProc <> 0 Then
        Call SetWindowLongPtr(SubClassedForm_hWnd, GWL_WNDPROC, _
                        SubClassedForm_OrigWndProc)
        SubClassedForm_OrigWndProc = 0
        For I = 0 To 5
            CtrlInstance_Ptr(I) = 0
        Next I
    End If
End Sub

Private Function VBFormWndProc(ByVal hWnd As Long, ByVal wMsg As Long, _
        ByVal wParam As Long, ByVal lParam As Long) As Long
    Dim oObject As UserControl1
    Dim I As Integer

    For I = 0 To 5
        If CtrlInstance_Ptr(I) > 0 Then
            Call CopyMemory(oObject, CtrlInstance_Ptr(I), 4)
            VBFormWndProc = oObject.HandleMessage(SubClassedForm_OrigWndProc, _
                        hWnd, wMsg, wParam, lParam)
            Call CopyMemory(oObject, 0&, 4)
        End If
    Next I
End Function
```

The major change to this module is that the *CtrlInstance_Ptr* member variable is now an array. Though this array is set to a size of five, the code could be changed to allow an unbounded number of controls to be placed on the form at any one time. I left this inflexibility in the code so that the code would stay lean and easier to read.

The *SubClass* function still uses only *SetWindowLongPtr* to subclass the form for the first instance of the control that is sited on the form. This function adds code to save a pointer to each instance of the control into the `CtrlInstance_Ptr` array.

The *UnSubClass* function calls *SetWindowLongPtr* to remove the subclass procedure for the control that installed the subclass procedure. Then, each element of the `CtrlInstance_Ptr` array is initialized back to zero.

The *VBFormWndProc* function is modified to iterate through the entire array of pointers to controls and call the *HandleMessage* function on each control.

No changes were made to the *UserControl1.ctl* module.

We now can place this control on a test form. Once again, we do not need to add any code to the form for the subclassing to work properly. Figure 6-7 shows a test form that hosts three controls.

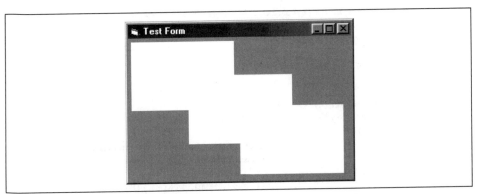

Figure 6-7. Screenshot of the test form hosting three of the new controls

When this application runs and the client area of the form is clicked, the background colors of each control now change color in unison. A small problem occurs, however, and we must remedy it: if the form is resized, moved, minimized, or maximized, the application goes haywire. The form and its controls will not paint properly, and the mouse cursor becomes stuck when the form is resized. These are just some of the problems. Rather than going on about *how* the application fails to work properly, I will show you *why* it fails to work properly.

Notice that the *VBFormWndProc* subclass procedure in Example 6-14 loops through all the controls that exist in the `CtrlInstance_Ptr` array and calls the *HandleMessage* function for each instance of the control. When the loop is done, it passes back the return value of the last call to *HandleMessage*. This value will almost always be zero unless only one control exists on the form. Remember that the *VBFormWndProc* function is the subclass procedure and the value that this function returns determines how the original window procedure handles this message. When a zero is returned, the original window procedure thinks the message was handled and no more processing should occur on that message. The operating system becomes confused about what it should do, if anything. This is why the form behaves oddly.

Creating the Third Version of the Control

To fix this problem, we can modify *VBFormWndProc*, as Example 6-15 shows. Essentially, this function now calls only the *HandleMessage* function for the instance of the control that subclassed the form; for all other instances of the control, it calls the *HandleOthers* method. This allows the return value of the control that actually subclassed the form to be retained. This value is then passed back by this function.

Example 6-15. The Third Version of the VBFormWndProc Procedure

```
Private Function VBFormWndProc(ByVal hWnd As Long, ByVal wMsg As Long, _
        ByVal wParam As Long, ByVal lParam As Long) As Long
    Dim oObject As UserControl1
    Dim I As Integer
    Dim RetVal As Long

    For I = 0 To 5
        If CtrlInstance_Ptr(I) <> 0 Then
            Call CopyMemory(oObject, CtrlInstance_Ptr(I), 4)
            If I = 0 Then
                RetVal = oObject.HandleMessage(SubClassedForm_OrigWndProc, _
                        hWnd, wMsg, wParam, lParam)
            Else
                Call oObject.HandleOthers(hWnd, wMsg, wParam, lParam)
            End If
            Call CopyMemory(oObject, 0&, 4)
        End If
    Next I

    'Otherwise this main subclass proc only returns zero!
    VBFormWndProc = RetVal
End Function
```

The *UserControl1.clt* module is modified, as Example 6-16 shows. Everything stays the same in this module except for the addition of the *HandleOthers* function. This function handles the messages passed to all the other controls that did not subclass the form. Notice that the only difference between the *HandleOthers* and *HandleMessage* functions is that the latter calls *CallWindowProc*. This allows the original window procedure to handle the message only once. If all controls called

the *HandleMessage* function, the message would be passed in to the original
window procedure once for every control instance. This is very bad and confuses
the window about what state it is in.

Example 6-16. The Third Version of the UserControl1.ctl Module

```
Private Const WM_LBUTTONDOWN = &H201
Private Const WM_LBUTTONUP = &H202

Private SubclassingCtrl As Boolean

Private Sub UserControl_Initialize()
    SubclassingCtrl = False
End Sub

Friend Function HandleOthers(ByVal hWnd As Long, ByVal wMsg As Long, _
        ByVal wParam As Long, ByVal lParam As Long) As Long
    Select Case wMsg
        Case WM_LBUTTONDOWN
            UserControl.BackColor = vbBlue
        Case WM_LBUTTONUP
            UserControl.BackColor = vbWhite
    End Select
End Function

Friend Function HandleMessage(ByVal OrigProc As Long, ByVal hWnd As Long, _
        ByVal wMsg As Long, ByVal wParam As Long, ByVal lParam As Long) As Long
    Select Case wMsg
        Case WM_LBUTTONDOWN
            UserControl.BackColor = vbBlue
        Case WM_LBUTTONUP
            UserControl.BackColor = vbWhite
    End Select

    HandleMessage = CallWindowProc(OrigProc, hWnd, wMsg, wParam, lParam)
End Function

Private Sub UserControl_ReadProperties(PropBag As PropertyBag)
    SubclassingCtrl = SubClass(UserControl.Parent.hWnd, Me)
End Sub

Private Sub UserControl_Terminate()
    If SubclassingCtrl Then Call UnSubClass
End Sub
```

As you can see, there are many different ways to use subclassing with ActiveX
controls. Which method you choose will depend on the application.

The real benefit of using subclassing with ActiveX controls is that you gain the
ability to drop a subclassing control onto a form, and nothing more needs to be
done. This encapsulation of the subclassing functionality is a wonderful thing.

7

Superclassing

This chapter is divided into two sections. The first section deals strictly with defining and comparing superclassing to subclassing. The second section takes a closer look at using only the Windows application programming interface (API) from within Visual Basic (VB) to create a window class and instantiate a window from that class. This material will not only discuss the use of several APIs required for superclassing within VB, but it will also give a better look into message loops and window creation. I will provide an example, written strictly in VB, to demonstrate superclassing from start to finish.

What Is Superclassing?

Superclassing, also known as class cloning, allows us to build upon an existing window class. See Figure 7-1 for an illustration of this technique. The existing class is called the *base class*. This can be any available class defined by the system or by an application. The base class information, obtained from its WNDCLASSEX structure, is copied into a second WNDCLASSEX structure. This second WNDCLASSEX structure is the beginning of our superclass. Before we have a usable superclass, we must do a couple of things to this new class structure. We must give it a new class name, a new instance handle, and a new window procedure. Also, we must register it with the system. After we do this we have a superclass that we can use to create new specialized windows for our applications.

The new window procedure we provide for the superclass defines the behavior of windows derived from this class. We can also modify members of the superclass's' WNDCLASSEX structure. For example, the *style* member can be modified to change the window's border, or the *hbrBackground* member can be changed to define the window's default background color. These modifications are left to the developer's discretion.

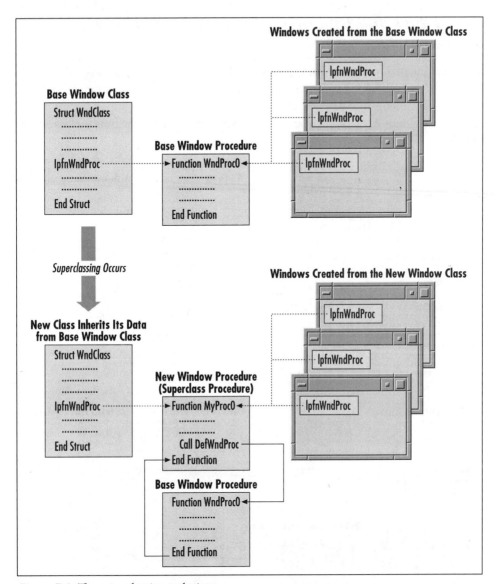

Figure 7-1. The superclassing technique

When the superclassing application terminates, it should remove all superclasses that it created from memory. It does this through a call to the *UnregisterClass* API function. When an application terminates, it automatically unregisters its classes, except for classes created by dynamic link libraries (DLLs) under Windows NT or Windows 2000. For this reason, you should always call *UnregisterClass*.

Similarities and Differences Between Subclassing and Superclassing

Superclassing has much in common with global subclassing; see Figure 7-1 and Figure 7-2 for this comparison. Each modifies a window class structure. Global subclassing modifies the original window class structure, while superclassing modifies a new window class created from the original, or base, window class structure.

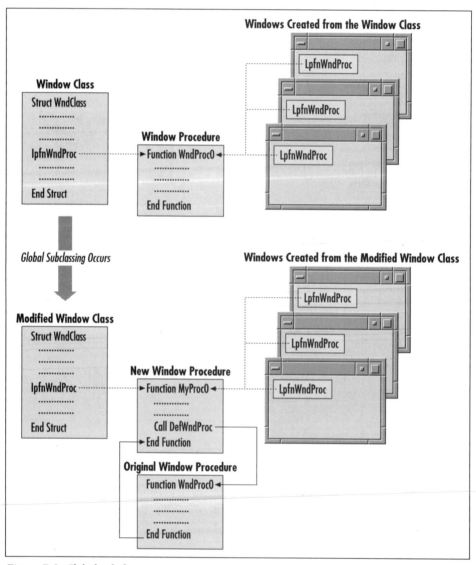

Figure 7-2. Global subclassing

Both the superclassing and global subclassing techniques modify the *lpfnWndProc* member function of the window class. Global subclassing modifies the *lpfnWndProc* member of the original window class. Superclassing modifies the *lpfnWndProc* member of the new superclass structure.

Because superclassing and global subclassing modify the window class, subsequent windows created from this modified class call the new window procedure, which we define. Therefore, we can use both techniques to modify the behavior of all windows belonging to a single window class. Instance subclassing allows only a single window instance to be modified.

Superclassing is very different from instance subclassing, as Figure 7-1 and Figure 7-3 show. Superclassing modifies the *lpfnWndProc* member of the class structure, while instance subclassing modifies the *lpfnWndProc* contained in the window itself. Remember, when the window is created, it receives a copy of the class structure information used to create it. In instance subclassing, the *lpfnWndProc* residing in the window is modified. Therefore, instance subclassing modifies the behavior of only a single window.

All types of subclassing require that the *lpfnWndClass* function pointer be restored to its original value. If this is not done, the subclassed window procedure will be destroyed while messages are still being sent to it through the *lpfnWndProc* function pointer. The *lpfnWndProc* becomes invalid at this point and causes your application to crash.

Superclassing, on the other hand, does not require the *lpfnWndProc* for any class or window be restored to its original state. Superclassing creates a new window class from the base class, but unlike global subclassing, it does not modify the base window class. Instead, superclassing modifies the new window class, and therefore, the *lpfnWndProc* of the base class is always valid. This means that there is no need to restore the member values of the base class when exiting the application. As for the superclass, any window the superclass creates will be destroyed before the superclass window procedure is destroyed. Therefore, the *lpfnWndProc* is valid as long as the window is in memory.

Superclassing allows the WM_CREATE and WM_NCCREATE window messages to be captured. Only global subclassing also gives you this ability. This works because the modified *lpfnWndProc* is inherited from the window class when a window is created. This forces all window creation messages to initially pass through our window procedure. We cannot capture window creation messages using instance subclassing because this technique does not operate on the window class. Instance subclassing is performed after a window has been created.

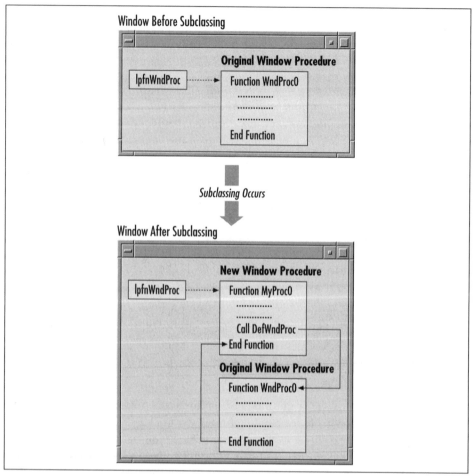

Figure 7-3. Instance subclassing

To recap, the following list compares superclassing with subclassing:

- Superclassing is similar to global subclassing in the following ways.
  - Both deal with a class structure.
  - Both modify the *lpfnWndProc* member of a window class structure.
  - Subsequent windows created from the modified class use the same developer-defined window procedure.
  - Both allow the capture of window creation messages.
- Superclassing is different from global subclassing in the following ways.
  - Superclassing creates a new window class and modifies it, while global subclassing modifies the original window class.

- — Applications incorporating superclassing "clean up" by calling *UnregisterClass* on all superclassed classes. Applications incorporating global subclassing "clean up" by calling *SetClassLongPtr* to restore the original window class to its initial state.

- — Superclassing requires that the *lpClassName* member of the window class structure be modified. You should not modify this member through global subclassing.

- Superclassing is completely different from instance subclassing in the following way.

  - — Superclassing modifies the behavior of all windows created from a single class. Instance subclassing modifies the behavior of a single window instance.

When to Use Superclassing

You should use superclassing instead of instance subclassing when you need to modify the behavior of all windows created from a single window class. Instance subclassing does not give us this ability. Although global subclassing also modifies the behavior of all windows created from a single class, there are subtle differences between superclassing and global subclassing.

The main advantage to using superclassing over global subclassing is that superclassing does not modify the base window class. Instead, it preserves the base window class information. This allows us to use both the base window class and the superclassed window class in our applications. This is not possible with global subclassing. Global subclassing directly modifies the window class structure so that all windows created after we have modified the *lpfnWndProc* member are necessarily subclassed.

How the Superclassing Example Works

To illustrate how you use superclassing, I will step through creating a relatively simple application which superclasses two existing window classes. I wrote the code completely in VB. However, I wrote it using Windows API functions. Visual C++ developers might recognize this code to be similar to the standard "hello world" application written in Visual C++.

The example will first superclass the `ThunderRt6FormDC` class that is used to create VB forms. The new class will be identified by the name `NewMainWindowClass`. It will have its own window procedure and will use the `IDC_UPARROW` mouse pointer as its default pointer. Normally, window classes use the `IDC_ARROW` for their mouse pointer. The `IDC_UPARROW` mouse pointer is simply an arrow pointer similar to the default mouse pointer, except that it points straight up instead of upward and to the left.

The caption for the first window created from the NewMainWindowClass super-class will be "Main Window", as Figure 7-4 shows. All subsequent windows created from this class will have the caption "New Window", as Figure 7-5 shows.

Figure 7-4. The main window

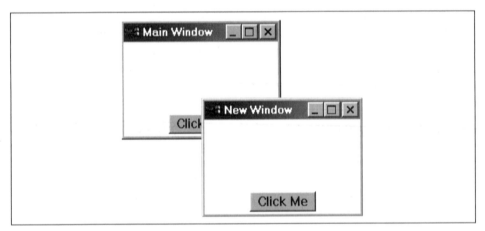

Figure 7-5. The new window

In addition to superclassing `ThunderRT6FormDC`, we'll also superclass the system-wide `BUTTON` window class. This is the class that creates the standard push button or command button control. We'll name the new `BUTTON` class `NewButtonClass` and define a new window procedure for it. This new window procedure will change the behavior of the `WM_LBUTTONUP` mouse button message. When the user clicks the left mouse button over this superclassed button, it will create a new window from the class `NewMainWindowClass` and then place a button created from the `NewButtonClass` class on the window.

When you start up the EXE for this example, it will initially create a superclassed `ThunderRT6FormDC` window containing a superclassed `BUTTON` control. When you click the button control, it will create a new form with a new button control.

The caption for this new window will be "New Window". The button on the newly created window also can create a new superclassed `ThunderRT6FormDC` window containing a superclassed `BUTTON` control.

The application terminates when you close the main window (the one with the "Main Window" caption). This closes all windows belonging to this application and shuts down the application.

The Code

It is not as easy to implement superclassing in VB as it is to implement sub-classing. VB does not allow the developer direct access to window classes or to the message loop. VB handles these things behind the scenes. This is why we need to incorporate several Windows API functions into our superclassing application. These Windows API functions give us the ability to create our own window classes, instantiate a window from that class, and create our own message loop.

The message loop that we create does not replace the message loop that VB provides. Instead, the message loop we create runs in parallel with the VB message loop. Both loops will be running in the same thread and will be grabbing messages from that thread's message queue. Remember, VB creates one thread for all its applications, and every thread creates a message queue and a message loop for itself. As such, both message loops, instead of only the thread's default message loop, will be running. It does not matter which loop receives a message because both loops will dispatch the message to the correct window for processing.

The project type for this application is a Standard EXE project and will contain a form (*Form1.frm*) that contains no controls and no code. Its only use is to provide the original class information that will be the foundation of our `NewMainWindowClass` class. This project also will contain a BAS module (*Module1.bas*) that contains all the code for this project.

The module-level declarations

The constants for the BAS module are defined as follows:

```
'Module Scope Const
Private Const SCButtonClassName = "NewBttnClass"
Private Const WindowClassName = "NewMainWndClass"
```

These two constants contain the class names of the superclassed button and form.

The variables for the BAS module are defined as follows:

```
'Module Scope Vars
Private m_hwndMain As Long
```

```
Private m_OrigBttnWinProc As Long
Private m_OrigWinProc As Long

Private m_CreatedWndHandles() As Long
```

m_hwndMain contains the handle to the first instance of the window created from
the `NewMainWndClass` class. *m_OrigBttnWinProc* contains the pointer to the
original window procedure of the `BUTTON` class. Likewise, *m_OrigWinProc* contains the pointer to the original window procedure of the `ThunderRT6FormDC`
class.

The *m_CreatedWndHandles* dynamic array will contain the hWnds of every new
superclassed window that is created when you click the superclassed button control. We use this array because we must terminate all the windows that we create
from the superclassed `ThunderRT6FormDC` class. If we do not, the *UnregisterClass*
function will not be able to remove the windows from memory before the application shuts down.

The Sub Main procedure

Because the project's startup object is set to Sub Main, the *Main* subroutine is the
first code executed in this example application. The code for the *Main* subroutine
appears in Example 7-1. The subroutine first loads a VB form, which we use to
retrieve the class information for the `ThunderRT6FormDC` class. Next, this subroutine calls the *RegisterFormClass* and *RegisterButtonClass* functions, which are
shown in Example 7-3 and Example 7-4, respectively. Both of these functions
create the superclassed classes from the `ThunderRT6FormDC` and `BUTTON` classes.
After we've superclassed both the VB form and the command button, the next
function, *CreateMainWindow*, which is shown in Example 7-5, calls
CreateWindowEx to create the initial window from the superclassed
`ThunderRT6FormDC` class. The *CreateSuperClsBttn* function, which is shown in
Example 7-6, calls *CreateWindowEx* to create the button control, which is placed
on the previously created window.

Example 7-1. The Main Subroutine
```
Public Sub Main()
    Dim structMsg As Msg
    Dim structAccel As Long     'Pointer to HACCEL structure

    'Initialization
    structAccel = 0                  'No accelerator tables in this project

    'Create window to steal class info from
    Load Form1

    'Register main window
    If RegisterFormClass = True Then
```

Example 7-1. The Main Subroutine (continued)

```
    'Register button superclass
    If RegisterButtonClass = True Then
        'Creation
        If CreateMainWindow = True Then          'Create main window
            If CreateSuperClsBttn = True Then    'Create button superclass
                'Message loop (Message pump)
                Do While GetMessage(structMsg, 0&, 0&, 0&)
                    If Not (TranslateAccelerator(structMsg.hwnd, structAccel, _
                        structMsg)) Then
                        Call TranslateMessage(structMsg)
                        Call DispatchMessage(structMsg)
                    End If
                Loop
            End If
        End If

        'Clean up
        Call UnregisterClass(SCButtonClassName, App.hInstance)
        Call UnregisterClass(WindowClassName, App.hInstance)
    End If
End If

    Unload Form1
End Sub
```

If each function returns successfully, the message loop is started. This loop runs until the WM_QUIT message is received. When the *GetMessage* function processes the WM_QUIT message, it automatically returns a FALSE value. This is the only message that produces a FALSE return value for the *GetMessage* function.

The code within this message loop first checks if this is an accelerator message. If so, *TranslateAccelerator* is the only function that processes the message. If the message is not an accelerator, the *TranslateMessage* and the *DispatchMessage* functions process the message and pass it on to the appropriate window procedure.

After the message loop receives the WM_QUIT message, the *GetMessage* function returns FALSE and the message loop is exited. Now that the application is terminating, the superclassed ThunderRT6FormDC and BUTTON classes must be destroyed to properly clean up the application. The *UnregisterClass* function destroys these classes. It is defined in VB as follows:

```
Public Declare Function UnregisterClass Lib "user32" Alias "UnregisterClassA" _
    (ByVal lpClassName As String, ByVal hInstance As Long) As Long
```

This function removes the class that the *RegisterClassEx* API function created from memory. It takes only two arguments; the first is the name of the class (*lpClassName*), and the second is the module handle for the class (*hInstance*). The value for the module handle argument, *hInstance*, is equivalent to the *hInstance* member of the WNDCLASSEX structure.

Lastly, the Form1 form is unloaded from memory. Because this is the last form left in the application, the application ends.

Note that VB considers this application to consist of only a single form, Form1. This is because, by using *CreateWindowEx* to create a window, we are circumventing VB's form creation methods. In doing so, VB will not keep a reference count of our windows created with *CreateWindowEx*.

Message loop operation

I added a message loop to this application to give you a better idea of how the loop works and where it fits into an application. We do not actually have to write this piece of code because VB creates its own message loop for each application. You can determine this by removing (or commenting out) the code that makes up the loop, as Example 7-2 shows, and running the application. As a note, you also will have to remove the line containing the code `Unload Form1` in this function. The application functions the same regardless of whether this loop is included in the code.

Example 7-2. The Main Subroutine

```
Public Sub Main()
    Dim structMsg As Msg
    Dim structAccel As Long      'Pointer to HACCEL structure

    'Initialization
    structAccel = 0                   'No accelerator tables in this project

    'Create window to steal class info from
    Load Form1

    'Register main window
    If RegisterFormClass = True Then
        'Register button superclass
        If RegisterButtonClass = True Then
            'Creation
            If CreateMainWindow = True Then          'Create main window
                If CreateSuperClsBttn = True Then    'Create button superclass
                End If
            End If
        End If
    End If
End Sub
```

If, however, we do add this message loop to the application, both message loops will be working in parallel to pull messages off the message queue, process them, and dispatch them to the correct window. Synchronization is not a problem because both message loops are running in the same thread. A thread executes code one line at a time. Therefore, only one message loop can be removing messages from the queue and dispatching them at any one time.

You write a complete message loop in VB code like this:

```
Do While GetMessage(structMsg, 0&, 0&, 0&)
    If Not (TranslateAccelerator(structMsg.hwnd, structAccel, structMsg)) Then
        If Not (IsDialogMessage(m_hwndModalDlg, structMsg)) Then
            Call TranslateMessage(structMsg)
            Call DispatchMessage(structMsg)
        End If
    End If
Loop
```

Many times, message loops in an application are written without calling the *IsDialogMessage* and *TranslateAccelerator* functions. In the case of our sample application, these functions are provided in the message loop for completeness. The *IsDialogMessage* function is used to process keystrokes for all nonmodal dialog boxes. Windows does not automatically do this processing for nonmodal dialogs. The *TranslateAccelerator* function allows menu accelerator keystrokes to be processed. If an accelerator table resource is loaded, this function will process these keystrokes as well. Applications that do not use any accelerator keystrokes and do not have any nonmodal dialog boxes (such as our sample application) do not need to call either of these two functions.

Class creation

The **WNDCLASSEX** structure makes up every window class. All the basic information needed to create any type of window, including windows, dialog boxes, controls, etc., is contained within this structure.

To create a superclass from a base window class, we first need to call the *GetClassInfoEx* function to extract the information from the base window class structure. We then can use the information from this function to create the superclass. *GetClassInfoEx* is defined as follows:

```
Public Declare Function GetClassInfoEx Lib "user32" Alias "GetClassInfoExA" _
        (ByVal hInstance As Long, ByVal lpClassName As String, _
        lpWndClass As WNDCLASSEX) As Long
```

Its parameters are:

hInstance
Handle to the application instance that created the class. This argument is **NULL** if the system created the class (system-wide class).

lpClassName
The name or class atom of a registered class.

lpWndClass
Pointer to a **WNDCLASSEX** structure, which is passed back to the calling function.

This function returns a nonzero value if it successfully returns a window class structure. It returns a zero if the function fails.

The WNDCLASSEX structure contains several items of particular interest, specifically the instance handle (*hInstance*), the menu name (*lpMenuName*), and the class name (*lpClassName*) members from the base window class structure. These members must be modified to create the superclass.

The *hInstance* member requires the instance handle of the application (*App. hInstance*) which creates and registers this new class. The *lpszMenuName* member contains the name of the default menu resource that is provided for every window created from this base class, or else it contains NULL to signify that no menu exists. This menu resource must be contained within the application creating the new class. Because a menu resource for a system-wide base class might not be available to the application, we must assign a new resource name to the *lpszMenuName* member. Finally, the *lpszClassName* member must contain a unique name identifying the new class. This name needs to be unique only within the application that created and registered it. Using the returned base class name will cause registration of this new class to fail because of a duplicate class name.

As we've mentioned, the first class that the application superclasses is ThunderRT6FormDC, the VB form. The *RegisterFormClass* function shown in Example 7-3 performs this task.

Example 7-3. The RegisterFormClass Function

```
Private Function RegisterFormClass() As Boolean
    Dim structOrigWinClass As WNDCLASSEX
    Dim structWinClass As WNDCLASSEX
    Dim lretval As Long
    Dim sClassName As String * 100
    Dim lRetLength As Long
    Dim myhInst As Long

    lRetLength = GetClassName(Form1.hwnd, sClassName, 100)
    myhInst = GetClassLong(Form1.hwnd, GCL_HMODULE)
    lretval = GetClassInfoEx(myhInst, Left$(sClassName, lRetLength), _
                        structOrigWinClass)
    If lretval = 0 Then
        MsgBox "Error in getting original form class information: " & Err.LastDllError
        RegisterFormClass = False
    Else
        'Get a copy of its elements
        CopyMemory structWinClass, structOrigWinClass, LenB(structOrigWinClass)

        'Get original form window procedure and save it
        m_OrigWinProc = structWinClass.lpfnWndProc

        'Place the original element values into the new superclassed form class
        With structWinClass
```

Example 7-3. The RegisterFormClass Function (continued)

```
            .cbSize = LenB(structWinClass)
            .lpszClassName = WindowClassName
            'Window procedure address
            .lpfnWndProc = GetProcAddr(AddressOf MainWndProc)
            .hInstance = App.hInstance
            .hCursor = LoadCursor(0, IDC_UPARROW)
        End With

        'Register this class
        If RegisterClassEx(structWinClass) <> 0 Then
            RegisterFormClass = True
        Else
            RegisterFormClass = False
        End If
    End If
End Function
```

In most cases, *GetClassInfoEx* can be called with a literal representing the class name in the second argument of the function, as in the following code fragment:

```
lretval = GetClassInfoEx(App.hInstance, "BUTTON", structOrigBttnClass)
```

For VB classes, this is not possible because the class name of a VB form is **Thunder*** when running in the IDE and **ThunderRT6*** when running as an executable. Consequently, we must first retrieve VB class names using the *GetClassName* API function:

```
lRetLength = GetClassName(Form1.hwnd, sClassName, 100)
```

Here is where the Form1 form comes into play. Using the handle of this form, we are able to retrieve its class name, which is placed in the *sClassName* string variable.

Next, we must retrieve the instance handle of the module that created the class. The *GetClassLong* API function allows us to get this information. Once again, the handle to Form1 is employed:

```
myhInst = GetClassLong(Form1.hwnd, GCL_HMODULE)
```

Instead of calling *GetClassLong*, you would expect that you could simply retrieve the instance handle from the App object's **hInstance** property and pass it to *GetClassInfoEx*. But the instance handle of the module that created the class is different from **App.hInstance** when an application is running as an executable. They are the same when running in the IDE. Using the Dependency Walker application that ships with Visual C++, we can see that the EXE module for the example application has an **hInstance** of &H00400000, and that *MSVBVM60.DLL* has an **hInstance** of &H66000000. The base class's **hInstance** member signifies which module created this class. In this case, the *MSVBVM60.DLL* module created it. This is also the module where its class window procedure resides. *MSVBVM60.*

DLL is the VB virtual machine. This file must exist on the machine if it is to run a
VB 6.0 application. Some of the items contained within this DLL are the controls
intrinsic to VB, the code that creates the **Thunder*** classes, and many other functions used by a VB application.

If **App.hInstance** had been used in the *hInstance* argument to *GetClassInfoEx*,
the function would have returned an error. This is because the function would
have looked in the wrong module for the class definition. It would have looked in
the EXE module instead of the *MSVBVM60.DLL* module.

Using *GetClassInfoEx*, we can obtain the class information. The instance handle
myhInst is used as the first argument, and *sClassName* is used as the second
argument:

```
lretval = GetClassInfoEx(myhInst, Left$(sClassName, lRetLength),
structOrigWinClass)
```

This function returns the **ThunderRT6FormDC** class information in the
structOrigWinClass variable, which is a pointer to the **WNDCLASSEX** structure.
CopyMemory is used to copy into the *structWinClass* variable the structure that
this pointer points to. This is our superclass.

Now that we have the **WNDCLASSEX** structure for the class, we need to make some
modifications to it:

```
With structWinClass
    .cbSize = LenB(structWinClass)
    .lpszClassName = "NewMainWndClass"
    .lpfnWndProc = GetProcAddr(AddressOf MainWndProc) 'Window procedure address
    .hInstance = App.hInstance
    .hCursor = LoadCursor(0, IDC_UPARROW)
End With
```

First the size is recalculated and placed in the *cbSize* member. A unique name
must be placed in the *lpszClassName* member for this class to register with the
system properly. This new class is named **NewMainWndClass**. The foremost reason
to use superclassing is to substitute our superclass procedure for that of the default
window procedure. We accomplish this by placing the function pointer to our
superclass procedure, *MainWndProc* (which is shown in Example 7-7), in the
lpfnWndProc member. We do this through the *GetProcAddr* function, which is
defined as follows:

```
Function GetProcAddress(lFunctionAddress as long)
    GetProcAddress = lFunctionAddress
End Function
```

The *hInstance* is changed to our application's instance handle using **App.**
hInstance. **App.hInstance** holds the instance handle to the .EXE module of
our application (&H00400000). The class uses this instance handle to determine in

which module to look for the superclass procedure. Therefore, it must be the application's instance handle because that is where the superclass procedure is located.

The last item modified is the *hCursor* member. We do not have to modify this member. For this example, I wanted every window created from this class to use the up-arrow mouse pointer as its default. We also can modify other members of the class structure, such as the style member, to change the look or feel of the window.

Two members that we must handle carefully are *cbClsExtra* and *cbWndExtra*. These two members contain extra information (in byte format) for the class and any window created from that class, respectively. We can add extra bytes to these two members, but we cannot take them away. Removing this information from the class structure might cause unpredictable behavior, depending on the original use of the extra window or class bytes.

Lastly, we register the new class with the system by using the *RegisterClassEx* function. This function is defined as follows:

```
Public Declare Function RegisterClassEx Lib "user32" Alias "RegisterClassExA" _
    (pcWndClassEx As WNDCLASSEX) As Integer
```

When we call *RegisterClassEx*, we place the new class structure in the *pcWndClassEx* argument of the *RegisterClassEx* function:

```
If RegisterClassEx(structWinClass) <> 0 Then
```

If this call is successful, the new class is registered with the system, and a unique integer identifying the new class, called a *class atom*, is returned. The registered class is now ready to be used to create new windows.

Next, we need to superclass the BUTTON class. We do this in the *RegisterButtonClass* function shown in Example 7-4. Retrieving the BUTTON class structure is more straightforward than retrieving the ThunderRT6FormDC class. This is because BUTTON is a system-wide class. The system registers this class for use by all applications, and because of this, the BUTTON class has an *hInstance* of NULL. When calling the *GetClassInfoEx* function, the first argument, *hInstance*, can be NULL or zero to signify that this is a system-wide class.

Example 7-4. The RegisterButtonClass Function

```
Private Function RegisterButtonClass() As Boolean
    Dim structOrigBttnClass As WNDCLASSEX
    Dim structBttnSuperClass As WNDCLASSEX
    Dim lretval As Long

    'Get original Window's button class
    lretval = GetClassInfoEx(0, "BUTTON", structOrigBttnClass)
```

Example 7-4. The RegisterButtonClass Function (continued)

```
    If lretval = 0 Then
        MsgBox "Error in getting original button class information"
        RegisterButtonClass = False
    Else
        'Get a copy of its elements
        CopyMemory structBttnSuperClass, structOrigBttnClass, _
                    LenB(structOrigBttnClass)

        'Get original button window procedure and save it
        m_OrigBttnWinProc = structBttnSuperClass.lpfnWndProc

        'Place the original element values into the new superclassed button class
        With structBttnSuperClass
            .cbSize = LenB(structBttnSuperClass)
            .lpszClassName = "NewBttnClass"
            .hInstance = App.hInstance
            .lpfnWndProc = GetProcAddr(AddressOf ButtonWndProc)
        End With

        'Register the class
        If RegisterClassEx(structBttnSuperClass) <> 0 Then
            RegisterButtonClass = True
        Else
            RegisterButtonClass = False
        End If
    End If
End Function
```

We use *CopyMemory* to convert the **structOrigBttnClass** pointer to a structure. The original class structure is stored in the **structBttnSuperClass** variable. Once again, the **lpfnWndProc** pointer of the original class structure is saved in the **m_OrigBttnWinProc** variable:

```
    m_OrigBttnWinProc = structBttnSuperClass.lpfnWndProc
```

The **cbSize**, **lpszClassName**, **hInstance**, and **lpfnWndProc** members also are modified as follows:

```
    With structBttnSuperClass
        .cbSize = LenB(structBttnSuperClass)
        .lpszClassName = "NewBttnClass"
        .hInstance = App.hInstance
        .lpfnWndProc = GetProcAddr(AddressOf ButtonWndProc)
    End With
```

The name for this new class is **NewBttnClass**. The other members are modified similar to the **ThunderRT6FormDC** superclass. Lastly, the class is registered.

Window creation

Now that we have our registered classes, from the code presented in the previous section we can create windows from them. The code in the *CreateMainWindow* function shown in Example 7-5 calls the *CreateWindowEx* function to create a window from the `NewMainWndClass` superclass.

Example 7-5. The CreateMainWindow Function

```
Private Function CreateMainWindow() As Boolean
    'Create main window
    m_hwndMain = CreateWindowEx(0, "NewMainWndClass", "Main Window", _
            WS_OVERLAPPEDWINDOW, CW_USEDEFAULT, CW_USEDEFAULT, _
            208, 150, 0, 0, App.hInstance, ByVal 0)

    If m_hwndMain > 0 Then
        'Show main window
        Call ShowWindow(m_hwndMain, SW_SHOWNORMAL)
        CreateMainWindow = True
    Else
        MsgBox "Main window could not be created"
        CreateMainWindow = False
    End If
End Function
```

The actual window creation in Example 7-5 is performed by the *CreateWindowEx* function. The declaration for *CreateWindowEx* is as follows:

```
Public Declare Function CreateWindowEx Lib "user32" Alias "CreateWindowExA" _
        (ByVal dwExStyle As Long, ByVal lpClassName As String, _
        ByVal lpWindowName As String, ByVal dwStyle As Long, _
        ByVal x As Long, ByVal y As Long, ByVal nWidth As Long, _
        ByVal nHeight As Long, ByVal hWndParent As Long, _
        ByVal hMenu As Long, ByVal hInstance As Long, lpParam As Any) As Long
```

The function has the following parameters:

dwExStyle

One or more of the following extended styles of the window ORed together:

`WS_EX_APPWINDOW`

A top-level window is placed on the taskbar when the window is visible

`WS_EX_CLIENTEDGE`

Specifies a window with a border and a sunken edge

`WS_EX_DLGMODALFRAME`

Specifies a window with a double border

`WS_EX_NOACTIVATE`

Used in Windows 2000 to specify a window that a user cannot cause to become the foreground window

`WS_EX_NOPARENTNOTIFY`

Specifies a child window that does not send the `WM_PARENTNOTIFY` message to its parent window

WS_EX_OVERLAPPEDWINDOW

    Equivalent to (WS_EX_CLIENTEDGE OR WS_EX_WINDOWEDGE)

WS_EX_STATICEDGE

    Specifies a window that has a three-dimensional border but does not take user input

WS_EX_TOPMOST

    Specifies a window that should always be placed on top of other windows that are set to be top-most windows

WS_EX_WINDOWEDGE

    Specifies a window with a border and a raised edge

lpClassName

    A string containing the name of the class from which this window inherits

lpWindowName

    A string displayed in the title bar of the window

dwStyle

    One or more of the following window styles or control styles ORed together:

WS_BORDER

    Specifies a window with a thin-line border.

WS_CAPTION

    Specifies a window with a title bar.

WS_CLIPCHILDREN

    Specifies a window that does not paint the area that contains a child window.

WS_CLIPSIBLINGS

    Specifies a window that does not paint all overlapping child windows outside the region of the child windows' client area

WS_DLGFRAME

    Specifies a window with a dialog box border and no caption.

WS_MINIMIZE

    The window is created in a minimized state.

WS_MINIMIZEBOX

    Specifies a window with a minimize button in the title bar.

WS_MAXIMIZE

    The window is created in a maximized state.

WS_MAXIMIZEBOX

    Specifies a window with a maximize button in the title bar.

WS_OVERLAPPED
>   Specifies a window with a title bar and a border.

WS_OVERLAPPEDWINDOW
>   Equivalent to (WS_OVERLAPPED OR WS_CAPTION OR WS_SYSMENU OR
>   WS_THICKFRAME OR WS_MINIMIZEBOX OR WS_MAXIMIZEBOX)

WS_POPUP
>   Specifies a pop-up window.

WS_POPUPWINDOW
>   Specifies a pop-up window with the styles (WS_BORDER OR WS_POPUP OR
>   WS_SYSMENU OR WS_CAPTION)

WS_SYSMENU
>   Specifies a window containing a window menu on its title bar.

WS_THICKFRAME
>   Specifies a window with a sizing border.

WS_TILED
>   Same as WS_OVERLAPPED.

WS_TILEDWINDOW
>   Same as WS_OVERLAPPEDWINDOW.

WS_VISIBLE
>   Specifies a window that is initially visible.

x
>   The position of the window with respect to the left side of the screen

y
>   The position of the window with respect to the top of the screen

nWidth
>   The width of the window

nHeight
>   The height of the window

hWndParent
>   Handle to the parent or owner window to this window

hMenu
>   Handle to the menu that is used by this window

hInstance
>   Handle of the module instance to be associated with this window

lpParam
>   Pointer to a value that can be passed in to the window through the
>   CREATESTRUCT structure

If this function succeeds in creating the window, a handle to that window is returned; otherwise, a zero is returned.

In the call to *CreateWindowEx* in Example 7-5, we define the new window's caption to be "Main Window", as Figure 7-4 shows.

The `lpClassName` argument receives the same value placed in the `lpszClassName` member of the `WNDCLASSEX` structure. The `hInstance` argument is ignored in Windows NT and Windows 2000. If you are using Windows 9x, you need to supply the instance handle of the module that is creating this window. For our example, we can use `App.hInstance` for this argument.

The constant `CW_USEDEFAULT` indicates that the system should set the default x and y coordinates of the new window. We also can use this constant in the `nHeight` and `nWidth` arguments to allow the system to set the default height and width of the new window.

A zero is provided for the `hWndParent` argument. This informs the new window that it has no parent or owning windows.

The *ShowWindow* function is called to display the window after it is successfully created because *CreateWindowEx* does not do this automatically. The declaration for *ShowWindow* is as follows:

```
Public Declare Function ShowWindow Lib "user32" _
        (ByVal hwnd As Long, ByVal nCmdShow As Long) As Long
```

ShowWindow has the following parameters:

hwnd
> The window handle.

nCmdShow
> Specifies how the window is displayed. It can be one of the following constants:

> SW_FORCEMINIMIZE
> > Displays a minimized window even if the thread that owns the window is hung.

> SW_HIDE
> > Hides the window and activates another window.

> SW_MAXIMIZE
> > Displays a maximized window.

> SW_MINIMIZE
> > Displays a minimized window.

> SW_RESTORE
> > Displays a window in its restored state.

SW_SHOW
> Activates a window.

SW_SHOWMAXIMIZED
> Activates and maximizes the window.

SW_SHOWMINIMIZED
> Activates and minimizes the window.

SW_SHOWMINNOACTIVE
> Displays a minimized window but does not activate it.

SW_SHOWNA
> Displays a window but does not activate it.

SW_SHOWNORMAL
> Activates and displays a window. If the window is minimized or maximized, it is first restored.

SW_SHOWNOACTIVATE
> Same as SW_SHOWNORMAL, but the window is not activated.

The return value of this function is zero if the window was previously hidden. If the window was previously visible, the return value is nonzero.

We create the button control created from the **NewBttnClass** superclass in a similar way. The *CreateSuperClsBttn* function shown in Example 7-6 creates this control. The button control has a caption of "Click Me" and is contained within the window created from the **NewMainWndClass** superclass, as Figure 7-4 shows. The window style WS_CHILD means that this control will be a child of the parent window whose hWnd is set in the *hWndParent* argument of the *CreateWindowEx* function. The *hWndParent* argument contains the handle to the main window, which we created previously. The **BS_PUSHBUTTON** style creates a push button instead of another button type, such as the checkbox style button. This button control also will have the same **hInstance** as the application.

Example 7-6. The CreateSuperClsBttn Function

```
Private Function CreateSuperClsBttn() As Boolean
    'Create superclassed button
    m_hwndSCBttn = CreateWindowEx(0, "NewBttnClass", "Click Me", _
            WS_CHILD Or WS_VISIBLE Or BS_PUSHBUTTON, _
            58, 90, 85, 25, m_hwndMain, 0, App.hInstance, 0)

    'Show the button
    If m_hwndSCBttn > 0 Then
        Call ShowWindow(m_hwndSCBttn, SW_SHOWNORMAL)
        CreateSuperClsBttn = True
    Else
        MsgBox "Superclassed button could not be created"
        CreateSuperClsBttn = False
```

Example 7-6. The CreateSuperClsBttn Function (continued)

```
    End If
End Function
```

After this control is successfully created, it is displayed on its parent window
through the call to *ShowWindow.*

The superclass procedures

Finally, we need to create the window procedures that are associated with our
superclasses. Such a window procedure is normally referred to as the *superclass
procedure.* The first superclass procedure is for the `NewMainWndClass` superclass
and is shown in Example 7-7.

Example 7-7. The MainWndProc Window Procedure

```
Public Function MainWndProc(ByVal hwnd As Long, ByVal uMsg As Long, _
        ByVal wParam As Long, ByVal lParam As Long) As Long
    Dim Count As Long

    Select Case uMsg
        Case WM_LBUTTONDOWN
            MsgBox "Window: " & hwnd & " was clicked."
        Case WM_DESTROY:
            'If we are destroying the main window
            '  then we will want to end the application
            If hwnd = m_hwndMain Then
                For Count = 0 To UBound(m_CreatedWndHandles) - 1
                    DestroyWindow (m_CreatedWndHandles(Count))
                Next

                'Exit the message loop and Stop the application
                Call PostQuitMessage(0&)
            End If
            Exit Function
    End Select

    'Let the main window behave as a normal window
    MainWndProc = DefWindowProc(hwnd, uMsg, wParam, lParam)
End Function
```

This function traps two messages. It changes the `WM_LBUTTONDOWN` message
behavior to display a message box containing the handle of the window that was
clicked. The `WM_DESTROY` message behavior is modified as well. This message
modification is very important to this application for it to shut down properly. If a
window other than the main window (which has the "Main Window" caption) is
being closed, the default window procedure simply closes only that window. If,
however, the main window is being closed, this message will first destroy all windows created from the `NewMainWndClass` superclass. We accomplish this by iterating through the *m_CreatedWndHandles* array of stored window handles and

calling the *DestroyWindow* function for all these windows. The *DestroyWindow* function sends the WM_DESTROY and WM_NCDESTROY messages to the respective windows to destroy them. After they are destroyed, the message queue is flushed of all messages pertaining to that window:

```
For Count = 0 To UBound(m_CreatedWndHandles) - 1
    DestroyWindow (m_CreatedWndHandles(Count))
Next
```

The *PostQuitMessage* function is then called to jump out of the message loop and close down the application.

It is necessary to destroy these windows in this manner to allow our application to shut down cleanly. If we did not destroy these windows, *UnregisterClass* would fail to destroy the NewMainWndClass and NewBttnClass superclasses. Most likely, the classes will be destroyed after the application finishes shutting down. But if a DLL were to register these classes on a Windows NT or a Windows 2000 system, the classes would not be unregistered and the memory used to store the class information would not be reclaimed. This causes a memory leak. To be safe, all classes registered by the application should be unregistered by that application before terminating.

Finally, this superclass procedure passes all messages except for WM_DESTROY to the default window procedure.

As you can see, there is no difference in the structure and operation of a super-class procedure compared to the window procedures we are used to working with.

Example 7-8 shows the superclass procedure for the NewBttnClass superclass. This superclass procedure traps the WM_LBUTTONUP message for the superclassed button control. When this message is received, a new window is created from the NewMainWndClass superclass, and a button control created from the NewBttnClass superclass is placed on this window, as Figure 7-5 shows. The *ShowWindow* function is called to display both windows. For all windows created in this manner, an entry is added to the *m_CreatedWindows* array. This allows us to cleanly destroy all windows created in this manner when the main window is closed.

Example 7-8. The ButtonWndProc Window Procedure

```
Public Function ButtonWndProc(ByVal hwnd As Long, ByVal uMsg As Long, _
        ByVal wParam As Long, ByVal lParam As Long) As Long
        Dim tempHwnd As Long
        Dim tempButtonHwnd As Long

    Select Case uMsg&
        Case WM_LBUTTONUP:
```

Example 7-8. The ButtonWndProc Window Procedure (continued)

```
            'Create a new window with the superclassed button on it
            tempHwnd = CreateWindowEx(0, "NewMainWndClass", "New Window", _
            WS_OVERLAPPEDWINDOW, CW_USEDEFAULT, CW_USEDEFAULT, 208, 150, _
            0, 0, CLng(App.hInstance), ByVal 0)

            tempButtonHwnd = CreateWindowEx(0, "NewBttnClass", "Click Me", _
            WS_CHILD Or WS_VISIBLE Or BS_PUSHBUTTON, _
            58, 90, 85, 25, tempHwnd, 0, CLng(App.hInstance), 0)

            'Show all new windows
            Call ShowWindow(tempHwnd, SW_SHOWNORMAL)
            Call ShowWindow(tempButtonHwnd, SW_SHOWNORMAL)

            'Add this window's hwnd to the list of created windows
            m_CreatedWndHandles(UBound(m_CreatedWndHandles)) = tempHwnd
            ReDim Preserve m_CreatedWndHandles(UBound(m_CreatedWndHandles) + 1)
    End Select

    'Pass messages on to original button window procedure
    ButtonWndProc = CallWindowProc(m_OrigBttnWinProc, hwnd, uMsg, wParam, lParam)
End Function
```

All messages are passed on to the original window procedure. It is interesting to note that we can use *CallWindowProc* to pass to the button class's original window procedure all the messages for the superclassed button control. We cannot do this with windows created from the superclassed ThunderRT6FormDC class. If we try using the *CallWindowProc* instead of the *DefWindowProc* function, a General Protection Fault (GPF) is generated inside the *MSVBVM60.DLL* module. The reason for this can be found in the way the classes are registered. The BUTTON class is registered as a global class. Its scope includes all modules in all running applications. This is not so with the ThunderRT6FormDC class; it is registered as an application local class. This is how you can determine the scope of class:

- If the *hInstance* member of the class structure is zero, the class is a system-wide class.

- If the CS_GLOBALCLASS style is included in the *style* member of the class structure, the class is an application global class.

- If the CS_GLOBALCLASS style is not included in the *style* member of the class structure, the class is an application-local class.

An application-local class is one that is created by a module only to be used by that module. The ThunderRT6FormDC class is designed to work only within the *MSVBVM60.DLL* module. Our superclass, which is created from the ThunderRT6FormDC base class, works fine until the original window procedure is called. The original window procedure is located in the *MSVBVM60.DLL* module, and the superclass procedure is located in the EXE module. The problem occurs when we try to call the original window procedure from within the EXE module, which has a different instance handle. The application will not allow this and subsequently throws a GPF.

To see this from a different angle, start Spy++ and compare the Instance Handle fields for all controls created directly from the `Thunder*` classes. They are all the same. The windows created from the `NewMainWindowClass` superclass all have the instance handle of the EXE module.

We can superclass the `BUTTON` class because it is a system-wide class. This class is available for use in all modules. This class also allows code within any module to call back to the window procedure of the original `BUTTON` class.

Peering into the Superclassing Application with Spy++

When using Spy++ to analyze this superclassing example application, we see several interesting things. Examining the window and window class information for each window of the application, we notice that all the information from the original class is copied over to the superclass. For example, the `ThunderRT6FormDC` base class information contains this data:

```
Class WndProc       6601FFCB
hInstance           66000000
Style               CS_DBLCLKS or CS_OWNDC
Class Extra Bytes   0
Wnd Extra Bytes     2
Menu                (none)
Icon Handle         (none)
Cursor Handle       IDC_ARROW
Bkgnd Brush         COLOR_WINDOW
```

Using *GetClassInfoEx* and *RegisterClassEx*, we made a copy of the `ThunderRT6FormDC` base class and registered it as the `NewMainWndClass` superclass. The `NewMainWndClass` superclass information contains this data:

```
Class WndProc       004032CE
hInstance           00400000
Style               CS_DBLCLKS or CS_OWNDC
Class Extra Bytes   0
Wnd Extra Bytes     2
Menu                (none)
Icon Handle         (none)
Cursor Handle       IDC_UPARROW
Bkgnd Brush         COLOR_WINDOW
```

The class name (*lpszClassName*), the class window procedure (*lpfnWndProc*), the instance handle (*hInstance*), and the Cursor Handle (*hCursor*) were the only class structure members modified. The above information reflects these changes. All other class information is copied into the `NewMainWndClass` superclass verbatim.

We superclass the `BUTTON` base class in a similar way, except *hCursor* is not modified. The global `BUTTON` base class contains this data:

```
Class WndProc        77E8BB63
hInstance            NULL
Style                CS_PARENTDC or CS_DBLCLKS or CS_HREDRAW or CS_VREDRAW
Class Extra Bytes    0
Wnd Extra Bytes      4
Menu                 (none)
Icon Handle          (none)
Cursor Handle        IDC_ARROW
Bkgnd Brush          (none)
```

Comparatively, the `NewBttnClass` superclass contains this data:

```
Class WndProc        00403C95
hInstance            00400000
Style                CS_PARENTDC or CS_DBLCLKS or CS_HREDRAW or CS_VREDRAW
Class Extra Bytes    0
Wnd Extra Bytes      4
Menu                 (none)
Icon Handle          (none)
Cursor Handle        IDC_ARROW
Bkgnd Brush          (none)
```

As a note, all superclassed windows have the same window procedure address. Every window created from the `NewMainWndClass` superclass inherits the window procedure address from the class it was created from. Therefore, all windows of this type will call the same superclass procedure (unless they themselves are subclassed). It is possible that one of these windows will need to process a message differently from the rest of the windows. To do this, simply check the hWnd passed into the superclass procedure for the window in question.

The example application for this chapter has an illustration of this problem. The application is shut down only when the main window is closed. The hWnd value is checked in the superclass procedure any time a window is closed. If the window handle matches the main window's handle, the application is shut down. Otherwise, only the window being closed is destroyed.

All superclassed button controls will call the same superclass procedure. This is similar to how the superclassed windows operate.

Using Spy++ to examine the windows as they are running in the VB IDE, as opposed to a compiled executable, we notice something of interest. First, the instance handles to all windows and window classes are the same when running in the IDE. While running in a compiled executable, all `Thunder*` classes have the instance handle of the *MSVBVM60.DLL* module, while all classes registered in the EXE module have the instance handle of the EXE.

This poses a problem when trying to run an application which superclasses **Thunder*** classes in the IDE and as a compiled executable. In the IDE, there is no problem using the **Thunder*** class name directly in the *GetClassInfoEx* function call. Remember to leave off the RT6 from the class name while running in the IDE. The following code will work while running within the IDE but not from a compiled executable:

```
lRetVal = GetClassInfoEx(App.hInstance, "ThunderFormDC", _
          structOrigWinClass)
```

The function cannot find the **ThunderFormDC** class from within the EXE module of a compiled application because the class does not exist in that module (the **App.hInstance** property contains the EXE module instance handle, not the *MSVBVM60.DLL* module instance handle).

To make our applications flexible enough to work both in the IDE and as a compiled EXE, we should use the following code:

```
lRetLength = GetClassName(Form1.hwnd, sClassName, 100)
myhInst = GetClassLong(Form1.hwnd, GCL_HMODULE)
lretval = GetClassInfoEx(myhInst, Left$(sClassName, lRetLength), _
structOrigWinClass)
```

The last item of interest is the order in which the **WM_DESTROY** and **WM_NCDESTROY** messages are sent to the various windows that make up this application. This will provide some insight on how the windows are systematically destroyed upon closing the application.

The following order of events is observed by using Spy++ to monitor messages for the example application presented in this chapter, while it is shutting down:

1. Main Window (client area)
2. New Window (client area)
3. New Window—Button (client area)
4. New Window—Button (nonclient area)
5. New Window (nonclient area)
6. Main Window—Button (client area)
7. Main Window—Button (nonclient area)
8. Main Window (nonclient area)
9. Form1 (client area)
10. Form1 (nonclient area)

11. ThunderRT6Main (client area)

12. VBFocusRT6 (client area)

13. VBFocusRT6 (nonclient area)

14. ThunderRT6Main (nonclient area)

15. VBMsoStdCompMgr (client area)

16. VBMsoStdCompMgr (nonclient area)

17. OleMainThreadWndClass (client area)

18. OleMainThreadWndClass (nonclient area)

The client area of a window is always destroyed before the nonclient area; therefore, the WM_DESTROY message is sent to a window before WM_NCDESTROY. This is the order in which this application's windows are destroyed. Note that the indented windows (Steps 2 through 5) must be destroyed before the Main Window's client area can be destroyed (Step 1). The Main Window's client area completes its destruction after all other open windows and their respective button controls are destroyed.

After the user closes the main window, the WM_DESTROY message is sent to that window. In response to that message, the superclass procedure loops through all other open windows and destroys each of them in turn. This is why the new windows and their button controls are being destroyed before the main window can finish destroying its own client area.

The button control on the main window is destroyed next (Steps 6 and 7), followed by the nonclient area of the main window (Step 8). The last action the code performs is to unload the Form1 window. This destroys both the client and nonclient areas of this form (Steps 9 and 10). This finishes the destruction of all forms that we generated in the application code.

The rest of the shutdown process involves destroying the windows that VB creates behind the scenes. The first is the ThunderRT6Main form (Step 11), which contains the VBFocusRT6 window. The VBFocusRT6 window must be completely destroyed (Steps 12 and 13) before the nonclient area of the ThunderRT6Main form can be destroyed (Step 14). The last two windows to be destroyed are VBMsoStdCompMgr (Steps 15 and 16) and OleMainThreadWndClass (Steps 17 and 18), in that order.

When the application is starting, it creates these windows in the reverse order.

Debugging Techniques
for Subclassing

Debugging an application that uses any type of subclassing or superclassing is difficult, at best. To aid you in this endeavor, this chapter will discuss the methods and tools useful in debugging instance subclassing, global subclassing, and superclassing applications.

The first section discusses ways to trace through your application's code to determine where a problem lies. The next section provides information on tools provided by Microsoft. The last section covers SmartCheck, a tool developed by NuMega to assist developers in debugging Visual Basic (VB) applications.

Where to Start

The most important thing that you should remember is to save your work often. I tell you this from experience. If your subclassing application crashes while running in the Visual Basic IDE, the entire VB environment including the running application is lost. All unsaved code also is lost.

There are reliable ways to debug subclassing applications. I will present the ones I use regularly here.

When writing a subclassing application, it is usually better to start simple. Write the subclassing code using only a minimal window procedure function. By this, I mean do not handle any messages within this function; only pass the messages on to the original window procedure. This is the code for a minimal window procedure:

```
Public Function WinProc(ByVal hwnd As Long, ByVal uMsg As Long, _
            ByVal wParam As Long, ByVal lParam As Long) As Long

   WinProc = CallWindowProc(OrigWndProc, hwnd, uMsg, wParam, lParam)
End Function
```

This allows you to test your subclassing code alone. After all problems are resolved with the subclassing code, you can proceed, adding the necessary code to the subclassed window procedure. If there is a problem after adding code to the subclassed window procedure, you can narrow it down to this new code.

Subclassing Checklist

Before running your subclassing application for the first time, it is a good idea to run through a basic checklist to verify that all pieces required for subclassing are accounted for. You can use the following checklists as guideline for verifying subclassing code:

1. The *SetWindowLongPtr* or *SetClassLongPtr* function used to initiate subclassing is present and all its parameters are correct. The `AddressOf` operator must reference a valid window procedure.

2. The original window procedure returned from the *SetWindowLongPtr* or *SetClassLongPtr* function is stored in a variable.

3. The subclass window procedure is accounted for and resides in a code (BAS) module.

4. The number and type of arguments for the subclass window procedure are correct.

5. The subclass window procedure contains a call to either *CallWindowProc* or *DefWindowProc* for default message processing.

6. The number and type of arguments for the *CallWindowProc* or *DefWindowProc* function are correct.

7. If *CallWindowProc* is used, the original window procedure passed as the first argument is valid.

8. The *SetWindowLongPtr* or *SetClassLongPtr* function used to terminate subclassing is present, and all its parameters are correct.

9. Before the subclassed window is closed, its original window procedure is replaced.

10. There are no **End** statements in the application.

11. Do not use *DoEvents*.

In addition, if you are performing global subclassing, add these items to the checklist:

1. A hidden window is created to initiate global subclassing. This window is destroyed only after global subclassing has been terminated.

2. Destroy all globally subclassed windows before terminating global subclassing.

If you are performing superclassing, add these items to the first checklist:

1. The pointer to the base class's window procedure is saved and used to provide the default processing for messages in the superclass procedure.

2. The superclass is given a new unique class name.

3. The superclass is given a valid instance handle.

This is a separate checklist you can use with common dialog box subclassing:

1. A valid dialog template resource is used.

2. The resource is correctly packaged as either a dynamic link library (DLL) or a resource (RES) file. You can use RES files only in compiled applications.

3. The correct structure is used to create the common dialog box.

4. The correct template resource and hook procedure have been added to the common dialog box structure.

5. The *hInstance* member of the common dialog box structure contains the handle to the module containing the dialog template resource.

6. The correct flags have been set in the *flags* member in the common dialog box structure.

7. The number and type of arguments for the dialog hook procedure are correct.

Stepping Through the Application

Although it is possible to set breakpoints in your subclassing application and step through the code, I do not recommend this practice. In many cases, this will cause your application and the VB environment to freeze or crash.

After subclassing is "turned on" for an application that you are stepping through, all messages sent to that window will cause the subclassed window procedure to be called. Unfortunately, there is a big problem with activation between your application's window and the code window within the IDE. As you are stepping through your code, the code window must be the active window. If you try to set your application window as the active window, the system will immediately start sending messages to that window to activate it, paint it on the screen, and so forth. Every message that is sent to the application window causes the code window to activate, allowing you to step through the code in the subclassed window procedure. As you step through the code you will notice that the subclassed window procedure is called a large number of times. Many of the messages being sent to this procedure are trying to position and paint the subclassed window on the screen. What is happening is that the code window of the IDE is contending with the subclassed window for activation. This will cause each window to paint on the screen in an erratic way. This will most likely end up freezing your application, and the only way out is to kill off the application's process and the VB IDE with it.

There are more robust ways of debugging your code. The main drawback is that you might not get the instant feedback that you can get by stepping through your application in the IDE, and you cannot change the code on the fly.

Log Files

The best way to trace execution in your subclassing application, short of using third-party tools, is to use the event logging capabilities of VB. This technique is simple and effective. The information you glean from these log files can tell you what your application was doing when it crashed, where it crashed, and even what made it crash.

I have used two different methods for implementing log files. The first is to provide a text box on a window that can receive messages and comments. At strategic locations throughout the code, I place lines that add information to this text box. For example, I might add a line in the code that writes the value of the original window procedure's function pointer to this text box. The line might look something like this:

```
Form1.Text1.Text = Form1.Text1.Text & "Original Window Proc: " & m_OrigWinProc & _
                    vbCrLf
```

This is a fast and easy way to get feedback on how your application is operating. There are two drawbacks to this method, however. The first is that you must supply the code to add messages to this text box throughout your code. This might take some trial and error to get all the information that you need to debug your application.

The other drawback is that if you are sending a large number of messages to this text box—say 400 lines—and your application crashes, you will not be able to see all the information in your text box. The fix for this problem is a slightly different method of logging messages. In addition, because it's debugging code, you have to remove it or comment it out in the production version. A common (and embarrassing) source of errors is to fail to remove all debugging code.

Instead of using a text box, you can write out information to the event log. Adding event logging to your applications is actually very easy. There is a single method of the App object, LogEvent, which is used when logging information from a VB application. The following code example demonstrates the use of this method:

```
Public Const vbLogEventTypeInformation = 4

Private Sub cmdCreateLog_Click()
    App.LogEvent "This is a test", vbLogEventTypeInformation
End Sub
```

The first parameter of the LogEvent method is the text string that is sent to the event log. The second parameter is one of following three values:

```
Public Const vbLogEventTypeError = 1        'Error message
Public Const vbLogEventTypeWarning = 2      'Warning message
Public Const vbLogEventTypeInformation = 4  'Informational message
```

It is important to keep the following in mind when using event logging:

- Event logging works only in compiled applications.

- The *Source* column in the Event Viewer for any VB application entry is always set to "VBRuntime".

- You can customize VB's logging behavior somewhat by calling the App object's StartLogging method, which has the following syntax:

  ```
  StartLogging sLogTarget, lLogModes
  ```

  where *sLogTarget* is a string containing the path and filename of the log file, and *lLogModes* is one or more of the following intrinsic constants:

  vbLogAuto *(0)*

  On Windows 9x, logs messages to the file specified in the *LogFile* property. On Windows NT/2000, logs messages to the Application Event Log, with "VBRunTime" used as the application source and App.Title appearing in the description.

  vbLogOff *(1)*

  Turns all logging off and causes subsequent calls to the LogEvent method to be ignored.

  vbLogToFile *(2)*

  Forces logging to a file specified by *LogPath*.

  VbLogToNT *(3)*

  Forces logging to the NT event log. If not running on Windows NT, or if the event log is unavailable, logging is ignored and the property is set to vbLogOff.

  VbLogOverwrite *(16)*

  For Windows 9x only, indicates that *logfile* should be re-created each time the application starts. (By default, items are appended to the log.) This value can be ORed with other constants.

  VbLogThreadID *(32)*

  Indicates that the current thread ID be prepended to the message, in the form "[T:0nnn]." This value can be ORed with other constants.

- If you do not use StartLogging to override the default settings for the Event Viewer, the log entries go to the event log on Windows NT/2000 and the *VBEvents.log* file in the %SystemRoot% directory on a Windows 9x system.

The beauty of using this method for logging information is that, if your application crashes, information can be written to the log file up to the point that it crashed or froze. Usually when an application crashes, it stops accepting messages. When this happens, the window fails to update properly. This prevents you from viewing the information sent to a text box immediately before the application crashed. The last lines of information in your log file are usually the most critical. They can help you pinpoint where the crash occurred and what values were contained in the variables before the crash.

Microsoft Tools

Microsoft provides some useful debugging tools along with its development products. You can find these tools on Microsoft's web site. They also are bundled with Visual C++ and VB.

Spy++

Spy++ is one of the most useful tools to give us insight on how our application is structured, as well as to allow us to examine the messages our application is receiving. I have provided an introduction to using this tool in Chapter 1. Throughout many of the chapters, I have described specific uses of this tool as it relates to each chapter's topic.

DBGWPROC.DLL

This tool, which Microsoft designed, is available at *http://msdn.microsoft.com/vbasic/downloads/controls.asp*. This tool is provided free of charge.

This is simply a Component Object Model (COM) DLL that you add to your application. You need to add very little code to allow your application to use this DLL.

To incorporate this DLL into your application, register it using *regsvr32.exe* and add it to your project references by checking the "Debug Object for AddressOf Subclassing" option in the References dialog. Click on the Make tab in the Project Properties dialog box. Add the text

```
DEBUGWINDOWPROC = -1 : USEGETPROP = -1
```

to the Conditional Compilation text box. For the release version of this application, you should change the −1 values to zeroes and remove the reference to *DBGWPROC.DLL*.

Next, you must create an object **m_DbgHook** from the *WindowProcHook* class.

```
#If DEBUGWINDOWPROC Then
     Private m_DbgHook As WindowProcHook
#End If
```

If we are not using *DBGWPROC.DLL*, we can call *SetWindowLongPtr* as we normally would to subclass a window. Otherwise, we set up *DBGWPROC.DLL* to control the subclassing, as in the following code:

```
#If DEBUGWINDOWPROC Then
    On Error Resume Next
    Set m_DbgHook = CreateWindowProcHook
    If Err Then
        MsgBox Err.Description
        Err.Clear
        DisableSubclass       'Replace with your own disable subclass function
        Exit Function
    End If
    On Error GoTo 0
    With m_DbgHook
        .SetMainProc AddressOf Module1.NewWndProc    'Replace with your win proc
        m_lOrigWndProc = SetWindowLongPtr(m_hwnd, GWLP_WNDPROC, .ProcAddress)
        .SetDebugProc m_lOrigWndProc
    End With
#Else
    m_lOrigWndProc = SetWindowLongPtr(m_hwnd, GWLP_WNDPROC, AddressOf Module1.
NewWndProc)
#End If
```

The most relevant code is within the `With m_DbgHook` code block. The first line in this block of code stores the address of your subclass window procedure in the DLL; in this case, it is the address of the *Module1.NewWndProc* function. The second line uses the familiar *SetWindowLongPtr* to initiate the subclassing, except that the address of the new window procedure is not our function; instead, it is set to *ProcAddress*, which is a read-only property of the DLL that contains an address to a function within the DLL. This is the actual subclass window procedure that is called for our window. Finally, the original window procedure is stored in the DLL through the *SetDebugProc* function.

This is how the DLL works:

1. Subclassing is initiated as in the previous code.

2. When a message is sent to the subclassed window, it arrives in the subclass window procedure defined by the *ProcAddress* property.

3. The subclassed window procedure then determines where to send the message:

   a. If the `AddressOf` operator returns a zero to the *SetMainProc* method, the original window procedure is called. The original window procedure function address was sent to the *SetDebugProc* method of the DLL.

   b. Otherwise our subclass window procedure is called. This is the function address sent to the *SetMainProc* method of the DLL.

The original intent of this DLL was to circumvent the error caused by the AddressOf operator returning a zero while running within the VB IDE. Oddly enough, I discovered that AddressOf returns a valid function pointer while running within the IDE, although, this might work differently for VB prior to Version 6.

You might be wondering why to even use this DLL for debugging if the AddressOf operator returns a valid function address. The answer is that using this DLL solves the problem of the code window and the application window competing to be the active window when stepping through the code. This makes it much easier and safer to step through code while in the VB IDE.

NuMega's SmartCheck

I have not mentioned this tool much, although I use it frequently. SmartCheck provides debug information about a VB application during runtime. This tool is invaluable in debugging application crashes, erroneous application programming interface (API) calls, and much more. You can set up this tool as an add-in to VB, and it is fairly intuitive to use.

Besides pointing out application errors, SmartCheck also displays API functions, function parameters, return values, and even the data to which a pointer points. This is very useful when determining if the string data or a structure pointed to by a pointer contains the correct information. Figure 8-1 displays a screenshot of SmartCheck.

To illustrate what type of information SmartCheck provides you with and what a VB subclassing application looks like on the inside, I will step through the output of a previous example application. The example application I will examine is the Minimize button subclassing example of Chapter 4. Figure 8-2 shows a screenshot of this application.

I will run this application under SmartCheck, subclass the Minimize button, remove the subclassing, and then shut down the application. Before shutting down the application, I will use Spy++ to get the window handles of all windows belonging to this application. The windows and their handles are listed in Table 8-1. Knowing this information allows us to determine on which window the action is taking place.

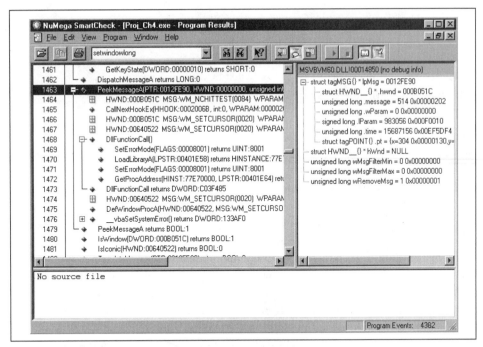

Figure 8-1. Screenshot of the SmartCheck debugging tool

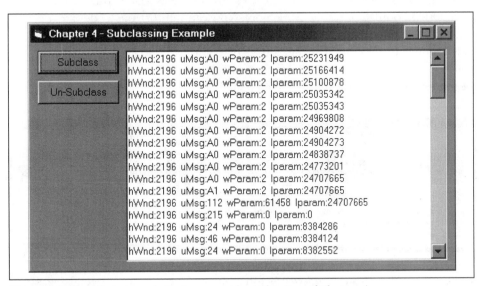

Figure 8-2. The Minimize subclassing example application of Chapter 4

Table 8-1. Window Handles for the Example Application

Hwnd	Window Description
&H640522	ThunderRT6FormDC—the only VB form in the project
&H8051A	ThunderRT6Edit—the only text box on the form
&HE0516	ThunderRT6CommandButton—the Un-Subclass button
&HB051C	ThunderRT6CommandButton—the Subclass button
&H290500	VBBubbleRT6
&H25050A	OleMainThreadWndName
&H160512	ThunderRT6Main
&H5050E	VBMsoStdCompMgr
&H6050C	VBFocusRT6

Examining the output from SmartCheck shows that one of the first things VB does is create the ThunderRT6Main window. This window owns the other application windows. After this window is destroyed, the application shuts down and unloads itself from memory. After this window is created, the initial form is created from the `ThunderRT6FormDC` class. This process is illustrated in Figure 8-3, in which a windowpane icon indicates a message that has been *handled* by a window procedure. A diamond icon indicates API calls. Lightning bolt icons indicate a VB event being fired. VB performs the call to *CreateWindowExA* (Line 814) to create the ThunderRT6FormDC window in memory. You can tell that this code is executing in the *MSVBVM60.DLL* module from the `hInstance` argument to this function (this argument and several others are displayed off the edge of the screen). It is 66000000, which is the same `hInstance` as this DLL. You can see this using the Dependency Walker tool supplied with Visual C++.

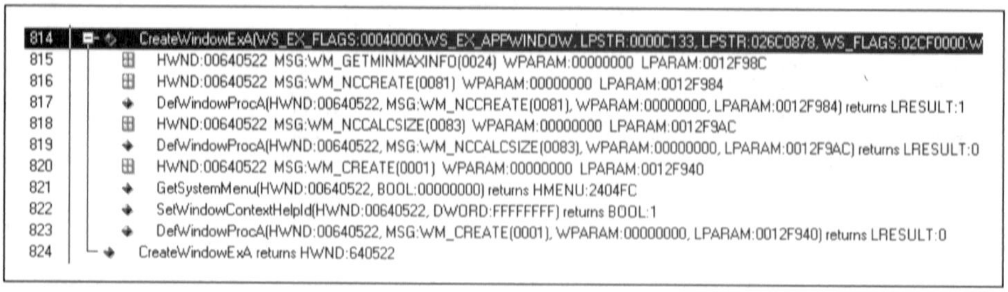

```
814    ⊞ ◈  CreateWindowExA(WS_EX_FLAGS:00040000:WS_EX_APPWINDOW, LPSTR:0000C133, LPSTR:026C0878, WS_FLAGS:02CF0000:W
815         ⊞  HWND:00640522 MSG:WM_GETMINMAXINFO(0024) WPARAM:00000000 LPARAM:0012F98C
816         ⊞  HWND:00640522 MSG:WM_NCCREATE(0081) WPARAM:00000000 LPARAM:0012F984
817         ◈  DefWindowProcA(HWND:00640522, MSG:WM_NCCREATE(0081), WPARAM:00000000, LPARAM:0012F984) returns LRESULT:1
818         ⊞  HWND:00640522 MSG:WM_NCCALCSIZE(0083) WPARAM:00000000 LPARAM:0012F9AC
819         ◈  DefWindowProcA(HWND:00640522, MSG:WM_NCCALCSIZE(0083), WPARAM:00000000, LPARAM:0012F9AC) returns LRESULT:0
820         ⊞  HWND:00640522 MSG:WM_CREATE(0001) WPARAM:00000000 LPARAM:0012F940
821         ◈  GetSystemMenu(HWND:00640522, BOOL:00000000) returns HMENU:2404FC
822         ◈  SetWindowContextHelpId(HWND:00640522, DWORD:FFFFFFFF) returns BOOL:1
823         ◈  DefWindowProcA(HWND:00640522, MSG:WM_CREATE(0001), WPARAM:00000000, LPARAM:0012F940) returns LRESULT:0
824      ◈  CreateWindowExA returns HWND:640522
```

Figure 8-3. SmartCheck output for creating a VB form

While within the *CreateWindowExA* function, we can see that several messages are handled and other API calls are made. First, the `WM_GETMINMAXINFO` message is sent to the newly created window. At this point, we know that the window procedure for this window was created because it is accepting this message. The next message that *CreateWindowExA* sends to this window procedure is the `WM_NCCREATE` message. Notice that after the window procedure processes this message, it passes it on to the *DefWindowProcA* function for default processing (Line 817). You will see the *DefWindowProcA* function called many times in an application because it contains the default functionality for all windows.

DefWindowProcA returns a 1 for the `WM_NCCREATE` message. This allows window creation to continue. If a zero was returned, the *CreateWindowExA* function would have stopped the creation of this window and returned control to the calling procedure.

Next, this new window processes the `WM_NCCALCSIZE` message (Line 818), followed by the `WM_CREATE` message (Line 820). When the window procedure processes the `WM_CREATE` message, it calls the *GetSystemMenu* and *SetWindowContextHelpId* functions before sending the message on to the *DefWindowProcA* function (Line 823). The *GetSystemMenu* function makes a copy of the system menu to be used by this window. The *SetWindowContextHelpId* function returns any help context ID for the window specified by the *hwnd* argument.

After the *DefWindowProcA* function returns successfully, the *CreateWindowExA* function returns execution to its calling function. The return value for this function is the handle of the newly created window (Line 824).

Figure 8-4 shows how a call can be nested within another function call. In this sample output, the main window is being activated. We know it is the main window from the *HWND* argument of the `WM_NCACTIVATE` message (Line 961). This message has completed its processing in the window procedure associated with this *HWND*. A call is then made to *DefWindowProcA* (Line 962). While within this function, the `WM_GETTEXT` message is sent to the window procedure of the main window via the *SendMessage* function (Line 963). We know that the *SendMessage* function is used because the message is immediately processed. If the message were posted, we would see it processed later on by the message loop. I will discuss the message loop later in this chapter.

```
961        ⊞      HWND:00640522 MSG:WM_NCACTIVATE(0086) WPARAM:00000001 LPARAM:00000000
962      ⊟ ◆    DefWindowProcA(HWND:00640522, MSG:WM_NCACTIVATE(0086), WPARAM:00000001, LPARAM:00000000)
963          ⊞      HWND:00640522 MSG:WM_GETTEXT(000D) WPARAM:000000FF LPARAM:0012F018
964          ◆    DefWindowProcA(HWND:00640522, MSG:WM_GETTEXT(000D), WPARAM:000000FF, LPARAM:0012F018) returns LRESULT:1F
965      └ ◆   DefWindowProcA returns LRESULT:1
966        ⊞      HWND:00640522 MSG:WM_ACTIVATE(0006) WPARAM:00000001 LPARAM:00000000
```

Figure 8-4. Nested function calls

The `WM_NCACTIVATE` message changes the nonclient area of a window to either an active or inactive state. The *wParam* of this message is set to **True**, telling us that the active title bar needs to be redrawn. Before redrawing the title bar, the system needs to get and store the window caption so that it can be replaced after the nonclient area is redrawn. To do this, the *DefWindowProcA* function sends the WM_GETTEXT message to retrieve the window caption of the main window (Line 963). *DefWindowProcA* is called again from within the window procedure while it is processing the WM_GETTEXT message (Line 964).

DefWindowProcA is a *reentrant* function. In other words, before the code in this function is finished executing, it could be called again. To be reentrant, the function needs to be able to save its state, process the nested function call, and then restore its state and continue executing.

After the inner *DefWindowProcA* function is finished (Line 964), it returns control to the outer *DefWindowProcA* function (Line 962). When the default processing is finished for the WM_NCACTIVATE message, the outer *DefWindowProcA* function returns, and then the application proceeds to activate its client area by sending the WM_ACTIVATE message (Line 966).

The next thing I want to show you is the VB message loop. The VB message loop, which is shown in Figure 8-5, is not quite like the message loops I have previously shown you. As you can see there is no GetMessage function in this loop. Instead PeekMessage is used (Line 1194). This function is defined as follows:

```
Public Declare Function PeekMessage Lib "user32" Alias "PeekMessageA" _
       (lpMsg As MSG, ByVal hwnd As Long, ByVal wMsgFilterMin As Long, _
       ByVal wMsgFilterMax As Long, ByVal wRemoveMsg As Long) As Long
```

Its parameters are:

lpMsg
  A long pointer to an MSG structure.

hwnd
  The handle of the window whose messages are to be read from the queue. If this is zero, all messages will be read.

wMsgFilterMin
  The minimum message value that is read from the message queue.

wMsgFilterMax
  The maximum message value that is retrieved from the message queue. If this value is zero, all messages starting with the *wMsgFilterMin* value are read from the message queue.

wRemoveMsg
  If this is set to 1, the message is read and then removed from the queue. If this is set to 0, the message is read but left on the queue.

If there are no messages on the queue, the return value for this function is zero. A nonzero return value means that a message was read from the queue.

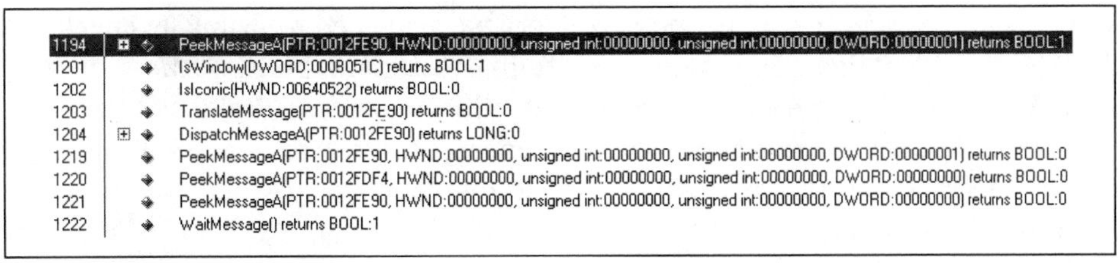

```
1194    ⊞ ⚡   PeekMessageA(PTR:0012FE90, HWND:00000000, unsigned int:00000000, unsigned int:00000000, DWORD:00000001) returns BOOL:1
1201      ⭢    IsWindow(DWORD:000B051C) returns BOOL:1
1202      ⭢    IsIconic(HWND:00640522) returns BOOL:0
1203      ⭢    TranslateMessage(PTR:0012FE90) returns BOOL:0
1204    ⊞ ⭢   DispatchMessageA(PTR:0012FE90) returns LONG:0
1219      ⭢    PeekMessageA(PTR:0012FE90, HWND:00000000, unsigned int:00000000, unsigned int:00000000, DWORD:00000001) returns BOOL:0
1220      ⭢    PeekMessageA(PTR:0012FDF4, HWND:00000000, unsigned int:00000000, unsigned int:00000000, DWORD:00000000) returns BOOL:0
1221      ⭢    PeekMessageA(PTR:0012FE90, HWND:00000000, unsigned int:00000000, unsigned int:00000000, DWORD:00000000) returns BOOL:0
1222      ⭢    WaitMessage() returns BOOL:1
```

Figure 8-5. The VB message loop

If we were to write this message loop in VB, it would look something like this:

```
Sub Main VBMessageLoop()

    While TRUE
        While PeekMessage(structMsg, 0, 0, 0, 1)
            If structMsg.message = WM_QUIT Then
                Exit Function
            Else
                If IsWindow And Not IsIconic() then
                    TranslateMessage (structMsg)
                    DispatchMessage (structMsg)
                End If
            End If
        Loop

        If BackgroundProcessingReady() Then
            DoBackGroundProcessing
        Else
            WaitMessage
        End If
    Loop
End Sub
```

PeekMessage is typically used in message loops for applications that need to do background processing. Both *PeekMessage* and *GetMessage* operate in a similar fashion—that is, until there are no more messages to be processed. When there are no more messages in the queue, the *GetMessage* function will not return control to the application and instead places the application in a sleep state. While an application is sleeping, it will not use up CPU processing cycles. Conversely, the *PeekMessage* function will return control to the application, and it will not place the application in a sleep state. If there are no messages to be processed, this loop will eat up CPU processing cycles that could be used by other applications. To stop this from happening, we can call the *WaitMessage* function. This function takes no arguments and returns only when a message is placed in the message queue. The return value of this function is of type Boolean. By putting the application to sleep with *WaitMessage*, we do not tie up the CPU with needless processing.

When using *PeekMessage* in the message loop, we also need to manually check for the WM_QUIT message. This messages returns **False** to both *GetMessage* and *PeekMessage*. *GetMessage* also will return this value and automatically exit the message loop. **PeekMessage** returns **True** when it processes this message and the message loop is not exited. *PeekMessage* returns **False** only when no messages are in the message queue.

Figure 8-6 shows another view of the VB message loop, only this time it is processing a WM_PAINT (&HF) message for the Edit control. *PeekMessage* in this loop found and removed a WM_PAINT message on the message queue (Line 1080). *IsWindow* and *IsIconic* are called to determine if this is the handle to an existing window, and if so, if it is in an iconic state (Lines 1081 and 1082). Because it is an existing window and this window is not iconized, execution continues to the *TranslateMessage* function (Line 1083). This is not a keyboard-input message, so this function returns without handling the message. Execution continues on to the *DispatchMessage* function. This function sends the message to the appropriate window procedure. Line 1085 of Figure 8-6 shows the WM_PAINT messages being processed by the Edit control. The processing of this message by the Edit control's window procedure causes the WM_CTLCOLOREDIT message to be sent to the control's parent window. Afterward, several other API functions are called, enabling the WM_PAINT message to complete.

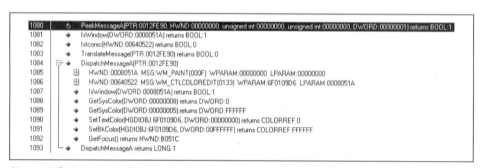

Figure 8-6. Processing the WM_PAINT message

Now that we have our window created and our message loop running, we can click the Subclassing button. Figure 8-7 shows what happens when the user clicks this button—VB fires the *_Click* event. This *_Click* event is in response to the *DispatchMessage* function sending the WM_LBUTTONUP message to the Subclass button. The *Click* event of the Subclass button calls a function, which calls the *SetWindowLongPtr* function. This function is mapped to the *SetWindowLongA* function because we are still using 32-bit Windows to perform the subclassing.

For VB to call this API function, it must use an internal method called *DllFunctionCall* to load the User32 library and get a pointer to the *SetWindowLongA* function within this library. The VB **Declare** statement for the

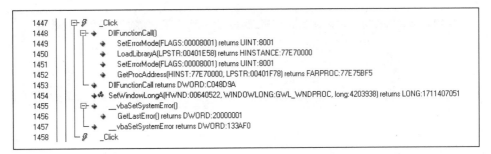

```
1447    ⊟ ⌀   _Click
1448      ⊟ ✦   DllFunctionCall()
1449          ✦    SetErrorMode(FLAGS:00008001) returns UINT:8001
1450          ✦    LoadLibraryA(LPSTR:00401E58) returns HINSTANCE:77E70000
1451          ✦    SetErrorMode(FLAGS:00008001) returns UINT:8001
1452          ✦    GetProcAddress(HINST:77E70000, LPSTR:00401F78) returns FARPROC:77E75BF5
1453      └ ✦   DllFunctionCall returns DWORD:C048D9A
1454        ✦✧ SetWindowLongA(HWND:00640522, WINDOWLONG:GWL_WNDPROC, long:4203938) returns LONG:1711407051
1455      ⊟ ✦   __vbaSetSystemError()
1456          ✦    GetLastError() returns DWORD:20000001
1457      └ ✦   __vbaSetSystemError returns DWORD:133AF0
1458    └ ⌀   _Click
```

Figure 8-7. Clicking the Subclass button

SetWindowLongPtr function provides the information used by *DllFunctionCall* to know which function in which library to use.

After it finds this function, VB calls the *SetWindowLongA* function (Line 1454). The new window procedure is put in place, and the address of the old procedure is returned. You should make a note of the old window procedure pointer and the new one. This information is useful when there is a problem with restoring the original window procedure. You can search through the SmartCheck output to determine when the last *SetWindowLongA* function was called. Compare the window procedure pointer that was set here to the original window procedure pointer. If they are not the same, you have a problem. You will need to determine why this happened. Perhaps you lost the original window procedure pointer, or *SetWindowLongA* was not called to restore the original window procedure before the application ended.

Next, VB performs some error checking and then returns from the *_Click* event.

At this point, our subclassed window procedure is being called. To keep the output of SmartCheck relatively simple, the only code I added to this function is *CallWindowProc*. Figure 8-8 shows this. The message loop's *PeekMessage* function grabs a WM_MOUSEMOVE event from the message queue (Line 1463). The WM_MOUSEMOVE message is contained within the PTR argument of the *PeekMessage* function. SmartCheck can display the value of this pointer as an MSG structure.

Because the mouse is moving across the Subclass button (hwnd &HB051C), the WM_NCHITTEST (Line 1464) and WM_SETCURSOR (Line 1466) messages are sent directly to this window. However, the WM_SETCURSOR message also is sent to the parent window of the Subclass button (Line 1467). The parent window is the window that we just subclassed. Because this is the first time that the subclassed window procedure is called, it will use the *DllFunctionCall* method (Line 1468) to look up the library and address for the *CallWindowProcA* function.

Immediately following the *DllFunctionCall* method, the same subclassed window (compare Line 1467 to Line 1474) processes the WM_SETCURSOR message a second

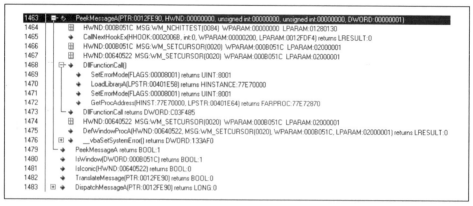

1463	PeekMessageA(PTR:0012FE90, HWND:00000000, unsigned int:00000000, unsigned int:00000000, DWORD:00000001)
1464	HWND:000B051C MSG:WM_NCHITTEST(0084) WPARAM:00000000 LPARAM:01280130
1465	CallNextHookEx(HHOOK:0002006B, int:0, WPARAM:00000200, LPARAM:0012FDF4) returns LRESULT:0
1466	HWND:000B051C MSG:WM_SETCURSOR(0020) WPARAM:000B051C LPARAM:02000001
1467	HWND:00640522 MSG:WM_SETCURSOR(0020) WPARAM:000B051C LPARAM:02000001
1468	DllFunctionCall()
1469	SetErrorMode(FLAGS:00008001) returns UINT:8001
1470	LoadLibraryA(LPSTR:00401E58) returns HINSTANCE:77E70000
1471	SetErrorMode(FLAGS:00008001) returns UINT:8001
1472	GetProcAddress(HINST:77E70000, LPSTR:00401E64) returns FARPROC:77E72870
1473	DllFunctionCall returns DWORD:C03F485
1474	HWND:00640522 MSG:WM_SETCURSOR(0020) WPARAM:000B051C LPARAM:02000001
1475	DefWindowProcA(HWND:00640522, MSG:WM_SETCURSOR(0020), WPARAM:000B051C, LPARAM:02000001) returns LRESULT:0
1476	__vbaSetSystemError() returns DWORD:133AF0
1479	PeekMessageA returns BOOL:1
1480	IsWindow(DWORD:000B051C) returns BOOL:1
1481	IsIconic(HWND:00640522) returns BOOL:0
1482	TranslateMessage(PTR:0012FE90) returns BOOL:0
1483	DispatchMessageA(PTR:0012FE90) returns LONG:0

Figure 8-8. Inside the subclassed window procedure

time. The first time the subclassed window procedure is processing the message. The second time the original window procedure is processing the message. After the original window procedure processes this message, it passes it along to the *DefWindowProcA* function (Line 1475).

This is the usual order of events in the subclass window procedure. If any event does not occur, you should examine the parameters for the functions, especially *DefWindowProcA* and *CallWindowProcA*. If the incorrect hWnd or the original window procedure is not being passed into these functions correctly, problems will occur. Also, if these functions are not called, the original window procedure will not process the messages. This will effectively cause the subclassed window to not respond to those messages that the original window procedure did not process.

Sometimes, the original window procedure is called at the wrong time. For example, if *CallWindowProcA* or *DefWindowProcA* is called ahead of the subclass window procedure, the window will process the message as it normally would, before the subclass window procedure gets a chance to process it. If the subclass window procedure modifies any message parameters, the parameters will never be passed into the original window procedure. To fix this problem, you need to place the *CallWindowProcA* or *DefWindowProcA* functions at the end of the subclass window procedure.

The last line is the *DispatchMessage* function. This function can now process the original message that *PeekMessage* pulled from the queue, which was the WM_MOUSEMOVE message for the Subclass button.

This output can be useful in determining the types of messages that the window procedure is processing and the order in which they are processed. If your application displays odd behavior, you can determine the message or messages that are being processed by the window procedure during the odd behavior. As I previously mentioned, some messages, as they are processed, can produce other messages. These new messages can cause the odd behavior.

It is even possible to get stuck in an infinite loop within the window procedure. This problem will most likely cause a stack overflow exception in your application and shut it down. Problems such as these can be tracked down fairly easily using SmartCheck.

In the next section of debugger output, I click the Un-Subclass button. The result is the output shown in Figure 8-9. The *PeekMessage* function (not shown) pulls the WM_LBUTTONUP message from the queue and passes it to *DispatchMessage* (Line 2183). This message is in response to the user clicking and releasing the left mouse button while over the Un-Subclass button. The *DispatchMessage* function then sends the WM_LBUTTONUP message to the window procedure of the Un-Subclass button. This causes a chain of events to occur, which ends up with the *_Click* event being raised for this button control (Line 2204). The code in this event simply calls the *SetWindowLongPtr* function to remove the subclassing (Line 2205).

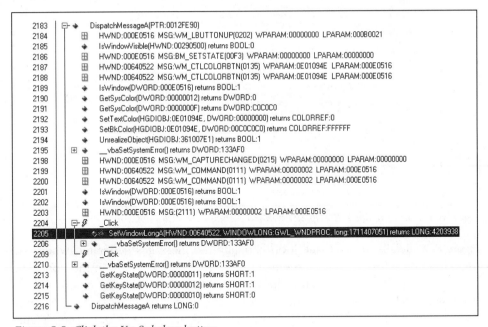

Figure 8-9. Click the Un-Subclass button

At this point, you should compare the original window procedure pointer that was replaced with the window procedure pointer that was set using *SetWindowLongPtr*. If they match, everything is fine; otherwise, you need to track down why the original window procedure pointer was not restored.

Notice that every time a message is sent to the subclassed window procedure, it is listed twice in the debugger output. The subclassed window procedure processes the first message, and the original window procedure processes the second message. You can see this on Lines 2187, 2188, 2199, and 2200.

The final processing that I want to examine is the destruction of a window. As Figure 8-10 shows, when the Close button on the main form is clicked, all windows in the application are destroyed and the application itself is shut down.

Figure 8-10. Shutting down the application via the window's Close button

Figure 8-10 details the message loop handling the messages generated when the user clicks the Close button on the main form. Any mouse action in the nonclient area of a window will first cause the WM_NCHITTEST message to be sent to that window's window procedure. The window handles this message (Line 3701) and then passes it on to the default window procedure (Line 3702). The default window procedure returns a value of &H14, which is the HTCLOSE code indicating that the window's Close button was clicked.

Windows will immediately send the WM_SETCURSOR message to that window to determine if the mouse cursor needs to be modified and, if so, modifies the cursor.

Because the left mouse button was clicked over the Close button of the window, the system posts the WM_NCLBUTTONDOWN message to that window, with the

HTCLOSE code in the *wParam* of this message (Line 3711). When this message is sent to the default window procedure (Line 3714), it sets off the following series of events:

1. Line 3716. This window is notified that it is losing the mouse capture window through the WM_CAPTURECHANGED message. The mouse capture window is the active window that receives mouse messages.

2. Line 3718. The WM_SYSCOMMAND message is sent to the window with the SC_CLOSE code in the *wParam* of this message.

3. Line 3719. The *_QueryUnload* event is raised. This equates to the form's *Form1_QueryUnload* event.

4. Line 3758. The Edit control on the form is destroyed.

5. Line 3774. The Un-Subclass button on the form is destroyed.

6. Line 3786. The Subclass button on the form is destroyed.

7. The main form is destroyed. Line 3797 of Figure 8-11 shows this.

Although the main form and all its controls were destroyed, the VB application still remains in memory. This is because not all of the application's windows were destroyed. VB continues its shutdown process by destroying the windows created from the VBBubbleRT6 class, the OleMainThreadWndName class, the VBMsoStdCompMgr class, the VBFocusRT6 class, and the ThunderRT6Main class. When these windows have been destroyed, the application can completely remove itself from memory.

Figure 8-11 details the *DestroyWindow* function for the main form, which is called in response to the user clicking the window's Close button. The *DestroyWindow* function immediately causes the WM_DESTROY message to be sent to the window being closed (Line 3798). This message calls the *SendMessageA* (Line 3799), *IsWindowVisible* (Line 3803), and *SelectObject* (Line 3804) functions.

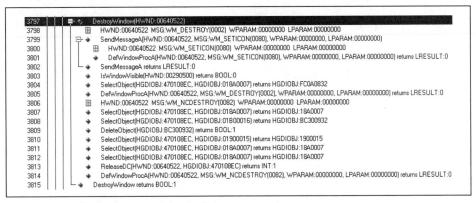

Figure 8-11. The destruction of the VB form

Notice the *SendMessageA* function (Line 3799); it sends the `WM_SETICON` message directly to the window procedure, which processes it and passes it on to *DefWindowProc*. Only after this processing is finished does the *SendMessageA* function return. This is how the *SendMessage* function operates.

After the default processing is finished for the `WM_DESTROY` message, the `WM_NCDESTROY` message is sent to the window (Line 3806). This message uses *SelectObject* to restore all GDI objects to their original state, and then it uses *DeleteObject* to remove any objects created by VB from memory. Finally, *ReleaseDC* frees up the device context memory for the window. The message is then sent to *DefWindowProc* (Line 3814) for default processing, and then the *DestroyWindow* function can return (Line 3815).

III

Hooking

This section devotes individual chapters to the following hooks:

WH_CALLWNDPROC
: Intercepts messages sent using the *SendMesssage* API function

WH_CALLWNDPROCRET
: Intercepts messages after they have been processed by their window procedure

WH_CBT
: Used to create Computer Based Training (CBT) applications

WH_DEBUG
: Intercepts calls to an installed hook's filter function

WH_FOREGROUNDIDLE
: Called when an application is about to enter an idle state

WH_GETMESSAGE
: Intercepts posted (and not sent) messages

WH_JOURNALPLAYBACK
: Posts prerecorded messages to the raw input thread's message queue so that they may be processed ("played back") by the system.

WH_JOURNALRECORD
: Intercept mouse, keyboard, and other hardware messages received by the system

WH_KEYBOARD *and* WH_KEYBOARD_LL
: Intercepts keyboard messages

WH_MOUSE *and* WH_MOUSE_LL
: Intercept mouse messages

WH_MSGFILTER

Intercepts sent messages produced by menus, dialog boxes, message boxes, and scroll bars

WH_SYSMSGFILTER

Intercepts sent messages produced by menus, dialog boxes, message boxes, and scroll bars on a system-wide basis

WH_SHELL

Intercepts messages that notify an application of actions occurring to it either through user intervention or through a change in the system's state

Each chapter will discuss a hook in detail. The chapters will begin by discussing the hook and providing relevant background information. I will use examples to aid in these discussions. Each chapter will end with a discussion of the problems to watch for while using the hook.

9

WH_CALLWNDPROC

The WH_CALLWNDPROC hook intercepts messages that you send through the *SendMessage* application programming interface (API) function. This hook ·can view messages, but it cannot modify or discard them. Normally, filter functions discard messages by not calling the *CallNextHookEx* function and returning a zero. But in the case of the WH_CALLWNDPROC hook, after the filter function is finished processing the message, it returns control to the *SendMessage* function, which then proceeds to send the message. For this reason, it is not possible to discard the sent message.

How WH_CALLWNDPROC Works

You also can use this hook to watch for any messages sent to a window. For instance, the Spy++ utility uses this hook when it watches for sent messages. This hook is also useful if you need to perform an action when a specific message is sent to one or more windows. For example, one application could broadcast a user-defined message. This message would then be picked up and acted upon by every other application that was using this hook to watch for that particular message.

You can use this hook as a thread-specific hook, or you can place it in a dynamic link library (DLL) and use it as a system-wide hook. A thread-specific hook intercepts all messages within the thread in which it is installed. When a hook is installed as a system-wide hook, it has to be placed in a DLL. This DLL is injected into every process so that the hook can operate on all messages in the system. Chapter 3 provides a thorough discussion of this technique.

Messages sent to windows through the *SendMessage* function are sent directly to the window procedure, bypassing both the system and thread message queues.

They do not go through the message queue, as a posted message does. As a result, these types of messages are processed before posted messages are. The following shows the order in which a message loop processes messages:

1. Sent messages

2. Posted messages

3. Input messages from hardware and internal system events

4. Sent messages (a second time)

5. `WM_PAINT` messages

6. `WM_TIMER` messages

As you can see, sent messages are processed not only first, but also fourth. A sent message is processed before any other messages to make sure that the sent message does not have to wait for the system to process any other type of messages before processing the next sent message. Sent messages are synchronous, therefore requiring the called window to return control before the caller sending the message can continue. If other messages, such as `WM_PAINT` messages, take a great deal of time to process, the function that sent the message cannot continue processing, at least not in a timely manner.

Next, posted messages are processed because they are usually critical to the application's operation. Posted message include messages about mouse movement, mouse button clicks, and keyboard events.

Input messages from hardware and internal system events include messages posted from other hardware attached to the system and from events such as low battery power on a laptop.

Sent messages are processed a second time to make sure they are processed before the `WM_PAINT` and `WM_TIMER` messages. This is because these two messages have a lower priority, and the `WM_PAINT` message takes considerable time to process.

When the `WH_CALLWNDPROC` hook is installed on a Windows 9x or NT 3.51 system, the hook's filter function is called when the *SendMessage* function is called. However, on NT 4.0 and Windows 2000 systems, the filter function is called immediately before the window procedure handles the sent message. Essentially, on a 9x or NT 3.51 system, the hook is called from within the context of the thread that called *SendMessage*. However, on an NT 4.0/2000 system, the hook's filter function is called within the context of the thread that contains the target window. This difference does not matter when you use this hook in a Visual Basic (VB) application with a thread-specific scope. This is because the filter function is always called from within the context of the same thread. However, this is not the case when multiple threads are created from within a VB application, or when messages are being sent between processes. Now the filter function can be called from within different threads, depending on the operating system used. This might cause problems if you are using the hook in a heterogeneous environment.

To aid in determining the source of the sent message, this hook sets the *wParam* parameter in its filter function to a zero or nonzero value. A nonzero value means that the message was sent from within the same thread that is handling the message. A zero value means that the message was sent from another thread. Distinguishing the source of the sent message allows you to handle it in an appropriate way. This is useful when you use a system-wide WH_CALLWNDPROC hook. In this case, your DLL containing the filter function is injected into all running processes. Using the *wParam* parameter, your code can determine where the message originated.

When using this hook, you should be aware of the different methods of sending messages. You can send a message using any one of six API functions: *SendMessage, SendMessageTimeout, SendNotifyMessage, SendMessageCallback, SendDlgItemMessage,* and *BroadcastSystemMessage.* These functions do not post messages to a thread's message queue; instead, they send the message directly to the window procedure or procedures. The main difference between these functions is the way control is returned back to the function that called *SendMessage* and whether the message is sent to one or more windows. The first of these functions is *SendMessage,* which has the following syntax in VB:

```
Public Declare Function SendMessage Lib "user32" Alias "SendMessageA" _
        (ByVal hwnd As Long, ByVal wMsg As Long, _
        ByVal wParam As Long, lParam As Any) As Long
```

Its parameters are:

hwnd

The handle of the target window, or HWND_BROADCAST if the message is to be sent to all top-level windows in the system

wMsg

The message to send to the target window

wParam

The first parameter of the message

lParam

The second parameter of the message

SendMessage simply sends a message to the specified target window. The return value depends on the message sent. The main drawback to using this function is that it is synchronous. This means that *SendMessage* will send the message and then wait for the target window procedure to return. If the target window procedure never returns, the function that called *SendMessage* can never continue processing. You can use several other API functions to solve this problem. The first of these is *SendMessageTimeout*:

```
Public Declare Function SendMessageTimeout Lib "user32" _
        Alias "SendMessageTimeoutA" _
    (ByVal hwnd As Long, ByVal Msg As Long, _
    ByVal wParam As Long, ByVal lParam As Long, _
    ByVal fuFlags As Long, ByVal uTimeout As Long, _
    lpdwResult As Long) As Long
```

Its parameters are:

hwnd

> The handle of the target window, or HWND_BROADCAST if the message is to be sent to all top-level windows in the system.

Msg

> The message to send to the target window.

wParam

> The first parameter of the message.

lParam

> The second parameter of the message.

fuFlags

> Determines how the message is sent. Valid values are as follows:

```
Public Const SMTO_NORMAL = &H0 until          'Does not block calling thread
                                              'function returns
Public Const SMTO_BLOCK = &H1                 'Blocks calling thread until
                                              'function returns
Public Const SMTO_ABORTIFHUNG = &H2           'Returns if app is hung
Public Const SMTO_NOTIMEOUTIFNOTHUNG = &H10   '(Win2000 only) Does not return
                                              'from the function if app is not
                                              'hung, even though the timeout
                                              'period may be expired
```

uTimeout

> The timeout value in milliseconds before the function times out and returns.

lpdwResult

> The result of processing the message.

SendMessageTimeout solves the problem of synchronously sending messages; it sends the message to the target window and then waits the number of milliseconds specified in the **uTimeout** parameter. The return value for this function is zero if the function succeeded and nonzero if it timed out or failed. Unfortunately, if you want to get a return value that depends on the message—similar to the return value of *SendMessage*—you are out of luck.

In addition to *SendMessageTimeout, SendNotifyMessage* also addresses the problem of sending a message synchronously. Its syntax is:

```
Public Declare Function SendNotifyMessage Lib "user32" _
        Alias "SendNotifyMessageA" _
        (ByVal hwnd As Long, ByVal Msg As Long, _
        ByVal wParam As Long, ByVal lParam As Long) As Long
```

Its parameters are:

hwnd

> The handle of the target window, or HWND_BROADCAST if the message is to be sent to all top-level windows in the system

wMsg

> The message to send to the target window

wParam

> The first parameter of the message

lParam

> The second parameter of the message

SendNotifyMessage works differently depending on whether the target thread is the same thread as the calling thread or is a different thread. If you use this function to send a message to a window in the same thread, the calling function halts processing until the *SendNotifyMessage* function returns, similar to the *SendMessage* function. If you send the message to a window in a different thread, the function returns immediately. This function returns only an error status (zero on failure, nonzero on success) and no other information.

The next Win32 API message function, *SendMessageCallback*, is asynchronous. It has the following VB declaration:

```
Public Declare Function SendMessageCallback Lib "user32" _
        Alias "SendMessageCallbackA" _
        (ByVal hwnd As Long, ByVal Msg As Long, _
        ByVal wParam As Long, ByVal lParam As Long, _
        ByVal lpResultCallBack As Long, ByVal dwData As Long) As Long
```

Its parameters are:

hwnd

> The handle of the target window, or HWND_BROADCAST if the message is to be sent to all top-level windows in the system

wMsg

> The message to send to the target window

wParam

> The first parameter of the message

lParam

   The second parameter of the message

lpResultCallBack

   The callback function address

dwData

   Data to be passed into the callback function

SendMessageCallback sends a message to a window and returns immediately. The return value is a success or failure (a zero or a nonzero value, respectively). However, this function uses a callback function to retrieve the message-dependent return value. This means that we can use *SendMessage* asynchronously and still get the message-dependent return value—similar to the return value of *SendMessage*.

The callback function is defined in this manner:

```
Public Sub DummyCallback(ByVal hwnd As Long, ByVal uMsg As Long, _
        ByVal dwData As Long, ByVal lResult As Long)
```

Its parameters are:

hwnd

   The handle of the target window

uMsg

   The message to send to the target window

dwData

   The value sent in the *dwData* parameter of the *SendMessageCallback* function

lResult

   The message-dependent result (similar to the result value from *SendMessage*)

Using the *lResult* parameter, we can obtain the same result value that the *SendMessage* function returns.

SendDlgItemMessage sends a message to a control on a dialog. This function has the following declaration:

```
Public Declare Function SendDlgItemMessage Lib "user32" _
        Alias "SendDlgItemMessageA" _
        (ByVal hDlg As Long, ByVal nIDDlgItem As Long, _
        ByVal wMsg As Long, ByVal wParam As Long, _
        ByVal lParam As Long) As Long
```

Its parameters are:

hDlg

   The handle of the target dialog box.

nIDDlgItem

The ID of the control on the dialog box that the *hDlg* handle specifies. You can find the control ID by using Spy++.

wMsg

The message to send to the target window.

wParam

The first parameter of the message.

lParam

The second parameter of the message.

SendDlgItemMessage operates similarly to the *SendMessage* function. Both are synchronous, and both return a value that depends on the message sent. The main difference between these two functions is that you can specify a control ID in *SendDlgItemMessage*. This means you can send a message to a control when you know its ID but not its hWnd.

The final function for sending messages that we will examine is *BroadcastSystemMessage*, which is defined as follows:

```
Public Declare Function BroadcastSystemMessage Lib "user32" _
    Alias "BroadcastSystemMessage" _
    (ByVal dw As Long, pdw As Long, ByVal un As Long, ByVal wParam As Long, _
    ByVal lParam As Long) As Long
```

Its parameters are:

dw

Specifies one of the following broadcasting flags:

BSF_ALLOWSFW

Enables the recipient to set the foreground window in the Windows 2000 system.

BSF_FLUSHDISK

Flushes the disk after each sent message is processed.

BSF_FORCEIFHUNG

Sends the message even if one or more recipients are hung.

BSF_IGNORECURRENTTASK

Prevents the sending application from receiving its own message.

BSF_NOHANG

Stops broadcasting messages if one recipient is hung.

BSF_NOTIMEOUTIFNOTHUNG

Does not time out unless a recipient is hung.

BSF_POSTMESSAGE
> Posts the message instead of sending it.

BSF_QUERY
> Each recipient must respond with a **True** value for the message to be sent to the next recipient.

BSF_SENDNOTIFYMESSAGE
> Uses the *SendNotifyMessage* function to send the message in the Windows 2000 system.

pdw
> Specifies a flag that determines the message recipients. It can be one of the following constants:

BSM_ALLCOMPONENTS
> Broadcasts to all components in the system

BSM_ALLDESKTOPS
> Broadcasts to all desktops in Windows NT/2000 systems

BSM_APPLICATIONS
> Broadcasts to all applications

BSM_INSTALLABLEDRIVERS
> Broadcasts to installable drivers in Windows 9x systems

BSM_NETDRIVER
> Broadcasts to network drivers in Windows 9x systems

BSM_VXDS
> Broadcasts to all system-level device drivers in Windows 9x systems

un
> The message identifier.

wParam
> Additional information for the message specified in *un.*

lParam
> Additional information for the message specified in *un.*

This function returns a positive value if it successfully sends the message to its recipients. It returns a –1 value if it was unable to send the message. Messages are sent to recipients as determined by the *pdw* parameter.

Filter Function Definition

The filter function prototype for this hook is written as follows:

```
Public Function WndProc(ByVal uCode As Long, ByVal wParam As Long, _
                        lParam As CWPSTRUCT) As Long
```

Its parameters are:

uCode

The code the system sends to this filter function. For a `WH_CALLWNDPROC` hook, the only hook code that it sent to this filter function is `HC_ACTION`, which is defined as follows:

```
Private Const HC_ACTION = 0
```

When the system sends this code to the filter function, the sent message can be processed. If `HC_ACTION` is not passed, you should skip message processing and call *CallNextHookEx* immediately.

wParam

If this is nonzero, the current thread sent the message; otherwise, another thread sent the message.

lParam

Pointer to a `CWPSTRUCT` structure.

The return value for this filter function should be the return value of the *CallNextHookEx* function. If this function is not called, the filter function should return a zero. I do not recommend skipping the call to *CallNextHookEx*, though. Failing to call this function will force other filter functions in the chain to not be called.

The `CWPSTRUCT` structure that the *lParam* parameter points to is defined as follows:

```
Public Type CWPSTRUCT
        lParam As Long
        wParam As Long
        message As Long
        hwnd As Long
End Type
```

Its members are:

lParam

The *lParam* parameter for this message

wParam

The *wParam* parameter for this message

message

The message identifier of the intercepted message

hwnd

The window handle that this message is directed to

This structure contains the message information that the *SendMessage* function sent. This is the same information contained in the parameters to the *SendMessage* function, as you can see by examining its prototype earlier in this chapter; there is a one-to-one correspondence between the *SendMessage* parameters and the CWPSTRUCT structure members.

Location of This Hook in the System

The WH_CALLWNDPROC hook is located within the *SendMessage* API function in the Windows 9x and Windows NT 3.51 operating systems. However, in the Windows NT 4.0 and Windows 2000 operating systems, the hook is located immediately before the window procedure. The hook also is located in the thread that receives the sent message. This is different from the Windows 9x and NT 3.51 operating systems, where the hook is fired from within the thread that sent the message. If the window procedure is subclassed, the hook is located before both the sub-classed window procedure and the original window procedure, as Figure 9-1 illustrates.

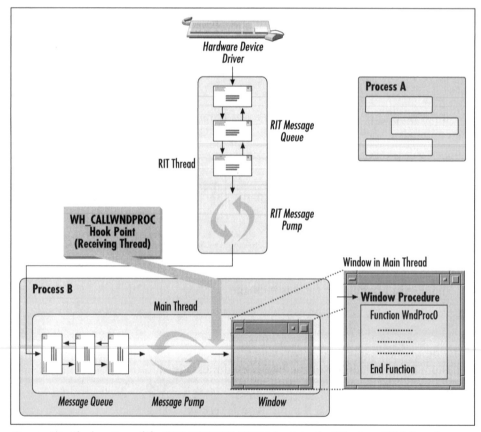

Figure 9-1. The location of the WH_CALLWNDPROC hook in the Windows NT 4.0 and Windows 2000 operating systems

This hook's dependency on the operating system could cause problems, especially when messages are sent from other processes. In this case you would not have access to the same process information from your filter function, depending on the operating system you were using. In both cases, however, the filter function is called before the destination window processes the sent message.

A Thread-Specific Example

The example presented here shows in more detail how to set up and use this hook. A single window is created in this example, which is shown in Figure 9-2. Table 9-1 defines the nondefault properties of the form and its controls. This window has a hook and an unhook button in the CALLWNDPROC frame. You use these buttons to install and remove the hook.

Table 9-1. Nondefault Property Values for the Form and Its Controls

Control	Property	Value
Form	Caption	WH_CALLWNDPROC Hook Test
cmdSendMsg	Caption	SendMsg
cmdSendMsgTO	Caption	SendMsgTO
cmdPostMessage	Caption	PostMessage
cmdSendMsgCB	Caption	SendMsgCB
cmdBroadcastMsg	Caption	BroadcastMsg
cmdSendDlgMsg	Caption	SendDlgMsg
Frame1	Caption	CallWndProc
Text1	MultiLine	True

Each button's functionality is defined as follows:

SendMsg
   Calls the *SendMessage* function.

SendMsgNotify
   Calls the *SendNotifyMessage* function.

SendMsgTO
   Calls the *SendMessageTimeout* function.

SendMsgCB
   Calls the *SendMessageCallback* function. The callback function is called *DummyCallback* and is located in the *Module2.bas* file.

SendDlgMsg
   Calls the *SendDlgItemMessage* function.

BroadcastMsg

Calls the *BroadcastSystemMessage* function.

PostMessage

Calls the *PostMessage* function.

You use the text box on this window to display the values of parameters passed to the WH_CALLWNDPROC filter function.

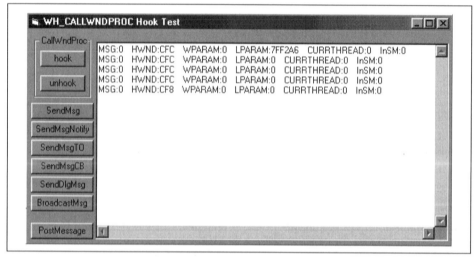

Figure 9-2. Screenshot of the WH_CALLWNDPROC hook example application

The centerpiece of the project is the code module, *Module2.bas*, which includes the following declaration of the *hHook* member variable and the *IsHooked* public variable:

```
Private hHook As Long
Public IsHooked As Boolean
```

You use the *hHook* member variable to hold the handle to the WH_CALLWNDPROC hook. The *IsHooked* global variable is a flag that is set to True while the hook is installed. This prevents us from installing the hook more than once and from shutting down the application before removing the hook. Either action can cause a General Protection Fault (GPF).

As Example 9-1 shows, *SetWndProcHook*, which is responsible for setting the hook in place, uses *SetWindowsHookEx* to install the WH_CALLWNDPROC hook as a thread-specific hook. The *IsHooked* flag is set to True, indicating that the hook is installed.

Example 9-1. Establishing a WH_CALLWNDPROC Hook With SetWndProcHook

```
Public Sub SetWndProcHook()
    If IsHooked Then
```

Example 9-1. Establishing a WH_CALLWNDPROC Hook With SetWndProcHook (continued)

```
        MsgBox "Don't hook CALLWNDPROC twice or you will be unable to unhook it."
    Else
        lpPrevWndProc = SetWindowsHookEx(WH_CALLWNDPROC, AddressOf WndProc, 0, _
                    App.ThreadID)
        IsHooked = True
    End If
End Sub
```

Example 9-2 shows the *RemoveWndProcHook* function, which uninstalls the WH_
CALLWNDPROC hook. It uses *UnhookWindowsHookEx* to remove the WH_
CALLWNDPROC hook from the hook chain. *IsHooked* is set to **False**, allowing the
hook to be reinstalled or the application to be shut down.

Example 9-2. The RemoveWndProcHook Procedure to Remove a WH_CALLWNDPROC Hook

```
Public Sub RemoveWndProcHook()
    Dim temp As Long
    temp = UnhookWindowsHookEx(lpPrevWndProc)
    IsHooked = False
End Sub
```

The *WndProc* function, which is shown in Example 9-3, is the filter function for
this hook. If the *uCode* parameter for this function contains the HC_ACTION code
and the message sent is WM_NULL, the *wParam* and *lParam* parameters for this
function are written to the text box on the form. The declaration of WM_NULL is as
follows:

```
    Const WM_NULL = &H0
```

Simply put, this message does nothing. This message allows the hook to watch for
a specific message that we intentionally send. This message will not adversely
affect our application.

The value that the *InSendMessage* function returns also is written to the text box to
show where the message originated. *InSendMessage* is defined in VB as follows:

```
    Public Declare Function InSendMessage Lib "user32" () As Long
```

This function takes no parameters and returns either a zero or a 1. If the function
returns a zero, the thread that received the message sent the message. If the function returns a 1, a separate thread sent the message.

The final line in this filter function calls *CallNextHookEx* to allow the other filter
functions in this hook chain to process the message.

There is a potential problem with this filter function. If the **If...Then** statement
that checks for the WM_NULL message is not present, the application will crash.
This is because the line that writes the messages to the Text1 text box causes a
WM_CTLCOLOREDIT message to be sent to the text box. This, in turn, causes the

WndProc filter function to be re-entered. Every time text is written to the Text1 text box, the function is re-entered and it never returns. This causes a stack overflow and a GPF. Using the `If...Then` statement to trap only the `WM_NULL` message allows all other messages to be bypassed and processed without the filter function intervening. When using hooks and subclassing, you should always be aware of any code within the subclass procedure or the filter function that could cause other messages to be fired.

Example 9-3. The WH_CALLWNDPROC Filter Function

```
Public Function WndProc(ByVal uCode As Long, ByVal wParam As Long, _
                         lParam As CWPSTRUCT) As Long
   If lParam.message = WM_NULL Then
      Select Case uCode
         Case HC_ACTION
            Form2.Text1.Text = Form2.Text1.Text & "MSG:" & Hex$(lParam.message) _
                           & "   HWND:" & Hex$(lParam.hwnd) _
                           & "   WPARAM:" & Hex$(lParam.wParam) _
                           & "   LPARAM:" & Hex$(lParam.lParam) _
                           & "   CURRTHREAD:" & wParam _
                           & "   InSM:" & InSendMessage() & vbNewLine
            DoEvents
         Case Else
      End Select
   End If

   'WndProc = 0  'Returning zero to try and discard the message does not work.
   WndProc = CallNextHookEx(lpPrevWndProc, uCode, wParam, lParam)
End Function
```

The *DummyCallback* function, which is shown in Example 9-4, is basically a stub function for *SendMessageCallback*, which you use to send a message when the user clicks the *SendMsgCB* button. It does no processing; its only reason for existing is to allow the receiving thread to properly call back to a callback function.

Example 9-4. The Callback Function for the SendMessageCallback Function

```
Public Sub DummyCallback(ByVal hwnd As Long, ByVal uMsg As Long, _
                          ByVal dwData As Long, ByVal lResult As Long)
   'Do nothing and return
End Sub
```

That is it for the code in the *Module2.bas* module. As Example 9-5 shows, most of the code in the *Form1.frm* module consists of event handlers for the command buttons. It also includes the *Form_QueryUnload* shutdown method.

Example 9-5. Source Code for the Form1.frm Module

```
'-----------
'START
```

Example 9-5. Source Code for the Form1.frm Module (continued)

```
'-----------
Private Sub cmdSubclass_Click()
    Text1.Text = ""
    Call SetWndProcHook
End Sub

Private Sub cmdUnSubclass_Click()
    Call RemoveWndProcHook
End Sub

Private Sub cmdSendMsgNotify_Click()
    Call SendNotifyMessage(Form2.hwnd, WM_NULL, 0, 0)
End Sub

Private Sub cmdSendMsg_Click()
    Call SendMessage(Form2.hwnd, WM_NULL, 0, 0)
End Sub

Private Sub cmdSendMsgTO_Click()
    Dim retval As Long
    Call SendMessageTimeout(Form2.hwnd, WM_NULL, 0, 0, SMTO_BLOCK, 2000, retval)
End Sub

Private Sub cmdPostMessage_Click()
    Call PostMessage(Form2.hwnd, WM_NULL, 0, 0)
End Sub

Private Sub cmdSendMsgCB_Click()
    Call SendMessageCallback(Form2.hwnd, WM_NULL, 0, 0, AddressOf DummyCallback, 0)
End Sub

Private Sub cmdBroadcastMsg_Click()
    Dim RetIndicator As Long
    RetIndicator = BroadcastSystemMessage(BSF_NOTIMEOUTIFNOTHUNG, _
            BSM_ALLCOMPONENTS, WM_NULL, 0, 0)
    MsgBox "The return value for BroadcastSystemMessage: " & Hex$(RetIndicator)
End Sub

Private Sub cmdSendDlgMsg_Click()
    Call SendDlgItemMessage(Form2.hwnd, 2, WM_NULL, 0, 0)
    'The control ID (2) can be found by using Spy++
End Sub

'-----------
'CLEANUP
'-----------
Private Sub Form_QueryUnload(Cancel As Integer, UnloadMode As Integer)
    If IsHooked Or IsDBGHooked Then
    Cancel = 1
    MsgBox "Unhook before closing, or the IDE will crash."
    End If
End Sub
```

The code behind the top two buttons installs and removes the WH_CALLWNDPROC hook. The other buttons call each *SendMessage* function, along with a *PostMessage* function. Notice that the *SendMessage* and *PostMessage* functions all send the WM_NULL message. This is because this message does nothing and, therefore, will not affect other applications adversely when broadcast. The *Form_QueryUnload* method stops the application from shutting down if the hook is still installed and presents a message to the user to remove the hook before shutting down.

To use the application, double-click its executable file and click the hook button. At this point the hook is in place and is watching for the WM_NULL message. Clicking the SendMsg, SendMsgNotify, SendMsgTO, SendMsgCB, or SendDlgMsg buttons will place a new line of text in the text box because each *SendMessage* function is sending the WM_NULL message to the Form2 window. The hook's filter function intercepts the message before it is sent and sends a line of information regarding the message to the Text1 text box. After the filter function returns, the *SendMessage* function can send the message to its destination window.

When you click the BroadcastMsg button, a single WM_NULL message is sent to all the top-level windows and device drivers in the system through *BroadcastSystemMessage*. A different line is added to the Text1 text box for each WM_NULL message sent. The window handle is displayed, indicating to which window the WM_NULL message was sent. (You also can send messages to top-level windows by using the HWND_BROADCAST constant in the *hwnd* parameter of the *SendMessage* function. Using this function will not send messages to device drivers, which is what happens when you use *BroadcastSystemMessage*.)

A return value is set in the *lpdwRecipients* parameter of the *BroadcastSystemMessage* function after the function returns. The return value defines what windows or device drivers received the message. ANDing this result with the following constants provides information about which windows or device drivers received the broadcast message:

```
Public Const BSM_ALLCOMPONENTS = &H0
Public Const BSM_VXDS = &H1
Public Const BSM_NETDRIVER = &H2
Public Const BSM_INSTALLABLEDRIVERS = &H4
Public Const BSM_APPLICATIONS = &H8
Public Const BSM_ALLDESKTOPS = &H10
```

Clicking the PostMessage button posts a message to this application's message queue. This will not display a new line in the Text1 text box. This is the correct behavior because the message is being posted and not sent through one of the *SendMessage* functions.

Substituting the BSF_POSTMESSAGE constant in the *dwFlags* parameter of the *BroadcastSystemMessage* function causes messages to be posted instead of sent to all windows and device drivers. If this substitution is made, the `WH_CALLWNDPROC` hook will not be able to intercept the posted message, and no text will be placed in the Text1 text box.

Caveats

The main thing to remember when using this hook is that it captures only messages that are sent using the *SendMessage* function. It will not capture messages that you post to the message queue using the *PostMessage* function. For the case of posted messages, you should use the `WH_GETMESSAGE` hook, which is discussed in Chapter 11.

You should take care when using any hook, as performance can be seriously degraded. Using a thread-specific hook can degrade performance for a single thread because it operates from within that thread only. A system-wide hook resides in a DLL that is injected into all running processes. Therefore, if the hook's filter function code puts undue strain on the system, every thread in the system can slow to a crawl. This causes the entire system to act sluggishly. When writing filter functions for hooks of either scope, you should exit the code as soon as possible. By this I mean that if the hook intercepts messages that are of no interest, you should exit the filter function immediately. As we saw earlier, windows are constantly being bombarded with messages. Spending time processing a few of those messages most likely will not put a strain on the system. However, spending time processing all messages will certainly place a strain on the system.

There is a bug using this hook on the Windows 95 operating system. This bug is described in article Q149862. In short, when this hook is installed as a system-wide hook and the user presses the ALT-ESC key combination, the DLL is injected into the *KERNEL32.DLL* process. When the hook is released, the hook DLL is not removed from the *KERNEL32.DLL* process. The only solution is to restart the machine.

10

WH_CALLWNDPROCRET

The next logical choice of hooks to discuss is the WH_CALLWNDPROCRET hook. This hook intercepts messages not only after the WH_CALLWNDPROC hook has intercepted the message, but also after the window procedure has processed the message. This chapter will discuss the WH_CALLWNDPROCRET hook and compare and contrast it with the WH_CALLWNDPROC hook, which was discussed in Chapter 9.

How WH_CALLWNDPROCRET Works

Like the WH_CALLWNDPROC hook, the WH_CALLWNDPROCRET hook is used to intercept messages sent through the various *SendMessage* function types. However, WH_CALLWNDPROCRET intercepts its messages later than WH_CALLWNDPROC does: whereas the latter intercepts messages before they are processed by their window procedure, the former intercepts messages only after the window procedure has processed them. As a result, you once again cannot modify or discard the message intercepted through this hook, in this case because message processing is largely complete.

You can use this hook to monitor sent messages, similar to the WH_CALLWNDPROC hook. However, the WH_CALLWNDPROCRET hook provides extra information that WH_CALLWNDPROC does not. First, it makes available the return value of the call to the *SendMessage* function. Second, the *wParam* specifies whether the sent message originates from the same process in which the hook is installed, or from another process. An application could use this hook to listen for a specific message that is broadcast from another application and take some action based on receiving that message.

You can use this hook as a thread-specific hook, or you can place it in a dynamic link library (DLL) and use it as a system-wide hook. A thread-specific hook intercepts all messages within the thread in which it is installed. When a hook is installed as a system-wide hook, it has to be placed in a DLL. This DLL is injected into every process so that the hook can operate on all messages in the system. See Chapter 3 for a thorough discussion of this topic.

Using the WH_CALLWNDPROC and WH_CALLWNDPROCRET hooks together, you have the ability to watch for sent messages and determine if any of their parameters were modified by a subclass procedure or possibly by a completely different hook that is installed. This is how it would operate:

1. The WH_CALLWNDPROC hook captures the message, where the message parameter values are stored in the application.

2. The window procedure and any subclass window procedures that might have been installed process the message.

3. The message is sent to the WH_CALLWNDPROCRET hook, where the message parameters are examined and compared to the original parameters that were sent to the WH_CALLWNDPROC hook. If they are different, you know that somewhere in the window procedure—or perhaps in a subclass window procedure—the message parameters were modified.

Filter Function Definition

The filter function prototype for this hook is written as follows:

```
Public Function WndProcRet(ByVal uCode As Long, _
                ByVal wParam As Long, _
                lParam As CWPRETSTRUCT) As Long
```

Its parameters are:

uCode

The code the system sends to this filter function. The HC_ACTION code is the only hook code that the system sends to this filter function. This code is defined as:

```
Private Const HC_ACTION = 0
```

When this code is sent to the filter function, the sent message can be processed. If HC_ACTION is not passed, you should skip message processing and call *CallNextHookEx* immediately.

wParam

Specifies which process the message originated from. If its value is 1, the message originated from a different process. If its value is zero, the message originated from the current process.

lParam

Holds a pointer to the CWPRETSTRUCT structure.

The return value for this filter function should be the return value of the *CallNextHookEx* function. If this function is not called, the filter function should return a zero. I do not recommend skipping the call to *CallNextHookEx*, though. Failing to call this function will force other filter functions in the chain to not be called.

The definition for the *uCode* parameter is exactly the same for this hook as it is for the WH_CALLWNDPROC hook. The *wParam* and *lParam* parameters of this hook contain different information compared to the WH_CALLWNDPROC hook. The WH_ CALLWNDPROCRET hook uses *wParam* to determine which process the message originated from. The WH_CALLWNDPROC hook uses it to determine which thread this message originated from. The *lParam* parameter for each hook contains a pointer to a structure specific to that hook.

The CWPRETSTRUCT structure that the *lParam* parameter points to is defined as follows:

```
Public Type CWPRETSTRUCT
        lResult As Long
        lParam As Long
        wParam As Long
        message As Long
        hwnd As Long
End Type
```

It has the following members:

lResult
   The return value of the window procedure after processing the message

lParam
   The second parameter of the message

wParam
   The first parameter of the message

message
   The message identifier

hwnd
   The window handle that the message is directed to

This structure is similar to the CWPSTRUCT structure that the WH_CALLWNDPROC hook uses, except that this structure contains an extra member, *lResult*. Because the hook intercepts the message after the window procedure returns, this value is available.

Location of This Hook in the System

This hook is located after the window procedure finishes processing the sent message, as Figure 10-1 shows. This hook intercepts the message from inside the thread that received the sent message.

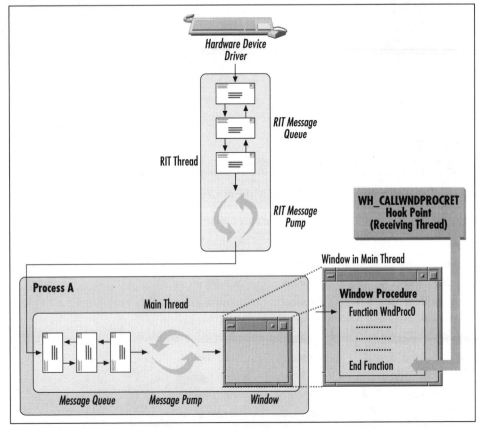

Figure 10-1. The location of the WH_CALLWNDPROCRET function in the messaging system

A Thread-Specific Example

To better illustrate this hook's function and position in the messaging system, I will modify the thread-specific example for the WH_CALLWNDPROC hook to incorporate the WH_CALLWNDPROCRET hook. As Figure 10-2 shows, the interface is similar to the example in Chapter 9, except for the output.

Table 10-1 defines the nondefault properties of the form and its controls.

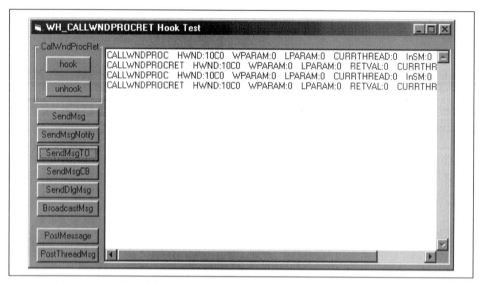

Figure 10-2. A screenshot of the WH_CALLWNDPROCRET example application

Table 10-1. Nondefault Property Values for the Form and Its Controls

Control	Property	Value
Form	Caption	WH_CALLWNDPROC Hook Test
cmdSendMsg	Caption	SendMsg
cmdSendMsgTO	Caption	SendMsgTO
cmdPostMessage	Caption	PostMessage
cmdPostThreadMsg	Caption	PostThreadMsg
cmdSendMsgCB	Caption	SendMsgCB
cmdBroadcastMsg	Caption	BroadcastMsg
cmdSendDlgMsg	Caption	SendDlgMsg
cmdSendMsgNotify	Caption	SendMsgNotify
Frame1	Caption	CallWndProc
Text1	MultiLine	True

The code for this example is very similar to the code for the WH_CALLWNDPROC example. I will focus the following discussion on the changes to the code, starting with the *Module2.bas* module.

A single private member variable, *bProcRetHook*, was added to the code (BAS) module to hold the hook handle for the WH_CALLWNDPROCRET hook. The public and module-level variables declared in the BAS module are now:

```
Private hProcRetHook As Long
Private hProcHook As Long

Public IsHooked As Boolean
```

The *SetHooks* function, which is shown in Example 10-1, adds a line of code that calls *SetWindowsHookEx* to set the WH_CALLWNDPROCRET hook.

Example 10-1. The SetHooks Function to Install the WH_CALLWNDPROCRET Hook

```
Public Sub SetHooks()
    If IsHooked Then
        MsgBox "Don't hook CALLWNDPROC twice or you will be unable to unhook it."
    Else
        hProcHook = SetWindowsHookEx(WH_CALLWNDPROC, AddressOf WndProc, 0, _
                    App.ThreadID)
        hProcRetHook = SetWindowsHookEx(WH_CALLWNDPROCRET, AddressOf WndProcRet, _
                    0, App.ThreadID)
        IsHooked = True
    End If
End Sub
```

The *RemoveHooks* function, which is shown in Example 10-2, adds a line of code that calls *UnhookWindowsHookEx* to remove the WH_CALLWNDPROCRET hook.

Example 10-2. The RemoveHooks Function to Remove the WH_CALLWNDPROCRET Hook

```
Public Sub RemoveHooks()
    Dim temp As Long
    temp = UnhookWindowsHookEx(hProcRetHook)
    temp = UnhookWindowsHookEx(hProcHook)
    IsHooked = False
End Sub
```

The *WndProcRet* function, which is shown in Example 10-3, is the filter function for the WH_CALLWNDPROCRET hook. This function outputs the name of the hook function, the *wParam* value, and the values of the CWPRETSTRUCT structure. A call is made to *CallNextHookEx* at the end of the function, and the value that this function returns is passed on as the return value of the filter function.

Example 10-3. The WndProcRet Filter Function for the WM_CALLWNDPROCRET Hook

```
Public Function WndProcRet(ByVal uCode As Long, ByVal wParam As Long, _
                    lParam As CWPRETSTRUCT) As Long
    If lParam.message = WM_NULL Then
        Select Case uCode
            Case HC_ACTION
                Form2.Text1.Text = Form2.Text1.Text & "CALLWNDPROCRET" _
                            & "   HWND:" & Hex$(lParam.hwnd) _
                            & "   WPARAM:" & Hex$(lParam.wParam) _
                            & "   LPARAM:" & Hex$(lParam.lParam) _
                            & "   RETVAL:" & Hex$(lParam.lResult) _
                            & "   CURRTHREAD:" & Hex$(wParam) _
                            & "   InSM:" & InSendMessage() & vbNewLine
                DoEvents
            Case Else
```

Example 10-3. The WndProcRet Filter Function for the WM_CALLWNDPROCRET Hook (continued)

```
      End Select
   End If


   WndProcRet = CallNextHookEx(hProcRetHook, uCode, wParam, lParam)
End Function
```

The *WndProc* function shown in Example 10-4 is the filter function for the WH_ CALLWNDPROC hook.

Example 10-4. The WndProc Filter Function for the WM_CALLWNDPROC Hook

```
Public Function WndProc(ByVal uCode As Long, ByVal wParam As Long, _
                        lParam As CWPSTRUCT) As Long
   If lParam.message = WM_NULL Then
      Select Case uCode
         Case HC_ACTION
            Form2.Text1.Text = Form2.Text1.Text & "CALLWNDPROC" _
                            & "    HWND:" & Hex$(lParam.hwnd) _
                            & "    WPARAM:" & Hex$(lParam.wParam) _
                            & "    LPARAM:" & Hex$(lParam.lParam) _
                            & "    CURRTHREAD:" & wParam _
                            & "    InSM:" & InSendMessage() & vbNewLine
          . DoEvents
         Case Else
      End Select
   End If


   WndProc = CallNextHookEx(hProcHook, uCode, wParam, lParam)
End Function
```

The *DummyCallback* function shown in Example 10-5 is basically a stub function for *SendMessageCallback*. It does no processing; its only reason for existing is to allow the receiving thread to properly call back to a callback function.

Example 10-5. The Callback Function for the SendMessageCallback API Function

```
Public Sub DummyCallback(ByVal hwnd As Long, ByVal uMsg As Long, _
               ByVal dwData As Long, ByVal lResult As Long)
   'Do nothing and return
End Sub
```

Example 10-6 shows the code contained in the *Form2.frm* module.

Example 10-6. Source Code for the Form2.frm Module

```
Option Explicit


Private Sub cmdHook_Click()
   Text1.Text = ""
   Call SetHooks
End Sub
```

Example 10-6. Source Code for the Form2.frm Module (continued)

```vb
Private Sub cmdUnHook_Click()
    Call RemoveHooks
End Sub

Private Sub cmdSendMsgNotify_Click()
    Call SendNotifyMessage(Form2.hwnd, WM_NULL, 0, 0)
End Sub

Private Sub cmdSendMsg_Click()
    Call SendMessage(Form2.hwnd, WM_NULL, 0, 0)        'HWND_TOPMOST
End Sub

Private Sub cmdSendMsgTO_Click()
    Dim retval As Long
    Call SendMessageTimeout(Form2.hwnd, WM_NULL, 0, 0, SMTO_BLOCK, 2000, _
                            retval)
End Sub

Private Sub cmdPostMessage_Click()
    Call PostMessage(Form2.hwnd, WM_NULL, 0, 0)
End Sub

Private Sub cmdSendMsgCB_Click()
    Call SendMessageCallback(Form2.hwnd, WM_NULL, 0, 0, _
                             AddressOf DummyCallback, 0)
End Sub

Private Sub cmdBroadcastMsg_Click()
    Dim RetIndicator As Long
    Call BroadcastSystemMessage(BSF_NOTIMEOUTIFNOTHUNG, RetIndicator, _
                                WM_NULL, 0, 0)
    MsgBox "The return value for BroadcastSystemMessage: " & Hex$(RetIndicator)
End Sub

Private Sub cmdSendDlgMsg_Click()
    Call SendDlgItemMessage(Form2.hwnd, 2, WM_NULL, 0, 0)
    'The control ID can be found by using Spy++
End Sub

Private Sub cmdPostThreadMsg_Click()
    Call PostThreadMessage(App.ThreadID, WM_NULL, 0, 0)
End Sub

'-----------
'CLEANUP
'-----------
Private Sub Form_QueryUnload(Cancel As Integer, UnloadMode As Integer)
    If IsHooked Then
    Cancel = 1
    MsgBox "Unhook before closing, or the application will crash."
    End If
End Sub
```

When you click the hook button, the WH_CALLWNDPROC and WH_CALLWNDPROCRET hooks are both installed. Clicking either the PostMessage or the PostThreadMsg buttons does not produce any output. Once again, this hook intercepts only sent messages, not posted messages.

When you click any of the SendMessage buttons, the output to the text box is as follows:

```
CALLWNDPROC
CALLWNDPROCRET
```

This is the expected output. We can see this by looking at the locations of each hook in the messaging system.

Initially, the *SendMessage* function is called. This function passes a message directly to the message loop of the thread that contains the destination window. The WH_CALLWNDPROC hook is called before the message is passed on to the window procedure; the operating system determines the location (see Chapter 9 for more information). After the WH_CALLWNDPROC hook returns, the message is passed on to the window procedure. If the window procedure happens to be sub-classed, the message is first passed to the subclass function(s) and then on to the window procedure. When the window procedure is finished processing the message, the function returns and the WH_CALLWNDPROCRET hook then intercepts the message and its return value. After this hook is finished processing, it passes the message on to the next hook in the hook chain, if one exists. After each hook has processed the message, control is returned to the *SendMessage* function. The *SendMessage* function then returns control to the code that called it—in this case, the Visual Basic (VB) code in the *Form2.frm* module.

To further investigate the order of events for both hooks, modify the above functions as follows. First modify the SendMessage button (*Command4_Click*) to appear as shown in Example 10-7; modified code is shown in boldface.

Example 10-7. The Modified Event Handler for the SendMsg Button

```
Private Sub Command4_Click()
    Call SendMessage(Text1.hwnd, WM_SETTEXT, 0, "Sent Text")
End Sub
```

Calling *SendMessage* in this manner will send the text "Sent Text" to the Text1 text box.

Next, modify the *WndProc* function so that it appears as shown in Example 10-8; once again, changed lines are shown in boldface.

Example 10-8. The Modified WndProc Function

```
Public Function WndProc(ByVal uCode As Long, ByVal wParam As Long, _
                 lParam As CWPSTRUCT) As Long
```

Example 10-8. The Modified WndProc Function (continued)

```
If lParam.message = WM_SETTEXT And lParam.hwnd = Form2.Text1.hwnd Then
    Select Case uCode
        Case HC_ACTION
            MsgBox "Inside the WH_CALLWNDPROC hook."
        Case Else
    End Select
End If

    WndProc = CallNextHookEx(hProcHook, uCode, wParam, lParam)
End Function
```

This filter function waits for the WM_SETTEXT message to be sent to the Text1 text box. When this message is sent, the filter function displays a message box with the text "Inside the WH_CALLWNDPROC hook". We would not want to try to place a message in the text box in this function because this would automatically cause a WM_SETTEXT message to be sent to the text box with the relevant text inside of the message structure. The filter function would then be re-entered when it detected this message. Therefore, the function would never return and would eventually GPF with a stack overflow. Using the message box circumvents this problem.

Finally, you should modify the *WndProcRet* function to appear as shown in Example 10-9 (modified lines are in boldface).

Example 10-9. The Modified WndProcRet Function

```
Public Function WndProcRet(ByVal uCode As Long, ByVal wParam As Long, _
                           lParam As CWPRETSTRUCT) As Long
    If lParam.message = WM_SETTEXT And lParam.hwnd = Form2.Text1.hwnd Then
        Select Case uCode
            Case HC_ACTION
                MsgBox "Inside the WH_CALLWNDPROCRET hook."
            Case Else
        End Select
    End If

    WndProcRet = CallNextHookEx(hProcRetHook, uCode, wParam, lParam)
End Function
```

Once again, we use the message box to declare that the code inside the WH_CALLWNDPROCRET filter function is being executed.

After you make these changes, compile the application and execute it. Before going any further, you need to start Spy++ and set it to watch for all WM_SETTEXT messages sent to this application's Text1 text box.

Click the hook button on the application to install both hooks. Next, click the SendMessage button. The events, as they occur, happen as follows:

1. The SendMessage function is called, sending the WM_SETTEXT message with the string "Sent Text" to the Text1 text box. In Figure 10-3, Spy++ shows that

the WM_SETTEXT message has been sent to the destination window. The third item displayed in Spy++ is an S, meaning that the *SendMessage* function has sent the message. An R means that the *SendMessage* function has returned.

2. The WH_CALLWNDPROC function intercepts the WM_SETTEXT message before it gets to the window procedure of the destination window.

3. The WH_CALLWNDPROC function displays the message box with the text "Inside the WH_CALLWNDPROC hook".

4. The WM_SETTEXT message is passed on to any other WH_CALLWNDPROC hooks in this hook chain.

5. The message is sent on to the window procedure to be processed. Processing this message sends the "Sent Text" string to the Text1 text box, as Figure 10-4 shows.

6. After exiting the window procedure, the WM_SETTEXT message is sent to the WH_CALLWNDPROCRET hook.

7. The filter function for the WH_CALLWNDPROCRET hook displays a message box with the string "Inside the WH_CALLWNDPROCRET hook". Examining Spy++ reveals that the *SendMessage* function has not returned at this point.

8. The WM_SETTEXT message is passed on to any other WH_CALLWNDPROCRET hooks in this hook chain.

9. Finally, the *SendMessage* function returns control to the code that executed it. As Figure 10-5 shows, Spy++ shows that the *SendMessage* function has indeed returned.

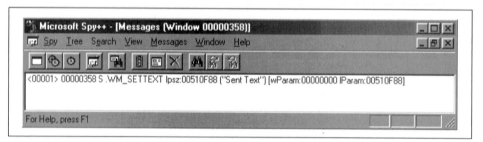

Figure 10-3. The state of the WM_SETTEXT message before the WH_CALLWNDPROC hook finishes processing it

Caveats

As with the WH_CALLWNDPROC hook, the main thing to remember is that this hook captures only messages that are sent using the *SendMessage* function. This function will not capture messages that are posted to the message queue using the *PostMessage* function. In the case of posted messages, you should use the WH_GETMESSAGE hook; this hook is discussed in Chapter 11.

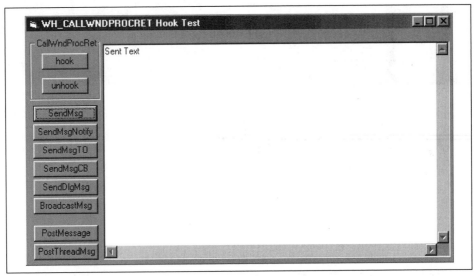

Figure 10-4. The output of the application after the window procedure has processed the WM_SETTEXT message

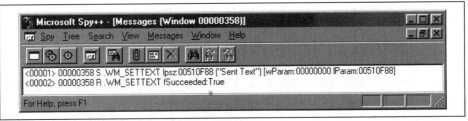

Figure 10-5. The state of the WM_SETTEXT message before the WH_CALLWNDPROCRET hook finishes processing it

The other thing to remember is that this hook captures messages after the window procedure has processed the message. The WH_CALLWNDPROC hook captures the sent message before the window procedure has processed it.

Take care when using any hook because performance can be seriously degraded. Using a thread-specific hook can degrade performance for a single thread because it operates from within that thread only. A system-wide hook resides in a DLL that is injected into all running processes. Therefore, if the hook's filter function code puts undue strain on the system, every thread in the system can slow to a crawl. This causes the entire system to act sluggishly. When writing filter functions for hooks of either scope, you should exit the code as early as possible. By this I mean that if the hook intercepts messages that are of no interest, you should exit the filter function immediately.

11

WH_GETMESSAGE

At first glance, the WH_GETMESSAGE hook seems to be similar to the WH_CALLWNDPROC and WH_CALLWNDPROCRET hooks. As we shall see, though, this hook is very different from the other two hooks. This chapter will focus on the WH_GETMESSAGE hook, while also comparing and contrasting it with the WH_CALLWNDPROC and WH_CALLWNDPROCRET hooks.

How WH_GETMESSAGE Works

You use the WH_GETMESSAGE hook to intercept only posted (and not sent) messages. Using this hook, you also can modify a message before the window procedure processes it. These are the two main differences between this hook and the WH_CALLWNDPROC and WH_CALLWNDPROCRET hooks. The WH_CALLWNDPROC and WH_CALLWNDPROCRET hooks only intercept sent messages and cannot modify the messages they intercept.

You can use this hook as a thread-specific hook, or you can place it in a dynamic link library (DLL) and use it as a system-wide hook. A thread-specific hook intercepts all messages within the thread in which it is installed. When you install a hook as a system-wide hook, you must place it in a DLL. This DLL is injected into every process so that the hook can operate on all messages in the system. Chapter 3 provides a thorough discussion of this concept.

Before explaining how this hook operates, I need to discuss both the *GetMessage* and the *PeekMessage* functions. *GetMessage* retrieves a single message from the message queue of the thread in which this function was called. This function is used mostly in a message loop for an application. *GetMessage* is defined as follows:

```
Public Declare Function GetMessage Lib "user32" Alias "GetMessageA" _
      (lpMsg As MSG, ByVal hwnd As Long, ByVal wMsgFilterMin As Long, _
      ByVal wMsgFilterMax As Long) As Long
```

GetMessage has the following parameters:

lpMsg

A Long pointer to an MSG structure that receives the message.

hwnd

The handle of the window whose messages are to be read from the queue. If this is zero, all messages will be read.

wMsgFilterMin

The minimum message value that is read from the message queue.

wMsgFilterMax

The maximum message value that is retrieved from the message queue. If this value is zero, all messages starting with the *wMsgFilterMin* value are read from the message queue.

If an error occurs, this function will return −1. If this function processes a WM_QUIT message, it will return a zero; otherwise, it returns a nonzero value. It also returns a zero when the WM_QUIT message is processed to allow the message loop to exit and the application to shut down.

PeekMessage is similar to *GetMessage* in that it gets a message from the message queue of the thread in which this function is called. The main difference is that *PeekMessage* does not automatically remove the message from the message queue, as *GetMessage* does. *PeekMessage* is defined as follows:

```
Public Declare Function PeekMessage Lib "user32" Alias "PeekMessageA" _
      (lpMsg As MSG, ByVal hwnd As Long, ByVal wMsgFilterMin As Long, _
      ByVal wMsgFilterMax As Long, ByVal wRemoveMsg As Long) As Long
```

Its parameters are:

lpMsg

A Long pointer to an MSG structure.

hwnd

The handle of the window whose messages are to be read from the queue. If this is zero, all messages will be read.

wMsgFilterMin

The minimum message value that is read from the message queue.

wMsgFilterMax

The maximum message value that is retrieved from the message queue. If this value is zero, all messages starting with the *wMsgFilterMin* value are read from the message queue.

wRemoveMsg

> If this is set to PM_REMOVE (1), the message is read and then removed from the queue. If this is set to PM_NOREMOVE (0), the message is read but left on the queue.

If no messages are on the queue, the return value for this function is zero. A non-zero return value means that a message was read from the queue. You can use the *PeekMessage* function in a message loop in place of the *GetMessage* function. You do this to allow background processing to be performed when the application has no more messages to process in its message queue. For a more detailed discussion of this technique, see Chapter 8.

The WH_GETMESSAGE hook intercepts messages as either the *GetMessage* or the *PeekMessage* functions are pulling them off of the message queue.

When using this hook, be concerned with performance. As you know, the raw input thread (RIT) posts mouse and keyboard input to each thread. At least one *GetMessage* and/or *PeekMessage* function is called for each message. That means these functions make the same number of calls to the WH_GETMESSAGE hook's filter function. Because the potential exists for messages, especially WM_MOUSEMOVE messages, to be posted at a furious rate to the thread or threads to which this hook is attached, we must take care to not execute unneeded code from within the filter function. Using WM_GETMESSAGE as a system-wide hook only compounds this problem. With a system-wide hook, the filter function is called every time a *GetMessage* or *PeekMessage* function is called throughout every thread in the system. This can very quickly cause performance to degrade.

Note also that the WH_GETMESSAGE hook only intercepts messages before the window procedure, or any subclass procedure, receives the message. There is no type of WH_GETMESSAGE hook that intercepts messages after the window procedure returns—similar to how the WH_CALLWNDPROCRET hook operates.

To better understand this hook as well as the example presented in this chapter, it is useful to understand what a posted message is and how it differs from a sent message. A posted message is a message that is placed at the end of a thread's message queue. The messages in the queue are processed in the order in which they are received. When an application posts a message, the application continues processing and does not wait to see if the posted message is processed correctly, or at all. In contrast, a sent message is sent directly to one or more windows, not to a thread's message queue. Bypassing the message queue allows the sent message to be processed immediately. Sent messages are usually processed synchronously; that is, the application that sends the message must wait until the target window finishes processing it. One function, *SendMessageCallback*, allows a sent message to be processed asynchronously. Sending a message allows the function that sent the message to receive a value indicating if the sent message was processed correctly. Chapter 9 discusses sending messages in greater detail.

The first and most commonly used method of posting messages is the *PostMessage* function. This function simply posts a message to the message queue of one or more threads. After posting the message, the *PostMessage* function returns. It does not wait for a response to the posted message, as does *SendMessage*. This function is defined as follows:

```
Public Declare Function PostMessage Lib "user32" Alias "PostMessageA" _
        (ByVal hwnd As Long, ByVal wMsg As Long, _
        ByVal wParam As Long, ByVal lParam As Long) As Long
```

PostMessage has the following parameters:

hwnd

> The window handle that the message is directed to. If this parameter is set to HWND_BROADCAST, the message is posted to all top-level windows in the system. If this parameter is set to NULL, the message is posted to the message queue of the thread in which this function was called.

uMsg

> The message identifier.

lParam

> The second parameter of the message.

wParam

> The first parameter of the message.

The return value is nonzero if the function succeeded in posting the message; otherwise, it returns a zero value.

The next method of posting messages is *PostThreadMessage*. Instead of using a window handle to determine which message queue is to receive the message, it uses the actual thread ID. This function also does not wait for a response to the posted message. This function is defined as follows:

```
Public Declare Function PostThreadMessage Lib "user32" _
        Alias "PostThreadMessageA" _
        (ByVal idThread As Long, ByVal msg As Long, _
        ByVal wParam As Long, ByVal lParam As Long) As Long
```

Its parameters are:

idThread

> The thread identifier that the message is posted to. You can determine this value using the Visual Basic (VB) App.ThreadID property, or by using either

of the *GetCurrentThreadID* or *GetWindowThreadProcessId* application programming interface (API) functions.

uMsg

The message identifier.

lParam

The second parameter of the message.

wParam

The first parameter of the message.

If the function succeeds in posting the message it returns a nonzero value; otherwise, it returns a zero value.

The last method is *PostQuitMessage*. This function simply posts a WM_QUIT message to the message queue of the thread in which it was called. The WM_QUIT message then causes the application to exit its message loop and shut down. I did not use this function in the example application for one reason. When the message loop receives the WM_QUIT message, it exits without first removing all the installed hooks, causing the application to crash. The syntax of *PostQuitMessage* is:

```
Public Declare Sub PostQuitMessage Lib "user32" Alias "PostQuitMessage" _
        (ByVal nExitCode As Long)
```

Its single parameter is:

nExitCode

A code that is sent to the **wParam** parameter of the WM_QUIT message.

No values are returned from this function.

 It might be helpful to note that Windows 2000 can contain up to 10,000 messages in any one message queue; this should be sufficient for any application. The lowest value that you can set for this size is 4,000 messages. You set this value through the following registry key:

```
HKEY_LOCAL_MACHINE\SOFTWARE\Microsoft\Windows NT\
CurrentVersion\Windows\USERPostMessageLimit
```

You should set the default value of this key to a number between 4,000 and 10,000.

Filter Function Definition

The filter function prototype for this hook is written as follows:

```
Public Function GetMsgProc(ByVal uCode As Long, ByVal wParam As Long, _
                lParam As MSG) As Long
```

Its parameters are:

uCode

> The code that the system sends to this filter function. HC_ACTION is the only hook code the system sends to this filter function. This code is defined as follows:

```
Private Const HC_ACTION = 0
```

> When the system sends this code to the filter function, the sent message can be processed. If HC_ACTION is not passed in, you should skip message processing and call *CallNextHookEx* immediately.

wParam

> Specifies whether the message was removed from the message queue. If this value is set to PM_NOREMOVE, the message was not removed from the message queue. If this value is set to PM_REMOVE, the message was removed from the message queue.

lParam

> Holds a pointer to an MSG structure.

The return value for this filter function should be the return value of the *CallNextHookEx* function. If this function is not called, the filter function should return a zero. I do not recommend skipping the call to *CallNextHookEx*, though. Failing to call this function will force other filter functions in the chain to not be called.

When the filter function returns, the *wParam* parameter of this filter function contains a value that specifies whether the message was removed from the message queue. If the value of this parameter is set to PM_REMOVE, either *GetMessage* was used or *PeekMessage* was used with the PM_REMOVE flag. If the value of this parameter is set to PM_NOREMOVE, *PeekMessage* was used with the PM_NOREMOVE flag.

The *lParam* parameter holds a pointer to an MSG structure, which is defined as follows:

```
Public Type MSG
    hwnd As Long
    message As Long
    wParam As Long
    lParam As Long
    time As Long
    pt As POINTAPI
End Type
```

The members of this structure are defined as follows:

hwnd

    Handle to the window that this message is directed to

message

    The ID of this message

wParam

    Value depends on the message sent

lParam

    Value depends on the message sent

time

    The time that this message was posted

pt

    The mouse x and y coordinates at the time this message was posted

Location of This Hook in the System

This hook is located inside both the *GetMessage* and *PeekMessage* functions. These functions make up part of the message loop for a thread, as Figure 11-1 shows. When either function retrieves a message from the message queue, the WH_ GETMESSAGE filter function is called. When the filter function returns, the *GetMessage* or *PeekMessage* function finishes its processing and then returns. If these functions are running within a message loop, the *DispatchMessage* function inside of the message loop passes the message on to the window procedure. This is why we cannot discard a message using this hook. Even though we try to discard the message from within the filter function, it is still passed on to *DispatchMessage* to be sent to the correct window procedure for processing. The filter function has no control over this.

You can use something of a hack to discard messages with this hook, however. Simply modify the message contained in the *lParam* parameter to a WM_NULL message. The WM_NULL message is then passed on to the window procedure, and not the original message. To do this, add this code before *CallNextHookEx* is called:

```
lParam.Message = WM_NULL
lParam.lParam = 0
lParam.wParam = 0
```

A Thread-Specific Example

The example presented here, which is shown in Figure 11-2, will build on what you learned in Chapter 9 and Chapter 10. By following this example, you will see

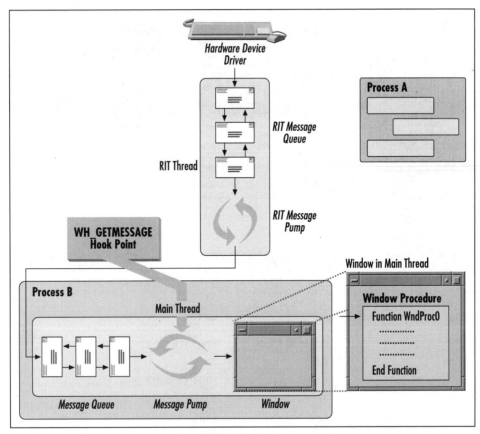

Figure 11-1. The location of the WH_GETMESSAGE function in the messaging system

the differences between the WH_CALLWNDPROC, WH_CALLWNDPROCRET, and WH_GETMESSAGE hooks. This example installs the three hooks. Now, when you click the PostMessage and PostThreadMsg buttons, you will see the WH_GETMESSAGE hook display messages in the text box.

Table 11-1 lists the nondefault properties of the form and its controls.

You use this application in the same way you used the sample applications in the previous two chapters. Click the hook button to install all three hooks, and then click each of the lower buttons shown in Figure 11-2 to send and post the WM_NULL message. The text box will indicate which hook intercepted the WM_NULL message, as well as the available parameters for that hook. There is no difference from the previous applications in output displayed when you click the SendMessage type buttons. When you click the PostMessage and PostThreadMsg buttons, the WH_GETMESSAGE hook now displays a line of text indicating that it has intercepted the posted message.

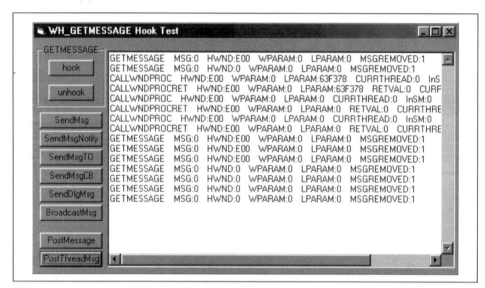

Figure 11-2. Screenshot of example application

Table 11-1. Nondefault Properties of the Form and Its Controls

Object Type	Property Name	Property Value
Form	Name	Form2
Form	Caption	"WH_GETMESSAGE Hook Test"
Form	Top	420
Form	Left	132
Form	Height	1572
Form	Width	6972
Text Box	Name	Text1
Text Box	Multiline	True
Text Box	Top	240
Text Box	Left	1440
Text Box	Height	1212
Text Box	Width	5412
Text Box	ScrollBars	3-Both
Frame	Caption	"GETMESSAGE"
Frame	Name	Frame1
Frame	Top	120
Frame	Left	120
Frame	Height	1335
Frame	Width	1155
Command Button1	Name	cmdHook

Table 11-1. Nondefault Properties of the Form and Its Controls (continued)

Object Type	Property Name	Property Value
Command Button1	Caption	"hook"
Command Button1	Top	300
Command Button1	Left	120
Command Button1	Height	315
Command Button1	Width	915
Command Button2	Name	cmdUnHook
Command Button2	Caption	"unhook"
Command Button2	Top	780
Command Button2	Left	120
Command Button2	Height	315
Command Button2	Width	915
Command Button3	Name	cmdSendMsg
Command Button3	Caption	"SendMsg"
Command Button3	Top	1440
Command Button3	Left	120
Command Button3	Height	315
Command Button3	Width	915
Command Button4	Name	cmdSendMsgNotify
Command Button4	Caption	"SendMsgNotify"
Command Button4	Top	1800
Command Button4	Left	120
Command Button4	Height	315
Command Button4	Width	915
Command Button5	Name	cmdSendMsgTO
Command Button5	Caption	"SendMsgTO"
Command Button5	Top	1275
Command Button5	Left	120
Command Button5	Height	315
Command Button5	Width	915
Command Button6	Name	cmdSendMsgCB
Command Button6	Caption	"SendMsgCB"
Command Button6	Top	2520
Command Button6	Left	120
Command Button6	Height	315
Command Button6	Width	915
Command Button7	Name	cmdSendDlgMsg

Table 11-1. Nondefault Properties of the Form and Its Controls (continued)

Object Type	Property Name	Property Value
Command Button7	Caption	"SendDlgMsg"
Command Button7	Top	2880
Command Button7	Left	120
Command Button7	Height	315
Command Button7	Width	915
Command Button8	Name	cmdBroadcastMsg
Command Button8	Caption	"BroadcastMsg"
Command Button8	Top	3240
Command Button8	Left	120
Command Button8	Height	315
Command Button8	Width	915
Command Button9	Name	cmdPostMessage
Command Button9	Caption	"PostMessage"
Command Button9	Top	3780
Command Button9	Left	120
Command Button9	Height	315
Command Button9	Width	915
Command Button10	Name	cmdPostThreadMsg
Command Button10	Caption	"PostThreadMsg"
Command Button10	Top	4140
Command Button10	Left	120
Command Button10	Height	315
Command Button10	Width	915

To implement the `WH_GETMESSAGE` hook, let's begin with the changes needed to the *Module2.bas* code module. (Throughout this discussion, the new lines of code that you must add to the project to implement the `WH_GETMESSAGE` hook will appear in boldface.) A new private member variable, *hGetMsgHook*, is added to store the `WH_GETMESSAGE` hook handle:

```
Private hProcRetHook As Long
Private hProcHook As Long
Private hGetMsgHook As Long

Public IsHooked As Boolean
```

The *SetHooks* function, which is shown in Example 11-1, contains a new line to install the `WH_GETMESSAGE` hook.

Example 11-1. The SetHooks Function to Install the WM_GETMESSAGE Hook

```
Public Sub SetHooks()
    If IsHooked Then
        MsgBox "Don't hook CALLWNDPROC twice or you will be unable to unhook it."
    Else
        hGetMsgHook = SetWindowsHookEx(WH_GETMESSAGE, AddressOf GetMsgProc, _
                        0, App.ThreadID)
        hProcHook = SetWindowsHookEx(WH_CALLWNDPROC, AddressOf WndProc, 0, _
                    App.ThreadID)
        hProcRetHook = SetWindowsHookEx(WH_CALLWNDPROCRET, AddressOf WndProcRet, _
                        0, App.ThreadID)
        IsHooked = True
    End If
End Sub
```

The *RemoveHooks* method, shown in Example 11-2, contains a new line to remove the WH_GETMESSAGE hook.

Example 11-2. The RemoveHooks Function to Remove the WM_GETMESSAGE Hook

```
Public Sub RemoveHooks()
    Dim temp As Long
    temp = UnhookWindowsHookEx(hGetMsgHook)
    temp = UnhookWindowsHookEx(hProcHook)
    temp = UnhookWindowsHookEx(hProcRetHook)
    IsHooked = False
End Sub
```

A new function shown in Example 11-3, GetMsgProc, is added to act as the filter function for the WH_GETMESSAGE hook. This filter function outputs a line of text to the Text1 text box when a WM_NULL message is posted to the message queue.

Example 11-3. The GetMsgProc Filter Function

```
Public Function GetMsgProc(ByVal uCode As Long, ByVal wParam As Long, _
                        lParam As MSG) As Long
    If lParam.message = WM_NULL Then
        Select Case uCode
            Case HC_ACTION
                Form2.Text1.Text = Form2.Text1.Text & "GETMESSAGE" _
                            & "   MSG:" & Hex$(lParam.message) _
                            & "   HWND:" & Hex$(lParam.hwnd) _
                            & "   WPARAM:" & Hex$(lParam.wParam) _
                            & "   LPARAM:" & Hex$(lParam.lParam) _
                            & "   MSGREMOVED:" & Hex$(wParam) & vbNewLine
            Case Else
        End Select
    End If

    GetMsgProc = CallNextHookEx(hGetMsgHook, uCode, wParam, lParam)
End Function
```

That is it for changes to this application. From these changes you can see how all three hooks are used and how they operate.

It is interesting to note that because *PeekMessage* can only read a message from the queue without removing it, you can call the WH_GETMESSAGE hook more than once for each message on the queue. You can observe this by running the example application included in this chapter from within the VB IDE and clicking the PostMessage button. First, you can see posted messages being read using the *PeekMessage* function with the PM_NOREMOVE flag. Next, the message is removed from the message queue using the *PeekMessage* function with the PM_REMOVE flag. See Figure 11-3 and Figure 11-4 for an example of this.

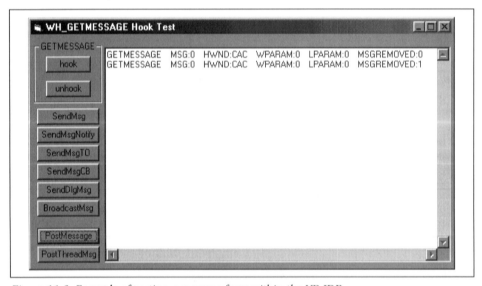

Figure 11-3. Example of posting a message from within the VB IDE

Other Uses of This Hook

The WH_GETMESSAGE hook is a very useful hook for many different applications. One application is watching for the WM_CANCELJOURNAL message, which is defined as follows:

```
Public Const WM_CANCELJOURNAL = &H4B
```

To fully understand why this is useful, you need to read Chapter 19 and Chapter 20, which cover the WH_JOURNALRECORD and WH_JOURNALPLAYBACK hooks, respectively. In short, the WM_CANCELJOURNAL message is posted to the message queue of the thread in which one of these hooks is installed when the user forcefully cancels journal recording or playback. The hooks are actually removed after this message is processed. By taking advantage of this, we can per-

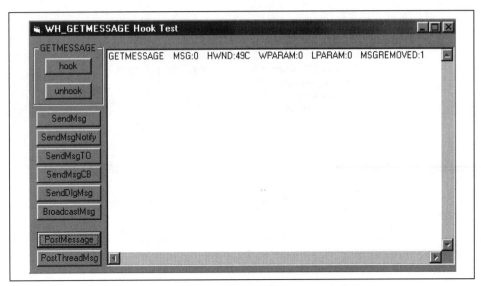

Figure 11-4. Example of posting a message from within a compiled EXE

form any cleanup required before the hook is actually removed. To do this, you can place the following **If...Then** statement inside the filter function for the **WM_GETMESSAGE** hook:

```
If lParam.message = WM_CANCELJOURNAL Then
     'Place cleanup code here.
End If
```

You also can use this hook to fix the problem of the Tab and Arrow keys not functioning as expected in a modeless dialog box and, more specifically, in the Find and Replace common dialog boxes. For a modeless dialog to work properly, Windows requires that you use the *IsDialogMessage* API function in the main message loop of the application. The *IsDialogMessage* API function basically does the work of the *TranslateMessage* and the *DispatchMessage* API functions, but for modeless dialog boxes. Therefore, if *IsDialogMessage* returns a **TRUE** value, it has processed the message and the *TranslateMessage* and the *DispatchMessage* API functions should not be called. The *IsDialogMessage* API function's main purpose is to provide default dialog keyboard processing for the modeless dialog box. Modal dialog boxes automatically support default dialog keyboard processing. You cannot add the *IsDialogMessage* API function to the main message loop of a VB application because it is located in ThunderRT6Main. To fix this problem, simply install a thread-specific **WM_GETMESSAGE** hook upon receiving the **WM_INITDIALOG** message in the common dialog box subclass procedure. Next, add to your code a **WH_GETMESSAGE** filter function similar to the following:

```
Public Function GetMsgProc(ByVal uCode As Long, ByVal wParam As Long, _
                    lParam As MSG) As Long
```

```
    If wParam = PM_REMOVE Then
        Select Case uCode
            Case HC_ACTION
                If lParam.message >= WM_KEYFIRST And lParam.message <= WM_KEYLAST Then
                    If IsDialogMessage(hwndCommDialog, lParam) Then
                        lParam.message = WM_NULL
                        lParam.wParam = 0
                        lParam.lParam = 0
                    End If
                End If
            Case Else
        End Select
    End If

    GetMsgProc = CallNextHookEx(hGetMsgHook, uCode, wParam, lParam)
End Function
```

This will, in effect, add the missing *IsDialogMessage* function to your message loop and cause the Tab and Arrow keys to be correctly processed. This problem was discussed in Chapter 5.

You can find several other examples of using this hook in the Microsoft Developer Network (MSDN). I have listed them in Table 11-2, along with brief descriptions.

Table 11-2. MSDN Articles on Using the WM_GETMESSAGE Hook

Article ID	Description
Q198439	How to jump to a specific property page sheet.
Q33690	How to alter keyboard messages (the WH_KEYBOARD hook cannot alter messages).
Q233263	How to process Tab and Arrow keys in a modeless dialog box.
Q238882	How to know when a screensaver activates.
Q125680	How to subclass a window in a different process.

Caveats

You must remember that this hook only intercepts posted messages. Any message sent to a window using *SendMessage*-type API calls will not be captured. Also, this hook might modify the message. Take care when modifying any message; verify that it will not adversely affect any other functionality.

This hook functions differently when running in the VB IDE than when running from inside an EXE. The difference is that while running in the IDE, an additional *PeekMessage* is performed with a PM_NOREMOVE flag. This simply examines the message and its details but does not remove it from the message queue. The message is removed from the message queue in a subsequent *PeekMessage* call. See Figure 11-1 and Figure 11-2 for examples of this.

As always, you must take performance into consideration when using this hook, especially when the hook is system-wide.

12

WH_KEYBOARD and WH_KEYBOARD_LL

This chapter deals first with the WH_KEYBOARD hook and then with the WH_KEYBOARD_LL hook. The LL stands for low-level. This chapter describes these hooks and discusses how keyboard messages are handled in the Windows messaging system. I will present examples using each hook.

How Keyboard Messaging Operates

When the user presses and releases a key on the keyboard, several hidden things happen within the messaging system. When the user presses a key on the keyboard, the keyboard sends a *scan code* to the keyboard device driver indicating that a specific key was pressed. This device driver converts the scan code to a virtual key code that Windows defines. A message structure is filled with either a WM_KEYDOWN or WM_SYSKEYDOWN message, according to the type of key the user pressed.

System key-down and key-up messages are produced in one of three ways:

- By pressing the F10 key, which causes the menu bar to activate
- By holding down the ALT key while pressing another key such as ALT-F4, which closes a window
- When no window in the system has the keyboard input focus, such as when all windows are minimized

System key messages are used mainly by the system and provide a standard keyboard interface for manipulating windows. For example, pressing ALT-F4 closes a window—you can find this key combination in a window's system menu. Other examples of system key combinations are:

CTRL-ESC

Opens the Windows Start menu (or the Task Manager under Windows NT)

ALT-ESC

Switches to the next running application in the Z-order

ALT-TAB

Switches to the next running application in the Z-order

ALT-DOWN ARROW

Opens a drop-down list box

ALT-SPACE

Displays the active window's system menu

ALT-F6

Switches between windows within the same application

A nonsystem key is a key that is pressed without the ALT key being pressed. Examples of nonsystem keys are ENTER, TAB, ESC, or any character key (a-z, A-Z) on the keyboard.

The MSG message structure as it pertains to keyboard messages is defined as follows:

```
Private Type MSG
    hwnd As Long
    message As Long
    wParam As Long
    lParam As Long
    time As Long
    pt As POINTAPI
End Type
```

Each member of this structure is defined as follows:

hwnd

Handle to the window that this message is directed to.

message

The message ID, either WM_KEYDOWN, WM_KEYUP, WM_SYSKEYDOWN, or WM_SYSKEYUP.

wParam

The virtual key code of the key pressed. Virtual key codes are usually defined as constants in code and have the prefix VK_.

lParam

Flags and other information about the key pressed. They include:

key repeat count

The number of times the key was repeated as a result of the user holding the key down.

scan code

This value depends on the original equipment manufacturer (OEM).

extended-key flag

Specifies whether the key pressed is a function key or a key on the keypad.

context code

Specifies if the ALT key was pressed.

previous key-state flag

Specifies if the automatic repeat feature of a keyboard generated this message.

transition-state flag

Specifies if the key is being pressed or released.

time

The time that this message was posted.

pt

The mouse x and y coordinates at the time this message was posted.

The system sends this message to the raw input thread (RIT), which passes it on to the message queue of the thread that has the keyboard input focus.

When the user releases the key, the keyboard sends a separate scan code to the device driver indicating that the key being pressed was released. The device driver then converts this scan code into a virtual key code. A message structure is filled with either a WM_KEYUP or WM_SYSKEYUP message, according to the type of key pressed. This message also is passed on to the RIT and then on to the message queue of the thread that has the keyboard input focus.

You might be wondering what the keyboard input focus refers to. The *keyboard input focus* is a property that each thread in the system contains. This property contains the window handle of a window within the thread that is currently set to receive all the keyboard input. Because all threads contain this property, each thread can have a window handle contained in this property. But the only window that actually receives keyboard input is the window that has the keyboard input focus and that is contained in the foreground thread. Even though other windows might have the keyboard input focus for their thread, they cannot receive keyboard input. When another thread becomes the foreground thread, the keyboard input focus property of the new thread will determine which window the keyboard messages will be sent to.

If you use Spy++ to watch keyboard messages, you will see that an extra message, WM_CHAR, is generated. This message contains the actual character code (equivalent to its ASCII value) in the *wParam* member of its MSG structure. The keyboard only generates these messages in this sequence:

```
WM_KEYUP
WM_KEYDOWN
```

But when the window procedure receives these messages, the WM_CHAR message mysteriously appears. The message sequence now looks like this:

```
WM_KEYUP
WM_CHAR
WM_KEYDOWN
```

The WM_CHAR message is generated inside the message loop of the destination thread. A simple message loop is written like this:

```
while (GetMessage(&msg, (HWND) NULL, 0, 0))
{
    TranslateMessage(&msg);
    DispatchMessage(&msg); }
}
```

The *TranslateMessage* function is key to understanding how WM_CHAR messages are generated. When the *GetMessage* function obtains a WM_KEYDOWN or WM_SYSKEYDOWN message from the message queue, it sends it to the *TranslateMessage* function. This function first determines if the virtual key code can be converted to a character code. If it can, it creates a WM_CHAR or WM_SYSCHAR message, depending on the type of key down message. The WM_CHAR or WM_SYSCHAR message structure will contain the character code of the key pressed in its *wParam* member. The *lParam* information from the WM_KEYDOWN or WM_SYSKEYDOWN message structures are passed on, unchanged, to the *lParam* member of the WM_CHAR or WM_SYSCHAR message structure.

The *TranslateMessage* function then takes the new WM_CHAR or WM_SYSCHAR message and places it at the head of the message queue. This means that after the *TranslateMessage* function obtains the WM_KEYDOWN or WM_SYSKEYDOWN message from the message queue, it will obtain either the WM_CHAR or WM_SYSCHAR message next. This occurs only if the *TranslateMessage* function can translate the virtual key code into a character key code; otherwise, it won't create WM_CHAR or WM_SYSCHAR messages.

You can use any of the following keys to generate WM_CHAR messages:

* BACKSPACE
* ENTER (carriage return)
* ESC
* SHIFT+ENTER (linefeed)

- TAB

- All characters in the ASCII value range of &H00 to &HFF

You can use either of the following keys to generate WM_SYSCHAR messages:

- F10

- ALT+{key}

The last step is to send the message to the correct window procedure. The keyboard input focus property of the thread determines which window procedure will receive the keyboard message. You can use the *GetFocus* function to determine which window has the keyboard focus for the thread in which this function is executed. You declare this function in Visual Basic (VB) as follows:

```
Private Declare Function GetFocus Lib "user32" Alias "GetFocus" () As Long
```

This function takes no parameters and returns the hWnd of the window with keyboard input focus. If no window has the keyboard input focus, this function returns a NULL.

Description of Hooks

The WH_KEYBOARD and WH_KEYBOARD_LL hooks intercept messages that relate to keyboard input. The main difference is that the WH_KEYBOARD_LL hook captures messages sooner in the messaging system than the WH_KEYBOARD hook does. This allows the WH_KEYBOARD_LL hook to capture certain keyboard messages that the WH_KEYBOARD hook cannot capture.

You can use the WH_KEYBOARD hook as a thread-specific hook, or you can place it in a dynamic link library (DLL) and use it as a system-wide hook. You can use the WH_KEYBOARD_LL hook only as a system-wide hook, however. A thread-specific hook intercepts all messages within the thread in which it is installed. When you install a hook as a system-wide hook, you must place it in a DLL. This DLL is injected into every process so that the hook can operate on all messages in the system. Chapter 3 discusses this in detail.

Both hooks can only monitor or remove a keyboard message; neither hook can modify the message. The WH_KEYBOARD hook can intercept two specific messages; they are WM_KEYDOWN and WM_KEYUP. The WH_KEYBOARD_LL hook can intercept these two messages as well as any WM_SYSKEYDOWN and WM_SYSKEYUP messages. There is one key combination that neither hook can remove; this is the CTRL-ALT-DEL key combination. By preventing this key combination from operating, you could open up security holes in the Windows NT/2000 operating systems. The WH_KEYBOARD_LL hook, unlike the WH_KEYBOARD hook, can detect the CTRL-ALT-DEL key combination, though.

Another difference between the two hooks is that the `WH_KEYBOARD_LL` hook can determine if the keyboard message actually originated at the keyboard, or if it was injected into the messaging system. You can inject a keyboard message into the messaging system by using the *SendInput* function, which is defined as follows:

```
UINT SendInput (UINT uInputs, LPINPUT pInput, UINT cbSize);
```

It has the following three parameters:

uInputs
: The number of `INPUT` structures in the array pointed to by *pInput*

pInput
: A pointer to an array of `INPUT` structures

cbSize
: The size of the `INPUT` structure

The `INPUT` structure contains members identifying the type of message (keyboard, mouse, or hardware) and a structure identifying the relevant data for the type of message identified.

The *SendInput* function replaces the *Keybd_event* function for all operating systems except Windows 95. Note that Windows NT must have Service Pack 3 or greater installed. You use *SendInput* to create messages and inject them into the message stream so that they are almost indistinguishable from normal messages. For example, you can use this function to create `WM_KEYUP` and `WM_KEYDOWN` messages to simulate keystrokes. Further discussion of this function is beyond the scope of this book.

One piece of information that only the `WM_KEYBOARD` hook can determine is the repeat count of the key being pressed. The *repeat count* is the number of times the same key has been repeated while the user is holding down the key. Instead of sending as a separate message every repeated key character the user sends to the system, the system sends one message with a repeat count property that determines how many times the key has repeated. You should use this feature of the keyboard message only when the application cannot process the individual messages quickly enough. To illustrate this, the messages produced from pressing and holding down a key normally look like this:

```
WM_KEYDOWN                          (Repeat count = 1)
WM_CHAR                             (Repeat count = 1)
WM_KEYDOWN                          (Repeat count = 1)
WM_CHAR                             (Repeat count = 1)
WM_KEYDOWN                          (Repeat count = 1)
WM_CHAR                             (Repeat count = 1)
WM_KEYDOWN                          (Repeat count = 1)
WM_CHAR                             (Repeat count = 1)
WM_KEYDOWN                          (Repeat count = 1)
```

```
WM_CHAR                               (Repeat count = 1)
WM_KEYDOWN                            (Repeat count = 1)
WM_CHAR                               (Repeat count = 1)
WM_KEYDOWN                            (Repeat count = 1)
WM_CHAR                               (Repeat count = 1)
WM_KEYUP                              (Repeat count = 1)
```

If the application is busy processing other messages and cannot process the WM_
KEYDOWN or WM_SYSKEYDOWN messages quickly enough, it uses the repeat count
property. The messages produced in this case would look like this:

```
WM_KEYDOWN                            (Repeat count = 10)
WM_CHAR                               (Repeat count = 10)
WM_KEYDOWN                            (Repeat count = 1)
```

This allows the system to more efficiently queue messages in the thread's message
queue.

The WH_KEYBOARD_LL hook captures messages before they have a chance to be
posted to any thread's message queue. With this hook, you also can capture
system keyboard messages (WM_SYSKEYUP and WM_SYSKEYDOWN).

WH_KEYBOARD_LL is an interesting exception because you can install it only as a
system-wide hook. As I previously mentioned, system-wide hooks must reside in a
DLL. However, this hook, as well as the WH_MOUSE_LL, WH_JOURNALPLAYBACK,
and WH_JOURNALRECORD hooks, can reside either in an EXE or DLL module. This
means that we can implement these four hooks within VB. This is because the
filter functions of these hooks are called from within the context of the thread that
has installed these types of hooks.

To understand why these hooks can reside in an EXE, we need to understand how
they manipulate the message processing of each thread running in the system.
Normally, every thread has its own message queue to which it is connected. These
message queues receive messages from the RIT. This architecture gives all 32-bit
Windows operating systems robust multithreading capability and prevents one
application from hanging the whole system. As we will see, however, installing the
WH_KEYBOARD_LL hook destroys this one-to-one relationship between a thread
and its message queue.

It is possible to force multiple threads to receive messages from a single message
queue. You can accomplish this by using the *AttachThreadInput* application programming interface (API) function. You declare this function in VB as follows:

```
Private Declare Function AttachThreadInput Lib "user32" _
        Alias "AttachThreadInput"
        (ByVal idAttach As Long, _
        ByVal idAttachTo As Long, _\
        ByVal fAttach As Long) As Long
```

Its parameters are:

idAttach

The thread ID of the thread to be attached to another thread's message queue.

idAttachTo

The thread ID of the thread containing the message queue to which the thread specified by *idAttach* is attached.

fAttach

True specifies to attach the two threads; **False** specifies to unattach the two threads.

A return value of zero indicates that this function failed; any other value indicates success. Note that you cannot attach a thread to the RIT, to itself, or to a thread in another desktop. The message queue that is used by the thread that *idAttach* specifies does not receive input after this thread is attached to the other message queue.

When you install a **WH_KEYBOARD_LL** hook in a thread, the system attaches all threads to the message queue of the thread that installed this hook. This is similar to calling *AttachThreadInput* for each thread and setting the value of *idAttach* to the thread ID for each individual thread, always setting *idAttachTo* to the thread ID of the thread that installed the journal hook, and always setting *fAttach* to **True**. The result is a single message queue for all threads in the system. Figure 12-1 illustrates this concept.

Because a single message queue is feeding all threads in the system, you can call these hooks from within the context of the thread that installed the hooks—which, in our case, is the VB application.

Ordinarily, DLLs are required for system-wide hooks because each thread has its own message queue. This DLL is injected into every process so that the hook can operate on all messages (and all message queues) in the system. An EXE, unlike a DLL, cannot be injected into every process, and hence cannot operate on all messages when there are multiple message queues. On the other hand, you can install **WH_KEYBOARD_LL** for a single thread and still receive every message the system generates because every message is being funneled through a single message queue.

Filter Function Definitions

The function prototype for the **WH_KEYBOARD** hook is defined as follows:

```
Public Function WndKeyBoardProc(ByVal uCode As Long, _
        ByVal wParam As Long, _
        ByVal lParam As Long) As Long
```

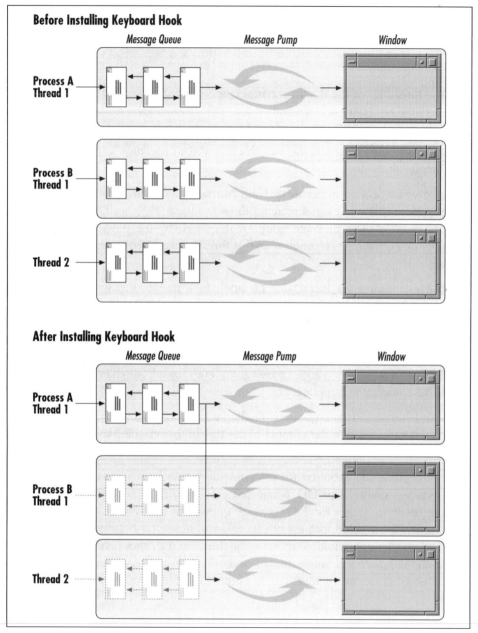

Figure 12-1. Thread state before and after a WH_KEYBOARD_LL hook is installed

Its parameters are:

uCode

> The code sent to this hook that informs the developer how to handle this keyboard message.

wParam

The virtual key code.

lParam

This member contains flags and other information about the key pressed. Information includes transition-state flag, previous key-state flag, context code, extended-key flag, scan code, and key repeat count.

The function prototype for the WH_KEYBOARD_LL hook is defined as follows:

```
Public Function WndKeyBoardProc_LL(ByVal uCode As Long, _
        ByVal wParam As Long, _
        ByVal lParam As Long) As Long
```

The hook's parameters are:

uCode

The code sent to this hook that informs the developer how to handle this keyboard message

wParam

The message ID (WM_KEYDOWN, WM_KEYUP, WM_SYSKEYDOWN, or WM_SYSKEYUP)

lParam

A pointer to a KBDLLHOOKSTRUCT structure

The KBDLLHOOKSTRUCT structure contains information specific to the WH_ KEYBOARD_LL hook, some of which you cannot obtain through the WH_KEYBOARD hook. This structure is defined in VB as follows:

```
Private Type KBDLLHOOKSTRUCT
    vkCode as Long
    scanCode as Long
    flags as Long
    time as Long
    dwExtraInfo as Long
End Type
```

The members of the KBDLLHOOKSTRUCT structure are:

vkCode

The virtual key code.

scanCode

The scan code.

flags

This member contains flags for the key pressed. The flags include extended key, injected message, context code, and transition state.

time

The time this message was posted.

dwExtraInfo
   A pointer to extra developer-defined information.

Explanation of Hook Codes

The system sends two codes to the *uCode* parameter of the WH_KEYBOARD hook's filter function: HC_ACTION and HC_NOREMOVE. The WH_KEYBOARD_LL, however, only receives the HC_ACTION code. There is no reason for the low-level keyboard hook to use the HC_NOREMOVE code because the messages have not yet been placed onto the message queue. Each code is defined here:

HC_ACTION
   The *wParam* and *lParam* parameters contain information about keyboard messages that have been removed from the message queue (*GetMessage*).

HC_NOREMOVE
   The *wParam* and *lParam* parameters contain information about keyboard messages that have been read but not removed from the message queue (*Peek-Message*).

Location of This Hook in the System

The WH_KEYBOARD hook is called in the message loop of a thread. This hook is located inside of the *GetMessage* and *PeekMessage* functions, as Figure 12-2 illustrates. Therefore, if the hook returns a 1, the system discards the message inside the *GetMessage* or *PeekMessage* function and the rest of the message loop does not process the message.

The WH_KEYBOARD_LL hook also is located immediately before a message is placed into the message queue of the thread that installed the hook, as Figure 12-2 illustrates. Remember that all message queues are attached to the message loop of this same thread.

A Thread-Specific Example

The first example using the WH_KEYBOARD hook will be thread-specific. This example will watch for the Windows key on the keyboard to be pressed, along with the "w" key. When the user presses this key combination, Internet Explorer starts. It is easy to change the key combination and the application that is started to suit your own purposes.

To use the application, simply click the Hook button in the WH_KEYBOARD frame on the VB form. Next, press the Windows key on the keyboard and hold it down

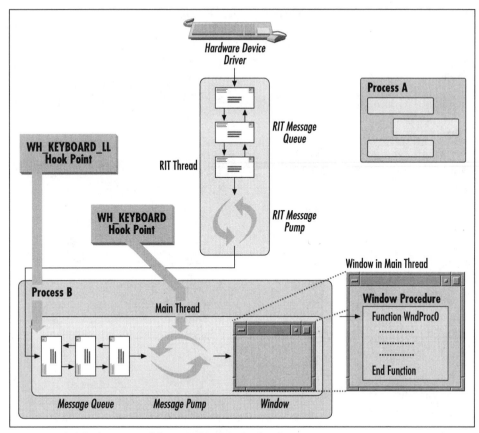

Figure 12-2. The location of the WH_KEYBOARD hook

while pressing the "w" key; Internet Explorer should start. Figure 12-3 shows a screenshot of the application's user interface (UI).

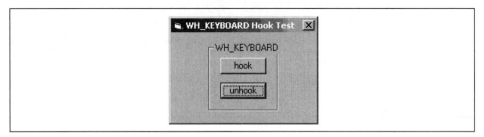

Figure 12-3. Screenshot of the thread-specific example

Table 12-1 lists the nondefault properties of the form and its controls.

Table 12-1. Nondefault Properties of the Form and Its Controls

Object Type	Property Name	Property Value
Form	Name	Form2
Form	Caption	"WH_KEYBOARD Hook Test"
Form	BorderStyle	3-Fixed Dialog
Form	Top	420
Form	Left	132
Form	Height	2100
Form	Width	2985
Frame	Caption	"WH_KEYBOARD"
Frame	Name	Frame1
Frame	Top	180
Frame	Left	751
Frame	Height	1335
Frame	Width	1392
Command Button1	Name	cmdHook
Command Button1	Caption	"hook"
Command Button1	Top	300
Command Button1	Left	240
Command Button1	Height	315
Command Button1	Width	915
Command Button2	Name	cmdUnHook
Command Button2	Caption	"unhook"
Command Button2	Top	780
Command Button2	Left	240
Command Button2	Height	315
Command Button2	Width	915

The application contains a hook button that installs the system-wide hook, and an unhook button that removes the hook. The VB code in Example 12-1 is placed behind each button in the *Form2.frm* module.

Example 12-1. Form2.frm Code

```
Private Sub cmdHook_Click()
    Call SetKeyboardHook
End Sub

Private Sub cmdUnHook_Click()
    Call RemoveKeyboardHook
End Sub
```

Example 12-1. Form2.frm Code (continued)

```
'-----------
'CLEANUP
'-----------
Private Sub Form_QueryUnload(Cancel As Integer, UnloadMode As Integer)
    If IsHooked Then
        Cancel = 1
        MsgBox "Unhook before closing, or the IDE will crash."
    End If
End Sub
```

The *Form_QueryUnload* event simply checks the *IsHooked* global flag to determine if the hook is still installed. If it is, the system displays a message warning the user that the hook is still in place and that shutting down the application is canceled. If the application were to shut down without removing the hook, it would suffer a General Protection Fault (GPF).

Example 12-2 presents the code for the *Module1.bas* module. A private variable, *hHook*, is declared to hold the handle to the hook. A global variable, *IsHooked*, is declared as a flag indicating whether the hook is installed.

Example 12-2. Module1.bas Code

```
Private hHook As Long
Public IsHooked As Boolean


'---------------------------
' SET MESSAGE FILTER HOOK
'---------------------------
Public Sub SetKeyboardHook()
    If IsHooked Then
        MsgBox "Don't hook WH_KEYBOARD twice or you will be unable to unhook it."
    Else
        hHook = SetWindowsHookEx(WH_KEYBOARD, AddressOf WndKeyBoardProc, 0, _
                              App.ThreadID)
        IsHooked = True
    End If
End Sub


'---------------------------
' REMOVE MESSAGE FILTER HOOK
'---------------------------
Public Sub RemoveKeyboardHook()
    Dim RetVal As Long
    RetVal = UnhookWindowsHookEx(hHook)
    IsHooked = False
End Sub


'---------------------------
' HOOK FILTER FUNCTION
'---------------------------
Public Function WndKeyBoardProc(ByVal uCode As Long, ByVal wParam As Long, _
```

Example 12-2. Module1.bas Code (continued)

```
      ByVal lParam As Long) As Long
  Dim bWinKeyDown As Boolean
  Dim bCharKeyUp As Boolean
  Dim iWinKeyState As Integer

  If uCode >= 0 Then
      Select Case uCode
          Case HC_ACTION
              iWinKeyState = GetAsyncKeyState(VK_LWIN)
              If (iWinKeyState And &H8000) = &H8000 Then
                  bWinKeyDown = True
              Else
                  bWinKeyDown = False
              End If

              If (lParam And &H80000000) = &H80000000 Then
                  'WM_KEYUP
                  bCharKeyUp = True
              Else
                  'WM_KEYDOWN
                  bCharKeyUp = False
              End If

              If ((Hex$(wParam) = "57") And bWinKeyDown And Not (bCharKeyUp)) Then
                  'If you do this on a keydown then you get 2-4 copies loaded
                  '  This only happens when the VB driver app is @ the foreground
                  Call Shell("C:\Program Files\Internet Explorer\Iexplore.exe", _
                          SW_SHOWNORMAL)

                  'Returning false disallows the w to be sent to the focus window
                  WndKeyBoardProc = 1
                  Exit Function
              End If
          Case HC_NOREMOVE
              'The message has not been removed from the message queue
          Case Else
              'Do nothing
      End Select
  End If

  WndKeyBoardProc = CallNextHookEx(hHook, uCode, wParam, lParam)
End Function
```

The *SetKeyboardHook* function uses the *SetWindowsHookEx* function to install the
WH_KEYBOARD hook and sets the *IsHooked* flag to True. The *SetWindowsHookEx*
function uses the WH_KEYBOARD constant to signify that a keyboard hook is to be
installed. The WH_KEYBOARD constant has a value of 2.

Example 12-2 shows how to code the filter function for the keyboard hook. In this
filter function, the processing is performed when the HC_ACTION code is passed in to
this function; otherwise, no processing occurs, and the next hook in the chain is

called. The first thing we must do when an HC_ACTION code is passed in to this function is to determine if the Windows key is currently pressed. To do this, we must pass in the virtual key code of the Windows key (VK_LWIN) to the *GetAsyncKeyState* function.

GetAsyncKeyState is declared in Visual Basic as follows:

```
Private Declare Function GetAsyncKeyState Lib "user32" (ByVal vKey As Long) _
        As Integer
```

Its single parameter is:

VKey
   The virtual key whose state is to be checked

The return value of this function is an integer. The most significant bit is set if the key associated with the *vKey* parameter is currently down; it is zero otherwise. The least significant bit is set if the user pressed the key after a prior call to *GetAsyncKey-State*. By ANDing the return value of this function with the value &H8000, we can determine if the most significant bit is set. If this bit is set, the Boolean *bWinKeyDown* flag is set to True, indicating that the left Windows key is currently being pressed.

The next thing to determine is the state of the most significant bit of the *lParam* parameter for this filter function. This bit is the transition flag for the keyboard event. If this bit is set, the user is releasing the key (WM_KEYUP); otherwise, the user is pressing it (WM_KEYDOWN). The system sets the Boolean *bCharKeyUp* flag to True when the user is releasing the key.

If the Windows key is pressed, next we can determine if the "w" key also is being pressed. The virtual key code for the "w" key is &H57. The *wParam* parameter of the filter function contains the virtual key code. The following line of code tests for this:

```
If ((Hex$(wParam) = "57") And bWinKeyDown And Not (bCharKeyUp)) Then
```

When this statement evaluates to True, the Internet Explorer application starts. We must do two more important things before we can exit this function. If the system does not throw out the message, it will still be sent to its original destination. This causes a problem when an edit window has the current keyboard input focus. If the message reaches its original window destination, the edit window, a "w" is displayed in the edit window. To stop this from happening, we simply throw out the message and stop any other keyboard hooks from processing the keyboard message. First, we set the return value for the filter function to 1. This causes the hook to throw out the keyboard message for the "w" key; therefore, it will never reach the intended window with keyboard focus. Second, the filter function is exited, and the next filter function in the hook chain is *not* called.

On the other hand, if the Windows and "w" keys are not pressed, we call *CallNext-HookEx* to pass the message on to the next installed filter function in the hook chain.

A System-Wide Example

Allowing a single application to make use of the Windows key is nice, but it would be better if we could add a system-wide Windows key function. Taking the previous example one step further, we could create the hook with a system-wide scope so that no matter which application you were in, you could always press the Windows key along with the "w" key, and Internet Explorer would start. This is similar in concept to Windows' default behavior of launching Windows Explorer when the user presses the Windows key along with the "e" key.

The UI for this application, which Figure 12-4 illustrates, is very simple. The Hook button simply installs the hook by injecting the C++ DLL containing the filter function into all running processes. Now we can press the Hook button and have Internet Explorer start when we press the Windows key and the "w" key. The Unhook button removes the hook from all running processes.

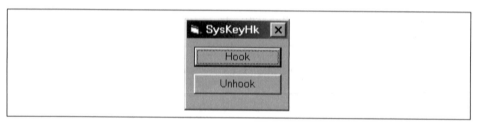

Figure 12-4. Screenshot of system-wide keyboard hook application

Table 12-2 presents the nondefault properties of the form and its controls.

Table 12-2. Nondefault Properties of the Form and Its Controls

Object Type	Property Name	Property Value
Form	Name	SysForm1
Form	Caption	"SysKeyHk"
Form	BorderStyle	3-Fixed Dialog
Form	Top	420
Form	Left	132
Form	Height	1455
Form	Width	1695
Command Button1	Name	cmdHook
Command Button1	Caption	"Hook"

Table 12-2. Nondefault Properties of the Form and Its Controls (continued)

Object Type	Property Name	Property Value
Command Button1	Top	120
Command Button1	Left	120
Command Button1	Height	315
Command Button1	Width	1395
Command Button2	Name	cmdUnHook
Command Button2	Caption	"Unhook"
Command Button2	Top	540
Command Button2	Left	120
Command Button2	Height	315
Command Button2	Width	1395

We don't need to write much VB code for the VB portion of this application. Example 12-3 shows the code for the *SysForm1.frm* module. The two external functions, *InstallFilterDLL* and *UnInstallFilterDLL*, are declared first. The Hook button simply calls *InstallFilterDLL* and the Unhook button calls *UnInstallFilterDLL*. Nothing else of importance happens in the VB code.

Example 12-3. VB SysForm1.frm Code for a System-wide Keyboard Hook

```
Private Declare Function InstallFilterDLL Lib ".\SysHook\Debug\MainHook.Dll" () _
        As Long
Private Declare Function UnInstallFilterDLL Lib ".\SysHook\Debug\MainHook.Dll" () _
        As Long

Public Sub cmdHook_Click ()
    Dim lRetVal As Long
    lRetVal = InstallFilterDLL()

    If lRetVal <> 1 Then
        MsgBox "Error Installing Keyboard Hook"
    End If
End Sub

Public Sub cmdUnhook_Click()
    Dim lRetVal As Long
    lRetVal = UnInstallFilterDLL()

    If lRetVal <> 1 Then
        MsgBox "Error removing Keyboard Hook"
    End If
End Sub
```

The DLL contains the main functionality. I wrote this code in C++ and placed it in a Win32 DLL. I did this because a system-wide hook must be placed in a DLL, and

VB cannot create true Win32 DLLs. The system injects this DLL into every process. Therefore, any process can call our hook function.

The DLL contains two exported functions, *InstallFilterDLL* and *UnInstallFilterDLL*, as well as the *KeyboardFunc* filter function. Example 12-4 shows the code added to the *MainHook.h* header file. The first line defines the *SysMsgProc* filter function as type **CALLBACK**. The rest of the code defines the two exported functions as **MAINHOOK_API**. **MAINHOOK_API** is, in turn, defined as **__decdlspec(dllexport)**.

Example 12-4. The MainHook.h Header File

```
#define MAINHOOK_API __declspec(dllexport)

 #define CCONV _stdcall
 #define NOMANGLE

/*
 * Define's and Structure used by WH_KEYBOARD_LL
 */
#define WH_KEYBOARD 2
#define HC_ACTION 0

typedef struct tagKBDLLHOOKSTRUCT {
 DWORD vkCode;
 DWORD scanCode;
 DWORD flags;
 DWORD time;
 DWORD dwExtraInfo;
} KBDLLHOOKSTRUCT, FAR *LPKBDLLHOOKSTRUCT, *PKBDLLHOOKSTRUCT;

// Function declarations
LRESULT CALLBACK KeyboardFunc (int nCode, WPARAM wParam, LPARAM lParam );

// These classes are exported from the MainHook.dll
#ifdef __cplusplus
extern "C" {
#endif
MAINHOOK_API int InstallFilterDLL(void);
MAINHOOK_API int UnInstallFilterDLL(void);
#ifdef __cplusplus
}
#endif
```

Example 12-5 shows the *MainHook.cpp* file.

Example 12-5. The MainHook.cpp Source File

```
#include "stdafx.h"
#include "MainHook.h"
#include "WINUSER.H"     //contains all these constants, structs, etc...

//-------------------------
// Global Variables
```

Example 12-5. The MainHook.cpp Source File (continued)

```
//------------------------
HANDLEhInstance; // Global instance handle forDLL
HHOOKhhookHooks; // Hook handle


//------------------------
// DLL Code
//------------------------
BOOL APIENTRY DllMain( HANDLE hModule,
                       DWORD  ul_reason_for_call,
                       LPVOID lpReserved
                       )
{
    hInstance = hModule;

    switch (ul_reason_for_call)
    {
        case DLL_PROCESS_ATTACH:
        case DLL_THREAD_ATTACH:
        case DLL_THREAD_DETACH:
        case DLL_PROCESS_DETACH:
            break;
    }
    return TRUE;
}


//------------------------------
// Thes are the exported functions.
//------------------------------
MAINHOOK_API int InstallFilterDLL(void)
{
    hhookHooks = SetWindowsHookEx(WH_KEYBOARD,(HOOKPROC) KeyboardFunc, (HINSTANCE)
                                  hInstance, 0);
    return 1;
}

MAINHOOK_API int UnInstallFilterDLL(void)
{
    UnhookWindowsHookEx(hhookHooks);
    return 1;
}


//-------------------------------------------------------------------------
// Filter function for WH_KEYBOARD
//-------------------------------------------------------------------------
LRESULT CALLBACK KeyboardFunc (int nCode, WPARAM wParam, LPARAM lParam )
{
    bool    bWinKeyDown = 0;
    bool    bKeyUp = 0;

    if ( nCode = HC_ACTION )
    {
```

Example 12-5. The MainHook.cpp Source File (continued)

```
    // Check to see if the CTRL key is pressed && the WM_KEYDOWN message was
    // passed in
    bWinKeyDown = GetAsyncKeyState (VK_LWIN) >> ((sizeof(SHORT) * 8) - 1);
    bKeyUp = (lParam >> ((sizeof(LPARAM) * 8) - 1));    //bKeyup=1   WM_KEYUP

    if ((wParam == 0x57) && bWinKeyDown && !bKeyUp)
    {
        WinExec("C:\\Program Files\\Internet Explorer\\Iexplore.exe", _
            SW_SHOWNORMAL);
        return 1;  //Returning false disallows the w to be sent
                   //to the focus window
    }
}

//Pass all messages on to the next hook in the chain
return( CallNextHookEx(hhookHooks, nCode, wParam, lParam));
}
```

To start, two variables that are global to each instance of the DLL are declared. To
share variables between all instances of a DLL, we must declare the variable in a
`#pragma data_seg` code block similar to the following:

```
#pragma data_seg("DLLSHARE")
    HWND hwndMain = NULL;
#pragma data_seg()
```

This causes a single *hwndMain* variable to be shared across the instances of this
DLL. For this application, there are two global variables, and no variables are
shared across DLL instances. These are the only two global variables that we need
to define:

```
HANDLE hInstance;        // Global instance handle for DLL
HHOOK hhookHooks;        // Hook handle
```

The *hInstance* variable contains the instance or module handle for the DLL. The
system passes this value to *DllMain*—the DLL's entry point—as the first parameter. We simply need to add the following code to the *DllMain* function:

```
hInstance = hModule;
```

The second global variable is *hhookHooks*. This variable contains the handle to
the installed hook, which the *SetWindowsHookEx* function passes back. As a note,
never share the hook handle across DLL instances. Each DLL will call its own
InstallFilterDLL function and obtain a unique hook handle. Using a single hook
handle across all DLL instances will cause a serious problem for running applications into which you have injected this DLL.

There are three main functions in the DLL, as Example 12-5 shows. The first is
InstallFilterDLL, which installs the keyboard hook. This function is exported from
the DLL. The second is *UnInstallFilterDLL*, which removes the hook. This function

is exported as well. The third function is *KeyboardFunc*, which is the filter function for the keyboard hook. Instead of being exported, this function is defined as a callback routine. The functionality within this filter function is similar to the thread-specific filter function in the VB example in Example 12-2.

A Low-Level Hook Example

The following example uses the `WH_KEYBOARD_LL` hook in a pure VB application, which is shown in Figure 12-5. You do not have to use C++ code to install and use this hook. In fact, in many instances you can substitute this hook for a system-wide `WH_KEYBOARD` hook; this way, you do not have to use any language other than VB.

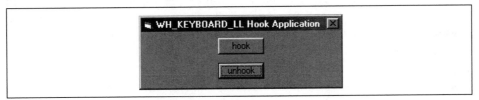

Figure 12-5. Screenshot of low-level keyboard hook application

Table 12-3 presents the nondefault properties of the form and its controls.

Table 12-3. Nondefault Properties of the Form and Its Controls

Object Type	Property Name	Property Value
Form	Name	Form2
Form	Caption	"WH_KEYBOARD_LL Hook Application"
Form	BorderStyle	3-Fixed Dialog
Form	Top	420
Form	Left	132
Form	Height	1440
Form	Width	4065
Command Button1	Name	cmdHook
Command Button1	Caption	"hook"
Command Button1	Top	120
Command Button1	Left	1530
Command Button1	Height	315
Command Button1	Width	915
Command Button2	Name	cmdUnHook
Command Button2	Caption	"unhook"

Table 12-3. Nondefault Properties of the Form and Its Controls (continued)

Object Type	Property Name	Property Value
Command Button2	Top	600
Command Button2	Left	1530
Command Button2	Height	315
Command Button2	Width	915

This application sets a system-wide, low-level keyboard hook and discards any DEL key presses. More specifically, it discards the `WM_KEYDOWN` and `WM_KEYUP` messages for the DEL key.

To see how this application operates, open up several copies of Notepad or another word processor. Click the hook button on the application window, which is shown in Figure 12-5, and then try to delete any characters in the word processing programs. Notice that the DEL key fails to do anything, not only for one word processor, but also for all word processors. Click the unhook button and then try to delete characters in any of the word processors. Now the DEL key works the way it should.

The application contains a hook button that installs the system-wide hook, and an unhook button that removes the hook. The VB code shown in Example 12-6 is placed behind each button in the *Form2.frm* module.

Example 12-6. Form2.frm Code

```
Private Sub cmdHook_Click()
    Call SetKeyboardHook
End Sub

Private Sub cmdUnHook_Click()
    Call RemoveKeyboardHook
End Sub

'-----------
'CLEANUP
'-----------
Private Sub Form_QueryUnload(Cancel As Integer, UnloadMode As Integer)
    If IsHooked Then
        Cancel = 1
        MsgBox "Unhook before closing, or the IDE will crash."
    End If
End Sub
```

Example 12-7 presents the code for the *Module1.bas* module.

Example 12-7. Module1.bas Code

```
Private hHook As Long
Public IsHooked As Boolean
```

Example 12-7. Module1.bas Code (continued)

```
'----------------------------
' SET HOOK
'----------------------------
Public Sub SetKeyboardHook()
    If IsHooked Then
        MsgBox "Don't hook WH_KEYBOARD_LL twice or you will be unable to unhook it."
    Else
        'This must be set up as a system-wide hook
        hHook = SetWindowsHookEx(WH_KEYBOARD_LL, AddressOf WndLLKeyBoardProc, _
                                 App.hInstance, 0)

        IsHooked = True
    End If
End Sub


'----------------------------
' REMOVE HOOK
'----------------------------
Public Sub RemoveKeyboardHook()
    Dim RetVal As Long
    RetVal = UnhookWindowsHookEx(hHook)
    IsHooked = False
End Sub


'----------------------------
' HOOK FILTER FUNCTION
'----------------------------
Public Function WndLLKeyBoardProc(ByVal uCode As Long, ByVal wParam As Long, _
        lParam As KBDLLHOOKSTRUCT) As Long
    Dim bCtrlKeyDown As Boolean
    Dim bAltKeyPressed As Boolean
    Dim iCtrlKeyState As Integer

    If uCode >= 0 Then
        Select Case uCode
            Case HC_ACTION
                'If a DELETE key is pulled from the queue then discard it.
                If Hex$(lParam.vkCode) = "2E" Then
                    WndLLKeyBoardProc = 1
                    Exit Function
                End If


'UNCOMMENT THIS SECTION TO SEE HOW THE CTRL+ALT+DEL KEY COMBINATION
'AFFECTS THIS HOOK
'
'                iCtrlKeyState = GetAsyncKeyState(VK_CONTROL)
'                If (iCtrlKeyState And &H8000) = &H8000 Then
'                    bCtrlKeyDown = True
'                Else
'                    bCtrlKeyDown = False
'                End If
'
```

Example 12-7. Module1.bas Code (continued)

```
'                  If (lParam.flags And LLKHF_ALTDOWN) = LLKHF_ALTDOWN Then
'                      bAltKeyPressed = True
'                  Else
'                      bAltKeyPressed = False
'                  End If
'
'                  If ((Hex$(lParam.vkCode) = "2E") And bCtrlKeyDown And
(bAltKeyPressed)) Then
'                      'Returning false still allows the CTRL-ALT-DEL to be sent
                       'to the system.
'                      'Returning false for any other characters disallows it to be sent
'                      'to the focus window.
'                      WndLLKeyBoardProc = 1
'                      Exit Function
'                  End If
              Case HC_NOREMOVE
                  'The message has not been removed from the message queue
          End Select
      End If

      WndLLKeyBoardProc = CallNextHookEx(hHook, uCode, wParam, lParam)
End Function
```

The code is similar to that for the previous thread-specific hooks, except for the way the hook is installed. Notice the *SetKeyboardHook* function, shown in Example 12-7, where the *SetWindowsHookEx* function is called. The last two arguments to this function are **App.Instance** and 0. This allows us to set the hook as a system-wide hook instead of a thread-specific one. In fact, if we tried to call this function with the last two parameters set to 0 and **App.ThreadID** (as we would do with thread-specific hooks) the function would fail and return a zero. Note that the system will not allow us to install this hook as a thread-specific hook because of the way that it reconfigures all the message queues to send messages to the message loop on the thread in which the hook was installed.

The *WndLLKeyBoardProc* function, which is also shown in Example 12-7, acts as the filter function for this hook. This function watches for the DEL **WM_KEYDOWN** or **WM_KEYUP** messages to be sent to the message queue. The virtual key code for this key is 2E. After the filter function finds this key code, it returns a 1 and does not call the next filter function in the chain. This prevents any other hook from acting on this key code so that both the **WM_KEYDOWN** and **WM_KEYUP** messages are discarded.

If you want to see that the CTRL-ALT-DEL key combination cannot be discarded, comment the previous code that discarded only the DEL key and uncomment the following code:

```
'UNCOMMENT THIS SECTION TO
'SEE HOW THIS HOOK AFFECTS
'THE CTRL+ALT+DEL KEY COMBINATION
```

When you run this application and install the hook, you can press the CTRL-ALT-DEL key combination. Even though we try, we will not succeed in discarding it.

Caveats

Performance might be an issue when you use the WH_KEYBOARD and WH_KEYBOARD_LL hooks, especially with system-wide and low-level keyboard hooks. You should use these hooks judiciously.

The low-level keyboard hook forces every thread to receive messages from a single queue. This is how 16-bit Windows operating systems work. Therefore, the operating system cannot take advantage of multitasking. A problem that occurs in all 16-bit Windows operating systems can now occur in 32-bit Windows operating systems: a single application can hang all applications, even the desktop.

Because low-level keyboard hooks serialize all input to all windows, there is a large performance penalty. You should be careful when using hooks such as these. When you use these hooks, install them for as little time as possible.

Also, when using the WH_KEYBOARD_LL low-level keyboard hook, note that the debug hook cannot receive the input to this hook before the hook is called. The debug hook works normally with the keyboard hook (WH_KEYBOARD). Chapter 21 describes the debug hook.

When using Windows NT or Windows 2000 along with the enhanced Windows keyboards, note that the keys, which are duplicated on the left and right, now have different virtual key codes. Here is a list of left and right virtual key codes:

VK_LWIN and VK_RWIN
  The left and right virtual key codes for the Windows keys

VK_LSHIFT and VK_RSHIFT
  The left and right virtual key codes for the shift keys

VK_LCONTROL and VK_RCONTROL
  The left and right virtual key codes for the control keys

VK_LMENU and VK_RMENU
  The left and right virtual key codes for the menu keys

A registry key is associated with low-level hooks such as WH_KEYBOARD_LL and WH_MOUSE_LL (WH_MOUSE_LL is described in Chapter 13). The DWORD value LowLevelHooksTimeout is located in the following registry key:

    HKEY_CURRENT_USER\Control Panel\Desktop

This registry key controls the timeout value for all low-level hooks. This value is expressed in milliseconds. If the filter function for a low-level hook does not return within this time span, the system will call the next low-level hook in the chain.

Although all 32-bit and 64-bit operating systems support the WH_KEYBOARD hook, all do not support the WH_KEYBOARD_LL hook. The WH_KEYBOARD_LL hook is found only in Windows NT (Service Pack 3 or higher) and Windows 2000; it is not found in Windows 9x.

13

WH_MOUSE and
WH_MOUSE_LL

This chapter deals first with the `WH_MOUSE` hook and then with the `WH_MOUSE_LL` hook. The `LL` stands for low-level. This chapter describes these hooks and discusses how the Windows messaging system handles mouse messages. I will provide examples using each hook.

How Mouse Messaging Operates

Unlike with keyboard messages, the system must be able to send mouse messages to any visible window in the system, even if it is not the active window. We can see this by using Spy++ to view mouse messages on a system-wide level. Start Spy++ and click the Spy → Messages . . . menu item. The Message Options dialog will appear. Check the All Windows In System checkbox on the Windows tab, and check the Mouse checkbox on the Messages tab. Finally, click the OK button. This will start Spy++ recording mouse messages. As you move the mouse cursor over windows in the system, you will see that a window does not have to be active to receive mouse messages. The Spy++ output looks similar to this:

```
WM_SETCURSOR        (Sent)
WM_SETCURSOR        (Returned)
WM_MOUSEMOVE        (Posted)
```

This series of messages is repeated over and over again as the user moves the mouse across any visible windows on the desktop. Right- or left-clicking any visible windows also sends the appropriate mouse messages to that window.

A window does have to be visible to the mouse cursor to receive messages, though. Any window or part of a window hidden behind another window in the Z-order will not be able to receive mouse messages. You might notice that the Windows desktop also receives and processes mouse messages. The only window that does not seem to receive messages at any time is the Spy++ window. Spy++ watches for messages that are directed to any of its own windows and will not display them. This is by design; you do not want any messages that the Spy++ application receives to clutter up the display of other messages.

If all visible windows did not receive mouse input at a system-wide level, it would be very difficult or even impossible to switch to another window simply by clicking it, and drag-and-drop actions would not be easy to implement as well. These other windows would not be able to receive the required mouse messages.

Using Spy++, we can conclude that the system directs mouse messages to the window that is directly under the mouse cursor—or, more specifically, the mouse cursor hot spot. Also, a window does not have to be active or have keyboard input focus to receive mouse messages; it only needs to be visible to the mouse cursor. There is an exception, though, which revolves around which window has the mouse capture.

The Mouse Capture

When a window has the mouse capture, the system redirects all mouse messages to that window, regardless of whether the mouse cursor is located inside or outside of the window's bounding rectangle. Only one window in the system can have the mouse capture at any one time.

A single data structure located within each running thread contains the mouse capture state for a window, along with other mouse information, such as cursor shape and visibility. This is the same data structure that contains the keyboard state information for each thread. As discussed in Chapter 12, you can set the window of one or more threads to have the keyboard input focus. This window must be owned by the thread that is setting its keyboard input focus state. But only the active foreground window can actually process keyboard messages. Mouse capture works similarly: at most, one window in the system can have this at any one time. However, normally, no windows in the system have the mouse capture. When no windows have the mouse capture, mouse messages are processed by the window under the mouse cursor, as they normally would be. When a window does have the mouse capture, the system sends all mouse messages to that one window, no matter which window the mouse cursor is over. Setting the mouse capture is mainly used for drag-and-drop and drawing applications, as we shall see.

The window having the mouse capture does not capture mouse messages in two situations. The first is when the window that the mouse cursor is over is not in the same process as the window that has the mouse capture. In this situation, the system sends mouse messages to the window in the separate process, not to the window that has the mouse capture. The second situation is when the mouse cursor is over a window that is in the same process as the window that has the mouse capture, but both windows are in separate threads. In this case, the system directs mouse messages to the window that has the mouse capture only when a mouse button is depressed; in all other circumstances, the system sends mouse messages to the window in the separate thread.

To set the mouse capture for a window, you need to call only the *SetCapture* function, which is declared in Visual Basic (VB) as follows:

```
Private Declare Function SetCapture Lib "user32" Alias "SetCapture" _
    (ByVal hwnd As Long) As Long
```

The single parameter of the *SetCapture* function is:

hwnd
> The window handle of the window that should receive all mouse input

This function will return the window handle of the window that previously had the mouse capture. If no window had the mouse capture, it returns a NULL. This function cannot set the mouse capture for a window that resides in a different thread. You should also note that when this function is successfully called, the menu hotkeys and keyboard accelerators will not work until the mouse capture is released. This is so that those operations using *SetCapture*, such as drawing and drag-and-drop, will not be interrupted.

The *GetCapture* function determines if a window currently has the mouse capture. This function is declared in VB in this manner:

```
Private Declare Function GetCapture Lib "user32" Alias "GetCapture" () As Long
```

This function takes no parameters and returns the window handle of the window that currently has the mouse capture. If no window has the mouse capture, it returns a NULL.

You can release the mouse capture for a window in several ways. The obvious first choice is to use *ReleaseCapture*. This function is declared in VB in this manner:

```
Private Declare Function ReleaseCapture Lib "user32" Alias "ReleaseCapture" () As
    Long
```

This function takes no parameters and returns a nonzero value if the function succeeds in releasing the mouse capture on the window, or a zero if the function fails. This function cannot release the mouse capture for a window in a different thread, only for windows within the thread in which this function was called. The second way is to call *SetCapture* a second time. This will cause the window that currently has the mouse input to lose it and then set the mouse capture to the window specified in the *hwnd* parameter of *SetCapture*. The third and final way is to click a window that does not have the mouse capture. This will cause any window that has the mouse capture to lose it.

To get a better understanding of mouse capture, consider the following example. A user clicks and drags an item from one window to a second window. The user must first click the item in the first window and drag it while holding the mouse down to the second window. After the item is over the second window, the user can release the mouse button to drop the item onto the second window. During this process, the user clicks and holds down the mouse button while over the item in the first window. At this point, the *SetCapture* function should be called, passing to it the handle of the first window. VB does this automatically for us, while you must do it manually in Visual C++. Now that you have set the mouse capture to the first window, the system will send all mouse messages to the first window even though the user moves the mouse over the second window. This allows the first window to know where the user is going to drop the item because the system is still directing mouse move and mouse click messages to the first window. This also allows the first window to define the mouse cursor shape at a system-wide level, overriding any mouse cursor shapes set at the thread level. When the user decides to drop the item onto the second window and releases the mouse button, two interesting things happen. First, the system sends the mouse button up message to the first window. Next, it releases the mouse capture from the first window—at this point, no window will have the mouse capture unless another call is made to *SetCapture*. All mouse messages are now directed to the window that the mouse pointer is directly over.

Mouse Click Messages

When a user single-clicks the left mouse button on a window, the system sends the following series of mouse messages:

```
WM_LBUTTONDOWN
WM_LBUTTONUP
```

When a user double-clicks the left mouse button on a window, one of two things can happen. The first occurs if all three of the following conditions are met:

1. The CS_DBLCLKS class style is set.

2. The second click happened within a set space around the cursor hot spot. This set space is defined by a rectangle with dimensions that you can obtain through *GetSystemMetrics* and by using the SM_CXDOUBLECLK and SM_CYDOUBLECLK flags.

3. The second click happened within a set time of the first click. You can obtain this set time by using the *GetDoubleClickTime* application programming interface (API) function with the SM_CYDOUBLECLK or SM_CXDOUBLECLK flags.

In this case, the system sends the following series of mouse messages to the window:

```
WM_LBUTTONDOWN
WM_LBUTTONUP
WM_LBUTTONDBLCLK            <-This is where the double click occurs
WM_LBUTTONUP
```

Otherwise, it sends this series of mouse messages to the window:

```
WM_LBUTTONDOWN
WM_LBUTTONUP
WM_LBUTTONDOWN             <-No double click occurs here
WM_LBUTTONUP
```

As you can see, in the second case, the system sends only the mouse down and mouse up messages, once for each click. Otherwise, it replaces the second WM_LBUTTONDOWN message with a WM_LBUTTONDBLCLK message.

Description of Hooks

You can use the WH_MOUSE hook as a thread-specific hook, or you can place it in a dynamic link library (DLL) and use it as a system-wide hook. A thread-specific hook intercepts all messages within the thread in which it is installed. When you install a hook as a system-wide hook, it has to be placed in a DLL. This DLL is injected into every process so that the hook can operate on all messages in the system. Chapter 3 provides a thorough discussion of this concept.

The WH_MOUSE hook allows us to only watch or discard mouse messages. You can use this hook to intercept messages for a single thread or for all running threads. This hook provides a large amount of control over the mouse and the way the user is able to use the mouse.

The second mouse hook, WH_MOUSE_LL, was introduced with Windows NT Service Pack 3 and higher. This hook is similar to the WH_MOUSE hook, except that it intercepts messages at a much earlier point in the Windows messaging system. This provides extra information about mouse messages that is not available through the WH_MOUSE hook. Table 13-1 describes the information that you can obtain from each type of mouse hook.

Table 13-1. Information Provided by WH_MOUSE and WH_MOUSE_LL Hooks

WH_MOUSE	WH_MOUSE_LL
Cursor coordinates (x,y)	Cursor coordinates (x,y)
Extra information	Extra information
Message ID	Message ID
MSLLHOOKSTRUCT	MOUSEHOOKSTRUCT

Table 13-1. Information Provided by WH_MOUSE and WH_MOUSE_LL Hooks (continued)

WH_MOUSE	WH_MOUSE_LL
Window hwnd	N/A
Hit-test value	N/A
N/A	Mouse wheel delta
N/A	Which XBUTTON was pressed
N/A	Flag to determine if the message was injected
N/A	Time the message was sent to the message queue

The WH_MOUSE_LL hook captures messages before they have a chance to be posted to a thread's message queue. Using this mouse hook, you can capture messages dealing with the mouse wheel and the xmouse buttons.

You install the WH_MOUSE_LL hook in a similar fashion to the WH_KEYBOARD_LL hook. You can place the code in either a Win32 DLL or a VB EXE.

The WH_MOUSE_LL hook is an interesting exception because you can install it only as a system-wide hook. As I previously mentioned, system-wide hooks must reside in a DLL. However, this hook, as well as the WH_KEYBOARD_LL, WH_JOURNALPLAYBACK, and WH_JOURNALRECORD hooks, can reside either in an EXE or DLL module. This means that we can implement these four hooks within VB. This is because the filter functions of these hooks are called from within the context of the thread that has installed these types of hooks.

To understand why these hooks can reside in an EXE, we need to understand how they manipulate the message processing of each thread running in the system. Normally, every thread has its own message queue to which it is connected. These message queues receive messages from the raw input thread (RIT). This architecture gives all 32-bit Windows operating systems robust multithreading capability and prevents one application from hanging the whole system. As we will see, however, installing the WH_MOUSE_LL hook destroys this one-to-one relationship between a thread and its message queue.

It is possible to force multiple threads to receive messages from a single message queue. You accomplish this by using the *AttachThreadInput* API function. This function is declared in VB as follows:

```
Private Declare Function AttachThreadInput Lib "user32" _
        Alias "AttachThreadInput" _
        (ByVal idAttach As Long, _
        ByVal idAttachTo As Long, _\
        ByVal fAttach As Long) As Long
```

Its parameters are:

idAttach

The thread ID of the thread to be attached to another thread's message queue.

idAttachTo
> The thread ID of the thread containing the message queue to which the thread specified by *idAttach* is attached.

fAttach
> True specifies to attach the two threads; False specifies to detach the two threads.

A return value of zero indicates that this function failed; any other value indicates success. Note that a thread cannot be attached to the RIT, to itself, or to a thread in another desktop. The message queue used by the thread that *idAttach* specifies does not receive input after this thread is attached to the other message queue.

When you install a WH_MOUSE_LL hook in a thread, the system attaches all threads to the message queue of the thread that installed this hook. This is similar to calling *AttachThreadInput* for each thread and setting the value of *idAttach* to the thread ID for each individual thread, always setting *idAttachTo* to the thread ID of the thread that installed the journal hook, and always setting *fAttach* to True. The result is a single message queue for all threads in the system. Figure 13-1 illustrates this concept.

Because a single message queue is feeding all threads in the system, you can call these hooks from within the context of the thread that installed the hook—which, in our case, is the VB application.

Ordinarily, DLLs are required for system-wide hooks because each thread has its own message queue. This DLL is injected into every process so that the hook can operate on all messages (and on all message queues) in the system. An EXE, unlike a DLL, cannot be injected into every process, and hence cannot operate on all messages when there are multiple message queues. On the other hand, you can install WH_MOUSE_LL for a single thread and still receive every message that the system generates because the system is funneling every message through a single message queue.

Filter Function Definitions

The filter function for each hook is similar, except for the *lParam* parameter. The WH_MOUSE hook filter function prototype is as follows:

```
Public Function MouseProc(ByVal uCode As Long, _
                ByVal wParam As Long, _
                lParam As MOUSEHOOKSTRUCT) As Long
```

Its parameters are:

uCode
> The hook code passed in by the system

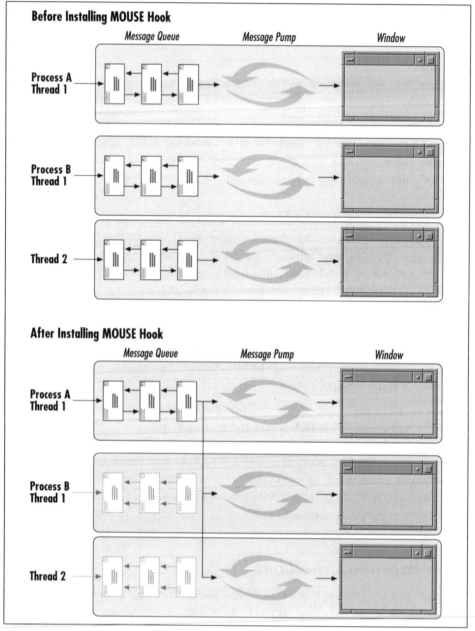

Figure 13-1. Thread state before and after a WH_MOUSE_LL hook is installed

wParam

    The mouse message identifier

lParam

    A pointer to the MOUSEHOOKSTRUCT structure

The MOUSEHOOKSTRUCT structure is defined in this manner:

```
Public Type MOUSEHOOKSTRUCT
        pt As POINTAPI
        hwnd As Long
        wHitTestCode As Long
        dwExtraInfo As Long
End Type
```

The members of the MOUSEHOOKSTRUCT structure are:

pt

> The x and y coordinates of the mouse pointer

hwnd

> The handle of the window that the mouse pointer was over when the mouse message was fired

wHitTestCode

> The hit test code detailing the nonclient area of the window that the mouse cursor is over

dwExtraInfo

> Extra information

If you are running Windows 2000 or higher, *lParam* instead points to the MOUSEHOOKSTRUCTEX structure, a structure that Windows 9x and Windows NT do not support. This structure is defined as follows:

```
Public Type MOUSEHOOKSTRUCTEX
        structMouseHook As MOUSEHOOKSTRUCT
        mousedata As Long
End Type
```

The members of MOUSEHOOKSTRUCTEX are:

structMouseHook

> A pointer to the MOUSEHOOKSTRUCT structure.

mousedata

> A Long integer that contains mouse wheel and xbutton information in the high-order word. The low-order word is reserved for system use.

> Newer mouse devices incorporate a mouse wheel to aid in scrolling. If the *MouseProc* filter function's *wParam* parameter specifies the WM_MOUSEWHEEL message, the *mousedata* member's high-order word contains the mouse wheel delta (a positive value means that the mouse wheel was rolled forward, a negative value means that it was rolled backward).

> Some newer mouse devices also incorporate extra buttons in addition to the left, right, and middle buttons. These buttons are called *xbuttons*. If the *MouseProc* filter function's *wParam* parameter specifies that an xbutton was

clicked, the *mousedata* member's high-order word determines whether the first or second xbutton was pressed. The system reserves the low-order word in both cases.

The low-level mouse hook filter function prototype is as follows:

```
Public Function LLMouseProc(ByVal uCode As Long, _
                ByVal wParam As Long, _
                lParam As MSLLHOOKSTRUCT) As Long
```

Its parameters are:

uCode

The hook code passed in by the system

wParam

The mouse message identifier

lParam

A pointer to the **MSLLHOOKSTRUCT** structure

The **MSLLHOOKSTRUCT** structure is defined in this manner:

```
Public Type MSLLHOOKSTRUCT
        pt As POINTAPI
        mousedata As Long
        flags As Long
        time As Long
        dwExtraInfo As Long
    End Type
```

The members of the **MSLLHOOKSTRUCT** structure are:

pt

The x and y coordinates of the mouse pointer.

mousedata

If the *wParam* parameter specifies the **WM_MOUSEWHEEL** message, this member's high-order word contains the mouse wheel delta (a positive value means that the mouse wheel was rolled forward, a negative value means that it was rolled backward). If the *wParam* parameter specifies that an xbutton was clicked, this member's high-order word determines whether the first or second xbutton was pressed. The system reserves the low-order word in both cases.

flags

Determines whether the message was injected. If ANDing this flag with 1 results in a 1 or **True**, this message was injected; otherwise, the message was not injected. You can inject a mouse message into the messaging system by using the *SendInput* function defined in Chapter 12.

time

The time that this message was posted to the message queue.

dwExtraInfo
Extra information.

As you can see, the main differences between these two function prototypes is the structure that *lParam* points to.

Explanation of Hook Codes

The system sends two codes to the *uCode* parameter of the mouse hook's filter function. These codes are HC_ACTION and HC_NOREMOVE. The WH_MOUSE_LL hook does not use the HC_NOREMOVE code because the mouse message has not yet been placed in the message queue. The meaning of the codes is as follows:

HC_ACTION
The *wParam* and *lParam* parameters contain information about mouse messages that have been removed from the message queue (using *GetMessage*).

HC_NOREMOVE
The *wParam* and *lParam* parameters contain information about mouse messages that have been read but not removed from the message queue (using *PeekMessage*).

Location of This Hook in the System

The WH_MOUSE hook is called in a thread's message loop, as Figure 13-2 shows. This hook is located inside the *GetMessage* and *PeekMessage* functions. Therefore, if the hook returns a 1, the message is discarded inside the *GetMessage* or *PeekMessage* function and the rest of the message loop does not process it.

The WH_MOUSE_LL hook is located immediately before a message is placed into the message queue of the thread that installed the hook. Remember that all message queues are attached to the message loop of this thread. Figure 13-2 illustrates the location of this hook.

A Single-Thread Example

The example presented here is simple in structure: it watches for all mouse messages and displays each message in the text box. Figure 13-3 shows a screenshot of this application. To use this application, simply click the hook button contained in the MOUSE frame. This will install the WH_MOUSE hook and start displaying the mouse messages in the text box. The text box will fill up rather quickly as the mouse messages are fired, even though the mouse must be within the borders of the window for this hook to capture a mouse message. A system-wide mouse hook will catch all mouse messages for all windows that are visible

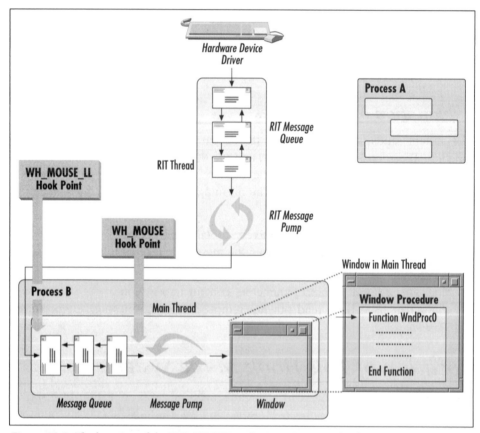

Figure 13-2. The location of the WH_MOUSE and WH_MOUSE_LL hooks

on the screen, including the desktop; had we implemented it, output from this hook to the text box would have been completely overwhelming.

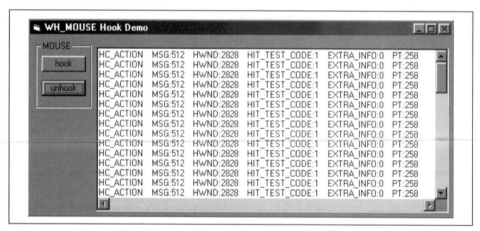

Figure 13-3. A screenshot of the single-threaded mouse hook application

Table 13-2 presents the nondefault properties of the form and its controls.

Table 13-2. Nondefault Properties of the Form and Its Controls

Object Type	Property Name	Property Value
Form	Name	Form2
Form	Caption	"WH_MOUSE Hook Demo"
Form	Top	420
Form	Left	132
Form	Height	3555
Form	Width	8655
Frame	Caption	"MOUSE"
Frame	Name	Frame1
Frame	Top	120
Frame	Left	120
Frame	Height	1335
Frame	Width	1155
TextBox	MultiLine	True
TextBox	Top	240
TextBox	Left	1380
TextBox	Height	3255
TextBox	Width	7215
Command Button1	Name	cmdHook
Command Button1	Caption	"hook"
Command Button1	Top	300
Command Button1	Left	240
Command Button1	Height	315
Command Button1	Width	915
Command Button2	Name	cmdUnHook
Command Button2	Caption	"unhook"
Command Button2	Top	780
Command Button2	Left	240
Command Button2	Height	315
Command Button2	Width	915

Before closing this application, you must click the unhook button to remove the
WH_MOUSE hook. If a hook is not removed properly, it will crash the application as
it is shutting down.

The *SetMouseHook* function, which is shown in Example 13-1, installs the thread-
specific WH_MOUSE hook using the *SetWindowsHookEx* function.

Example 13-1. The SetMouseHook Function

```
Public Sub SetMouseHook()
    If IsHooked Then
        MsgBox "Don't hook the MOUSE twice, or you will be unable to unhook it."
    Else
        lpPrevWndProc = SetWindowsHookEx(WH_MOUSE, _
                        AddressOf MouseProc, _
                        0, App.ThreadID)
        IsHooked = True
    End If
End Sub
```

The *RemoveMouseHook* function, which is shown in Example 13-2, uses the *UnhookWindowsHookEx* function to remove the WH_MOUSE hook.

Example 13-2. The RemoveMouseHook Function

```
Public Sub RemoveMouseHook()
    Dim temp As Long
    temp = UnhookWindowsHookEx(lpPrevWndProc)
    IsHooked = False
End Sub
```

Finally, the *MouseProc* function shown in Example 13-3 serves as the filter function.

Example 13-3. The MouseProc Function

```
Public Function MouseProc(ByVal uCode As Long, _
                ByVal wParam As Long, _
                lParam As MOUSEHOOKSTRUCT) As Long
    If uCode < 0 Then
        MouseProc = CallNextHookEx(lpPrevWndProc, uCode, wParam, lParam)
    Else
        Select Case uCode
            Case HC_ACTION
                Form2.Text1.Text = Form2.Text1.Text & "HC_ACTION    MSG:" & wParam _
                    & "    HWND:" & lParam.hwnd _
                    & "    HIT_TEST_CODE:" & lParam.wHitTestCode _
                    & "    EXTRA_INFO:" & lParam.dwExtraInfo _
                    & "    PT:" & CStr(lParam.pt.y) & vbNewLine
            Case HC_NOREMOVE
                Form2.Text1.Text = Form2.Text1.Text & "HC_NOREMOVE    MSG:" & wParam _
                    & "    HWND:" & lParam.hwnd _
                    & "    HIT_TEST_CODE:" & lParam.wHitTestCode _
                    & "    EXTRA_INFO:" & lParam.dwExtraInfo _
                    & "    PT:" & CStr(lParam.pt.y) & vbNewLine
            Case Else
        End Select

        MouseProc = CallNextHookEx(lpPrevWndProc, uCode, wParam, lParam)
    End If
End Function
```

As with all filter functions, when the *uCode* parameter is less than 1, you should skip the function's code and call *CallNextHookEx* immediately. When *uCode* is equal to HC_ACTION or HC_NOREMOVE, this code, along with several other parameters, is written to the text box. Finally, to allow other hooks in this chain to be called, the *CallNextHookEx* function is called.

An interesting thing happens when you run this application from within the VB IDE as opposed to a straight EXE. When you run it in the IDE, the output that is displayed in the text box is similar to the following:

```
HC_NOREMOVE  MSG:512   HWND:25192   HIT_TEST_CODE:1   EXTRA_INFO:0   PT:56
HC_ACTION    MSG:512   HWND:25192   HIT_TEST_CODE:1   EXTRA_INFO:0   PT:56
HC_NOREMOVE  MSG:512   HWND:25192   HIT_TEST_CODE:1   EXTRA_INFO:0   PT:57
HC_ACTION    MSG:512   HWND:25192   HIT_TEST_CODE:1   EXTRA_INFO:0   PT:57
HC_NOREMOVE  MSG:512   HWND:25192   HIT_TEST_CODE:1   EXTRA_INFO:0   PT:58
HC_ACTION    MSG:512   HWND:25192   HIT_TEST_CODE:1   EXTRA_INFO:0   PT:58
```

The first thing you might notice is that messages are captured when the mouse is over not only the application, but also the IDE. This occurs because the windows of the IDE and the application are all within the same thread and, therefore, share the same message queue and mouse hook. Using Spy++, we can see that the VB6 process contains two threads, one of which contains both the IDE and the running application.

The second thing you might notice is that the HC_NOREMOVE and HC_ACTION codes are repeated for each mouse message. This occurs because a *PeekMessage* is performed on the mouse message in the message queue, and then the mouse message is removed using *GetMessage*.

When you run the output as a standalone executable, it is similar to the following:

```
HC_ACTION    MSG:512   HWND:20840   HIT_TEST_CODE:1   EXTRA_INFO:0   PT:59
HC_ACTION    MSG:512   HWND:20840   HIT_TEST_CODE:1   EXTRA_INFO:0   PT:64
HC_ACTION    MSG:512   HWND:20840   HIT_TEST_CODE:1   EXTRA_INFO:0   PT:67
```

This output is somewhat different from that produced by running the code in the Visual Basic IDE. It displays only one code for each mouse message. In this instance, *PeekMessage* is not called for mouse messages placed on the message queue.

A System-Wide Hook Example

If you installed the WH_MOUSE hook as a system-wide hook, you would need to create a Win32 DLL to house the filter function as well as the code required to install and remove the hook. This is because a system-wide hook must be placed in a DLL, and VB cannot create true Win32 DLLs. The system injects this DLL into every process. Therefore, any process can call our hook function.

The DLL contains two exported functions, *InstallFilterDLL* and *UnInstallFilterDLL*, as well as the filter function, *MouseFunc*. Example 13-4 shows the code added to the *MainHook.h* header file. The first line defines the *MouseFunc* filter function as type CALLBACK. The rest of the code defines the two exported functions as MAINHOOK_API. MAINHOOK_API is, in turn, defined as __decdlspec(dllexport).

Example 13-4. The MainHook.h Header File

```
#define MAINHOOK_API  __declspec(dllexport)

  #define CCONV _stdcall
  #define NOMANGLE

/*
 * Define's and Structure used by WH_KEYBOARD_LL
 */
#define WH_MOUSE      7
#define HC_ACTION 0

typedef struct tagMOUSEHOOKSTRUCT {
    POINT    pt;
    HWND     hwnd;
    UINT     wHitTestCode;
    DWORD    dwExtraInfo;
} MOUSEHOOKSTRUCT, FAR *LPMOUSEHOOKSTRUCT, *PMOUSEHOOKSTRUCT;

// Function declarations
LRESULT CALLBACK MouseFunc (int nCode, WPARAM wParam, LPARAM lParam );


// These classes are exported from the MainHook.dll
#ifdef __cplusplus
extern "C" {
#endif
MAINHOOK_API int InstallFilterDLL(void);
MAINHOOK_API int UnInstallFilterDLL(void);
#ifdef __cplusplus
}
#endif
```

Example 13-5 shows the *MainHook.cpp* file.

Example 13-5. The MainHook.cpp Source File

```
#include "stdafx.h"
#include "MainHook.h"
#include "WINUSER.H"      //contains all these constants, structs, etc...

//-------------------------
// Global Variables
//-------------------------
HANDLEhInstance; // Global instance handle forDLL
HHOOKhhookHooks; // Hook handle
```

Example 13-5. The MainHook.cpp Source File (continued)

```cpp
//------------------------
// DLL Code
//------------------------
BOOL APIENTRY DllMain( HANDLE hModule,
                       DWORD  ul_reason_for_call,
                       LPVOID lpReserved
                       )
{
    hInstance = hModule;

    switch (ul_reason_for_call)
    {
        case DLL_PROCESS_ATTACH:
        case DLL_THREAD_ATTACH:
        case DLL_THREAD_DETACH:
        case DLL_PROCESS_DETACH:
            break;
    }
    return TRUE;
}


//-------------------------------
// Thes are the exported functions.
//-------------------------------
MAINHOOK_API int InstallFilterDLL(void)
{
    hhookHooks = SetWindowsHookEx(WH_MOUSE,(HOOKPROC) MouseFunc,
                                  (HINSTANCE) hInstance, 0);
    return 1;
}

MAINHOOK_API int UnInstallFilterDLL(void)
{
    UnhookWindowsHookEx(hhookHooks);
    return 1;
}


//--------------------------------------------------------------------------
// Filter function for WH_MOUSE
//--------------------------------------------------------------------------
LRESULT CALLBACK MouseFunc (int nCode, WPARAM wParam, LPARAM lParam )
{
    //Pass all messages on to the next hook in the chain
    return( CallNextHookEx(hhookHooks, nCode, wParam, lParam));
}
```

MainHook.cpp in Example 13-5 begins by declaring two global variables, *hInstance* and *hhookHooks*. These variables are global to this DLL and not to all DLLs. To share variables between all instances of a DLL, you must declare the variable in a #pragma data_seg code block similar to the following:

```
#pragma data_seg("DLLSHARE")
    HWND hwndMain = NULL;
#pragma data_seg()
```

This causes a single *hwndMain* variable to be shared across all instances of this
DLL. For this application, there are two global variables, and no variables are
shared across DLL instances. These are the only two global variables that need to
be defined:

```
HANDLE      hInstance;                     // Global instance handle for DLL
HHOOK       hhookHooks;                    // Hook handle
```

The *hInstance* variable contains the instance or module handle for the DLL. This
value is passed in to *DllMain*—the DLL's entry point—as the first parameter. We
simply need to add the following code to the *DllMain* function:

```
hInstance = hModule;
```

The second global variable is *hhookHooks*. This variable contains the handle to
the installed hook, which is passed back from the *SetWindowsHookEx* function. As
a note, never share the hook handle across DLL instances. Each DLL will call its
own *InstallFilterDLL* function and obtain a unique hook handle. Using a single
hook handle across all DLL instances will cause a serious problem for running
applications into which you have injected this DLL.

There are three main functions in the DLL; Example 13-5 shows the source code
for all three. The first is *InstallFilterDLL*, which installs the mouse hook. This function is exported from the DLL. The second function is *UnInstallFilterDLL*, which
removes the hook. This function is also exported. The third function is
MouseFunc, which is the filter function for the mouse hook. Instead of being
exported, this function is defined as a callback routine. The functionality within
this filter function is similar to the thread-specific filter function in Example 13-3.

Now that we have our DLL, we need to call the *InstallFilterDLL* function to install
this hook. To do this, simply create a VB EXE with one form. Place two command
buttons on the form, and place the code shown in Example 13-6 into the *Form1.
frm* module.

The two functions exported from our DLL, *InstallFilterDLL* and *UnInstallFilterDLL*,
are declared first. The Hook button simply calls *InstallFilterDLL*, and the Unhook
button calls *UnInstallFilterDLL*. Nothing else of importance happens in the VB
code.

Example 13-6. VB Form1.frm Code for a System-Wide Mouse Hook

```
Private Declare Function InstallFilterDLL Lib MainHook.Dll" () As Long
Private Declare Function UnInstallFilterDLL Lib MainHook.Dll" () As Long
```

Example 13-6. VB Form1.frm Code for a System-Wide Mouse Hook (continued)

```
Public Sub Command1_Click ()
    Dim lRetVal As Long
    lRetVal = InstallFilterDLL()

    If lRetVal <> 1 Then
        MsgBox "Error Installing mouse Hook"
    End If
End Sub

Public Sub Command2_Click()
    Dim lRetVal As Long
    lRetVal = UnInstallFilterDLL()

    If lRetVal <> 1 Then
        MsgBox "Error removing mouse Hook"
    End If
End Sub
```

Low-Level Mouse Hook Example

This example describes how to use the WH_MOUSE_LL hook in a pure VB application. You do not have to use any C++ code to install and use this hook. In fact, in many instances you can substitute this hook for a system-wide WH_MOUSE hook; this way, you do not have to use any language other than VB. Figure 13-4 shows the hooking application.

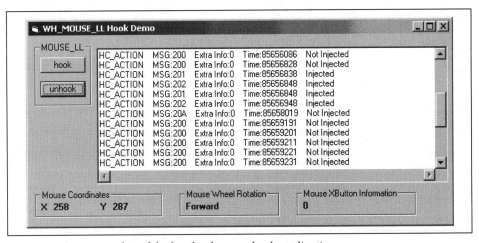

Figure 13-4. A screenshot of the low-level mouse hook application

Table 13-3 presents the nondefault properties of the form and its controls.

Table 13-3. Nondefault Properties of the Form and Its Controls

Object Type	Property Name	Property Value
Form	Name	Form2
Form	Caption	"WH_MOUSE_LL Hook Demo"
Form	Top	420
Form	Left	132
Form	Height	3765
Form	Width	8655
Frame1	Caption	"MOUSE_LL"
Frame1	Name	Frame1
Frame1	Top	120
Frame1	Left	120
Frame1	Height	1335
Frame1	Width	1155
Frame2	Caption	"Mouse Coordinates"
Frame2	Name	Frame1
Frame2	Top	3060
Frame2	Left	120
Frame2	Height	555
Frame2	Width	2595
Frame3	Caption	"Mouse Wheel Rotation"
Frame3	Name	Frame1
Frame3	Top	3060
Frame3	Left	3060
Frame3	Height	1335
Frame3	Width	2055
Frame4	Caption	"Mouse XButton Information"
Frame4	Name	Frame1
Frame4	Top	3060
Frame4	Left	5460
Frame4	Height	555
Frame4	Width	2475
TextBox	MultiLine	True
TextBox	Top	240
TextBox	Left	1380
TextBox	Height	2715
TextBox	Width	7215

Table 13-3. Nondefault Properties of the Form and Its Controls (continued)

Object Type	Property Name	Property Value
Command Button1	Name	cmdHook
Command Button1	Caption	"hook"
Command Button1	Top	300
Command Button1	Left	120
Command Button1	Height	315
Command Button1	Width	915
Command Button2	Name	cmdUnHook
Command Button2	Caption	"unhook"
Command Button2	Top	780
Command Button2	Left	120
Command Button2	Height	315
Command Button2	Width	915
Label1	Name	lblBttnInfo
Label1	Caption	""
Label1	Top	240
Label1	Left	120
Label1	Height	195
Label1	Width	2295
Label2	Name	lblwheelInfo
Label2	Caption	""
Label2	Top	240
Label2	Left	120
Label2	Height	195
Label2	Width	1815
Label3	Name	lblX
Label3	Caption	"X: "
Label3	Top	240
Label3	Left	1320
Label3	Height	195
Label3	Width	135
Label4	Name	lblY
Label4	Caption	"Y: "
Label4	Top	240
Label4	Left	1560
Label4	Height	195
Label4	Width	855

To use this application, click the hook button in the MOUSE_LL frame control. This will install the hook and immediately start displaying mouse messages when the system receives them. You can move the mouse pointer over any window, and the hook will still receive messages even though you installed the hook in an EXE.

The system captures the mouse pointer's coordinates and places them in the Mouse Coordinates frame control. The Mouse Wheel Rotation frame control describes any movements of the mouse wheel. Every time the mouse wheel is moved forward or backward, the direction of the movement is placed in this frame. As a note, one WM_MOUSEWHEEL message carries the information to describe the direction of the mouse wheel, and this message also is considered one change in the wheel rotation or wheel delta, as it is commonly referred to. A wheel delta is defined in code as WHEEL_DELTA, which is a constant equal to 120. Any time the user clicks one of the xbuttons on the mouse, the Mouse XButton Information frame will contain the value of the xbutton that was clicked.

Every mouse message that this hook intercepts has a flag indicating whether this message was injected into the messaging stream. Most of the time, device drivers inject mouse or keyboard messages into the message stream to synthetically produce a mouse or keyboard message. These synthetic messages cannot be detected except by a bit in the *flags* member of the MSLLHOOKSTRUCT structure that is passed to this hook. The *flags* member can be ANDed with the LLMHF_INJECTED constant to determine whether the message was injected.

If you are using the Microsoft IntelliSense mouse driver, you will notice injected messages appearing for specific events. For example, if you set your mouse wheel to reproduce a double-click, when it is clicked—that is, *clicked*, not *rotated*—you will notice a series of messages that are injected for this action. What happens is that the mouse driver detects that the mouse wheel has been clicked and injects the following messages:

```
WM_LBUTTONDOWN
WM_LBUTTONUP
WM_LBUTTONDOWN
WM_LBUTTONUP
```

If the window class where the double-click occurred is set to receive double-click events, the previous four messages are converted to the following:

```
WM_LBUTTONDOWN
WM_LBUTTONUP
WM_LBUTTONDBLCLK          <-This is where the double click occurs
WM_LBUTTONUP
```

This is one example of an injected message. Other device drivers or applications that might want to synthetically create mouse or keyboard messages also can inject messages into the message stream.

The code to install and remove this hook is similar to the code used in the WH_ KEYBOARD_LL hook application; it is shown in Example 13-7. The point of interest is that the *SetWindowsHookEx* installs WH_MOUSE_LL as a system-wide rather than a thread-specific hook. Note the last two parameters of the *SetWindowsHookEx* function. In this example, the *hMod* parameter of the *SetWIndowsHookEx* function is set equal to App.hInstance, which is the instance handle of this application. This value must be equal to the handle of the module in which the filter function resides. The final parameter, *dwThreadId*, is set to zero, meaning that this hook will monitor every thread in the system for mouse messages.

Example 13-7. Installing and Removing the WH_MOUSE_LL Hook

```
Private hHook As Long
Public IsHooked As Boolean

Public Sub SetMouseHook()
    If IsHooked Then
        MsgBox "Don't hook the MOUSE_LL hook twice or you will be unable to unhook it."
    Else
        'This has to be set up as a system-wide hook
        hHook = SetWindowsHookEx(WH_MOUSE_LL, AddressOf MouseProc, App.hInstance, 0)
        IsHooked = True
    End If
End Sub

Public Sub RemoveMouseHook()
    Dim temp As Long
    temp = UnhookWindowsHookEx(hHook)
    IsHooked = False
End Sub
```

The *MouseProc* function, which is shown in Example 13-8, acts as the filter function for this hook. This function simply displays the following information that the hook provides:

- The text box displays the hook code, message ID, extra information associated with the message, the time the message was created, and whether the message was injected.

- The Mouse Coordinates frame receives the x and y coordinates derived from the message. The x and y coordinates are stored in the POINT structure within the MSLLHOOKSTRUCT structure.

- The Mouse Wheel Rotation frame displays the direction (forward or backward) that the mouse wheel is rotating. If the *wParam* parameter indicates that a WM_MOUSEWHEEL message has been intercepted, you can use the high-order word of the *mouseData* member of the MSLLHOOKSTRUCT structure to determine the direction of this rotation. If this value is positive, the mouse wheel is being rotated forward; otherwise, it is being rotated backward.

- The Mouse XButton Information frame receives a value indicating which mouse xbutton was pressed or released. You can obtain the xbutton information from the high-order word of the *mouseData* member of the MSLLHOOKSTRUCT structure, but only when *wParam* contains one of the following messages:

  — WM_XBUTTONDOWN

  — WM_XBUTTONUP

  — WM_XBUTTONDBLCLK

  — WM_NCXBUTTONDOWN

  — WM_NCXBUTTONUP

  — WM_NCXBUTTONDBLCLK

Example 13-8. The MouseProc Filter Function

```
Public Function MouseProc(ByVal uCode As Long, ByVal wParam As Long, _
            lParam As MSLLHOOKSTRUCT) As Long
    Dim strInjected As String

    If uCode >= 0 Then
        If LLMHF_INJECTED And lParam.flags Then
            strInjected = "Injected"
        Else
            strInjected = "Not Injected"
        End If

        If wParam = WM_MOUSEWHEEL Then
            If CLng(lParam.mouseData And &HFFFF0000) > 0 Then
                Form2.lblWheelInfo = "Forward"
            Else
                Form2.lblWheelInfo = "Backwards"
            End If
        Else
            Form2.lblBttnInfo = CStr(lParam.mouseData And &HFFFF0000)
        End If

        Form2.lblX.Caption = lParam.pt.x
        Form2.lblY.Caption = lParam.pt.y

        Select Case uCode
            Case HC_ACTION
                Form2.Text1.Text = Form2.Text1.Text & "HC_ACTION      MSG:" & _
                Hex$(wParam) & "     Extra Info:" & lParam.dwExtraInfo & _
                "  Time:" & lParam.time & "   " & strInjected & vbNewLine
            Case HC_NOREMOVE
                Form2.Text1.Text = Form2.Text1.Text & "HC_NOREMOVE    MSG:" & _
                Hex$(wParam) & "     Extra Info:" & lParam.dwExtraInfo & _
                "  Time:" & lParam.time & "   " & strInjected & vbNewLine
            Case Else
        End Select
```

Example 13-8. The MouseProc Filter Function (continued)

```
    Else
        Form2.Text1.Text = "NA" & vbNewLine
    End If

    MouseProc = CallNextHookEx(hHook, uCode, wParam, lParam)
End Function
```

Caveats

Once again, performance might be an issue with the use of the WH_MOUSE or WH_MOUSE_LL hook, especially with system-wide and low-level mouse hooks. You should use these hooks judiciously. For more information on the problems with low-level hooks, refer to the "Caveats" section of Chapter 12.

When using the low-level mouse hook (WH_MOUSE_LL), note that the debug hook cannot receive the input to this hook before the hook is called. The debug hook works normally with the mouse hook (WH_MOUSE). The debug hook is described in Chapter 21.

A registry key is associated with low-level hooks, such as WH_MOUSE_LL and WH_KEYBOARD_LL (see Chapter 12). The numeric registry value LowLevelHooksTimeout is located in the following registry key:

```
    HKEY_CURRENT_USER\Control Panel\Desktop
```

This value controls the timeout period in milliseconds for all low-level hooks. If the filter function for a low-level hook does not return within this time span, the system will call the next low-level hook in the chain.

Although all 32-bit and 64-bit operating systems support the WH_MOUSE hook, all do not support the WH_MOUSE_LL hook. The WH_MOUSE_LL hook is found only in Windows NT (Service Pack 3 or higher) and Windows 2000; it is not found in Windows 9x.

As one final caution, there is a bug when using the mouse hooks from within a VB user control. Article Q238672 in the Microsoft Developer Network (MSDN) details the bug and how to work around it (Visual Studio 6, Service Pack 4 solves this problem).

14

WH_FOREGROUNDIDLE

This chapter covers the `WH_FOREGROUNDIDLE` hook. The chapter provides a description of the hook and an explanation of how it is used. It also provides an example to demonstrate this hook's use in an application. The chapter ends with a discussion of some considerations to keep in mind when using this hook.

Description

You use the `WH_FOREGROUNDIDLE` hook mainly to allow an application to do background processing when it is about to go into an idle state. This type of processing is normally called *background processing* because it occurs after other more important processing has finished. An application achieves an idle state when it has no more messages in the message queue to process.

To be more specific, the system calls this hook when the foreground thread is about to enter an idle state. Every application has one foreground thread; any other thread is considered a background thread. Because Visual Basic (VB) applications run in a single thread, this thread is considered the foreground thread. If a VB application creates multiple threads, the system will call the hook only when the main or foreground thread is about to go into an idle state.

When the application is about to enter an idle state, the system will check to see if any `WH_FOREGROUNDIDLE` hooks were installed. If so, the system calls the first filter function installed in the chain for this hook.

You can use this hook as a thread-specific hook, or you can place it in a dynamic link library (DLL) and use it as a system-wide hook. A thread-specific hook intercepts all messages within the thread in which it is installed. When you install a hook as a system-wide hook, you must place it in a DLL. This DLL is injected into every process so that the hook can operate on all messages in the system. Chapter 3 discusses this in detail.

The *wParam* and *lParam* arguments are not used for this hook, which makes this hook one of the simpler to implement.

Location of This Hook in the System

The system calls the filter function for this hook only when the application has determined that there are no more pending messages in the queue but immediately before the thread yields itself to other waiting threads. This hook is called from within the message loop function.

A typical message loop is written like this:

```
while( GetMessage( &msg, NULL, 0, 0 ) )
{
    TranslateMessage( &msg );
    DispatchMessage( &msg );
}
```

When no more messages are present in the message queue, the *GetMessage* function puts the application into an idle state. An application in an idle state will yield control of the CPU to other applications. While the application is idle, *GetMessage* watches for any new messages placed in the queue. After a new message is placed there, *GetMessage* takes the application out of its idle state and proceeds to process this new message.

A VB message loop looks something like this:

```
While TRUE
    While PeekMessage(structMsg, 0, 0, 0, 1)
        If structMsg.message = WM_QUIT Then
            Exit Function
        Else
            If IsWindow And Not IsIconic() then
                TranslateMessage (structMsg)
                DispatchMessage (structMsg)
            End If
        End If
    Loop

    If BackgroundProcessingReady() Then
        DoBackGroundProcessing
    Else
        WaitMessage
    End If
Loop
```

Instead of using a *GetMessage* message loop, VB applications use a *PeekMessage* message loop. In doing so, the application must call the *WaitMessage* function to tell the system that it is in an idle state. The *WaitMessage* function places the application in an idle state when no messages are in the message queue, and it does not return until a new message is placed in the queue, similar to the way *GetMessage* works.

If we had access to this code, we could simply add our background processing function immediately before or after the *DoBackgroundProcessing* function. Because we do not have access to this code, we must use the WH_FOREGROUNDIDLE hook if we are to do any background processing.

Using NuMega's SmartCheck utility, we can see exactly where this hook is called, as Figure 14-1 illustrates.

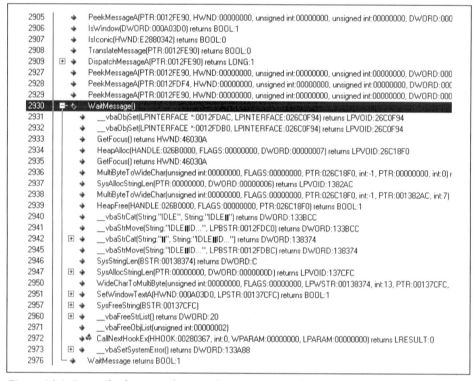

Figure 14-1. SmartCheck output showing the message loop for this application

Line 2905 is the start of the *PeekMessage* loop. Line 2909 shows the *DispatchMessage* function sending the message on to the correct window procedure. Line 2930 shows the *WaitMessage* function being called. It is here that the WH_FOREGROUNDIDLE hook is called. Lines 2931 through 2971 mainly deal with the code within the filter function which increments the counter in the text box on the application's main form. Line 2972 is where the *CallNextHookEx* function calls the next WH_FOREGROUNDIDLE hook in the hook chain.

Figure 14-2 illustrates where the hook point exists in the Windows messaging system.

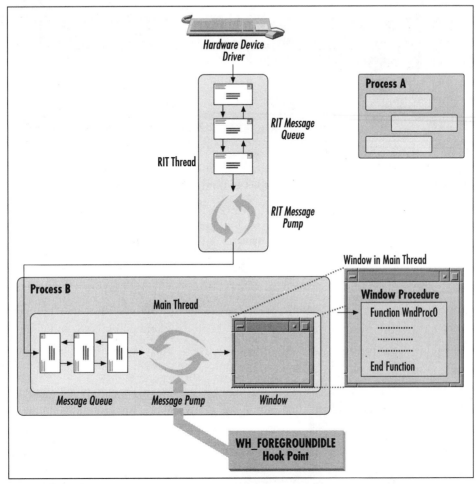

Figure 14-2. The location of the WH_FOREGROUNDIDLE hook in the messaging system

The system calls this hook when either the *GetMessage* or *WaitMessage* functions are about to place the foreground thread into an idle state.

Background Processing Example

The WH_FOREGROUNDIDLE hook example for this chapter will simply increment a number in a text box. Figure 14-3 shows a screenshot of the example application. This application has two buttons. The hook button will install the hook, and the unhook button will remove the hook. If the user tries to close the application before removing the hook, the application will display a message box informing the user to first click the unhook button and then shut down the application.

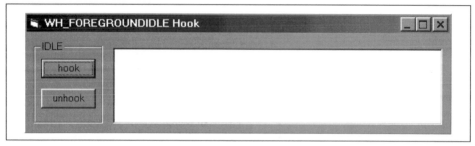

Figure 14-3. A screenshot of the example application

Table 14-1 lists the nondefault properties of the form and its controls.

Table 14-1. Nondefault Properties of the Form and Its Controls

Object Type	Property Name	Property Value
Form	Name	Form1
Form	Caption	"WH_FOREGROUNDIDLE Hook"
Form	Top	420
Form	Left	132
Form	Height	1572
Form	Width	6972
Text Box	Name	Text1
Text Box	Top	240
Text Box	Left	1440
Text Box	Height	1212
Text Box	Width	5412
Text Box	ScrollBars	3-Both
Frame	Caption	"IDLE"
Frame	Name	Frame1
Frame	Top	120
Frame	Left	120
Frame	Height	1335
Frame	Width	1155
Command Button	Name	Command1
Command Button	Caption	"hook"
Command Button	Top	300
Command Button	Left	120

Table 14-1. Nondefault Properties of the Form and Its Controls (continued)

Object Type	Property Name	Property Value
Command Button	Height	315
Command Button	Width	915
Command Button	Name	Command2
Command Button	Caption	"unhook"
Command Button	Top	780
Command Button	Left	120
Command Button	Height	315
Command Button	Width	915

When the user clicks the hook button, the application will increment a number in the text box from 0 to 100,000 whenever it enters its idle state. When it reaches 100,000 it will start over at zero.

Example 14-1 presents the code contained in the declaration section of the *Module1.bas* module.

Example 14-1. The Declaration Section for the Module1.bas Module

```
Private Declare Function SetWindowsHookEx Lib "user32" Alias "SetWindowsHookExA" _
    (ByVal idHook As Long, ByVal lpfn As Long, ByVal hmod As Long, _
    ByVal dwThreadId As Long) As Long
Private Declare Function UnhookWindowsHookEx Lib "user32" _
    ByVal hHook As Long) As Long
Private Declare Function CallNextHookEx Lib "user32" (ByVal hHook As Long, _
    ByVal ncode As Long, ByVal wParam As Long, lParam As Any) As Long

Private Const WH_FOREGROUNDIDLE = 11
Private Const HC_ACTION = 0

Private hHook As Long
Private IsHooked as Boolean
```

The **WH_FOREGROUNDIDLE** constant is the identifier for this hook type. The **HC_ACTION** constant is compared to the *uCode* argument sent to the filter function. If the *uCode* argument is equal to or greater than **HC_ACTION**, we can execute our functionality; otherwise, we need to skip it.

Next, we need to define a module-level variable, *hHook*, to hold the hook handle that we get from *SetWindowsHookEx*. We will need the hook handle to call the next hook in the chain, as well as to remove the hook when we are finished using it.

The final module-level variable that we need to create is *IsHooked*. This variable will act as a flag to signify whether the hook has been installed. This will prevent us from installing a second, duplicate hook.

Example 14-2 presents the code for the *Module1.bas* module.

Example 14-2. The Module1.bas Module

```
Public Sub SetIdleHook()
    If IsHooked Then
        MsgBox "Don't hook it twice without unhooking or you " & _
                "will be unable to unhook it."
    Else
        hHook = SetWindowsHookEx(WH_FOREGROUNDIDLE, AddressOf IdleProc, 0,_
                                 App.ThreadID)

        IsHooked = True
    End If
End Sub


Public Sub RemoveIdleHook()
    Dim temp As Long
    temp = UnhookWindowsHookEx(hHook)
    IsHooked = False
End Sub


Public Function IdleProc(ByVal uCode As Long, ByVal wParam As Long, _
                         lParam As Long) As Long
    If uCode >= HC_ACTION Then
        If IsNumeric(Form2.Text1.Text) Then
            If CDbl(Form2.Text1.Text) > 100000 Then
                Form2.Text1.Text = "0"
            Else
                Form2.Text1.Text = CDbl(Form2.Text1.Text) + 1
            End If
        End If
    Else
        'Skip processing
    End If

    IdleProc = CallNextHookEx(hHook, uCode, wParam, lParam)
End Function
```

The *SetIdleHook* routine in Example 14-2 shows the code to install the hook. To set the hook, we call *SetWindowsHookEx* with the WH_FOREGROUNDIDLE constant in the first argument and the address of the filter function in the second argument. The third argument is a zero because the filter function is not located within a DLL module. The fourth argument is set equal to App.ThreadID. This is the identifier of the thread in which the filter function is located.

Notice how the *IsHooked* variable prevents the user from setting the hook a second time.

The second function that we need to write releases the hook; it is named *RemoveIdleHook* and is shown in Example 14-2. This function will simply call the

UnHookWindowsHookEx function and then set the *IsHooked* flag to False, indicating that the hook has been removed.

The last function that we need to write is the filter function for the hook, which also is shown in Example 14-2. The system initially passes the *uCode* argument into this function. When your filter function receives a value less than zero, you must not perform any processing and call *CallNextHookEx* to call any other filter functions in the chain. If the *uCode* argument contains a value greater than or equal to HC_ACTION (this is a constant that is equal to zero), you can perform any processing from inside your filter function and then call the next filter function in the chain.

As you can see, the code to increment the number displayed in the text box is executed only when *uCode* is greater than or equal to HC_ACTION; otherwise, we need to skip the processing and call the next hook in the chain. Placing the *CallNextHookEx* function at the end of this function assures us that the system will call the next hook in the chain.

Example 14-3 shows the code in the *Form1.frm* module. The Command1 button sets the value in the text box to zero and calls *SetIdleHook* to install the hook. The Command2 button simply calls *RemoveIdleHook* to remove the installed hook. Finally, the *Form_QueryUnload* event procedure tests the *IsHooked* flag to determine if the hook is still installed. If it is, a message box is displayed informing the user to click the unhook button before shutting down the application. If this test was not performed and the application was shut down with the hook still installed, a General Protection Fault (GPF) would occur.

Example 14-3. Source Code for the Form1.frm Module

```
Private Sub Command1_Click()
    Text1.Text = "0"
    Call SetIdleHook
End Sub

Private Sub Command2_Click()
    Call RemoveIdleHook
End Sub


'-----------
'CLEANUP
'-----------
Private Sub Form_QueryUnload(Cancel As Integer, UnloadMode As Integer)
    If IsHooked Then
        Cancel = 1
        MsgBox "Unhook before closing, or the application will crash."
    End If
End Sub
```

Caveats

While running the example application provided with this chapter, you might notice that the number stops incrementing when another application is brought to the foreground. If you make the example application the active window, the number continues to increment. This is because the main thread of our application is considered the foreground thread when the application is active. A foreground thread is the main thread of an application that is currently activated. All other threads are considered background threads. This design allows the system to give more CPU time to this thread, thus boosting the performance of the active application. When our application is deactivated, another application's main thread will become the foreground thread, and the main thread of our application will become a background thread. After our application's main thread ceases to be a foreground thread, the system will not call the hook installed on that thread.

The system calls the WH_FOREGROUNDIDLE hook only immediately before the application goes into an idle state, not while the application is in an idle state. Therefore, this hook can prevent the application from going into an idle state if the code within the hook causes a message to be sent to the window's message queue. The *WaitMessage* function will see this new message and return, preventing the application from entering an idle state. You can see evidence of this in our sample application: the number in the text box keeps incrementing when the window is the active window but no input is being sent to it. This happens because our code is writing the incremented number to the text box, effectively sending several messages to the text box control on our form. One of these messages is the WM_CTLCOLOREDIT, which is sent to inform the parent window, our form, that the text box is going to repaint itself. The system places this message on the message queue, and when this happens, the application comes out of its idle state and begins to process this new message. When finished, it once again tries to enter an idle state. The system calls our hook function and increments the number in the text box. This once again sends the WM_CTLCOLOREDIT message to the main form, preventing our application from entering an idle state.

As another test, you can replace the following code in the *SetIdleProc* filter function:

```
If IsNumeric(Form2.Text1.Text) Then
    If CDbl(Form2.Text1.Text) > 100000 Then
        Form2.Text1.Text = "0"
    Else
        Form2.Text1.Text = CDbl(Form2.Text1.Text) + 1
    End If
End If
```

with this code:

```
If Form2.Left > 0 then
    Form2.Left = Form2.Left - 1
End If
If Form2.Top > 0 then
    Form2.Top = Form2.Top - 1
End If
```

This code checks the location of the form to see if its top left corner is at the 0,0 coordinates on the screen. If the form is not at this location, the code will proceed to move the form closer to the top left corner one pixel at a time. This produces the annoying effect of the form constantly moving while you are trying to use it.

If you run this code, you will notice that the form moves only when messages are being sent to the window. For example, move the mouse across the form. The form will move closer to the top left corner of the screen. Stop moving the mouse and the form will cease moving. This again proves that the code in the filter function is being called only immediately before the application goes into an idle state.

15

WH_MSGFILTER

This chapter will discuss the WH_MSGFILTER hook and will include a thread-specific example to demonstrate its setup and use. The WH_MSGFILTER hook is a special type of hook that intercepts only a specific subset of sent messages. This hook has a very close cousin, the WH_SYSMSGFILTER hook. The WH_SYSMSGFILTER hook intercepts the same type of messages but at a system-wide level only. Chapter 16 will discuss the WH_SYSMSGFILTER hook and compare and contrast it with the WH_MSGFILTER hook.

Description

The WH_MSGFILTER hook intercepts only sent messages (and not posted messages) that menus, dialog boxes, message boxes, and scrollbars produce. For a more detailed discussion of sent messages versus posted messages, see Chapter 9 and Chapter 11. You can implement the WH_MSGFILTER hook with either thread-specific or system-wide scope. You can implement the cousin of this hook, WH_SYSMSGFILTER, only with system-wide scope.

You can use the WH_MSGFILTER hook as a thread-specific hook, or you can place it in a dynamic link library (DLL) and use it as a system-wide hook. A thread-specific hook intercepts all messages within the thread in which it is installed. When you install a hook as a system-wide hook, you must place it in a DLL. This DLL is injected into every process so that the hook can operate on all messages in the system. Chapter 3 discusses this in detail.

You might be wondering why this hook intercepts a seemingly arbitrary set of messages. To understand why, we need to understand what a modal loop is and how it affects messages that you send and post to a thread.

The Modal Loop

Microsoft defines a *modal loop* as follows:

> A message-processing loop during which the system retrieves and dispatches messages without allowing an application the opportunity to filter the messages in its main message loop.

In other words, when certain events occur in the system (e.g., a menu is opened, a window is moved/sized, a modal dialog is displayed, or a scrollbar is moved), the thread enters a loop in its own messaging system. This loop is called a *modal loop*. Note that when a window enters a modal loop, it affects only the thread that the window belongs to.

During this loop, the window procedure receives messages pertaining only to the specific type of event that occurred (e.g., to the menu that was opened, to the window being moved or resized, to the modal dialog being displayed, or to the scrollbar being moved). Posted messages are not retrieved from the message queue during this modal loop. To end the loop, the user must perform an action that causes the modal loop to terminate. This action can be any of the following:

- Clicking a menu item, which closes the menu, terminates the modal loop, and performs the menu action the user chose.

- Releasing the left mouse button during a moving or sizing operation on a window, which causes the moving or sizing operation to cease and the modal loop to terminate.

- Releasing the left mouse button after moving the thumb on a scrollbar, which stops the scrolling action and ends the modal loop.

- Clicking the OK or Cancel buttons on a modal dialog or message box, which closes the modal window and ends the modal loop.

- Pressing the ESC key, which causes a modal loop to terminate.

- Switching to a different window, which causes the modal loop to terminate, except when a modal dialog box or message box is displayed; in this case, the user needs to close the modal window to end the modal loop.

When the modal loop ends, the window can once again receive posted messages from the message queue.

To see this in action, let's first examine a modal loop that the user initiates when he clicks a menu item. Figure 15-1 displays the Spy++ output from this action. First, the user clicks the left mouse button on a top-level menu item. This corresponds to Line 40 of the Spy++ output. This action causes the WM_NCLBUTTONDOWN message to be posted with a *HitTest* value of HTMENU. The *HitTest* value comes from the *wParam* parameter of this message and provides information on where the mouse is positioned when the left mouse button is depressed. A value of HTMENU indicates that the mouse is positioned over a menu. Eventually, the *DefWindowProc* function receives this message after the specific window procedure processes it. The *DefWindowProc* function uses the *HitTest* value to determine if any other actions need to be performed before returning. Because of this *HitTest* value, *DefWindowProc* in Line 41 sends a WM_SYSCOMMAND message with an SC_MOUSEMENU flag to the window that owns the menu. When *DefWindowProc* receives the WM_SYSCOMMAND message, it sends a WM_ENTERMENULOOP message in Line 42 to the window that owns the menu. The WM_ENTERMENULOOP message is a notification type message that informs the window owning this menu that a modal loop is being entered. Notice that the *DefWindowProc* function has not returned from processing the initial WM_SYSCOMMAND message. Until it returns from this message, it cannot process any posted messages. The *DefWindowProc* function finally returns from this call in Line 78. In between Lines 41 and 78, you can see all the nested messages that have been sent and returned. All these messages are in response to specific events occurring in the menu from the mouse and keyboard. All the messages sent within the modal loop are either being sent from the *DefWindowProc* or directly from the menu.

Figure 15-1. Spy++ output during a menu modal loop

You might be wondering how mouse and keyboard messages—which are only posted—still work while the window is in a modal loop. It seems like the modal loop would prevent the mouse and keyboard from functioning while inside the menu. Here's how Windows gets around that problem. When a mouse or keyboard message is posted, the parent window of the menu pulls the message off of the message queue. It then sends a WM_NOTIFY message with the appropriate notification code to the menu. The menu is then notified of mouse and keyboard events as they occur. Some of the notification codes that are used for mouse and keyboard input are:

- NM_KEYDOWN
- NM_HITTEST
- NM_RCLICK
- NM_CLICK
- NM_CHAR

As I mentioned previously, menus are not the only things that can cause a modal loop to occur. A moving or sizing operation on a window can cause this as well. Note that a minimize, restore, or maximize action also will cause a sizing modal loop to occur. As we can see in Figure 15-2, a window enters a modal loop for a moving action on Line 65 of the Spy++ output. This is in response to the user clicking and dragging the window. Line 64 shows the user beginning the moving action. Once again, the WM_NCLBUTTONDOWN message is sent. This time the message contains a *HitTest* value of HTCAPTION, which causes the *DefWindowProc* to send a WM_SYSCOMMAND message with an SC_MOVE flag to the window being moved. The user releases the mouse button, causing the WM_SYSCOMMAND message to return. You might notice that the WM_NCLBUTTONUP message is not being posted. This is because during a modal loop, no messages can be posted to the thread's message queue. Instead, it is notified that the action is ending. Releasing the mouse button causes the *DefWindowProc* to allow the WM_SYSCOMMAND message to return, ending the modal loop.

In most instances, the modal loop for a moving operation is very long. To show this, another move modal loop begins on Line 74 of Figure 15-2. The move modal loop ends on Line 139 of Figure 15-3. Actually, since many other messages—such as mouse movement, notification, and painting messages—are being fired, I chose to eliminate these from the output to allow for easier reading.

Creating and displaying a modal dialog or message box causes another modal loop. Figure 15-4 shows the creation of a message box and the subsequent modal loop. In this case, the *MsgBox* command in Visual Basic (VB) causes the WM_COMMAND message to be sent in Line 54. This starts the modal loop for the modal message box. A series of messages follow to create, size, position, and paint the message box on the screen. The modal loop is finally exited on Line 207 of Figure 15-5. The modal loop is exited only after the message box is closed.

Figure 15-2. Spy++ output for a modal loop caused by a moving operation

Figure 15-3. Spy++ output for ending a modal loop caused by the user releasing the left mouse button

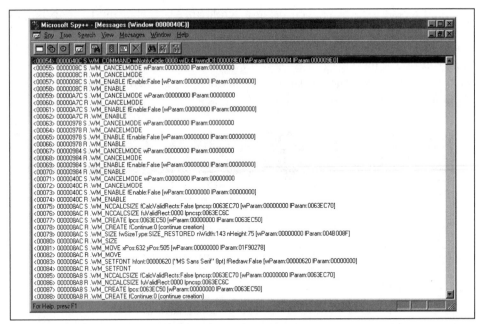

Figure 15-4. Spy++ output for beginning a message box modal loop

Figure 15-5. Spy++ output for ending a message box modal loop

The final modal loop deals with using a scrollbar. A scrollbar modal loop begins on Line 47 of Figure 15-6. Once again, the WM_NCLBUTTONDOWN message is fired when the user clicks on the scrollbar and drags it to move it. The WM_NCLBUTTONDOWN message causes *DefWindowProc* to send a WM_SYSCOMMAND with the SC_VSCROLL flag. The modal loop ends on Line 71 when the user releases the left mouse button.

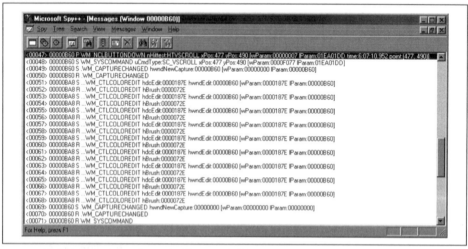

Figure 15-6. Spy++ output for a scrollbar modal loop

You can see other examples of modal loops by checking the "Show window contents while dragging" option in the Effects tab of the Display Properties dialog box; you can access this dialog box by selecting the Control Panel's Display applet. After you check this option, open Notepad and start typing. As you might already have guessed, the keyboard posts messages to Notepad, and Notepad displays them. Now click the title bar and drag the window around the screen. While you are doing this and before releasing the button, try typing. The cursor is still blinking in the client area of Notepad, but no keyboard messages are being posted to the window. When you release the left mouse button, ending the moving operation, you will notice that none of the keys you typed is displayed. The keyboard messages were discarded from the message queue while the window was inside the modal loop. This shows another important aspect of modal loops. During a modal loop, the thread will process any posted messages and send them as notifications to the modal loop. Because the modal loop will not allow the characters to be displayed on the screen, the keypresses are discarded. Doing this ensures that the modal loop and, thus, the moving operation are not interrupted.

The modal loop is the main reason for having the WH_MSGFILTER hook. Using this hook, we can perform processing during a modal loop. Using the WH_CALLWNDPROC hook, we can intercept all messages sent to the window procedure, but using the `WH_MSGFILTER` hook, we intercept only a subset of those messages. It can be a big performance booster if you can use a `WH_MSGFILTER` hook instead of a `WH_CALLWNDPROC` hook.

Filter Function Definition

The filter function prototype for this hook is written as follows:

```
Public Function MessageProc (ByVal uCode As Long, _
                             ByVal wParam As Long, _
                             lParam As MSG) As Long
```

The parameters passed to it are:

uCode

The code the system sends to this filter function.

wParam

This parameter is not used.

lParam

A pointer to the `MSG` structure.

The return value for this filter function should be the return value of the *CallNextHookEx* function, which ordinarily is zero. If this function is not called, the filter function returns a zero. I do not recommend skipping the call to *CallNextHookEx*, though. Failing to call this function will force other filter functions in the chain to not be called.

Explanation of Hook Codes

The *uCode* parameter of the filter function will receive a hook code. There are four codes that may be sent to this filter function. The codes are:

MSGF_DIALOGBOX

An input event—such as a mouse or keyboard message—has been sent to a message box or a dialog box. For the similarities and differences between windows, message boxes, and dialog boxes, see Chapter 2. You declare this constant as follows:

```
Public Const MSGF_DIALOGBOX = 0
```

MSGF_SCROLLBAR

An input event occurred in a scrollbar. This constant defined as follows:

```
Public Const MSGF_SCROLLBAR = 5
```

MSGF_MENU

An input event has occurred in a menu. This constant is defined as follows:

```
Public Const MSGF_MENU = 2
```

MSGF_DDEMGR

An input event has occurred while the Dynamic Data Exchange Management Library (DDEML) was in the process of waiting for a synchronous transaction to complete. The DDEML is a Win32 interface that allows developers to add Dynamic Data Exchange (DDE) to their applications. DDE is a data transfer mechanism that allows multiple applications to communicate through a defined set of methods. DDE is not state-of-the-art technology, and it never gained widespread acceptance. This constant is defined as follows:

```
Public Const MSGF_DDEMGR = &H8001
```

If none of these codes is passed in, message processing should be skipped, and *CallNextHookEx* should be called immediately.

Location of This Hook in the System

This hook is located inside a thread's message loop, as Figure 15-7 illustrates. The hook is called before the message is passed on to the window procedure or to any installed subclass procedure.

A Thread-Specific Example

The example application presented here is similar to previous examples. The application provides one button for installing the WH_MSGFILTER hook and one for uninstalling the hook. After you install the hook, messages that the WH_MSGFILTER hook intercepts are displayed, along with the members of the MSG structure for each message, as Figure 15-8 shows.

Table 15-1 presents the nondefault properties of the form and its controls.

Three items are present in the sample application to test this hook. The first is a menu that contains a single menu item. When the hook is installed and this menu is used, the hook will intercept messages related to actions performed on the menu and display them in the text box provided. Menu messages to the filter function with a code of MSGF_MENU. As a note, you can right-click the text box or the window title bar to produce a pop-up menu. The hook also will intercept messages related to these types of menus.

The second item is a button that displays a message box. When the message box is displayed, the WH_MSGFILTER hook will intercept messages related to the message box. Message box messages are sent to the filter function with a code of MSGF_DIALOGBOX. When the user clicks the OK button, the hook ceases to intercept messages for the message box.

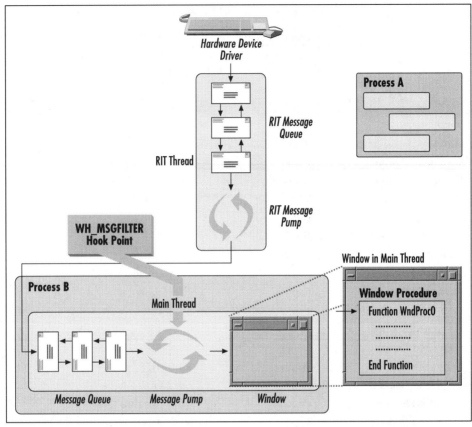

Figure 15-7. The location of the WH_MSGFILTER hook in the messaging system

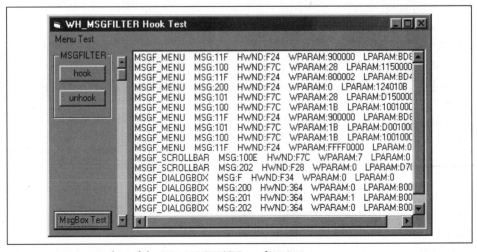

Figure 15-8. Screenshot of the WH_MSGFILTER application

Table 15-1. Nondefault Properties of the Form and Its Controls

Object	Property Name	Property Value
Form	Caption	"WH_MSGFILTER Hook Test"
Form	Top	735
Form	Left	165
Form	Height	3630
Form	Width	7575
Command Button1	Name	Command1
Command Button1	Caption	"hook"
Command Button1	Top	300
Command Button1	Left	120
Command Button1	Height	315
Command Button1	Width	915
Command Button2	Name	Command2
Command Button2	Caption	"unhook"
Command Button2	Top	780
Command Button2	Left	120
Command Button2	Height	315
Command Button2	Width	915
Command Button3	Name	cmdUnhook
Command Button3	Caption	"MsgBox Test"
Command Button3	Top	3180
Command Button3	Left	60
Command Button3	Height	315
Command Button3	Width	1155
ScrollBar	Top	180
ScrollBar	Left	1320
ScrollBar	Height	3315
ScrollBar	Width	195
TextBox	MultiLine	True
TextBox	ScrollBars	3-Both
TextBox	Top	60
TextBox	Left	1620
TextBox	Height	3495
TextBox	Width	5895
Top-Level Menu	Caption	"Menu Test"
Sub-Menu	Caption	"Do Nothing"

The final item provided is a scrollbar situated to the left of the text box. When you use this scroll bar—or the ones the text box provides—messages pertaining to the scrollbar are displayed. Scrollbar messages are sent to the filter function with a code of `MSGF_SCROLLBAR`.

Let's examine the code for this application by starting with the *Module2.bas* module. The code in this module starts with the declaration of a private member variable, *hHook*, that stores the handle of the `WH_MSGFILTER` hook, and of a public member variable, *IsHooked*, a Boolean flag indicating whether the hook has been installed. The following code declares these two variables:

```
Private hHook As Long
Public IsHooked As Boolean
```

Next, as Example 15-1 shows, the *SetWindowsHookEx* function installs the `WH_MSGFILTER` hook and sets the *IsHooked* flag to `True` to indicate that the hook is installed.

Example 15-1. Installing the WH_MSGFILTER Hook

```
Public Sub SetMessageHook()
    If IsHooked Then
        MsgBox "Don't install the hook twice or you will be unable to unhook it."
    Else
        hHook = SetWindowsHookEx(WH_MSGFILTER, AddressOf MessageProc, 0, App.ThreadID)
        IsHooked = True
    End If
End Sub
```

The *RemoveMessageHook* function, which Example 15-2 illustrates, removes the `WH_MSGFILTER` hook.

Example 15-2. Removing the WH_MSGFILTER Hook

```
Public Sub RemoveMessageHook()
    Dim temp As Long
    temp = UnhookWindowsHookEx(hHook)
    IsHooked = False
End Sub
```

The *MessageProc* function, which Example 15-3 shows, acts as the filter function for the `WH_MSGFILTER` hook.

Example 15-3. The WH_MSGFILTER Hook's Filter Function

```
Public Function MessageProc(ByVal uCode As Long, ByVal wParam As Long, _
                        lParam As MSG) As Long
    Select Case uCode
        Case MSGF_DIALOGBOX
            Form2.Text1.Text = Form2.Text1.Text & "MSGF_DIALOGBOX MSG:" & _
                            Hex$(lParam.message) & _
        "       HWND:" & Hex$(lParam.hwnd) & _
        "     WPARAM:" & Hex$(lParam.wParam) & _
```

Example 15-3. The WH_MSGFILTER Hook's Filter Function (continued)

```
            "     LPARAM:" & Hex$(lParam.lParam) & vbNewLine
      Case MSGF_MENU
            Form2.Text1.Text = Form2.Text1.Text & "MSGF_MENU MSG:" & _
                              Hex$(lParam.message) & _
            "     HWND:" & Hex$(lParam.hwnd) & _
            "     WPARAM:" & Hex$(lParam.wParam) & _
            "     LPARAM:" & Hex$(lParam.lParam) & vbNewLine
      Case MSGF_SCROLLBAR
            Form2.Text1.Text = Form2.Text1.Text & "MSGF_SCROLLBAR MSG:" & _
                              Hex$(lParam.message) & _
            "     HWND:" & Hex$(lParam.hwnd) & _
            "     WPARAM:" & Hex$(lParam.wParam) & _
            "     LPARAM:" & Hex$(lParam.lParam) & vbNewLine
      Case MSGF_DDEMGR
            Form2.Text1.Text = Form2.Text1.Text & "MSGF_DDEMGR MSG:" & _
                              Hex$(lParam.message) & _
            "     HWND:" & Hex$(lParam.hwnd) & _
            "     WPARAM:" & Hex$(lParam.wParam) & _
            "     LPARAM:" & Hex$(lParam.lParam) & vbNewLine
      Case Else
            Form2.Text1.Text = Form2.Text1.Text & "ELSE: " & uCode
   End Select

   DoEvents
   MessageProc = CallNextHookEx(hHook, uCode, wParam, lParam)
End Function
```

This filter function simply displays the messages that are funneled through it and categorizes them by the *uCode* parameter. The *DoEvents* function is called to give the text box time to display the line of text before proceeding. You must include *DoEvents* if you change the last line of code in the function from this:

```
   MessageProc = CallNextHookEx(hHook, uCode, wParam, lParam)
```

to this:

```
   MessageProc = 1
```

After making this change, compile and run the application. Do not run this application in this state inside the IDE because you might have to shut down the IDE along with the application if it locks up. Note that in some cases you might have to terminate the process manually through the Task Manager. After running the application, click the hook button for the WH_MSGFILTER hook and then try to use the provided menu, scrollbar, or message box button. As you can see, after the modal loop is started for any of these items, the application stays in the modal loop until it is manually forced to exit it.

This change causes all messages that pass through this filter function to be discarded. If this filter function returns a nonzero, the message will be discarded. Be very careful when discarding a message in this filter function. If the messages that cause a modal loop to end are discarded, the application cannot exit the modal loop, and your application will be stuck inside the loop. Note that switching to a different application and then switching back to the original stalled application will usually force the modal loop to be exited. The one instance where this does not hold true is when a message box is displayed.

Example 15-4 shows the code in the *Form2.frm* module. The Command1 button clears the text box of all information and calls *SetMessageHook* to install the hook. The Command2 button simply calls *RemoveMessageHook* to remove the installed hook. The cmdMessage button displays a message box so that you can test the effects of this hook with a message box. Finally, the *Form_QueryUnload* event procedure tests the *IsHooked* flag to determine if the hook is still installed. If so, a message box is displayed informing the user to click the unhook button before shutting down the application. If the procedure did not perform this test and you shut down the application with the hook still installed, a General Protection Fault (GPF) would result.

Example 15-4. Code for the Form2.frm Module

```
Option Explicit

Private Sub Command1_Click()
    Text1.Text = ""
    Call SetMessageHook
End Sub

Private Sub Command2_Click()
    Call RemoveMessageHook
End Sub

Private Sub cmdMessage_Click()
    MsgBox "Message Filter Hook Test"
End Sub



'-----------
'CLEANUP
'-----------
Private Sub Form_QueryUnload(Cancel As Integer, UnloadMode As Integer)
    If IsHooked Then
        Cancel = 1
        MsgBox "Unhook before closing or the IDE will crash."
    End If
End Sub
```

Caveats

You should remember that this hook intercepts sent messages only. During the modal loop, no messages can be posted to the thread's message queue.

Some additional **MSGF_** messages are defined in *Winuser.h*, but this hook does not currently implement them. These messages are listed here:

```
Public Const MSGF_MAINLOOP = 8        'Not used with MsgFilter Hook
Public Const MSGF_MAX = 8             'Not used with MsgFilter Hook
Public Const MSGF_MESSAGEBOX = 1      'Not used with MsgFilter Hook
Public Const MSGF_MOVE = 3            'Not used with MsgFilter Hook
Public Const MSGF_SIZE = 4            'Not used with MsgFilter Hook
Public Const MSGF_USER = 4096         'Not used with MsgFilter Hook
Public Const MSGF_NEXTWINDOW = 6      'Not used with MsgFilter Hook
```

Even though this hook intercepts a subset of the messages that hooks such as **WH_CALLWNDPROC** or **WH_CALLWNDPROCRET** intercept, you should still watch how this hook affects your application's performance.

16

WH_SYSMSGFILTER

The WH_SYSMSGFILTER hook is a close relative of the WH_MSGFILTER hook, as I mentioned in Chapter 15. These hooks are very similar in appearance, but as you will see, they each have their own peculiarities. In this chapter I will compare and contrast these two hooks and present an example using the WH_SYSMSGFILTER hook.

Description

Both the WH_SYSMSGFILTER and the WH_MSGFILTER hooks allow you to monitor or discard messages dealing with menus, modal dialog boxes, message boxes, and scrollbars. These messages are intercepted before the window procedure or any subclass procedure processes them. As mentioned in Chapter 15, the WH_SYSMSGFILTER hook intercepts messages only belonging to this set of items because they all operate within a modal loop. See Chapter 15 for more information about the modal loop and how it operates.

You cannot use this hook as a thread-specific hook, you must place it in a dynamic link library (DLL) and use it as a system-wide hook. When you install a hook as a system-wide hook, you must place it in a DLL. This DLL is injected into every process so that the hook can operate on all messages in the system. Chapter 3 discusses this in detail.

A big difference between the WH_SYSMSGFILTER hook and the WH_MSGFILTER hook is that you can use the WH_SYSMSGFILTER hook only as a system-wide hook, whereas you can use the WH_MSGFILTER hook as both a system-wide and a thread-specific hook.

Table 16-1 compares the WH_SYSMSGFILTER and WH_MSGFILTER hooks. Looking at this table, we can determine that the WH_SYSMSGFILTER hook essentially contains a subset of the functionality of the WH_MSGFILTER hook. However, note the order in which the system calls these two hooks. WH_SYSMSGFILTER hooks are always called before WH_MSGFILTER hooks. The thing to remember here is that if any of the WH_SYSMSGFILTER hooks returns a zero (TRUE), none of the WH_MSGFILTER hooks is called.

Table 16-1. A Comparison of the WH_SYSMSGFILTER and WH_MSGFILTER Hooks

WH_SYSMSGFILTER	WH_MSGFILTER
Monitors and discards messages	Monitors and discards messages
Intercepts menu messages	Intercepts menu messages
Intercepts modal dialog box messages	Intercepts modal dialog box messages
Intercepts message box messages	Intercepts message box messages
Intercepts scrollbar messages	Intercepts scrollbar messages
Does not intercept Dynamic Data Exchange Management Library (DDEML) messages	Intercepts DDEML messages while in a synchronous transaction
Used only as a system-wide hook	Can be used as both as system-wide and a thread-specific hook
Available hook codes: MSGF_DIALOGBOX, MSGF_SCROLLBAR, and MSGF_MENU	Available hook codes: MSGF_DDEML, MSGF_DIALOGBOX, MSGF_SCROLLBAR, and MSGF_MENU
The *wParam* is not used	The *wParam* is not used
The *lParam* contains a pointer to an MSG structure	The *lParam* contains a pointer to an MSG structure
Intercepts messages before they are processed	Intercepts messages before they are processed

Filter Function Definition

The filter function prototype for the WH_SYSMSGFILTER hook is:

```
LRESULT CALLBACK SysMsgProc (int nCode, WPARAM wParam, LPARAM lParam )
```

Its parameters are:

uCode

The code the system sends to this filter function.

wParam

This parameter is not used.

lParam

A pointer to an MSG structure.

I've presented this function prototype in C++ because the filter function can reside only in a Win32 DLL. You cannot create a Win32 DLL using Visual Basic (VB). If you translated this function prototype into VB code, it would look like this.

```
Public Function SysMsgProc (ByVal uCode As Long, _
                        ByVal wParam As Long, _
                        ByVal lParam As Long) As Long
```

The return value for this filter function should be the return value of the *CallNextHookEx* function. If this function is not called, the filter function should return a zero. I do not recommend skipping the call to *CallNextHookEx*, though. Failing to call this function will force other filter functions in the chain to not be called.

Explanation of Hook Codes

The *uCode* parameter of the filter function will receive a hook code. The following three codes can be sent to this filter function:

MSGF_DIALOGBOX

> An input event—such as a mouse or keyboard message—has been sent to a message box or a dialog box. For the similarities and differences between windows, message boxes, and dialog boxes, see Chapter 2. The constant is defined as follows:
>
> ```
> Public Const MSGF_DIALOGBOX = 0
> ```

MSGF_SCROLLBAR

> An input event occurred in a scrollbar. The constant is declared as follows:
>
> ```
> Public Const MSGF_SCROLLBAR = 5
> ```

MSGF_MENU

> An input event occurred in a menu. The constant is defined as follows:
>
> ```
> Public Const MSGF_MENU = 2
> ```

If none of these codes is passed in, you should skip the message processing and call *CallNextHookEx* immediately.

Location of This Hook in the System

The filter function for this hook is called from within the message loop of all running threads, as Figure 16-1 shows. The hook is called before the message is passed on to the window procedure or to any subclass procedure that has been installed.

A System-Wide Example

This example shows how to set up and install a system-wide WH_SYSMSGFILTER hook. You must place the filter function and the functions that install and remove the hook in a Win32 DLL. First I will show you the code contained in the VB EXE that loads and uses the DLL. Figure 16-2 shows a screenshot of the VB application.

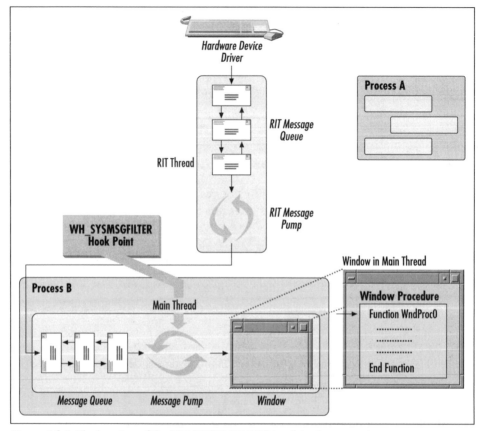

Figure 16-1. The location of the WH_SYSMSGFILTER hook in the messaging system

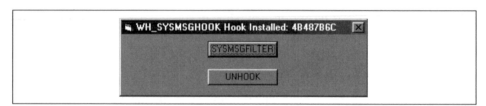

Figure 16-2. Screenshot of the VB EXE

Table 16-2 presents the nondefault properties of the form and its controls.

Table 16-2. Nondefault Properties of the Form and Its Controls

Object	Property Name	Property Value
Form	BorderStyle	3-Fixed Dialog
Form	Caption	"No Hooks Installed"
Form	Top	330
Form	Left	45

Table 16-2. Nondefault Properties of the Form and Its Controls (continued)

Object	Property Name	Property Value
Form	Height	1155
Form	Width	4905
Command Button1	Name	cmdHook
Command Button1	Caption	"SYSMSGFILTER"
Command Button1	Top	120
Command Button1	Left	1755
Command Button1	Height	315
Command Button1	Width	1395
Command Button2	Name	cmdUnhook
Command Button2	Caption	"UNHOOK"
Command Button2	Top	660
Command Button2	Left	1755
Command Button2	Height	315
Command Button2	Width	1395

The application contains a SYSMSGFILTER button that installs the system-wide hook and an UNHOOK button that removes the hook. The VB code that Example 16-1 illustrates is placed behind each button in the *SysForm2.frm* module.

Example 16-1. Event Procedures for the cmdHook and cmdUnhook Buttons

```
Private Sub cmdHook_Click()
    Call Install
End Sub

Private Sub cmdUnhook_Click()
    Call UnInstall
End Sub
```

Example 16-2 shows the code behind the *SysModule1.bas* module. The code includes the declarations of two external functions, *InstallFilterDLL* and *UnInstallFilterDLL*, that are located in the Win32 *MainHook.Dll* module and that are to be called from VB code. The two other functions, *Install* and *UnInstall*, call the two functions that the DLL defines. Example 16-1 and Example 16-2 list all the code that the EXE contains.

Example 16-2. The SysModule1.bas Module

```
Public Declare Function InstallFilterDLL Lib ".\MainHook\Debug\MainHook.Dll" () _
                As Long
Public Declare Function UnInstallFilterDLL Lib ".\MainHook\Debug\MainHook.Dll" () _
                As Long
```

Example 16-2. The SysModule1.bas Module (continued)

```
Public Sub Install()
    Dim lRetVal As Long

    lRetVal = Install ()

    If lRetVal <> 0 Then
        SysForm1.Caption = "WH_SYSMSGHOOK Hook Installed: " & Hex$(lRetVal)
    Else
        SysForm1.Caption = "Error Installing Hook: " & Hex$(lRetVal)
    End If
End Sub

Public Sub UnInstall ()
    Dim lRetVal As Long

    lRetVal = UnInstallFilterDLL

    MsgBox lRetVal

    If lRetVal = 1 Then
        SysForm1.Caption = "No Hooks Installed"
    End If
End Sub
```

The DLL contains two exported functions, *InstallFilterDLL* and *UnInstallFilterDLL*, as well as the filter function *SysMsgProc*. Example 16-3 shows the code added to the *MainHook.h* header file. The first line defines the *SysMsgProc* filter function as type CALLBACK. The rest of the code defines the two exported functions as MAINHOOK_API. MAINHOOK_API is, in turn, defined as __decdlspec(dllexport).

Example 16-3. The MainHook.h Header File

```
// Function declarations
LRESULT CALLBACK SysMsgProc (int nCode, WPARAM wParam, LPARAM lParam );

// Exported classes from the MainHook.dll
#ifdef __cplusplus
    extern "C" {
#endif
#define MAINHOOK_API __declspec(dllexport)
MAINHOOK_API int InstallFilterDLL(void);
MAINHOOK_API int UnInstallFilterDLL(void);
#ifdef __cplusplus
}
#endif
```

Example 16-4 shows the *MainHook.cpp* file. First, the code defines two global variables, *hInstance* and *hHook*. The *hInstance* variable holds the module handle that is passed in to *DllMain*, the DLL's entry point. The *SetWindowsHookEx* function uses this variable to install this hook as a system-wide hook. The *hHook* vari-

able contains the handle to the installed hook. The *SetWindowsHookEx* function
returns this handle and it is used throughout the code. Next, the shared data section is included in case any data needs to be shared between all instances of the
DLL; in our example, however, there is no shared data. Following the shared data
section is the source code for *DllMain*, the entry point to this DLL.

Example 16-4. The MainHook.cpp Source File

```
#include "stdafx.h"
#include "MainHook.h"
#include "WINUSER.H"      //contains all these constants, structs, etc...



//------------------------
// Global Variables
//------------------------
HANDLEhInstance;         // Global instance handle forDLL
HHOOKhHook;                   // Hook handle
//------------------------
// Shared DATA
//------------------------
#pragma data_seg("SHARDATA")
#pragma data_seg()
//------------------------
// DLL Code
//------------------------
BOOL APIENTRY DllMain( HANDLE hModule,
                       DWORD  ul_reason_for_call,
                       LPVOID lpReserved
                       )
{
    hInstance = hModule;

    switch (ul_reason_for_call)
    {
        case DLL_PROCESS_ATTACH:
        case DLL_THREAD_ATTACH:
        case DLL_THREAD_DETACH:
        case DLL_PROCESS_DETACH:
            break;
    }
    return TRUE;
}
//----------------------------
// This is an exported function
//   used to install the hook.
//----------------------------
MAINHOOK_API int InstallFilterDLL()
{
    hHook = SetWindowsHookEx(WH_SYSMSGFILTER,
            (HOOKPROC) SysMsgProc, (HINSTANCE) hInstance, 0);

    return (int)hHook;
```

Example 16-4. The MainHook.cpp Source File (continued)

```
}
//-----------------------------
// This is an exported function
//   used to uninstall the hook.
//-----------------------------
MAINHOOK_API int UnInstallFilterDLL(void)
{
    return UnhookWindowsHookEx(hHook);
}
//------------------------------------------------------------------------
// Filter function for the WH_SYSMSGFILTER hook
//------------------------------------------------------------------------
LRESULT CALLBACK SysMsgProc (int nCode, WPARAM wParam, LPARAM lParam )
{
    MSG      *lpMsg;
    lpMsg = (MSG *) lParam;

    switch (nCode)
    {
        case MSGF_DIALOGBOX:
            // TODO: Add code to deal with modal dialog boxes and message boxes
            break;
        case MSGF_MENU:
            // TODO: Add code to deal with menus
            break;
        case MSGF_SCROLLBAR:
            // TODO: Add code to deal with scroll bars
            break;
        default:
            break;
    }

    //Pass messages on to the next hook in the chain
    return CallNextHookEx(hHook, nCode, wParam, lParam);
}
```

The exported function *InstallFilterDLL*, which is located after the *DllMain* function, installs the WH_SYSMSGFILTER hook by calling the *SetWindowsHookEx* function. To modify this DLL to install the WH_MSGFILTER function, simply replace the WH_SYSMSGFILTER constant with the WH_MSGFILTER constant. (The constants themselves are defined in the *winuser.h* header file, which is included by the third #include directive.)

The second exported function, *UnInstallFilterDLL*, uses the *UnhookWindowsHookEx* function to remove the WH_SYSMSGFILTER hook from the process space in which the DLL resides.

Finally, the *SysMsgProc* function acts as the filter function for this hook. A switch statement (equivalent to the VB Select Case statement) is provided to deal with each type of code that this hook can return. You can add code to each TODO section to deal with modal dialog boxes, message boxes, menus, and scrollbars. The function ends by calling *CallNextHookEx* to allow other installed filter functions to be called.

Example 16-5 shows the *MainHook.def* file. Its **EXPORTS** section lists the DLL's exported functions. This allows other applications and libraries, including our VB application, to use these functions.

Example 16-5. The MainHook.def File

```
LIBRARY MainHook

EXPORTS
    InstallFilterDLL@1
    UnInstallFilterDLL@2
```

Caveats

This hook's most outstanding feature is that you can use it only as a system-wide hook. This means that the filter function must reside in a Win32 DLL. This DLL is injected into every running process. Therefore, this hook carries with it a bigger performance penalty than thread-specific hooks.

You should remember that this hook intercepts sent messages only. During the modal loop, no messages can be posted to the thread's message queue.

Watch your return values because a returned zero will prevent any other **WH_MSGFILTER** hook from operating. Because this hook is installed only as a system-wide hook, if a zero is returned, it means that no **WH_MSGFILTER** hooks will be called from within any thread. This could cause other applications that rely on these hooks to fail.

Some additional **MSGF_** messages are defined in *Winuser.h*, but this hook currently is not implementing them. These messages are:

```
Public Const MSGF_MAINLOOP = 8       'Not used with SysMsgFilter Hook
Public Const MSGF_MAX = 8            'Not used with SysMsgFilter Hook
Public Const MSGF_MESSAGEBOX = 1     'Not used with SysMsgFilter Hook
Public Const MSGF_MOVE = 3           'Not used with SysMsgFilter Hook
Public Const MSGF_SIZE = 4           'Not used with SysMsgFilter Hook
Public Const MSGF_USER = 4096        'Not used with SysMsgFilter Hook
Public Const MSGF_NEXTWINDOW = 6     'Not used with SysMsgFilter Hook
```

Even though this hook intercepts a subset of the messages that hooks such as **WH_CALLWNDPROC** or **WH_CALLWNDPROCRET** intercept, you should still watch how this hook affects your application's performance.

17

WH_SHELL

This chapter deals with the WH_SHELL hook. In this chapter, I will compare and contrast this hook with WH_CBT, a similar hook that will be discussed in Chapter 18.

Description

The WH_SHELL hook is a notification hook. That is, you can use it to notify an application of actions occurring to it, either through user intervention or through a change in the system's state. Examples of user intervention include a user minimizing a window, pressing an application command button on the mouse or keyboard, or even activating a window.

Newer keyboards and mice can include extra application buttons. These extra buttons allow the user to open applications, control media applications, and open and control Internet browsers. Using this hook, an application developer can add support for these new application buttons to one or more of her applications.

Examples of a change in system state include a change in the keyboard language, a change in the accessibility state, or the system redrawing the window title text in the task bar. The following is a complete list of events for which the WH_SHELL hook can provide notification:

HSHELL_ACCESSIBILITYSTATE
    The accessibility state has changed. This is a notification for Windows 2000 and greater operation systems.

HSHELL_ACTIVATESHELLWINDOW

The shell should activate the next application's main window in the Z-order of current windows.

HSHELL_APPCOMMAND

The user has pressed an application command button on the mouse or on the keyboard and the application did not handle this command button event. An application command button can either be extra buttons added to a keyboard, usually used to control multimedia devices, or extra buttons added to a mouse beyond the left, middle, and right buttons. This is a notification for Windows 2000 and greater operating systems.

HSHELL_GETMINRECT

The user is either minimizing or maximizing the window that is hooked.

HSHELL_LANGUAGE

The keyboard language or a new keyboard layout was loaded.

HSHELL_REDRAW

The title of a window in the Windows task bar (not the title in the window title bar) has been redrawn.

HSHELL_TASKMAN

The user has started the Windows task list.

HSHELL_WINDOWACTIVATED

The active window has changed from a different top-level unowned window—the main window of an application, which does not have a handle to a parent window—to the current window (i.e., a user has switched to the current window to make it the active window).

HSHELL_WINDOWCREATED

A top-level unowned window has been created. The window still exists when the hook's filter function receives this hook notification.

HSHELL_WIDNOWDESTROYED

A top-level unowned window is about to be destroyed. The window still exists when the hook's filter function receives this hook notification.

This hook does not allow the intercepted messages to be discarded or modified in any way. There is one exception to this rule: returning a TRUE from the hook's filter function when it receives the HSHELL_TASKMAN notification will prevent the task manager from being displayed.

In most cases, the action has already occurred before the WH_SHELL hook is notified. The only two exceptions are when a window is destroyed, and when it is minimized/maximized. During window destruction, the window still exists when this hook is notified, and then it is removed from the screen and destroyed after the hook's filter function has been called. When a window is being minimized or maximized, this hook is notified through the HSHELL_GETMINRECT hook code before the window is actually minimized or maximized.

You can use this hook as a thread-specific hook, or you can place it in a dynamic link library (DLL) and use it as a system-wide hook. A thread-specific hook intercepts all messages within the thread in which it is installed. When you install a hook as a system-wide hook, you must place it in a DLL. This DLL is injected into every process so that the hook can operate on all messages in the system. Chapter 3 discusses this in detail.

Filter Function Definition

The filter function prototype for this hook is written as follows:

```
Public Function ShellProc(ByVal uCode As Long, ByVal wParam As Long, _
                          ByVal lParam As Long) As Long
```

Its parameters are:

uCode

> The code the system sends to this filter function. I discuss the *uCode* value in greater detail in the following section, "Explanation of Hook Codes."

wParam

> This parameter depends on the *uCode*.

lParam

> This parameter depends on the *uCode*.

The return value for this filter function should be the return value of the *CallNextHookEx* function. Forcing the return value of this filter function to another value will not affect the outcome of the hook, except in the case of HSHELL_TASKMAN. In this case, returning a value of TRUE will prevent the task manager from being displayed.

Explanation of Hook Codes

The *uCode* parameter of the filter function will receive a hook code. There are 10 codes that can be sent to this filter function. The codes are defined as follows:

HSHELL_ACCESSIBILITYSTATE

> For Windows 2000 and greater operating systems, this code indicates that the accessibility state has changed. Accessibility is provided in Windows to allow people with disabilities to better use Windows. The code is defined as follows:
>
> ```
> Public Const HSHELL_ACCESSIBILITYSTATE = 11
> ```

The *lParam* parameter is not used for this code, but the *wParam* parameter of this code contains one of the following three constants:

Public Const ACCESS_STICKYKEYS = &H1

Indicates a change in the stickykeys state. *Stickykeys* is a feature that allows the user to press either the SHIFT, CTRL, or ALT key once and then press another key in sequence, as opposed to pressing each key at the same time. Pressing one of these three modifier keys once effectively locks the key in the down state until the user presses it again to unlock it, or until the user clicks a mouse button. Pressing the modifier key twice in succession locks the key in the down state; you press it a third time to unlock it. This feature helps people with motor-skill disabilities to type more easily. You turn this feature on or off by pressing the SHIFT key five times.

Public Const ACCESS_FILTERKEYS = &H2

Indicates that one of the following keyboard properties has been changed:

— Time delay before a key is accepted

— Time delay before a key is repeated

— Using sound as a feedback mechanism

This feature also is available to people with motor-skill disabilities. You turn it on or off by pressing and holding the RIGHT SHIFT key for 8 seconds.

Public Const ACCESS_MOUSEKEYS = &H3

Indicates that a change in the mousekeys state has occurred. The *mousekeys* feature allows the user to use the numeric keypad rather than the mouse to control the mouse. This feature is once again available to people with motor-skill disabilities. You turn this feature on or off by pressing the LEFT ALT + LEFT SHIFT + NUM LOCK keys at the same time.

HSHELL_WINDOWCREATED

Indicates that a top-level unowned window has been created and displayed. It is important to remember that the window exists when the hook is called with this code. The constant is defined as follows:

```
Public Const HSHELL_WINDOWCREATED = 1
```

The *lParam* parameter is not used for this code, but the *wParam* parameter of this code contains the handle to the newly created window.

HSHELL_WINDOWDESTROYED

Indicates that a top-level unowned window is about to be destroyed. It is important to remember that the window has not been destroyed at this point; in fact, it is still being displayed on the screen. The window is actually removed from the screen and destroyed after the hook's filter function—and any other installed filter functions for this hook—have processed this code. This constant is defined as follows:

```
Public Const HSHELL_WINDOWDESTROYED = 2
```

The *lParam* parameter is not used for this code, but the *wParam* parameter of this code contains the handle to the window about to be destroyed.

HSHELL_ACTIVATESHELLWINDOW

Indicates that the shell should activate its main window. The *lParam* and *wParam* parameters are not used for this code. The constant is defined as follows:

```
Public Const HSHELL_ACTIVATESHELLWINDOW = 3
```

HSHELL_APPCOMMAND

For Windows 2000 and greater operating systems, this code indicates that the user has pressed either a mouse or a keyboard application button. The constant is defined as follows:

```
Public Const HSHELL_APPCOMMAND = 12
```

There are two very important things to understand when using this code. First, this code is sent to the hook only when the application does not process the WM_APPCOMMAND message that either the mouse or keyboard application button generated. Second, if the filter function handles this code, it should not call *CallNextHookEx*, and instead should return TRUE. This allows only this filter function to handle the HSHELL_APPCOMMAND message and prevents other filter functions from also handling this message.

The *wParam* parameter contains the handle of the window that was the original WM_APPCOMMAND message destination.

The *lParam* parameter contains three specific values pertaining to the WM_APPCOMMAND message. The first is the APPCOMMAND value, which you can derive as follows:

```
Public Function GetAppCommand_lParam(ByRef Value As Long) As Long
    GetAppCommand_lParam = ((Value And &HFFFF0000) And &H7FFF0000
End Function
```

This value is equivalent to the application command that corresponds to the mouse or keyboard input. The value for this can be any of the constants listed in Table 17-1.

Table 17-1. APPCOMMAND Value Constants

Constant	Literal	Definition
APPCOMMAND_BASS_BOOST	20	Toggle the bass boost on and off
APPCOMMAND_BASS_DOWN	19	Decrease the bass

Table 17-1. APPCOMMAND Value Constants (continued)

Constant	Literal	Definition
APPCOMMAND_BASS_UP	21	Increase the bass
APPCOMMAND_BROWSER_BACKWARD	1	Navigate backward
APPCOMMAND_BROWSER_FAVORITES	6	Open favorites
APPCOMMAND_BROWSER_FORWARD	2	Navigate forward
APPCOMMAND_BROWSER_HOME	7	Navigate home
APPCOMMAND_BROWSER_REFRESH	3	Refresh the page
APPCOMMAND_BROWSER_SEARCH	5	Open search
APPCOMMAND_BROWSER_STOP	4	Stop the download
APPCOMMAND_LAUNCH_APP1	17	Start App1
APPCOMMAND_LAUNCH_APP2	18	Start App2
APPCOMMAND_LAUNCH_MAIL	15	Open mail
APPCOMMAND_MEDIA_NEXTTRACK	11	Go to the next track
APPCOMMAND_MEDIA_PLAY_PAUSE	14	Play or pause playback
APPCOMMAND_MEDIA_PREVIOUSTRACK	12	Go to the previous track
APPCOMMAND_MEDIA_STOP	4	Stop playback
APPCOMMAND_TREBLE_DOWN	22	Decrease the treble
APPCOMMAND_TREBLE_UP	23	Increase the treble
APPCOMMAND_VOLUME_DOWN	9	Lower the volume
APPCOMMAND_VOLUME_MUTE	8	Mute the volume
APPCOMMAND_VOLUME_UP	10	Raise the volume

The next part of the *lParam* is the DEVICE value that describes where this input originated. You obtain this value through the following code function:

```
Public Function GetDevice_lParam(ByRef Value As Long) As Long
    GetDevice_lParam = ((Value And &HFFFF0000) And &H8000&)
End Function
```

Most likely, the device will be the mouse or keyboard. You can use any of the constants in Table 17-2 as its value.

Table 17-2. DEVICE Constants

Constant	Literal	Definition
FAPPCOMMAND_KEY	&H0	User pressed a key
FAPPCOMMAND_MOUSE	&H8000	User clicked a mouse button
FAPPCOMMAND_OEM	&H1000	An unidentified hardware source generated the event. It could be a mouse or a keyboard event.

The final part of *lParam* is the FLAGS value, which indicates if the user pressed a CTRL or SHIFT key while pressing the mouse or keyboard application button. It also indicates which mouse button the user pressed. You obtain this value through the C++ GET_FLAGS_LPARAM(lParam) macro. You can use any of the constants in Table 17-3 as its value.

Table 17-3. FLAGS Constants

Constant	Literal	Definition
MK_CONTROL	&H8	The CTRL key is down
MK_SHIFT	&H4	The SHIFT key is down
MK_LBUTTON	&H1	The left mouse button is down
MK_MBUTTON	&H10	The middle mouse button is down
MK_RBUTTON	&H2	The right mouse button is down
MK_XBUTTON1	&H20	The first X button is down
MK_XBUTTON2	&H40	The second X button is down

HSHELL_WINDOWACTIVATED

The current window has been changed to the active window. This is only for top-level unowned windows. The *wParam* parameter for this code contains the handle of the activated window. The *lParam* parameter for this code contains TRUE if the window is maximized or FALSE if it is not. This constant is defined as follows:

```
Public Const HSHELL_WINDOWACTIVATED = 4
```

HSHELL_GETMINRECT

Indicates that the user has either minimized or maximized the active window. This constant is defined as follows:

```
Public Const HSHELL_GETMINRECT = 5
```

Note that this code does not indicate that the user is resizing or moving the window. The *wParam* parameter for this code contains the handle to the window that the user minimized or maximized. The *lParam* parameter contains a pointer to a RECT structure that defines the window size. You should use *CopyMemory* to copy into a structure of type RECT the information that the pointer points to. A RECT structure is defined in Visual Basic (VB) as follows:

```
Public Type RECT
        Left As Long
        Top As Long
        Right As Long
        Bottom As Long
End Type
```

HSHELL_REDRAW

Indicates that the window title displayed in the Windows task bar has been redrawn. This code is not sent to the filter function when a window title is redrawn in the window title bar as a result of the user moving or sizing the window. This constant is defined as follows:

```
Public Const HSHELL_REDRAW = 6
```

The *wParam* parameter contains the handle to the window whose title the system redrew in the task bar. The *lParam* parameter contains **TRUE** if the window is flashing or **FALSE** otherwise.

HSHELL_TASKMAN

Indicates that the user has opened the Windows task manager. Returning **TRUE** from the filter function will prevent the system from displaying the task manager. This is useful if you want to replace the task manager with one of your own design or if you want to prevent the user from displaying the task manager altogether. This constant is defined as follows:

```
Public Const HSHELL_TASKMAN = 7
```

The *wParam* and *lParam* parameters are not used for this hook code.

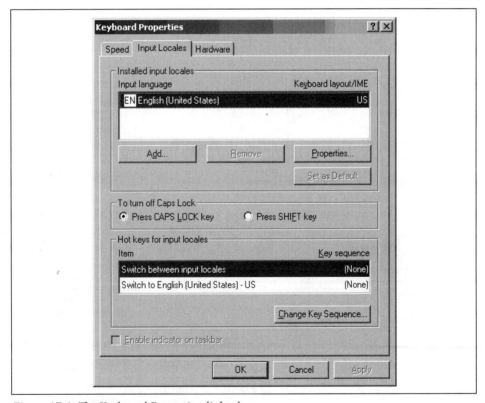

Figure 17-1. The Keyboard Properties dialog box

HSHELL_LANGUAGE

Indicates that the user has changed the keyboard language or layout. The user does this using the Input Locales tab of the Control Panel's Keyboard applet, which Figure 17-1 illustrates. This constant is defined as follows:

```
Public Const HSHELL_LANGUAGE = 8
```

Switching languages either through this dialog box or by using one of the keyboard shortcuts (Left ALT+SHIFT or CTRL+SHIFT) sends this code to this hook's filter function.

If none of these codes is passed in, you should skip message processing and call *CallNextHookEx* immediately.

Location of This Hook in the System

The filter function for this hook is called from within the message loop of the thread or threads in which this hook has been installed. Figure 17-2 illustrates this.

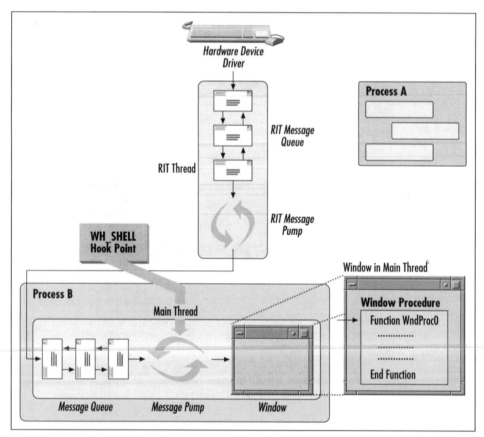

Figure 17-2. The location of the WH_SHELL hook in the system

A Thread-Specific Example

The example presented here is a thread-specific example that installs the WH_ SHELL hook and displays shell notification messages as they occur. Figure 17-3 provides a screenshot of the example application.

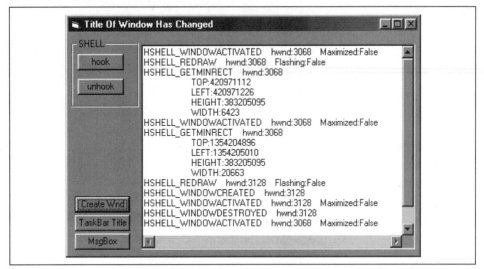

Figure 17-3. Screenshot of example application

Table 17-4 presents the nondefault properties of the form and its controls.

Using the Application

The application works like the previous examples. Click the hook button to install the hook and the unhook button to remove the hook. The hook and unhook buttons in the SHELL frame deal with the WH_SHELL hook. The following three extra buttons are included as well:

Create Wnd
Creates and displays a form using the code Load Form1.

TaskBar Title
Changes the text in the window title bar from "WH_SHELL Example" to "Title of Window Has Changed". Note that changing the top-level unowned window's title text causes the same text to be displayed in the task bar for this window.

MsgBox
Displays a simple message box.

Table 17-4. Nondefault Properties of the Form and Its Controls

Object	Property Name	Property Value
Form1	Name	Form2
Form1	Caption	"WH_SHELL Example"
Form1	Top	330
Form1	Left	105
Form1	Height	4710
Form1	Width	7095
Form2	Name	Form1
Form2	Caption	"NEW FORM"
Command Button1	Name	cmdHook
Command Button1	Caption	"hook"
Command Button1	Top	120
Command Button1	Left	120
Command Button1	Height	300
Command Button1	Width	915
Command Button2	Name	cmdUnhook
Command Button2	Caption	"unhook"
Command Button2	Top	780
Command Button2	Left	120
Command Button2	Height	300
Command Button2	Width	915
Command Button3	Name	cmdCreateWnd
Command Button3	Caption	"CreateWnd"
Command Button3	Top	3180
Command Button3	Left	120
Command Button3	Height	315
Command Button3	Width	1395
Command Button3	Name	cmdTaskBarTitle
Command Button4	Caption	"TaskBar Title"
Command Button4	Top	3540
Command Button4	Left	120
Command Button4	Height	315
Command Button4	Width	1395
Command Button4	Name	cmdMsgBox
Command Button5	Caption	"MsgBox"
Command Button5	Top	3900
Command Button5	Left	120

Table 17-4. Nondefault Properties of the Form and Its Controls (continued)

Object	Property Name	Property Value
Command Button5	Height	315
Command Button5	Width	1395
TextBox	MultiLine	True
TextBox	Top	240
TextBox	Left	1440
TextBox	Height	3975
TextBox	Width	5475

Clicking the Create Wnd button loads and displays a new VB form. This fires the following hook codes:

```
HSHELL_REDRAW               hwnd:3128      Flashing:False
HSHELL_WINDOWCREATED        hwnd:3128
HSHELL_WINDOWACTIVATED      hwnd:3128      Maximized:False
```

What has happened is that the HSHELL_REDRAW code was fired when the title text of the new window was redrawn in the task bar. Next, the HSHELL_WINDOWCREATED code is fired once the new window was created and displayed. Finally, the HSHELL_WINDOWACTIVATED code was fired when the newly created window became the active window.

When this window is destroyed, the following text is displayed in the application's text box:

```
HSHELL_WINDOWDESTROYED      hwnd:3128
HSHELL_WINDOWACTIVATED      hwnd:3068      Maximized:False
HSHELL_REDRAW               hwnd:3128      Flashing:False
```

HSHELL_WINDOWDESTROYED indicates that the window is about to be destroyed. At this point, though, the window is still being displayed on the screen. Next, the window is removed from the screen and destroyed. When this happens, the next window in the Z-order for this application, which is our initial main window, becomes active. This causes the HSHELL_WINDOWACTIVATED code to be fired. Finally, the HSHELL_REDRAW code is fired, indicating that the window title text of the recently destroyed window was removed from the task bar.

Clicking the MsgBox button does not fire any WH_SHELL hook codes. This is because these windows are not top-level unowned windows. Remember that this hook intercepts only actions taken on top-level unowned windows.

When the user clicks the TaskBar Title button, the following text appears in the application's text box:

```
HSHELL_REDRAW   hwnd:3068   Flashing:False
```

The window title text is modified on the window as well as on the task bar. After the text has been redrawn in the task bar, the HSHELL_REDRAW hook code is fired.

Bringing up the Windows task manager will cause the following text to be displayed in the application's text box:

    HSHELL_TASKMAN

The HSHELL_TASKMAN code is fired, indicating that the user is in the process of opening the task manager but the task manager itself has not yet been opened. Because the task manager has not been opened, it is possible to return a TRUE value from the filter function to prevent Windows from opening the task manager.

Minimizing the main window causes the system to display the following text in the text box:

    HSHELL_GETMINRECT   hwnd:3068
                            TOP:1363116648
                            LEFT:1363116762
                            HEIGHT:383205095
                            WIDTH:20799

The HSHELL_GETMINRECT code is fired in response to this action. This code provides a RECT structure in its *lParam* parameter indicating the top, left, height, and width of the window rectangle.

Restoring the main window from its minimized state causes the following text to be displayed in the text box:

    HSHELL_WINDOWACTIVATED   hwnd:3068   Maximized:False
    HSHELL_GETMINRECT   hwnd:3068
                                 TOP:707233504
                                 LEFT:707233618
                                 HEIGHT:383205095
                                 WIDTH:10791

The first hook code that is fired is HSHELL_WINDOWACTIVATED. This indicates that the window being maximized is first set as the active window. Next, HSHELL_ GETMINRECT is fired in response to the window's restoration. This code provides a RECT structure in its *lParam* parameter indicating the top, left, height, and width of the window rectangle.

Modifying the keyboard language or layout causes the following text to be displayed in the text box.

    HSHELL_LANGUAGE   hwnd:3068   Keybd Handle:67699766

After the new keyboard language or layout is loaded, this hook code is fired. The Keybd Handle contains a handle for the new keyboard language or layout.

If the user presses an application button on the mouse or the keyboard, the following hook code is fired:

```
HSHELL_APPCOMMAND          Destination:3068     APP_CMD:6560768
```

The **Destination** value is the window handle of the main window in our application. The **APP_CMD** value is a combination of the application command, the device that generated the command, and a flag value. Using this information, the developer can cause specific actions to occur in response to the click of application buttons on keyboards and mice.

If the user changes the accessibility state, the text box displays one of the following lines of text:

```
HSHELL_ACCESSIBILITYSTATE     wParam:FILTERKEYS
HSHELL_ACCESSIBILITYSTATE     wParam:STICKYKEYS
HSHELL_ACCESSIBILITYSTATE     wParam:MOUSEKEYS
```

The value that the *wParam* field displays in depends on what type of accessibility state the user changed.

The Code

This application consists of a code module named *Module2.bas*, as well as forms named Form1 and Form2; the latter is the application's startup form. The *Module2. bas* module of the application declares two private member variables:

```
Private hHook As Long
Public IsHooked As Boolean
```

The *hHook* variable contains the handle to the installed **WH_SHELL** hook. The *SetWindowHookEx* function returns this value. The **IsHooked** flag indicates whether this hook has been installed.

The *SetShellHook* installs the **WH_SHELL** hook by calling the *SetWindowsHookEx* function, as Example 17-1 shows.

Example 17-1. Installing the WH_SHELL Hook

```
Public Sub SetShellHook()
    If IsHooked Then
        MsgBox "Don't hook SHELL twice or you will be unable to unhook it."
    Else
        hHook = SetWindowsHookEx(WH_SHELL, AddressOf ShellProc, 0, App.ThreadID)
        IsHooked = True
    End If
End Sub
```

The *RemoveShellHook*, shown in Example 17-2, removes the **WH_SHELL** hook by calling the *UnhookWindowsHookEx* function.

Example 17-2. Uninstalling the WH_SHELL Hook

```
Public Sub RemoveShellHook()
    Dim temp As Long
    temp = UnhookWindowsHookEx(hHook)
    IsHooked = False
End Sub
```

The *ShellProc* function in Example 17-3 acts as the filter function for the WH_SHELL hook. The second argument of the *SetWindowsHookEx* function (in this case, AddressOf ShellProc) defines the filter function. This function simply prints out the various hook codes and their parameters in the Text1 text box on this application's main window.

Example 17-3. The WH_SHELL Filter Function

```
Public Function ShellProc(ByVal uCode As Long, ByVal wParam As Long, _
                          ByVal lParam As Long) As Long
    Dim structWindowSize As RECT

    Select Case uCode
        Case HSHELL_ACTIVATESHELLWINDOW
            Form2.Text1.Text = Form2.Text1.Text & "HSHELL_ACTIVATESHELLWINDOW" & _
                               vbNewLine
        Case HSHELL_WINDOWCREATED
            'wParam == Handle to the created window
            Form2.Text1.Text = Form2.Text1.Text & "HSHELL_WINDOWCREATED    hwnd:" _
                               & wParam & vbNewLine
        Case HSHELL_WINDOWDESTROYED
            'wParam == Handle to the destroyed window
            Form2.Text1.Text = Form2.Text1.Text & "HSHELL_WINDOWDESTROYED    hwnd:" _
                               & wParam & vbNewLine
        Case HSHELL_WINDOWACTIVATED
            'wParam == Handle to the activated window
            'lParam == The value is TRUE if the window is in full-screen mode,
            'or FALSE otherwise
            Form2.Text1.Text = Form2.Text1.Text & "HSHELL_WINDOWACTIVATED    hwnd:" _
                               & wParam & "    Maximized:" & CBool(lParam) & vbNewLine
        Case HSHELL_GETMINRECT
            'wParam == Handle to the minimized or maximized window
            'lParam == Pointer to a RECT structure
            CopyMemory structWindowSize, lParam, Len(structWindowSize)
            Form2.Text1.Text = Form2.Text1.Text & "HSHELL_GETMINRECT    hwnd:" & _
                               wParam & vbNewLine
            Form2.Text1.Text = Form2.Text1.Text & "                         TOP:" _
                               & structWindowSize.Top & vbNewLine
            Form2.Text1.Text = Form2.Text1.Text & "                         LEFT:" _
                               & structWindowSize.Left & vbNewLine
            Form2.Text1.Text = Form2.Text1.Text & "                         HEIGHT:" _
                               & structWindowSize.Right & vbNewLine
            Form2.Text1.Text = Form2.Text1.Text & "                         WIDTH:" _
                               & structWindowSize.Bottom & vbNewLine
        Case HSHELL_REDRAW
```

Example 17-3. The WH_SHELL Filter Function (continued)

```
                'wParam == Handle to the redrawn window
                'lParam == The value is TRUE if the window is flashing, or FALSE otherwise
                Form2.Text1.Text = Form2.Text1.Text & "HSHELL_REDRAW    hwnd:" & wParam _
                               & "  Flashing:" & CBool(lParam) & vbNewLine
        Case HSHELL_TASKMAN
                Form2.Text1.Text = Form2.Text1.Text & "HSHELL_TASKMAN" & vbNewLine
        Case HSHELL_LANGUAGE
                'wParam == Handle to the window
                'lParam == Handle to a keyboard layout
                Form2.Text1.Text = Form2.Text1.Text & "HSHELL_LANGUAGE    hwnd:" & _
                               wParam & "   Keybd Handle:" & lParam & vbNewLine
        Case HSHELL_ACCESSIBILITYSTATE
                'wParam == ACCESS_FILTERKEYS, ACCESS_MOUSEKEYS, or ACCESS_STICKYKEYS
                Form2.Text1.Text = Form2.Text1.Text & _
                                   "HSHELL_ACCESSIBILITYSTATE wParam:""
                If wParam = ACCESS_FILTERKEYS Then
                        Form2.Text1.Text = Form2.Text1.Text & "FILTERKEYS" & vbNewLine
                ElseIf wParam = ACCESS_MOUSEKEYS Then
                        Form2.Text1.Text = Form2.Text1.Text & "MOUSEKEYS" & vbNewLine
                ElseIf wParam = ACCESS_STICKYKEYS Then
                        Form2.Text1.Text = Form2.Text1.Text & "STICKYKEYS" & vbNewLine
                End If
        Case HSHELL_APPCOMMAND
                'wParam == Windows 2000: Where the WM_APPCOMMAND message was
                'originally sent
                'lParam == application command corresponding to the input event
                Form2.Text1.Text = Form2.Text1.Text & "HSHELLAPPCOMMAND    " & _
                                   "Destination:" & wParam & " APP_CMD:" & _
                                   lParam & vbNewLine
                'Since we handle this message we should prevent it from being
                'handled elsewhere
                ShellProc = True
                Exit Function
    End Select

    ShellProc = CallNextHookEx(hHook, uCode, wParam, lParam)
End Function
```

This filter function has two points of interest. The first is the code that handles the **HSHELL_GETMINRECT** case. It uses *CopyMemory* to get the **RECT** structure from the returned pointer in the *lParam* parameter. This is something that we have seen before. The second is the **HSHELL_APPCOMMAND** case. If we handle this hook code, we need to return a **TRUE** value and exit the function at this point. Doing this prevents any other installed **WH_SHELL** filter functions from handling this hook code. The code behind the *Form2.frm* module, which is shown in Example 17-4, simply calls the functions in the *Module1.bas* module to install and remove the **WH_SHELL** hook. The Command5 button creates and displays a new form, the Command6 button changes the title of the main window, and the Command7 button displays a message box. These two buttons allow you to test several of the WH_SHELL hook codes.

Example 17-4. The Code for Form2.frm

```
Private Sub Command1_Click()
    Text1.Text = ""
    Call SetShellHook
End Sub

Private Sub Command2_Click()
    Call RemoveShellHook
End Sub


Private Sub Command5_Click()
    Form1.Show
End Sub

Private Sub Command6_Click()
    If Me.Caption = "Title Of Window Has Changed" Then
        Me.Caption = "WH_SHELL Example"
    Else
        Me.Caption = "Title Of Window Has Changed"
    End If
End Sub

Private Sub Command7_Click()
    MsgBox "The WH_SHELL hook does not acknowledge the creation of this message box."
End Sub

'-----------
'CLEANUP
'-----------
Private Sub Form_QueryUnload(Cancel As Integer, UnloadMode As Integer)
    If IsHooked Or IsDBGHooked Then
    Cancel = 1
    MsgBox "Unhook before closing, or the IDE will crash."
    End If
End Sub
```

Caveats

As with all hooks, performance needs to be a top consideration, although this hook carries a smaller performance penalty than most other hooks. This is because this hook intercepts fewer messages than other hooks do. For example, the WH_MOUSE hook intercepts many messages every second—mainly messages such as WM_MOUSEMOVE. The WH_SHELL hook intercepts messages at a higher level. By this I mean that instead of calling the hook's filter function for all messages that are either sent or posted to create a window, it waits until the window has been created and then at that point its filter function is called.

Two of the codes that this hook implements work only on Windows 2000 and greater operating systems. These codes are:

```
HSHELL_ACCESSIBILITYSTATE
HSHELL_APPCOMMAND
```

We should pay attention to when the hook's filter function is called. For instance, when window is created, the HSHELL_WINDOWCREATED code is fired *after* the window is created and displayed. However, if the window is being destroyed, the HSHELL_WINDOWDESTROYED code is fired before the window is removed from the screen and destroyed.

The HSHELL_TASKMAN code is fired before the Windows task manager is opened. This is the only hook code that allows you to return a TRUE value to prevent the action from occurring. No other hook codes have this ability.

It is important to remember that the HSHELL_APPCOMMAND hook code is fired only if the application itself has not processed the WM_APPCOMMAND message. Also keep in mind that if the filter function processes this message, you should immediately return a TRUE to prevent the *CallNextHookEx* function from being called.

And remember, this hook operates only on top-level unowned windows. This hook ignores message boxes and other various owned or child windows.

18

WH_CBT

You use the WH_CBT hook primarily for building Computer Based Training (CBT) applications. A *CBT application* trains a user to use an application. Usually, it will present a text-based set of instructions for using the application; however, it also can contain multimedia demonstrations. But the real power of CBT is its ability to walk the user through specific pieces of the application in which the user is being trained. The real magic behind CBT is the WH_CBT hook, although you can typically use other hooks as well, including the WH_JOURNALPLAYBACK hook and the WH_MOUSE and WH_KEYBOARD hooks.

Let's step through a portion of an example CBT application—in this case, a simple one in which the user is learning how to save an Excel spreadsheet. When the CBT application starts an Excel application and opens a sample spreadsheet, it gathers some general information about the application that will tell it what the user is doing in Excel, including:

- The ProcessID
- The handle to the top-level window
- The handle to the main menu
- The position of the top-level window

Next, the application presents the user with instructions on how to save a spreadsheet, possibly including a multimedia presentation as well. After reading the explanation, the user is prompted to perform the Save operation on the running instance of Excel. This is where the WH_CBT hook comes into play: the hook is installed before the user actually performs the Save operation and is released after the user is finished performing the operation and the hook is no longer needed. While it is installed, the hook makes it possible to watch key actions that the user makes. (The CBT might also need to install the WH_MOUSE and/or WH_KEYBOARD hooks so that it can be notified of more specific actions that the user is per-forming, which the WH_CBT hook might not be able to see.)

Using the WH_CBT hook, the CBT application can watch the user select the File menu item and then click the Save menu item. If this is the first time the spread-sheet is being saved, a Save dialog will be displayed allowing the user to choose where and how to save the spreadsheet. The WH_CBT hook also can see the Save dialog being displayed and will follow the user's actions within the Save dialog. If the user deviates from the way that the CBT application wants the user to save a spreadsheet, then the CBT application can raise a warning stating that the user is not following the correct procedure. This is a difficult process for the CBT applica-tion to perform because the user can perform many different actions, and even save the spreadsheet in many different ways. For example, the user could use the Ctrl-S key combination, or the File → Save or File → Save As menu commands to save the spreadsheet. This is the real challenge of creating a CBT application.

If the user completes the Save operation correctly, the CBT application can dis-play a congratulatory message. However, if the user fails to complete the opera-tion correctly or in the right order, the CBT application can prompt the user to show the correct process. This is where the WH_JOURNALPLAYBACK hook comes into play. You install and use this hook to play back a prerecorded string of mes-sages against the Excel application. This string of messages might look something like this:

1. Position the mouse pointer over the Excel application's File menu.

2. Click the File menu.

3. Position the mouse pointer over the Save menu item.

4. Click the Save menu item. The Save dialog box is displayed here with the focus on the "File name" text box.

5. A filename is typed into the "File name" text box in the Save dialog box.

6. The correct directory in which to save the file is chosen.

7. The Save button is clicked.

After this string of prerecorded messages is played back, the WH_ JOURNALPLAYBACK hook is released and the user can retry the operation or go back to reread the finer points of saving a spreadsheet.

As you can see, the WH_CBT hook is central to writing CBT applications. But because of the amount of functionality built into this hook, you might find many other interesting uses for this hook as well.

With the description of CBT out of the way, let's get into the nuts and bolts of the WH_CBT hook.

Description

The WH_CBT hook captures a wide variety of information about the actions a user is performing on the system. The system notifies the WH_CBT hook *before* any of the following actions occur:

- A window is created.

- A window is destroyed.

- A window is activated.

- A window is moved.

- A window is sized.

- A window is minimized.

- A window is maximized.

- The input focus is set to a different window.

- A user completes a system command. *System commands* originate from a window's system menu, maximize button, minimize button, restore button, or close button.

- A mouse message is removed from the raw input thread (RIT).

- A keyboard message is removed from the RIT.

- The current thread is synchronized with the RIT.

Because this notification occurs before any of these actions, you can prevent the action from occurring by passing back a nonzero return value from the filter function.

You can use this hook as a thread-specific hook, or you can place it in a dynamic link library (DLL) and use it as a system-wide hook. A thread-specific hook intercepts all messages within the thread in which it is installed. When you install a hook as a system-wide hook, you must place it in a DLL. This DLL is injected into every process so that the hook can operate on all messages in the system. Chapter 3 discusses this in detail.

Filter Function Definition

The filter function for the WH_CBT hook is defined as follows:

```
Public Function CBTProc(ByVal uCode As Long, ByVal wParam As Long, _
                ByVal lParam As Long) As Long
```

The filter function's parameters are defined as follows:

uCode

The code the system passes in to the function. The next section explains the valid codes for this hook.

wParam

The value depends on the *uCode* that is passed to the function.

lParam

The value depends on the *uCode* that is passed to the function.

The return value for this filter function should be the return value of the *CallNextHookEx* function. If this function is not called, return a zero. To prevent the action from occurring, return a 1. I do not recommend skipping the call to *CallNextHookEx*, though. Failing to call this function will prevent other filter functions in the chain from being called.

The *uCode* sent to this function will either be one of the HCBT_* codes specifically used with this hook, or a negative number. If any of the HCBT_* codes is passed as an argument, the filter function should process the information passed to it. If the *uCode* argument is a negative number, you should call *CallNextHookEx* immediately, and the filter function should not process any information passed to it.

Explanation of Hook Codes

The system can send the following 10 hook codes to this hook. Because the *lParam* and *wParam* parameters for this hook function depend on the hook code, each code description also contains a definition of the code's corresponding *lParam* and *wParam* parameters. The codes are:

HCBT_SETFOCUS

Notifies the hook that the user is causing a new control contained in a window to receive the focus. In this case, a *window* refers only to a control contained within a parent window. Therefore, the WH_CBT hook will be sent this code whenever the user changes the active control on a window to a new control, but not when the user changes the active window to a different window. The filter function can return a nonzero value to prevent the new control from gaining the focus. The other parameters passed to the filter function are:

wParam

The hWnd of the window gaining the focus

lParam

The hWnd of the window losing the focus

The HCBT_SETFOCUS constant is defined as follows:

```
Public Const HCBT_SETFOCUS = 9
```

HCBT_ACTIVATE

Notifies the hook that the user is activating a different window. In this case, the hook is notified only when a window—i.e., a Visual Basic (VB) form rather than a control—is activated; use HCBT_SETFOCUS to determine when a control receives the focus. Note, however, that usually a control is given the focus on a newly activated window. In these cases, you will see HCBT_ ACTIVATE followed immediately by HCBT_SETFOCUS. The filter function can return a nonzero value to prevent the window from being activated. The other parameters passed to the filter function are:

wParam

The hWnd of the window that is about to become active.

lParam

A pointer to a **CBTACTIVATESTRUCT** structure, which is defined as follows:

```
Public Type CBTACTIVATESTRUCT
    fMouse As Long
    hWndActive As Long
End Type
```

Table 18-1 describes the members of the **CBTACTIVATESTRUCT** structure.

Table 18-1. Members of the CBTACTIVATESTRUCT Structure

Member	Description
fMouse	True if a mouse click activated the window; otherwise False, indicating that something else, such as an ALT-TAB key combination, activated the window
hWndActive	The hwnd of the active window

This constant is defined as follows:

```
Public Const HCBT_ACTIVATE = 5
```

HCBT_MINMAX

Notifies the hook that the user is about to minimize or maximize a window. The filter function can return a nonzero value to prevent the minimize or maximize operation. The other parameters passed to the filter function are:

wParam

The hWnd to the window that the user is minimizing or maximizing.

lParam

The low-order word of this parameter is one of the following values:

```
Public Const SW_MAXIMIZE = 3        'Maximizes the window
Public Const SW_MINIMIZE = 6        'Minimizes the window
Public Const SW_SHOWMAXIMIZED = 3   'Activates and minimizes the window
```

```
Public Const SW_SHOWMINIMIZED = 2    'Activates and maximizes the window
Public Const SW_SHOWMINNOACTIVE = 7 'Minimizes the window and
                                     'does not activate it
```

The high-order word of this parameter is undefined. To find the low-order word of *lParam*, simply AND *lParam* with the value &HFFFF.

The HCBT_MINMAX constant is defined as follows:

```
Public Const HCBT_MINMAX = 1
```

HCBT_MOVESIZE

Notifies the hook that the user is about to move or size a window. The filter function can return a nonzero value to prevent the window from being moved or sized. The other parameters passed to the filter function are:

wParam

The hWnd of the window that the user is moving or sizing.

lParam

Pointer to a RECT structure, which is defined as follows:

```
Public Type RECT
    Left As Long
    Top As Long
    Right As Long
    Bottom As Long
End Type
```

.You can modify the values in this structure to control the final destination of a window when the user is moving it, or the final size of a window when the user is sizing it.

The HCBT_MOVESIZE constant is defined as follows:

```
Public Const HCBT_MOVESIZE = 0
```

HCBT_DESTROYWND

Notifies the hook that a window is about to be destroyed. The filter function can return a nonzero value to prevent the window's destruction. The other parameters passed to the filter function are:

wParam

The hWnd to the window about to be destroyed

lParam

Not used

The constant is defined as follows:

```
Public Const HCBT_DESTROYWND = 4
```

HCBT_CREATEWND

Notifies the hook that the user is about to create a window . The other parameters passed to the filter function are:

wParam

The hWnd of the window that the user is about to create

lParam

A pointer to a **CBT_CREATEWND** structure, which is defined as follows:

```
Public Type CBT_CREATEWND
lpcs As CREATESTRUCT
hWndInsertAfter As Long
End Type
```

Table 18-2 shows the members of the **CBT_CREATEWND** structure.

Table 18-2. Members of the CBT_CREATEWND Structure

Member	Description

lpcs	Pointer to a CREATESTRUCT structure, which is defined as follows:
	
	 ```Public Type CREATESTRUCT```
	     ```lpCreateParams As Long```
	     ```hInstance As Long```
	     ```hMenu As Long```
	     ```hWndParent As Long```
	     ```cy As Long```
	     ```cx As Long```
	     ```y As Long```
	     ```x As Long```
	     ```style As Long```
	     ```lpszName As String```
	     ```lpszClass As String```
	     ```ExStyle As Long```
	 ```End Type```
	
	 I discussed this structure in detail in Chapter 2. You can modify the members of this structure to change the properties of the new window. For instance, you can substitute a new menu handle in the *hMenu* member, or you can modify the *x*, *y*, *cx*, and *cy* members to change the initial position and size of the window.

hWndInsertAfter	The hWnd of the window whose position in the Z-order is to precede the window being created. You can modify *hWndInsertAfter* to change the position in the Z-order of the window that is being created.

The **HCBT_CREATEWND** constant is defined as follows:

```
Public Const HCBT_CREATEWND = 3
```

HCBT_SYSCOMMAND

Notifies the hook that a system command is about to be processed. The filter function can return a nonzero value to disable the system command that the user selects. The other parameters passed to the filter function are:

wParam

The type of system command that the user selected. Valid values for this parameter are:

```
Public Const SC_CLOSE = &HF060&          'Close the window
Public Const SC_HOTKEY = &HF150&         'Activates wnd associated with
                                         'the hotkey
Public Const SC_HSCROLL = &HF080&        'Scroll horizontally
Public Const SC_KEYMENU = &HF100&        'Gets wnd menu as the result of a
                                         'keypress
Public Const SC_MONITORPOWER = &H10      'Forces the display to a low-power
                                         'or off setting
Public Const SC_MAXIMIZE = &HF030&       'Maximize the window
Public Const SC_MINIMIZE = &HF020&       'Minimize the window
Public Const SC_MOUSEMENU = &HF090&      'Gets wnd menu as the result of a
                                         'mouse click
Public Const SC_MOVE = &HF010&           'Move the window
Public Const SC_NEXTWINDOW = &HF040&     'Activates the next window
Public Const SC_PREVWINDOW = &HF050&     'Activates the previous window
Public Const SC_RESTORE = &HF120&        'Restores the current window to its
                                         'original state
Public Const SC_SCREENSAVE = &HF140&     'Starts the screensaver
Public Const SC_SIZE = &HF000&           'Sizes the window
Public Const SC_TASKLIST = &HF130&       'Activates the Start menu
Public Const SC_VSCROLL = &HF070&        'Scroll vertically
Public Const SC_ICON = SC_MINIMIZE       'The window is being minimized
Public Const SC_ZOOM = SC_MAXIMIZE       'The window is being maximized
```

lParam

If the user used the mouse to select the system command from the window menu, the low-order word of this parameter contains the mouse pointer's x coordinate, and the high-order word contains the mouse pointer's y coordinate. If the user did not use the mouse, the low-order word of this parameter is not used, and the high-order word is –1 if a system accelerator key was used, or zero if a mnemonic was used. The following function will return the high-order word:

```
Public Function GetHiWord(ByRef Value As Long) As Long
    If (Value And &H80000000) = &H80000000 Then
        GetHiWord = ((Value And &H7FFF0000) \ &H10000) Or &H8000&
    Else
        GetHiWord = (Value And &HFFFF0000) \ &H10000
    End If
End Function
```

The **HCBT_SYSCOMMAND** constant is defined as follows:

```
Public Const HCBT_SYSCOMMAND = 8
```

HCBT_QS

Used by the hook to synchronize between messages that a **WH_ JOURNALPLAYBACK** hook plays back and messages that the mouse and keyboard normally send. (I provide more information about how to use this code later in this chapter.) The system ignores this hook's return value. The other parameters passed to the filter function are:

wParam

Not used

lParam

Not used

The constant is defined as follows:

```
Public Const HCBT_QS = 2
```

HCBT_KEYSKIPPED

Indicates that a keyboard message has been removed from the RIT. (I provide more information about how to use this code later in this chapter.) The system ignores this hook's return value. The other parameters passed to the filter function are:

wParam

The virtual key code of the key that the user typed.

lParam

The repeat count, scan code, extended-key flag, context code, previous key-state flag, and transition-state flag of the key that the user typed. The *lParam* parameter is divided into the bit fields shown in Table 18-3.

Table 18-3. Bit Fields of the lParam Parameter for the HCBT_KEYSKIPPED Code

Bit Positions	Description
0-15	The repeat count.
16-23	The scan code.
24	If 1, this is an extended key; if 0, this is not an extended key.
25-28	Reserved.
29	The context code. This value is 0 for WM_KEYUP messages.
30	The previous key state. This value is 0 for WM_KEYUP messages.
31	The Transition state. This value is 0 for WM_KEYUP messages.

The HCBT_KEYSKIPPED constant is defined as follows:

```
Public Const HCBT_KEYSKIPPED = 7
```

HCBT_CLICKSKIPPED

Indicates that a mouse message has been removed from the RIT. (I provide more information about how to use this code later in this chapter.) The system ignores this hook's return value. The other parameters passed to the filter function are:

wParam

The mouse message that was removed from the RIT.

lParam

Pointer to a **MOUSEHOOKSTRUCT** structure, which is defined as follows:

```
Public Type MOUSEHOOKSTRUCT
pt As POINTAPI
hwnd As Long
wHitTestCode As Long
dwExtraInfo As Long
End Type
```

Table 18-4 shows the members of the **MOUSEHOOKSTRUCT** structure.

Table 18-4. Members of the MOUSEHOOKSTRUCT Structure

Member	Description

pt	A pointer to a POINTAPI structure, which is defined as follows:
	   Public Type POINTAPI
	   x As Long
	   y As Long
	   End Type

hwnd	Handle of the window that is to receive the mouse message
wHitTestCode	The hit test value
dwExtraInfo	Contains any extra information associated with the message

The **HCBT_CLICKSKIPPED** constant is defined as follows:

```
Public Const HCBT_CLICKSKIPPED = 6
```

Comparing WH_SHELL to WH_CBT

The closest relative to the WH_CBT hook is the WH_SHELL hook. Chapter 17 describes the WH_SHELL hook in detail. Generally speaking, you use the WH_SHELL hook to retrieve information from top-level windows and the WH_CBT hook to create CBT applications. That is not to say that each hook is confined to only working on top-level windows or on CBT applications; the use of each hook is limited only by the developer's imagination.

The two hooks are compared in Table 18-5. As you can see, the hooks' hook codes overlap somewhat. But in terms of functionality, the WH_CBT hook has more flexibility and power than the WH_SHELL hook. The WH_CBT hook is notified of events that occur on all windows, not just on top-level unowned windows, as is the case with the WH_SHELL hook. Possibly of more importance, though, is the WH_CBT hook's ability to actually prevent the event from occurring by returning a nonzero value from the filter function. This occurs because the WH_CBT hook is notified of the event before it has taken place, whereas the WH_SHELL hook in most instances is notified after the event has taken place. The sole exception to this rule is the WH_SHELL hook's HSHELL_WINDOWDESTROYED hook code, which intercepts the window destruction before it occurs.

Table 18-5. Comparison of the WH_CBT Hook to the WH_SHELL Hook

WH_CBT Hook Code	Comparison to WH_SHELL
HCBT_ACTIVATE	The WH_SHELL hook uses the HSHELL_WINDOWACTIVATED hook code to notify itself that a different top-level unowned window has become the active window. This notification is sent after the window has become the active window instead of before, as is the case with the HCBT_ACTIVATE code. Also, the HCBT_ACTIVATE hook code notifies the WH_CBT hook of any windows that change activation, not only of top-level unowned windows.
HCBT_SETFOCUS	WH_SHELL has no comparable hook code.
HCBT_CLICKSKIPPED	WH_SHELL has no comparable hook code.
HCBT_CREATEWND	The WH_SHELL hook uses the HSHELL_WINDOWCREATED hook code to notify itself that a top-level unowned window has already been created. The window exists when the WH_SHELL hook filter function is called. The HCBT_CREATEWND hook code is sent to the WH_CBT hook before the window is actually created. This allows the WH_CBT hook to modify the window's properties before the window is displayed, or even to prevent the window from being created at all. HCBT_CREATEWND notifies the WH_CBT hook of any window being created, not just of top-level unowned windows.
HCBT_DESTROYWND	The WH_SHELL hook uses the HSHELL_WINDOWDESTROYED hook code to notify itself that a top-level unowned window is about to be destroyed. The window exists when the WH_SHELL hook receives this notification. Both this hook code and the HCBT_DESTROYWND code for the WH_CBT hook notify the filter function before the window is actually destroyed. The HCBT_DESTROYWND code notifies the WH_CBT hook of any window being destroyed, not just of top-level unowned windows.
HCBT_KEYSKIPPED	WH_SHELL has no comparable hook code.
HCBT_MINMAX	The WH_SHELL hook uses the HSHELL_GETMINRECT hook code to notify itself that a window is being minimized or maximized. The HCBT_MINMAX code contains a show window value (SW_*) that provides more detail on the minimization or maximization operation, which the HSHELL_GETMINRECT hook code lacks. The HCBT_MINMAX code notifies the WH_CBT hook of any window being destroyed, not just of top-level unowned windows.
HCBT_MOVESIZE	WH_SHELL has no comparable hook code.
HCBT_QS	WH_SHELL has no comparable hook code.
HCBT_SYSCOMMAND	WH_SHELL has no comparable hook code.

A Thread-Specific Example

This first example illustrates the information that you can obtain from the `WH_CBT` hook. Figure 18-1 shows a screenshot of the application. This application contains a menu bar with the Test menu item, a CreateWnd button, and a MSGBOX button. Each item will aid in our understanding of this hook.

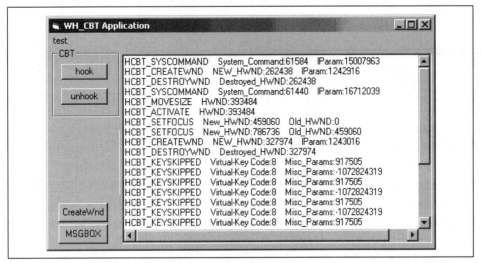

Figure 18-1. Screenshot of the WH_CBT application

Table 18-6 presents the nondefault properties of the form and its controls.

Table 18-6. Nondefault Properties of the Form and Its Controls

Object	Property Name	Property Value
Form1	Name	Form2
Form1	Caption	"WH_CBT Application"
Form1	Top	330
Form1	Left	105
Form1	Height	4710
Form1	Width	7095
Form2	Name	Form1
Form2	Caption	"NEW FORM"
Command Button1	Name	cmdHook
Command Button1	Caption	"hook"
Command Button1	Top	120
Command Button1	Left	120
Command Button1	Height	300

Table 18-6. Nondefault Properties of the Form and Its Controls (continued)

Object	Property Name	Property Value
Command Button1	Width	915
Command Button2	Name	cmdUnhook
Command Button2	Caption	"unhook"
Command Button2	Top	780
Command Button2	Left	120
Command Button2	Height	300
Command Button2	Width	915
Command Button3	Name	cmdCreateWnd
Command Button3	Caption	"CreateWnd"
Command Button3	Top	3180
Command Button3	Left	120
Command Button3	Height	315
Command Button3	Width	1395
Command Button4	Name	cmdMsgBox
Command Button4	Caption	"MsgBox"
Command Button4	Top	3900
Command Button4	Left	120
Command Button4	Height	315
Command Button4	Width	1395
TextBox	Name	Text1
TextBox	MultiLine	True
TextBox	Top	240
TextBox	Left	1440
TextBox	Height	3975
TextBox	Width	5475

To install this hook, simply click the hook button contained in the CBT frame control. After the hook is installed, begin experimenting with it by clicking the CreateWnd and MSGBOX buttons, as well as the Test menu item. You will notice some interesting things, including the following:

• When you create a pop-up menu by right-clicking either a text box or the title bar, the WH_CBT hook is sent a HCBT_CREATEWND code when it appears and a HCBT_DESTROYWND code when it is closed.

• If the pop-up menu is a system menu and the user chooses an item in the menu, a HCBT_SYSCOMMAND code is sent to the hook after the HCBT_DESTROYWND code is sent.

- When you minimize a window by clicking the Minimize button in the window's title bar, an HCBT_SYSCOMMAND code is sent. This code is followed by the HCBT_MINMAX code, and then by the HCBT_SETFOCUS code. The HCBT_SETFOCUS code indicates that the focus has shifted from the minimized window to another window. If the *wParam* of the HCBT_SETFOCUS code is zero, the desktop window is receiving the focus.

- If you deactivate the application's main window, no codes are sent to the hook, but if you activate the application's main window, the HCBT_ACTIVATE code is sent, followed by an HCBT_SETFOCUS code. This HCBT_SETFOCUS code indicates which control on the window got the focus. The control that gets the focus is the last control to have the focus before the window was deactivated.

- If clicking its title bar activates the application's main window, the HCBT_ACTIVATE code is sent, followed by the HCBT_SETFOCUS code, which we saw in the previous bullet. The HCBT_SYSCOMMAND code is then sent with the SC_MOVE value in the *wParam* parameter, indicating that the title bar was clicked. If an SC_SIZE value is in the *wParam* parameter, you clicked a sizing border when you activated the window.

- When you create a window, regardless of whether it is a message box, a dialog box, or a top-level window, a series of codes are sent to this hook. The HCBT_CREATEWND code is sent for the window and for every control that is created on the window. Then the HCBT_SETFOCUS code is sent, indicating which control gets the focus on the new window. Finally, the HCBT_ACTIVATE code is sent, indicating that the window is being activated.

- When you destroy a window, regardless of whether it is a message box, a dialog box, or a top-level window, a series of codes are sent to this hook. First, the HCBT_ACTIVATE code is sent, indicating that a new window is about to be activated. Next, the HCBT_SETFOCUS code is sent, indicating that a control on the newly activated window is about to receive the focus. Finally, the controls on the window about to be destroyed are destroyed, along with the window.

- The form is always created first; the controls are created in an order defined by the control's control ID. The control with a control ID of 1 is always created first. The VBFocusRT6 window has a control ID of zero. There is always one of these windows for each VB application; therefore, you will notice that the control IDs start at 1 and increase from there when a window is created or destroyed in a VB application.

- The controls are always destroyed in the same order in which they were created. This also depends on the control's control ID. Therefore, the control with an ID of 1 is always created first and destroyed first. The form is destroyed last.

- When you move or size a window, an HCBT_SYSCOMMAND code is sent to the hook first with a *wParam* of SC_MOVE or SC_SIZE, respectively. Next, the HCBT_MOVESIZE code is sent to the hook.

- When you minimize, maximize, or restore the window, an HCBT_SYSCOMMAND code is sent with a *wParam* value of SC_MINIMIZE, SC_MAXIMIZE, or SC_RESTORE, respectively. Next, the HCBT_MINMAX code is sent with a show-window value in the low-order word of the *lParam* parameter. This show-window value can be SW_MINIMIZE, SW_MAXIMIZE, or SW_RESTORE.

- If you use the TAB key to set the focus to another control, the HCBT_SETFOCUS code is sent to the hook. However, if a WH_KEYBOARD hook is set, the HCBT_KEYSKIPPED code also is sent to the hook both before and after the HCBT_SETFOCUS code. The two HCBT_KEYSKIPPED codes indicate the key being pressed and the key being released.

Example 18-1 lists the code behind the *Form2.frm* module. The *cmdHook_Click* and *cmdUnHook_Click* events install and remove the CBT hook, respectively. The *cmdMsgBox_Click* event displays a message box, and the *cmdCreateWnd_Click* event shows the Form1 form. These last two button-click events allow us to test the CBT hook's functionality.

Example 18-1. Code Contained in the Form2.frm Module

```
Private Sub cmdHook_Click()
    Text1.Text = ""
    Call SetCBTHook
End Sub

Private Sub cmdUnHook_Click()
    Call RemoveCBTHook
End Sub


Private Sub cmdMsgBox_Click()
    MsgBox "test"
End Sub


Private Sub cmdCreateWnd_Click()
    Form1.Show
End Sub

'-----------
'CLEANUP
'-----------
Private Sub Form_QueryUnload(Cancel As Integer, UnloadMode As Integer)
    If IsHooked Then
```

Example 18-1. Code Contained in the Form2.frm Module (continued)

```
        Cancel = 1
        MsgBox "Unhook before closing, or the IDE will crash."
    End If
End Sub
```

The *Form_QueryUnload* event tests the *IsHooked* flag to determine if the CBT hook is still installed. If it is, a message is displayed warning that this hook is still installed and that the application cannot shut down. Without this check, if the application were to shut down with the hook still installed, the application would suffer a General Protection Fault (GPF) upon closing.

You set up this hook in much the same way as you do the previous hooks. The code in Example 18-2 contains a function to install the hook, a function to remove the hook, and the CBT filter function. The code in Example 18-2 is contained in the *Module1.bas* module.

Example 18-2. Code Contained in the Module1.bas Module

```
Private hHook As Long
Public IsHooked as Boolean

Public Sub SetCBTHook()
    If IsHooked Then
        MsgBox "Don't hook CBT twice or you will be unable to unhook it."
    Else
        hHook = SetWindowsHookEx(WH_CBT, AddressOf CBTProc, 0, App.ThreadID)
        IsHooked = True
    End If
End Sub

Public Sub RemoveCBTHook()
    Dim temp As Long
    temp = UnhookWindowsHookEx(hHook)
    IsHooked = False
End Sub

Public Function CBTProc(ByVal uCode As Long, ByVal wParam As Long, _
                        ByVal lParam As Long) As Long
    If uCode >= 0 Then
        Select Case uCode
            Case HCBT_ACTIVATE
                'wParam == Specifies the handle to the window about to be activated
                'lParam == Pointer to the CBTACTIVATESTRUCT struct
                Form2.Text1.Text = Form2.Text1.Text & "HCBT_ACTIVATE   HWND:" & _
                                wParam & vbNewLine
            Case HCBT_CLICKSKIPPED
                'wParam == Specifies the mouse message removed from the
                '             system message queue
                'lParam == Pointer to the MOUSEHOOKSTRUCT struct
                Form2.Text1.Text = Form2.Text1.Text & "HCBT_CLICKSKIPPED  MouseMsg:" & _
                                wParam & vbNewLine
```

Example 18-2. Code Contained in the Module1.bas Module (continued)

```
        Case HCBT_CREATEWND
           'wParam == Specifies the handle to the new window
           'lParam == Pointer to the CBT_CREATEWND struct
           Form2.Text1.Text = Form2.Text1.Text & "HCBT_CREATEWND    NEW_HWND:" & _
                            wParam & "    lParam:" & lParam & vbNewLine
               Exit Function 'Otherwise a GPF occurs in the CallNextHookEx function
        Case HCBT_DESTROYWND
           'wParam == Specifies the handle to the window about to be destroyed
           'lParam == 0
           Form2.Text1.Text = Form2.Text1.Text & "HCBT_DESTROYWND     " & _
                            "Destroyed_HWND:" & wParam & vbNewLine
        Case HCBT_KEYSKIPPED
           'wParam == Specifies the virtual-key code
           'lParam == Specifies the repeat count, scan code, key-transition code,
           '          previous key state, and context code
           Form2.Text1.Text = Form2.Text1.Text & _
                            "HCBT_KEYSKIPPED    Virtual-Key Code:" & _
                            wParam & "    Misc_Params:" & lParam & vbNewLine
        Case HCBT_MINMAX
           'wParam == Specifies the handle to the window being minimized
           '          or maximized
           'lParam == Specifies, in the low-order word, a show-window value (SW_)
           '          specifying the operation, the high order word is undefined
           Form2.Text1.Text = Form2.Text1.Text & "HCBT_MINMAX    HWND:" & wParam & _
                            "    lParam:" & (&HFFFF And lParam) & vbNewLine
        Case HCBT_MOVESIZE
           'wParam == Specifies the handle to the window to be moved or sized
           'lParam == Pointer to a RECT struct
           Form2.Text1.Text = Form2.Text1.Text & "HCBT_MOVESIZE    HWND:" & _
                            wParam & vbNewLine
        Case HCBT_QS
           'wParam == 0
           'lParam == 0
           Form2.Text1.Text = Form2.Text1.Text & "HCBT_QS" & vbNewLine
        Case HCBT_SETFOCUS
           'wParam == Specifies the handle to the window gaining the keyboard focus
           'lParam == Specifies the handle to the window losing the keyboard focus
           Form2.Text1.Text = Form2.Text1.Text & "HCBT_SETFOCUS    New_HWND:" & _
                            wParam & "    Old_HWND:" & lParam & vbNewLine
        Case HCBT_SYSCOMMAND
           'wParam == Specifies a system-command value (SC_*)
           'lParam == Contains the same data as the lParam value of a
           '          WM_SYSCOMMAND message
           Form2.Text1.Text = Form2.Text1.Text & "HCBT_SYSCOMMAND    " & _
                            "System_Command:" & wParam & _
                            "    lParam:" & lParam & vbNewLine
    End Select
End If

If uCode = HCBT_MOVESIZE Then
   CBTProc = 1
Else
```

Example 18-2. Code Contained in the Module1.bas Module (continued)

```
    CBTProc = CallNextHookEx(hHook, uCode, wParam, lParam)
  End If
End Function
```

The *CBTProc* filter function, shown in Example 18-2, displays the events that this hook captures as they occur in the Text1 text box. The one interesting thing about this function is that after this hook is installed, the application's main window cannot be moved or sized. This is because the function returns a nonzero value whenever the `HCBT_MOVESIZE` hook code is sent to this function. This causes the window's x and y coordinates to be replaced with their original values after the user finishes the move operation. This also causes the height and width of the window to be replaced with their original values after the user finishes the resize operation.

Using the WH_JOURNALPLAYBACK Hook with a CBT

To allow the CBT application to take control of the system for the purpose of showing the user how to perform a specific task, you must incorporate into the application several hooks that work together. Ordinarily, you install a `WH_CBT` hook along with a `WH_KEYBOARD` hook and/or a `WH_MOUSE` hook. The `WH_KEYBOARD` and `WH_MOUSE` hooks' duties include watching for a specific set of events; in response to those events a `WH_JOURNALPLAYBACK` hook is installed. This `WH_JOURNALPLAYBACK` hook plays back a prerecorded set of mouse and keyboard messages to show the user how to perform a specific task.

Let's see how to do this by adding to the last example application the playback of a prerecorded set of messages to the user. When the `WH_CBT` application is installed, a `WH_KEYBOARD` hook is installed at the same time. Installing the `WH_KEYBOARD` hook allows the `HCBT_KEYSKIPPED` code to be sent to the `WH_CBT` hook's filter function. If a `WH_MOUSE` hook is installed, the `HCBT_CLICKSKIPPED` code is sent to the filter function.

To use this example, first click the hook button to install the CBT hook. Next, click the CreateWnd button to create and display the Form1 form; this form has the caption "WH_CBT Test Form," as in Figure 18-2. Finally, with the Form1 form as the active window, press and release the ESC key. You will see the text "test" displayed in the text box on Form1.

The code in the CBT's filter function tests for the ESC key being released when the `HCBT_KEYSKIPPED` code is sent to the `WH_CBT` hook's filter function. In response to this action, a `WH_JOURNALPLAYBACK` hook is installed and a series of messages is played back to send the word "test" to the text box in the Form2 window, as shown in Figure 18-2.

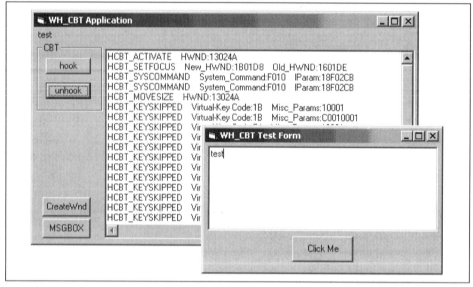

Figure 18-2. The word "test" is sent to the text box when the user releases the ESC key

As a note, if we did not test for the ESC key being released, the word "test" would be printed twice in the text box, once for the `WM_KEYDOWN` message and once for the `WM_KEYUP` message.

Let's see how to modify the code from the previous example application to add journal playback capabilities. Just add the following to the *Form2.frm* module:

```
Private Sub Form2_Load()
    Call Init()
End Sub
```

You must call the *Init* function once during application startup. I will describe this function in detail shortly.

Example 18-3 shows the additional variable and array declarations.

Example 18-3. The Modified Version of the Declarations of Module1.bas

```
Private hRecordHook As Long
Private hPlaybackHook As Long
Private MsgArray() As Long
Private StartTime As Long
Private CurrMSG As Long

Private hHook As Long
Private hKbdHook As Long
```

Example 18-3. The Modified Version of the Declarations of Module1.bas (continued)

```
Public IsHooked As Boolean
Public IsPBHooked As Boolean
```

As Example 18-4 shows, an extra *SetWindowsHookEx* function call was added to
the *SetCBTHook* function to install the WH_KEYBOARD hook.

Example 18-4. The Modified Version of the SetCBTHook Installation Routine

```
Public Sub SetCBTHook()
    If IsHooked Then
        MsgBox "Don't hook CBT twice or you will be unable to unhook it."
    Else
        hHook = SetWindowsHookEx(WH_CBT, AddressOf CBTProc, 0, App.ThreadID)
        hKbdHook = SetWindowsHookEx(WH_KEYBOARD, AddressOf KbdProc, 0, App.ThreadID)
        IsHooked = True
    End If
End Sub
```

Because we are installing a second hook, we must also remove that hook in the
RemoveCBTHook function, as Example 18-5 shows.

Example 18-5. The Modified Version of the RemoveCBTHook Routine

```
Public Sub RemoveCBTHook()
    Dim temp As Long
    temp = UnhookWindowsHookEx(hHook)
    temp = UnhookWindowsHookEx(hKbdHook)
    IsHooked = False
End Sub
```

We add three lines of code to the *CBTProc* filter function. The added code is highlighted in Example 18-6.

Example 18-6. The Modified Version of the CBTProc Filter Function

```
Public Function CBTProc(ByVal uCode As Long, ByVal wParam As Long, _
                        ByVal lParam As Long) As Long
    If uCode >= 0 Then
        Select Case uCode
            Case HCBT_ACTIVATE
                'wParam == Specifies the handle to the window about to be activated
                'lParam == Pointer to the CBTACTIVATESTRUCT struct
                Form2.Text1.Text = Form2.Text1.Text & "HCBT_ACTIVATE  HWND:" & _
                                    wParam & vbNewLine
            Case HCBT_CLICKSKIPPED
                'wParam == Specifies the mouse message removed from the
                            system message queue
                'lParam == Pointer to the MOUSEHOOKSTRUCT struct
                Form2.Text1.Text = Form2.Text1.Text & "HCBT_CLICKSKIPPED  " & _
                                    MouseMsg:" & wParam & vbNewLine
            Case HCBT_CREATEWND
                'wParam == Specifies the handle to the new window
```

Example 18-6. The Modified Version of the CBTProc Filter Function (continued)

```
                'lParam == Pointer to the CBT_CREATEWND struct
                Form2.Text1.Text = Form2.Text1.Text & "HCBT_CREATEWND    " & _
                            NEW_HWND:" & wParam & _
                            "   lParam:" & lParam & vbNewLine
            Exit Function 'Otherwise a GPF occurs in the CallNextHookEx function
        Case HCBT_DESTROYWND
            'wParam == Specifies the handle to the window about to be destroyed
            'lParam == 0
            Form2.Text1.Text = Form2.Text1.Text & "HCBT_DESTROYWND     " & _
                        Destroyed_HWND:" & wParam & vbNewLine
        Case HCBT_KEYSKIPPED
            'wParam == Specifies the virtual-key code
            'lParam == Specifies the repeat count, scan code, key-transition
                    code, previous key state, and context code
            Form2.Text1.Text = Form2.Text1.Text & "HCBT_KEYSKIPPED     " & _
                        "Virtual-Key Code:" & wParam & _
                        "   Misc_Params:" & lParam & vbNewLine

            If wParam = VK_ESCAPE And (lParam And &H80000000) Then
                Call SetPlaybackHook
            End If
        Case HCBT_MINMAX
            'wParam == Specifies the handle to the window being minimized
                    or maximized
            'lParam == The low-order word specifies a show-window value
                    (SW_) defining the operation, the high order word is
                    undefined
            Form2.Text1.Text = Form2.Text1.Text & "HCBT_MINMAX     HWND:" & _
                        wParam & "     lParam:" & _
                        (&HFFFF And lParam) & vbNewLine
        Case HCBT_MOVESIZE
            'wParam == Specifies the handle to the window to be moved or sized
            'lParam == Pointer to a RECT struct
            Form2.Text1.Text = Form2.Text1.Text & "HCBT_MOVESIZE     HWND:" & _
                        wParam & vbNewLine
        Case HCBT_QS
            'wParam == 0
            'lParam == 0
            Form2.Text1.Text = Form2.Text1.Text & "HCBT_QS" & vbNewLine
        Case HCBT_SETFOCUS
            'wParam == Specifies the handle to the window gaining the
                    keyboard focus
            'lParam == Specifies the handle to the window losing the
                    keyboard focus
            Form2.Text1.Text = Form2.Text1.Text & "HCBT_SETFOCUS     New_HWND:" _
                        & wParam & "     Old_HWND:" & lParam & vbNewLine
        Case HCBT_SYSCOMMAND
            'wParam == A system-command value (SC_*)
            'lParam == Contains the same data as the lParam value of a
                    WM_SYSCOMMAND message
            Form2.Text1.Text = Form2.Text1.Text & "HCBT_SYSCOMMAND     " & 
                        "System_Command:" & wParam & _
```

Example 18-6. The Modified Version of the CBTProc Filter Function (continued)

```
                                     "    lParam:" & lParam & vbNewLine
            End Select
        End If

        If uCode = HCBT_MOVESIZE Then
            CBTProc = 1
        Else
            CBTProc = CallNextHookEx(hHook, uCode, wParam, lParam)
        End If
End Function
```

The **Case** statement that evaluates the *uCode* parameter for the **HCBT_KEYSKIPPED** constant contains an **If...Then** statement that watches for the ESC key to be released. When the most significant bit of the *lParam* parameter is on, the ESC key is being released. You test for this by ANDing *lParam* with the value &H80000000. When the ESC key is being released, a **WH_JOURNALPLAYBACK** hook is installed to play back a prerecorded set of messages.

The code in Example 18-7 shows the *Init* function that is contained in *Module1. bas*. This function initializes an *MsgArray* array with the window messages that the **WH_JOURNALPLAYBACK** hook will play back. The array elements contain the following information:

MsgArray(1,x)

The window message that the **WH_JOURNALPLAYBACK** hook is to play back.

MsgArray(2,x)

The hWnd of the window in which to play back the hook

MsgArray(3,x)

The *wParam* for the message contained in array element MsgArray(1,x)

MsgArray(4,x)

The *lParam* for the message contained in array element MsgArray(1,x)

MsgArray(5,x)

The time delay in which to play back the message

This array starts and ends with the **WM_QUEUESYNC** message—more about this message shortly. The rest of the array contains a **WM_KEYDOWN** and **WM_KEYUP** message for each letter of the word "test".

Example 18-7. The Init Procedure to Initialize Messages for Playback

```
Public Sub Init()
    ReDim MsgArray(6, 10) As Long

    'WM_QUEUESYNC
    MsgArray(0, 0) = 0
    MsgArray(1, 0) = WM_QUEUESYNC
```

Example 18-7. The Init Procedure to Initialize Messages for Playback (continued)

```
MsgArray(2, 0) = Form2.hWnd
MsgArray(3, 0) = 0
MsgArray(4, 0) = 0
MsgArray(5, 0) = 0

'T
MsgArray(0, 1) = 0
MsgArray(1, 1) = WM_KEYDOWN
MsgArray(2, 1) = Form2.hWnd
MsgArray(3, 1) = 1
MsgArray(4, 1) = 5204
MsgArray(5, 1) = 1152

MsgArray(0, 2) = 0
MsgArray(1, 2) = WM_KEYUP
MsgArray(2, 2) = Form2.hWnd
MsgArray(3, 2) = 1
MsgArray(4, 2) = 5204
MsgArray(5, 2) = 1251

'E
MsgArray(0, 3) = 0
MsgArray(1, 3) = WM_KEYDOWN
MsgArray(2, 3) = Form2.hWnd
MsgArray(3, 3) = 1
MsgArray(4, 3) = 4677
MsgArray(5, 3) = 1501

MsgArray(0, 4) = 0
MsgArray(1, 4) = WM_KEYUP
MsgArray(2, 4) = Form2.hWnd
MsgArray(3, 4) = 1
MsgArray(4, 4) = 4677
MsgArray(5, 4) = 1589

'S
MsgArray(0, 5) = 0
MsgArray(1, 5) = WM_KEYDOWN
MsgArray(2, 5) = Form2.hWnd
MsgArray(3, 5) = 1
MsgArray(4, 5) = 8019
MsgArray(5, 5) = 1834

MsgArray(0, 6) = 0
MsgArray(1, 6) = WM_KEYUP
MsgArray(2, 6) = Form2.hWnd
MsgArray(3, 6) = 1
MsgArray(4, 6) = 8019
MsgArray(5, 6) = 1898

'T
MsgArray(0, 7) = 0
```

Example 18-7. The Init Procedure to Initialize Messages for Playback (continued)

```
    MsgArray(1, 7) = WM_KEYDOWN
    MsgArray(2, 7) = Form2.hWnd
    MsgArray(3, 7) = 1
    MsgArray(4, 7) = 5204
    MsgArray(5, 7) = 2252

    MsgArray(0, 8) = 0
    MsgArray(1, 8) = WM_KEYUP
    MsgArray(2, 8) = Form2.hWnd
    MsgArray(3, 8) = 1
    MsgArray(4, 8) = 5204
    MsgArray(5, 8) = 2351

    'WM_QUEUESYNC
    MsgArray(0, 9) = 0
    MsgArray(1, 9) = WM_QUEUESYNC
    MsgArray(2, 9) = Form2.hWnd
    MsgArray(3, 9) = 0
    MsgArray(4, 9) = 0
    MsgArray(5, 9) = 2451
End Sub
```

You might notice that there is one problem with using the `WH_JOURNALPLAYBACK` hook. You do not want the `WH_CBT` hook to operate on the actions that are being played back through the `WH_JOURNALPLAYBACK` hook. To differentiate between the user's actions and the playback of messages through the `WH_JOURNALPLAYBACK` hook, the `WM_QUEUESYNC` message is used. This message is always the first and the last message to be played back through the `WH_JOURNALPLAYBACK` hook. When the `WH_CBT` hook intercepts this message, it sends the `HCBT_QS` code to the `WH_CBT` hook. The `WH_CBT` hook can set a flag indicating that a `WH_JOURNALPLAYBACK` hook is installed. The last message that the `WH_JOURNALPLAYBACK` hook plays is the `WM_QUEUESYNC` message. The `HCBT_QS` code is sent to the `WH_CBT` hook. The `WH_CBT` hook can then reset the flag to its initial state, indicating that the `WH_JOURNALPLAYBACK` hook is finished. This flag that the `WH_CBT` hook sets is used to tell this hook that it should do no processing while it is set. In this way, the `WH_CBT` hook can differentiate between a user's actions and actions being played back through a `WH_JOURNALPLAYBACK` hook.

The block of code in Example 18-8 is added to the BAS module of the example application to install and remove the `WH_JOURNALPLAYBACK` hook.

Example 18-8. Code to Install and Remove the WH_JOURNALPLAYBACK Hook

```
Public Sub SetPlaybackHook()
    If IsPBHooked Then
        'Don't hook WH_JOURNALPLAYBACK twice without unhooking.
    Else
        StartTime = GetTickCount
```

Example 18-8. Code to Install and Remove the WH_JOURNALPLAYBACK Hook (continued)

```
        CurrMSG = 0
        hPlaybackHook = SetWindowsHookEx(WH_JOURNALPLAYBACK, _
                AddressOf JournalPlaybackProc, App.hInstance, 0)
        IsPBHooked = True
    End If
End Sub

Public Sub RemovePlaybackHook()
    Dim lRetVal As Long
    lRetVal = UnhookWindowsHookEx(hPlaybackHook)
    IsPBHooked = False
End Sub
```

Example 18-9 shows the filter function for the WH_JOURNALPLAYBACK hook. This code is almost identical to the filter function used in the example application in Chapter 20, which covers the WH_JOURNALPLAYBACK hook. The main difference is indicated in boldface in the *JournalPlaybackProc* function. This If...Then...Else block of code makes sure that the first message played back is timed correctly.

Example 18-9. The Filter Function for the WH_JOURNALPLAYBACK Hook

```
Public Function JournalPlaybackProc(ByVal uCode As Long, ByVal wParam As Long, _
                            lParam As EVENTMSG) As Long
    If uCode = HC_GETNEXT Then          'play the current message
        If CurrMSG >= 10 Then
            'No more messages to play, remove the hook and restore control
            'to the user gracefully
            Call RemovePlaybackHook
        Else
            lParam.message = MsgArray(1, CurrMSG)
            lParam.hwnd = MsgArray(2, CurrMSG)
            lParam.paramH = MsgArray(3, CurrMSG)
            lParam.paramL = MsgArray(4, CurrMSG)
            If CurrMSG = 0 Then
                lParam.time = MsgArray(5, CurrMSG)
                JournalPlaybackProc = MsgArray(5, CurrMSG)
            Else
                lParam.time = MsgArray(5, CurrMSG) - MsgArray(5, CurrMSG - 1)
                JournalPlaybackProc = MsgArray(5, CurrMSG) - MsgArray(5, CurrMSG - 1)
            End If
        End If
    ElseIf uCode = HC_SKIP Then         'retrieve the next message
        If CurrMSG >= 10 Then
            'No more messages to play, remove the hook and restore control
            'to the user gracefully
            Call RemovePlaybackHook
        End If

        CurrMSG = CurrMSG + 1
    ElseIf uCode = HC_NOREMOVE Then
        'Skip Playback - an app has called PeekMessage.
    ElseIf uCode = HC_SYSMODALON Then
```

Example 18-9. The Filter Function for the WH_JOURNALPLAYBACK Hook (continued)

```
        'Skip playback
    ElseIf uCode = HC_SYSMODALOFF Then
        'Skip playback
    End If

    JournalPlaybackProc = CallNextHookEx(hPlaybackHook, uCode, wParam, lParam)
End Function
```

Caveats

This hook hampers system performance considerably because it intercepts many common events that occur in the system, such as changing a control's focus or manipulating a window. Unlike the WH_SHELL hook, this hook works for all windows and not just the top-level unowned windows in the system. If you can solve a problem with the WH_SHELL hook instead of with the WH_CBT hook, by all means use the WH_SHELL hook. The WH_SHELL hook puts less of a strain on the system because not all window events are intercepted—just those of top-level unowned windows.

If you want to use the HCBT_KEYSKIPPED code, you must install a WM_KEYBOARD hook. Likewise, if you want to use the HCBT_CLICKSKIPPED code, you must install a WM_MOUSE hook.

If you use the HCBT_KEYSKIPPED code to initiate an action for a keystroke, you should also test for either the WM_KEYUP or WM_KEYDOWN message and then initiate the action for one of these messages. Otherwise, the action will be performed twice, once for each message.

Most likely, when using the WH_CBT hook, you also will use one or more other hooks to augment it. When doing so, verify that you release each hook not only before the application ends, but also before it is reinstalled. You can install the WH_JOURNALPLAYBACK hook multiple times in a single CBT application's lifetime. It is imperative that you release this hook after it is finished or it might seem as if your application has locked up.

There is an article in the Microsoft Developer Network (MSDN) called "'PRB: CBT_CREATEWND Struct Returns Invalid Class Name ID: Q106079,'" which indicates that there is a potential problem with retrieving the class name of a window when the WH_CBT hook receives the HCBT_CREATEWND code. This code contains a pointer to a CBT_CREATEWND structure in its *lParam* parameter. This structure contains a nested structure, CREATESTRUCT, that contains the class name *lpszClass*. The *lpszClass* member does not always contain the most reliable information, especially when an internal system window is being created. The recommended workaround is to use the *GetClassName* function instead of the CBT_CREATEWND structure.

19

WH_JOURNALRECORD

This is the first of two chapters that will examine journaling hooks. To illustrate how these hooks operate, we will build a macro recorder application that is similar to the macro recorder that shipped with Windows 3x. In this chapter, we will use the WH_JOURNALRECORD hook to build the piece of the application that records a macro. In Chapter 20 we will use the WH_JOURNALPLAYBACK hook to build the piece of the application that plays back the recorded macro.

Description

You use the WH_JOURNALRECORD hook to intercept mouse, keyboard, and other hardware messages that the system receives. The system redirects these messages to this hook's filter function. The filter function can then either monitor the message or copy it to memory for later use; it cannot modify the message in any way. After the filter function is finished processing the message, it passes the message on to the message loop of the thread for which it was originally destined.

When you use this hook to copy messages to memory, you can play them back using the WH_JOURNALPLAYBACK hook, which we discuss in Chapter 20. Typically, you refer to these two hooks, WH_JOURNALRECORD and WH_JOURNALPLAYBACK, as *journaling hooks*.

The function prototype for the WH_JOURNALRECORD hook's filter function is:

```
Public Function JournalProc(ByVal uCode As Long, _
              ByVal wParam As Long, _
              lParam As EVENTMSG) As Long
```

The *uCode* parameter contains a special code that informs the filter function of the actions that it can take on each message. The codes passed in to the *uCode* argument are discussed later in this section. An EVENTMSG structure is always passed in to the *lParam* argument of this filter function. The *wParam* argument of this function is not used.

A message is passed into this hook's filter function through the EVENTMSG structure, which is defined as follows:

```
Private Type EVENTMSG
        message As Long
        paramL As Long
        paramH As Long
        time As Long
        hwnd As Long
    End Type
```

The members of the EVENTMSG structure are:

message

The message identifier.

paramL

A message parameter. The message type defines the meaning for this member.

paramH

A message parameter. The message type defines the meaning for this member.

time

The time that this message was posted.

hwnd

The handle of the window to which this

message is to be sent.

Compare this structure to the MSG structure defined in Chapter 11:

```
Private Type MSG
    hwnd As Long
    message As Long
    wParam As Long
    lParam As Long
    time As Long
    pt As POINTAPI
End Type
```

The MSG structure is the complete message sent to the raw input thread (RIT) and dispatched to the relevant message queue. There are a couple of differences between it and the EVENTMSG structure:

- The *wParam* member of the MSG structure maps to the *paramL* member for the EVENTMSG structure.

- The *lParam* member of the MSG structure maps to the *paramH* member of the EVENTMSG structure.

- The MSG structure has a *pt* member, and the EVENTMSG structure does not. The *pt* member is a POINTAPI structure that contains the x and y coordinates of the mouse pointer at the time this message was sent. This structure is defined as follows:

```
Private Type POINTAPI
    x As Long
    y As Long
End Type
```

You do not need this member in the EVENTMSG structure because it is irrelevant to the message's playback. The time member is relevant because it is used to synchronize the playback of each message. We will see how this works in Chapter 20.

Stopping This Hook

Windows has a built-in way of canceling the operation of any type of journaling hook. The two key combinations that do this are CTRL-ESC and CTRL-ALT-DEL. When the user enters one of these key combinations, the system immediately stops and removes all journaling hooks. This override is necessary because a single misbehaving application can cause the system to hang.

When you install this hook, it forces all input to be serialized. In other words, all applications will take turns reading from their message queues. This allows the hook to record messages in an orderly fashion. Otherwise, messages might be recorded out of sequence, and unpredictable behavior might result when the WH_ JOURNALPLAYBACK hook plays them back. If one application hangs, all other applications must wait until the hung application returns, if it ever does. If it does not return, the user must use either the CTRL-ESC or the CTRL-ALT-DEL key combinations to stop the journaling hooks and return control back to the user.

To determine if a user has stopped journaling through one of these key combinations, the application can watch for the WM_CANCELJOURNAL message either by adding code to the message loop (this can be done only in a C++ application), or by installing a WH_GETMESSAGE hook.

The WM_CANCELJOURNAL message is sent with its *hwnd* member set to NULL. This causes the *DispatchMessage* function in the message loop not to send this message to any window. For this reason, we cannot use any type of subclassing method to watch for this message because subclassing captures messages after they have been dispatched to the appropriate window procedure.

The Microsoft documentation for journaling hooks recommends using the CTRL-BREAK key combination to gracefully stop the journaling hook. The system does not automatically implement this key combination to stop and remove the journaling hooks; therefore, we must manually implement it in our code. This key combination has the virtual key code VK_CANCEL. This code is defined in Visual Basic (VB) in this manner:

```
Private Const VK_CANCEL = &H3
```

Implementing this key combination to cancel the recording process is not very hard. This code example demonstrates how to do it:

```
If lParam.message = WM_KEYDOWN And GetLowByte(lParam.paramL) = VK_CANCEL Then
    Call RemoveJournalHook
End If
```

Whenever the filter function receives the WM_KEYDOWN message, the EVENTMSG structure's *paramL* member determines if the CTRL-BREAK key combination is pressed. The VK_CANCEL value is contained within the low-order byte of the *paramL* member of the EVENTMSG structure. If the VK_CANCEL key combination is found, the code simply calls the function to remove this hook. Note that no code is executed after the call to *RemoveJournalHook*. This is because the filter function is removed from the system whenever the hook is removed, and therefore the code also is removed. To test this, place an *MsgBox* function after the call to *RemoveJournalHook*. When you press the CTRL-BREAK key combination, the *MsgBox* function never executes.

Trapping this key combination to stop the hook will allow you to remove the hook gracefully. You can perform any cleanup here, or even inform the main application that the user canceled the recording. The CTRL-ESC or CTRL-ALT-DEL key combinations will stop recording immediately, without informing your code, and giving you a chance to clean up before the hook is removed. The CTRL-BREAK key combination is just a recommendation; it is not a rule.

Explanation of Hook Codes

There are three specific hook codes that can be passed in to this hook's filter function. The *uCode* argument of the filter function will receive any of the following codes:

HC_ACTION

Informs us that the RIT has dispatched a message and that this hook has intercepted it. The message is contained in the EVENTMSG structure. The constant is defined as follows:

```
Const HC_ACTION = 0
```

HC_SYSMODALON

Informs us that a system modal dialog box has been displayed. Any time a system modal dialog box is displayed, we must pause the message recording function until that dialog box has been shut down. The constant is defined as follows:

```
Const HC_SYSMODALON = 4
```

HC_SYSMODALOFF

Informs us that the system modal dialog box has been shut down. At this time, we can resume our recording. The constant is defined as follows:

```
Const HC_SYSMODALOFF = 5
```

We can ignore the **HC_SYSMODALON** and **HC_SYSMODALOFF** codes because these two codes were held over from the Win16 days. In Win32, there cannot be a true system modal window, since this would cause all windows in all threads to stop receiving input until the system modal window is shut down. Win32 does not allow this to happen because it is a true multitasking system. Although you can add the **vbSystemModal** setting to a VB message box, this setting will not act as a system modal window in the Win32 environment. Messages will still be sent to other windows. For example, the code:

```
MsgBox "Test", vbSystemModal
```

causes the message box to appear at the top of the window Z-order. The only window that does not receive messages until this message box is closed is the window that created the message box.

The Win32 *MessageBoxEx* application programming interface (API) function also has **MB_SYSTEMMODAL**, a constant similar to the VB **vbSystemModal** setting. Message boxes with this type of setting work in a fashion similar to VB message boxes with the **vbSystemModal** setting.

As usual, we should skip our hook processing and immediately call *CallNextHookEx* if the *uCode* argument is less than zero.

Location of This Hook in the System

This hook is located at the point inside the thread that installed the journal hook. Figure 19-1 shows where the main thread of process B has installed the WH_JOURNALRECORD hook.

As with the **WH_JOURNALPLAYBACK**, **WH_KEYBOARD_LL**, and **WH_MOUSE_LL** hooks, you can install the **WH_JOURNALRECORD** hook only as a system-wide hook. To review, these hooks can reside either in an EXE or dynamic link library (DLL) module. This means that we can implement these hooks solely within VB. This is because the hooks' filter functions are called from within the context of the thread that has installed these two types of hooks.

Ordinarily, when you install a hook as a system-wide hook, you must place it in a DLL. This DLL is injected into every process so that the hook can operate on all messages in the system. However, in the case of these four hooks, the hook can be installed for a single thread and still receive every message that the system generates because every message is being funneled through a single message queue.

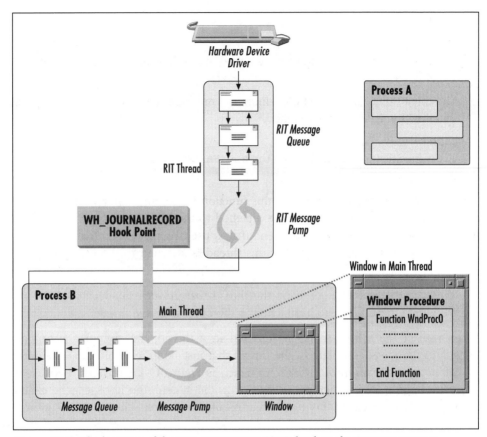

Figure 19-1. The location of the WH_JOURNALRECORD hook in the messaging system

As a result, the hook does not have to reside in a DLL; it can reside in an EXE as well.

Normally, every thread is connected to its own message queue. These message queues receive messages from the RIT. This architecture gives all 32-bit Windows operating systems robust multithreading capability and prevents one application from hanging the whole system.

You can force multiple threads to receive messages from a single message queue. You do this by calling the *AttachThreadInput* API function. This function is declared in VB as follows:

```
Private Declare Function AttachThreadInput Lib "user32" _
        Alias "AttachThreadInput" _
        (ByVal idAttach As Long, _
        ByVal idAttachTo As Long, _
        ByVal fAttach As Long) As Long
```

Its parameters are:

idAttach

> The thread ID of the thread to be attached to another thread's message queue.

idAttachTo

> The thread ID of the thread containing the message queue to which the thread specified by *idAttach* is attached.

fAttach

> True specifies to attach the two threads; False specifies to unattach the two threads.

A return value of zero indicates that this function failed; any other value indicates success. Note that a thread cannot be attached to the RIT, to itself, or to a thread in another desktop. The message queue that is used by the thread that *idAttach* specifies does not receive input after this thread is attached to the other message queue.

The message queue that is used by the thread that *idAttach* specifies does not receive input after this thread is attached to the other message queue.

When one of these four hooks is installed in a thread, the system attaches all threads to the message queue of the thread that installed the hook. This is similar to calling *AttachThreadInput* for each thread, as Figure 19-2 illustrates. Because a single message queue is feeding all threads in the system, the hook can be called from within the context of the thread that installed the hook—the VB application.

The Macro Recorder Example

As mentioned previously, the example demonstrating this hook is an application that records user actions. You can play back these actions later using a different hook—see the example in Chapter 20, where we'll complete this portion of our application. Figure 19-3 displays a screenshot of this application.

Table 19-1 presents the nondefault properties of the form and its controls.

The RECORD frame on this form holds two buttons. The hook button will install the WH_JOURNALRECORD hook, and the unhook button will remove this hook. The TEST AREA frame includes an MSG BOX button that displays a test message box with an OK button. A text box and a checkbox also are included. You can use these controls to record some simple macros. You also can record actions taken on other applications.

To operate this application, click the hook button and then perform some actions. These actions could be clicking the MSG BOX button to create a message box,

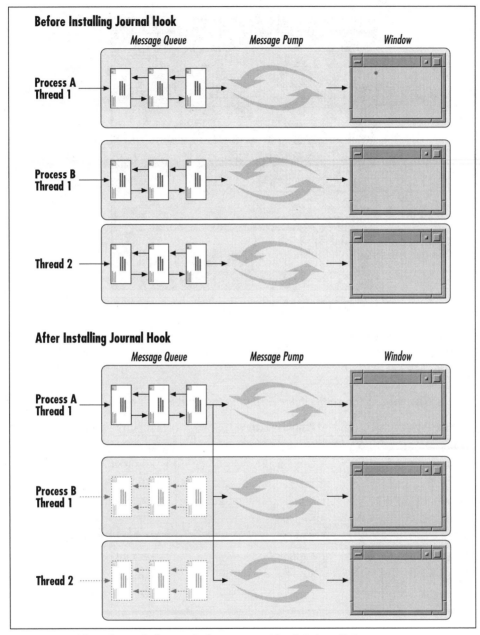

Figure 19-2. Thread state before and after a journal hook is installed

checking and unchecking the checkbox, or even performing actions on a separate application. To stop the recording, click the unhook button.

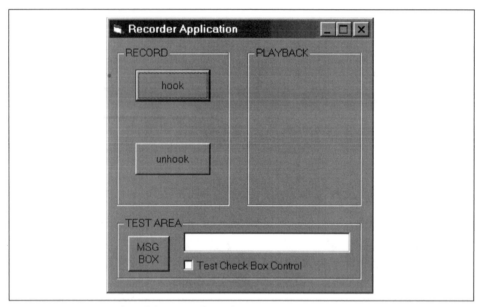

Figure 19-3. A screenshot of the example application

Initially this application will not do much. Chapter 20, which introduces the WH_
JOURNALPLAYBACK hook, will complete the functionality for this macro recorder
application.

Table 19-1. Nondefault Properties of the Form and Its Controls

Object Type	Property Name	Property Value
Form	Name	Form2
Form	Caption	"Recorder Application"
Form	Top	420
Form	Left	132
Form	Height	4305
Form	Width	4290
Frame	Caption	"RECORD"
Frame	Name	Frame1
Frame	Top	120
Frame	Left	120
Frame	Height	1335
Frame	Width	1155
Frame	Caption	"PLAYBACK"
Frame	Name	Frame2
Frame	Top	120

Table 19-1. Nondefault Properties of the Form and Its Controls (continued)

Object Type	Property Name	Property Value
Frame	Left	120
Frame	Height	2475
Frame	Width	1815
Frame	Caption	"TEST AREA"
Frame	Name	Frame3
Frame	Top	120
Frame	Left	2220
Frame	Height	2475
Frame	Width	1815
TextBox	Top	240
TextBox	Left	1080
TextBox	Height	315
TextBox	Width	2655
Command Button1	Name	cmdHook
Command Button1	Caption	"hook"
Command Button1	Top	360
Command Button1	Left	300
Command Button1	Height	495
Command Button1	Width	1215
Command Button2	Name	cmdUnHook
Command Button2	Caption	"unhook"
Command Button2	Top	1500
Command Button2	Left	300
Command Button2	Height	495
Command Button2	Width	1215
Command Button2	Caption	"MSG BOX"
Command Button2	Top	300
Command Button2	Left	180
Command Button2	Height	555
Command Button2	Width	675
CheckBox	Caption	"Test Check Box Control"
CheckBox	Top	660
CheckBox	Left	1080
CheckBox	Height	195
CheckBox	Width	2655

Let's start examining the application's code by looking at *Module2.bas*, the application's code module. We must initially define several variables for this application:

```
Private hRecordHook As Long
Private MsgArray() As Long
Private StartTime As Long

Public IsHooked As Boolean
```

The *hRecordHook* variable will hold the hook handle, which is returned from the *SetWindowsHookEx* function and is used in several other functions. For this reason, it is declared as a module-level variable. The *UnHookWindowsHookEx* function uses this handle when removing a hook, and the *CallNextHookEx* function uses it when calling the next hook in the hook chain.

The *MsgArray* variable is a multidimensional dynamic array that contains the messages that this hook records. The WM_JOURNALPLAYBACK hook uses this array to play back the messages. You could store these messages in a text file or in a database if they become excessively large.

The *StartTime* variable will hold the time in which the hook started recording. This value is subtracted from the *time* member in the EVENTMSG structure to get the amount of time between when the hook was installed and the message was dispatched to its respective thread. The purpose of this will become apparent when we attempt to play back these messages at the same pace at which they were recorded.

The Boolean *IsHooked* variable is used as a flag to determine whether the hook has been set. This will prevent us from installing this hook more than once.

The first function that we need is the filter function. This function is named *JournalProc* and is defined in Example 19-1. This function records a message only when the *uCode* argument is equal to HC_ACTION. Before actually recording the message, the function will test to determine whether the user pressed the CTRL-BREAK key combination. If the user did press this key combination, the code will clean up after itself and remove the hook. If the user did not, the code will copy the structure members to which the *lParam* argument pointed into the dynamic array *MsgArray*. Notice that the time copied into this array is the current time minus the time that the recording was started. The last thing that this filter function does is call *CallNextHookEx* to pass this information to the next filter function in the hook chain.

Example 19-1. The JournalProc Filter Function

```
Public Function JournalProc(ByVal uCode As Long, _
              ByVal wParam As Long, _
              lParam As EVENTMSG) As Long
```

Example 19-1. The JournalProc Filter Function (continued)

```
    If uCode = HC_ACTION Then
        If lParam.message = WM_KEYDOWN And GetLowByte(lParam.paramL) = VK_CANCEL Then
            'Place clean up code here
            Call RemoveJournalHook
            'Code placed here will not be executed
        End If
        MsgArray(0, UBound(MsgArray, 2)) = uCode
        MsgArray(1, UBound(MsgArray, 2)) = lParam.message
        MsgArray(2, UBound(MsgArray, 2)) = lParam.hwnd
        MsgArray(3, UBound(MsgArray, 2)) = lParam.paramH
        MsgArray(4, UBound(MsgArray, 2)) = lParam.paramL
        MsgArray(5, UBound(MsgArray, 2)) = (lParam.time - StartTime)

        ReDim Preserve MsgArray(6, (UBound(MsgArray, 2) + 1)) As Long
    ElseIf uCode = HC_SYSMODALON Then
        'Skip recording
    ElseIf uCode = HC_SYSMODALOFF Then
        'Skip recording
    End If

    JournalProc = CallNextHookEx(hRecordHook, uCode, wParam, lParam)
End Function
```

The *SetJournalHook* subroutine shown in Example 19-2 sets up and installs this journaling hook. The *IsHooked* flag is checked to determine if the hook has already been installed. If it has not, the *MsgArray* array is initialized, the *StartTime* variable is set to the current system time, and the *SetWindowsHookEx* function installs the hook. Notice that this hook is installed similar to a system-wide hook, even though its filter function resides in this application and not in a DLL.

Example 19-2. Installing the WH_JOURNALRECORD Hook

```
Public Sub SetJournalHook()
    If IsHooked Then
        MsgBox "Don't hook it twice without unhooking or you will be unable " & _
                "to unhook it."
    Else
        ReDim MsgArray(6, 1) As Long
        StartTime = GetTickCount
        hRecordHook = SetWindowsHookEx(WH_JOURNALRECORD, _
                    AddressOf JournalProc, App.hInstance, 0)
        IsHooked = True
    End If
End Sub
```

To remove the hook, the *RemoveJournalHook* subroutine shown in Example 19-3 calls *UnhookWindowsHookEx* with the hook's handle. The *lRetVal* return value for this function is tested for a success or failure to remove the hook. If successful, the *IsHooked* flag is set to FALSE.

Example 19-3. Removing the WH_JOURNALRECORD Hook

```
Public Sub RemoveJournalHook()
    Dim lRetVal As Long
    lRetVal = UnhookWindowsHookEx(hRecordHook)
    IsHooked = False
End Sub
```

GetLowByte is a function that the hook procedure calls that returns the low-order byte of the *lValue* argument, as Example 19-4 illustrates. You need this function to get the virtual key code from the *paramL* member of the EVENTMSG structure that was passed in to the filter function.

Example 19-4. The GetLowByte Function

```
Public Function GetLowByte(ByRef lValue As Long) As Long
    GetLowByte = (lValue And &HFF&)
End Function
```

Finally, Example 19-5 shows the code that is placed in the form module. The subroutines under the RECORD section of the form module code install and remove the hook. The subroutine under the TEST section simply displays a message box, which can be used in the recording process. The CLEANUP section contains the *QueryUnload* subroutine, which tests for an active hook. If the hook is installed, a warning is displayed informing the user to remove the hook before closing the application. Instead of this message, we could call the *RemoveJournalHook* function to automatically remove the hook.

Example 19-5. The Source Code for Form2.frm

```
'-----------
'RECORD
'-----------
Private Sub cmdHook_Click()
    Call InitArray
    Call SetJournalHook
End Sub


Private Sub cmdUnHook_Click()
    Call RemoveJournalHook
End Sub



'-----------
'TEST
'-----------
Private Sub Command3_Click()
    MsgBox "Journaling Test Message Box."
End Sub
```

Example 19-5. The Source Code for Form2.frm (continued)

```
'-----------
'CLEANUP
'-----------
Private Sub Form_QueryUnload(Cancel As Integer, UnloadMode As Integer)
    If IsHooked Then
        Cancel = 1
        MsgBox "Unhook before closing or the application may crash."
    End If
End Sub
```

You don't need much code to create this example. The WM_JOURNALPLAYBACK hook, discussed in Chapter 20, is slightly more involved.

Caveats

This hook, in effect, forces every thread to receive messages from a single queue. This is how the 16-bit Windows operating systems works. Therefore, the operating system cannot take advantage of multitasking. A problem that occurs in all 16-bit Windows operating systems can now occur in 32-bit Windows operating systems: a single application can hang all applications, even the desktop. This is the reason for having the CTRL-ESC and CTRL-ALT-DEL key combinations built into the system to remove any journal hooks.

Because this hook serializes all input to all windows, there is a large performance penalty. You should use hooks such as this cautiously. When you do use such hooks, you should install them for as little time as possible. Windows cannot take advantage of its multitasking power when this hook is installed.

When you use this hook, you might encounter a problem with the mouse wheel. This problem is recorded under *ID: Q186942PRB: WM_MOUSEWHEEL Delta Values Not Supported by Journal Hooks*, in the Microsoft Developer Network (MSDN). In short, this hook does not record the wheel delta value. Therefore, when the messages are played back through the WH_JOURNALPLAYBACK hook, the mouse wheel rotations are not played back. This is because the wheel delta value is placed in the *wParam* member of the WM_MOUSEWHEEL message, which this hook does not record. The rest of the WM_MOUSEWHEEL message, however, is recorded and played back.

This hook cannot record the CTRL-ESC and CTRL-ALT-DEL key combinations. Similarly, any key or key combination that you might use to gracefully exit the hook should not be recorded.

20

WH_JOURNALPLAYBACK

Chapter 19 discussed the `WH_JOURNALRECORD` hook and how you can use it to record mouse and keyboard input messages. This chapter will cover the `WH_JOURNALPLAYBACK` hook, which is the counterpart to the `WH_JOURNALRECORD` hook that you can use to play back mouse and keyboard messages. After discussing the `WH_JOURNALPLAYBACK` hook, I will demonstrate how you can use this hook to finish the macro recorder example application that we began in Chapter 19.

Description

The `WH_JOURNALPLAYBACK` hook provides a way to play back messages to the Windows operating system. When I say "play back messages," I mean to post pre-recorded messages to the raw input thread (RIT) message queue so that the system can process them. From the system's point of view, messages played back in this manner are no different from messages input through a keyboard or mouse.

This hook works differently than the other hooks do. Instead of intercepting messages within the message stream, this hook posts messages to the RIT message queue. After you install this hook, the message loop in the RIT ceases to remove messages from its message queue that were placed there by normal keyboard and mouse input, and it starts accepting only messages from the hook's filter function. More specifically, it receives the actual message from the filter function's *lParam* argument. This is why the system seems as though it is not accepting input from the keyboard or mouse while the hook is installed.

While this hook is installed, events that the mouse and keyboard produce are placed in the RIT's message queue, as they normally would be. These queued messages are not passed on to the RIT's message loop until the `WH_`

JOURNALPLAYBACK hook is removed. After this hook is removed, the queued messages are sent to their respective windows. The memory space that can be allocated for the message queue is not infinite; therefore, mouse or keyboard events are lost after this queue is filled.

The prototype for the WH_JOURNALPLAYBACK hook is:

```
Public Function JournalPlaybackProc(ByVal uCode As Long, _
                    ByVal wParam As Long, _
                    lParam As EVENTMSG) As Long
```

The system can send one of several codes to this filter function's *uCode* argument. The two most important codes are HC_GETNEXT and HC_SKIP. I will discuss these and the remaining codes in the next section.

This hook does not use the *wParam* argument. The *lParam* argument contains a pointer to the EVENTMSG structure. This is the same structure that I described in Chapter 19. The difference between the *lParam* argument of this hook and of the WH_JOURNALRECORD hook is that for this hook, the developer must fill the *lParam* argument with a valid EVENTMSG structure. The WH_JOURNALRECORD hook provides a message structure in the *lParam* so that the developer can monitor or record the message. The EVENTMSG structure is then converted to an MSG structure and the RIT dispatches it to the appropriate thread.

An installed WH_JOURNALPLAYBACK hook will accept messages through its filter function's *lParam* argument. When this filter function returns, it causes the message to be placed at the head of the message queue. The RIT's message loop then processes this message and sends it to the correct window.

The filter function's return value is used for timing purposes. If a developer sets the return value to zero, there is no delay between messages being sent and processed. If a developer sets the return value to any value greater than zero, a delay is introduced between the sending of messages. The return value is equal to the number of clock ticks that the hook must wait before sending the next message. This return value is used only if the *uCode* argument is equal to HC_GETNEXT; otherwise, it is ignored.

This hook is similar to the WH_JOURNALRECORD hook in the following ways:

- Both are system-wide hooks that you can place in an EXE or in a dynamic link library (DLL) module.

- Both hooks' filter functions are called from within the context of the thread in which they reside.

- You can stop both hooks using the CTRL-ESC or CTRL-ALT-DELETE key combinations.

- When you stop either hook using the aforementioned key combinations, the **WM_CANCELJOURNAL** message is sent to the hooking application.

- Microsoft recommends adding the CTRL-BREAK key combination to allow the user to gracefully stop either hook.

- You can ignore the **HC_SYSMODALON** and **HC_SYSMODALOFF** codes for either hook.

Explanation of Hook Codes

The filter function's *uCode* argument can receive any of five different codes. These codes are:

HC_GETNEXT

> When the filter function receives this code, the function must place the next message to be played into the **EVENTMSG** structure. If a message is repeated many times, this code will be sent in succession, one time for each repeated message.
>
> The return value for the filter function determines how long to wait before sending the current message. Because messages are sent only for the **HC_GETNEXT** code, the return value for the filter function will cause the system to wait only when this code is received.
>
> The **HC_GETNEXT** constant is defined as follows:
>
> ```
> Const HC_GETNEXT = 1
> ```

HC_SKIP

> When the filter function receives this code, the function must prepare to place the next message into the **EVENTMSG** structure. This message will be played the next time this function receives the **HC_GETNEXT** code.
>
> The **HC_SKIP** code is sent to the filter function when the RIT's message loop has processed and sent to its destination thread the message sent on the previous **HC_GETNEXT** code. Usually, the **HC_GETNEXT** and **HC_SKIP** codes are interlaced, as shown here:
>
> ```
> HC_GETNEXT         (Play message #1)
> HC_SKIP            (Prepare to play message #2)
> HC_GETNEXT         (Play message #2)
> HC_SKIP            (Prepare to play message #3)
> HC_GETNEXT         (Play message #3)
> HC_SKIP            (Prepare to play message #4)
> HC_GETNEXT         (Play message #4)
> HC_SKIP            (Prepare to play message #5)
> HC_GETNEXT         (Play message #5)
> ```

If a message is repeated, though, **HC_GETNEXT** is called each time the message is repeated without an interlaced call to **HC_SKIP**, as shown here:

```
HC_GETNEXT        (Play message #1)
HC_SKIP           (Prepare to play message #2)
HC_GETNEXT        (Play message #2 - First time message #2 is played)
HC_GETNEXT        (Play message #2 - First repeat of message #2)
HC_GETNEXT        (Play message #2 - Second repeat of message #2)
HC_SKIP           (Prepare to play message #3)
HC_GETNEXT        (Play message #3)
```

The **HC_SKIP** constant is defined as follows:

```
Const HC_SKIP = 2
```

HC_NOREMOVE

Indicates that a thread has called the *PeekMessage* function on its message queue. The *PeekMessage* function did not remove the message from the queue. The **HC_NOREMOVE** constant is defined as follows:

```
Const HC_NOREMOVE = 3
```

HC_SYSMODALON

Informs us that a system modal dialog box has been displayed. Any time a system modal dialog box is displayed, we must pause the message recording function until that dialog box has been shut down. The **HC_SYSMODALON** constant is defined as follows:

```
Const HC_SYSMODALON = 4
```

HC_SYSMODALOFF

Informs us that the system modal dialog box has been shut down. At this time, we can resume our recording. Our code can ignore both the **HC_SYSMODALON** and **HC_SYSMODALOFF** codes. These apply to the Win16 environment. The **HC_SYSMODALOFF** constant is defined as follows:

```
Const HC_SYSMODALOFF = 5
```

As with the **WH_JOURNALRECORD** hook, we should skip our hook processing and immediately call *CallNextHookEx* if the *uCode* argument is less than zero.

Location of This Hook in the System

This hook is located at the point in the system where messages are retrieved from the RIT's message queue. The diagram in Figure 20-1 illustrates this.

As with the **WH_JOURNALRECORD**, **WH_KEYBOARD_LL**, and **WH_MOUSE_LL** hooks, you can install this hook only as a system-wide hook. To review, these hooks can reside either in an EXE or DLL module. This means that we can implement these hooks solely within Visual Basic (VB). This is because these hooks' filter functions are called from within the context of the thread that has installed them.

Ordinarily, when you install a hook as a system-wide hook, you must place it in a DLL. This DLL is injected into every process so that the hook can operate on all

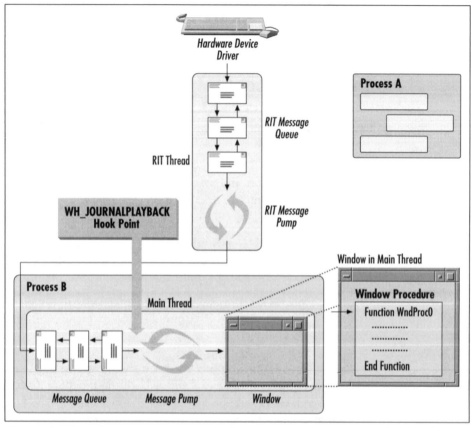

Figure 20-1. Point in the messaging system where WH_JOURNALPLAYBACK hook resides

messages in the system. However, in the case of these four hooks, the hook can
be installed for a single thread and still receive every message that the system generates because every message is being funneled through a single message queue.
As a result, the hook does not have to reside in a DLL; it can reside in an EXE as
well. For a detailed discussion of this, see Chapter 19.

The Macro Recorder/Playback Example

This example application looks and operates the same as the example in the previous chapter. The only difference is that we have added two new buttons, hook
and unhook, to the PLAYBACK frame. The code in this chapter will concentrate
on these new buttons. Figure 20-2 presents a screenshot of this example application.

Table 20-1 presents the nondefault properties of the form and its controls.

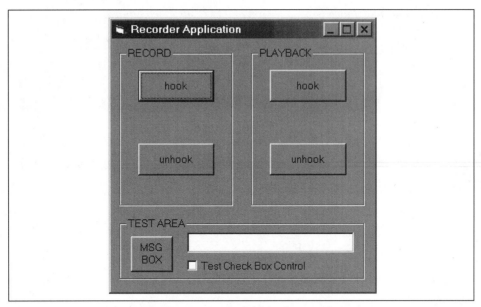

Figure 20-2. Screenshot of the Macro Recorder/Playback example application

Table 20-1. Nondefault Properties of the Form and Its Controls

Object Type	Property Name	Property Value
Form	Name	Form2
Form	Caption	"Recorder Application"
Form	Top	420
Form	Left	132
Form	Height	4305
Form	Width	4290
Frame	Caption	"RECORD"
Frame	Name	Frame1
Frame	Top	120
Frame	Left	120
Frame	Height	1335
Frame	Width	1155
Frame	Caption	"PLAYBACK"
Frame	Name	Frame2
Frame	Top	120
Frame	Left	120
Frame	Height	2475
Frame	Width	1815
Frame	Caption	"TEST AREA"

Table 20-1. Nondefault Properties of the Form and Its Controls (continued)

Object Type	Property Name	Property Value
Frame	Name	Frame3
Frame	Top	120
Frame	Left	2220
Frame	Height	2475
Frame	Width	1815
TextBox	Top	240
TextBox	Left	1080
TextBox	Height	315
TextBox	Width	2655
Command Button1	Name	cmdHook
Command Button1	Caption	"hook"
Command Button1	Top	360
Command Button1	Left	300
Command Button1	Height	495
Command Button1	Width	1215
Command Button2	Name	cmdUnHook
Command Button2	Caption	"unhook"
Command Button2	Top	1500
Command Button2	Left	300
Command Button2	Height	495
Command Button2	Width	1215
Command Button3	Caption	"MSG BOX"
Command Button3	Top	300
Command Button3	Left	180
Command Button3	Height	555
Command Button3	Width	675
Command Button4	Name	cmdPlaybackHook
Command Button4	Caption	"hook"
Command Button4	Top	360
Command Button4	Left	300
Command Button4	Height	495
Command Button4	Width	1215
Command Button5	Name	cmdPlaybackUnHook
Command Button5	Caption	"unhook"
Command Button5	Top	360
Command Button5	Left	300

Table 20-1. Nondefault Properties of the Form and Its Controls (continued)

Object Type	Property Name	Property Value
Command Button5	Height	495
Command Button5	Width	1215
CheckBox	Caption	"Test CheckBox Control"
CheckBox	Top	660
CheckBox	Left	1080
CheckBox	Height	195
CheckBox	Width	2655

The hook button that we add to the PLAYBACK frame installs the WH_
JOURNALPLAYBACK hook. After this hook is installed, it takes over and plays back
the recorded macro. While the macro is playing back, mouse and keyboard input
is placed in the RIT's message queue but not processed.

When the macro is finished playing, the hook is removed and system control is
returned to the user. The user does not have to click the unhook button before
taking an action such as recording another macro or exiting the application.

If the user presses the CTRL-ESC key combination or any other key combination
that stops the hook, the user must click the unhook button in the PLAYBACK
frame to remove the hook. This is because the *IsPBHooked* flag is still set for the
hook. Clicking the unhook button will set this flag to FALSE so that the application can be exited.

To fix this problem we could add a WH_GETMESSAGE hook to our code that would
watch for the WM_CANCELJOURNAL message and set the *IsPBHooked* flag to FALSE
automatically.

To record and play back a complete macro, follow these steps:

1. Click the hook button in the RECORD frame.
2. Record the macro.
3. Click the unhook button in the RECORD frame.
4. Click the hook button in the PLAYBACK frame.
5. Watch as your macro is played back.

This chapter will present only the new code that has been added to this project,
rather than repeat the code presented in Chapter 19. Once again, I will start with
the new variables that we must declare, which are shown in boldface:

```
Private hRecordHook As Long
Private hPlaybackHook As Long
Private MsgArray() As Long
```

```
Private StartTime As Long
Private CurrMSG As Long

Public IsHooked As Boolean
Public IsPBHooked As Boolean
```

The *hPlaybackHook* variable contains the handle to the WH_JOURNALPLAYBACK hook. This variable operates like the *hRecordHook* variable does.

The *CurrMSG* variable indicates which message in the *MsgArray* array is the one currently being sent to the WH_JOURNALPLAYBACK filter function. The filter function uses this variable to get the information from the *MsgArray* array into the EVENTMSG structure.

The *IsPBHooked* Boolean variable is a flag indicating whether the WH_JOURNALPLAYBACK hook has been installed. This variable works similar to the *IsHooked* Boolean flag.

Example 20-1 shows the WH_JOURNALPLAYBACK hook filter function.

Example 20-1. The JournalPlaybackProc Filter Function

```
Public Function JournalPlaybackProc(ByVal uCode As Long, ByVal wParam As Long, _
                    lParam As EVENTMSG) As Long
    If uCode = HC_GETNEXT Then        'You should play the current message
        If CurrMSG >= UBound(MsgArray, 2) Then
            'No more messages to play, remove the hook and restore control
            'to the user gracefully
            Call RemovePlaybackHook
        Else
            lParam.message = MsgArray(1, CurrMSG)
            lParam.hwnd = MsgArray(2, CurrMSG)
            lParam.paramH = MsgArray(3, CurrMSG)
            lParam.paramL = MsgArray(4, CurrMSG)
            lParam.time = MsgArray(5, CurrMSG) - MsgArray(5, CurrMSG - 1)

            JournalPlaybackProc = lParam.time
        End If
    ElseIf uCode = HC_SKIP Then        'You should retrieve the next message
        If CurrMSG >= UBound(MsgArray, 2) Then
            'No more messages to play, remove the hook and restore control
            'to the user gracefully
            Call RemovePlaybackHook
        End If

        CurrMSG = CurrMSG + 1
    ElseIf uCode = HC_NOREMOVE Then
        'Skip Playback - an app has called PeekMessage.
    ElseIf uCode = HC_SYSMODALON Then
        'Skip playback
    ElseIf uCode = HC_SYSMODALOFF Then
        'Skip playback
    End If
```

Example 20-1. The JournalPlaybackProc Filter Function (continued)

```
    JournalPlaybackProc = CallNextHookEx(hPlaybackHook, uCode, wParam, lParam)
End Function
```

The filter function focuses on two codes: HC_GETNEXT and HC_SKIP. The other codes are of no concern to us. The HC_GETNEXT code allows us to pass a message on to this filter function's *lParam* argument. First, though, we must determine if any more messages must be processed. We do this by checking if the value of the *CurrMsg* variable is greater than or equal to the upper bounds of the *MsgArray* array. If it is, the hook will be removed; otherwise, processing continues.

The next section of code within the HC_GETNEXT code block passes a message into the EVENTMSG structure. Notice that all elements of the *MsgArray* array are passed in unchanged, except for the *time* element.

We use the *time* element to synchronize message playback. If we passed back zero instead of the *lParam.time* member from the *JournalPlaybackProc* filter function, there would be no delays between messages. The messages would be played back at an extremely fast pace. There might be some instances in which the accelerated playback of messages is desirable. To make this happen, simply modify the line in the Filter function from:

```
    JournalPlaybackProc = lParam.time
```

to:

```
    JournalPlaybackProc = 0
```

If instead you want the playback of messages to occur at the same rate as the user recorded them, you need to find the difference in time between the current message and the previous message. You accomplish this through this line of code:

```
    lParam.time = MsgArray(5, CurrMSG) - MsgArray(5, CurrMSG - 1)
```

The number 5 in the *MsgArray* array represents the fifth member in the EVENTMSG structure or the time member. The result of this time difference is placed in the *lParam.time* member of the EVENTMSG structure and the filter function returns it.

Initially, the WH_JOURNALRECORD hook filter function determines the value placed in MsgArray(5, n) (equivalent to the time member of the EVENTMSG structure). Looking back at Chapter 19, we can see that we set the StartTime variable to the current time using the *GetTickCount* application programming interface (API) function at the point when the WH_JOURNALRECORD hook is installed:

```
    StartTime = GetTickCount
```

This variable gives us our baseline. The value in StartTime is subtracted from the current time each message is played using this line of code:

```
MsgArray(5, UBound(MsgArray, 2)) = (lParam.time - StartTime)
```

Now, the *time* member of each message in MsgArray contains the difference in time between when the WH_JOURNALRECORD hook was first installed and the message was played.

When we play back the message using the WH_JOURNALPLAYBACK hook, we use this line of code to get the amount of time for the WH_JOURNALPLAYBACK hook to wait before sending the next message:

```
lParam.time = MsgArray(5, CurrMSG) - MsgArray(5, CurrMSG - 1)
```

This line takes the time it took for the previous message to be recorded and subtracts that value from the time it took for the current message to be recorded. The result is the amount of time between messages.

Figure 20-3 shows the time calculation in graphical form. The line identified by the letter A is the time at which message #1 is recorded. The line identified by the letter B is the time at which message #2 is recorded. Therefore, the dotted lines A and B both represent the time that has lapsed between installing the WH_JOURNALRECORD hook and the actual message being sent. To find the value of Lines A and B, in CPU clock cycles, use the following equation in the WH_JOURNALRECORD hook filter function:

```
(lParam.time - StartTime)
```

Line C is the difference between the times at which messages #1 and #2 were recorded. This value is the time that the WH_JOURNALPLAYBACK function must wait between playing message #1 and message #2. You find Line C using this equation in the WH_JOURNALPLAYBACK hook filter function:

```
MsgArray(5, CurrMSG) - MsgArray(5, CurrMSG - 1):
```

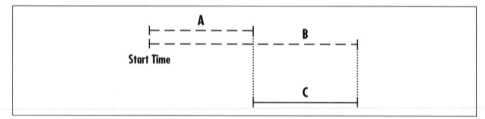

Figure 20-3. How to get the amount of time to wait between sending messages

After the EVENTMSG structure is filled in, the filter function returns the same value that was placed in the time member of the EVENTMSG structure. This causes the system to wait the number of clock cycles that this function returns before sending the next message.

If an `HC_SKIP` code is passed in to the filter function, we first determine if there are any more messages to play in the *MsgArray* array. If there are, we simply increment the *CurrMSG* variable by 1. Now our filter function is ready to play the next message in the array.

Finally, *CallNextHookEx* is called to allow any other installed `WH_ JOURNALPLAYBACK` hooks in the hook chain to execute.

You use the *SetPlaybackHook* function shown in Example 20-2 to install the `WH_ JOURNALPLAYBACK` hook. There is nothing new here except that the *CurrMSG* variable is initialized in the function.

Example 20-2. Installing the WH_JOURNALPLAYBACK Hook

```
Public Sub SetPlaybackHook()
    If IsPBHooked Or IsHooked Then
        MsgBox "Don't hook it twice without unhooking or " & _
               "you will be unable to remove the hook."
    Else
        StartTime = GetTickCount
        CurrMSG = 1

        hPlaybackHook = SetWindowsHookEx(WH_JOURNALPLAYBACK, _
                            AddressOf JournalPlaybackProc, _
                            App.hInstance, 0)

        IsPBHooked = True
    End If
End Sub
```

You use the *RemovePlaybackHook* function, which Example 20-3 illustrates, to remove the installed `WH_JOURNALPLAYBACK` hook.

Example 20-3. Removing the WH_JOURNALPLAYBACK Hook

```
Public Sub RemovePlaybackHook()
    Dim lRetVal As Long
    lRetVal = UnhookWindowsHookEx(hPlaybackHook)
    IsPBHooked = False
End Sub
```

Finally, the code shown in Example 20-4 is added to the form module to enable the user to play back the previous recorded message.

Example 20-4. Source Code for the Form2.frm Module

```
'-----------
'PLAYBACK
'-----------
```

Example 20-4. Source Code for the Form2.frm Module (continued)

```
Private Sub cmdPlaybackHook_Click()
    Call SetPlaybackHook
End Sub

Private Sub cmdPlaybackUnHook_Click()
    Call RemovePlaybackHook
End Sub

'-----------
'CLEANUP
'-----------
Private Sub Form_QueryUnload(Cancel As Integer, UnloadMode As Integer)
    If IsHooked Then
        Cancel = 1
        MsgBox "Unhook the WM_JOURNALRECORD hook before closing " & _
            "or the application may crash."
    End If

    If IsPBHooked Then
        Cancel = 1
        MsgBox "Unhook the WM_JOURNALPLAYBACK hook before closing or " & _
            "the application may crash."
    End If
End Sub
```

We have added the *Click* event handlers for the hook and unhook buttons in the PLAYBACK frame. Also, we have added code to the *Form_QueryUnload* event handler to check to see whether the WH_JOURNALPLAYBACK hook was removed before the application unloaded. Ending the application before unhooking any hooks can cause a crash.

Caveats

You must watch several things carefully when using the WH_JOURNALPLAYBACK hook. First, you must watch for different screen resolutions. A macro recorded in one resolution might not play back correctly in a different resolution. As a test, record a macro using the application you built in this chapter at a resolution of 640x480. Then, switch to a higher resolution, such as 1024x768. You will notice that the x and y coordinates of the mouse during playback at the higher resolution are scaled down, as if the system still thinks the resolution is 640x480.

You also must watch for a window changing locations when the macro is played back. The played back macro still assumes that the window is in its original position and plays back the macro accordingly. Similar problems arise with windows that become covered by another window, windows that become hidden, or windows that become destroyed.

Macros recorded in one operating system (Windows 9x, NT, or 2000) can have problems when played back in a different operating system. Some causes for these problems might be:

- The messages that are recorded in one operating system might not exist on the operating system in which that the macro is being played back.

- Different resolutions.

- Different desktop layouts.

- Different mouse setups (e.g., if a snap-to or wrapping option is set for the mouse in one operating system and not in the other).

Problems also could arise after the macro has finished playing. Remember that messages are still being placed into the message queue (except for WM_MOUSEMOVE messages), even though the WH_JOURNALPLAYBACK hook is installed. When the hook is removed, the queued messages will be sent to their corresponding window procedure to be acted upon.

You can record a macro that installs a WH_JOURNALPLAYBACK hook, which in turn plays back a different macro, although doing so might cause unpredictable results because either macro can do something to affect the other macro. You can simulate this by recording a macro with the macro recorder application you built in this chapter and then recording a second macro that installs the WH_JOURNALPLAYBACK hook. You accomplish this by clicking the hook button in the PLAYBACK frame on the user interface while recording a macro. You should always verify that the WH_JOURNALPLAYBACK hook is removed before ending the macro.

Finally, pressing the Windows key, present on many keyboards, has the same effect as pressing the CTRL-ESC key combination—the Windows Start menu is displayed and any installed journal hooks are removed. Pressing the Windows key on the keyboard sends the CTRL-ESC key combination to the system at some point. If this key combination is used or if the Windows key is pressed, the installed journal hook will be removed.

21

WH_DEBUG

This chapter deals with the WH_DEBUG hook. Along with describing how this hook operates, I also will discuss how to use it to aid in debugging other hooks you have installed in your application.

Description

The main purpose of the WH_DEBUG hook, as its name implies, is for debugging other hooks. When you install this hook, it intercepts the call to an installed hook's filter function before the call is actually made. For the sake of simplicity, I will refer to the hook that is being debugged as the target hook. Figure 21-1 illustrates the relationship of the WH_DEBUG hook to the operating system and the target hook.

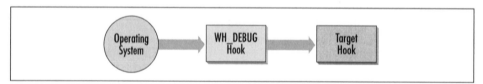

Figure 21-1. The WH_DEBUG hook is called before the target hook

You can install this hook as a thread-specific hook in a Visual Basic (VB) application, or you can install it as a system-wide hook in a Win32 dynamic link library (DLL). When you install it as a thread-specific hook, the system will call it before calling any installed hook filter functions within that specific thread. As a note, the WH_DEBUG hook will not intercept messages sent to the WH_MOUSE_LL and WH_ KEYBOARD_LL hook filter functions, since these low-level hook filter functions are called earlier in the messaging system. When you install the WH_DEBUG hook as a system-wide hook, the system will call it before calling any installed hook filter functions within the system, once again excluding all WH_MOUSE_LL and WH_KEYBOARD_LL hooks.

As you can see, any installed filter functions for the WH_DEBUG hook are always called before calling any other hook's filter function. If several hooks are installed at one time along with the WH_DEBUG hook, the WH_DEBUG hook will be flooded by calls to various hook filter functions. Determining which hook's filter function is being called can become quite confusing, but by using the *wParam* parameter of the WH_DEBUG hook, we can determine the type of hook that is being called.

When you want to debug a thread-specific hook with the WH_DEBUG hook, you must install the WH_DEBUG hook in the same thread as the thread-specific target hook. Otherwise, you will never be able to intercept the system's calls to the target hook. You can install a system-wide WH_DEBUG hook, but then you will see all calls made to every installed hook in the system. This can introduce more noise than is helpful. You should keep the WH_DEBUG hook to a thread-specific scope if at all possible. After all, debugging consists of focusing in on the problem; in most instances, it will be harder to focus in on a hook problem with a system-wide WH_DEBUG hook.

Another important point about this hook is that it will capture information about each hook installed in a hook chain. For example, if three keyboard hooks are installed, the WH_DEBUG hook will be called once for each keyboard hook. Also remember that the last hook installed is the first hook that is called in the hook chain.

Filter Function Definition

The filter function for the WH_DEBUG hook is defined as follows:

```
Public Function DebugProc(ByVal uCode As Long, _
                ByVal wParam As Long, _
                lParam As DEBUGHOOKINFO) As Long
```

The filter function's parameters are:

uCode

> The code the system sends to this filter function. Possible *uCode* values are discussed in the "Explanation of Hook Codes" section later in this chapter.

wParam

> This value specifies the hook ID (that is, the type of hook) that is being called. Hook IDs can be any of the following:

```
WH_MSGFILTER = (-1)
WH_JOURNALRECORD = 0
WH_JOURNALPLAYBACK = 1
WH_KEYBOARD = 2
```

```
WH_GETMESSAGE = 3
WH_CALLWNDPROC = 4
WH_CBT = 5
WH_SYSMSGFILTER = 6
WH_MOUSE = 7
WH_HARDWARE = 8
WH_SHELL = 10
WH_FOREGROUNDIDLE = 11
WH_CALLWNDPROCRET = 12
```

lParam

A pointer to a DEBUGHOOKINFO structure. This structure gives the WH_DEBUG hook access to the information that is to be passed to the target hook and aids in identifying the target hook. You cannot modify this information.

The DEBUGHOOKINFO structure is defined as follows:

```
Public Type DEBUGHOOKINFO
       idThread As Long
       idThreadInstaller As Long
       lParam As Long
       wParam As Long
       code As Long
End Type
```

Its members are:

idThread

Handle to the thread containing the filter function of the hook that is about to be called

idThreadInstaller

Handle to the thread that installed the WH_DEBUG hook filter function

lParam

Value of the *lParam* that is to be sent to the filter function of the hook that is about to be called

wParam

Value of the *wParam* that is to be sent to the filter function of the hook that is about to be called

code

Value of the *uCode* that is to be sent to the filter function of the hook that is about to be called

As you can see, the *code*, *lParam*, and *wParam* members contain the same information that is sent to the target hook's filter function. All hook filter functions take these three parameters. The *idThread* member contains the handle to the thread where the hook's filter function is installed. The *idThreadInstaller* member contains the handle to the thread that installed the hook. These two handles can provide information on the installed hook's scope. If these two handles contain different values, you can be certain that this is a system-wide hook. However, if the two handles contain the same value, the target hook could have either thread-specific or system-wide scope; it is impossible to differentiate the scope using only these two thread handles. This is because a system-wide hook is installed in every process in the system, even the one that caused the hook to be installed in the first place.

The return value for this filter function should be the return value of the *CallNextHookEx* function. If this function is not called, return a zero. I do not recommend skipping the call to *CallNextHookEx*, though. Failing to call it prevents other filter functions in the chain from being called. However, forcing a nonzero number to be returned will cause the destination hook's filter function to not be called.

It is important to note that Windows 9x does not support the `WH_DEBUG` hook and the `DEBUGHOOKINFO` structure. Although you can install and run it in Windows 98 Second Edition (I used build 4.10.2222A), I do not recommend doing so. I was able to get it to run, but the information it produced was not reliable. In most instances, the `WH_DEBUG` hook was being called at odd times, sometimes even after the target hook finished processing.

Explanation of Hook Codes

The filter function's *uCode* parameter receives only one hook code: `HC_ACTION`. This code is defined as follows:

```
Private Const HC_ACTION = 0
```

When this code is sent to the filter function, the sent message can be processed. If `HC_ACTION` is not passed in, you should skip message processing and call *CallNextHookEx* immediately.

A Thread-Specific Example

This example uses the `WH_SHELL` example that was presented in Chapter 17. Figure 21-2 shows the application's user interface. As you can see, a checkbox labeled Discard Msg has been added to the example. When checked, it causes the `WH_DEBUG` hook to return a nonzero value, effectively preventing the target hook from being called. Otherwise, all messages will safely pass through this hook to the target hook.

Table 21-1 presents the nondefault properties of the form and its controls.

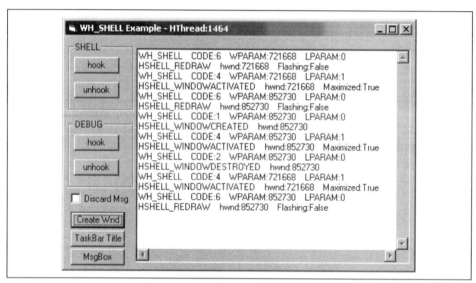

Figure 21-2. A screenshot of the WH_SHELL/WH_DEBUG example

Table 21-1. Nondefault Properties of the Form and Its Controls

Object	Property Name	Property Value
Form1	Name	Form2
Form1	Caption	"WH_SHELL Example"
Form1	Top	330
Form1	Left	105
Form1	Height	4710
Form1	Width	7095
Form2	Name	Form1
Form2	Caption	"NEW FORM"
Command Button1	Name	cmdHook
Command Button1	Caption	"hook"
Command Button1	Top	120
Command Button1	Left	120
Command Button1	Height	300
Command Button1	Width	915
Command Button2	Name	cmdUnhook
Command Button2	Caption	"unhook"
Command Button2	Top	780
Command Button2	Left	120

Table 21-1. Nondefault Properties of the Form and Its Controls (continued)

Object	Property Name	Property Value
Command Button2	Height	300
Command Button2	Width	915
Command Button3	Name	cmdCreateWnd
Command Button3	Caption	"CreateWnd"
Command Button3	Top	3180
Command Button3	Left	120
Command Button3	Height	315
Command Button3	Width	1395
Command Button4	Name	cmdTaskBarTitle
Command Button4	Caption	"TaskBar Title"
Command Button4	Top	3540
Command Button4	Left	120
Command Button4	Height	315
Command Button4	Width	1395
Command Button5	Name	cmdMsgBox
Command Button5	Caption	"MsgBox"
Command Button5	Top	3900
Command Button5	Left	120
Command Button5	Height	315
Command Button5	Width	1395
Command Button6	Name	cmdDBGHook
Command Button6	Caption	"hook"
Command Button6	Top	3900
Command Button6	Left	120
Command Button6	Height	315
Command Button6	Width	1395
Command Button7	Name	cmdDBGUnHook
Command Button7	Caption	"unhook"
Command Button7	Top	3900
Command Button7	Left	120
Command Button7	Height	315
Command Button7	Width	1395
CheckBox	Name	chkDiscardMsg
CheckBox	Caption	"Discard Msg"

Table 21-1. Nondefault Properties of the Form and Its Controls (continued)

Object	Property Name	Property Value
CheckBox	Top	3060
CheckBox	Left	120
CheckBox	Height	195
CheckBox	Width	1215
TextBox	Name	Text1
TextBox	MultiLine	True
TextBox	Top	240
TextBox	Left	1440
TextBox	Height	3975
TextBox	Width	5475

To use this application, click the hook button for the WH_SHELL hook, and then click the hook button for the WH_DEBUG hook. When the WH_SHELL hook is called, output to the text box will always show that the WH_DEBUG hook is called immediately before it.

If you check the Discard Msg checkbox, you will notice that only the WH_DEBUG hook is called. The WH_SHELL hook is not called because the WH_DEBUG hook function returns 1.

It is interesting to note that when the WH_DEBUG hook is installed and you do not explicitly install any other hooks, you might receive notifications that certain hooks are about to fire. For example, if you are using a third-party mouse or keyboard that contains extra input devices, you might notice that the WH_MOUSE, the WH_KEYBOARD, or even the WH_GETMESSAGE hooks are being fired, even though you did not install them. What is happening is that the software that you installed with these devices installs one or more system-wide hooks. These hooks are usually installed at boot time. This way, they can add extra capabilities to all processes running in the system by installing extra code—the hook's filter function—into each running process. For example, in Figure 21-3, you can see the system-wide hooks being called from within the thread that installed the WH_DEBUG hook.

Example 21-1 presents the code behind the form. The *Form_QueryUnload* function performs a final check to determine if any hooks are still installed. If any are installed, application shutdown is canceled. If the application were shut down before removing all hooks, the application would suffer a General Protection Fault (GPF).

Installing the WH_DEBUG hook is similar to installing any other thread-specific hook. The *SetDebugHook* function in Example 21-2 installs the WH_DEBUG hook.

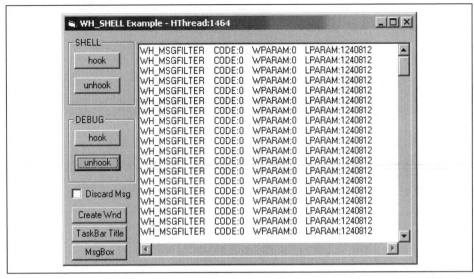

Figure 21-3. Installing only the WH_DEBUG book will inform you of any system-wide books that another application might have installed in your system

Example 21-1. Installing the WH_DEBUG Hook

```
Private Sub cmdHook_Click()
    Text1.Text = ""
    Call SetShellHook
End Sub

Private Sub cmdUnhook_Click()
    Call RemoveShellHook
End Sub


Private Sub cmdDBGHook_Click()
    Call SetDebugHook
End Sub

Private Sub cmdDBGUhHook_Click()
    Call RemoveDebugHook
End Sub


Private Sub cmdCreateWnd_Click()
    Form1.Show
End Sub


Private Sub cmdTaskBarTitle_Click()
    If Me.Caption = "Title Of Window Has Changed" Then
        Me.Caption = "WH_SHELL Example"
    Else
        Me.Caption = "Title Of Window Has Changed"
```

Example 21-1. Installing the WH_DEBUG Hook (continued)

```
    End If
End Sub

Private Sub cmdMsgBox_Click()
    MsgBox "The WH_SHELL hook does not acknowledge the creation of this message box."
End Sub

'-----------
'CLEANUP
'-----------
Private Sub Form_QueryUnload(Cancel As Integer, UnloadMode As Integer)
    If IsHooked Or IsDBGHooked Then
        Cancel = 1
        MsgBox "Unhook before closing, or the IDE will crash."
    End If
End Sub
```

Example 21-2. Installing the WH_DEBUG Hook

```
Public Sub SetDebugHook()
    If IsDBGHooked Then
        MsgBox "Don't hook DEBUG twice or you will be unable to unhook it."
    Else
        hHookDBG = SetWindowsHookEx(WH_DEBUG, AddressOf DebugProc, 0, _
                    App.ThreadID)
        IsDBGHooked = True
    End If
End Sub
```

You remove the hook using *UnhookWindowsHookEx*. The *RemoveDebugHook* function in Example 21-3 shows how you remove this hook.

Example 21-3. Removing the WH_DEBUG Hook

```
Public Sub RemoveDebugHook()
    Dim temp As Long
    temp = UnhookWindowsHookEx(hHookDBG)
    IsDBGHooked = False
End Sub
```

The *DebugProc* function acts as the filter function for this hook, as Example 21-4 illustrates. This function writes a line of text to the Text1 text box whenever each type of hook is called. This can work fine for a simple example that demonstrates how to use the WH_DEBUG hook, but in a real-world application it might cause problems.

Example 21-4. The WH_DEBUG Filter Function

```
Public Function DebugProc(ByVal uCode As Long, ByVal wParam As Long, _
                    lParam As DEBUGHOOKINFO) As Long
    If uCode >= 0 Then
```

Example 21-4. The WH_DEBUG Filter Function (continued)

```
Select Case wParam
    Case WH_CALLWNDPROCRET
        Form2.Text1.Text = Form2.Text1.Text & "WH_CALLWNDPROCRET    CODE:" & _
            lParam.code & "    WPARAM:" & lParam.wParam & _
            "    LPARAM:" & lParam.lParam & vbNewLine
    Case WH_CBT
        Form2.Text1.Text = Form2.Text1.Text & "WH_CBT     CODE:" & _
            lParam.code & "    WPARAM:" & lParam.wParam & _
            "    LPARAM:" & lParam.lParam & vbNewLine
    Case WH_FOREGROUNDIDLE
        Form2.Text1.Text = Form2.Text1.Text & "WH_FOREGROUNDIDLE     CODE:" & _
            lParam.code & "    WPARAM:" & lParam.wParam & _
            "    LPARAM:" & lParam.lParam & vbNewLine
    Case WH_JOURNALPLAYBACK
        Form2.Text1.Text = Form2.Text1.Text & "WH_JOURNALPLAYBACK  CODE:" & _
            lParam.code & "    WPARAM:" & lParam.wParam & "    LPARAM:" & _
            lParam.lParam & vbNewLine
    Case WH_JOURNALRECORD
        Form2.Text1.Text = Form2.Text1.Text & "WH_JOURNALRECORD" & vbNewLine
    Case WH_SYSMSGFILTER
        Form2.Text1.Text = Form2.Text1.Text & "WH_SYSMSGFILTER     CODE:" & _
            lParam.code & "    WPARAM:" & lParam.wParam & _
            "    LPARAM:" & lParam.lParam & vbNewLine
    Case WH_MSGFILTER
        Form2.Text1.Text = Form2.Text1.Text & "WH_MSGFILTER     CODE:" & _
            lParam.code & "    WPARAM:" & lParam.wParam & _
            "    LPARAM:" & lParam.lParam & vbNewLine
    Case WH_GETMESSAGE
        Form2.Text1.Text = Form2.Text1.Text & "WH_GETMESSAGE     CODE:" & _
            lParam.code & "    WPARAM:" & lParam.wParam & "    LPARAM:" _
            & lParam.lParam & " TID_ContainsFF:" & lParam.hModuleHook & _
            " TID_InstallFF:" & lParam.Reserved & bNewLine
    Case WH_KEYBOARD
        Form2.Text1.Text = Form2.Text1.Text & "WH_KEYBOARD     CODE:" & _
            lParam.code & "    WPARAM:" & lParam.wParam & _
            "    LPARAM:" & lParam.lParam & vbNewLine
    Case WH_MOUSE    ' This will fire many times
        Form2.Text1.Text = Form2.Text1.Text & "WH_MOUSE     CODE:" & _
            lParam.code & "    WPARAM:" & lParam.wParam & _
            "    LPARAM:" & lParam.lParam & vbNewLine
    Case WH_SHELL
        Form2.Text1.Text = Form2.Text1.Text & "WH_SHELL     CODE:" & _
            lParam.code & "    WPARAM:" & lParam.wParam & _
            "    LPARAM:" & lParam.lParam & vbNewLine
    Case WH_CALLWNDPROC
        'This one GPF's since everytime the text is added to the text box
        'another message is intercepted creating an infinite loop
        'Form2.Text1.Text = Form2.Text1.Text & "WH_CALLWNDPROC     CODE:" _
            & lParam.code & "    WPARAM:" & lParam.wParam & _
            "    LPARAM:" & lParam.lParam & vbNewLine
End Select
```

Example 21-4. The WH_DEBUG Filter Function (continued)

```
      If Form2.chkDiscardMsg.Value = 1 Then
          'To prevent the system from calling the hook,
          ' this hook procedure must return a nonzero value
          DebugProc = 1
          Exit Function
      Else
          DebugProc = CallNextHookEx(hHookDBG, uCode, wParam, lParam)
      End If
   End If
End Function
```

The biggest problem with this method of displaying information occurs when the WH_CALLWNDPROC hook is called. If you notice, I have commented out the code that writes the information for this hook to the text box. Initially when I left this code uncommented and ran this application, it immediately crashed. This occurred because a WH_CALLWNDPROC hook installed as either a system-wide or thread-specific hook is called whenever anything is written to the text box. This causes the filter function to be reentered before it can finish. This, in turn, causes a stack overflow, and the application crashes.

One way to get around this is to use the *OutputDebugString* application programming interface (API) function and the DBMon utility to monitor the WH_DEBUG hook instead of the text box method. The *OutputDebugString* function is defined as follows:

```
   Public Declare Sub c Lib "kernel32" Alias "OutputDebugStringA" _
          (ByVal lpOutputString As String)
```

Its single parameter is:

lpOutputString
    The string that will be sent to the debugger hooked up to the current application

This subroutine takes one parameter and does not have a return value. The *lpOutputString* parameter is displayed in the debugger for the current application. If no debugger is present, nothing happens. When you run the DBMon utility alongside your application, you can display output from *OutputDebugString*.

To make this change in the *DebugProc* filter function, simply change each line of code that sent a line of text to the Text1 text box from this:

```
   Form2.Text1.Text = Form2.Text1.Text & "WH_SHELL    CODE:" & lParam.code & " _
                    "   WPARAM:" & lParam.wParam & _
                    "   LPARAM:" & lParam.lParam & vbNewLine
```

to this:

```
   OutputDebugString("WH_SHELL    CODE:" & lParam.code & " _
          "   WPARAM:" & lParam.wParam & "    LPARAM:" & lParam.lParam)
```

This method prevents a stack overflow crash from occurring in your `WH_DEBUG` hook.

We can modify this application slightly to show the effects of the `WH_DEBUG` hook on a single type of hook installed multiple times. You would modify the *SetDebugHook* function as shown in Example 21-5. Two new calls to *SetWindowsHookEx* are added to this function. Notice that this set of calls installs the `WH_GETMESSAGE` hook twice. Two new filter functions are added to the BAS module to handle these two hooks, as Example 21-6 illustrates.

Example 21-5. Installing a Hook Multiple Times

```
Public Sub SetShellHook()
    If IsHooked Then
        MsgBox "Don't hook SHELL twice or you will be unable to unhook it."
    Else
        'hHookShell = SetWindowsHookEx(WH_SHELL, AddressOf ShellProc, 0, _
                    App.ThreadID)
        hHookGetMsg1 = SetWindowsHookEx(WH_GETMESSAGE, AddressOf GMProc, 0, _
                    App.ThreadID)
        hHookGetMsg2 = SetWindowsHookEx(WH_GETMESSAGE, AddressOf GMProc2, 0, _
                    App.ThreadID)

        IsHooked = True
    End If
End Sub
```

Example 21-6. The Two WH_GETMESSAGE Filter Functions

```
Public Function GMProc(ByVal uCode As Long, ByVal wParam As Long, _
                    ByVal lParam As Long) As Long
    Form2.Text1.Text = Form2.Text1.Text & "My first installed " & _
                    "WH_GETMESSAGE Hook Called" & vbNewLine
    GMProc = CallNextHookEx(hHookGetMsg1, uCode, wParam, lParam)
End Function

Public Function GMProc2(ByVal uCode As Long, ByVal wParam As Long, _
                    ByVal lParam As Long) As Long
    Form2.Text1.Text = Form2.Text1.Text & "My second installed " & _
                    "WH_GETMESSAGE Hook Called" & vbNewLine
    GMProc2 = CallNextHookEx(hHookGetMsg2, uCode, wParam, lParam)
End Function
```

As Example 21-7 shows, two calls to *UnhookWindowsHookEx* are added to the *RemoveDebugHook* function to remove the hooks and allow our application to stop gracefully.

Example 21-7. Removing Multiple WH_GETMESSAGE Hooks

```
Public Sub RemoveShellHook()
    Dim temp As Long
    'temp = UnhookWindowsHookEx(hHookShell)
```

Example 21-7. Removing Multiple WH_GETMESSAGE Hooks (continued)

```
    temp = UnhookWindowsHookEx(hHookGetMsg1)
    temp = UnhookWindowsHookEx(hHookGetMsg2)
    IsHooked = False
End Sub
```

Now, run the application and install the `WH_GETMESSAGE` hooks but not the `WH_DEBUG` hook. Figure 21-4 shows a screenshot of the application running. The output in the Text1 text box looks similar to the following:

```
    My second installed WH_GETMESSAGE Hook Called
    My first installed WH_GETMESSAGE Hook Called
    My second installed WH_GETMESSAGE Hook Called
    My first installed WH_GETMESSAGE Hook Called
```

As you can see, the last hook we installed is getting called first, followed by the first hook that we installed. This follows the calling pattern that occurs in filter function chains.

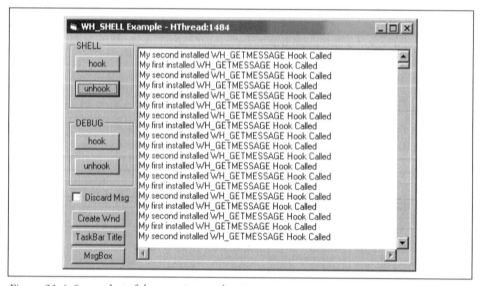

Figure 21-4. Screenshot of the running application

Next, install the `WH_DEBUG` hook. Figure 21-5 displays a screenshot of the running application. When you install this hook, the output looks similar to the following:

```
    WH_GETMESSGE Code:0  WPARAM:1   LPARAM:1244656
    My second installed WH_GETMESSAGE Hook Called
    WH_GETMESSGE Code:0  WPARAM:1   LPARAM:1244292
    My first installed WH_GETMESSAGE Hook Called
    WH_GETMESSGE Code:0  WPARAM:1   LPARAM:1243928
    WH_GETMESSGE Code:0  WPARAM:1   LPARAM:1244656
    My second installed WH_GETMESSAGE Hook Called
    WH_GETMESSGE Code:0  WPARAM:1   LPARAM:1244292
```

```
My first installed WH_GETMESSAGE Hook Called
WH_GETMESSGE Code:0  WPARAM:1   LPARAM:1243928
```

As you can see, the output shows that the WH_DEBUG hook is called before the last hook that we installed. Next, the last hook we installed is called. Once again, the WH_DEBUG hook is called, this time for the first hook that we installed. After this, our first hook is called. Now something strange happens: the WH_DEBUG hook is again called for no apparent reason.

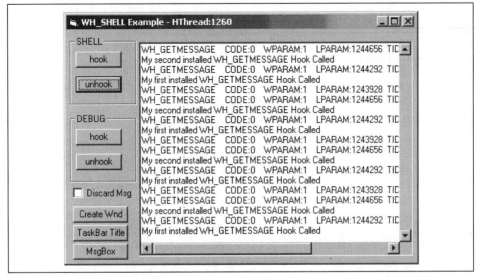

Figure 21-5. Screenshot of the running application with the WH_DEBUG hook installed

The third call to the WH_DEBUG hook is due to a third-party application installing a system-wide WH_GETMESSAGE hook prior to our application installing the other two WH_GETMESSAGE hooks. The WH_DEBUG hook is called in the context of the thread in which our application is running because the system-wide hook also is called from this thread. This might not occur on your system exactly as it did on my machine because a third-party application might not have installed this hook.

Some WH_DEBUG Scenarios

In this section, we'll examine some common problems that arise when debugging hooks, and show how you can use the WH_DEBUG hook to diagnose and solve them.

Problem: Misbehaving System-Wide Hook

Sometimes a misbehaving system-wide hook can interfere with your hook's operation. Consider the situation in which your application installs a system-wide keyboard hook when the system first boots up. Later on, a third-party application installs a keyboard hook. This keyboard hook, however, does not call the *CallNextHookEx* function at the end of its filter function, as a well-behaved hook should. When your application is running, you notice that your hook does not work, or worse, that it works intermittently.

To determine the cause, you can install a WH_DEBUG hook on the same thread as the target hook, and only watch for calls to any keyboard hooks. Watching for the WH_KEYBOARD constant in the *wParam* parameter of the WH_DEBUG hook allows you to watch calls that are made to the WH_KEYBOARD hook's filter function. This WH_DEBUG hook will intercept hooks installed with system-wide scope, or those installed from the same thread as the WH_DEBUG hook.

After you install the WH_DEBUG hook, you notice that it is capturing information about a hook that has the same *idThread* as the thread that contains your WH_ DEBUG hook as well as your keyboard hook. But when you inspect the *idThreadInstaller* member, you notice that it is different from the *idThread* value. This indicates that the next keyboard hook to be called was installed by a different process, but the filter function—which exists inside a DLL—has been injected into your application's process.

Investigating with Spy++ or some other process viewer, you find that this thread handle belongs to a third-party application. The next step is to prevent that third-party application from installing. It is also a good idea to reboot just to make sure the system-wide keyboard hook that it installed is removed from all processes. After you do this, you can restart your test with your application. If another system-wide hook is installed, you should remove this one as well. After you have removed all hooks, you should see the call to your installed keyboard hook appear inside the WH_DEBUG hook's filter function. If you don't, verify that the hook is being installed properly—*SetWindowsHookEx* should be returning a non-zero number.

Problem: Determining if Hooks Are Interfering with Each Other

One nice feature that the WH_DEBUG hook provides is the ability to prevent the target hook from being called. To do this, you only need to return a nonzero value from the WH_DEBUG hook's filter function, and the target hook will not be called.

Preventing the system from calling the target hook is especially useful when you are installing more than one hook and you need to determine if and why the hooks are interfering with each other. For example, a keyboard hook might be causing a message to be posted to a window, which is, in turn, intercepted by a *GetMessage* hook. You might not be expecting your *GetMessage* hook to be called at this time, and unexpected behavior might result. These are hard errors to find, but the `WH_DEBUG` hook allows you to trace the order and number of times a hook is called.

Simply install the `WH_DEBUG` hook and watch only for these two hooks to be called. If any system-wide hooks are installed that duplicate the hooks that you want to debug, you should follow the procedure discussed previously to eliminate them.

As you operate your application, you should watch the order in which the two hooks are being called. If the *GetMessage* hook is being called immediately after the keyboard hook at specific times, you should focus in on the actions the user performed when this happens.

Next, you should examine the *uCode*, *lParam*, and *wParam* parameters that are being sent to the target hooks. The information that these parameters contain should provide some insight about where the problem lies.

Problem: Performance Degradation

Another instance in which the `WH_DEBUG` hook comes in handy is when application performance slows when one or more hooks are installed. The `WH_DEBUG` hook can monitor the installed hooks and determine how many times a hook is called.

In this case, you might want to set up a counter inside the `WH_DEBUG` hook's filter function that indicates the number of times a hook is called. You would also want to be able to start and stop this counter at will—in other words, to install and remove the `WH_DEBUG` hook whenever you want. This way, you can gather information at specific points of execution in the application and compare them. If your hook is being called a large number of times at certain points in your application, you need to examine your application to see what is causing the hook to be called.

Unoptimized filter functions used in hooks such as `WH_MOUSE`, `WH_CALLWINDOWPROC`, `WH_GETMESSAGE`, `WH_FOREGROUNDIDLE`, `WH_MSGFILTER`, or `WH_SYSMSGFILTER` can hurt application performance because these types of hooks can potentially intercept a huge number of messages every second. The more time that is spent in the filter function, the less time the application has to do its regular processing. In this case, you might also want to profile your filter function to determine how much time is spent inside the filter function.

Caveats

With every other hook I have discussed thus far, I have warned about strongly considering performance when writing the filter functions. You do not have to take performance into consideration when using this hook, however, because this hook is a tool used for debugging purposes. You most likely would not want to release debugging code in the final release of your product.

I'm sure someone out there will find a legitimate reason for keeping a `WH_DEBUG` hook in the final release of your application. In this case, I would place performance at the forefront when designing this hook's filter function, because this hook is called once for every hook that you install in your system, plus for every system-wide hook. If your `WH_DEBUG` hook is a system-wide hook, you intercept calls made to every hook in every thread running in the system. That is a great deal of overhead for an application. In cases such as this, I would force the code to fall through and immediately call *CallNextHookEx* whenever you encounter a call to a target hook which you do not care about.

Here are a couple of things to remember:

- The `WH_DEBUG` hook is called once for every filter function that is installed in a filter function chain.

- If you install a thread-specific `WH_DEBUG` hook and it starts picking up calls to hooks that you have not installed, these extra hook calls are caused by another application installing a system-wide hook.

- Using *OutputDebugString* and the DBMon utility are far better than writing trace information to a text box within the hooked application.

- Returning a nonzero value from a `WH_DEBUG` hook filter function will prevent the target hook from being called.

- You should not use this hook in Window 9x, even if it appears to be working. The output is not always correct.

Also remember that the `WH_DEBUG` hook does not intercept calls to low-level hooks, such as `WH_KEYBOARD_LL` and `WH_MOUSE_LL`, because these hooks are called early on in message processing and the `WH_DEBUG` hook cannot see the calls to these hooks.

IV

The .NET Platform

Chapter 22 and Chapter 23 will explain how to implement subclassing and hooks using VB.NET. These chapters assume a familiarity with the VB.NET language as well as with the information contained in Chapter 2 and Chapter 3.

22

Subclassing .NET WinForms

This is the first of two chapters covering the techniques of subclassing and hooking as they apply to VB.NET. This chapter will cover how to subclass a Win-Form. The next chapter will explain how to implement hooks in VB.NET.

What Is a WinForm?

Simply, a *WinForm* is analogous to a Visual Basic (VB) 6 .FRM form module. On the exterior, both types of forms operate in a similar fashion, look the same, and are used as containers to display controls. Internally, however, they are very different.

You create a WinForm from the Form class within the .NET framework. This class exists in the `System.WinForms` namespace, which is contained within the *System.Winforms.DLL* file. The Form class inherits from several other classes. The following listing shows the class hierarchy for the Form class:

```
Object
MarshalByRefObject
MarshalByRefComponent
Control
RichControl
ScrollableControl
ContainerControl
Form
```

The Object class is the ultimate base class of the Form class, as well as all other classes contained in the .NET framework. A brief description of each class follows:

Object
    The base class of every object in the .NET framework.

MarshalByRefObject

> Contains base implementation for use by objects that need remoting ability.

MarshalByRefComponent

> Contains base implementation for use by all controls that can be sited on a form.

Control

> Contains base implementation for use by all objects that have a user interface. This class handles keyboard and mouse input, as well as message routing and security. This class is central to subclassing.

RichControl

> Extends the Control class by adding the ability to paint itself, to control context menus, and to handle docking and anchoring of its window.

ScrollableControl

> Adds the ability for a window to display and handle vertical and horizontal scrollbars, used to scroll the client area of the window.

ContainerControl

> Adds the ability for a window to contain other controls, as well as to handle control focus.

Form

> Used to create a Single Document Interface (SDI) window, Multiple Document Interface (MDI) window, dialog box, tool window, borderless window, or floating window.

You also can use many of these classes to construct controls, such as buttons, labels, and list boxes.

The WinForm is more robust and contains more functionality than the forms in previous versions of VB. Before subclassing a WinForm or a control, it is a good idea to research the previous list of classes to determine if the functionality you need is already built-in.

Using a WinForm

To use a WinForm in VB.NET, you must first import the `System.Winforms` namespace into your application. You do this by using the `Imports` statement, as shown here:

```
Imports System.WinForms
```

You must place the `Imports` statement before any other code in the .VB file. You must import two other namespaces as well; they are:

```
Imports System.ComponentModel
Imports System.Drawing
```

The `System.ComponentModel` namespace contains core component functionality such as containment, licensing, and attribute handling, as well as many others. The `System.Drawing` namespace contains functionality to paint objects on the screen.

After you import this namespace into the application, you need to create a class that inherits from the Form class. You accomplish this by using the following code:

```
Public Class Form1
    Inherits System.WinForms.Form

    'Place form code here
End Class
```

To allow your project to use this form, you must specify in the project properties dialog box that the StartupObject property is equal to *<project name>*.Form1, where *<project name>* is the name of your project. This will cause Form1 to be the startup form for this project; that is, the application will create and display this form first upon startup.

If you use the Visual Studio.NET (VS.NET) wizard to create a VB.NET WinForms application, it will set up your project to contain a single .VB file called Form1. It also will automatically create other project files, but we are not concerned with these files. The code in this file looks similar to the code presented in Example 22-1.

Example 22-1. VS.NET Wizard Created Code for a WinForm Application

```
Imports System.ComponentModel
Imports System.Drawing
Imports System.WinForms


Public Class Form1
    Inherits System.WinForms.Form

    Public Sub New()
        MyBase.New
        Form1 = Me

        'This call is required by the Win Form Designer.
        InitializeComponent

        'TODO: Add any initialization after the InitializeComponent() call
    End Sub

    'Form overrides dispose to clean up the component list.
    Overrides Public Sub Dispose()
        MyBase.Dispose
        components.Dispose
    End Sub

#Region " Windows Form Designer generated code "
```

Example 22-1. VS.NET Wizard Created Code for a WinForm Application (continued)

```
'Required by the Windows Form Designer
Private components As System.ComponentModel.Container

Dim WithEvents Form1 As System.WinForms.Form

'NOTE: The following procedure is required by the Windows Form Designer
'It can be modified using the Windows Form Designer.
'Do not modify it using the code editor.
Private Sub InitializeComponent()
    components = New System.ComponentModel.Container
    Me.Text = "Form1"
End Sub
```

```
#End Region
```

```
End Class
```

The *Sub New* subroutine is the constructor for this class. The form constructor replaces the familiar *Form_Load* event in previous versions of VB. This constructor initially calls the constructor of the base class and then immediately sets the **Me** reference to itself. This **Me** reference operates similar to the **Me** reference in previous versions of VB. Last, the constructor calls the InitializeComponent method, shown at the bottom of Example 22-1. The InitializeComponent method initializes the form as a container for controls and sets its caption to "Form1".

The wizard also adds a *Dispose* subroutine to allow the form to clean up after itself and to free any resources it is holding onto in a timely manner, instead of waiting for the Garbage Collector to perform this step at some undetermined later time.

The form designer writes the code between the `#Region` ... `#End Region` as you add, remove, or modify controls on this form. The `#Region` preprocessor directive allows you to collapse this block of code so that your editor screen can remain uncluttered.

Instance Subclassing

Subclassing a WinForm is much simpler and less error-prone than subclassing a VB 5 or 6 form module because Microsoft has written all the lower-level subclassing code for you. Now, all you really have to worry about is the code that you will write for your subclass window procedure.

To understand this better, we need to look behind the scenes at a window being created in a WinForm application. As soon as this window is created in memory, the *GetWindowLongW* application programming interface (API) function is called to replace the original window procedure with a new one. The original window procedure is stored so that it can be replaced when the window is destroyed. For more detail, see the "Behind the Scenes With Spy++" section later in this chapter.

Because the WinForm automatically takes care of subclassing and unsubclassing itself—not to mention storing the original window procedure for later use—we have fewer headaches to worry about when implementing subclassing. One thing that the WinForm does not automatically do, however, is write the empty subclass procedure.

Even though the WinForm handles much of the subclassing automatically, you must still follow the same rules as you did previously when writing your sub-classed window procedure. For example, long complex code in the window pro-cedure—including displaying a message box or dialog box for user input—will severely degrade your application's performance. Also, you must call the original window procedure of the subclassed WinForm so that default window processing can occur on the message.

A major benefit of subclassing a WinForm is that you do not have to worry about storing the original window procedure's address and using it to call and restore the original window procedure. We will see how this works in the first example application.

 This method of subclassing is available when using any .NET lan-guage, such as C# or managed C++. The only requirement is that you use the WinForms classes when creating the windows.

The messaging flow in a WinForm follows the same path as do messages in a typ-ical subclassed window. First the message is placed in the thread's message queue, where the message loop retrieves it and sends it on to the subclassed window pro-cedure. This subclassed window procedure is the one that the WinForm automati-cally inserts for you. Next, the message is sent on to the original window procedure and then on to the default window procedure. The following list speci-fies the order in which the message is handled:

1. Thread Message Queue

2. Message loop

3. Subclassed window procedure (inserted by .NET)

4. Original window procedure

5. DefaultWinProc → Return.

Next, I will present several examples showing how you can subclass a WinForm. It is interesting to note that there are three ways to subclass a WinForm in VB.NET. I will describe each technique in the next three examples.

Technique #1: Overriding the WinProc Method

The first technique for subclassing a WinForm is the simplest to write. It involves using the object-oriented capabilities of the WinForm classes to override the Wnd-Proc method. The WndProc method is the subclassed window procedure for the WinForm. This procedure is contained within the Control class from which the Form class inherits. The function declaration for WndProc is as follows:

```
Overridable Protected Sub WndProc(ByRef m as Message)
```

This function is marked as **Overridable**, which means that classes inheriting from the Control class can override the functionality in the Control.WndProc method to provide their own implementation. The **Protected** modifier indicates that the Control class, and any classes inheriting from this class, can access only the Wnd-Proc method. This protects the WndProc method from being accessed outside of the form.

The WndProc method takes only one parameter, *m*, which is of type **Message**. You will notice that it is marked as **ByRef**, which means that the WndProc can modify the message before it is passed back to the original window procedure.

In a VB 6 application, you can declare a subclassed window procedure as follows:

```
Public Function WndProc(hWnd As Long, Msg As Long, wParam As Long, _
                        lParam As Long) as Long
```

The VB.NET WndProc method is missing all the parameters, including the return value. All these parameters are now encapsulated in the **Message** type. The **Message** type is a structure that contains the following fields relating to a window's message:

Public hWnd As Integer
  Window handle to which the message is directed

Public msg As Integer
  ID of the message

Public lParam As Integer
  Meaning is determined by the message

Public wParam As Integer
  Meaning is determined by the message

Public result As Integer
  Return value of the message after the function processes it

You cannot create the **Message** structure simply by instantiating a new instance of the **Message** type. To create a new instance, the **Message** structure contains a public static method called Create—in VB.NET, static functions are declared as **Shared**. The declaration of this method is as follows:

```
Public Shared Function Create(ByVal hWnd As Integer, ByVal msg As Integer, _
    ByVal wParam As Integer, ByVal lParam As Integer) As Message
```

The reason for this method call instead of instantiating a new object is that the .NET framework creates a pool of **Message** structures available to the developer. The Create method returns a **Message** structure from this pool, thus improving the application's efficiency. When a Create method tries to return a **Message** structure and none is available, the system will create a new one.

To override a base class's function in VB.NET, you need to use the **Overrides** keyword. The following code overrides the Control class's WndProc method:

```
Protected Overrides Sub WndProc(ByRef m As Message)
    'Subclassing code goes here.

    MyBase.WndProc(m)
End Sub
```

When overriding a method—especially the WndProc method—you need to call the overridden, or base, method to complete the processing. In VB 6, we would use the following API function to return the message to the original window procedure:

```
WndProc = CallWindowProc(OrigWndProc, hwnd, uMsg, wParam, lParam)
```

In the case of the WndProc method, you must call the base WndProc method contained in the Control class. If you don't, the original window procedure will not process the message. To call the base class method, we need to use the **MyBase** keyword as follows:

```
MyBase.WndProc(m)
```

The **Message** structure (*m*) is sent to the overridden base class to complete its processing by the original window procedure. If we left out this line of code, we would, in effect, be preventing the window from finishing processing the message.

The application

The application you need to create to demonstrate this technique is simple. The only control on the form is a text box, as Figure 22-1 illustrates. Table 22-1 lists the nondefault properties of the form and the text box control.

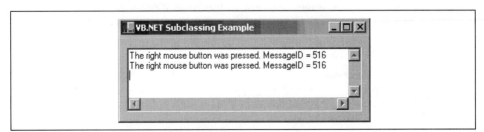

Figure 22-1. The application using the first technique of subclassing

Table 22-1. Nondefault Properties of the Form and Its Controls

Object	Property Name	Property Value
Form	Caption	"VB.NET Subclassing Example"
Form	Height	357
Form	Width	328
TextBox	Multiline	True
TextBox	Scrollbars	True
TextBox	WordWrap	False
TextBox	Top	16
TextBox	Left	8
TextBox	Height	144
TextBox	Width	312

The subclassed window procedure for this application watches for the right mouse button to be pressed while the mouse is over the form's client area. When the user clicks it, a message is placed in the text box indicating that the right mouse button was clicked and listing that message's ID. From the screenshot of the application in Figure 22-1, we can see that the right mouse button was clicked on the form twice. (As a note, the subclassed window procedure cannot see messages that are sent to nonclient areas of the form.)

The first difference you might notice between this application and the subclassing applications in previous chapters is that there are no Subclass and UnSubclass buttons on the form. When overriding the WndProc method, the WinForm is subclassed when it is created, and the subclassing cannot be removed until the form is destroyed. The system removes the subclassing immediately before the form is destroyed.

The .VB file

Example 22-2 presents the code for this technique. The code added to subclass the WinForm is highlighted. The code in the WndProc method watches for the WM_ RBUTTONDOWN message to be passed to it. When it receives this message, some text indicating that the right button was pressed is written to the text box. Upon completing its task, all messages are sent to the base WndProc method for default processing.

Example 22-2. The Form1.vb File Using Subclassing Technique #1

```
Imports System.ComponentModel
Imports System.Drawing
Imports System.WinForms
```

Example 22-2. The Form1.vb File Using Subclassing Technique #1 (continued)

```
Public Class Form1
    Inherits System.WinForms.Form

    Public Sub New()
        MyBase.New()
        Form1 = Me
        InitializeComponent()
    End Sub

    'Form overrides dispose to clean up the component list.
    Public Overrides Sub Dispose()
        MyBase.Dispose()
        components.Dispose()
    End Sub

#Region " Windows Form Designer generated code "

    'Required by the Windows Form Designer
    Private components As System.ComponentModel.Container

    Private WithEvents TextBox1 As System.WinForms.TextBox

    Dim WithEvents Form1 As System.WinForms.Form

    'NOTE: The following procedure is required by the Windows Form Designer
    'It can be modified using the Windows Form Designer.
    'Do not modify it using the code editor.
    Private Sub InitializeComponent()
        Me.components = New System.ComponentModel.Container()
        Me.TextBox1 = New System.WinForms.TextBox()

        '@design Me.TrayHeight = 0
        '@design Me.TrayLargeIcon = False
        '@design Me.TrayAutoArrange = True
        TextBox1.Location = New System.Drawing.Point(8, 16)
        TextBox1.Multiline = True
        TextBox1.ScrollBars = System.WinForms.ScrollBars.Both
        TextBox1.WordWrap = False
        TextBox1.TabIndex = 2
        TextBox1.Size = New System.Drawing.Size(312, 144)
        Me.Text = "VB.NET Subclassing Example"
        Me.AutoScaleBaseSize = New System.Drawing.Size(5, 13)
        Me.ClientSize = New System.Drawing.Size(328, 357)

        Me.Controls.Add(TextBox1)
    End Sub

    'SUBCLASSING TECHNIQUE #1
    Protected Overrides Sub WndProc(ByRef m As Message)
        If m.msg = microsoft.Win32.Interop.win.WM_RBUTTONDOWN Then
            textbox1.Text = textbox1.Text & "The right mouse button was " & _
                "pressed. MessageID = " + m.msg.ToString() & chr(13) & chr(10)
```

Example 22-2. The Form1.vb File Using Subclassing Technique #1 (continued)

```
        End If

        MyBase.WndProc(m)
    End Sub
#End Region
End Class
```

Technique #2: Binding to a NativeWindow Class Instance

This technique requires a little more code than the first technique, but you gain the ability to turn subclassing on and off at will. This technique will help optimize your application by allowing you to decide when the subclassing should be performed.

To use this second technique, we must first create a class that inherits from the NativeWindow class. This new class will contain the WndProc method as well as an event handler that is called when subclassing is turned on and off.

The NativeWindow class is a wrapper around an hWnd and a window procedure of the WinForm to which it is bound. To bind a NativeWindow to a WinForm, we use the NativeWindow.AssignHandle method. This method is declared as follows:

```
    Overridable Public Sub Assignhandle (handle As Integer)
```

To bind a WinForm to a NativeWindow class, we set the *handle* parameter of this method equal to the hWnd of the WinForm that we are subclassing. The Win-Form class has a read-only property called Handle, which is inherited from the Control class. By setting the *handle* parameter of the AssignHandle method to the WinForm Handle property value, we can bind the WinForm to the NativeWindow. The following code fragment performs this operation:

```
    Dim sc As New MySubClass()
    sc.AssignHandle(Form1.Handle)
```

In this code fragment, the MySubClass class inherits from the NativeWindow class and contains an overridden WndProc method. The NativeWindow object (*sc*) is created and its AssignHandle method is called with its *handle* parameter set to the Form1 form's Handle property.

At this point, whenever the application's message loop retrieves a message from the message queue, the message loop will examine the message's hWnd value and direct it to our instance of the NativeWindow class (*sc*) that contains our subclassed window procedure.

To remove the subclassing, we need to call the NativeWindow class's Release-Handle method. This function is declared as follows:

```
    Overridable Public Sub ReleaseHandle()
```

This method takes no parameters and does not return a value. To determine if this method executed successfully, you can check the Handle property of the object that inherited from the NativeWindow class. If the Handle property is set to zero, the ReleaseHandle method executed correctly. However, if the Handle property still contains the hWnd value of the WinForm, the method did not execute correctly. The code to remove the subclassing and check the Handle value is as follows:

```
sc.ReleaseHandle()
If sc.Handle = 0 Then
    'Executed Correctly
Else
    'Did not execute correctly
End If
```

You also can determine whether a call to AssignHandle or ReleaseHandle has succeeded by coding the NativeWindow object's *OnHandleChange* event procedure. This event is called whenever the Handle property of the `NativeWindow` class instance is modified. In this event procedure, you can check the value of the NativeWindow.Handle property to determine whether the WinForm is subclassed. If the Handle property is zero, the `NativeWindow` is not subclassed; otherwise, it is.

To subclass the WinForm in our application, we will call the AssignHandle method in the Subclass button's *Click* event. To remove the subclassing, we will call the ReleaseHandle method in the UnSubclass button's *Click* event.

As a note, the NativeWindow class has two methods, CreateHandle and Destroy-Handle, that you should *not* use when subclassing. The DestroyHandle method sets the Handle property of the NativeWindow class to zero and proceeds with shutting down the window. After the window is shut down, it is eligible for garbage collection. The CreateHandle method creates a new window from an existing window class.

It is interesting to note that when you use this subclassing technique in tandem with the first subclassing technique, they will each intercept messages sent to the WinForm. Therefore, you can override the Form class's WndProc method as well as bind the Form to a NativeWindow class and override its WndProc method. This, in effect, subclasses the WinForm twice. If you need to subclass the WinForm twice, this is the way to do it because the system automatically takes care of removing both subclassed window procedures and replacing the WinForm's original window procedure before the window is destroyed. To subclass the WinForm twice, add to the Form1 class the following code from Technique #1:

```
Protected Overrides Sub WndProc(ByRef m As Message)
    'Place subclassing code here.

    MyBase.WndProc(m)
End Sub
```

A really nice side benefit of using this technique is that if you fail to unsubclass the WinForm, your application will not crash. Failing to unsubclass a form before it was destroyed in a previous version of VB would cause your application to suffer a General Protection Fault (GPF). The system takes care of any cleanup that is required of a subclassed WinForm before it is destroyed.

The application

This application operates similarly to the example presented in the section entitled "Technique #1," with one exception: Subclass and UnSubclass buttons are added to the form. Figure 22-2 shows the application.

This application will place the same message used in the Technique #1 example in the text box whenever the right mouse button is clicked on the form's client area. The difference is that you must click the Subclass button to subclass the WinForm and intercept the WM_RBUTTONDOWN message. When you click the UnSubclass button, the subclassing is removed and the WinForm will no longer be able to intercept the WM_RBUTTONDOWN message.

Table 22-2 lists the nondefault properties of the form and its controls.

Table 22-2. Nondefault Properties of the Form and Its Controls

Object	Property Name	Property Value
Form	Caption	"VB.NET Subclassing Example"
Form	Height	357
Form	Width	504
TextBox	Multiline	True
TextBox	Scrollbars	True
TextBox	WordWrap	False
TextBox	Top	16
TextBox	Left	88
TextBox	Height	336
TextBox	Width	408
Button1	Caption	"SubClass"
Button1	Top	16
Button1	Left	8
Button1	Height	23
Button1	Width	75
Button2	Caption	"UnSubClass"
Button2	Top	48
Button2	Left	8
Button2	Height	23
Button2	Width	75

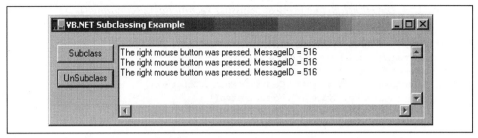

Figure 22-2. The application using the second technique of subclassing

The .VB file

Example 22-3 presents the code for this technique. The code added to subclass the WinForm is highlighted.

Example 22-3. The Form1.vb File Using Subclassing Technique #2

```vb
Imports System.ComponentModel
Imports System.Drawing
Imports System.WinForms


Public Class Form1
    Inherits System.WinForms.Form

    Private Dim sc As New MySubClass()

    Public Sub New()
        MyBase.New()
        Form1 = Me
        InitializeComponent()

        sc.SetRefToForm(Me)
    End Sub

    'Form overrides dispose to clean up the component list.
    Public Overrides Sub Dispose()
        MyBase.Dispose()
        components.Dispose()
    End Sub

#Region " Windows Form Designer generated code "

    'Required by the Windows Form Designer
    Private components As System.ComponentModel.Container

    Private WithEvents TextBox1 As System.WinForms.TextBox
    Private WithEvents Button2 As System.WinForms.Button
    Private WithEvents Button1 As System.WinForms.Button

    Dim WithEvents Form1 As System.WinForms.Form
```

Example 22-3. The Form1.vb File Using Subclassing Technique #2 (continued)

```
'NOTE: The following procedure is required by the Windows Form Designer
'It can be modified using the Windows Form Designer.
'Do not modify it using the code editor.
Private Sub InitializeComponent()
    Me.components = New System.ComponentModel.Container()
    Me.Button1 = New System.WinForms.Button()
    Me.Button2 = New System.WinForms.Button()
    Me.TextBox1 = New System.WinForms.TextBox()

    '@design Me.TrayHeight = 0
    '@design Me.TrayLargeIcon = False
    '@design Me.TrayAutoArrange = True
    Button1.Location = New System.Drawing.Point(8, 16)
    Button1.Size = New System.Drawing.Size(75, 23)
    Button1.TabIndex = 0
    Button1.Text = "Subclass"

    Button2.Location = New System.Drawing.Point(8, 48)
    Button2.Size = New System.Drawing.Size(75, 23)
    Button2.TabIndex = 1
    Button2.Text = "UnSubclass"

    TextBox1.Location = New System.Drawing.Point(88, 16)
    TextBox1.Multiline = True
    TextBox1.ScrollBars = System.WinForms.ScrollBars.Both
    TextBox1.WordWrap = False
    TextBox1.TabIndex = 2
    TextBox1.Size = New System.Drawing.Size(408, 336)

    Me.Text = "VB.NET Subclassing Example"
    Me.AutoScaleBaseSize = New System.Drawing.Size(5, 13)
    Me.ClientSize = New System.Drawing.Size(504, 357)

    Me.Controls.Add(TextBox1)
    Me.Controls.Add(Button2)
    Me.Controls.Add(Button1)
End Sub
#End Region




'SUBCLASS TECHNIQUE #2
Protected Sub Button1_Click(ByVal sender As Object, _
                            ByVal e As System.EventArgs)
    If sc.Handle() = 0 Then
        sc.AssignHandle(Me.Handle)
    Else
        msgbox("Don't try to subclass this window more than once")
    End If
End Sub


Protected Sub Button2_Click(ByVal sender As Object, _
```

Example 22-3. The Form1.vb File Using Subclassing Technique #2 (continued)

```
                              ByVal e As System.EventArgs)
        sc.ReleaseHandle()
        'The sc.Handle property reverts back to 0
    End Sub


    Public Class MySubclass
        Inherits NativeWindow

        Dim m_MainWindow As Form1

        Public Sub SetRefToForm(ByVal MainWindow As Form1)
            m_MainWindow = MainWindow
        End Sub

        Protected Overrides Sub WndProc(ByRef m As Message)
            If m.msg = microsoft.Win32.Interop.win.WM_RBUTTONDOWN Then
                m_MainWindow.textbox1.Text = m_MainWindow.textbox1.Text & _
                "The right mouse button was pressed. MessageID = " + _
                m.msg.ToString() & chr(13) & chr(10)
            End If

            MyBase.WndProc(m)
        End Sub

        Protected Overrides Sub OnHandleChange()
            msgbox("Handle has changed")
        End Sub
    End Class
End Class
```

The MySubclass public class is added at the bottom of this example code and inherits from the NativeWindow class. It is instantiated as a private field in the Form1 class. When the Form1 class constructor is called, a Me reference to Form1 is passed in to the SetRefToForm method in the MySubclass class. This reference allows text to be written to the text box contained in Form1 from the instance of the MySubclass class. Unlike in previous versions of VB, controls are now private to Form classes. Therefore, you need a mechanism such as this to write text to a text box from outside the Form class.

The code in the overridden WndProc method of MySubclass is almost identical to the overridden WndProc method in the Technique #1 example.

The protected overridden method, OnHandleChange, is an event handler that is fired whenever the handle to the Form1 window is modified. This method simply displays a message box indicating that the handle has changed.

When the Subclass button is clicked, the *Button1_Click* event is fired. This event determines whether a handle has been assigned to the instance of MySubclass, indicating that the form is subclassed. If a handle has not been assigned, the

AssignHandle method of the MySubclass class is called to assign Form1's handle to the MySubclass instance.

However, if a handle is already assigned and the user clicks the Subclass button a second time before clicking the UnSubclass button, a message is displayed indicating that the Form1 form cannot be subclassed a second time. Trying to assign a new handle to an instance of the NativeWindow class that has a handle assigned to it is similar to the problem in VB 6 of subclassing a form twice. To subclass a form more than once, you must keep track of all the pointers to the previous window procedures. Unfortunately, the .NET framework hides the window procedure pointers quite well, which makes it difficult at best to keep track of the previous window procedure pointers. The .NET framework prevents subclassing the form more than once by throwing a System.Exception error, indicating that the call to AssignHandle failed.

While the WinForm is subclassed, all messages sent to it are routed first through the MySubClass object's WndProc. After this function is finished processing the message, it passes the message on to the form's window procedure through the use of the `MyBase` keyword.

When the user clicks the UnSubclass button, the *Button2_Click* event is fired. This event simply calls the MySubclass class's ReleaseHandle method, which releases the handle assigned to the MySubclass instance and resets it back to zero.

Technique #3: The IMessageFilter Interface

A third technique to subclass a WinForm uses the `IMessageFilter` interface. This technique will not actually create a subclass window procedure that is placed before the original window procedure. Instead, it adds a function to the message loop, which intercepts each message before it is dispatched to its destination window procedure. A subclass window procedure would intercept the message after it has been dispatched to its destination window, but before that window's original window procedure has a chance to process the message. Therefore, by using this technique, we can intercept all messages sent to all windows that exist within a single thread. This can be a powerful technique, but be aware that you will be intercepting far more messages than a single subclass window procedure would. This can degrade system and application performance drastically. To offset the performance hit you are taking by using this technique, you should do as little work as possible in the function that will be inserted into the message loop, as well as exit this function as soon as possible.

This technique is similar in structure to Technique #2. In this technique, a new class is created that implements the `IMessageFilter` interface. This class must contain a method called PreFilterMessage, which is similar to a subclass window procedure. This is the method that will be placed inside the message loop of the thread in which this window resides. The declaration of the PreFilterMessage method is similar to that of the WndProc method and is as follows:

```
'[VB]
Public Function PreFilterMessage (ByVal m As Message) As Boolean _
        Implements System.WinForms.IMessageFilter.PreFilterMessage
```

The one difference between this method and the WndProc method is that this method returns a Boolean value. If this method returns a **False**, the message is sent on to the original window procedure. However, if it returns a **True**, the message is discarded and never sent on to the original window procedure.

To intercept messages before they are dispatched to a WinForm and its controls, you must instantiate an instance of the class that implements the **IMessageFilter** interface. The following code fragment does this:

```
Private MyMsgFilter As New TestMessageFilter()
```

Now that we have an instance of the MyMsgFilter class, we can pass it into the AddMessageFilter method of the Application class to subclass the WinForm. The AddMessageFilter method is declared as follows:

```
Public Shared Sub AddMessageFilter(ByVal value AS IMessageFilter)
```

This method is declared as static, which in VB.NET is a Shared method. This method also takes a parameter of type **IMessageFilter**. The code to call the AddMessageFilter method is as follows:

```
Application.AddMessageFilter(MyMsgFilter);
```

There is a complementary method to AddMessageFilter, called RemoveMessage-Filter. This method is declared as follows:

```
Public Shared Sub RemoveMessageFilter(ByVal value As IMessageFilter)
```

This method also takes parameter of type **IMessageFilter**. To remove our procedure from the message loop, we simply call RemoveMessageFilter as follows:

```
Application.RemoveMessageFilter(MyMsgFilter);
```

The application

The application for this technique is simple. The only control on the form is a text box, as Figure 22-3 shows. Table 22-3 lists the nondefault properties of the form and the text box control.

Table 22-3. Nondefault Properties of the Form and Its Controls

Object	Property Name	Property Value
Form	Caption	"C# Subclassing Example"
Form	Height	405
Form	Width	384
TextBox	Multiline	True
TextBox	Scrollbars	True
TextBox	WordWrap	False
TextBox	Top	8
TextBox	Left	8
TextBox	Height	232
TextBox	Width	368

The PreFilterMessage method watches for the left mouse button to be pressed while the mouse is over the client area of the form. (As we mentioned earlier, this method cannot see messages that are sent to nonclient areas of the form.) When the user clicks the right mouse button over the client area of the form or the text box, a message is placed in the text box indicating that the right mouse button was clicked.

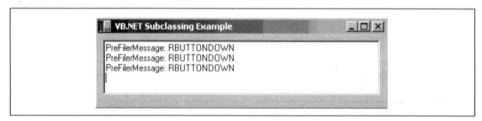

Figure 22-3. The C# application using the third technique of subclassing

This application is very similar to the one created in the "Technique #1: Overriding the WinProc Method" section. When the user clicks the right mouse button over the WinForm's client area, a message is written to the text box indicating that the right mouse button was clicked. The difference between this example and Example 22-2 is that when you click the right mouse button in the text box control, the PreFilterMessage method will intercept that message as well. Therefore, using the PreFilterMessage technique of subclassing allows us to intercept messages for not only all WinForms within a thread, but also all controls on each WinForm. On the other hand, overriding the WndProc method of a particular WinForm only allows us to intercept messages directed to that WinForm.

The .VB file

Example 22-4 presents the VB code for this technique. The code added to sub-class the WinForm appears in boldface.

Example 22-4. The Form1.vb File Using Subclassing Technique #3

```
Imports System
Imports System.ComponentModel
Imports System.Drawing
Imports System.WinForms

Public Class Form1
    Inherits System.WinForms.Form

    Private myMsgFilter As New TestMessageFilter()

    Public Sub New()
        MyBase.New()
        Form1 = Me
        InitializeComponent()

        myMsgFilter.SetRefToTextBox(Me)

        'SUBCLASSING TECHNIQUE #3
        System.WinForms.Application.AddMessageFilter(myMsgFilter)
    End Sub

    Public Sub WriteToTextBox(ByVal Message As String)
        TextBox1.Text += Message + chr(13) + chr(10)
    End Sub

    'Form overrides dispose to clean up the component list.
    Public Overrides Sub Dispose()
        MyBase.Dispose()
        components.Dispose()
    End Sub

#Region " Windows Form Designer generated code "

    'Required by the Windows Form Designer
    Private components As System.ComponentModel.Container
    Private WithEvents TextBox1 As System.WinForms.TextBox

    Dim WithEvents Form1 As System.WinForms.Form

    'NOTE: The following procedure is required by the Windows Form Designer
    'It can be modified using the Windows Form Designer.
    'Do not modify it using the code editor.
    Private Sub InitializeComponent()
        Me.components = New System.ComponentModel.Container()
        Me.TextBox1 = New System.WinForms.TextBox()

        '@design Me.TrayHeight = 0
```

Example 22-4. The Form1.vb File Using Subclassing Technique #3 (continued)

```
        '@design Me.TrayLargeIcon = False
        '@design Me.TrayAutoArrange = True
        TextBox1.Location = New System.Drawing.Point(8, 8)
        TextBox1.Multiline = True
        TextBox1.ScrollBars = System.WinForms.ScrollBars.Both
        TextBox1.WordWrap = False
        TextBox1.TabIndex = 2
        TextBox1.Size = New System.Drawing.Size(408, 200)
        Me.Text = "VB.NET Subclassing Example"
        Me.AutoScaleBaseSize = New System.Drawing.Size(5, 13)
        Me.ClientSize = New System.Drawing.Size(424, 357)

        Me.Controls.Add(TextBox1)
    End Sub
#End Region
End Class


'SUBCLASSING TECHNIQUE #3 (CONTINUED)
Public Class TestMessageFilter
    Implements System.WinForms.IMessageFilter

    Dim m_MainWindow As Form1

    Public Sub SetRefToTextBox(ByVal MainWindow As Form1)
        m_MainWindow = MainWindow
    End Sub

    Public Const WM_RBUTTONDOWN = &H204

    Function PreFilterMessage(ByRef m As System.WinForms.Message) As Boolean _
      Implements System.WinForms.IMessageFilter.PreFilterMessage
        If m.msg = WM_RBUTTONDOWN Then
            m_MainWindow.WriteToTextBox("PreFilterMessage: RBUTTONDOWN")
        End If

        PreFilterMessage = False
    End Function
End Class
```

The *MyMsgFilter* variable is declared as a private field to the Form1 WinForm. This variable is of type TestMessageFilter, a class declared at the bottom of the code example. In the constructor of Form1, a new instance of *MyMsgFilter* is created and a Me pointer is sent to its constructor. *MyMsgFilter* stores the Me pointer as a reference back to the Form1 WinForm so that it can write text into the text box that resides on Form1.

After the *MyMsgFilter* instance is created in the constructor, the shared Application.AddMessageFilter method is called to place the MyMsgFilter.PreFilterMessage method in the message loop, right before the message is dispatched.

The PreFilterMessage method in the TestMessageFilter class contains code that watches for the **WM_RBUTTONDOWN** message in the message loop. When it finds this message, it displays a message in the text box on Form1 with the following text: "PreFilterMessage: RBUTTONDOWN". The return value of this method is **False**, allowing the message loop to dispatch the message. If the return value were set to **True**, the message would not be dispatched.

Subclassing a Control

Like WinForm subclassing, control subclassing is much easier in VB.NET. In fact, to subclass a control, we can take the example application presented in the "Technique #2: Binding to a NativeWindow Class Instance" section and change one line of code. To subclass a control, all you have to do is assign its Handle property value to a class that inherits from the NativeWindow class. This subclass will contain an overridden implementation of the WndProc method, which contains the actual subclassing code.

The application

The application presented in this section is exactly the same as the one presented in the "Technique #2: Binding to a NativeWindow Class Instance" section. The only differences are that the window caption has changed to "VB.NET Control Subclassing Example," and one line of code also has changed. I will discuss the code modification shortly. Figure 22-4 presents a screenshot of this application.

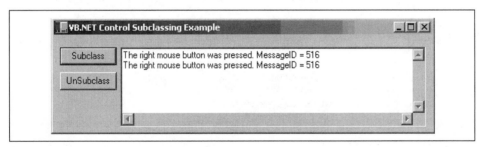

Figure 22-4. Subclassing a text box control

The .VB file

Example 22-5 presents the code for this technique. The modified code appears in boldface.

Example 22-5. The Form1.vb File Using the Control Subclassing Technique

```
Imports System.ComponentModel
Imports System.Drawing
Imports System.WinForms
```

Example 22-5. The Form1.vb File Using the Control Subclassing Technique (continued)

```
Public Class Form1
    Inherits System.WinForms.Form

    Dim sc As New MySubClass()

    Public Sub New()
        MyBase.New()
        Form1 = Me
        InitializeComponent()

        sc.SetRefToTextBox(Me)
    End Sub

    'Form overrides dispose to clean up the component list.
    Public Overrides Sub Dispose()
        MyBase.Dispose()
        components.Dispose()
    End Sub

#Region " Windows Form Designer generated code "

    'Required by the Windows Form Designer
    Private components As System.ComponentModel.Container

    Private WithEvents TextBox1 As System.WinForms.TextBox
    Private WithEvents Button2 As System.WinForms.Button
    Private WithEvents Button1 As System.WinForms.Button

    Dim WithEvents Form1 As System.WinForms.Form

    'NOTE: The following procedure is required by the Windows Form Designer
    'It can be modified using the Windows Form Designer.
    'Do not modify it using the code editor.
    Private Sub InitializeComponent()
        Me.components = New System.ComponentModel.Container()
        Me.Button1 = New System.WinForms.Button()
        Me.Button2 = New System.WinForms.Button()
        Me.TextBox1 = New System.WinForms.TextBox()

        '@design Me.TrayHeight = 0
        '@design Me.TrayLargeIcon = False
        '@design Me.TrayAutoArrange = True
        Button1.Location = New System.Drawing.Point(8, 16)
        Button1.Size = New System.Drawing.Size(75, 23)
        Button1.TabIndex = 0
        Button1.Text = "Subclass"

        Button2.Location = New System.Drawing.Point(8, 48)
        Button2.Size = New System.Drawing.Size(75, 23)
        Button2.TabIndex = 1
        Button2.Text = "UnSubclass"
```

Example 22-5. The Form1.vb File Using the Control Subclassing Technique (continued)

```
        TextBox1.Location = New System.Drawing.Point(88, 16)
        TextBox1.Multiline = True
        TextBox1.ScrollBars = System.WinForms.ScrollBars.Both
        TextBox1.WordWrap = False
        TextBox1.TabIndex = 2
        TextBox1.Size = New System.Drawing.Size(408, 336)

        Me.Text = "VB.NET Control Subclassing Example"
        Me.AutoScaleBaseSize = New System.Drawing.Size(5, 13)
        Me.ClientSize = New System.Drawing.Size(504, 357)

        Me.Controls.Add(TextBox1)
        Me.Controls.Add(Button2)
        Me.Controls.Add(Button1)
    End Sub
#End Region


    Protected Sub Button1_Click(ByVal sender As Object, ByVal e As System.EventArgs)
        If sc.Handle() = 0 Then
            sc.AssignHandle(TextBox1.Handle)
        Else
            msgbox("Don't try to subclass this control more than once")
        End If
    End Sub


    Protected Sub Button2_Click(ByVal sender As Object, ByVal e As System.EventArgs)
        sc.ReleaseHandle()
    End Sub


    Public Class MySubclass
        Inherits NativeWindow

        Dim m_MainWindow As Form1

        Public Sub SetRefToTextBox(ByVal MainWindow As Form1)
            m_MainWindow = MainWindow
        End Sub

        Protected Overrides Sub WndProc(ByRef m As Message)
            If m.msg = microsoft.Win32.Interop.win.WM_RBUTTONDOWN Then
                m_MainWindow.textbox1.Text = m_MainWindow.textbox1.Text & _
                    "The right mouse button was pressed. MessageID = " + _
                    m.msg.ToString() & chr(13) & chr(10)
            End If

            MyBase.WndProc(m)
        End Sub

        Protected Overrides Sub OnHandleChange()
            msgbox("Control Handle has changed")
```

Example 22-5. The Form1.vb File Using the Control Subclassing Technique (continued)

```
        End Sub
    End Class
End Class
```

The first code modification changes the WinForm caption. The second modification, which is what we are really interested in, is the following line of code:

```
    sc.AssignHandle(TextBox1.Handle)
```

Basically, this line uses a handle to bind the TextBox1 control to the instance of the MySubclass class, which inherits from the NativeWindow class. Now, whenever a message is sent to the TextBox1 control, the overridden WndProc method in the MySubclass class instance intercepts it. In the WndProc method, we watch for the WM_RBUTTONDOWN message. Whenever this message is intercepted, we display some text in the TextBox1 text box indicating that this action has occurred.

Superclassing

Superclassing was introduced in Chapter 4. Basically, superclassing involves creating a new base class—or superclass—that we then use to create one or more new superclassed windows. Each superclassed window retains the base class's properties and window procedure. This allows us to easily create many windows that look and operate similarly.

Due to the object-oriented nature of WinForms, we can easily perform superclassing using VB.NET or, for that matter, any other .NET language. The first step is to create a window that will act as our superclass, as Example 22-6 shows. We will use this superclass window to inherit from and create our own window, as Example 22-7 shows. It is just that simple—more so than implementing superclassing in a previous version of VB.

The application

The application that we will build to implement superclassing contains two WinForms. The first WinForm, called Form1, is the base, or superclass, WinForm. The second WinForm, called Superclass_Ex, inherits from Form1.

The code for Form1 is taken from the application in Example 22-3. To this code I have added a button that has the caption "Create Wnd". We will use this button to create new windows from the Superclass_Ex WinForm.

Table 22-4 lists the nondefault properties of the superclass form and its controls. Table 22-5 lists the nondefault properties for the Superclass_Ex WinForm. This form does not contain any controls; all controls are inherited from Form1.

Table 22-4. Nondefault Properties of the Form1 WinFform and Its Controls

Object	Property Name	Property Value
Form	Caption	"VB.NET Subclassing Example"
Form	Height	357
Form	Width	504
TextBox	Multiline	True
TextBox	Scrollbars	True
TextBox	WordWrap	False
TextBox	Top	16
TextBox	Left	88
TextBox	Height	336
TextBox	Width	408
Button1	Caption	"SubClass"
Button1	Top	16
Button1	Left	8
Button1	Height	23
Button1	Width	75
Button2	Caption	"UnSubClass"
Button2	Top	48
Button2	Left	8
Button2	Height	23
Button2	Width	75
Button3	Caption	"Create Wnd"
Button3	Top	104
Button3	Left	8
Button3	Height	23
Button3	Width	75

Table 22-5. Nondefault Properties of the Superclass_Ex WinFform and Its Controls

Item	Property Name	Property Value
Form	Caption	"Superclass_Ex"
Form	Color	"Bisque"

To use this application, simply click the Create Wnd button several times. This action will cause one Superclass_Ex form to be created and displayed for each button click. Figure 22-5 shows the application with three Superclass_Ex windows.

Notice that each Superclass_Ex WinForm takes on the characteristics of its superclass WinForm, Form1. In the Superclass_Ex WinForm, the background color has been overridden to display as Bisque. The Subclass and UnSubclass buttons work

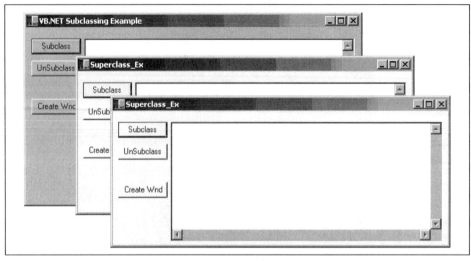

Figure 22-5. The superclassing example application

independently of each other. That is, you can click the Subclass button of one
WinForm and only that WinForm is subclassed. All other WinForms remain in their
previous state. Also, if you close the Form1 WinForm, which is the superclass Win-
Form, all other forms that inherit from that form also will be closed.

The .VB file

Example 22-6 presents the code for this technique. The code added to subclass the
WinForm appears in boldface. This code should be familiar to you from the code
in the "Technique #2: Binding to a NativeWindow Class Instance" section. A *Click*
event has been added for the Button3 control, which is the button labeled "Create
Wnd". This code simply creates a new instance of the Superclass_Ex WinForm and
calls its Show method so that it will display itself.

Example 22-6. The Form1.vb File that Acts as the Superclass WinForm

```
imports System.ComponentModel
Imports System.Drawing
Imports System.WinForms


Public Class Form1
    Inherits System.WinForms.Form

    Dim sc As MySubClass

    Public Sub New()
        MyBase.New()
        Form1 = Me
        InitializeComponent()
```

Example 22-6. The Form1.vb File that Acts as the Superclass WinForm (continued)

```vb
        sc = New MySubClass()
    End Sub

    'Form overrides dispose to clean up the component list.
    Public Overrides Sub Dispose()
        MyBase.Dispose()
        components.Dispose()
    End Sub

#Region " Windows Form Designer generated code "

    'Required by the Windows Form Designer
    Private components As System.ComponentModel.Container
        Private WithEvents Button3 As System.WinForms.Button

    Private WithEvents TextBox1 As System.WinForms.TextBox
    Private WithEvents Button2 As System.WinForms.Button
    Private WithEvents Button1 As System.WinForms.Button

    Dim WithEvents Form1 As System.WinForms.Form

    'NOTE: The following procedure is required by the Windows Form Designer
    'It can be modified using the Windows Form Designer.
    'Do not modify it using the code editor.
    Private Sub InitializeComponent()
        Me.components = New System.ComponentModel.Container
        Me.Button1 = New System.WinForms.Button
        Me.Button2 = New System.WinForms.Button
        Me.Button3 = New System.WinForms.Button
        Me.TextBox1 = New System.WinForms.TextBox

        '@design Me.TrayHeight = 0
        '@design Me.TrayLargeIcon = False
        '@design Me.TrayAutoArrange = True
        Button1.Location = New System.Drawing.Point(8, 16)
        Button1.Size = New System.Drawing.Size(75, 23)
        Button1.TabIndex = 0
        Button1.Text = "Subclass"

        Button2.Location = New System.Drawing.Point(8, 48)
        Button2.Size = New System.Drawing.Size(75, 23)
        Button2.TabIndex = 1
        Button2.Text = "UnSubclass"

        Button3.Location = New System.Drawing.Point(8, 104)
        Button3.Size = New System.Drawing.Size(75, 23)
        Button3.TabIndex = 3
        Button3.Text = "Create Wnd"

        TextBox1.Location = New System.Drawing.Point(88, 16)
        TextBox1.Multiline = True
        TextBox1.ScrollBars = System.WinForms.ScrollBars.Both
```

Example 22-6. The Form1.vb File that Acts as the Superclass WinForm (continued)

```vb
            TextBox1.WordWrap = False
            TextBox1.TabIndex = 2
            TextBox1.Size = New System.Drawing.Size(408, 336)
            Me.Text = "VB.NET Subclassing Example"
            Me.AutoScaleBaseSize = New System.Drawing.Size(5, 13)
            Me.ClientSize = New System.Drawing.Size(504, 357)

            Me.Controls.Add(Button3)
            Me.Controls.Add(TextBox1)
            Me.Controls.Add(Button2)
            Me.Controls.Add(Button1)
        End Sub
#End Region

    Protected Sub Button3_Click(ByVal sender As Object, ByVal e As System.EventArgs)
        Dim x As New Superclass_Ex()
        x.Show()
    End Sub


    'SUBCLASS TECHNIQUE #2
    Protected Sub Button1_Click(ByVal sender As Object, ByVal e As System.EventArgs)
        If sc.Handle() = 0 Then
            sc.AssignHandle(Me.Handle)
        Else
            msgbox("Don't try to subclass this window more than once")
        End If
    End Sub

    Protected Sub Button2_Click(ByVal sender As Object, ByVal e As System.EventArgs)
        sc.ReleaseHandle()
    End Sub


    Public Class MySubclass
        Inherits NativeWindow

        Protected Overrides Sub WndProc(ByRef m As Message)
            If m.msg = microsoft.Win32.Interop.win.WM_RBUTTONDOWN Then
                msgbox(m.msg.ToString())
            End If

            MyBase.WndProc(m)
        End Sub

        Protected Overrides Sub OnHandleChange()
            msgbox("Handle has changed")
        End Sub
    End Class
End Class
```

Example 22-7 presents the code for the Subclass_Ex WinForm. This code is much shorter than the first, simply because the Subclass_Ex WinForm inherits most of its functionality from the Form1 WinForm class. The highlighted line of code overrides the original background color of the Form1 WinForm. This allows us to more easily distinguish the superclass and subclass windows on the screen.

Example 22-7. The Superclass_Ex.vb File Using the Superclassing Technique

```
Imports System.Drawing
Imports System.WinForms
Imports System.ComponentModel


Public Class Superclass_Ex
    Inherits Form1

    Public Sub New()
        MyBase.New
        Superclass_Ex = Me
        InitializeComponent()

        'TODO: Add any initialization after the InitializeComponent() call
        Me.BackColor = System.Drawing.Color.Bisque()
    End Sub

    'Form overrides dispose to clean up the component list.
    Overrides Public Sub Dispose()
        MyBase.Dispose
        components.Dispose
    End Sub

#Region " Windows Form Designer generated code "
    Private components As System.ComponentModel.Container

    Dim WithEvents Superclass_Ex As System.WinForms.Form

    Private Sub InitializeComponent()
        components = New System.ComponentModel.Container
        Me.Text = "Superclass_Ex"
    End Sub
#End Region

End Class
```

The main thing to notice in this code example is that Superclass_Ex inherits from Form1. This is what allows us to perform superclassing so easily.

Superclassing a Control

Superclassing a control is similar to superclassing a WinForm. First, you write a new class that inherits from the control that you want to superclass; for the fol-

lowing example, it will be a button control. Next, you override the WndProc for
the control and add your own functionality.

The application

This example application contains a text box and a superclassed button control on
the WinForm. Table 22-6 lists the nondefault properties of the form and its controls. Figure 22-6 presents a screenshot of the application. When you right-click
the superclassed button, a message box is displayed indicating that the button
was, in fact, right-clicked.

Table 22-6. Nondefault Properties of the Form and Its Controls

Object	Property Name	Property Value
Form	Caption	"VB.NET Control Superclassing Example"
Form	Height	357
Form	Width	328
SCButton	Caption	"SC"
SCButton	Top	170
SCButton	Left	8
SCButton	Height	40
SCButton	Width	40

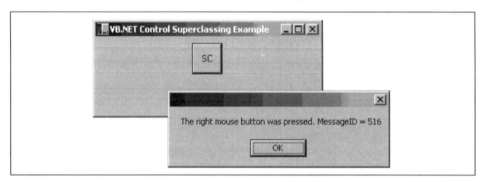

Figure 22-6. The application containing the superclassed button control

The .VB file

Example 22-8 presents the code for this technique. The important modifications to
the code are in boldface.

Example 22-8. The Form1.vb File for Superclassing a Button Control

```
Imports System.ComponentModel
Imports System.Drawing
Imports System.WinForms
```

Example 22-8. The Form1.vb File for Superclassing a Button Control (continued)

```
Public Class Form1
    Inherits System.WinForms.Form

    Public Sub New()
        MyBase.New()
        Form1 = Me
        InitializeComponent()
    End Sub

    'Form overrides dispose to clean up the component list.
    Public Overrides Sub Dispose()
        MyBase.Dispose()
        components.Dispose()
    End Sub

#Region " Windows Form Designer generated code "

    'Required by the Windows Form Designer
    Private components As System.ComponentModel.Container

    Private WithEvents scButton As SubCButton

    Dim WithEvents Form1 As System.WinForms.Form

    'NOTE: The following procedure is required by the Windows Form Designer
    'It can be modified using the Windows Form Designer.
    'Do not modify it using the code editor.
    Private Sub InitializeComponent()
        Me.components = New System.ComponentModel.Container()
        Me.scButton = New SuperButton()

        '@design Me.TrayHeight = 0
        '@design Me.TrayLargeIcon = False
        '@design Me.TrayAutoArrange = True
        scButton.Location = New System.Drawing.Point(130, 8)
        scButton.Size = New System.Drawing.Size(40, 40)
        scButton.Text = "SC"

        Me.Text = "VB.NET Control Superclassing Example"
        Me.AutoScaleBaseSize = New System.Drawing.Size(5, 13)
        Me.ClientSize = New System.Drawing.Size(300, 100)

        Me.Controls.Add(scButton)
    End Sub
#End Region
End Class

Public Class SuperButton
    Inherits System.WinForms.Button

    Protected Overrides Sub WndProc(ByRef m As Message)
        If m.msg = microsoft.Win32.Interop.win.WM_RBUTTONDOWN Then
```

```
        MessageBox.Show("The right mouse button was pressed. MessageID = " & _
                        m.msg.ToString())
    End If


    MyBase.WndProc(m)
  End Sub
End Class
```

A new class is created, called SuperButton, which contains the overridden Wnd-Proc method. It is in this WndProc method that we place our superclassing code. This code simply watches for the WM_RBUTTONDOWN message and then displays a message box indicating that this message was intercepted.

To instantiate and use this superclassed button control, we must add some extra code to the code block between the #Region...#End Region preprocessor directives. First we add the following code to hook up the events for this control:

```
    Private WithEvents scButton As SubCButton
```

Next, we instantiate the button control and set its properties in the InitializeComponent method:

```
    Me.scButton = New SuperButton()

    scButton.Location = New System.Drawing.Point(130, 8)
    scButton.Size = New System.Drawing.Size(40, 40)
    scButton.Text = "SC"
```

The Location property sets the Top and Left coordinates, and the Size property sets the Height and Width values. The Text property sets the button's caption.

Finally, we add the control to the WinForm's control array through the following line of code:

```
    Me.Controls.Add(scButton)
```

That is all there is to it.

Intercepting Keystrokes in a WinForm

I want to cover one final method of intercepting messages in a WinForm. There are nine built-in methods in the Control class that you can override to capture keystroke messages. If you need to capture only keyboard messages, using one or more of these methods will allow you to intercept the messages without having to subclass the WinForm.

The messages that you can intercept are:

```
    WM_CHAR
    WM_KEYDOWN
```

```
WM_KEYUP
WM_SYSKEYDOWN
WM_SYSKEYUP
```

The nine methods that you can override are:

ProcessKeyPreview

A child control calls this method before processing a keyboard message. If the child control does not process the message, it is sent on to the parent control. If no parent control exists, this method returns **True**, indicating that this message is not to be processed any longer.

PreProcessMessage

This method is called from the thread's message loop, before the message is dispatched. The processing that this method performs depends on the message received:

WM_KEYDOWN *and* WM_SYSKEYDOWN

ProcessCmdKey is first called to determine if the keyboard message is an accelerator or menu shortcut. If *ProcessCmdKey* returns **False**, *IsInputKey* is called to determine if the keyboard message is being sent as input to the control, such as characters being typed into a text box control. Finally, if *IsInputKey* returns **False**, the keyboard message is sent to *ProcessDialogKey*. *ProcessDialogKey* determines if the key is a dialog type key such as a TAB, an arrow, or mnemonics.

WM_CHAR

IsInputChar is first called to determine if the keyboard message is being sent as input to the control, such as characters being typed into a text box control. If *IsInputChar* returns **False**, *ProcessDialogChar* is called. *ProcessDialogChar* processes dialog characters, such as a TAB, an arrow, or mnemonics.

WM_SYSCHAR

ProcessDialogChar is called to determine if the key is a dialog type key such as a TAB, an arrow, or mnemonics.

WM_KEYUP *and* WM_SYSKEYUP

No processing is performed on these messages.

If this method returns **True**, the keyboard message is not dispatched; otherwise, it is dispatched.

IsInputChar

Determines if the keyboard message is one that the control is looking for, such as a mnemonic. If this method returns **True**, the message is sent directly to the control; otherwise, it is dispatched to the destination window procedure.

IsInputKey

Determines whether the keyboard message should be preprocessed or sent directly to the control. This method looks for the TAB, arrow, ESC, and RETURN keys. If this method returns True, the message is sent directly to the control; otherwise, it is dispatched to the destination window procedure.

ProcessCmdKey

Allows processing of command keys such as accelerators and menu shortcuts. If this method returns True, the message is discarded; otherwise, the message continues to be preprocessed.

ProcessDialogChar

Processes dialog box characters such as mnemonics. If this method returns True, the message is discarded; otherwise, the message continues to be preprocessed.

ProcessDialogKey

Processes dialog box keys, such as the TAB, arrow, ESC, and RETURN keys. If this method returns True, the message is discarded; otherwise, the message continues to be preprocessed.

ProcessKeyEventArgs

Processes messages sent to controls. This method calls the control's *OnKey-Down*, *OnKeyPress*, and *OnKeyUp* events. In addition to the previously mentioned keyboard messages, this method also processes the WM_IMECHAR message. If this method returns True, the message is discarded; otherwise, the message continues to be preprocessed.

ProcessMnemonic

This method processes a mnemonic character for a control. If it finds a mnemonic, this method should perform the action for the mnemonic and return a value of True. If this method returns True, the message is discarded; otherwise, the message continues to be preprocessed.

The application

This application allows you to watch each overridden method as it is called when you press and release keys individually or in combination. Each overridden method writes a brief message indicating that it has been called to a read-only text box, which is provided to prevent confusing output when the user tries to type a character into a text box.

Table 22-7 lists the nondefault properties of the superclass form and its controls. Figure 22-7 presents a screenshot of the example application.

Table 22-7. Nondefault Properties of the Form1 WinFform and Its Controls

Object	Property Name	Property Value
Form	Caption	"VB.NET Process Keys Example"
Form	Height	357
Form	Width	504
TextBox1	Multiline	True
TextBox1	Scrollbars	True
TextBox1	WordWrap	False
TextBox1	Top	16
TextBox1	Left	88
TextBox1	Height	336
TextBox1	Width	408
TextBox2	Top	72
TextBox2	Left	8
TextBox2	Height	20
TextBox2	Width	72
Button1	Caption	"Clear"
Button1	Top	16
Button1	Left	8
Button1	Height	23
Button1	Width	75

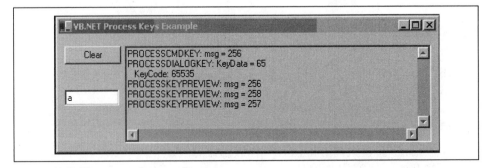

Figure 22-7. The process keys application

This example application overrides each of the nine methods that intercept keyboard messages. Whenever a key is pressed, each overridden method will output some text to a read-only text box—the text output depends on the method that was called. The Clear button is provided to allow you to clear the text box. A smaller text box is provided to allow you to enter characters to see how the system processes each character.

In the screenshot in Figure 22-7, the "a" key was pressed while the focus was in the small text box. If we press the "a" key while the focus is on the Clear button, we get the following text output to the text box:

```
PROCESSCMDKEY: msg = 256
PROCESSDIALOGKEY: KeyData = 65
 KeyCode: 65535
PROCESSKEYPREVIEW: msg = 256
PROCESSDIALOGCHAR: CharCode = a
PROCESSMNEMONIC: CharCode = a
PROCESSKEYPREVIEW: msg = 258
PROCESSKEYPREVIEW: msg = 257
```

The ProcessDialogChar and ProcessMnemonic methods were called, in addition to the methods that were called when the focus was on the text box. This is because a button control can have a mnemonic character and a text box control cannot.

The .VB file

Example 22-9 presents the code for this sample application. The code for the overridden methods appears in boldface.

Example 22-9. The Form1.cs File for Superclassing a Button Control

```
Imports System.ComponentModel
Imports System.Drawing
Imports System.WinForms


Public Class Form1
    Inherits System.WinForms.Form

    Public Sub New()
        MyBase.New()
        Form1 = Me
        InitializeComponent()
    End Sub

    'Form overrides dispose to clean up the component list.
    Public Overrides Sub Dispose()
        MyBase.Dispose()
        components.Dispose()
    End Sub

#Region " Windows Form Designer generated code "

    'Required by the Windows Form Designer
    Private components As System.ComponentModel.Container
    Private WithEvents TextBox2 As System.WinForms.TextBox
    Private WithEvents Button1 As System.WinForms.Button
```

Example 22-9. The Form1.cs File for Superclassing a Button Control (continued)

```
Private WithEvents TextBox1 As System.WinForms.TextBox

Dim WithEvents Form1 As System.WinForms.Form

'NOTE: The following procedure is required by the Windows Form Designer
'It can be modified using the Windows Form Designer.
'Do not modify it using the code editor.
Private Sub InitializeComponent()
    Me.components = New System.ComponentModel.Container()
    Me.Button1 = New System.WinForms.Button()
    Me.TextBox2 = New System.WinForms.TextBox()
    Me.TextBox1 = New System.WinForms.TextBox()

    '@design Me.TrayHeight = 0
    '@design Me.TrayLargeIcon = False
    '@design Me.TrayAutoArrange = True
    Button1.Location = New System.Drawing.Point(8, 16)
    Button1.Size = New System.Drawing.Size(75, 23)
    Button1.TabIndex = 3
    Button1.TabStop = False
    Button1.Text = "Clear"

    TextBox2.Location = New System.Drawing.Point(8, 72)
    TextBox2.TabIndex = 4
    TextBox2.Size = New System.Drawing.Size(72, 20)

    TextBox1.Location = New System.Drawing.Point(88, 16)
    TextBox1.ReadOnly = True
    TextBox1.Multiline = True
    TextBox1.ScrollBars = System.WinForms.ScrollBars.Both
    TextBox1.WordWrap = False
    TextBox1.TabIndex = 2
    TextBox1.TabStop = False
    TextBox1.Size = New System.Drawing.Size(408, 336)

    Me.Text = "VB.NET Subclassing Example"
    Me.AutoScaleBaseSize = New System.Drawing.Size(5, 13)
    Me.ClientSize = New System.Drawing.Size(504, 357)

    Me.Controls.Add(TextBox2)
    Me.Controls.Add(Button1)
    Me.Controls.Add(TextBox1)
End Sub

Protected Overrides Function ProcessKeyPreview(ByRef m As Message) As Boolean
    textbox1.Text = textbox1.Text & "PROCESSKEYPREVIEW: msg = " & _
    m.msg.ToString() & chr(13) & chr(10)
    ProcessKeyPreview = MyBase.ProcessKeyPreview(m)
End Function

Public Overrides Function PreProcessMessage(ByVal msg As _
    Microsoft.Win32.Interop.MSG) As Boolean
```

Example 22-9. The Form1.cs File for Superclassing a Button Control (continued)

```
    As Boolean
      textbox1.Text = textbox1.Text & "PREPROCESSMESSAGE: msg = " & _
        msg.message.ToString() & chr(13) & chr(10)
      PreProcessMessage = MyBase.PreProcessMessage(msg)
  End Function

  Protected Overrides Function IsInputChar(ByVal CharCode As Char) As Boolean
      textbox1.Text = textbox1.Text & "ISINPUTCHAR: CharCode = " & _
        CharCode.ToString() & chr(13) & chr(10)
      IsInputChar = MyBase.IsInputChar(CharCode)
  End Function

  Protected Overrides Function IsInputKey(ByVal KeyData As Keys) As Boolean
      textbox1.Text = textbox1.Text & "ISINPUTKEY: KeyData = " & _
        KeyData.ToString() & chr(13) & chr(10)
      textbox1.Text = textbox1.Text & "   KeyCode: " & KeyData.KeyCode.ToString() _
                    & chr(13) & chr(10)
      IsInputKey = MyBase.IsInputKey(Keydata)
  End Function

  Protected Overrides Function ProcessCmdKey(ByVal msg As _
          Microsoft.Win32.Interop.MSG, ByVal KeyData As Keys) As Boolean
    ByVal KeyData As Keys) As Boolean
      textbox1.Text = textbox1.Text & "PROCESSCMDKEY: msg = " & _
        msg.message.ToString() & chr(13) & chr(10)
      ProcessCmdKey = MyBase.ProcessCmdKey(msg, KeyData)
  End Function

  Protected Overrides Function ProcessDialogChar(ByVal CharCode As Char) As Boolean
      textbox1.Text = textbox1.Text & "PROCESSDIALOGCHAR: CharCode = " & _
        CharCode.ToString() & chr(13) & chr(10)
      ProcessDialogChar = MyBase.ProcessDialogChar(CharCode)
  End Function

  Protected Overrides Function ProcessDialogKey(ByVal KeyData As Keys) As Boolean
      textbox1.Text = textbox1.Text & "PROCESSDIALOGKEY: KeyData = " & _
        KeyData.ToString() & chr(13) & chr(10)
      textbox1.Text = textbox1.Text & "   KeyCode: " & KeyData.KeyCode.ToString() _
                    & chr(13) & chr(10)
      ProcessDialogKey = MyBase.ProcessDialogKey(KeyData)
  End Function

  Protected Overrides Function ProcessKeyEventArgs(ByRef m As Message) As Boolean
      textbox1.Text = textbox1.Text & "PROCESSKEYEVENTARGS: msg = " & _
        m.msg.ToString() & chr(13) & chr(10)
      ProcessKeyEventArgs = MyBase.ProcessKeyEventArgs(m)
  End Function

  Protected Overrides Function ProcessMnemonic(ByVal CharCode As Char) As Boolean
      textbox1.Text = textbox1.Text & "PROCESSMNEMONIC: CharCode = " & _
        CharCode.ToString() & chr(13) & chr(10)
      ProcessMnemonic = MyBase.ProcessMnemonic(CharCode)
```

Example 22-9. The Form1.cs File for Superclassing a Button Control (continued)

```
    End Function
#End Region

    Protected Sub Button1_Click(ByVal sender As Object, ByVal e As System.EventArgs)
        textbox1.Text = ""
    End Sub
End Class
```

Note that the overridden method's base class is called at the end of each over-ridden method. These overridden methods also return the value that the base class method returns.

Behind the Scenes with Spy++

To understand more of what is happening when we subclass a WinForm, we will use the Spy++ utility to see what is happening to our application before, during, and after we subclass an application.

To start, we will run the example application that we created in the "Technique #1: Overriding the WinProc Method" section. After starting Spy++ and finding the application, we immediately notice several things, as Figure 22-8 illustrates.

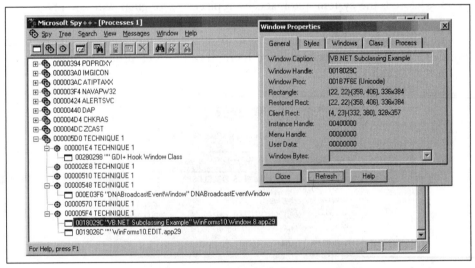

Figure 22-8. Using Spy++ to examine our VB.NET subclassing application created using Technique #1

The first thing of interest is that six threads are automatically created when a VB.NET application starts. Our application code runs in thread 0, which has a handle of &H5F4 in Figure 22-8. Using the Threading classes in the .NET framework, you can create even more threads. The examples presented here do not create multiple threads. However, if you create more threads using the Threading classes, you should be aware that the subclassing techniques described in this chapter work only within the thread that uses these techniques.

The other item of interest is the class names of the WinForm and its controls. Gone are the familiar `Thunder*` classes; even the standard windows classes, such as `BUTTON` and `EDIT`, are gone. Languages that run under the .NET framework, such as VB.NET and C#, use classes such as `WinForms10.Window.8.app29` for a WinForm, `WinForms10.BUTTON.app29` for button controls, and `WinForms10.EDIT.app29` for edit controls. Each WinForm control in the .NET framework has a new window class name. As a note, these class names might change after Beta 1.

If we double-click our application's WinForm (the WinForm item has a handle of &H18029C), the Window Properties dialog box is displayed, as Figure 22-9 shows. Note that the Window Proc field on this dialog box is set to &H1b7F6E. Now click the Class tab and look at the Window Proc field value, which Figure 22-9 shows. This tab reports that the class window procedure is set to &H1B7DEE, which is not the same as the WinForm's window procedure. This means that the system subclassed the window automatically. In fact, SetWindowLongW is called when the WinForm is first created to subclass its original window procedure. When the WinForm is closed, the system automatically replaces its original window procedure, which allows the WinForm to shut down gracefully. This is a big help for us when we are subclassing a WinForm. The system subclasses the WinForm, keeps track of its original window procedure, and then replaces it before it is completely shut down.

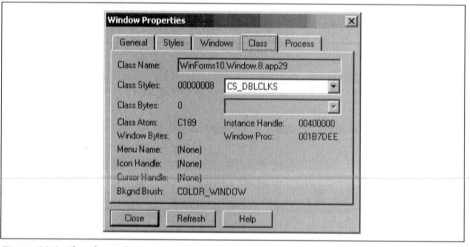

Figure 22-9. The Class tab properties for our VB.NET subclassing application created using Technique #1

WinForms are not the only windows that are subclassed in this manner; all .NET controls—at least the ones that I have checked out—are subclassed in this manner. You can check this out for yourself by comparing the Window Proc fields on the General and Class tabs of the Window Properties dialog box, as we did in Figure 22-8 and Figure 22-9. If the values are different, the control has been subclassed; otherwise, it has not. You should note that if you place an unmanaged ActiveX control on a WinForm, it is not automatically subclassed.

Continuing on, we will examine the application that we created in the "Technique #2: Binding to a NativeWindow Class Instance" section in the same manner. After starting the application and Spy++, we notice that the WinForm and its controls have been subclassed in the same manner as we saw with the previous application. If you notice in Figure 22-10 and Figure 22-11, the Window Proc fields of the General and Class tabs are different.

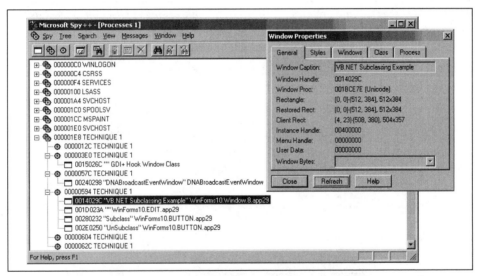

Figure 22-10. Using Spy++ to examine our VB.NET subclassing application created using Technique #2

This application uses a different technique to subclass a WinForm than the first application does. This application subclasses the WinForm only when we click the Subclass button. If we proceed to click the Subclass button, we notice that the Window Proc field on the General tab has been modified, as Figure 22-12 shows.

Now the WinForm is effectively subclassed twice, once by the system and once by our code calling the AssignHandle method on the NativeWindow class in our project. If you remember, the code in the Subclass button *Click* event looks like this:

```
Protected Sub Button1_Click(ByVal sender As Object, ByVal e As System.EventArgs)
```

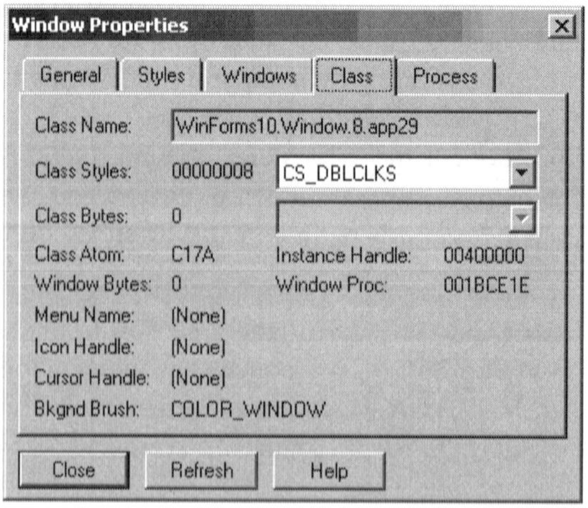

Figure 22-11. The Class tab properties for our VB.NET subclassing application created using Technique #2

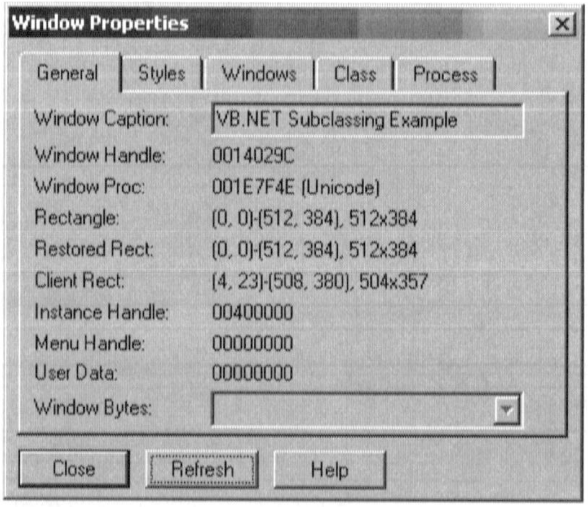

Figure 22-12. The Class tab properties for our VB.NET subclassing application after clicking the Subclass button

```
If sc.Handle() = 0 Then
    sc.AssignHandle(Me.Handle)
Else
    msgbox("Don't try to subclass this window more than once")
End If
End Sub
```

When the UnSubclass button is clicked, the subclassing is removed. If you look back at the Window Proc field on the General tab, you will notice that it reverts back to its previous value. The code behind the *Click* event of the UnSubclass button looks like this:

```
Protected Sub Button2_Click(ByVal sender As Object, ByVal e As System.EventArgs)
    sc.ReleaseHandle()
End Sub
```

From this information, we can plainly see that the system takes care of a lot of the details of subclassing for us. This is why a WinForm will not crash when we shut it down without removing the subclass procedure. As we will see in Chapter 23, the system does not help us out when implementing hooks as much as it does with subclassing and superclassing.

23

Implementing Hooks in VB.NET

This chapter covers the implementation of Windows hooks within a VB.NET application. It is assumed that you have read and understand the concepts laid out in Chapter 2 and Chapter 3. It also is assumed that you have a working knowledge of how to write VB.NET code.

Hooks and VB.NET

Unlike subclassing and superclassing, VB.NET does not readily support the use of the standard Windows hooks within the language.

 None of the .NET languages make any special concessions to easily implement Windows hooks. To implement hooks within other .NET languages, such as C#, follow the same steps as are outlined in this chapter.

Actually, more code is involved with implementing hooks in VB.NET than in the previous versions of Visual Basic (VB). This is because we must use delegates to implement the filter function callback mechanism that hooks rely on. I discuss delegates in more detail in the next section.

The example applications that we will create in this chapter will install thread-specific hooks. Unfortunately, as with VB 6 dynamic link libraries (DLLs), you cannot use VB.NET DLLs to install system-wide hooks. To install a system-wide hook, you must place the code to install and remove the hook, as well as the filter function itself, within a Win32 DLL. You can write this DLL using Visual C++ 6 or Visual C++.NET. Note that if you are using Visual C++.NET, you must write the DLL as unmanaged code.

As a note, the following functions will be removed after Beta 1:

> *Microsoft.Win32.Interop.Windows.SetWindowsHookEx*
> *Microsoft.Win32.Interop.Windows.UnhookWindowsHookEx*
> *Microsoft.Win32.Interop.Windows.CallNextHookEx*

Instead of using these functions, you should use the normal method of declaring application programming interface (API) functions that you have become accustomed to in VB 6. You should use the following declarations:

```
Public Declare Function SetWindowsHookEx Lib "user32" Alias "SetWindowsHookExA" _
    (ByVal HookID As Integer, ByVal lpfn As HookCallback, _
    ByVal hModule As Integer, ByVal ThreadId As Integer) As Integer

Public Declare Function UnhookWindowsHookEx Lib "user32" _
    Alias "UnhookWindowsHookEx" _
    (ByVal hHook As Integer) As Integer

Public Declare Function CallNextHookEx Lib "user32" Alias "CallNextHookEx" _
    (ByVal hHook As Integer, ByVal Code As Integer, ByVal wParam As Integer, _
    ByVal lParam As Integer) As Integer
```

Datatypes have also changed from VB 6 to VB.NET. The Long type in VB 6 was changed to an Integer in VB.NET. Also, the Any type that is sometimes used in API declarations is now gone, as are Variants. Instead of using the Any or Variant datatypes, you should declare the specific type that you will be using. In most instances, you will be working with pointers; therefore, you should use the Integer datatype.

Delegates

Delegates are one of the latest additions to the VB.NET language. *Delegates* are classes that inherit from either System.Delegate or System.MulticastDelegate. In VB.NET, delegates by default inherit from System.MulticastDelegate. A delegate is a class that acts as a wrapper around a function pointer. This allows function pointers, or delegates, to be object-oriented, typesafe, and secure.

A delegate can point to both a shared function and one that is associated with an instance of a class. A delegate that inherits from the System.Delegate class can only point to a single function at any one time. The delegate that inherits from the System.MulticastDelegate class, however, can point to a list of functions, all of which are called in succession when this type of delegate is used. The thing to watch out for when using multicast delegates is that, if the functions the delegate points to have a return value, the delegate's final return value is the return value of the last function the delegate calls. For this reason, you should use delegates that point to a single function when implementing hooks.

A Simple Example Using Delegates

To better understand delegates, let's examine a simple example that shows how to set up and use both the delegate and multicast delegate. Figure 23-1 presents a screenshot of this example application. Table 23-1 presents the nondefault properties of the form and its controls.

Table 23-1. Nondefault Properties of the Example Application's Form and Its Controls

Control	Property Name	Value
Form1	Caption	"Delegate Example"
Form1	Height	320
Form1	Width	269
Button1	Caption	"Single"
Button1	Top	8
Button1	Left	8
Button1	Height	23
Button1	Width	72
Button2	Caption	"Combine"
Button2	Top	40
Button2	Left	8
Button2	Height	23
Button2	Width	72
TextBox	MultiLine	True
TextBox	WordWrap	False
TextBox	ScrollBars	Both
TextBox	Top	8
TextBox	Left	40
TextBox	Height	256
TextBox	Width	224

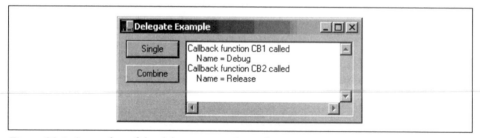

Figure 23-1. Screenshot of the delegate example application

This application contains two buttons and a text box, which displays the output from the delegate calls. The Single button creates a delegate, binds it to a single function, and then calls this delegate. This callback function writes the following text to the text box:

```
Callback function CB1 called
    Name = Debug
```

Within this same call, the delegate is set to point to a different function and the delegate is once again called. This second callback function writes the following text to the text box:

```
Callback function CB2 called
    Name = Release
```

When you click the Combine button, it creates two delegates and then combines them to form a third multicast delegate, which it then calls. The following text is written to the text box when the multicast delegate is called:

```
Callback function CB1 called
  Name = Multi-Fire Delegate
Callback function CB2 called
  Name = Multi-Fire Delegate
```

Example 23-1 presents the code to perform these tasks. The code in boldface shows how you set up and use the delegates.

Example 23-1. Code in the Form1.vb File for the Delegate Example Application

```
Imports System.ComponentModel
Imports System.Drawing
Imports System.WinForms


Public Class Form1
    Inherits System.WinForms.Form

    Public Sub New()
        MyBase.New
        Form1 = Me
        'This call is required by the Win Form Designer.
        InitializeComponent
    End Sub

    'Form overrides dispose to clean up the component list.
    Overrides Public Sub Dispose()
        MyBase.Dispose
        components.Dispose
    End Sub

#Region " Windows Form Designer generated code "
```

Example 23-1. Code in the Form1.vb File for the Delegate Example Application (continued)

```
'Required by the Windows Form Designer
Private components As System.ComponentModel.Container
Private WithEvents Button2 As System.WinForms.Button
Private WithEvents Button1 As System.WinForms.Button
Private WithEvents TextBox1 As System.WinForms.TextBox

Dim WithEvents Form1 As System.WinForms.Form

'NOTE: The following procedure is required by the Windows Form Designer
'It can be modified using the Windows Form Designer.
'Do not modify it using the code editor.
Private Sub InitializeComponent()
    Me.components = New System.ComponentModel.Container()
    Me.Button1 = New System.WinForms.Button()
    Me.Button2 = New System.WinForms.Button()
    Me.TextBox1 = New System.WinForms.TextBox()

    '@design Me.TrayHeight = 0
    '@design Me.TrayLargeIcon = False
    '@design Me.TrayAutoArrange = True
    Button1.Location = New System.Drawing.Point(8, 8)
    Button1.Size = New System.Drawing.Size(72, 23)
    Button1.TabIndex = 1
    Button1.Text = "Single"

    Button2.Location = New System.Drawing.Point(8, 40)
    Button2.Size = New System.Drawing.Size(72, 23)
    Button2.TabIndex = 2
    Button2.Text = "Combine"

    TextBox1.Location = New System.Drawing.Point(88, 8)
    TextBox1.Multiline = True
    TextBox1.ScrollBars = System.WinForms.ScrollBars.Both
    TextBox1.WordWrap = False
    TextBox1.TabIndex = 0
    TextBox1.Size = New System.Drawing.Size(224, 256)

    Me.Text = "Delegate Example"
    Me.AutoScaleBaseSize = New System.Drawing.Size(5, 13)
    Me.ClientSize = New System.Drawing.Size(320, 269)

    Me.Controls.Add(Button2)
    Me.Controls.Add(Button1)
    Me.Controls.Add(TextBox1)
End Sub

#End Region

    'Create the delegate
    Delegate Sub MyCallBack(ByVal Name As String)
```

Example 23-1. Code in the Form1.vb File for the Delegate Example Application (continued)

```
'Callback function #1
Public Sub CB1(ByVal Name As String)
    Textbox1.Text += "Callback function CB1 called" + chr(13) & chr(10)
    Textbox1.Text += "    Name = " & Name & chr(13) & chr(10)
End Sub

'Callback function #2
Public Sub CB2(ByVal Name As String)
    Textbox1.Text += "Callback function CB2 called" & chr(13) & chr(10)
    Textbox1.Text += "    Name = " & Name & chr(13) & chr(10)
End Sub

'Call delegate
Protected Sub Button1_Click(ByVal sender As Object, ByVal e As System.EventArgs)
    Dim MyDelegate As MyCallBack

    'Point the delegate to function CB1 and call it
    MyDelegate = AddressOf CB1
    MyDelegate("Debug")

    'Now, point the delegate to function CB2 and call it
    MyDelegate = AddressOf CB2
    MyDelegate("Release")
End Sub

Protected Sub Button2_Click(ByVal sender As Object, ByVal e As System.EventArgs)
    Dim MyDelegate1 As MyCallBack
    Dim MyDelegate2 As MyCallBack
    Dim MyDelegate3 As MyCallBack

    'Point delegates to their respective function
    MyDelegate1 = AddressOf CB1
    MyDelegate2 = AddressOf CB2

    'Create a delegate that combines the first two delegates and call it
    MyDelegate3 = CType(System.Delegate.Combine(MyDelegate1, MyDelegate2), _
                MyCallback)
    MyDelegate3("Multi-Fire Delegate")
End Sub
End Class
```

We are most interested in the code at the bottom of Example 23-1, in which a delegate named MyCallback is created. The following line of code creates this delegate:

```
Delegate Sub MyCallBack(ByVal Name As String)
```

The IL (or intermediate language) code that the line of code that creates the delegate generates is as follows:

```
.class auto ansi sealed nested public Form1$MyCallBack
        extends [mscorlib]System.MulticastDelegate
{
} // end of class Form1$MyCallBack
```

As we see here, a delegate is truly a class that inherits from System. MulticastDelegate.

Next, two subroutines, *CB1* and *CB2*, are declared that match the delegate's parameters. Notice that both functions also are declared as Subs, exactly as the delegate was previously declared.

In the *Button1_Click* event, an instance of the delegate is created as follows:

```
Dim MyDelegate As MyCallBack
```

The *MyDelegate* reference to the MyCallBack delegate is bound to the *CB1* function by using the AddressOf keyword. The code to perform this is as follows:

```
MyDelegate = AddressOf CB1
```

After the delegate is bound to the function, we can call the function through the reference to our delegate object. The code to perform this is as follows:

```
MyDelegate("Debug")
```

In the *Button2_Click* event, three delegates are declared. The first and second delegates are bound to functions *CB1* and *CB2*, respectively. The third delegate, however, uses the Combine method to add the first two delegates to the list of delegates that it must call. The code to perform this is as follows:

```
MyDelegate3 = CType(System.Delegate.Combine(MyDelegate1, MyDelegate2), MyCallback)
```

The Combine method takes two delegates as parameters, combines them into a single multicast delegate, and returns this multicast delegate. The *CType* function converts the returned delegate value from the Combine method into a MyCallBack datatype.

Now, when you use the MyDelegate3 delegate, the functions that MyDelegate1 and MyDelegate2 point to are called successively.

Implementing the WH_KEYBOARD Hook

When implementing any type of hook in VB.NET, you should follow the rules stated in Chapter 3 for setting up and using hooks. I noticed that if a hook is not removed before the application ends—using the *UnHookWindowsHookEx* API function—the application does not crash, as it normally would in a previous version of VB. However, I always incorporate code to remove a hook after it is installed.

Remember, you can install hooks on one thread at a time, or on every thread in the system. Therefore, if you create multiple threads in your application and you install a thread-specific hook, the hook will capture information only for that specific thread. If you want to capture information for more than one thread in your application, you must install the hook on each thread. Remember to remove the hook from each thread before the thread is destroyed.

The Application

Figure 23-2 presents the WH_KEYBOARD hook application's user interface (UI). Table 23-2 presents the nondefault properties of the form and its controls. This application is fairly simple. There are two buttons and a text box on the form. The Hook button calls *SetWindowsHookEx* to install the WH_KEYBOARD hook, and the UnHook button calls *UnhookWindowsHookEx* to remove the hook. The textbox displays the three parameters of the hook's filter function: `Code`, `lParam`, and `wParam`.

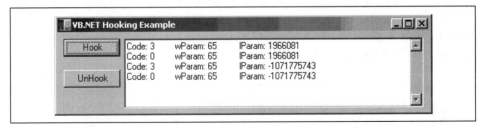

Figure 23-2. The WH_KEYBOARD hook example application screenshot

Table 23-2. Nondefault Properties of the Example Application's Form and Its Controls

Control	Property Name	Value
Form1	Caption	"VB.NET Hooking Example"
Form1	Height	381
Form1	Width	496
Button1	Caption	"Hook"
Button1	Top	8
Button1	Left	8
Button1	Height	23

*Table 23-2. Nondefault Properties of the Example Application's Form and Its
Controls (continued)*

Control	Property Name	Value
Button1	Width	72
Button2	Caption	"UnHook"
Button2	Top	48
Button2	Left	8
Button2	Height	23
Button2	Width	72
TextBox	MultiLine	True
TextBox	WordWrap	False
TextBox	ScrollBars	Both
TextBox	Top	8
TextBox	Left	88
TextBox	Height	368
TextBox	Width	400

To use the application, click the Hook button. Next, type in some text, making
sure that the text box does not have the focus. If the text box has the focus, the
text will overwrite itself as you type, making for a very messy display. However, if
you simply click the Hook button and immediately start to type, you will see the
filter function's parameters displayed. When you are done, click the UnHook
button and close the application.

For more information on how the WH_KEYBOARD hook works, see
Chapter 12.

The .VB File

Example 23-2 presents the code contained in the *Form1.vb* file.

*Example 23-2. The Code Contained in the Form1.vb File for the WH_KEYBOARD Hook
Example Application*

```
Imports System.ComponentModel
Imports System.Drawing
Imports System.WinForms
Imports System.Runtime.InteropServices
```

Example 23-2. The Code Contained in the Form1.vb File for the WH_KEYBOARD Hook
Example Application (continued)

```vb
'**************************************************
'MODULE SECTION
'**************************************************
Public Module mod1
    'declare delegate object
    Delegate Function HookCallback(ByVal Code As Integer, ByVal wParam As Integer, _
      ByVal lParam As Integer) As Integer

    'declare API's
    Public Declare Function SetWindowsHookEx Lib "user32" _
        Alias "SetWindowsHookExA" _
        (ByVal HookID As Integer, ByVal lpfn As HookCallback, _
        ByVal hModule As Integer, ByVal ThreadId As Integer) As Integer
    Public Declare Function UnhookWindowsHookEx Lib "user32" _
        Alias "UnhookWindowsHookEx" _
        (ByVal hHook As Integer) As Integer
    Public Declare Function CallNextHookEx Lib "user32" Alias "CallNextHookEx" _
        (ByVal hHook As Integer, ByVal Code As Integer, ByVal wParam As Integer, _
        ByVal lParam As Integer) As Integer

    'Global constants
    Public Const WH_KEYBOARD As Integer = 2

    Private m_hHook As Integer

    'Property to access hook handle
    Property hHook() As Integer
        Set
            If m_hHook <> 0 And Value <> 0 Then
                'Don't overwrite the handle
                '   Unless it is being reset to 0
            Else
                m_hHook = Value
            End If
        End Set

        Get
            hHook = m_hHook
        End Get
    End Property
End Module


'**************************************************
'FORM SECTION
'**************************************************
Public Class Form1
    Inherits System.WinForms.Form

    'declare nested class var
    Public hk As Hook
```

Example 23-2. The Code Contained in the Form1.vb File for the WH_KEYBOARD Hook Example Application (continued)

```
'declare delegate object
Public cb As HookCallback


'**************************************************
'NESTED CLASS-containing the callback HookProc
'**************************************************
Public Class Hook
    'reference back to the form
    Private TheWin As Form1

    'ctor - used to get a reference to the main window
    '       in order to write info to the textbox1 text box
    Public Sub New(ByVal MainWnd As Form1)
        TheWin = MainWnd
    End Sub

    'HOOK PROC
    Public Function HookProc(ByVal Code As Integer, ByVal wParam As Integer, _
      ByVal lParam As Integer) As Integer
        TheWin.PrintTxt("Code: " & Code & "          wParam: " & wParam & _
          "          lParam: " & lParam)
        HookProc = CallNextHookEx(hHook, Code, wParam, lParam)
    End Function
End Class


'START HERE - default ctor for Form1 class
Public Sub New()
    MyBase.New()
    Form1 = Me
    'This call is required by the Win Form Designer.
    InitializeComponent()

    'instantiate a new nested Hook class and pass in a reference to this form
    hk = New Hook(Me)

    'instantiate a new delegate object pointing to the HookProc function
    '   in the nested class
    cb = New HookCallback(AddressOf hk.HookProc)
End Sub

'used by Form1 to add text to the textbox1 text box, called by HookProc
Public Sub PrintTxt(ByVal strOutput As String)
    txtOutput.Text = txtOutput.Text & strOutput & chr(13) & chr(10)
End Sub

'Form overrides dispose to clean up the component list.
Public Overrides Sub Dispose()
    MyBase.Dispose()
    components.Dispose()
End Sub
```

Example 23-2. The Code Contained in the Form1.vb File for the WH_KEYBOARD Hook Example Application (continued)

```
'**************************************************
'REGULAR WINDOWS .NET STUFF
'**************************************************
#Region " Windows Form Designer generated code "
    'Required by the Windows Form Designer
    Private components As System.ComponentModel.Container
    Private WithEvents btnUnHook As System.WinForms.Button
    Private WithEvents btnHook As System.WinForms.Button
    Private WithEvents txtOutput As System.WinForms.TextBox

    Dim WithEvents Form1 As System.WinForms.Form

    'NOTE: The following procedure is required by the Windows Form Designer
    'It can be modified using the Windows Form Designer.
    'Do not modify it using the code editor.
    Private Sub InitializeComponent()
        Me.components = New System.ComponentModel.Container()
        Me.txtOutput = New System.WinForms.TextBox()
        Me.btnUnHook = New System.WinForms.Button()
        Me.btnHook = New System.WinForms.Button()

        '@design Me.TrayHeight = 0
        '@design Me.TrayLargeIcon = False
        '@design Me.TrayAutoArrange = True
        txtOutput.Location = New System.Drawing.Point(88, 8)
        txtOutput.Multiline = True
        txtOutput.ScrollBars = System.WinForms.ScrollBars.Both
        txtOutput.TabIndex = 0
        txtOutput.Size = New System.Drawing.Size(400, 368)

        btnUnHook.Location = New System.Drawing.Point(8, 48)
        btnUnHook.Size = New System.Drawing.Size(75, 23)
        btnUnHook.TabIndex = 2
        btnUnHook.Text = "UnHook"

        btnHook.Location = New System.Drawing.Point(8, 8)
        btnHook.Size = New System.Drawing.Size(75, 23)
        btnHook.TabIndex = 1
        btnHook.Text = "Hook"
        Me.Text = "VB.NET Hooking Example"
        Me.AutoScaleBaseSize = New System.Drawing.Size(5, 13)
        Me.ClientSize = New System.Drawing.Size(496, 381)

        Me.Controls.Add(btnUnHook)
        Me.Controls.Add(btnHook)
        Me.Controls.Add(txtOutput)
    End Sub
#End Region

'**************************************************
'EVENT HANDLERS FOR BUTTON CONTROLS
```

Example 23-2. The Code Contained in the Form1.vb File for the WH_KEYBOARD Hook Example Application (continued)

```
'**************************************************
Protected Sub btnUnHook_Click(ByVal sender As Object, _
                              ByVal e As System.EventArgs)
    'Install hook
    msgbox("UnhookWindowsHookEx returned: " & UnhookWindowsHookEx(hHook))
    hHook = 0
End Sub

Protected Sub btnHook_Click(ByVal sender As Object, ByVal e As System.EventArgs)
    'Remove hook
    hHook = SetWindowsHookEx(WH_KEYBOARD, cb, 0, appdomain.GetCurrentThreadId)
    msgbox("SetWindowsHookEx returned: " & hHook)
End Sub
End Class
```

Three classes are included with the code for this example. The first is a public module called mod1. This module contains the delegate declaration, the Win32 API function declarations, the WH_KEYBOARD hook constant, the hook handle variable (*m_hHook*), and a property used to access the hook handle (hHook).

The compiler actually converts module types declared in VB.NET applications to simple public class types. The mod1 module type is converted to the following IL:

```
.class public auto ansi mod1
       extends [mscorlib]System.Object
{
  .custom instance void [Microsoft.VisualBasic]Microsoft.
VisualBasic.Globals/Globals$StandardModuleAttribute::.ctor()
= ( 01 00 00 00 )
} // end of class mod1
```

Module types inherit from System.Object, and you usually use them to declare global types.

The second class declared is Form1. Form1 inherits from the System.WinForms. Form class and is the only window in our application. This class contains the code that the VB.NET application wizard automatically creates for you, the event handlers for each button control, and a nested class named Hook. This class is instantiated by Form1's constructor. You use this class mainly to contain the filter function for your WH_KEYBOARD hook function (*HookProc*).

When you start this application, the constructor of the Form1 class is called. This constructor creates a new instance of the Hook class and passes it a reference to the Form1 class (Me). Next, the constructor creates a new instance of the Hook-

Callback delegate and binds it to the *HookProc* filter function contained in the Hook class. This code is presented here:

```
'instantiate a new nested Hook class and pass in a reference to this form
hk = New Hook(Me)

'instantiate a new delegate object pointing to the HookProc function
'in the nested class
cb = New HookCallback(AddressOf hk.HookProc)
```

The reference to the Hook object (*hk*) is declared as a public member variable of the Form1 class. The reference to the delegate object (*cb*) also is declared as a public member variable of the Form1 class.

When the reference to the Hook object (*hk*) is created in the constructor of the Form1 class, the constructor of the Hook class is immediately called with a reference to the Form1 object as a parameter. The reference to the Form1 object is passed to the Hook object so that the filter function contained within the Hook class can write text out to the text box contained in the Form1 object. All controls within a Form object are set to Private access; therefore, no class, nested or otherwise, can access these controls. In previous versions of VB, the form controls had public access, and we did not have this problem.

After the Form1 form is displayed, the user can click the Hook button. This fires the *btnHook_Click* event, which calls *SetWindowsHookEx* to install the WH_ KEYBOARD's filter function. A message box is displayed following this call to display the handle to the hook. A hook value other than zero means that the hook has successfully been installed.

At this point, whenever the user presses a key on the keyboard, the *HookProc* filter function is called. This function calls the PrintTxt method in the Form1 object, which displays some text in the text box on the form. The text displayed includes the parameters to the filter function.

When the user clicks the UnHook button, the *BtnHook_Click* event is fired. This event causes *UnhookWindowsHookEx* to be called, removing the WH_KEYBOARD filter function. A message box is displayed showing the return value of this function call; a value other than zero means that the hook has successfully been removed.

Implementing the WH_MOUSE Hook

I also chose to include a WH_MOUSE hook example because it requires the use of a user-defined type. In VB.NET, user-defined types are gone and are replaced by structures. The example presented here will explain how to use a structure in place of a user-defined type.

If you are going to port any of this code to C#, you must add an attribute to the structure definition. The following is an example of this:

```
[StructLayout(LayoutKind.Sequential)]
public struct MOUSEHOOKSTRUCT
{
            public pt As POINTAPI
            public hwnd As Integer
            public wHitTestCode As Integer
            public dwExtraInfo As Integer
}
```

Examining the IL that the VB.NET application generated, we see the following

```
.class value sequential ansi sealed nested public
modl$POINTAPI
                extends [mscorlib]System.ValueType
{
} // end of class modl$POINTAPI
```

The structure is actually created as a class that inherits from the System.Value.Type class—the word extends in the previous IL code implies "inherits from." VB.NET automatically marks this class as sequential.

The Application

This application's UI is laid out exactly as in the previous example of the WH_KEYBOARD hook, which Figure 23-2 shows. The Hook button installs the WH_MOUSE hook, and the UnHook button removes this hook.

The filter function values are printed to the text box on the form whenever this hook is called. To see messages written out to this text box, move the mouse or click one of its buttons.

The .VB File

Example 23-3 presents the code contained in the *Form1.vb* file; the modifications needed to use structures with the MH_MOUSE hook appear in boldface.

Example 23-3. The Code Contained in the Form1.vb File for the WH_MOUSE Hook Example Application

```
Imports System.Drawing
Imports System.WinForms
Imports System.Runtime.InteropServices
Imports System.ComponentModel
```

Example 23-3. The Code Contained in the Form1.vb File for the WH_MOUSE Hook Example Application (continued)

```
'**************************************************
'MODULE SECTION
'**************************************************
Public Module mod1
    'declare delegate object
    Delegate Function HookCallback(ByVal Code As Integer, ByVal wParam As Integer, _
        ByVal lParam As Integer) As Integer

    'declare API's
    Public Declare Function SetWindowsHookEx Lib "user32" Alias "SetWindowsHookExA" _
        (ByVal HookID As Integer, ByVal lpfn As HookCallback, _
        ByVal hModule As Integer, ByVal ThreadId As Integer) As Integer
    Public Declare Function UnhookWindowsHookEx Lib "user32" _
        Alias "UnhookWindowsHookEx" _
        (ByVal hHook As Integer) As Integer
    Public Declare Function CallNextHookEx Lib "user32" Alias "CallNextHookEx" _
        (ByVal hHook As Integer, ByVal Code As Integer, ByVal wParam As Integer, _
        ByVal lParam As Integer) As Integer
    Public Declare Sub CopyMemory Lib "kernel32" Alias "RtlMoveMemory" _
        (ByRef Destination As mod1.MOUSEHOOKSTRUCT, ByVal Source As Integer, _
        ByVal Length As Integer)

    'Global constants
    Public Const WH_MOUSE As Integer = 7

    Structure POINTAPI
        Public x As Integer
        Public y As Integer
    End Structure

    Structure MOUSEHOOKSTRUCT
        Public pt As POINTAPI
        Public hwnd As Integer
        Public wHitTestCode As Integer
        Public dwExtraInfo As Integer
    End Structure

    Private m_hHook As Integer

    'Property to access hook handle
    Property hHook() As Integer
        Set
            If m_hHook <> 0 And Value <> 0 Then
                'Don't overwrite the handle
                '   Unless it is being reset to 0
            Else
                m_hHook = Value
            End If
        End Set

        Get
            hHook = m_hHook
```

*Example 23-3. The Code Contained in the Form1.vb File for the WH_MOUSE Hook Example
Application (continued)*

```
        End Get
    End Property
End Module



'**************************************************
'FORM SECTION
'**************************************************
Public Class frmHook
    Inherits System.WinForms.Form

    'declare nested class var
    Public hk As Hook

    'declare delegate object
    Public cb As HookCallback


    '**************************************************
    'NESTED CLASS-containing the callback HookProc
    '**************************************************
    Public Class Hook
        'reference back to the form
        Private TheWin As frmHook

        'ctor - used to get a reference to the main window
        '       in order to write info to the textbox1 text box
        Public Sub New(ByVal MainWnd As frmHook)
            TheWin = MainWnd
        End Sub

        'HOOK PROC
        Public Function HookProc(ByVal Code As Integer, ByVal wParam As Integer, _
          ByVal lParam As Integer) As Integer
            Dim Dest As New mod1.MOUSEHOOKSTRUCT()

            CopyMemory(Dest, lParam, sizeof(Dest))
            TheWin.PrintTxt(Dest.hwnd & " : " & Dest.pt.x & " : " & Dest.pt.y & _
              " : " & Dest.wHitTestCode)

            HookProc = CallNextHookEx(hHook, Code, wParam, lParam)
        End Function
    End Class
End Class

    'START HERE - default ctor for Form1 class
    Public Sub New()
        MyBase.New()
        frmHook = Me
        InitializeComponent()

        'instantiate a new nested Hook class passing in a reference to this form
```

Example 23-3. The Code Contained in the Form1.vb File for the WH_MOUSE Hook Example Application (continued)

```
        hk = New Hook(Me)

        'instantiate a new delegate object pointing to the HookProc function
        '   in the nested class
        cb = New HookCallback(AddressOf hk.HookProc)
    End Sub

    'used by Form1 to add text to the textbox1 text box, called by HookProc
    Public Sub PrintTxt(ByVal ip As String)
        textBox1.Text = TextBox1.Text & ip & chr(13) & chr(10)
    End Sub


    '**********************************************
    'REGULAR WINDOWS .NET STUFF
    '**********************************************
#Region " Windows Form Designer generated code "

    'Required by the Windows Form Designer
    Private components As System.ComponentModel.Container
    Private WithEvents Button2 As System.WinForms.Button
    Private WithEvents Button1 As System.WinForms.Button
    Private WithEvents TextBox1 As System.WinForms.TextBox

    Dim WithEvents Hook_Try2 As System.WinForms.Form

    'NOTE: The following procedure is required by the Windows Form Designer
    'It can be modified using the Windows Form Designer.
    'Do not modify it using the code editor.
    Private Sub InitializeComponent()
        Me.components = New System.ComponentModel.Container()
        Me.Button1 = New System.WinForms.Button()
        Me.Button2 = New System.WinForms.Button()
        Me.TextBox1 = New System.WinForms.TextBox()

        '@design Me.TrayHeight = 0
        '@design Me.TrayLargeIcon = False
        '@design Me.TrayAutoArrange = True
        Button1.Location = New System.Drawing.Point(8, 8)
        Button1.Size = New System.Drawing.Size(75, 23)
        Button1.TabIndex = 1
        Button1.Text = "Hook"

        Button2.Location = New System.Drawing.Point(8, 40)
        Button2.Size = New System.Drawing.Size(75, 23)
        Button2.TabIndex = 2
        Button2.Text = "UnHook"

        TextBox1.Location = New System.Drawing.Point(88, 0)
        TextBox1.Multiline = True
        TextBox1.ScrollBars = System.WinForms.ScrollBars.Both
        TextBox1.TabIndex = 0
```

Example 23-3. The Code Contained in the Form1.vb File for the WH_MOUSE Hook Example Application (continued)

```
        TextBox1.Size = New System.Drawing.Size(448, 620)

        Me.Text = "VB.NET Hooking Example"
        Me.AutoScaleBaseSize = New System.Drawing.Size(5, 13)
        Me.ClientSize = New System.Drawing.Size(536, 617)

        Me.Controls.Add(Button2)
        Me.Controls.Add(Button1)
        Me.Controls.Add(TextBox1)
    End Sub

#End Region

    'Form overrides dispose to clean up the component list.
    Public Overrides Sub Dispose()
        MyBase.Dispose()
        components.Dispose()
    End Sub

    '**************************************************
    'EVENT HANDLERS FOR BUTTON CONTROLS
    '**************************************************
    Protected Sub Button1_Click(ByVal sender As Object, ByVal e As System.EventArgs)
        'Install hook
        hHook = SetWindowsHookEx(WH_MOUSE, cb, 0, appdomain.GetCurrentThreadId)
        msgbox(hHook)
    End Sub
    Protected Sub Button2_Click(ByVal sender As Object, ByVal e As System.EventArgs)
        'Release hook
        msgbox(UnhookWindowsHookEx(hHook))
        hHook = 0
    End Sub
End Class
```

Using structures in place of user-defined types is actually not a major change. The main thing that you must do is instantiate the structure, which you did not have to do when using user-defined types. The MOUSEHOOKSTRUCT structure for the WH_MOUSE hook is instantiated in the *HookProc* function.

The first modification that we need to make to the previous WH_KEYBOARD hook code to convert it to use the WH_MOUSE hook is located in the mod1 module. We need to declare the familiar *CopyMemory* API function. Once again, this function is used to obtain a structure from a pointer that the filter function returns. We will see more of this in a moment. Next, the WH_MOUSE constant is declared, along with the POINTAPI and MOUSEHOOKSTRUCT structures.

The next modification is in the *HookProc* filter function. The following two lines of code are used to get a structure from a pointer contained in the *lParam* parameter:

```
Dim Dest As New mod1.MOUSEHOOKSTRUCT()
CopyMemory(Dest, lParam, sizeof(Dest))
```

The first line creates a new instance of the MOUSEHOOKSTRUCT structure defined in the mod1 module. Now that the *Dest* structure is created in memory, we can use the *CopyMemory* function to copy into the *Dest* structure the block of memory that the *lParam* parameter points to. At this point, we can use the *Dest* structure to access its members, as in the following line of code:

```
TheWin.PrintTxt(Dest.hwnd & " : " & Dest.pt.x & " : " & Dest.pt.y & " : " & _
              Dest.wHitTestCode)
```

After the *Dest* structure goes out of scope, it is marked for garbage collection. The memory for the *Dest* structure is automatically freed at a later time, when the Garbage Collector runs.

We make our final modification to the first parameter in the call to *SetWindowsHookEx* within the *Button1_Click* event. The WH_MOUSE constant is substituted for the WH_KEYBOARD constant.

As you can see, there is some more work involved with using hooks in VB.NET. The majority of this work is in writing the delegate that contains the pointer to the filter function. Some extra work also is needed when the filter function contains a pointer to a structure in one or more of its parameters.

Hooks can be just as powerful as they were in previous versions of VB. It is imperative that you be aware of the pitfalls of hooks—which are outlined in Chapter 3—before you start implementing hooks in your own applications. Failing to heed these warnings can cause your application to fail or, at best, operate inefficiently.

V

Appendixes

This section contains three appendixes that list Windows messages that you're likely to encounter and want to handle in your own subclassing and hooking applications, Win32 API calls used in this book, and constants and structures used in these API calls. Hence, these appendixes serve as a handy reference that you can use to look up details while you're writing code to perform subclassing or hooking.

Messages

This appendix lists the messages used in this book.

Window Messages

Public Const WM_NULL = &H0

wParam
　Unused.

lParam
　Unused.

Description
　This message does not affect the system.

Return Value
　Not used.

Public Const WM_CREATE = &H1

wParam
　Unused.

lParam
　Pointer to a CREATESTRUCT structure, defined in Appendix C.

Description
　Sent in response to a call to either the *CreateWindowEx* or *CreateWindow* API function, defined in Appendix B.

Return Value

   0 to continue window creation, -1 to cancel window creation so that *CreateWindowEx* returns a NULL.

Public Const WM_DESTROY = &H2

wParam

   Unused.

lParam

   Unused.

Description

   Sent to a window when it is being destroyed.

Return Value

   0 only if the application processes this message.

Public Const WM_MOVE = &H3

wParam

   Unused.

lParam

   Low-order word contains the x coordinate of the top of the window; high-order word contains the y coordinate of the top of the window.

Description

   Sent after the window is moved.

Return Value

   0 only if the application processes this message.

Public Const WM_SIZE = &H5

wParam

   Specifies the type of resizing.

lParam

   Low-order word contains the final width of the window; high-order word contains the final height of the window.

Description

   Sent after the window is resized; can be any one of the following constants, defined in Appendix C:

       SIZE_MAXHIDE
       SIZE_MAXIMIZED
       SIZE_MAXSHOW

```
        SIZE_MINIMIZED
        SIZE_RESTORED
```

Return Value

   0 only if the application processes this message.

Public Const WM_ACTIVATE = &H6

wParam

   Low-order word can be one of the following constants, defined in Appendix C:

```
        WA_ACTIVE
        WA_CLICKACTIVE
        WA_INACTIVE
```

   The high-order word contains a 0 if the window is minimized, a nonzero value otherwise.

lParam

   hWnd of the window being activated or deactivated.

Description

   Sent to the window being deactivated and then to the window being activated.

Return Value

   0 only if the application processes this message.

Public Const WM_SETFOCUS = &H7

wParam

   hWnd of the window that lost the keyboard focus.

lParam

   Unused.

Description

   Sent to a window that gained the keyboard focus.

Return Value

   0 only if the application processes this message.

Public Const WM_KILLFOCUS = &H8

wParam

   hWnd of the window that received the keyboard focus.

lParam

   Unused.

Description

Sent to a window before losing the keyboard focus.

Return Value

0 only if the application processes this message.

Public Const WM_SETTEXT = &HC

wParam

Unused.

lParam

Pointer to a null-terminated string containing the window's text.

Description

Forces the window's text to be drawn on the window's caption.

Return Value

True when the text is successfully drawn; False otherwise.

Public Const WM_PAINT = &HF

wParam

Unused.

lParam

Unused.

Description

Sent to inform the window to repaint all or part of itself.

Return Value

0 only if the application processes this message.

Public Const WM_QUIT = &H12

wParam

Contains an exit code that he *PostQuitMessage* API function provides, which is defined in Appendix B.

lParam

Unused.

Description

Causes an application to shut down; sent in response to a call to the *PostQuitMessage* API function.

Return Value

Unused.

Public Const WM_ERASEBKGND = &H14
wParam

The window's device context handle.

lParam

Unused.

Description

Sent to indicate that the window's background should be erased.

Return Value

Nonzero if the background is erased; otherwise a zero is returned.

Public Const WM_SHOWWINDOW = &H18
wParam

`True` if the window is being shown; `False` otherwise.

lParam

Status of the window that is shown; can be one of the following values, defined in Appendix C:

```
SW_OTHERUNZOOM
SW_OTHERZOOM
SW_PARENTCLOSING
SW_PARENTOPENING
```

Description

Sent to a window before it is shown or hidden.

Return Value

0 only if the application processes this message.

Public Const WM_SETCURSOR = &H20
wParam

hWnd of the window that the mouse cursor is over.

lParam

The low-order word contains the hit-test code; the high-order word contains the message ID.

Description

Sent when a mouse moves over a window that currently does not have the mouse capture.

Return Value

`True` only if the application processes this message; `False` otherwise.

Public Const WM_QUEUESYNC = &H23

wParam

Unused.

lParam

Unused.

Description

Sent by an application implementing a `WH_CBT` hook to distinguish between user input and input played back from a `WH_JOURNALPLAYBACK` hook.

Return Value

0 only if the application processes this message.

Public Const WM_GETMINMAXINFO = &H24

wParam

Unused.

lParam

Pointer to a `MINMAXINFO` structure, defined in Appendix C.

Description

Sent to a window before its location or size changes.

Return Value

0 only if the application processes this message.

Public Const WM_WINDOWPOSCHANGING = &H46

wParam

Unused.

lParam

Pointer to a `WINDOWPOS` structure, defined in Appendix C.

Description

Sent to a window before its location, size, or position in the Z-order changes.

Return Value

0 only if the application processes this message.

Public Const WM_WINDOWPOSCHANGED = &H47

wParam

Unused.

lParam

Pointer to a `WINDOWPOS` structure, defined in Appendix C.

Description

Sent to a window after its location, size, or position in the Z-order changes.

Return Value

0 only if the application processes this message.

Public Const WM_CANCELJOURNAL = &H4B

wParam

Unused.

lParam

Unused.

Description

Posted to an application when the user cancels a journaling hook.

Return Value

Unused.

Public Const WM_NCCREATE = &H81

wParam

Unused.

lParam

Pointer to a CREATESTRUCT structure, defined in Appendix C.

Description

Sent when the nonclient area of a window is created.

Return Value

True to continue the window creation; False otherwise.

Public Const WM_NCDESTROY = &H82

wParam

Unused.

lParam

Unused.

Description

Informs the window that its nonclient area is being destroyed. Sent by the *DestroyWindow* API function, which is defined in Appendix B.

Return Value

0 only if the application processes this message.

Public Const WM_NCCALCSIZE = &H83

wParam

If True, the window needs to define the area that does not need repainting. If False, the entire window is repainted.

lParam

If *wParam* is True, this parameter contains a pointer to an NCCALCSIZE_PARAMS structure, defined in Appendix C. If *wParam* is False, this parameter contains a pointer to a RECT structure, defined in Appendix C.

Description

Indicates that the client area must be resized.

Return Value

If *wParam* is True, the return value is one or more of the following, defined in Appendix C:

> WVR_ALIGNTOP
>
> WVR_ALIGNLEFT
>
> WVR_ALIGNBOTTOM
>
> WVR_HREDRAW
>
> WVR_VREDRAW
>
> WVR_REDRAW
>
> WVR_VALIDRECTS

If *wParam* is False, the return value is 0.

Public Const WM_NCHITTEST = &H84

wParam

Unused.

lParam

The low-order word contains the x coordinate of the mouse pointer. The high-order word contains the y coordinate of the mouse pointer.

Description

Sent whenever the mouse pointer is moved or a mouse button is pressed while over a window.

Return Value

Indicates the general location of the mouse pointer while over a window; it can be one of the following, defined in Appendix C:

> HTBORDER
>
> HTBOTTOM
>
> HTBOTTOMLEFT

HTBOTTOMRIGHT
HTCATPTION
HTCLIENT
HTCLOSE
HTERROR
HTGROWBOX
HT HELP
HTHSCROLL
HTLEFT
HTMENU
HTMAXBUTTON
HTMINBUTTON
HTNOWHERE
HTREDUCE
HTRIGHT
HTSIZE
HTSYSMENU
NTTTOP
HTTOPLEFT
HTTOPRIGHT
HTTRANSPARENT
HTVSCROLL
HTZOOM

Public Const WM_NCPAINT = &H85

wParam

Handle to a device context for the window's nonclient area.

lParam

Unused.

Description

Indicates that the window's nonclient area must be repainted.

Return Value

0 only if the application processes this message.

Public Const WM_NCACTIVATE = &H86

wParam

If True, the nonclient area of a window should be repainted to indicate an active window. If False, the nonclient area should be repainted to indicate an inactive state.

lParam

Unused.

Description

Indicates that the nonclient area of a window should be repainted to show an active or inactive state.

Return Value

If *wParam* is True, the return value is not used. If *wParam* is False, the return value should be True if the window should continue to change state; otherwise, a False should be returned to stop the window from changing state.

Public Const WM_GETDLGCODE = &H87

wParam

Unused.

lParam

Pointer to an MSG structure, defined in Appendix C.

Description

Indicates which messages a control wants to process itself instead of having the system process them. This message is used only for controls on a dialog box.

Return Value

Indicates the type of input messages the control's window procedure should process; can be one or more of the following, defined in Appendix C:

DLGC_BUTTON
DLGC_DEFPUSHBUTTON
DLGC_HASSETSEL
DLGC_RADIOBUTTON
DLGC_STATIC
DLGC_UNDEFPUSHBUTTON
DLGC_WANTALLKEYS
DLGC_WANTARROWS
DLGC_WANTCHARS
DLGC_WANTMESSAGE
DLGC_WANTTAB

Public Const WM_NCMOUSEMOVE = &HA0

wParam

Contains a hit test value; for a list of hit test values see the WM_NCHITTEST message.

lParam

Points to a POINTS structure, defined in Appendix C.

Description

Posted to a window to indicate that the mouse is moving over the window's nonclient area.

Return Value

0 only if the application processes this message.

Public Const WM_NCLBUTTONDOWN = &HA1

wParam

Contains a hit test value; for a list of hit test values, see the WM_NCHITTEST message.

lParam

Points to a POINTS structure, defined in Appendix C.

Description

Indicates that the left mouse button is pressed while the mouse pointer is over the nonclient portion of a window.

Return Value

0 only if the application processes this message.

Public Const WM_NCLBUTTONUP = &HA2

wParam

Contains a hit test value; for a list of hit test values, see the WM_NCHITTEST message.

lParam

Points to a POINTS structure, defined in Appendix C.

Description

Indicates that the left mouse button is released while the mouse pointer is over the nonclient portion of a window.

Return Value

0 only if the application processes this message.

Public Const WM_NCLBUTTONDBLCLK = &HA3

wParam

Contains a hit test value; for a list of hit test values, see the WM_NCHITTEST message.

lParam

Points to a POINTS structure, defined in Appendix C.

Description

Indicates that the left mouse button is double-clicked while the mouse pointer is over the nonclient portion of a window.

Return Value

0 only if the application processes this message.

Public Const WM_NCRBUTTONDOWN = &HA4

wParam

Contains a hit test value; for a list of hit test values, see the `WM_NCHITTEST` message.

lParam

Points to a `POINTS` structure, defined in Appendix C.

Description

Indicates that the right mouse button is pressed while the mouse pointer is over the nonclient portion of a window.

Return Value

0 only if the application processes this message.

Public Const WM_NCRBUTTONUP = &HA5

wParam

Contains a hit test value; for a list of hit test values, see the `WM_NCHITTEST` message.

lParam

Points to a `POINTS` structure, defined in Appendix C.

Description

Indicates that the right mouse button is released while the mouse pointer is over the nonclient portion of a window.

Return Value

0 only if the application processes this message.

Public Const WM_NCRBUTTONDBLCLK = &HA6

wParam

Contains a hit test value; for a list of hit test values, see the `WM_NCHITTEST` message.

lParam

Points to a `POINTS` structure, defined in Appendix C.

Description

Indicates that the right mouse button is double-clicked while the mouse pointer is over the nonclient portion of a window.

Return Value

0 only if the application processes this message.

Public Const WM_NCMBUTTONDOWN = &HA7

wParam

Contains a hit test value; for a list of hit test values, see the WM_NCHITTEST message.

lParam

Points to a POINTS structure, defined in Appendix C.

Description

Indicates that the middle mouse button is pressed while the mouse pointer is over the nonclient portion of a window.

Return Value

0 only if the application processes this message.

Public Const WM_NCMBUTTONUP = &HA8

wParam

Contains a hit test value; for a list of hit test values, see the WM_NCHITTEST message.

lParam

Points to a POINTS structure, defined in Appendix C.

Description

Indicates that the middle mouse button is released while the mouse pointer is over the nonclient portion of a window.

Return Value

0 only if the application processes this message.

Public Const WM_NCMBUTTONDBLCLK = &HA9

wParam

Contains a hit test value; for a list of hit test values, see the WM_NCHITTEST message.

lParam

Points to a POINTS structure, defined in Appendix C.

Description

Indicates that the middle mouse button is double-clicked while the mouse pointer is over the nonclient portion of a window.

Return Value

0 only if the application processes this message.

Public Const WM_NCXBUTTONDOWN = &HAB

wParam

The low-order word contains a hit test value; for a list of hit test values, see the WM_NCHITTEST message. The high-order word contains the mouse button that was pressed; it can be one of the following, defined in Appendix C:

    XBUTTON1
    XBUTTON2

lParam

Points to a POINTS structure, defined in Appendix C.

Description

Indicates that either the first or second x-button on the mouse is pressed while the mouse pointer is over the nonclient portion of a window.

Return Value

0 only if the application processes this message.

Public Const WM_NCXBUTTONUP = &HAC

wParam

The low-order word contains a hit test value; for a list of hit test values, see the WM_NCHITTEST message. The high-order word contains the mouse button that was pressed; it can be one of the following, defined in Appendix C:

    XBUTTON1
    XBUTTON2

lParam

Points to a POINTS structure, defined in Appendix C.

Description

Indicates that either the first or second x-button on the mouse is released while the mouse pointer is over the nonclient portion of a window.

Return Value

0 only if the application processes this message.

Public Const WM_NCXBUTTONDBLCLK = &HAD

wParam

> The low-order word contains a hit test value; for a list of hit test values, see the WM_NCHITTEST message. The high-order word contains the mouse button that was pressed; it can be one of the following, defined in Appendix C:

> > XBUTTON1
> > XBUTTON2

lParam

> Points to a POINTS structure, defined in Appendix C.

Description

> Indicates that either the first or second x-button on the mouse is double-clicked while the mouse pointer is over the nonclient portion of a window.

Return Value

> 0 only if the application processes this message.

Public Const WM_KEYDOWN = &H100

wParam

> Contains the virtual key code of the key pressed.

lParam

> Contains bit flags for the key pressed. The bit flags are defined as follows:

> *0-15*

> > Number of times the key is repeated

> *16-23*

> > Scan code

> *24*

> > Indicates if the key pressed is an extended key

> *25-28*

> > Reserved

> *29*

> > Always 0 for WM_KEYDOWN messages

> *30*

> > The previous key state; 1 if the key was already pressed before this message was posted, 0 otherwise

> *31*

> > Always 1 for WM_KEYDOWN messages

Description

  Posted to a window indicating that a non-system key was pressed (a non-system key is one that is pressed while the ALT key is not being pressed).

Return Value

  0 only if the application processes this message.

Public Const WM_KEYUP = &H101

wParam

  Contains the virtual key code of the key released.

lParam

  Contains bit flags for the key released. The bit flags are defined as follows:

  0-15

    Number of times the key is repeated

  16-23

    Scan code

  24

    Indicates if the key pressed is an extended key

  25-28

    Reserved

  29

    Always 0 for `WM_KEYUP` messages

  30

    Always 1 for `WM_KEYUP` messages

  31

    Always 1 for `WM_KEYUP` messages

Description

  Posted to a window to indicate that a nonsystem key was pressed (a non-system key is one that is pressed while the ALT key is not being pressed).

Return Value

  0 only if the application processes this message.

Public Const WM_CHAR = &H102

wParam

  Contains the virtual key code of the key pressed.

lParam

  Contains bit flags for the key pressed. The bit flags are as follows:

0-15

Number of times the key is repeated

16-23

Scan code

24

Indicates if the key pressed is an extended key

25-28

Reserved

29

1 if the ALT key is pressed along with this key; 0 otherwise

30

The previous key state; 1 if the key was already pressed before this message was posted, 0 otherwise

31

1 if the key is released; 0 otherwise

Description

Posted to a window to indicate that a nonsystem key was pressed (a nonsystem key is one that is pressed while the ALT key is not being pressed).

Return Value

0 only if the application processes this message.

Public Const WM_SYSKEYDOWN = &H104

wParam

Contains the virtual key code of the key pressed.

lParam

Contains bit flags for the key pressed. The bit flags are as follows:

0-15

Number of times the key is repeated

16-23

Scan code

24

Indicates if the key pressed is an extended key

25-28

Reserved

29

Always 0 for WM_SYSKEYDOWN messages

30

The previous key state; 1 if the key was already pressed before this message was posted, 0 otherwise

31

Always 1 for WM_SYSKEYDOWN messages

Description

Posted to a window indicating that a system key was pressed (a *system key* is the F10 key or one that is pressed while the ALT key is being pressed).

Return Value

0 only if the application processes this message.

Public Const WM_SYSKEYUP = &H105

wParam

Contains the virtual key code of the key released.

lParam

Contains bit flags for the key released. The bit flags are defined as follows:

0-15

Number of times the key is repeated

16-23

Scan code

24

Indicates if the key pressed is an extended key

25-28

Reserved

29

Always 0 for WM_SYSKEYUP messages

30

Always 1 for WM_SYSKEYUP messages

31

Always 1 for WM_SYSKEYUP messages

Description

Posted to a window to indicate that a system key was released (a system key is the F10 key or one that is pressed while the ALT key is being pressed).

Return Value

0 only if the application processes this message.

Public Const WM_SYSCHAR = &H106

wParam

Contains the virtual key code of the key pressed.

lParam

Contains bit flags for the key pressed. The bit flags are as follows:

0-15

Number of times the key is repeated

16-23

Scan code

24

Indicates if the key pressed is an extended key

25-28

Reserved

29

1 if the ALT key is pressed along with this key; 0 otherwise

30

The previous key state; 1 if the key was already pressed before this message was posted, 0 otherwise

31

1 if the key is released; 0 otherwise

Description

Posted to a window to indicate that a system key was pressed (a system key is the F10 key or one that is pressed while the ALT key is being pressed).

Return Value

0 only if the application processes this message.

Public Const WM_INITDIALOG = &H110

wParam

hWnd of the control that should receive the initial focus.

lParam

Contains additional information.

Description

Sent to the dialog box before it is displayed.

Return Value

True if the focus should be set to the control specified in *wParam*, otherwise, a False should be returned.

Public Const WM_COMMAND = &H111

wParam

The low-order word contains the menu item, accelerator key, or control ID. The high-order word indicates whether the notification message is from an accelerator key, control, or menu item.

lParam

hWnd of the control sending the notification message.

Description

Sent if an accelerator key is pressed, a command menu item is selected, or a control sends a notification message to its parent.

Return Value

0 only if the application processes this message.

Public Const WM_SYSCOMMAND = &H112

wParam

Indicates the action initiated by the user; can be one of the following, defined in Appendix C:

    SC_CLOSE
    SC_CONTEXTHELP
    SC_DEFAULT
    SC_HOTKEY
    SC_HSCROLL
    SC_KEYMENU
    SC_MAXIMIZE
    SC_MINIMIZE
    SC_MONITORPOWER
    SC_MOUSEMENU
    SC_MOVE
    SC_NEXTWINDOW
    SC_PREVWINDOW
    SC_RESTORE
    SC_SCREENSAVE
    SC_SIZE
    SC_TASKLIST
    SC_VSCROLL

lParam

The low-order word contains the x-coordinate of the mouse pointer if a menu item is selected; otherwise, it is not used. The high-order word contains the y-coordinate of the mouse pointer if a menu item is selected by the mouse; it is

−1 if an accelerator is used to access the menu item, or it is 0 if a mnemonic is used to access the menu item.

Description

Sent when a menu item is selected from the Window menu, the Minimize button is clicked, the Maximize button is clicked, the Restore button is clicked, or the Close button is clicked.

Return Value

0 only if the application processes this message.

Public Const WM_ENTERIDLE = &H121

wParam

Indicates whether the window is entering the idle state due to a menu item or dialog box being displayed; can be one of the following, defined in Appendix C:

    MSGF_DIALOGBOX
    MSGF_MENU

lParam

hWnd to the dialog box or menu.

Description

Sent to a window that is entering the idle state.

Return Value

0 only if the application processes this message.

Public Const WM_CTLCOLOREDIT = &H133

wParam

The edit control's device context handle.

lParam

hWnd of the edit control.

Description

Sent to the parent window of a control to indicate that it is going to repaint itself.

Return Value

The brush handle, only if the application processes this message.

Public Const WM_CTLCOLORLISTBOX = &H134

wParam

The list box's device context handle.

lParam

hWnd of list box control.

Description

Sent to the parent window of a control to indicate that the control is going to repaint itself.

Return Value

The brush handle, only if the application processes this message.

Public Const WM_CTLCOLORBTN = &H135

wParam

The button's device context handle.

lParam

hWnd of the button control.

Description

Sent to the parent window of a control to indicate that it is going to repaint itself.

Return Value

The brush handle, only if the application processes this message.

Public Const WM_CTLCOLORDLG = &H136

wParam

The dialog box's device context handle.

lParam

hWnd of the dialog box.

Description

Sent to the dialog box to indicate that it is going to repaint itself.

Return Value

The brush handle, only if the application processes this message.

Public Const WM_CTLCOLORSCROLLBAR = &H137

wParam

The scrollbar's device context handle.

lParam

hWnd of the scrollbar control.

Description

Sent to the parent window of a control to indicate that it is going to repaint itself.

Return Value

The brush handle, only if the application processes this message.

Public Const WM_CTLCOLORSTATIC = &H138

`wParam`

A static control's device context handle.

`lParam`

hWnd of a static control.

Description

Sent to the parent window of a control to indicate that it is going to repaint itself.

Return Value

The brush handle, only if the application processes this message.

Public Const WM_MOUSEMOVE = &H200

`wParam`

Contains the virtual keys pressed when this message is posted; can be one or more of the following, defined in Appendix C:

```
MK_CONTROL
MK_LBUTTON
MK_RBUTTON
MK_MBUTTON
MK_SHIFT
MK_XBUTTON1
MK_XBUTTON2
```

`lParam`

The low-order word contains the x-coordinate of the mouse pointer; the high-order word contains the y-coordinate of the mouse pointer.

Description

Posted to the window over which the mouse moved.

Return Value

0 only if the application processes this message.

Public Const WM_LBUTTONDOWN = &H201

`wParam`

Contains the virtual keys pressed when this message is posted; can be one or more of the following, defined in Appendix C:

```
MK_CONTROL
MK_LBUTTON
```

```
MK_RBUTTON
MK_MBUTTON
MK_SHIFT
MK_XBUTTON1
MK_XBUTTON2
```

lParam

The low-order word contains the x-coordinate of the mouse pointer; the high-order word contains the y-coordinate of the mouse pointer.

Description

Posted to the window over which the left mouse button is pressed.

Return Value

0 only if the application processes this message.

Public Const WM_LBUTTONUP = &H202

wParam

Contains the virtual keys pressed when this message is posted; can be one or more of the following, defined in Appendix C:

```
MK_CONTROL
MK_LBUTTON
MK_RBUTTON
MK_MBUTTON
MK_SHIFT
MK_XBUTTON1
MK_XBUTTON2
```

lParam

The low-order word contains the x-coordinate of the mouse pointer; the high-order word contains the y-coordinate of the mouse pointer.

Description

Posted to the window over which the left mouse button is released.

Return Value

0 only if the application processes this message.

Public Const WM_LBUTTONDBLCLK = &H203

wParam

Contains the virtual keys pressed when this message is posted; can be one or more of the following, defined in Appendix C:

```
MK_CONTROL
MK_LBUTTON
```

```
        MK_RBUTTON
        MK_MBUTTON
        MK_SHIFT
        MK_XBUTTON1
        MK_XBUTTON2
```

lParam

The low-order word contains the x-coordinate of the mouse pointer; the high-order word contains the y-coordinate of the mouse pointer.

Description

Posted to the window over which the left mouse button is double-clicked.

Return Value

0 only if the application processes this message.

Public Const WM_RBUTTONDOWN = &H204

wParam

Contains the virtual keys pressed when this message is posted; can be one or more of the following, defined in Appendix C:

```
        MK_CONTROL
        MK_LBUTTON
        MK_RBUTTON
        MK_MBUTTON
        MK_SHIFT
        MK_XBUTTON1
        MK_XBUTTON2
```

lParam

The low-order word contains the x-coordinate of the mouse pointer; the high-order word contains the y-coordinate of the mouse pointer.

Description

Posted to the window over which the right mouse button is pressed.

Return Value

0 only if the application processes this message.

Public Const WM_RBUTTONUP = &H205

wParam

Contains the virtual keys pressed when this message is posted; can be one or more of the following, defined in Appendix C:

```
        MK_CONTROL
        MK_LBUTTON
```

        MK_RBUTTON
        MK_MBUTTON
        MK_SHIFT
        MK_XBUTTON1
        MK_XBUTTON2

lParam

The low-order word contains the x-coordinate of the mouse pointer; the high-order word contains the y-coordinate of the mouse pointer.

Description

Posted to the window over which the right mouse button is released.

Return Value

0 only if the application processes this message.

Public Const WM_RBUTTONDBLCLK = &H206

wParam

Contains the virtual keys pressed when this message is posted; can be one or more of the following, defined in Appendix C:

        MK_CONTROL
        MK_LBUTTON
        MK_RBUTTON
        MK_MBUTTON
        MK_SHIFT
        MK_XBUTTON1
        MK_XBUTTON2

lParam

The low-order word contains the x-coordinate of the mouse pointer; the high-order word contains the y-coordinate of the mouse pointer.

Description

Posted to the window over which the right mouse button is double-clicked.

Return Value

0 only if the application processes this message.

Public Const WM_MBUTTONDOWN = &H207

wParam

Contains the virtual keys pressed when this message is posted; can be one or more of the following, defined in Appendix C:

        MK_CONTROL
        MK_LBUTTON

       MK_RBUTTON
       MK_MBUTTON
       MK_SHIFT
       MK_XBUTTON1
       MK_XBUTTON2

lParam

The low-order word contains the x-coordinate of the mouse pointer; the high-order word contains the y-coordinate of the mouse pointer.

Description

Posted to the window over which the middle mouse button is pressed.

Return Value

0 only if the application processes this message.

Public Const WM_MBUTTONUP = &H208

wParam

Contains the virtual keys pressed when this message is posted; can be one or more of the following, defined in Appendix C:

       MK_CONTROL
       MK_LBUTTON
       MK_RBUTTON
       MK_MBUTTON
       MK_SHIFT
       MK_XBUTTON1
       MK_XBUTTON2

lParam

The low-order word contains the x-coordinate of the mouse pointer; the high-order word contains the y-coordinate of the mouse pointer.

Description

Posted to the window over which the middle mouse button is released.

Return Value

0 only if the application processes this message.

Public Const WM_MBUTTONDBLCLK = &H209

wParam

Contains the virtual keys pressed when this message is posted; can be one or more of the following, defined in Appendix C:

       MK_CONTROL
       MK_LBUTTON

```
MK_RBUTTON
MK_MBUTTON
MK_SHIFT
MK_XBUTTON1
MK_XBUTTON2
```

lParam

The low-order word contains the x-coordinate of the mouse pointer; the high-order word contains the y-coordinate of the mouse pointer.

Description

Posted to the window over which the middle mouse button is double-clicked.

Return Value

0 only if the application processes this message.

Public Const WM_XBUTTONDOWN = &H20B

wParam

The low-order word contains the virtual keys pressed when this message is posted; it can be one or more of the following, defined in Appendix C:

```
MK_CONTROL
MK_LBUTTON
MK_RBUTTON
MK_MBUTTON
MK_SHIFT
MK_XBUTTON1
MK_XBUTTON2
```

The high-order word contains the x-button that was pressed; it can be one of the following, defined in Appendix C:

```
XBUTTON1
XBUTTON2
```

lParam

The low-order word contains the x-coordinate of the mouse pointer; the high-order word contains the y-coordinate of the mouse pointer.

Description

Posted to the window over which the mouse's x-button is pressed.

Return Value

0 only if the application processes this message.

Public Const WM_XBUTTONUP = &H20C

wParam

The low-order word contains the virtual keys pressed when this message is posted; can be one or more of the following, defined in Appendix C:

```
MK_CONTROL
MK_LBUTTON
MK_RBUTTON
MK_MBUTTON
MK_SHIFT
MK_XBUTTON1
MK_XBUTTON2
```

The high-order word contains the x-button that was released; it can be one of the following, defined in Appendix C:

```
XBUTTON1
XBUTTON2
```

lParam

The low-order word contains the x-coordinate of the mouse pointer; the high-order word contains the y-coordinate of the mouse pointer.

Description

Posted to the window over which the mouse's x-button is released.

Return Value

0 only if the application processes this message.

Public Const WM_XBUTTONDBLCLK = &H20D

wParam

The low-order word contains the virtual keys pressed when this message is posted; it can be one or more of the following, defined in Appendix C:

```
MK_CONTROL
MK_LBUTTON
MK_RBUTTON
MK_MBUTTON
MK_SHIFT
MK_XBUTTON1
MK_XBUTTON2
```

The high-order word contains the x-button that was double-clicked; it can be one of the following, defined in Appendix C:

      XBUTTON1

      XBUTTON2

lParam

> The low-order word contains the x-coordinate of the mouse pointer; the high-order word contains the y-coordinate of the mouse pointer.

Description

> Posted to the window over which the mouse's x-button is double-clicked.

Return Value

> 0 only if the application processes this message.

Public Const WM_PARENTNOTIFY = &H210

wParam

> The low-order word contains the action for which the parent is being notified; it can be one of the following:

      WM_CREATE

      WM_DESTROY

      WM_LBUTTONDOWN

      WM_MBUTTONDOWN

      WM_RBUTTONDOWN

      WM_XBUTTONDOWN

> The high-order word contains a value that depends on the low-order word of *wParam*; it can be one of the following:

      WM_CREATE

      WM_DESTROY

      WM_LBUTTONDOWN

      WM_MBUTTONDOWN

      WM_RBUTTONDOWN

      WM_XBUTTONDOWN

lParam

> Value depends on the low-order word of *wParam*; it can be one of the following:

      WM_CREATE

      WM_DESTROY

      WM_LBUTTONDOWN

      WM_MBUTTONDOWN

      WM_RBUTTONDOWN

      WM_XBUTTONDOWN

Description

> Notifies the parent of an action occurring in a child control.

Return Value

　0 only if the application processes this message.

Public Const WM_ENTERMENULOOP = &H211

wParam

　True if the menu was activated using the *TrackPopupMenu* API function, defined in Appendix B.

lParam

　Unused.

Description

　Indicates that a menu modal loop has been entered.

Return Value

　0 only if the application processes this message.

Public Const WM_EXITMENULOOP = &H212

wParam

　True if a shortcut menu was activated; False otherwise.

lParam

　Unused.

Description

　Indicates that a menu modal loop has been exited.

Return Value

　0 only if the application processes this message.

Public Const WM_SIZING = &H214

wParam

　Indicates the window edge that is being sized; can be one or more of the following, defined in Appendix C:

```
WMSZ_BOTTOM
WMSZ_BOTTOMLEFT
WMSZ_BOTTOMRIGHT
WMSZ_LEFT
WMSZ_RIGHT
WMSZ_TOP
WMSZ_TOPLEFT
WMSZ_TOPRIGHT
```

lParam

　Pointer to a RECT structure, defined in Appendix C.

Description

Sent to a window currently being resized.

Return Value

0 only if the application processes this message.

Public Const WM_CAPTURECHANGED = &H215

`wParam`

Unused.

`lParam`

hWnd of the window gaining the mouse capture.

Description

Sent to a window that lost the mouse capture.

Return Value

0 only if the application processes this message.

Public Const WM_MOVING = &H216

`wParam`

Indicates the window edge that is being moved; it can be one or more of the following, defined in Appendix C:

```
WMSZ_BOTTOM
WMSZ_BOTTOMLEFT
WMSZ_BOTTOMRIGHT
WMSZ_LEFT
WMSZ_RIGHT
WMSZ_TOP
WMSZ_TOPLEFT
WMSZ_TOPRIGHT
```

`lParam`

Pointer to a RECT structure, defined in Appendix C.

Description

Sent to a window currently being moved.

Return Value

0 only if the application processes this message.

Public Const WM_ENTERSIZEMOVE = &H231

`wParam`

Unused.

lParam

    Unused.

Description

    Indicates that a sizing modal loop has been entered.

Return Value

    0 only if the application processes this message.

Public Const WM_EXITSIZEMOVE = &H232

wParam

    Unused.

lParam

    Unused.

Description

    Indicates that a sizing modal loop has been exited.

Return Value

    0 only if the application processes this message.

Public Const WM_HOTKEY = &H312

wParam

    Indicates the hot key ID that generated the message; can be one of the following, defined in Appendix C:

```
IDHOT_SNAPDESKTOP
IDHOT_SNAPWINDOW
```

lParam

    The high-order word contains the hot key's virtual key code. The low-order word indicates the keys pressed in combination with the hot key. It can be one of the following, defined in Appendix C:

```
MOD_ALT
MOD_CONTROL
MOD_SHIFT
MOD_WIN
```

Description

    Posted when a hot key is pressed.

Return Value

    0 only if the application processes this message.

Button Control-Specific Messages

Public Const BM_GETCHECK = &HF0
wParam

   Unused.

lParam

   Unused.

Description

   Gets the state of the checkbox or radio button (checked or unchecked).

Return Value

   Indicates the state of the control; can be one of the following, defined in
   Appendix C:

      BST_CHECKED
      BST_INDETERMINATE
      BST_UNCHECKED

Public Const BM_SETCHECK = &HF1
wParam

   Sets the state of the checkbox or radio button; can be one of the following,
   defined in Appendix C:

      BST_CHECKED
      BST_INDETERMINATE
      BST_UNCHECKED

lParam

   Unused.

Description

   Sets the state of the control.

Return Value

   Always 0.

Public Const BM_CLICK = &HF5
wParam

   Unused.

lParam

   Unused.

Description

    Forces a button to be clicked.

Return Value

    Unused.

Combo Box-Specific Messages

Public Const CB_ADDSTRING = &H143

`wParam`

    Unused.

`lParam`

    Pointer to a null-terminated string.

Description

    Places a string in the text box portion of a combo box.

Return Value

    A 0-based index to the string to add to the combo box.

Public Const CB_DELETESTRING = &H144

`wParam`

    A 0-based index to the combo box item to delete.

`lParam`

    Unused.

Description

    Removes an item from a combo box.

Return Value

    Number of items left in the combo box after this item is deleted.

Public Const CB_GETCOUNT = &H146

`wParam`

    Unused.

`lParam`

    Unused.

Description

    Retrieves the number of items in a combo box.

Return Value

    The number of items in a combo box.

Public Const CB_GETCURSEL = &H147

wParam

   Unused.

lParam

   Unused.

Description

   Retrieves the currently selected item in a combo box.

Return Value

   The 0-based index of the selected item.

Edit Control-Specific Messages

Public Const EM_GETLINE = &HC4

wParam

   The 0-based index of the line to retrieve from the text box.

lParam

   Pointer to a buffer that will receive the string.

Description

   Retrieves a string from a particular line in a text box.

Return Value

   Number of characters returned.

Public Const EM_CANUNDO = &HC6

wParam

   Unused.

lParam

   Unused.

Description

   Determines whether any actions can be undone in a text box.

Return Value

   0 if no actions can be undone; nonzero otherwise.

Public Const EM_UNDO = &HC7

wParam

   Unused.

lParam

   Unused.

Description

   Undoes the last action in a text control.

Return Value

   A single-line text box always returns `True`. A multiline text box returns `True` if
   the last action was undone; otherwise, it returns `False`.

Listbox-Specific Messages

Public Const LB_ADDSTRING = &H180
wParam

   Unused.

lParam

   Pointer to a null-terminated string to add to the list box.

Description

   Adds a string to a list box.

Return Value

   0-based index of the position that the string is added to the list box.

Public Const LB_DELETESTRING = &H182
wParam

   0-based index of the position in the list box to delete the string.

lParam

   Unused.

Description

   Removes a string from a list box.

Return Value

   Number of items remaining in the list box.

Public Const LB_SETSEL = &H185
wParam

   `True` to highlight an item, `False` to remove the highlighting.

lParam

   0-based index of the item to select.

Description

   Selects an item in a list box.

Return Value

   Unused, unless an error occurs, in which case `LB_ERR` is returned.

Public Const LB_GETSEL = &H187

wParam

   0-based index of the item to select.

lParam

   Unused.

Description

   Gets the item that is selected in a list box.

Return Value

   0 if an item is not selected; nonzero otherwise.

Scroll Bar-Specific Messages

Public Const SBM_SETPOS = &HE0

wParam

   The new position of the scrollbox.

lParam

   `True` to redraw the control; `False` to prevent the control from redrawing.

Description

   Sets the position of the scrollbox in a scrollbar control.

Return Value

   The previous position of the scrollbox; 0 if the scrollbox did not move.

Public Const SBM_GETPOS = &HE1

wParam

   Unused.

lParam

   Unused.

Description

   Retrieves the current position of the scrollbox in a scrollbar control.

Return Value

   Position of the scrollbox.

Public Const SBM_SETRANGE = &HE2

wParam

   The minimum scroll range.

lParam

   The maximum scroll range.

Description

   Sets the maximum and minimum scroll ranges of the scrollbar control.

Return Value

   The previous position of the scrollbox; 0 if the scrollbox did not move.

Public Const SBM_GETRANGE = &HE3

wParam

   Pointer to a buffer that gets the minimum scroll range.

lParam

   Pointer to a buffer that gets the maximum scroll range.

Description

   Gets the maximum and minimum scroll ranges of the scrollbar control.

Return Value

   Unused.

Messages Specific to the Common Dialog Boxes

Public Const CDM_GETFILEPATH = (CDM_FIRST + &H1)

wParam

   Size of the buffer pointed to by *lParam.*

lParam

   Pointer to a buffer, which gets the path and filename.

Description

   Gets the path and filename selected in an Open or Save As common dialog box.

Return Value

   A negative number indicates failure; otherwise, the number indicates the length of the path, filename, and a terminating null character.

Public Const CDM_GETFOLDERPATH = (CDM_FIRST + &H2)

wParam

   Size of the buffer pointed to by *lParam.*

lParam

Pointer to a buffer, which gets the path and filename.

Description

Gets the path of the opened folder in an Open or Save As common dialog box.

Return Value

A negative number indicates failure; otherwise, the number indicates the length of the path, filename, and terminating null character.

Public Const CDM_GETSPEC = (CDM_FIRST + &H0)

wParam

Size of the buffer pointed to by *lParam.*

lParam

Pointer to a buffer, which gets the path and filename.

Description

Gets only the filename of the selected file in an Open or Save As common dialog box.

Return Value

A negative number indicates failure; otherwise, the number indicates the length of the path, filename, and a terminating null character.

Public Const CDM_HIDECONTROL = (CDM_FIRST + &H5)

wParam

Control ID.

lParam

Unused.

Description

Hides a control in an Open or Save As common dialog box.

Return Value

Unused.

Public Const CDM_SETCONTROLTEXT = (CDM_FIRST + &H4)

wParam

Control ID.

lParam

Pointer to a null-terminated string containing the text for the control.

Description

Sets the text of a control specified in *wParam*.

Return Value

Unused.

Public Const CDM_SETDEFEXT = (CDM_FIRST + &H6)

wParam

Unused.

lParam

Pointer to a null-terminated string containing the filename extension

Description

Sets the default filename extension for an Open or Save As common dialog box.

Return Value

Unused.

Messages Specific to the Font Common Dialog Box

Public Const WM_CHOOSEFONT_GETLOGFONT = _USER + 1)

wParam

Unused.

lParam

Pointer to a LOGFONT structure, defined in Appendix C.

Description

Gets information on the current font selection in the Font common dialog box.

Return Value

Unused.

Public Const WM_CHOOSEFONT_SETLOGFONT = (WM_USER + 101)

wParam

Unused.

lParam

Pointer to a LOGFONT structure, defined in Appendix C.

Description

Sets the current font in a Font common dialog box.

Return Value

Unused.

Public Const WM_CHOOSEFONT_SETFLAGS = (WM_USER + 102)

wParam

Unused.

lParam

Pointer to a CHOOSEFONT structure, defined in Appendix C.

Description

Sets the flags to specify how the Font common dialog box is displayed.

Return Value

Unused.

Messages Specific to the Page Setup Common Dialog Box

Note: if the PSD_ENABLEPAGEPAINTHOOK flag is set in the PAGESETUPDLG flags member, you can implement a second hook function. This hook function intercepts the following messages, which modify the look of the sample page image at the top of this common dialog box.

Public Const WM_PSD_PAGESETUPDLG = (WM_USER)

wParam

The low-order word contains the paper size; the high-order word contains the orientation of the paper and whether the printer is a dot matrix or a Hewlett-Packard Printer Control Language device.

lParam

Pointer to a PAGESETUPDLG structure, defined in Appendix C.

Description

Notifies the Page Setup common dialog box *PagePaintHook* hook procedure that the sample page contents are about to be drawn on the screen.

Return Value

True if the image is to be drawn on the screen; False otherwise.

Public Const WM_PSD_FULLPAGERECT = (WM_USER+1)

wParam

Device context handle to the sample page image.

lParam

Pointer to a RECT structure, defined in Appendix C.

Description

Notifies the Page Setup common dialog box hook *PagePaintHook* procedure that the return address rectangle is about to be drawn on the screen.

Return Value

True if the image is to be drawn on the screen; False otherwise.

Public Const WM_PSD_MINMARGINRECT = (WM_USER+2)

wParam

Device context handle to the sample page image.

lParam

Pointer to a RECT structure, defined in Appendix C.

Description

Notifies the Page Setup common dialog box *PagePaintHook* hook procedure that the sample page is about to be drawn on the screen.

Return Value

True if the image is to be drawn on the screen; False otherwise.

Public Const WM_PSD_MARGINRECT = (WM_USER+3)

wParam

Device context handle to the sample page image.

lParam

Pointer to a RECT structure, defined in Appendix C.

Description

Notifies the Page Setup common dialog box hook *PagePaintHook* procedure that the margin rectangle is about to be drawn on the screen.

Return Value

True if the image is to be drawn on the screen; False otherwise.

Public Const WM_PSD_ENVSTAMPRECT = (WM_USER+5)

wParam

Device context handle to the sample page image.

lParam

Pointer to a RECT structure, defined in Appendix C.

Description

Notifies the Page Setup common dialog box hook *PagePaintHook* procedure that the envelope stamp rectangle is about to be drawn on the screen.

Return Value

    True if the image is to be drawn on the screen; False otherwise.

Public Const WM_PSD_FULLPAGERECT = (WM_USER+6)

wParam

    Device context handle to the sample page image.

lParam

    Pointer to a RECT structure, defined in Appendix C.

Description

    Notifies the Page Setup common dialog box hook *PagePaintHook* procedure that the sample page rectangle is about to be drawn on the screen.

Return Value

    True if the image is to be drawn on the screen; False otherwise.

B

API Functions

This appendix lists the Windows API functions used in this book, along with their syntax and a description of their parameters.

AttachThreadInput

Forces multiple threads to receive messages from a single message queue:

```
Private Declare Function AttachThreadInput Lib "user32" _
    Alias "AttachThreadInput" _
    (ByVal idAttach As Long, _
    ByVal idAttachTo As Long, _\
    ByVal fAttach As Long) As Long
```

Parameters

idAttach

The thread ID of the thread to be attached to another thread's message queue.

idAttachTo

The thread ID of the thread containing the message queue to which the thread specified by *idAttach* is attached.

fAttach

`True` specifies to attach the two threads; `False` specifies to detach the two threads.

Return Value

0 indicates that the function failed; any other value indicates success.

BroadcastSystemMessage

Sends a message to multiple recipients. The recipients are specified in the pdw parameter of this function:

```
Public Declare Function BroadcastSystemMessage Lib "user32" _
    Alias "BroadcastSystemMessage" _
    (ByVal dw As Long, pdw As Long, ByVal un As Long, ByVal wParam As Long, _
    ByVal lParam As Long) As Long
```

Parameters

dw

Specifies one or more of the following broadcasting flags:

BSF_ALLOWSFW

Enables the foreground window to be set by the recipient in the Windows 2000 system.

BSF_FLUSHDISK

Flushes the disk after each sent message is processed.

BSF_FORCEIFHUNG

Message is sent even if one or more recipients are hung.

BSF_IGNORECURRENTTASK

Prevents the sending application from receiving its own message.

BSF_NOHANG

Stops broadcasting messages if one recipient is hung.

BSF_NOTIMEOUTIFNOTHUNG

Does not time out unless a recipient is hung.

BSF_POSTMESSAGE

Posts the message instead of sending it.

BSF_QUERY

Each recipient must respond with a **True** value for the message to be sent to the next recipient.

BSF_SENDNOTIFYMESSAGE

Uses the *SendNotifyMessage* function to send the message in the Windows 2000 system.

pdw

Specifies one or more of the following flags that determines the recipients of the message:

BSM_ALLCOMPONENTS

Broadcasts to all components in the system

BSM_ALLDESKTOPS

>Broadcasts to all desktops in Windows NT/2000 systems

BSM_APPLICATIONS

>Broadcasts to all applications

BSM_INSTALLABLEDRIVERS

>Broadcasts to installable drivers in Windows 9x systems

BSM_NETDRIVER

>Broadcasts to network drivers in Windows 9x systems

BSM_VXDS

>Broadcasts to all system-level device drivers in Windows 9x systems

un

>Message identifier

wParam

>Additional information for the message specified in *un*

lParam

>Additional information for the message specified in *un*

Return Value

Returns a positive value if the message is successfully sent to its recipients. Returns a –1 if the function was unable to send the message. Messages are sent to recipients determined by the **pdw** parameter.

CallNextHookEx

Used in a hook's filter function to send information on to the next hook in the chain:

```
Private Declare Function CallNextHookEx Lib "user32"_
        (ByVal hHook As Long, _
        ByVal ncode As Long, _
        ByVal wParam As Long, _
        lParam As Any) As Long
```

Parameters

hHook

>The handle to the hook. The *SetWindowHookEx* function returns this hook handle.

ncode

>A constant identifying the hook code.

wParam

> The *wParam* argument passed in to the hook filter function. The value of this argument depends on the message that it is associated with.

lParam

> The *lParam* argument passed in to the hook filter function. The value of this argument depends on the message that it is associated with.

Return Value

The return value depends on the type of hook that is installed.

CallWindowProc

Used to call a function specified by the *lpPrevWndFunc* function pointer:

```
Public Declare Function CallWindowProc Lib "user32" Alias "CallWindowProcA" _
        (ByVal lpPrevWndFunc As Long, _
        ByVal hWnd As Long, _
        ByVal Msg As Long, _
        ByVal wParam As Long, _
        ByVal lParam As Long) As Long
```

Parameters

lPrevWndFunc

> A pointer to the window procedure to be called

hWnd

> The handle of a window

Msg

> The message to send to the target window procedure

wParam

> The first parameter of the message

lParam

> The second parameter of the message

Return Value

This function's return value depends on the type of message (identified by the *Msg* argument) processed.

ChooseColor

Displays the Color common dialog box:

```
Public Declare Function ChooseColor Lib "comdlg32.dll" Alias "ChooseColorA" _
        (pChoosecolor As CHOOSECOLOR) As Long
```

Parameters

pChoosecolor
A pointer to a CHOOSECOLOR structure

Return Value

Returns 0 if there is an error, the Close button on the title bar was clicked, or the Cancel button was clicked. Otherwise, returns a nonzero value.

ChooseFont

Displays the Font common dialog box:

```
Public Declare Function ChooseFont Lib "comdlg32.dll" Alias "ChooseFontA" _
        (pChoosefont As CHOOSEFONT) As Long
```

Parameters

pChoosefont
A pointer to a CHOOSEFONT structure

Return Value

Returns 0 if there is an error, the Close button on the title bar was clicked, or the Cancel button was clicked. Otherwise, returns a nonzero value.

CopyMemory

Copies the contents of one memory location to another memory location:

```
Public Declare Sub CopyMemory Lib "kernel32" Alias "RtlMoveMemory" _
        (Destination As Any, Source As Any, ByVal Length As Long)
```

Parameters

Destination
The destination address to which the information is to be copied

Source
The source address from which the information is to be copied

Length
The length in bytes of the information to be copied

Return Value

None

CreateWindowEx

Creates a window:

```
Public Declare Function CreateWindowEx Lib "user32" Alias "CreateWindowExA" _
        (ByVal dwExStyle As Long, ByVal lpClassName As String, _
        ByVal lpWindowName As String, ByVal dwStyle As Long, _
        ByVal x As Long, ByVal y As Long, ByVal nWidth As Long, _
        ByVal nHeight As Long, ByVal hWndParent As Long, _
        ByVal hMenu As Long, ByVal hInstance As Long, lpParam As Any) As Long
```

dwExStyle

One or more extended styles of the window ORed together

WS_EX_APPWINDOW

A top-level window is placed on the taskbar when the window is visible.

WS_EX_CLIENTEDGE

Specifies a window with a border and a sunken edge.

WS_EX_DLGMODALFRAME

Specifies a window with a double border.

WS_EX_NOACTIVATE

Used in Windows 2000 to specify a window that a user cannot make the foreground window.

WS_EX_NOPARENTNOTIFY

Specifies a child window that does not send the WM_PARENTNOTIFY message to its parent window.

WS_EX_OVERLAPPEDWINDOW

Equivalent to (WS_EX_CLIENTEDGE OR WS_EX_WINDOWEDGE).

WS_EX_STATICEDGE

Specifies a window that has a three-dimensional border but does not take user input.

WS_EX_TOPMOST

Specifies a window that should always be placed on top of other windows that are set to be top-most windows.

WS_EX_WINDOWEDGE

Specifies a window with a border and a raised edge.

lpClassName

A string containing the name of the class from which this window inherits

lpWindowName

A string displayed in the title bar of the window

dwStyle

One or more window styles or control styles ORed together

WS_BORDER
Specifies a window with a thin-line border.

WS_CAPTION
Specifies a window with a title bar.

WS_CLIPCHILDREN
Specifies a window that does not paint the area that contains a child window.

WS_CLIPSIBLINGS
Specifies a window that does not paint all overlapping child windows outside the region of the child window's client area.

WS_DLGFRAME
Specifies a window with a dialog box border and no caption.

WS_MINIMIZE
The window is created in a minimized state.

WS_MINIMIZEBOX
Specifies a window with a minimize button in the title bar.

WS_MAXIMIZE
The window is created in a maximized state.

WS_MAXIMIZEBOX
Specifies a window with a maximized button in the title bar.

WS_OVERLAPPED
Specifies a window with a title bar and a border.

WS_OVERLAPPEDWINDOW
Equivalent to (WS_OVERLAPPED OR WS_CAPTION OR WS_SYSMENU OR WS_THICKFRAME OR WS_MINIMIZEBOX OR WS_MAXIMIZEBOX).

WS_POPUP
Specifies a pop-up window.

WS_POPUPWINDOW
Specifies a pop-up window with these properties (WS_BORDER OR WS_POPUP OR WS_SYSMENU OR WS_CAPTION).

WS_SYSMENU
Specifies a window containing a window menu on its title bar.

WS_THICKFRAME
Specifies a window with a sizing border.

WS_TILED
Same as WS_OVERLAPPED.

WS_TILEDWINDOW

 Same as WS_OVERLAPPEDWINDOW.

WS_VISIBLE

 Specifies a window that is initially visible.

x

 The position of the window with respect to the left side of the screen

y

 The position of the window with respect to the top of the screen

nWidth

 The width of the window

nHeight

 The height of the window

hWndParent

 Handle to the parent or owner window to this window

hMenu

 Handle to the menu that is used by this window

hInstance

 Handle of the module instance to be associated with this window

lpParam

 Pointer to a value that can be passed in to the window through the CREATESTRUCT structure

Return Value

If this function succeeds in creating the window, a handle to that window is passed back; otherwise, a 0 is returned.

DefWindowProc

Passes a message to the default window procedure for default processing:

```
Public Declare Function DefWindowProc Lib "user32" _
        Alias "DefWindowProcA" _
        (ByVal hwnd As Long, ByVal wMsg As Long, _
        ByVal wParam As Long, ByVal lParam As Long) As Long
```

Parameters

hwnd

 The handle of the window to which the message is directed.

uMsg

 A constant that identifies the message being sent.

wParam

> Extra information that the message can contain. This value is determined by the message.

lParam

> Extra information that the message can contain. This value is determined by the message.

Return Value

The return value depends on the message.

EnumChildWindows

Enumerates the child windows belonging to a specific parent window:

```
Public Declare Function EnumChildWindows Lib "user32" Alias "EnumChildWindows" _
    (ByVal hWndParent As Long, ByVal lpEnumFunc As Long, _
    ByVal lParam As Long) As Long
```

Parameters

hWndParent

> The handle to the parent window whose child windows we want to enumerate

lpEnumFunc

> A pointer to a callback function

lParam

> Any other data that needs to be sent to the callback function

Return Value

Returns 0 if the function fails; any other value indicates success.

FindText

Displays the Find common dialog box:

```
Public Declare Function FindText Lib "comdlg32.dll" Alias "FindTextA " _
    (pFindreplace As FINDREPLACE) As Long
```

Parameters

pFindreplace

> A pointer to a **FINDREPLACE** structure

Return Value

Returns 0 if there is an error, the Close button on the title bar was clicked, or the Cancel button was clicked. Otherwise, returns a nonzero value.

FindWindow

Searches for the specified top-level window:

```
Public Declare Function FindWindow Lib "user32" Alias "FindWindowA" _
       (ByVal lpClassName As String, ByVal lpWindowName As String) As Long
```

Parameters

lpClassName

> A string that contains the window class name of the window being searched for

lpWindowName

> A string that contains the window name of the window being searched for

Return Value

Returns the hWnd of the first top-level window that matches the criteria. Returns 0 if no windows match the specified criteria. If more than one window is found, it returns the window highest in the Z-order.

FindWindowEx

Searches for a specified child window:

```
Private Declare Function FindWindowEx Lib "user32" Alias "FindWindowExA" _
       (ByVal hWnd1 As Long, ByVal hWnd2 As Long, _
       ByVal lpsz1 As String, ByVal lpsz2 As String) As Long
```

Parameters

hWnd1

> The hWnd of the parent window to the window that you want to find. The function uses this parameter as a starting point for searching for the target window. If Null, the function uses the desktop as the parent window.

hWnd2

> The hWnd of any child windows to the window specified by the *hWnd1* parameter. If a valid child window handle is provided, this function starts searching through all the windows that are children to the window specified by this parameter.

lpsz1

> The class name or class atom of the window that we are searching for.

lpsz2

> The caption of the window that we are searching for.

Return Value

If this function succeeds, the hWnd of the window is returned; otherwise, it returns a 0, indicating failure.

GetClassInfoEx

Returns information about the specified class:

```
Public Declare Function GetClassInfoEx Lib "user32" Alias "GetClassInfoExA" _
        (ByVal hInstance As Long, ByVal lpClassName As String, _
        lpWndClass As WNDCLASSEX) As Long
```

Parameters

hInstance

Handle to the application instance that created the class. This argument is NULL if the system created the class (system-wide class).

lpClassName

The name or class atom of a registered class.

lpWndClass

Pointer to a WNDCLASSEX structure, which is passed back to the calling function.

Return Value

Returns a nonzero value if it successfully returns a window class structure. Returns 0 if the function fails.

GetDeskTopWindow

Returns an hWnd to the desktop window:

```
Public Declare Function GetDesktopWindow Lib "user32" _
        Alias "GetDesktopWindow" () As Long
```

Parameters

This function takes no arguments.

Return Value

Returns the desktop window handle.

GetDlgItem

Returns a handle to a specified control in a dialog box:

```
Public Declare Function GetDlgItem Lib "user32" Alias "GetDlgItem" _
        (ByVal hDlg As Long, ByVal nIDDlgItem As Long) As Long
```

Parameters

hDlg

The handle to the dialog box where the control is located. This can be either the default common dialog box or the child dialog box.

nIDDlgItem

The ID of the control in the resource file.

Return Value

Returns the handle of the control that you specify. Otherwise, returns a 0.

GetMessage

Retrieves a single message from the message queue of the thread in which this function was called:

```
Public Declare Function GetMessage Lib "user32" Alias "GetMessageA" _
    (lpMsg As MSG, ByVal hwnd As Long, ByVal wMsgFilterMin As Long,
    ByVal wMsgFilterMax As Long) As Long
```

Parameters

lpMsg

A Long pointer to an MSG structure that receives the message.

hwnd

The handle of the window whose messages are to be read from the queue. If this is zero, all messages will be read.

wMsgFilterMin

The minimum message value that is read from the message queue.

wMsgFilterMax

The maximum message value that is retrieved from the message queue. If this value is zero, all messages starting with the *wMsgFilterMin* value are read from the message queue.

Return Value

If an error occurs, this function will return a −1. If this function processes a WM_QUIT message, it will return a 0. Otherwise, it will return a nonzero value.

GetParent

Returns an hWnd of the parent window to the specified window:

```
Public Declare Function GetParent Lib "user32" Alias "GetParent" _
    (ByVal hwnd As Long) As Long
```

Parameters

hwnd

> The handle of the child window

Return Value

The handle of that child's parent window

GetSaveFileName

Displays the Save As common dialog box:

```
Private Declare Function GetSaveFileName Lib "comdlg32.dll" _
    Alias "GetSaveFileNameA" (pSavefilename As OPENFILENAME) As Long
```

Parameters

pSaveFilename

> A pointer to an **OPENFILENAME** structure

Return Value

Returns 0 if there is an error, the Close button on the title bar was clicked, or the Cancel button was clicked. Otherwise, returns a nonzero value.

GetWindow

By first using the *GetDesktopWindow* or the *FindWindow* functions, you can obtain a handle that the *GetWindow* function can use to find a related window:

```
Public Declare Function GetWindow Lib "user32" Alias "GetWindow" _
        (ByVal hwnd As Long, ByVal wCmd As Long) As Long
```

Parameters

hwnd

> The handle of a window used as a starting point.

wCmd

> Defines the relationship between the window provided by the *hwnd* argument and the window handle to be returned by this function. Possible values of the *wCmd* parameter are described in greater detail below. The *wCmd* argument can contain any of the following values:

GW_CHILD *(5)*

> The returned window handle is the first child window found in the Z-order.

GW_ENABLEDPOPUP *(6)*

> The returned window handle is a pop-up window owned by the window represented by the *hwnd* argument. For Windows 2000 only.

GW_HWNDFIRST *(0)*

The returned window handle is the first in the Z-order with the same window type (topmost, top-level, or child) as the window represented by the *hwnd* argument.

GW_HWNDLAST *(1)*

The returned window handle is the last in the Z-order with the same window type (topmost, top-level, or child) as the window represented by the *hwnd* argument.

GW_HWNDNEXT *(2)*

The returned window handle is next in the Z-order with the same window type (topmost, top-level, or child) as the window represented by the *hwnd* argument.

GW_HWNDPREV *(3)*

The returned window handle is previous in the Z-order with the same window type (topmost, top-level, or child) as the window represented by the *hwnd* argument.

GW_OWNER *(4)*

The returned window handle is the owner of the window represented by the *hwnd* argument.

Return Value

A window handle is returned based on its relationship with the window provided in the *hwnd* argument. The *wCmd* constant determines this relationship; if no window meets the criterion defined by *wCmd*, the function returns either 0 or *hwnd*.

GetWindowLong

Returns the specified information about a window:

```
Public Declare Function GetWindowLong Lib "user32" _
       Alias "GetWindowLongA" _
       (ByVal hwnd As Long, ByVal nIndex As Long) As Long
```

Parameters

hwnd

A window handle.

nIndex

A constant that determines the type of value that this function will return. The GWL_HINSTANCE constant (or –6) must be provided to the *nIndex* parameter to return the application's instance handle.

Return Value

If successful, returns the value requested. Otherwise, returns a zero.

GetWindowRect

Returns the top, left, height, and width of the specified window's bounding rectangle:

```
Private Declare Function GetWindowRect Lib "user32" _
        (ByVal hwnd As Long, lpRect As RECT) As Long
```

Parameters

hwnd

   The handle of the window

lpRect

   A pointer to a RECT structure

Return Value

If successful, returns a nonzero value. Otherwise, returns a zero.

OutputDebugStringA

Displays the specified string in a debugging window:

```
Public Declare Sub OutputDebugStringA Lib "kernel32" Alias "OutputDebugStringA" _
        (ByVal lpOutputString As String)
```

Parameters

lpOutputString

   The string that will be sent to the debugger hooked up to the current application

Return Value

None

PageSetupDlg

Displays a Page Setup common dialog box:

```
Public Declare Function PageSetupDlg Lib "comdlg32.dll" Alias "PageSetupDlgA" _
        (pPagesetupdlg As PAGESETUPDLG) As Long
```

Parameters

pPagesetupdlg

   A pointer to a PAGESETUPDLF structure

Return Value

Returns 0 if there is an error, the Close button on the title bar was clicked, or the Cancel button was clicked. Otherwise, returns a nonzero value.

PeekMessage

PeekMessage is similar to *GetMessage* in that it gets a message from the message queue of the thread that calls this. The main difference is that *PeekMessage* does not automatically remove the message from the message queue, and *GetMessage* does.

```
Public Declare Function PeekMessage Lib "user32" Alias "PeekMessageA" _
        (lpMsg As MSG, ByVal hwnd As Long, ByVal wMsgFilterMin As Long, _
        ByVal wMsgFilterMax As Long, ByVal wRemoveMsg As Long) As Long
```

Parameters

lpMsg

A Long pointer to an MSG structure.

hwnd

The handle of the window whose messages are to be read from the queue. If this is zero, all messages will be read.

wMsgFilterMin

The minimum message value that is read from the message queue.

wMsgFilterMax

The maximum message value that is retrieved from the message queue. If this value is zero, all messages starting with the *wMsgFilterMin* value are read from the message queue.

wRemoveMsg

If this is set to 1, the message is read and then removed from the queue. If this is set to 0, the message is read but left on the queue.

Return Value

If there are no messages on the queue, the return value for this function is zero. A nonzero return value means that a message has been read from the queue.

PostMessage

This function simply posts a message to the message queue of one or more threads. After posting the message, the *PostMessage* function returns; it does not wait for a response to the posted message, as does *SendMessage*.

```
Public Declare Function PostMessage Lib "user32" Alias "PostMessageA" _
        (ByVal hwnd As Long, ByVal wMsg As Long, _
        ByVal wParam As Long, ByVal lParam As Long) As Long
```

Parameters

hwnd

The window handle that the message is directed to. If this parameter is set to HWND_BROADCAST, the message is posted to all top-level windows in the system. If this parameter is set to NULL, the message is posted to the message queue of the thread in which this function was called.

uMsg

The message identifier.

lParam

The second parameter of the message.

wParam

The first parameter of the message.

Return Value

The return value is nonzero if the function succeeded in posting the message; otherwise, returns a zero value.

PostQuitMessage

Posts a WM_QUIT message to the message queue of the thread that called this function:

```
Public Declare Sub PostQuitMessage Lib "user32" Alias "PostQuitMessage" _
        (ByVal nExitCode As Long)
```

Parameters

nExitCode

A code that is sent to the *wParam* parameter of the WM_QUIT message

Return Value

None

PostThreadMessage

This function uses the actual thread ID to determine which message queue is to receive the message. This function also does not wait for a response to the posted message. This function is defined as follows:

```
Public Declare Function PostThreadMessage Lib "user32" _
        Alias "PostThreadMessageA" _
        (ByVal idThread As Long, ByVal msg As Long, _
        ByVal wParam As Long, ByVal lParam As Long) As Long
```

Parameters

idThread

> The thread identifier that the message is posted to. You can determine this value using the Visual Basic App.ThreadID method, or by using either of the *GetCurrentThreadID* or *GetWindowThreadProcessId* API functions.

uMsg

> The message identifier.

lParam

> The second parameter of the message.

wParam

> The first parameter of the message.

Return Value

The return value is nonzero if the function succeeded in posting the message; otherwise, returns a zero value.

PrintDlg

Displays the Print common dialog box:

```
Public Declare Function PrintDlg Lib "comdlg32.dll" Alias "PrintDlgA" _
        (pPrintdlg As PRINTDLG) As Long
```

Parameters

pPrintdlg

> A pointer to a **PRINTDLG** structure

Return Value

Returns 0 if there is an error, the Close button on the title bar was clicked, or the Cancel button was clicked. Otherwise, returns a nonzero value.

PrintDlgEx

Displays the Print Property Sheet common dialog box:

```
Public Declare Function PrintDlgEx Lib "comdlg32.dll" Alias "PrintDlgA" _
        (pPrintdlg As PRINTDLGEX) As Long
```

Parameters

pPringdlg

> A pointer to a **PRINTDLGEX** structure

Return Value

Returns 0 if there is an error, the Close button on the title bar was clicked, or the Cancel button was clicked. Otherwise, returns a nonzero value.

RegisterClassEx

Registers a new windows class so that it can be used in subsequent window creation:

```
Public Declare Function RegisterClassEx Lib "user32" _
        Alias "RegisterClassExA" _
        (pcWndClassEx As WNDCLASSEX) As Integer
```

Parameters

pcWndClassEx

A pointer to the WNDCLASSEX structure

Return Value

Returns a class atom, which is a unique identifier to the newly registered class. A return value of 0 indicates failure.

RegisterWindowMessage

Registers a new message that the system can use:

```
Public Declare Function RegisterWindowMessage Lib "user32" _
        Alias "RegisterWindowMessageA" _
        (ByVal lpString As String) As Long
```

Parameters

lpString

A null-terminated string that identifies the new message

Return Value

Returns a unique number identifying the message in the range of &HC000 to &HFFFF. Messages in this range are global to the system; therefore, after a message is registered, any application can use it. If a 0 is returned, the message failed to register.

ReleaseCapture

Releases the mouse capture for a window:

```
Private Declare Function ReleaseCapture Lib "user32" _
        Alias "ReleaseCapture" () As Long
```

Parameters

This function takes no parameters.

Return Value

Returns a nonzero value if the function succeeds in releasing the mouse capture on the window, or a 0 if the function failed.

ReplaceText

Displays the Replace common dialog box:

```
Public Declare Function ReplaceText Lib "comdlg32.dll" Alias "ReplaceTextA" _
        (pFindreplace As FINDREPLACE) As Long
```

Parameters

pFindreplace

A pointer to a **FINDREPLACE** structure

Return Value

Returns 0 if there is an error, the Close button on the title bar was clicked, or the Cancel button was clicked. Otherwise, returns a nonzero value.

SendDlgItemMessage

SendDlgItemMessage operates similarly to *SendMessage*. Both functions are synchronous, and both return a value that depends on the message sent. The main difference between these two functions is that you can specify a control ID in *SendDlgItemMessage*. This allows a message to be sent to a control when you know its ID but not its hwnd:

```
Public Declare Function SendDlgItemMessage Lib "user32" _
        Alias "SendDlgItemMessageA" _
        (ByVal hDlg As Long, ByVal nIDDlgItem As Long, _
        ByVal wMsg As Long, ByVal wParam As Long, _
        ByVal lParam As Long) As Long
```

Parameters

hDlg

The handle of the target dialog box.

nIDDlgItem

The ID of the control on the dialog box specified by the *hDlg* handle. You can find the control ID by using Spy++.

wMsg

The message to send to the target window.

wParam

> The first parameter of the message.

lParam

> The second parameter of the message.

Return Value

The return value depends on the message sent.

SendMessage

Sends a message to the specified target window:

```
Public Declare Function SendMessage Lib "user32" Alias "SendMessageA" _
        (ByVal hwnd As Long, ByVal wMsg As Long, _
        ByVal wParam As Long, lParam As Any) As Long
```

Parameters

hwnd

> The handle of the target window, or HWND_BROADCAST if the message is to be sent to all top-level windows in the system

wMsg

> The message to send to the target window

wParam

> The first parameter of the message

lParam

> The second parameter of the message

Return Value

The return value depends on the message sent.

SendMessageCallback

Sends a message to a window and returns immediately:

```
Public Declare Function SendMessageCallback Lib "user32" _
        Alias "SendMessageCallbackA" _
        (ByVal hwnd As Long, ByVal Msg As Long, _
        ByVal wParam As Long, ByVal lParam As Long, _
        ByVal lpResultCallBack As Long, ByVal dwData As Long) As Long
```

Parameters

hwnd

> The handle of the target window, or HWND_BROADCAST if the message is to be sent to all top-level windows in the system

wMsg

   The message to send to the target window

wParam

   The first parameter of the message

lParam

   The second parameter of the message

lpResultCallBack

   The callback function address

dwData

   Data to be passed into the callback function

Return Value

The return value is a success or failure (a zero or a nonzero value, respectively). However, this function uses a callback function to retrieve the message-dependent return value.

SendMessageTimeout

Sends the message to the target window and then waits the number of milliseconds specified in the *uTimeout* parameter:

```
Public Declare Function SendMessageTimeout Lib "user32" _
    Alias "SendMessageTimeoutA" _
    (ByVal hwnd As Long, ByVal Msg As Long, _
    ByVal wParam As Long, ByVal lParam As Long, _
    ByVal fuFlags As Long, ByVal uTimeout As Long, _
    lpdwResult As Long) As Long
```

Parameters

hwnd

   The handle of the target window, or HWND_BROADCAST if the message is to be sent to all top-level windows in the system.

Msg

   The message to send to the target window.

wParam

   The first parameter of the message.

lParam

   The second parameter of the message.

fuFlags

   Determines how the message is sent. Valid values are as follows:

SMTO_NORMAL *(&H0)*

Does not block calling thread until function returns

SMTO_BLOCK *(&H1)*

Blocks calling thread until function returns

SMTO_ABORTIFHUNG *(&H2)*

Returns if the application is hung

SMTO_NOTIMEOUTIFNOTHUNG *(&H10)*

(Win2000 only) Does not return from the function if the application is not hung, even though the timeout period might be expired

uTimeout

The timeout value in milliseconds before the function times out and returns.

lpdwResult

The result of processing the message.

Return Value

Returns 0 if the function succeeded, and nonzero if it timed out or failed.

SendNotifyMessage

If this function is used to send a message to a window in the same thread, the calling function halts processing until the *SendNotifyMessage* function returns, similar to the *SendMessage* function. If the message is sent to a window in a different thread, the function returns immediately:

```
Public Declare Function SendNotifyMessage Lib "user32" _
        Alias "SendNotifyMessageA" _
        (ByVal hwnd As Long, ByVal Msg As Long, _
        ByVal wParam As Long, ByVal lParam As Long) As Long
```

Parameters

hwnd

The handle of the target window, or HWND_BROADCAST if the message is to be sent to all top-level windows in the system

wMsg

The message to send to the target window

wParam

The first parameter of the message

lParam

The second parameter of the message

Return Value

This function returns only an error status (zero on failure, nonzero on success) and no other information.

SetCapture

Sets the mouse capture for a window:

```
Private Declare Function SetCapture Lib "user32" Alias "SetCapture" _
    (ByVal hwnd As Long) As Long
```

Parameters

hwnd

The window handle of the window that should receive all mouse input

Return Value

Returns the window handle of the window that previously had the mouse capture. If no window had the mouse capture, returns a NULL.

SetClassLongPtr

Replaces the specified member of the WNDCLASSEX structure of a window:

```
Public Declare Function SetClassLongPtr Lib "user32" Alias "SetClassLongA" _
    (ByVal hwnd As Long, ByVal nIndex As Long, _
    ByVal dwNewLong As Long) As Long
```

Parameters

hwnd

The handle to a window that was created using the class we want to modify. You can obtain it by retrieving the value of a form or control's hWnd property.

nIndex

A Long indicating the window attribute to be modified. A number of values are possible, though the value used to modify the window procedure is GCLP_WNDPROC, or −24.

dwNewLong

The replacement value. For a subclassed window, this parameter represents the address of the new window procedure. You can get the address of your new window procedure by passing its name as an argument to the AddressOf operator.

Return Value

The return value of this function will be the original value in the class structure that was replaced with the value in the *dwNewLong* argument. For our purposes, this function will return a zero if an error occurred, or the address of the original class window procedure if it was successful.

SetWindowLongPtr

Modifies the properties of a window:

```
Declare Function SetWindowLongPtr Lib "user32" Alias "SetWindowLongA" _
        (ByVal hwnd As Long, _
        ByVal nIndex As Long, _
        ByVal dwNewLong As Long) As Long
```

Parameters

hwnd

The handle of the window whose attribute is to be modified. You can obtain it by retrieving the value of a form or control's hWnd property.

nIndex

A Long indicating the window attribute to be modified. A number of values are possible, though the value used to replace a window procedure is GWLP_WNDPROC, or –4.

dwNewLong

The replacement value. For a subclassed window, this parameter represents the address of the new window procedure. You can get the address of your new window procedure by passing its name as an argument to the AddressOf operator.

Return Value

If successful, the function returns the original value before replacement (in this case, the original address of the window procedure). If it fails, it returns 0.

SetWindowPos

Allows a window's size, position, or location in the window Z-order to be modified:

```
Public Declare Function SetWindowPos Lib "user32" Alias "SetWindowPos" _
        (ByVal hwnd As Long, ByVal hWndInsertAfter As Long, _
        ByVal x As Long, ByVal y As Long, ByVal cx As Long, _
        ByVal cy As Long, ByVal wFlags As Long) As Long
```

Parameters

hwnd

The handle of the window being modified.

hWndInsertAfter

> The handle of the window that comes before this window in the Z-order. This argument also can take the following constants:

> HWND_BOTTOM (1)
>> Places the window at the bottom of the Z-order.

> HWND_NOTOPMOST (-2)
>> For topmost windows, places the window above all non-topmost windows (that is, behind all topmost windows). For non-topmost windows, the flag has no effect.

> HWND_TOP (0)
>> Places the window at the top of the Z-order.

> HWND_TOPMOST (-1)
>> Places the window above all non-topmost windows and maintains the window's topmost position, even if it loses the focus (an option typically indicated on menus as "always on top").

x

> Equivalent to the Left property in Visual Basic.

y

> Equivalent to the Top property in Visual Basic.

cx

> Equivalent to the Width property in Visual Basic.

cy

> Equivalent to the Height property in Visual Basic.

wFlags

> Flags that specify the sizing and positioning attributes. If multiple flags are present, you can logically Or them together. Some of the possible flags are:

> SWP_DRAWFRAME *(32)*
>> Draws a frame around the window.

> SWP_HIDEWINDOW *(128)*
>> Hides the window.

> SWP_NOACTIVATE *(16)*
>> Does not activate the window. Otherwise, *SetWindowPos* by default activates the window.

> SWP_NOMOVE *(2)*
>> Retains the window's current position (i.e., ignores the *x* and *y* parameters).

> SWP_NOOWNERZORDER *(512)*
>> Leaves the owner window's position in the Z-order unchanged.

SWP_NOREPOSITION *(512)*

The same as the **SWP_NOOWNERZORDER** flag.

SWP_NOSIZE *(1)*

Retains the current window size (ignores the *cx* and *cy* parameters).

SWP_NOZORDER *(4)*

Retains the current Z-order (ignores the *hWndInsertAfter* parameter).

SWP_SHOWWINDOW *(64)*

Displays the window.

Return Value

A return value of nonzero indicates success; a return value of zero indicates failure.

SetWindowsHookEx

Installs the specified window's hook:

```
Public Declare Function SetWindowsHookEx Lib "user32" _
    Alias "SetWindowsHookExA" _
    (ByVal idHook As Long, ByVal lpfn As Long, _
    ByVal hmod As Long, ByVal dwThreadId As Long) As Long
```

Parameters

idHook

This is the identifier of the type of hook that is being installed.

lpfn

Function pointer that points to the hook callback function.

hmod

The handle of the DLL containing the hook callback function. If this is NULL, the hook callback function is not contained within a DLL. Instead, it is contained in the application's (EXE's) code.

dwThreadId

The application's thread that contains the hook callback function. If this is NULL, the hook callback function is contained within a DLL (see *hmod*).

Return Value

Returns the handle to the newly created hook. A return value of zero indicates failure.

ShowWindow

Determines how the window is displayed:

```
Public Declare Function ShowWindow Lib "user32" _
        (ByVal hwnd As Long, ByVal nCmdShow As Long) As Long
```

Parameters

hwnd

> Window handle

nCmdShow

> Specifies how the window is displayed:

> SW_FORCEMINIMIZE
>
>> Displays a minimized window even if the thread that owns the window is hung.

> SW_HIDE
>
>> Hides the window and activates another window.

> SW_MAXIMIZE
>
>> Displays a maximized window.

> SW_MINIMIZE
>
>> Displays a minimized window.

> SW_RESTORE
>
>> Displays a window in its restored state.

> SW_SHOW
>
>> Activates a window.

> SW_SHOWMAXIMIZED
>
>> Activates and maximizes the window.

> SW_SHOWMINIMIZED
>
>> Activates and minimizes the window.

> SW_SHOWMINNOACTIVE
>
>> Displays a minimized window, but does not activate it.

> SW_SHOWNA
>
>> Displays a window, but does not activate it.

> SW_SHOWNORMAL
>
>> Activates and displays a window. If the window is minimized or maximized, it is first restored.

> SW_SHOWNOACTIVATE
>
>> Same as SW_SHOWNORMAL, but the window is not activated.

Return Value

Returns 0 if the window was previously hidden. Returns nonzero if the window was previously visible.

UnhookWindowsHookEx

Removes the specified window's hook:

```
Private Declare Function UnhookWindowsHookEx Lib "user32" _
                  (ByVal hHook As Long) As Long
```

Parameters

hHook
> The handle to the hook. The *SetWindowHookEx* function returns this hook handle.

Return Value

A return value of zero indicates failure; otherwise, the hook is removed.

UnregisterClass

Removes the class that the *RegisterClassEx* API function created from memory:

```
Public Declare Function UnregisterClass Lib "user32" Alias "UnregisterClassA" _
          (ByVal lpClassName As String, ByVal hInstance As Long) As Long
```

Parameters

lpClassName
> Name of the class

hInstance
> Module handle for the class

Return Value

A return value of zero indicates failure; otherwise, the class is unregistered and its memory is freed.

C

Structures and Constants

This appendix first lists the structures used in this book, and then finishes by listing the constants used in this book.

CBT_CREATEWND

Contains information used by the **WH_CBT** hook when a window is created:

```
Public Type CBT_CREATEWND
    lpcs As CREATESTRUCT
    hWndInsertAfter As Long
End Type
```

Structure Members

lpcs

Pointer to a **CREATESTRUCT** structure, which is defined as follows:

```
Public Type CREATESTRUCT
    lpCreateParams As Long
    hInstance As Long
    hMenu As Long
    hWndParent As Long
    cy As Long
    cx As Long
    y As Long
    x As Long
    style As Long
    lpszName As String
    lpszClass As String
    ExStyle As Long
End Type
```

hWndInsertAfter

hWnd of the window whose position in the Z-order is to precede the window being created. Youc an modify *hWndInsertAfter* to change the position in the Z-order of the window that is being created.

CBTACTIVATESTRUCT

Contains information used by the WH_CBT hook when a window is activated:

```
Public Type CBTACTIVATESTRUCT
    fMouse As Long
    hWndActive As Long
End Type
```

Structure Members

fMouse

True if the window was activated by a mouse click; otherwise False, indicating that the window was activated by some other means, such as an ALT-TAB key combination.

hWndActive

The hWnd of the active window.

CHOOSECOLOR

Used to define the Color common dialog box when it is created:

```
Public Type CHOOSECOLOR
        lStructSize As Long
        hwndOwner As Long
        hInstance As Long
        rgbResult As Long
        lpCustColors As Long
        flags As Long
        lCustData As Long
        lpfnHook As Long
        lpTemplateName As long
End Type
```

Structure Members

lStructSize

Size of this structure.

hwndOwner

Owning window.

hInstance

The instance handle of the object that contains the dialog resource. You usually set this equal to the App.hInstance property.

rgbResult

User-selected color returned to the application.

lpCustColors

Pointer to array of COLORREF structures.

flags

Flags describing this common dialog box. You must set the CC_ ENABLETEMPLATE and CC_ENABLEHOOK flags to use a modified template and a dialog hook function.

lCustData

Application-defined data passed in to the hook.

lpfnHook

A pointer to the developer-defined dialog hook function.

lpTemplateName

The ID of the modified dialog resource.

CHOOSEFONT

Used to define the Font common dialog box when it is created:

```
Public Type CHOOSEFONT
        lStructSize As Long
        hwndOwner As Long
        hdc As Long
        lpLogFont As Long
        iPointSize As Long
        flags As Long
        rgbColors As Long
        lCustData As Long
        lpfnHook As Long
        lpTemplateName As String
        hInstance As Long
        lpszStyle As String
        nFontType As Integer
        MISSING_ALIGNMENT As Integer
        nSizeMin As Long
        nSizeMax As Long
    End Type
```

Structure Members

lStructSize

Size of this structure.

hwndOwner

    Calling window's handle.

hdc

    Printer DC/IC.

lpLogFont

    Pointer to the **LOGFONT** structure.

iPointSize

    10 * size in points of selected font.

flags

    Flags describing this common dialog box. You must set the **CF_ENABLETEMPLATE** and **CF_ENABLEHOOK** flags must be set to use a modified template and a dialog hook function.

rgbColors

    Returned text color.

lCustData

    Application-defined data passed in to the hook.

lpfnHook

    A pointer to the developer-defined dialog hook function.

lpTemplateName

    The ID of the modified dialog resource.

hInstance

    The instance handle of the object that contains the dialog resource. This is usually set equal to the **App.hInstance** property.

lpszStyle

    Style field here must be **LF_FACESIZE** or larger.

nFontType

    Same value reported to the *EnumFonts* callback with the extra **FONTTYPE** bits added.

nSizeMin

    Minimum point size allowed.

nSizeMax

    Maximum point size allowed.

CWPRETSTRUCT

Contains information that the **WH_CALLWNDPROCRET** hook uses. This structure is similar to the **CWPSTRUCT** structure that the **WH_CALLWNDPROC** hook uses, except that this structure contains an extra member, *lResult*:

```
Public Type CWPRETSTRUCT
        lResult As Long
        lParam As Long
        wParam As Long
        message As Long
        hwnd As Long
End Type
```

Structure Members

lResult

   The return value of the window procedure after processing the message

lParam

   The second parameter of the message

wParam

   The first parameter of the message

message

   The message identifier

hwnd

   The window handle that the message is directed to

CWPSTRUCT

Contains information used by the WH_CALLWNDPROC hook:

```
Public Type CWPSTRUCT
        lParam As Long
        wParam As Long
        message As Long
        hwnd As Long
End Type
```

Structure Members

lParam

   The *lParam* parameter for this message

wParam

   The *wParam* parameter for this message

message

   The message identifier of the intercepted message

hwnd

   The window handle that this message is directed to

DEBUGHOOKINFO

Contains information used with the WH_DEBUG hook:

```
Public Type DEBUGHOOKINFO
        idThread As Long
        idThreadInstaller As Long
        lParam As Long
        wParam As Long
        code As Long
End Type
```

Structure Members

idThread

> Handle to the thread containing the filter function of the hook that is about to be called

idThreadInstaller

> Handle to the thread that installed the WH_DEBUG hook filter function.

lParam

> Value of the *lParam* that is to be sent to the filter function of the hook that is about to be called

wParam

> Value of the *wParam* that is to be sent to the filter function of the hook that is about to be called

code

> Value of the *uCode* that is to be sent to the filter function of the hook that is about to be called

EVENTMSG

Contains information used with the WH_JOURNALRECORD hook:

```
Private Type EVENTMSG
        message As Long
        paramL As Long
        paramH As Long
        time As Long
        hwnd As Long
End Type
```

Structure Members

message

> The message identifier.

paramL

> A message parameter. The message type defines the meaning for this member.

paramH

A message parameter. The message type defines the meaning for this member.

time

The time that this message was posted.

hwnd

The handle of the window to which this message is to be sent.

FINDREPLACE

Used to define the Find and Replace common dialog boxes when they are created:

```
Public Type FINDREPLACE
        lStructSize As Long
        hwndOwner As Long
        hInstance As Long
        flags As Long
        lpstrFindWhat As String
        lpstrReplaceWith As String
        wFindWhatLen As Integer
        wReplaceWithLen As Integer
        lCustData As Long
        lpfnHook As Long
        lpTemplateName As Long
    End Type
```

Structure Members

lStructSize

Size of this structure.

hwndOwner

Calling window's handle.

hinstance

The instance handle of the object that contains the dialog resource. This is usually set equal to the **App.hInstance** property.

flags

Flags describing this common dialog box. You must set the FR_ ENABLETEMPLATE and FR_ENABLEHOOK flags to use a modified template and a dialog hook function.

lpstrFindWhat

Pointer to search string.

lpstrReplaceWith

Pointer to replace string.

wFindWhatLen

Size of find buffer.

wReplaceWithLen

Size of replace buffer.

lCustData

Custom data passed to this hook function.

lpfnHook

The pointer to the developer-defined dialog hook function.

lpTemplateName

The ID of the modified dialog resource.

KBDLLHOOKSTRUCT

Contains information used by the **WH_KEYBOARD_LL** hook:

```
Private Type KBDLLHOOKSTRUCT
    vkCode as Long
    scanCode as Long
    flags as Long
    time as Long
    dwExtraInfo as Long
End Type
```

Structure Members

vkCode

The virtual key code.

scanCode

The scan code.

flags

This member contains flags for the key pressed. The flags include extended key, injected message, context code, and transition state.

time

The time this message was posted.

dwExtraInfo

A pointer to extra developer-defined information.

MOUSEHOOKSTRUCT

Contains information used by the **WH_MOUSE** hook:

```
Public Type MOUSEHOOKSTRUCT
        pt As POINTAPI
        hwnd As Long
        wHitTestCode As Long
        dwExtraInfo As Long
End Type
```

Structure Members

pt

   The x and y coordinates of the mouse pointer

hwnd

   The handle of the window that the mouse pointer was over when the mouse
   message was fired

wHitTextCode

   The hit test code detailing the nonclient area of the window that the mouse
   cursor is over

dwExtraInfo

   Extra information

MOUSEHOOKSTRUCTEX

Contains information used by the WH_MOUSE hook. This structure contains extra
information that the MOUSEHOOKSTRUCT does not contain:

```
Public Type MOUSEHOOKSTRUCTEX
    structMouseHook As MOUSEHOOKSTRUCT
    mousedata As Long
End Type
```

Structure Members

structMouseHook

   A pointer to the MOUSEHOOKSTRUCT structure.

mousedata

   A Long integer that contains mouse wheel and XButton information in the
   high-order word. The low-order word is reserved for system use.

MSG

Contains all information that defines a Windows message:

```
Public Type MSG
    hwnd As Long
    message As Long
    wParam As Long
    lParam As Long
    time As Long
    pt As POINTAPI
End Type
```

Structure Members

hwnd

The handle of the window to which the message is directed.

message

The message to be passed to this window. All window messages are constants and are defined in the Win32 Software Development Kit (SDK) header files. The header files *WINUSER.H* and *WINABLE.H* contain most of these constants.

wParam and lParam

Many messages use the *wParam* and *lParam* elements to pass extra information to the receiving window procedure. This extra information depends on the message. For example, it could indicate which mouse button was pressed, or if the Ctrl key was pressed in combination with the currently pressed key. Some messages need to pass much more information than is possible with the *wParam* and *lParam* arguments. To get around this limitation, some messages have special structures associated with them. Pointers to these structures are passed in either the *lParam* or the *wParam* elements.

Each message has its own identity—that is, the way one message fills in the **MSG** structure is not the way every message will fill it in. Most messages have their own information that must be passed on to the receiving window. Therefore, become familiar with the message that you are going to be trapping before you write the code or you might be in for a surprise.

time

Represents when the message was posted. *time* is equal to the number of clock ticks since the computer has been running. So, to find the amount of time that has elapsed between messages, just subtract the previous message's time member from the current message's time member. The time member plays an important role when using journal hooks.

pt

A pointer to a **POINT** structure. The *pt* member points to a structure containing the mouse cursor coordinates when this message was generated.

MSLLHOOKSTRUCT

Contains information used by the **WH_MOUSE_LL** hook:

```
Public Type MSLLHOOKSTRUCT
        pt As POINTAPI
        mousedata As Long
        flags As Long
```

```
        time As Long
        dwExtraInfo As Long
    End Type
```

Structure Members

pt

The x and y coordinates of the mouse pointer.

mousedata

If the *wParam* parameter specifies the WM_MOUSEWHEEL message, the high-order word of this member contains the mouse wheel delta (a positive value means that the mouse wheel was rolled forward, a negative value means that it was rolled backward). If the *wParam* parameter specifies that an XButton was clicked, the high-order word of this member determines whether the first or second XButton was pressed. The low-order word is reserved by the system in both cases.

flags

Determines whether the message was injected. If ANDing this flag with 1 results in a 1 or True, this message was injected; otherwise, the message was not injected. You can inject a mouse message into the messaging system by using the *SendInput* function defined in Chapter 12.

time

The time that this message was posted to the message queue.

dwExtraInfo

Extra information.

NMHDR

Contains information used by notification messages:

```
    Private Type NMHDR
        hwndFrom As Long
        idfrom As Long
        code As Long
    End Type
```

Structure Members

hwndFrom

The handle to the control sending this notification message

idFrom

The identifier of the control sending this notification message

code

A code identifying the type of notification

OPENFILENAME

Defines the Open and Save As common dialog boxes:

```
Private Type OPENFILENAME
    lStructSize As Long
    hwndOwner As Long
    hInstance As Long
    lpstrFilter As String
    lpstrCustomFilter As String
    nMaxCustFilter As Long
    nFilterIndex As Long
    lpstrFile As String
    nMaxFile As Long
    lpstrFileTitle As String
    nMaxFileTitle As Long
    lpstrInitialDir As String
    lpstrTitle As String
    flags As Long
    nFileOffset As Integer
    nFileExtension As Integer
    lpstrDefExt As String
    lCustData As Long
    lpfnHook As Long
    lpTemplateName As String
    pvReserved As Long
    dwReserved As Long
    FlagsEx As Long
End Type
```

Structure Members

lStructSize

Size of this structure. You should set it to Len(OPENFILENAME).

hwndOwner

The handle of the dialog's owning window. Can be 0 if no window owns this dialog.

hInstance

The handle to the object that contains the dialog template resource. If the dialog template resource resides in a DLL, use the *LoadLibrary* API function. The function takes one parameter, the path and filename of the DLL. *LoadLibrary* returns the handle to the DLL.

lpstrFilter

A string defining the filters, if any, used in the dialog box's Save As Type drop-down list. The filter is in the format {filter name}|{filter}. The filter name is a name for the filter such as "All Files". The filter is an expression used to describe the filter, such as "*.*". Therefore, the code to describe this filter would look like the following:

```
OPENFILENAME.lpstrFilter = "AllFiles | *.*"
```

lpstrCustomFilter

>   Contains the last filter chosen by the user.

nMaxCustFilter

>   Contains the size of *lpstrCustomFilter*.

nFilterIndex

>   Contains the index of the chosen filter.

lpstrFile

>   When initializing the dialog, this member contains the default text for the File Name edit control. When the user selects a file and exits the dialog box, this member contains the complete path for the selected file.

nMaxFile

>   Contains the size of *lpstrFile*.

lpstrFileTitle

>   The filename and extension only of the returned file.

nMaxFileTitle

>   Contains the size of *lpstrFileTitle*.

lpstrInitialDir

>   Contains the default path for the dialog box when it is initialized.

lpstrTitle

>   The title of the dialog box.

flags

>   Various flags used to initialize the dialog box. These are some of the more commonly used flags:
>
>   OFN_ALLOWMULTISELECT
>
>   >   Allows the user to select more than one file.
>
>   OFN_EXPLORER
>
>   >   Create a new explorer-style common dialog box.
>
>   OFN_FILEMUSTEXIST
>
>   >   To open a file, the file must exist or an error is raised.
>
>   OFN_HIDEREADONLY
>
>   >   The Read Only checkbox on the dialog is hidden.
>
>   OFN_NOVALIDATE
>
>   >   The file and path are not validated during processing by the dialog.
>
>   OFN_PATHMUSTEXIST
>
>   >   The path chosen in the dialog must exist or an error is raised.
>
>   OFN_SHOWHELP
>
>   >   The Help button is displayed.

OFN_ENABLEHOOK

Used for subclassing; enables the use of a dialog hook procedure.

OFN_ENABLETEMPLATE

Used for subclassing; enables the use of a resource in either a .RES or .DLL format.

OFN_ENABLETEMPLATEHANDLE

Used for subclassing; enables the use of a resource stored in memory.

OFN_ENABLEINCLUDENOTIFY

Used for subclassing; enables the dialog to send the CDN_INCLUDEITEM notification.

nFileOffset

Contains the position of the first character of the filename in *lpstrFile*. This member is zero-based.

nFileExtension

Contains the position of the first character of the filename extension in *lpstrFile*. This member is zero-based.

lpstrDefExt

The file extension appended to the filename if one is not provided.

lCustData

Extra data that can be sent to the dialog hook procedure via the WM_INITDIALOG message. When this message is sent to the hook procedure, it contains a pointer to this structure in the *lParam* parameter of this message.

lpfnHook

The pointer to our dialog hook procedure.

lpTemplateName

The dialog template resource ID.

pvReserved

Reserved by the system.

dwReserved

Reserved by the system.

FlagsEx

Setting this flag to zero allows the Places Bar to be displayed on the common dialog box; setting this flag to any other number prevents this bar from displaying. The Places Bar is located on the lefthand side of the Open and Save As common dialog boxes under Windows 2000. This bar contains shortcuts to commonly used folders, such as Desktop, History, My Documents, My Computer, and My Network Places.

PAGESETUPDLG

Defines the Page Setup common dialog box:

```
Public Type PAGESETUPDLG
        lStructSize As Long
        hwndOwner As Long
        hDevMode As Long
        hDevNames As Long
         flags As Long
        ptPaperSize As POINTAPI
        rtMinMargin As Rect
        rtMargin As Rect
        hInstance As Long
        lCustData As Long
        lpfnPageSetupHook As Long
        lpfnPagePaintHook As Long
        lpPageSetupTemplateName As String
        hPageSetupTemplate As Long
    End Type
```

Structure Members

lStructSize

> Size of this structure.

hwndOwner

> Handle of the owning window.

hDevMode

> Pointer to a DEVMODE structure.

hDevNames

> Pointer to a DEVNAMES structure.

flags

> Flags describing this common dialog box. You must set the PSD_ ENABLEPAGESETUPTEMPLATE flag to use a modified template. You must set the PSD_ENABLEPAGESETUPHOOK flag to use the page setup hook that the *lpfnPageSetupHook* function pointer points to. You must set the PSD_ ENABLEPAGEPAINTHOOK flag to use the page setup hook that the *lpfnPagePaintHook* function pointer points to

ptPaperSize

> Pointer to a POINTAPI structure.

rtMinMargin

> Minimum sizes of the margins.

rtMargin

> Actual sizes of the margins.

hInstance

> The instance handle of the object that contains the dialog resource. This is usually set equal to the **App.hInstance** property.

lCustData

> Application-defined data passed in to the hook.

lpfnPageSetupHook

> A pointer to the developer-defined dialog hook function.

lpfnPagePaintHook

> A pointer to the developer-defined dialog hook function, which specifically intercepts the painting messages for the sample page object on this dialog box.

lpPageSetupTemplateName

> Page setup template name.

hPageSetupTemplate

> Handle to the page setup template.

POINTAPI

Defines a point on an x and y coordinate plane:

```
Public Type POINTAPI
        x As Long
        y As Long
End Type
```

Structure Members

x

> x coordinate of a point

y

> y coordinate of a point

PRINTDLG

Defines the Print common dialog box:

```
Public Type PRINTDLG
        lStructSize As Long
        hwndOwner As Long
        hDevMode As Long
        hDevNames As Long
        hdc As Long
        flags As Long
        nFromPage As Integer
        nToPage As Integer
```

```
            nMinPage As Integer
            nMaxPage As Integer
            nCopies As Integer
            hInstance As Long
            lCustData As Long
            lpfnPrintHook As Long
            lpfnSetupHook As Long
            lpPrintTemplateName As String
            lpSetupTemplateName As String
            hPrintTemplate As Long
            hSetupTemplate As Long
        End Type
```

Structure Members

lStructSize

Size of this structure.

hwndOwner

Handle of the owning window.

hDevMode

Pointer to a DEVMODE structure.

hDevNames

Pointer to a DEVNAMES structure.

hdc

Handle to a device context.

flags

Flags describing this common dialog box. You must set the PD_
ENABLEPRINTTEMPLATE flag to use a modified template for the Print dialog
box. You must set the PD_ENABLESETUPTEMPLATE flag to use a modified template for the Print Setup dialog box.

nFromPage

Starting page.

nToPage

Ending page.

nMinPage

Minimum starting page number.

nMaxPage

Maximum ending page number.

nCopies

Number of copies.

hInstance

The instance handle of the object that contains the dialog resource. This is
usually set equal to the App.hInstance property.

lCustData
    Application-defined data passed in to the hook.

lpfnPrintHook
    A pointer to the developer-defined dialog hook function.

lpfnSetupHook
    A pointer to the developer-defined Print Setup dialog hook function.

lpPrintTemplateName
    The ID of the modified Print dialog resource.

lpSetupTemplate
    The ID of the modified Print Setup dialog resource.

hPrintTemplate
    Print template name (in memory object).

hSetupTemplate
    Setup template name (in memory object).

PRINTDLGEX

Defines a Print Property Sheet common dialog box:

```
Public Type PRINTDLGEX
        lStructSize As Long
        hwndOwner As Long
        hDevMode As Long
        hDevNames As Long
        hdc As Long
        flags As Long
        flags2 As Long
        Exclusionflags As Long
        nPageRanges As Long
        nMaxPageRanges As Long
        lpPageRanges As Long
        nMinPage As Long
        nMaxPage As Long
        nCopies As Long
        hInstance As Long
        lpPrintTemplateName As Long
        lpCallback As Long
        nPropertyPages As Long
        lphPropertyPagesAs String
        nnStartPage As Long
        dwResultAction As Long
    End Type
```

Structure Members

lStructSize
    Size of this structure.

hwndOwner

    Handle of the owning window.

hDevMode

    Pointer to a DEVMODE structure.

hDevNames

    Pointer to a DEVNAMES structure.

hdc

    Handle to a device context.

flags

    Flags describing this common dialog box. You must set the PD_ ENABLEPRINTTEMPLATE flag to use a modified dialog template for the General tab.

flags2

    Must be set to zero.

Exclusionflags

    Excludes controls from the Print Driver Property page.

nPageRanges

    Number of page ranges.

nMaxPageRanges

    Size of *lpPageRanges.*

lpPageRanges

    Pointer to array of PRINTPAGERANGE structures.

nMinPage

    Minimum starting page number.

nMaxPage

    Maximum ending page number.

nCopies

    Number of copies.

hInstance

    The instance handle of the object that contains the dialog resource. This is usually set equal to the App.hInstance property.

lpPrintTemplateName

    The ID of the modified dialog resource for the General tab.

lpCallback

    A pointer to the developer-defined dialog hook function.

nPropertyPages

    Number of property page handles.

lphPropertyPagesAs
> Pointer to array of property page handles.

nnStartPage
> Property page initially displayed.

dwResultAction
> Contains the results of actions performed in this dialog

RECT

Defines the boundaries of a rectangular shape:

```
Public Type RECT
        Left As Long
        Top As Long
        Right As Long
        Bottom As Long
End Type
```

Structure Members

Left
> Equal to the Left property of a form

Top
> Equal to the Top property of a form

Right
> Equal to the Width property of a form

Bottom
> Equal to the Height property of a form

WNDCLASSEX

Defines a window's class:

```
Public Type WNDCLASSEX
    cbSize As Long
    style As Long
    lpfnWndProc As Long
    cbClsExtra As Long
    cbWndExtra As Long
    hInstance As Long
    hIcon As Long
    hCursor As Long
    hbrBackground As Long
    lpszMenuName As String
    lpszClassName As String
    hIconSm As Long
End Type
```

Structure Members

cbSize

The size of this structure. You should set it to `Len(WNDCLASSEX)`.

style

A combination of class style constants ORed together. These styles determine the fundamental look and operation of a window created from this class. For example, the CS_NOCLOSE constant disables the Close option on the class's window menu, while the CS_HREDRAW constant forces a redraw of the window whenever the width of its client area changes.

lpfnWndProc

The function pointer to the window procedure for this class.

cbClsExtra

Amount of extra space to add to the end of the class structure. The developer uses this to store class-related information.

cbWndExtra

Amount of extra space to add to the end of the window structure. The developer uses this to store window-related information.

hInstance

The instance handle of the module that contains the window procedure for this class.

hIcon

Handle to an icon resource.

hCursor

Handle to a cursor resource.

hbrBackGround

The handle to a brush or a color value used to paint the background of the window created from this class.

lpszMenuName

The null-terminated string that defines the menu resource.

lpszClassName

The null-terminated string or class atom defining the name of the class. This value must be unique.

hIconSm

Handle to the small icon resource.

Message (.NET Structure)

Defines a Windows message:

```
Public Structure Message
```

Public Shared Methods

Create
Creates a new Message structure.

Public Instance Fields

hwnd
The handle to which this message is sent.

msg
The identifier for this message.

lParam
Definition depends on message.

wParam
Definition depends on message.

result
Return value for this message.

Public Instance Methods

Equals
Determines if this Message structure is equal to another object.

GetHashCode
Returns a hash code value for the instance of this structure.

GetLParam
Casts the lParam field to an Object type.

GetType
Returns this structure's type.

ToString
Returns the name of this structure.

Protected Instance Methods

Finalize
The destructor for this class.

MemberwiseClone
Returns a shallow copy of this structure's instance.

Constants

BroadcastSystemMessage Function Masks

```
Public Const BSM_ALLCOMPONENTS = &H0
Public Const BSM_VXDS = &H1
Public Const BSM_NETDRIVER = &H2
Public Const BSM_INSTALLABLEDRIVERS = &H4
Public Const BSM_APPLICATIONS = &H8
Public Const BSM_ALLDESKTOPS = &H10
```

Common Dialog Box Error Messages

```
Private Const CDERR_DIALOGFAILURE = &HFFFF
Private Const CDERR_FINDRESFAILURE = &H6
Private Const CDERR_GENERALCODES = &H0
Private Const CDERR_INITIALIZATION = &H2
Private Const CDERR_LOADRESFAILURE = &H7
Private Const CDERR_LOADSTRFAILURE = &H5
Private Const CDERR_LOCKRESFAILURE = &H8
Private Const CDERR_MEMALLOCFAILURE = &H9
Private Const CDERR_MEMLOCKFAILURE = &HA
Private Const CDERR_NOHINSTANCE = &H4
Private Const CDERR_NOHOOK = &HB
Private Const CDERR_NOTEMPLATE = &H3
Private Const CDERR_REGISTERMSGFAIL = &HC
Private Const CDERR_STRUCTSIZE = &H1
```

Common Dialog Box Notification Messages

```
Public Const CDN_INITDONE = -601
Public Const CDN_SELCHANGE = -602
Public Const CDN_FOLDERCHANGE = -603
Public Const CDN_SHAREVIOLATION = -604
Public Const CDN_HELP = -605
Public Const CDN_FILEOK = -606
Public Const CDN_TYPECHANGE = -607
Public Const CDN_INCLUDEITEM = -608
```

Class Styles

```
Public Const CS_VREDRAW = &H1
Public Const CS_HREDRAW = &H2
Public Const CS_KEYCVTWINDOW = &H4
Public Const CS_DBLCLKS = &H8
Public Const CS_OWNDC = &H20
Public Const CS_CLASSDC = &H40
Public Const CS_PARENTDC = &H80
Public Const CS_NOKEYCVT = &H100
Public Const CS_NOCLOSE = &H200
```

```
Public Const CS_SAVEBITS = &H800
Public Const CS_BYTEALIGNCLIENT = &H1000
Public Const CS_BYTEALIGNWINDOW = &H2000
Public Const CS_PUBLICCLASS = &H4000
```

Edit Control Notification Codes

```
Public Const EN_SETFOCUS = &H100
Public Const EN_KILLFOCUS = &H0200
Public Const EN_CHANGE = &H300
Public Const EN_UPDATE = &H400
Public Const EN_ERRSPACE = &H500
Public Const EN_MAXTEXT = &H501
Public Const EN_HSCROLL = &H601
Public Const EN_VSCROLL = &H602
Public Const EN_ALIGN_LTR_EC = &H700
Public Const EN_ALIGN_RTL_EC = &H701
```

Extended Window Styles

```
Public Const WS_EX_DLGMODALFRAME = &H1&
Public Const WS_EX_NOPARENTNOTIFY = &H4&
Public Const WS_EX_TOPMOST = &H8&
Public Const WS_EX_ACCEPTFILES = &H10&
Public Const WS_EX_TRANSPARENT = &H20&
```

GetClassLongPtr Function Constants

```
Public Const GCLP_MENUNAME = (-8)
Public Const GCLP_HBRBACKGROUND = (-10)
Public Const GCLP_HCURSOR = (-12)
Public Const GCLP_HICONSM = (-34)
Public Const GCLP_HMODULE = (-16)
Public Const GCLP_WNDPROC = (-24)
```

GetWindow API Function Constants

```
Public Const GW_HWNDFIRST = 0
Public Const GW_HWNDLAST = 1
Public Const GW_HWNDNEXT = 2
Public Const GW_HWNDPREV = 3
Public Const GW_OWNER = 4
Public Const GW_CHILD = 5
```

GetWindowLongPtr Function Constants

```
Public Const GWLP_HINSTANCE = (-6)
Public Const GWLP_WNDPROC = (-4)
Public Const GWLP_USERDATA = (-21)
Public Const GWLP_HWNDPARENT = (-8)
```

Hook Codes

General

```
Public Const HC_ACTION = 0
Public Const HC_GETNEXT = 1
Public Const HC_SKIP = 2
Public Const HC_NOREMOVE = 3
Public Const HC_NOREM = HC_NOREMOVE
Public Const HC_SYSMODALON = 4
Public Const HC_SYSMODALOFF = 5
```

Computer-based training (CBT) hook codes

```
Public Const HCBT_MOVESIZE = 0
Public Const HCBT_MINMAX = 1
Public Const HCBT_QS = 2
Public Const HCBT_CREATEWND = 3
Public Const HCBT_DESTROYWND = 4
Public Const HCBT_ACTIVATE = 5
Public Const HCBT_CLICKSKIPPED = 6
Public Const HCBT_KEYSKIPPED = 7
Public Const HCBT_SYSCOMMAND = 8
Public Const HCBT_SETFOCUS = 9
```

WH_MSGFILTER hook codes

```
Public Const MSGF_DIALOGBOX = 0
Public Const MSGF_MESSAGEBOX = 1
Public Const MSGF_MENU = 2
Public Const MSGF_MOVE = 3
Public Const MSGF_SIZE = 4
Public Const MSGF_SCROLLBAR = 5
Public Const MSGF_NEXTWINDOW = 6
Public Const MSGF_MAINLOOP = 8
Public Const MSGF_MAX = 8
Public Const MSGF_USER = 4096
```

WH_SHELL hook codes

```
Public Const HSHELL_WINDOWCREATED = 1
Public Const HSHELL_WINDOWDESTROYED = 2
Public Const HSHELL_ACTIVATESHELLWINDOW = 3
Public Const HSHELL_WINDOWACTIVATED = 4
Public Const HSHELL_GETMINRECT = 5
Public Const HSHELL_REDRAW =6
Public Const HSHELL_TASKMAN = 7
Public Const HSHELL_LANGUAGE = 8
Public Const HSHELL_ACCESSIBILITYSTATE = 11
Public Const HSHELL_APPCOMMAND = 12
```

HSHELL_ACCESSIBILITYSTATE Constants

```
Public Const ACCESS_STICKYKEYS = &H1
Public Const ACCESS_FILTERKEYS = &H2
Public Const ACCESS_MOUSEKEYS = &H3
```

Key State Masks for Mouse Messages

```
Public Const MK_LBUTTON = &H1
Public Const MK_RBUTTON = &H2
Public Const MK_SHIFT = &H4
Public Const MK_CONTROL = &H8
Public Const MK_MBUTTON = &H10
Public Const MK_XBUTTON1 = &H20
Public Const MK_XBUTTON2 = &H40
```

Low-Level Hook Constants

```
Public Const KF_EXTENDED = &H100
Public Const KF_ALTDOWN = &H2000
Public Const KF_UP = &H8000
Public Const LLKHF_EXTENDED = (KF_EXTENDED >> 8)
Public Const LLKHF_INJECTED = &H10
Public Const LLKHF_ALTDOWN = (KF_ALTDOWN >> 8)
Public Const LLKHF_UP = (KF_UP >> 8)
Public Const LLMHF_INJECTED = &H1
```

Mouse Wheel Constant

```
Public Const WHEEL_DELTA = 120
```

Open and Save As Common Dialog Box Notification Codes

```
Public Const OFN_ALLOWMULTISELECT = &H200
Public Const OFN_CREATEPROMPT = &H2000
Public Const OFN_ENABLEHOOK = &H20
Public Const OFN_ENABLETEMPLATE = &H40
Public Const OFN_ENABLETEMPLATEHANDLE = &H80
Public Const OFN_EXPLORER = &H80000
Public Const OFN_EXTENSIONDIFFERENT = &H400
Public Const OFN_FILEMUSTEXIST = &H1000
Public Const OFN_HIDEREADONLY = &H4
Public Const OFN_LONGNAMES = &H200000
Public Const OFN_NOCHANGEDIR = &H8
Public Const OFN_NODEREFERENCELINKS = &H100000
Public Const OFN_NOLONGNAMES = &H40000
Public Const OFN_NONETWORKBUTTON = &H20000
Public Const OFN_NOREADONLYRETURN = &H8000
```

```
Public Const OFN_NOTESTFILECREATE = &H10000
Public Const OFN_NOVALIDATE = &H100
Public Const OFN_OVERWRITEPROMPT = &H2
Public Const OFN_PATHMUSTEXIST = &H800
Public Const OFN_READONLY = &H1
Public Const OFN_SHAREAWARE = &H4000
Public Const OFN_SHAREFALLTHROUGH = 2
Public Const OFN_SHARENOWARN = 1
Public Const OFN_SHAREWARN = 0
Public Const OFN_SHOWHELP = &H10
Public Const OFN_ENABLEINCLUDENOTIFY = &H400000
```

PeekMessage Function Options

```
Public Const PM_NOREMOVE = &H0
Public Const PM_REMOVE = &H1
Public Const PM_NOYIELD = &H2
```

PostMessage and SendMessage Function Constants

```
Public Const HWND_BROADCAST = &HFFFF&
Public Const HWND_DESKTOP = 0
```

Predefined Control ID Values for the Open and Save As Common Dialog Boxes

```
Public Const chx1 = &H410
Public Const cmb1 = &H470
Public Const cmb2 = &H471
Public Const cmb13 = &H47C
Public Const edt1 = &H480
Public Const lst1 = &H460
Public Const stc1 = &H440
Public Const stc2 = &H441
Public Const stc3 = &H442
Public Const stc4 = &H443
Public Const IDOK = 1
Public Const IDCANCEL = 2
Public Const IDABORT = 3
Public Const IDRETRY = 4
Public Const IDYES = 6
Public Const IDNO = 7
Public Const IDCLOSE = 8
Public Const IDHELP = 9
Public Const pshHelp = psh15
```

SendMessageTimeout API Function Constants

```
Public Const SMTO_NORMAL = &H0
Public Const SMTO_BLOCK = &H1
Public Const SMTO_ABORTIFHUNG = &H2
Public Const SMTO_NOTIMEOUTIFNOTHUNG = &H8
```

SetWindowLongPtr/GetWindowLongPtr Function Constants

```
Public Const DWLP_MSGRESULT = 0
Public Const DWLP_DLGPROC = 4
Public Const DWLP_USER = 8
```

SetWindowPos Function Constants

```
Public Const SWP_NOSIZE = &H1
Public Const SWP_NOMOVE = &H2
Public Const SWP_NOZORDER = &H4
Public Const SWP_NOREDRAW = &H8
Public Const SWP_NOACTIVATE = &H10
Public Const SWP_FRAMECHANGED = &H20
Public Const SWP_SHOWWINDOW = &H40
Public Const SWP_HIDEWINDOW = &H80
Public Const SWP_NOCOPYBITS = &H100
Public Const SWP_NOOWNERZORDER = &H200
Public Const SWP_DRAWFRAME = SWP_FRAMECHANGED
Public Const SWP_NOREPOSITION = SWP_NOOWNERZORDER
Public Const HWND_TOP = 0
Public Const HWND_BOTTOM = 1
Public Const HWND_TOPMOST = -1
Public Const HWND_NOTOPMOST = -2
Public Const DLGWINDOWEXTRA = 30
```

ShowWindow Function Constants

```
Public Const SW_MAXIMIZE = 3
Public Const SW_MINIMIZE = 6
Public Const SW_SHOWMAXIMIZED = 3
Public Const SW_SHOWMINIMIZED = 2
Public Const SW_SHOWMINNOACTIVE = 7
```

User Button Notification Codes

```
Public Const BN_CLICKED = 0
Public Const BN_PAINT = 1
Public Const BN_HILITE = 2
Public Const BN_UNHILITE = 3
Public Const BN_DISABLE = 4
Public Const BN_DOUBLECLICKED = 5
Public Const BN_PUSHED = BN_HILITE
Public Const BN_UNPUSHED = BN_UNHILITE
Public Const BN_DBLCLK = BN_DOUBLECLICKED
Public Const BN_SETFOCUS = 6
Public Const BN_KILLFOCUS = 7
```

Virtual Key Codes

```
Public Const VK_LBUTTON = &H1
Public Const VK_RBUTTON = &H2
```

```
Public Const VK_CANCEL = &H3
Public Const VK_MBUTTON = &H4
Public Const VK_XBUTTON1 = &H5
Public Const VK_XBUTTON2 = &H6
Public Const VK_BACK = &H8
Public Const VK_TAB = &H9
Public Const VK_CLEAR = &HC
Public Const VK_RETURN = &HD
Public Const VK_SHIFT = &H10
Public Const VK_CONTROL = &H11
Public Const VK_MENU = &H12
Public Const VK_PAUSE = &H13
Public Const VK_CAPITAL = &H14
Public Const VK_ESCAPE = &H1B
Public Const VK_SPACE = &H20
Public Const VK_PRIOR = &H21
Public Const VK_NEXT = &H22
Public Const VK_END = &H23
Public Const VK_HOME = &H24
Public Const VK_LEFT = &H25
Public Const VK_UP = &H26
Public Const VK_RIGHT = &H27
Public Const VK_DOWN = &H28
Public Const VK_SELECT = &H29
Public Const VK_PRINT = &H2A
Public Const VK_EXECUTE = &H2B
Public Const VK_SNAPSHOT = &H2C
Public Const VK_INSERT = &H2D
Public Const VK_DELETE = &H2E
Public Const VK_HELP = &H2F
Public Const VK_NUMPAD0 = &H60
Public Const VK_NUMPAD1 = &H61
Public Const VK_NUMPAD2 = &H62
Public Const VK_NUMPAD3 = &H63
Public Const VK_NUMPAD4 = &H64
Public Const VK_NUMPAD5 = &H65
Public Const VK_NUMPAD6 = &H66
Public Const VK_NUMPAD7 = &H67
Public Const VK_NUMPAD8 = &H68
Public Const VK_NUMPAD9 = &H69
Public Const VK_MULTIPLY = &H6A
Public Const VK_ADD = &H6B
Public Const VK_SEPARATOR = &H6C
Public Const VK_SUBTRACT = &H6D
Public Const VK_DECIMAL = &H6E
Public Const VK_DIVIDE = &H6F
Public Const VK_F1 = &H70
Public Const VK_F2 = &H71
Public Const VK_F3 = &H72
Public Const VK_F4 = &H73
Public Const VK_F5 = &H74
Public Const VK_F6 = &H75
Public Const VK_F7 = &H76
Public Const VK_F8 = &H77
```

```
Public Const VK_F9 = &H78
Public Const VK_F10 = &H79
Public Const VK_F11 = &H7A
Public Const VK_F12 = &H7B
Public Const VK_F13 = &H7C
Public Const VK_F14 = &H7D
Public Const VK_F15 = &H7E
Public Const VK_F16 = &H7F
Public Const VK_F17 = &H80
Public Const VK_F18 = &H81
Public Const VK_F19 = &H82
Public Const VK_F20 = &H83
Public Const VK_F21 = &H84
Public Const VK_F22 = &H85
Public Const VK_F23 = &H86
Public Const VK_F24 = &H87
Public Const VK_NUMLOCK = &H90
Public Const VK_SCROLL = &H91
Public Const VK_LSHIFT = &HA0
Public Const VK_RSHIFT = &HA1
Public Const VK_LCONTROL = &HA2
Public Const VK_RCONTROL = &HA3
Public Const VK_LMENU = &HA4
Public Const VK_RMENU = &HA5
Public Const VK_ATTN = &HF6
Public Const VK_CRSEL = &HF7
Public Const VK_EXSEL = &HF8
Public Const VK_EREOF = &HF9
Public Const VK_PLAY = &HFA
Public Const VK_ZOOM = &HFB
Public Const VK_NONAME = &HFC
Public Const VK_PA1 = &HFD
Public Const VK_OEM_CLEAR = &HFE

'VK_A thru VK_Z are the same as their ASCII equivalents: 'A' thru 'Z'
'VK_0 thru VK_9 are the same as their ASCII equivalents: '0' thru '9'
```

Window Hook Constants

```
Public Const WH_MIN = (-1)
Public Const WH_MSGFILTER = (-1)
Public Const WH_JOURNALRECORD = 0
Public Const WH_JOURNALPLAYBACK = 1
Public Const WH_KEYBOARD = 2
Public Const WH_GETMESSAGE = 3
Public Const WH_CALLWNDPROC = 4
Public Const WH_CBT = 5
Public Const WH_SYSMSGFILTER = 6
Public Const WH_MOUSE = 7
Public Const WH_HARDWARE = 8
Public Const WH_DEBUG = 9
Public Const WH_SHELL = 10
Public Const WH_FOREGROUNDIDLE = 11
Public Const WH_MAX = 11
```

Window Styles

```
Public Const WS_OVERLAPPED = &H0&
Public Const WS_POPUP = &H80000000
Public Const WS_CHILD = &H40000000
Public Const WS_MINIMIZE = &H20000000
Public Const WS_VISIBLE = &H10000000
Public Const WS_DISABLED = &H8000000
Public Const WS_CLIPSIBLINGS = &H4000000
Public Const WS_CLIPCHILDREN = &H2000000
Public Const WS_MAXIMIZE = &H1000000
Public Const WS_CAPTION = &HC00000
Public Const WS_BORDER = &H800000
Public Const WS_DLGFRAME = &H400000
Public Const WS_VSCROLL = &H200000
Public Const WS_HSCROLL = &H100000
Public Const WS_SYSMENU = &H80000
Public Const WS_THICKFRAME = &H40000
Public Const WS_GROUP = &H20000
Public Const WS_TABSTOP = &H10000
Public Const WS_MINIMIZEBOX = &H20000
Public Const WS_MAXIMIZEBOX = &H10000
Public Const WS_TILED = WS_OVERLAPPED
Public Const WS_ICONIC = WS_MINIMIZE
Public Const WS_SIZEBOX = WS_THICKFRAME
Public Const WS_TILEDWINDOW = WS_OVERLAPPEDWINDOW
Public Const WS_POPUPWINDOW = (WS_POPUP Or WS_BORDER Or WS_SYSMENU)
Public Const WS_CHILDWINDOW = (WS_CHILD)
Public Const WS_OVERLAPPEDWINDOW = (WS_OVERLAPPED Or WS_CAPTION Or WS_SYSMENU Or
                                    WS_THICKFRAME Or WS_MINIMIZEBOX
                                    Or WS_MAXIMIZEBOX)
```

WM_KEYUP, WM_DOWN, and WM_CHAR lParam HIWORD Flags

```
Public Const KF_EXTENDED = &H100
Public Const KF_DLGMODE = &H800
Public Const KF_MENUMODE = &H1000
Public Const KF_ALTDOWN = &H2000
Public Const KF_REPEAT = &H4000
Public Const KF_UP = &H8000
```

WM_NCHITTEST Codes

```
Public Const HTERROR = (-2)
Public Const HTTRANSPARENT = (-1)
Public Const HTNOWHERE = 0
Public Const HTCLIENT = 1
Public Const HTCAPTION = 2
Public Const HTSYSMENU = 3
Public Const HTGROWBOX = 4
Public Const HTSIZE = HTGROWBOX
```

```
Public Const HTMENU = 5
Public Const HTHSCROLL = 6
Public Const HTVSCROLL = 7
Public Const HTMINBUTTON = 8
Public Const HTMAXBUTTON = 9
Public Const HTLEFT = 10
Public Const HTRIGHT = 11
Public Const HTTOP = 12
Public Const HTTOPLEFT = 13
Public Const HTTOPRIGHT = 14
Public Const HTBOTTOM = 15
Public Const HTBOTTOMLEFT = 16
Public Const HTBOTTOMRIGHT = 17
Public Const HTBORDER = 18
Public Const HTREDUCE = HTMINBUTTON
Public Const HTZOOM = HTMAXBUTTON
Public Const HTSIZEFIRST = HTLEFT
Public Const HTSIZELAST = HTBOTTOMRIGHT
```

WH_SHELL Codes for the HSHELL_APPCOMMAND Hook Code

```
Public Const APPCOMMAND_BASS_BOOST = 20
Public Const APPCOMMAND_BASS_DOWN = 19
Public Const APPCOMMAND_BASS_UP = 21
Public Const APPCOMMAND_BROWSER_BACKWARD = 1
Public Const APPCOMMAND_BROWSER_FAVORITES = 6
Public Const APPCOMMAND_BROWSER_FORWARD = 2
Public Const APPCOMMAND_BROWSER_HOME = 7
Public Const APPCOMMAND_BROWSER_REFRESH = 3
Public Const APPCOMMAND_BROWSER_SEARCH = 5
Public Const APPCOMMAND_BROWSER_STOP = 4
Public Const APPCOMMAND_LAUNCH_APP1 = 17
Public Const APPCOMMAND_LAUNCH_APP2 = 18
Public Const APPCOMMAND_LAUNCH_MAIL = 15
Public Const APPCOMMAND_MEDIA_NEXTTRACK = 11
Public Const APPCOMMAND_MEDIA_PLAY_PAUSE = 14
Public Const APPCOMMAND_MEDIA_PREVIOUSTRACK = 12
Public Const APPCOMMAND_MEDIA_STOP = 4
Public Const APPCOMMAND_TREBLE_DOWN = 22
Public Const APPCOMMAND_TREBLE_UP = 23
Public Const APPCOMMAND_VOLUME_DOWN = 9
Public Const APPCOMMAND_VOLUME_MUTE = 8
Public Const APPCOMMAND_VOLUME_UP = 10
Public Const FAPPCOMMAND_KEY = &H0
Public Const FAPPCOMMAND_MOUSE = &H8000
Public Const FAPPCOMMAND_OEM = &H1000
```

WM_SIZE Message wParam Values

```
Public Const SIZE_RESTORED = 0
Public Const SIZE_MINIMIZED = 1
Public Const SIZE_MAXIMIZED = 2
```

```
Public Const SIZE_MAXSHOW = 3
Public Const SIZE_MAXHIDE = 4
```

WM_SYSCOMMAND Message wParam Constants

```
Public Const SC_MINIMIZE = &HF020&
Public Const SC_CLOSE = &HF060&
Public Const SC_HOTKEY = &HF150&
Public Const SC_HSCROLL = &HF080&
Public Const SC_KEYMENU = &HF100&
Public Const SC_MONITORPOWER = &H10
Public Const SC_MAXIMIZE = &HF030&
Public Const SC_MINIMIZE = &HF020&
Public Const SC_MOUSEMENU = &HF090&
Public Const SC_MOVE = &HF010&
Public Const SC_NEXTWINDOW = &HF040&
Public Const SC_PREVWINDOW = &HF050&
Public Const SC_RESTORE = &HF120&
Public Const SC_SCREENSAVE = &HF140&
Public Const SC_SIZE = &HF000&
Public Const SC_TASKLIST = &HF130&
Public Const SC_VSCROLL = &HF070&
Public Const SC_ICON = SC_MINIMIZE
Public Const SC_ZOOM = SC_MAXIMIZE
```

XButton Constants

```
Public Const XBUTTON1      0x0001
Public Const XBUTTON2      0x0002
```

Index

Numbers

3D-look checkbox, dialog box
    window, 148
64-bit Windows operating system,
    compatibility, 54–56

A

ABM message prefix, 47
activating windows, 20
active windows
    user input, 18
    Z-order, 18–19
ActiveX controls
    CallWindowProc function, 195
    compiling to, 212
    containers, 199
    creating, 198–199
    EXE project, 208
    hosting, 208–209
    subclassing other windows, 209–217
    third-party, 195–196
    UserControl and, 204–208
    UserControl_Initialize event, 205
    UserControl_Terminate event, 205
    VB-created, 196–202
        UserControl and, 202–209
    (see also controls)
addresses, window procedures
    saving, 98
    variables, 205

AddressOf operator, 53, 83–90
    BAS module and, 85
    FRM module and, 85
    function pointers and, 89–90
    placement, 84
    rules for using, 84–86
    subclassing and, 89–90
ALT-DOWN ARROW key combination, 315
ALT-ESC key combination, 315
ALT-F6 key combination, 315
ALT-SPACE key combination, 315
ALT-TAB key combination, 315
always on top windows, 20
API (application programming
    interface), 10
API functions, 10, 23
    AttachThreadInput, 320, 346, 601
    BAS module and, 100–103
    BroadcastSystemMessage, 275–276,
        602–603
    ByVal, 49
    calling errors, 49
    CallNextHookEx, 74, 603–604
    calls, 64-bit Windows, 54
    CallWindowProc, 56–57, 604
    ChooseColor, 179, 604–605
    ChooseFont, 605
    ChooseFontDlg, 180
    CopyMemory, 36, 37, 605
    CreateThread, 73
    CreateWindow, 606–608

About the Author

Stephen Teilhet earned a degree in Electrical Engineering, but soon afterwards began writing software for the Windows platform. For the last eight years, he has worked for several consulting firms on a wide range of projects, specializing in Visual Basic, Visual C++, MTS, COM, MSMQ, and SQL Server. Stephen currently works for Compuware Numega Labs in Nashua, New Hampshire, where he is immersed in the Microsoft .NET technologies.

His interest in understanding the underlying mechanisms of software, rather than just using the software, is what led him to write this book. In addition to this book he has also written for the *Visual Basic Programmers Journal*. Currently, his two main interests involve studying the inner workings of compilers and understanding the intricacies and operation of the .NET framework and languages.

Colophon

Our look is the result of reader comments, our own experimentation, and feedback from distribution channels. Distinctive covers complement our distinctive approach to technical topics, breathing personality and life into potentially dry subjects.

The animals on the cover of *Subclassing and Hooking with Visual Basic* are common brushtail possums (*Trichosurus vulpecula*). These small Australian marsupials are about one-sixth the size of a housecat. They have big ears, long whiskers, and a pointy snout tipped with a pink nose; their fur color ranges from light gray to dark brown. A brushtail possum pregnancy lasts only about 17 days, but, after birth, the single infant spends up to 5 months in his mother's pouch and then is dependent on mom for another 1 to 2 months longer.

Ordinarily, brushtail possums are tree-dwellers; their long, prehensile tails and opposable digits are ideal for grasping tree branches. They dine on leaves, fruits, and flowers and were once common all over Australia. But now they're largely absent from the interior of the country, and they can too often be found living in the eaves and attics of suburban houses, raiding trash cans for their dinners. Introduced to New Zealand in 1840, they're a major pest species in that country as well, and population control efforts include attempts to popularize possum-fur garments.

Leanne Soylemez and Matt Hutchinson were the production editors for *Subclassing and Hooking with Visual Basic*. Leanne Soylemez was the proofreader. Audrey Doyle was the copyeditor. Linley Dolby provided quality control. Johnna VanHoose Dinse and Brenda Miller wrote the index. Ellie Volckhausen designed the cover of this book, based on a series design by Edie Freedman. The cover image is from *The Illustrated Natural History: Mammalia*. Emma Colby produced the cover layout with QuarkXPress 4.1 using Adobe's ITC Garamond font. David Futato designed the interior layout based on a series design by Nancy Priest. Anne-Marie Vaduva converted the files from Microsoft Word to FrameMaker 5.5.6 using tools created by Mike Sierra. The text and heading fonts are ITC Garamond Light and Garamond Book; the code font is Constant Willison. The illustrations that appear in the book were produced by Robert Romano and Jessamyn Read using Macromedia FreeHand 9 and Adobe Photoshop 6. This colophon was written by Leanne Soylemez.

Whenever possible, our books use a durable and flexible lay-flat binding. If the page count exceeds this binding's limit, perfect binding is used.